ILLUSTRATED GUIDE TO THE SOUTHERN AFRICAN COAST

Illustrated Guide to the Southern African Coast

Published by AA The Motorist Publications (Pty) Limited
for The Automobile Association of South Africa

Illustrated Guide to the Southern African Coast was edited and designed by
AA The Motorist Publications (Pty) Ltd,
130 Strand Street, Cape Town 8001

EDITOR Cecile Reynierse
ART EDITOR Neville Poulter
RESEARCH EDITOR Judy Beyer
PROJECT CO-ORDINATOR Carol Adams
CONTRIBUTORS Lynnath Beckley, David Bristow, Monica Fairall,
Vivien Horler, Brian Johnson Barker, George
Maclay, Tim O'Hagan, Charles Riddle,
Paul Tingay, San Vivier

First Edition © 1988 AA The Motorist Publications (Pty) Ltd

ISBN 0 947008 47 0

Complete guide to the coast

Everyone loves the seaside — and South Africa has one of the loveliest coastlines in the world, from the endless gleaming sands of the west coast, around to the secret, palm-fringed beaches of Natal. *Illustrated Guide to the Southern African Coast* will open your eyes to the wonderful variety and richness of this world, telling you where to go, what to do (and how to do it), and what to see.

● Where to go
The heart of the book is 'Exploring the coast', a step-by-step guide to the coastline from the Kunene River on the northern Namibian border, to Kosi Bay just south of Mozambique. The coast is divided into 32 separate regions, each accompa-nied by a detailed map with the region's main attractions numbered.

● What to do
Each of the 32 regional sections is accompanied by a special feature detailing 'Things to do' in the area: an easy, alphabetical list of activities such as angling, beachcombing, boating, walking, etc.

● How to do it
'Seaside sense' at the back of the book contains practical information designed to help you make the most of the coast, with tips on angling, what you need to know about diving, and how to ride the waves. Most importantly, it gives general advice on first aid and safety at the beach.

● What to see
The book begins with 'The living seashore', telling you what you might see at the seaside — and how to understand and appreciate the fascinating world between waves and shore.

● A word of caution
Remember that water is not man's natural element and bathing can never be considered entirely safe. While we have tried to identify coastal areas generally considered less dangerous for swimming than others, the designation of 'safe' must be understood with this in mind. The publishers cannot be held responsible for any difficulties that may arise as a result of consulting this book.

THIS PAGE *Churchhaven, on the lovely sprawl of the west coast's Langebaan Lagoon.* (Photograph: Walter Knirr)

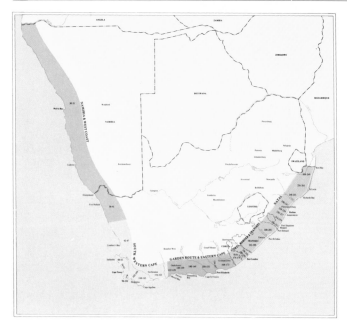

Contents

PART ONE

THE LIVING SEASHORE *8*

PART TWO

EXPLORING THE COAST *28*

PART THREE

SEASIDE SENSE *270*

The living seashore

CONSTANTLY BEING RESHAPED by the mighty hand of the sea and wind, the seashore is neither wholly of the sea nor of the land, but an ever-changing blend of the two as tides ebb and flow. The plants and animals that live between the waves and the sun need to be infinitely adaptable, a never-ending wonder for the naturalist and beachcomber. Here is a canvas for everyone to appreciate. Explore the shore at low tide, sifting through seaweed and pottering about rock pools to discover a world in miniature; paddle in the shallows of an estuary, tracing the wake of the waders that flock to feed there; or head for the coastal heights, and while sea birds wheel above you, scour the sea for the telltale water spout of a calving whale.

RIGHT *The interplay of elements that create the kaleidoscopic coast.*

The making of the coast

The forces of nature are constantly at work, shaping and reshaping the coastline.

THE FAMILIAR COASTLINE of southern Africa has taken millions of years to reach its present form, its ever-changing shape sculpted by continental drift, changes in sea level and the contrary forces of erosion and 'accretion' — the accumulation of new material added by waves, currents and wind — giving us a coastline of fascinating variety: from wave-formed rock platforms, cliffs, beaches of sand, shingle or boulders, to estuaries, vleis and coastal lakes.

Continental drift

An intergalactic traveller looking down on our earth about 200-million years ago would have seen a very different world to the one we know today: instead of the familiar continents, there was just one landmass, known to scientists as Pangaea, and the rest was ocean.

In the course of time, the heat from the molten centre of the earth moved outwards to vent its fury on the surface as volcanos and earthquakes. Slowly, inexorably, a rift began to open in the land, the ocean pouring in, and the two halves, like giant ice floes floating on the molten substance of the earth below, began to drift apart to form two new

 Direction of movement

 Rifts

 New ocean floor

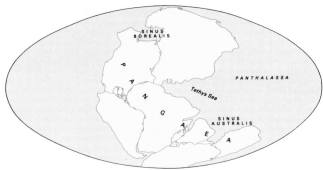

About 200-million years ago the universal landmass, Pangaea, probably looked like this, with the Tethys Sea separating Africa from Eurasia.

By 180-million years ago, Laurasia and Gondwanaland had split, and India and the Australia-Antarctica landmass were being liberated.

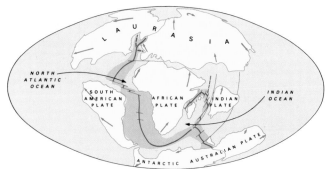

By 65-million years ago, the continent of Africa — with Madagascar breaking away — had been born.

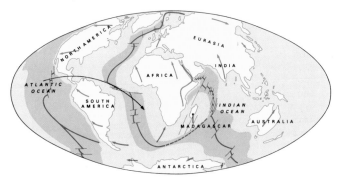

The world as it is today, with India part of Asia and Antarctica and Australia two separate continents.

supercontinents: Gondwanaland, consisting of present-day Africa, South America, India, Australia and Antarctica, in the southern hemisphere; and Laurasia, consisting of North America, Greenland, Europe and Asia, in the northern hemisphere.

The forces that had split Pangaea were still at work; about 180-million years ago the same process was repeated in Gondwanaland. The land parted, liberating India (to start its drift to the northern hemisphere) and the Australia-Antarctica landmass from the Africa-South America landmass, and opening up the Indian Ocean between them.

Then, about 130-million years ago, South America broke away from Africa, creating the South Atlantic Ocean. Madagascar followed about 65-million years ago and Africa, with its relatively sheer coastline, was born.

Continental drift continues even today: Africa and South America are still drifting apart at a rate of about 10 cm a year; and it is predicted that 50-million years from now the South Atlantic and Indian oceans will be much larger and Australia will have begun drifting northwards.

The changing level of the sea

Changes in the sea level during different periods in the earth's history have also played a part, extending and retracting the land as the level has dropped and then risen again — up to 500 m lower and 300 m higher than at present.

These changes can be ascribed to two main causes: rises and falls of the sea bed, which have forced the water level up or down; and successive ice ages, which have locked the oceans around the poles into great wildernesses of ice, thus lowering the sea level. As the earth warmed between the ice ages, and the icecaps retreated, the sea level rose.

At present the earth is between ice ages, and the current sea level was reached only 4 000 years ago; before that, many of southern Africa's coastal towns and cities — had they existed at the time — would have been much further from the coast than they are today. Go back even further and cities such as Cape Town, Durban and Port Elizabeth would have been under water!

Erosion and deposits

Coasts formed by continental drift are known to scientists as 'primary' coasts. But the story does not end there: the erosive action of waves, currents and tides also plays an important part in shaping the shore, notably in determining the particular nature or type of coast: a sandy beach, a shelving cliff and so on.

The rate of coastal wear and tear depends on many factors, including the type and uniformity of the rock along the shore and its degree of exposure to large waves. If the coastal rock is of a uniform hardness, then pounding waves are likely to straighten the coast into cliffs. However, if the rocks are made up of varying degrees of hardness, the waves cut indentations — or bays — into the

softer material, leaving the more resistant rocks protruding as points, such as at Algoa Bay, St Francis Bay, Plettenberg Bay and Mossel Bay, all characterised by east-jutting capes of Table Mountain Sandstone.

Waves and currents not only erode, they can also deposit sand and other sediments along the shore, adding to the land. This so-called 'accretion' is very limited in South Africa, although it does occur in such places as St Helena Bay, Yzerfontein, St Sebastian Bay and Mtunzini.

The wind can also assist in building up the shore. Along the south coast, wind-blown sand spills eastwards across the headlands of the bays to maintain the adjacent beaches. In some cases this natural sand supply has been disrupted because the source of supply — nearby sand dunes — has either been stabilised by the planting of vegetation or by building.

For example, near Port Elizabeth, development at Cape Recife has stabilised the dunes to such an extent that sand no longer blows across to the beaches at Summerstrand — with the result that sand lost from the beaches by the action of the sea is not replaced, leaving the once-sparkling beaches as bare rock. The sand carried away by the sea

piles up against the south-eastern harbour breakwater and enlarges nearby King's Beach. Similarly, in Durban groynes and piers along the beachfront have impeded the natural movement of sediment along the shore — which is why some beaches are being built up, while adjacent ones are being eroded so fast that the sand has to be replaced by the municipality.

Coasts may also be built up by marine organisms, such as oysters, mangroves and salt marsh plants. The most spectacular of these so-called 'deposition' coasts are coral reefs, colonies of tiny, interconnected animals, housed in a complex lime skeleton. When the polyps die, their skeletons remain intact, providing a base on which future generations of polyps develop, building up the reefs. In the right conditions, ideally clear, warm waters, corals may develop as fringing reefs (those growing outward from the coast), barrier reefs (a reef chain parallel to the coast) or atolls (a ring of reefs).

Coral reefs are generally confined to tropical areas, but they do occur off the northern Natal and KwaZulu coast, where the southern limits of the East African fringing reefs extend out to a depth of 25 to 30 m ●

THE CONTINENTAL SHELF

Surrounding the continents is a shallow, submerged platform — the continental shelf — extending from the shore outwards to the continental slope, where the sea floor drops steeply downwards to the ocean depths (abyssal plain).

The continental shelf around southern Africa varies around the coast, from a narrow shelf off the east coast, 10 to 40 km wide and less than 200 m deep, to the Agulhas Bank off the south coast, where the 200 m depth contour is found some 270 km offshore. Around the Cape Peninsula the shelf is again

relatively narrow, but northwards it broadens considerably to about 200 km off the mouth of the Orange River.

The continental shelf is covered with sediments: the inner shelf mainly with sand and shell material, and the outer shelf with different kinds of gravel.

Off the east coast of southern Africa submarine dunes, driven by the Agulhas Current, migrate southwards; while the Agulhas Bank off the south coast is cut by river valleys formed when part of the shelf was still dry land.

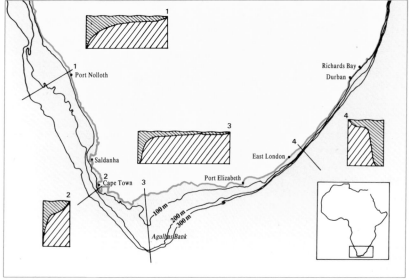

Southern Africa's continental shelf, with insets showing the varying profile.

The weather, wind and waves

A characteristic breaker off the dramatic Tsitsikamma coast, the foaming crest curling and spilling forcefully down the wave face.

WEATHER AND WIND at the coast unite to create a seemingly infinite spectrum of conditions, from balmy unrippled seas bathed in sunshine, to galeforce winds, driving rain and huge storm waves lashing the shore. Knowing how the weather conditions — from place to place, and season to season — differ, can help you to select the ideal time to visit the coastal resort of your choice.

All weather stems from differences in air temperature and pressure. Heated air will expand and lose pressure, cooled air will contract and gain pressure, and all the while, the air will seek to equalise pressure by flowing from an area of high pressure to one of low pressure.

The tapering subcontinent of Africa is particularly vulnerable to the influence of the sea on weather. Bounded by the Atlantic, Southern and Indian oceans, it projects southwards to 35°S, placing it within the southern hemisphere belt of high-pressure cells, where it is skirted to the south by the cold air that surrounds the pole.

The weather pattern along the coast can be said to consist of a succession of cyclones or depressions (moving air of low atmospheric pressure) and anticyclones (moving air of high atmospheric pressure). Fine and dry conditions generally occur when the high-pressure anticyclone centres over the continent, but may be disrupted by temperate disturbances (low-pressure cyclonic systems moving from west to east) or tropical disturbances (such as subtropical lows and tropical cyclones).

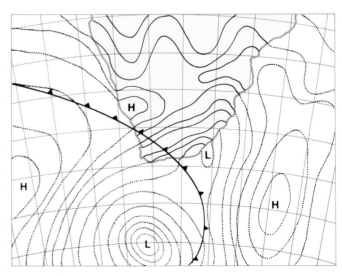

A synoptic weather map, with an eastward-moving cold front bringing cloudy, wet conditions to the southern and eastern Cape, and later Natal.

MAKING WAVES

When a gust of wind blows over still water, it immediately causes a ripple effect on the water surface. This is how waves are generated, both by distant storms that drive swells in to shore and by local coastal winds whipping up the water.

All waves have certain characteristics, determined by the strength of the wind, the length of time for which it blows and the distance over which it blows (called the fetch). Each wave is characterised by its length (the distance between successive crests), wave period (the time taken for successive crests to pass a fixed point) and speed (wavelength divided by wave period), as well as by its height (the distance between trough and crest).

Waves merely reflect the shape of the water surface and are not a forward-flowing movement of water. Within each wave, the motion of individual water particles is quite distinct: as a wave passes, each particle rotates through a circle, beginning and ending its rotation at virtually the same spot. When waves reach shallow water, the friction of the sea floor slows the waves so that they bunch up, increasing wave height. At a certain point, this interrupts the circular motion of the water particles and the wave crest topples forward, breaking on the shore.

There are three basic types of breakers: surging, plunging and spilling. Surging breakers usually have a low wave height and break on steep shores, in a smooth, gliding movement up the beach. Opposed to these are the spilling breakers, associated with high wave height and gently sloping beaches; these break a considerable distance from the shore, their foaming crests tumbling down the wave face. Plunging breakers (a lower wave height and occurring generally on steeper beach slopes) are also known as dumpers, because of their tendency to curl dangerously into a tube before thudding into shallow water.

Wave heights differ around the coast, according to how the waves are generated in a particular area. Off the west coast of the Cape Peninsula, waves of up to 10 m have been recorded, the biggest on the whole coast. (These stem from the storms moving eastwards in the depression belt south of the continent.) The wave height decreases up both the west and east coasts, so that off Walvis Bay and Richards Bay the maximum recorded heights are 4 and 6 m respectively, while at least half the deep-sea waves arriving on the south coast are lower than 2,5 m.

The direction of waves may be changed by topographical features of the sea bed and the coast. In particular areas, this concentrates the waves and creates extremely dangerous conditions, such as those found near the Gordon's Bay, Robberg and Tsitsikamma cliffs. Similarly, waves may become dangerous when strong winds blow against a current. For example, along the edge of the continental shelf on the east coast, short wavelength waves generated locally by galeforce south-westerly winds come up against the strong southward-flowing Agulhas Current. The wave height is increased, and if any of these waves become superimposed on the large, long wavelength swells generated by westerly storms south of the continent, then massive waves of up to 20 m in height can result. These freak waves may present an awesome hazard to shipping.

The most destructive of all waves is the Pacific tsunami, often called a tidal wave but actually the result of a volcano or an earthquake. When such movements in the earth's crust cause the sudden displacement of vast amounts of water, low shock waves are formed, which travel at great speed and sometimes over vast distances before striking land.

Weather and wind

Southern Africa has five major coastal climatic regions: the west, south-west, south, south-east and east coasts. These are distinguished by seasonal differences in temperature and in the amounts of sunshine and rain they receive.

The winds around the coast are determined largely by the South Atlantic and South Indian high-pressure systems (around which the winds blow in an anticlockwise direction) and the low-pressure systems moving from west to east south of the continent (around which winds blow in a clockwise direction). In general, they tend to blow along the coastline. The weather follows a pattern from west to east: as a cold front passes by (the boundary between a warm and a cold airmass), winds back from north-westerly to south-westerly, and then swing through southerlies to south-easterly or north-easterly as the high-pressure system ridges in.

West coast. The arid Namib region is characterised by frequent fog, caused by the

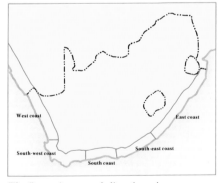

The five major coastal climatic regions.

proximity of the cold Benguela Current. The fog — which is also the main form of precipitation — keeps the sunshine levels low all year round, despite the fact that the western interior receives the most sunshine across the land. The cold Benguela Current keeps the mean annual temperature fairly low (about 15°C at 30°S).

The strongest winds occur in midsummer, and

the least amount of wind in autumn and early winter. In both summer and winter, wind speed reaches its daily maximum in the afternoon. Land and sea breezes cause a daily variation in wind direction. This is slight in summer, but in winter offshore north-easterly winds blow at night and in the morning, while diametrically opposite south-westerly winds blow in the afternoon.

South-west coast. The south-western Cape has warm, dry summers and most of its rainfall in winter. In summer it basks in levels of seventy to eighty per cent sunshine, but only about fifty per cent in winter. Maximum cloudiness occurs in the morning, which is also when rain generally falls. Again, the Benguela Current keeps mean temperatures fairly low.

Prevailing wind directions are north-west and south-east, with the latter — galeforce summer south-easters, accompanied by white cloud pouring down the mountains — the most distinctive. The strongest winds are again in midsummer, the least amount of wind occurs in autumn and early winter, and top daily wind speeds all year are reached in the afternoon. The least daily variation in wind direction occurs in the south-western Cape.

South coast. This region has a warm temperate climate and receives rain throughout the year, peaking in spring and autumn and falling mainly at night. The strongest winds generally occur in spring, with autumn and early winter again being relatively free of wind. Throughout the year, the wind blows strongest in the afternoons.

South-east coast. This warm, temperate region has a summer rainy season. The region receives only fifty per cent of the possible sunshine in summer, but this improves in winter. Spring is again the peak season for wind, and autumn and early winter the quiet seasons. The wind reaches it maximum daily speed in the afternoon and there is a pronounced daily variation in wind direction.

East coast. The Natal/KwaZulu coastal region has a warm, humid climate with rain in summer, often in the form of thundershowers. In summer it receives only fifty per cent of the possible sunshine, but during winter it receives seventy to eighty per cent. Maximum cloudiness occurs in the afternoon, and most rainfall occurs in the late afternoon. The annual mean temperature at latitude 30°S is about 21°C, due to the warm Agulhas Current.

Prevailing wind directions are south-west and north-east, with the most characteristic being the south-westerly 'busters', associated with the backs of coastal lows preceding cold fronts up the coast.

As is the case elsewhere, the strongest winds generally occur in spring, and the least wind occurs in autumn and early winter. Wind speed again reaches its daily maximum in the afternoon, and daily variations in wind direction are marked ●

Tides and currents

ABOVE *The malleable sea, its surface worked into a living sculpture by nature's forces.* BELOW *The effects of the sun and moon on tides.*

THE FATHOMLESS OCEANS of the world are never still. Daily, sea level rises and falls rhythmically with high and low tide, while the greatest streams on earth, the ocean currents, move massive quantities of water over vast distances.

Tides

Tides are caused by two main forces acting on the waters of the earth: the gravitational pull of the moon and the sun, and the contrary centrifugal force generated by the moon and earth spinning around together. The gravitational force of the moon draws the waters of the oceans towards the moon so they 'bulge' out on the side facing the moon, creating a high tide. At the same time, there is a high tide on the opposite side of the earth, with the outward-acting centrifugal force causing the waters there too to bulge. For the water to bulge at two points of the earth, it must be drawn away from other areas, creating low tides. This means there are two equal high tides on opposite sides of the earth, with two equal low tides between them.

Because the earth rotates daily on its own axis, any point on the earth's surface experiences two high tides every day, but not at the same time each day. It takes 28 days for the moon to orbit the earth, so every day the moon must move a further 28th of its total orbiting distance around the earth. This causes a slight delay in the tides each day (25 minutes per tide).

The sun's gravitational pull on the oceans is less than that of the moon, because it is so much further than the moon from the earth. Its role becomes significant, however, during new and full moon, when the sun, earth and moon lie in a straight line and the pull of the sun reinforces that of the moon. This causes extra-high tides and corresponding extra-low tides. These are the spring tides and they occur once every two weeks. (The sun's influence is at its height when it is overhead at the equator, so the highest tides of all occur during the equinoxes in late March and September.) During the first and last quarters of the moon, the gravitational forces of the sun and moon on the earth's oceans are at right angles to each other and the tides then become less marked. During these so-called neap tides, sea level does not rise as high or fall as low.

Along the coast of southern Africa tides are regular and the difference between high and low tide is a fairly consistent 2 m. (Tidal levels are measured by gauges in the major ports.) While times and heights of high and low tides can be predicted, these are not always met, because of the effects of atmospheric pressure and onshore or

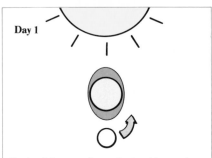

Day 1

During full moon, the gravitational forces of sun and moon are on opposite sides of the earth and reinforce high tides, creating spring tides.

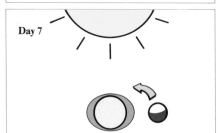

Day 7

During the last quarter, sun and moon are at right angles and cancel each other's gravitational pull, creating neap tides.

offshore winds. Generally, though, spring high tides occur around 03h00 and 15h00, and spring low tides around 09h00 and 21h00. (Tides in estuaries, however, are delayed by channel constriction and the outflow of river water through the mouth.)

Currents

Ocean currents are watermasses that move in response to prevailing global wind patterns and/or to differences in salinity and temperature. They differ from the currents associated with waves and tides, and from those that develop locally in coastal waters under the influence of strong winds.

In both the South Indian and South Atlantic oceans, south-east trade winds blow towards the west at the equator, while westerly winds blow towards the east around 40°S. The stress of these winds on the surface of the sea churns up great anticyclonic (anticlockwise) gyres or spirals of water circulating in these oceans.

The Agulhas Current on the east coast of southern Africa forms part of the Indian Ocean gyre. This warm current is deep (0-2000 m) and fast-flowing (4-7 km/h), and its core (the region of maximum speed), which is usually found just seaward of the continental slope, has a temperature of 25°C.

The Agulhas Current is closest to the coast between Durban and East London, where the continental shelf is very narrow, but in the south it diverges from the coast, following the edge of the Agulhas Bank. South-west of Port Elizabeth most of the current heads back eastwards in a U-turn known as the Agulhas retroflection, but some

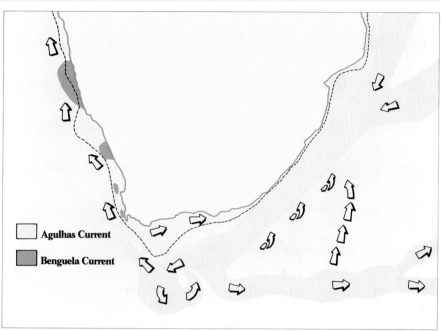

The course of the Agulhas and Benguela currents, with areas of upwelling off the west coast.

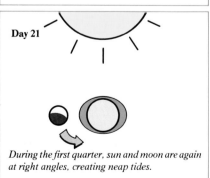

At new moon, sun and moon are again aligned to produce spring tides.

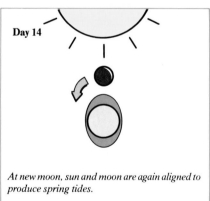

During the first quarter, sun and moon are again at right angles, creating neap tides.

warm water extends around Cape Agulhas and occasionally even up the west coast.

Off the west coast the south-east trade wind gyre results in oceanic water being moved northwards. Along the coast locally strong south and south-east winds, coupled with the so-called Coriolis force, act on the coastal waters to create the north-flowing Benguela Current. (Coriolis force results from the rotation of the earth and causes a moving body to be deflected to the left of its path in the southern hemisphere, and to the right in the northern.) The wind drives the surface waters almost parallel to the coast, but because of the Coriolis force, they are deflected away from the coast. To replace this, deep cold water upwells.

Upwelling off the west Cape coast is most pronounced during summer when south-easters prevail; then sea temperatures as low as 10°C off the beaches are not uncommon! South of the Orange River upwelling is concentrated in three main plumes of cold water, and off the coast of Namibia in two semipermanent plumes of cold water. Between the cold (8-14°C) inshore water and the warm (16-20°C) blue oceanic water of these upwelling regions, there are fronts marked by north-flowing jet currents.

Currents play a role in marine life cycles by transporting many plants and animals — from minute spores to lumbering turtles. The Agulhas Current transports a host of tropical species southwards, including fish and the larvae of species such as elf and leervis. It also sweeps sea beans (*Entada pursaetha*) — the seeds of a creeper growing around rivers in tropical Africa — all the way down the east coast as far as False Bay.

Inshore currents differ from ocean currents by being driven mainly by local winds. They too may be extremely important in the distribution and

transportation of the seeds, eggs, larvae and juveniles of coastal plants and animals. Inshore of the Agulhas Current on the east coast, northward-flowing countercurrents occur frequently during south-westerly winds, while within the bays of the south coast, the circulation inshore is generally cyclonic (clockwise). In False Bay various circulation patterns occur, depending on wind and tidal conditions. On the west Cape coast during the north-west winds of winter there is an onshore movement of water, with southward-flowing currents recorded off Melkbosstrand and Lambert's Bay.

A third kind of current is the so-called rip current, familiar to many bathers because it is so dangerous. Waves breaking on beaches transport a mass of water ashore. This build-up of water is transferred into currents moving alongshore, on the beach side of the breakers, and these currents form the narrow zones of offshore movement called rip currents. They are particularly common along sandy beaches where the wave action is heavy, and can usually be recognised as plumes of foam extending seawards. Rip current systems are important off the sandy beaches of the eastern Cape, where they maintain large blooms of diatoms (algae).

Less obvious along the southern African coast are tidal currents, which are produced by the ebb and flow of tides. Alternating in direction and strongest where the flow is channelled, they are significant only at the entrances of estuaries and lagoons such as Knysna and Langebaan, where they can present a danger to swimmers and sailors. Tidal currents, which are at their strongest midway between high and low tides, are used by the fry of numerous fish to enter protected, food-rich estuarine nurseries ●

The changing coastline

Sandy shores, seemingly bare of life, make up nearly half the southern African coastline.

THE CHARACTER of the southern African coastline alternates between sandy beaches and rocky shores. These, respectively making up 42 and 27 per cent of the total, are interspersed with mixed shores, which are mainly wave-cut rocky platforms, overlain with sand. Backing the coast in places are extensive dunefields and in others soaring rock cliffs, while yet other shores are incised by the estuaries of the numerous rivers threading their way to the sea.

The coast, no matter what its nature, supports a kaleidoscope of marine life, arranged to an almost fixed pattern according to the fierceness of the sea's onslaught.

Sandy beaches

Beaches may seem the most unlikely landforms to face the open sea: they are, after all, merely piles of loose sand. Yet it is this that allows them to remain intact — by changing shape — on an exposed coastline where the waves can reduce concrete breakwaters to rubble in a short time.

A beach extends from the surf zone to the high-water mark. Its profile depends on the steepness and size of the waves breaking on the shore, and in general southern African beaches are rather exposed. They are made up of deposits of different sized sand grains, with the coarser grains found on beaches where wave action is heavy, and the finer grains on sheltered beaches. Silica quartz grains are the main beach sediments, but where a lot of shells are found, the lime content of the sediment may be higher.

Most of the west coast consists of exposed sandy beaches, while in the south-western Cape there are pocket beaches between rocky areas. The south coast is characterised by several very long stretches of exposed beach, backed by dunes, in the half-heart bays, while in Transkei there are again numerous pocket beaches between rocky headlands. Towards Durban the beaches are steep and coarse-grained with plunging waves, and these give way to the northern beaches characterised by a moderate slope, wide surf zone and medium-sized sand grains.

Sandy beaches may at first seem lifeless as there are no attached plants and the animals are apt to burrow into the sand. There are, however, distinct communities of animals occupying the upper, mid- and lower shore. Although the species of animals differ around the coast, the upper shore animals are generally air-breathing scavengers that feed on decaying matter washed up on the beach. Ghost crabs dominate this zone on the east coast, while countless sand hoppers are found among the stranded kelp on the west coast. The midshore region is characterised by carnivorous animals such as the plough snails (*Bullia*), which migrate up and down the beach with the tide. The lower shore is dominated by filter-feeding animals such as the white sand mussels (*Donax*). In the surf zone, prawns and mysid shrimps are common and predators such as sand sharks and fish occur.

Rocky shores

The rocky shores along our coast assume a variety of forms, ranging from steep cliffs and projecting headlands to wave-cut platforms and boulder beaches. Gullies, running parallel or at right angles to the coast, often cut rocky shores, and tidal pools frequently occur between high and low tide levels. Rocky areas on the west and east coasts are generally sandstone, while around the Cape Peninsula granite is common. On the south coast quartzite is typical, though limestone, slates and shales are also found.

Plants and animals living on rocky shores arrange themselves in horizontal zones according to their ability to withstand exposure to air with the rise and fall of the tides: those living high on the shore must be more tolerant than those living low on the shore. Throughout the world, four distinct zones of rocky shores are recognised: the infratidal zone (at spring low tide level); the lower and upper balanoid zones (named for the barnacle species found between the neap low and high tide levels); and the littorina zone (named for the tiny snail found on the upper shore between the neap and spring high tide levels).

Along the west coast the upper shore is dominated by *Littorina* snails and the flat, sheetlike, purple seaweed *Porphyra*. Barnacles and various limpet species occupy the upper balanoid zone, and seaweeds, black mussels and *Gunnarea* tube worms the lower balanoid. An additional zone, the cochlear zone, consisting of the pear-shaped limpets *Patella cochlear* and pink encrusting coralline algae, is found at the low-water neap tide level. The infratidal zone is dominated by the large kelps *Ecklonia* and *Laminaria*. A whole community of organisms — ranging from seaweeds to ribbed mussels, sea

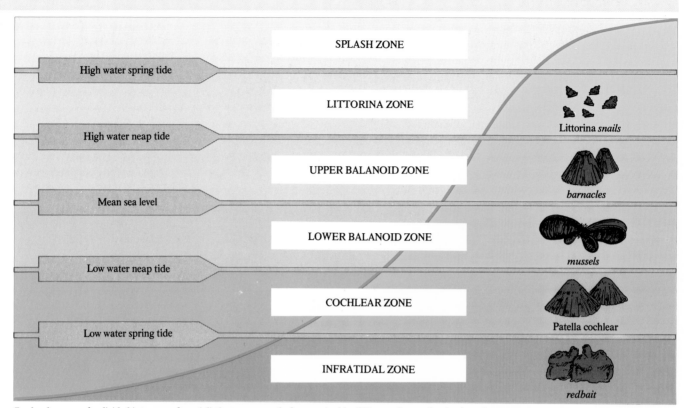

High water spring tide	SPLASH ZONE
	LITTORINA ZONE
High water neap tide	*Littorina snails*
	UPPER BALANOID ZONE
Mean sea level	*barnacles*
	LOWER BALANOID ZONE
Low water neap tide	*mussels*
	COCHLEAR ZONE
Low water spring tide	*Patella cochlear*
	INFRATIDAL ZONE
	redbait

Rocky shores can be divided into a number of distinct zones, each characterised by different plant and animal species.

urchins, perlemoen and rock lobsters — is associated with the west coast kelp beds.

Along the warm temperate south coast, zonation is similar to the west coast. The upper shore is dominated by a single *Littorina* species, and the upper balanoid supports various species of barnacles and limpets, as well as the seaweeds *Ulva* and *Gelidium*. The lower balanoid is dominated by brown mussels and seaweeds. The cochlear zone is again present, with the infratidal zone supporting redbait and various seaweeds.

The east coast upper shore is dominated by a few species of small *Littorina* snails. Below this is a band of Natal rock oysters, followed by a mixed upper balanoid zone of barnacles and limpets. The lower balanoid zone comprises brown mussels and zoanthid corals, and the infratidal fringe is dominated by seaweeds and redbait.

Estuaries

Formed where rivers meet the sea, estuaries are influenced by both tides and river flow, and their salinity ranges widely. Southern Africa is characterised by many small estuaries that are seasonally closed off from the sea due to the accumulation of sand in times of low rainfall. The larger estuaries include the St Lucia (the biggest, with a water area of 360 km²), Kosi Bay and Wilderness systems. Most local estuaries are quite shallow (less than 5 m deep), with the Msikaba estuary in Transkei, reaching 35 m, the deepest. Like large, swift-flowing rivers the world over, the region's largest rivers — the Orange and Tugela

— have only brief estuarine phases and are fresh all the way to the sea for most of the year.

Because estuaries are such variable environments, the plants and animals associated with them must be able to tolerate a wide range of conditions in order to survive. Most estuaries have extensive areas made up of soft sediments, ranging from muds to sands. Generally the mouth and upper reaches of the river have coarser sediments (because of river and tidal currents), while the middle reaches have mudflats.

Mangroves occur along the banks of east coast estuaries as far south as Transkei. Salt marshes with their wide variety of plants fringe the middle reaches of most south coast estuaries, and beds of eelgrass are common from the low tide level downwards. The animals associated with the soft sediments of estuaries are chiefly burrowing crabs, prawns, molluscs and worms. Some of these feed on detritus (decaying matter), and others — particularly bivalve molluscs — filter suspended particles and plankton out of the water.

As estuaries provide food and shelter they are frequently used as nursery areas by juvenile animals (e.g., swimming prawns, in the estuaries of Natal and KwaZulu). Although few fish species actually breed in estuaries, the juveniles of many species enter estuaries as tiny fry to develop there before returning to the sea to breed. Birds, especially waders (many of them migrants), are particularly plentiful in estuaries because of the

RIGHT *The delicate balance at Langebaan.*

rich pickings from the soft sediments.

Estuarine environments in southern Africa are under threat. The dams and weirs constructed to tap the region's limited freshwater resources for agriculture, mining, industry and urban areas, affect the natural flushing of the estuaries, and poor farming and engineering practices lead to a build-up of sand that undoes the natural balance necessary to support life there ●

The 60 cm-long kelp gull (Larus dominicanus) *is the region's largest.*

Coastal birds

BIRDS ARE PROBABLY THE EASIEST of the coastal inhabitants to spot. Southern Africa boasts about 900 bird species — a generous tenth of the world population — and of these, more than 130 are endemic.

Of the birds that derive their living solely from the sea and shore, about twenty species are resident, breeding in colonies on offshore islands or at remote coastal spots. Prominent among these are the Cape cormorant, Cape gannet and jackass penguin. The resident numbers are swelled each summer by nonbreeding migrant shore birds (mainly waders) from the northern hemisphere, as well as some migrants (notably terns) that spend the northern winter off the coast. In addition, during the southern winter, some sea birds migrate north from their Antarctic breeding grounds; these include albatrosses, petrels and shearwaters.

The determining factor in the distribution and abundance of birds is the availability of food. While this can be seen offshore (e.g., by the way the fish-rich Benguela Current off the west coast draws thousands of birds), it is perhaps more apparent on the shore. There are three main coastal habitats: sandy beaches, rocky shores, and lagoons and estuaries. The first is the least attractive, with birds such as the whitefronted plover forced to feed only on the outgoing and incoming tide, when the animal life is closest to the surface rather than buried under water or deep in the sand. Rocky shores, while rich in marine life, pose their own problems because the birds that feed there (such as black oystercatchers) must either have specialised bills for opening shells or have to probe the awkward rock crevices for softer-bodied creatures. Lagoons and estuaries, on the other hand, are ideal feeding grounds: the limited wave action allows the formation of extensive and organically rich mudbanks able to support large numbers of worms, molluscs and crustaceans, and — in turn — large numbers of birds.

The birds shown on these pages, while only a fraction of the total number, have been selected as an introduction to some of the fascinating species you might hope to spot along the southern African coast. (Note that these, and all the illustrations that follow, are not all drawn to the same scale.)

ABOVE *White pelican* (Pelecanus onocrotalus). *Large (140-178 cm) plunge-diving bird, widely distributed in Africa. The smaller pinkbacked pelican is found on the east coast.* RIGHT *Cape cormorant* (Phalacrocorax capensis). *Colonial bird (61-64 cm long) found all along coast. Other species include the bank, whitebreasted, reed and crowned cormorant.*

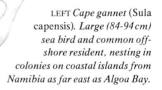

LEFT *Cape gannet* (Sula capensis). *Large (84-94 cm) sea bird and common off-shore resident, nesting in colonies on coastal islands from Namibia as far east as Algoa Bay.*

Common tern (Sterna hirundo). *A small (32-38 cm) migrant. Other terns include the Damara (endemic to the west coast) and the swift tern.*

Blacknecked grebe (Podiceps nigricollis). *A species (28 cm long) found in dense flocks off the Namibian coast during winter.*

Greater flamingo (Phoenicopterus ruber). *Large (140 cm) species frequenting coastal areas and salt pans throughout southern Africa; the lesser flamingo is also found throughout but is less common.*

Pied kingfisher (Ceryle rudis). *A widely distributed species (25-29 cm long) preying on fish in rivers, estuaries and along the shore; other species include the giant, malachite and mangrove kingfishers.*

Jackass penguin (Spheniscus demersus). *Colonial species (60 cm), breeding on offshore islands from Namibia to Algoa Bay. An endangered species particularly vulnerable to oil pollution because of inability to fly.*

Curlew sandpiper (Calidris ferruginea). *A common migrant (20 cm long), occurring in large flocks and probing for worms and crustaceans on muddy banks.*

Turnstone (Arenaria interpres). *A common migrant (23 cm long), found feeding in the intertidal zone, mainly on rocky shores.*

Redknobbed coot (Fulica cristata). *A species (43 cm long) common in coastal lakes, where it is often found swimming in large flocks.*

Little egret (Egretta garzetta). *Resident species (64 cm long) found throughout southern Africa; usually solitary when feeding along estuary banks or the seashore, but gregarious when nesting.*

Cape teal (Anas capensis). *This species (46 cm long) may sometimes be found in small groups in estuaries around the southern African coast.*

Greyheaded gull (Larus cirrocephalus). *A resident species (41-43 cm long) on the east coast; the similar-looking Hartlaub's gull occurs in the south-western Cape; mixed flocks occur in Namibia.*

ABOVE RIGHT *African black oystercatcher* (Haematopus moquini). *A rocky and sandy shore resident (41 cm long) from Namibia to Transkei.* LEFT *African fish eagle* (Haliaeetus vocifer). *A species (63-73 cm long) found on rivers, estuaries and lagoons.*

Klipfish (Clinus superciliosus). *Many species of these cryptic (camouflaged) fish (about 20 cm long) occur around the coast, mainly in rocky areas and tidal pools; they bear live young.*

ABOVE *Goby* (Caffrogobius caffer). *Small (15 cm) mottled fish found all around the coast, mainly in tidal pools but some species also in estuaries, mangrove swamps, sandy areas and reefs.* LEFT *This beautiful tropical lutjanid species explores the wonders of the underwater world. These fish are generally brightly coloured and are often also gaily patterned.*

Coastal fish

SOUTHERN AFRICA IS wonderfully rich in marine fish life, with more than 2 000 different species occurring in coastal waters. This diversity is largely due to the two opposing currents that flow around its coast: the cold Benguela Current which occurs up the west coast, and the warm Agulhas Current which flows down the east coast.

On the west coast the water is cold (but rich in nutrients), and although it supports relatively few species, they are so numerous that these waters have become the subcontinent's most commercially valuable. From the Cape Peninsula to the vicinity of East London the water is more temperate, and the number of species increases. From this point northwards, the sea becomes warmer and there is an explosion in the variety of fish, including many brightly coloured tropical species and some fine angling species.

Most marine fish are seen in their natural environment only by divers. The fish selected here are, on the whole, those most familiar to anglers. (Sizes given are maximum lengths attained.)

Yellowbelly rockcod (Epinephalus guaza). *Sought-after angling species (150 cm long) occurring along rocky shores and over deep reefs all along the coast; other species confined to east coast. SA angling record 25,5 kg.*

Kabeljou/kob (Argyrosomus hololepidotus). *Common species (200 cm long) all around coast. SA angling record 73,5 kg.*

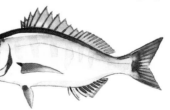

LEFT *White steenbras* (Lithognathus lithognathus). *Prime (100 cm) angling species caught in estuaries (a juvenile nursery) and from sandy beaches from south-western Cape to southern Natal. SA angling record 29,9 kg.*

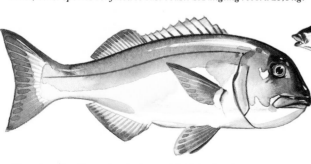

Musselcracker (Sparodon durbanensis). *Prized rock angling species (120 cm long) with large head and powerful jaws, four prominent incisors and rows of crushing molars. SA angling record 23,1 kg.*

RIGHT *Stonefish* (Synanceja verrucosa). *A well-camouflaged dangerous species (40 cm long) with venom sacs; found from Natal northwards on reefs.*

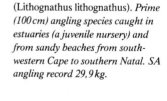

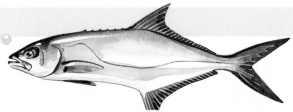

Leervis/garrick (Lichia amia). Predator (150 cm long) occurring all around coast along surf backline and in estuaries. SA angling record 32,2 kg.

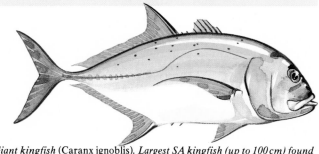

Giant kingfish (Caranx ignoblis). Largest SA kingfish (up to 100 cm) found from Algoa Bay northwards. SA angling record 55,3 kg.

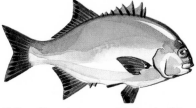

Galjoen (Coracinus capensis). Species (80 cm long) found off rocky shores from Namibia to southern Natal. SA angling record 6,5 kg.

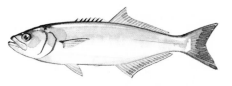

Elf/shad (Pomatomus saltatrix). Esteemed sport fish (100 cm long) occurring all around the coast. SA angling record 10,2 kg.

Mullet/harder (Liza richardsonii). Occurs from Namibia to East London in estuaries and along sandy beaches (60 cm long). SA angling record 0,5 kg.

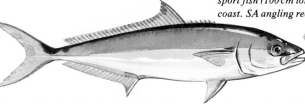

Yellowtail (Seriola lalandi). Game fish (150 cm) occurring from Namibia to Natal, often in shoals. SA angling record 33,1 kg.

Blacktail/dassie (Diplodus sargus). Common fish (40 cm long) right around the coast. SA angling record 2,9 kg.

Cape stumpnose (Rhabdosargus holubi). Species (40 cm long) found from Mossel Bay to Maputo. SA angling record 2,3 kg.

Spotted grunter (Pomadasys commersonnii). Species (80 cm long) found from south-western Cape to KwaZulu. SA angling record 9,5 kg.

Blaasop (Amblyrhyncotes honckenii). Poisonous fish (30 cm long) found from False Bay to KwaZulu.

Zebra/wildeperd (Diplodus cervinus). Fish (50 cm long) found in rocky areas from False Bay to Natal. SA angling record 6,3 kg.

ABOVE *Hottentot (Pachymetopon blochii). West coast kelp bed species (35 cm long). SA angling record 2,6 kg.* RIGHT *Strepie (Sarpa salpa). Small fish (30 cm long) common from south-western Cape to KwaZulu. SA angling record 1,3 kg.*

Sea barbel (Galeichthys feliceps). Spiny species (45 cm long). SA angling record 3,8 kg.

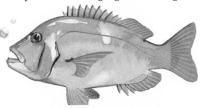

Roman (Chrysoblephus laticeps). Scarlet reef fish (50 cm long) occurring chiefly in southern Cape. SA angling record 4,1 kg.

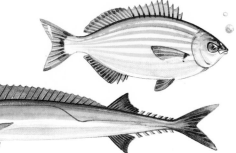

Snoek (Thyrsites atun). Large (110 cm) predatory fish occurring from Namibia to Algoa Bay. SA angling record 8,6 kg.

Dusky dolphin (Lagenorhyncus obscurus). *Small (2 m) dolphins found in the temperate southern hemisphere and characterised by two black 'brush' markings on the side; they are playful and frequently ride the bow waves of ships. Other species include the similarly sized common and humpback dolphins, and the larger Indian and Atlantic Ocean bottlenosed dolphins.*

LEFT *and* RIGHT *Cape fur seal* (Arctocephalus pusillus). *Large (2,15 m; 200 kg) brown seals (the females are smaller), with characteristic small pointed ears; occur from Angola to the east coast, with more than ninety per cent on west coast islands and a few mainland sites.*

Marine mammals, reptiles, sharks and rays

THE 'MAMMOTHS' of the animal kingdom today are the whales, which are among the most highly specialised of all mammals. Capable of diving repeatedly to great depths, these giants of the ocean nonetheless retain the characteristics of suckling their young and breathing air, for which they have to surface periodically. (The well-known 'blow' is caused by warm, moist air from the lungs being forced out through the blowhole or nostrils and condensing as water droplets.)

Dolphins, the smaller whales, are generally better known because they can easily be viewed in oceanariums. Their adaptability to captivity and ability to be schooled in certain behaviour seem to indicate intelligence, perhaps borne out (as with whales) in the area of communication. There is evidence that sperm whales emit clicks not only for echolocation, but also to communicate their presence (across several kilometres) to other individuals in a pod. Bottlenosed dolphins emit a whole range of sounds, from whistles to moans, including a distress call to summon help.

Seals, the third of the marine mammal types, are represented in southern African waters by the Cape fur seal, which breeds off the west coast, although six other species occur as vagrants. Indiscriminate exploitation of these seals for their valuable skins led to a decrease in their number, but today hunting is controlled by legislation.

Only a few reptiles are found in local waters, and they are not frequently seen. There is just one sea snake, which may be washed ashore and stranded. Five marine turtles occur in these waters, with two breeding on the northern Natal/KwaZulu coast and the others preferring the Mozambique coast and islands further to the north.

Sharks and rays differ from other fish in that they have a cartilaginous rather than bony skeleton. More than a hundred species of shark are found in these

Sea snake (Pelamis platurus). *Front-fanged venomous Indo-Pacific snake reaching about 75 cm in length; it has an eel-like head but the tail is laterally flattened and paddlelike, with mottled yellow and black markings.*

Leatherback turtle (Dermochelys coriacea). *Heaviest living reptile (2,5 m; 645 kg), with disconnected shell plates embedded in tough skin; a rare species breeding on the northern Natal/KwaZulu coast. Other species include the loggerhead , hawksbill, green and olive Ridley turtles.*

waters, and while only a handful are dangerous to man, they have developed a rather fearsome reputation. Sharks are usually torpedo-shaped, quite different from the flattened rays, adapted for living on the bottom of the sea. Notable among the rays (many of which, as in the case of sharks, are popular angling fish) are the stingrays and electric rays.

Southern right whale (Balaena glacialis). *Large (14-18 m; mass of up to 67 000 kg) black baleen whales with no dorsal fin and a distinct V-shaped blow; the broad tail flukes (lobes) show when diving. Named for the fact that these were the 'right' whales to catch (because they floated after being killed, and had long baleen or whalebone plates and a high oil yield), these mammals visit the bays of the Cape coast during winter and spring to calve and mate and then return to Antarctic waters.*

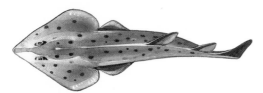

LEFT *Great white shark* (Carcharodon carcharias). *A large (6 m) powerful predator and man-eater, grey-blue in colour with broad, triangular, serrated teeth; found worldwide, often around islands with seal populations. SA angling record 753 kg.*

RIGHT *Hammerhead shark* (Sphyrna zygaena). *A medium-sized (3,5 m) common pelagic shark. (Large schools of juveniles are often seen near the surface in local waters.) This species and two others found here are characterised by peculiarly flattened and laterally protruding heads; they have slanting triangular teeth. SA angling record 136 kg.*

Sand shark (Rhinobatus annulatus). *A common, smallish (1,2 m) surf-zone species with blunt, coffee-grinder teeth for crushing molluscs and crabs; found from Langebaan Lagoon to the east coast, with two other species in Natal. SA angling record 27,7 kg.*

Bronze whaler shark (Carcharinus brachyurus). *A medium-sized (3 m) brown shark with slender, pointed, triangular teeth; primarily a shallow water species, favouring colder to temperate waters from Namibia to southern Natal. SA angling record 192 kg.*

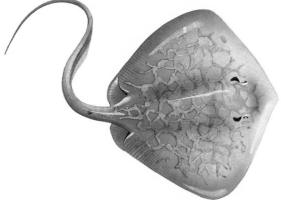

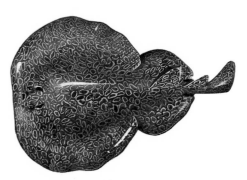

Blue stingray (Dasyatis pastinaca). *This mottled blue-and-brown ray, which can reach a disc width of up to 75 cm, has a sharp, poisonous spine on the tail which can inflict a painful wound; a common coastal species from Namibia to Natal. SA angling record 24,5 kg.*

Marbled electric ray (Torpedo sinuspersici). *A blotchy ray (disc width up to 90 cm) that can generate powerful shocks from large, paired electric organs in the pectoral fins; found in shallow sandy areas and estuaries. SA angling record 10,4 kg.*

This wave-lashed rocky shore hosts a variety of marine life.

Sponge (Haliclona stilensis). These colourful, primitive animals, found in tidal pools, gullies and on reefs, have various forms (including encrusting, tubular and fan-shaped species); they filter food from water drawn through the numerous pores in their bodies.

Zoanthus natalensis. Zoanthids are colonial sea anemones linked together by a fleshy layer of tissue. They are common in tropical seas, with many colourful species occurring on the Natal and KwaZulu coasts where they typically carpet the rocks of the lower shore.

Coral (Pocillophora). Hard corals (which include branched, platelike and ball-shaped species) are colonies of polyps that secrete a skeleton of calcium carbonate; these are tropical species forming reefs from the Natal/KwaZulu coast northwards.

Sea anemone (Pseudactina flagellifera). Most of these soft, fleshy, cylindrical polyps, with tentacles surrounding the mouth, are carnivorous and have stinging cells or nematocysts for immobilising their prey. This species is common from Namibia to Natal, with many others occurring on rocky shores and reefs around the coast.

Sea fan (Lophogorgia flammea). This sea fan (a soft coral) is common in gullies and subtidal reefs on the south and east coast, where it is often washed ashore; it consists of a colony of small, carnivorous polyps embedded in a layer of tissue surrounding a horny axis.

Marine and estuarine invertebrates

THE LOWLIEST OF creatures, those without a backbone, are also those that perhaps best illustrate the unique nature of the seashore. The ebbing and flowing tides create an environment so changeable that each creature must cling tenaciously to life there. When the tide comes in and covers the shore, molluscs, worms and others emerge from the security of seaweed tufts, rock crevices or sandy burrows to search for food. As the tide recedes, they must retreat again to avoid drying out in the sun and air, and being unnecessarily exposed to sharp-eyed predatory birds.

Their ability to conceal themselves for protection makes these invertebrates all the more intriguing to the beachcomber, because it takes patient study to detect them. The reward is an unimaginable richness and diversity of life.

At the bottom of the range are the sponges — porous animals with no organs. Then there are the sea anemones, corals, bluebottles and jellyfish, with only a single opening to their bodies and often growing together in colonies. The worms include flatworms, also with only one opening to their bodies, and the segmented worms whose bodies are divided into rings.

The next division contains the crustaceans, which are segmented and covered by a hard outer skeleton. The familiar molluscs have soft, unsegmented bodies, covered usually by a hard shell. Next there are the starfish, sea urchins and sea cucumbers, with their five-rayed bodies often covered by rough or spiky skin, and finally the sea squirts, which as larvae attach themselves to rocks where they metamorphose into sedentary adults.

RIGHT *Jellyfish (Aurelia). These slightly buoyant, disc- or bell-shaped animals, often cast up on our beaches, have a ventral mouth, often fringed by tentacles. The related box jellies are smaller and have very powerful stinging cells dangerous to man.*

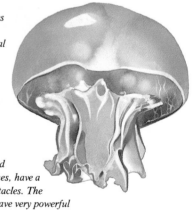

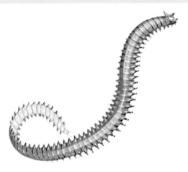

Musselworm (Pseudonereis variegata). This segmented worm is found on rocky shores among mussels and barnacles and is a favourite bait (but beware of the sharp teeth at the end of the proboscis). Other related worms include the fan worms and bloodworms.

Acorn barnacle (Octomeris angulosus). Barnacles are crustaceans enclosed in hard, platelike shells. Numerous species include the dirty white Octomeris, found in large sheets on the midshore from Port Nolloth to Durban; the small, star-shaped Chthamalus dentatus, occurring on the upper shore; and the grey volcano-shaped Tetraclita squamosa, found on the midshore on the south and east coasts.

Sand hopper (Talorchestia capensis). Occurs on sandy beaches and emerges at night to feed on washed-up seaweed. A common rocky shore species is Hyale grandicornis, which shelters among seaweeds and barnacles.

Sand shrimp (Palaemon pacificus). Found in tidal pools and weed beds in estuaries from Namibia to East London.

Fiddler crab (Uca urvillei). Three species of these burrowing crabs characterised by large nippers are found in mangroves and sandbanks of estuaries on the east coast.

Mud prawn (Upogebia africana) and sand prawn (Callianassa kraussi). Two sought-after bait species found respectively in muddy and sandy areas in estuaries from the west coast to KwaZulu. Six species of swimming prawn are found on the east coast and are distinguished by the number of teeth on the rostrum (the structure projecting between the eyes).

Cape rock lobster (Jasus lalandii). The west coast rock lobster is found chiefly on the west and south-west coasts in kelp beds and on rocky reefs; it grows by a series of moults, taking about nine years to reach the minimum legal size for capture. The similar-looking Natal rock lobster (Panulirus homarus) is found from Port Elizabeth to KwaZulu.

Shore crab (Cyclograpsus punctatus). One of the commonest species on rocky shores, sheltering under stones on the high shore. The giant mud crab (Scylla serrata), which may reach 40 cm, makes deep burrows in estuaries from Knysna northwards and migrates to sea to breed.

Cape rock crab (Plagusia chabrus). An active scavenger and swimmer, occurring from Namibia to Natal in tidal pools and subtidally.

Hermit crab (Clibanarius virescens). Highly modified crustaceans that reside in the empty shells of gastropod molluscs; this species, easily identified by the yellow bands at the base of its legs, is found abundantly along the rocky shores of the east coast. Although hermit crabs never eject living gastropods from their shells, their growing bodies force them into fierce battles with other hermit crabs for new and larger homes.

Giant chiton (Dinoplax gigas). *Characterised by its articulated shell plates, this chiton is found from False Bay to Transkei in crevices on rocky shores; it is used as bait.*

White mussel (Donax serra). *These large bivalves live in the intertidal zone of sandy beaches on the west and south coasts.*

Black mussel (Choromytilus meridionalis). *These filter-feeders occur on the west coast in intertidal and subtidal rocky areas.*

Natal oyster (Saccostrea cuccullata). *Characterised by interlocking projections on the shell, this species is found in dense beds in the intertidal zone from Transkei northwards.*

Limpet (Patella cochlear). *Found on the lower shore from the west coast to Natal, these limpets form a characteristic mosaic among pink encrusting coralline algae; other species include* P. granularis, *with a bumpy shell.*

Perlemoen (Haliotis midae). *These large (20 cm) herbivorous gastropods occur subtidally from St Helena Bay to East London and are particularly common in kelp beds; they are fished commercially on the south-west coast.*

Tiger cowrie (Cypraea tigris). *This species is found in Natal and KwaZulu; in general these molluscs, with their characteristic glossy shells, are found in warm tropical waters in the subtidal region.*

Plough shell (Bullia rhodostoma). *These scavenging molluscs have a large foot to surf up the beach on the tide. Three main species are found on sandy beaches around the coast:* B. digitalis *on the west coast,* B. rhodostoma *on the south coast and* B. natalensis *on the east coast.*

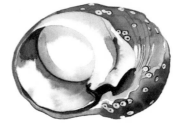

Alikreukel (Turbo sarmaticus). *This fairly large (10 cm) herbivorous species, characterised by its buttonlike operculum with granular white structures, is considered to be a delicacy. It occurs at the low tide mark from the south-western Cape to Natal.*

ABOVE LEFT *Whelk* (Burnupena cinta). *Common scavengers from the west coast to Transkei in the mid-tide zone.* ABOVE RIGHT *Winkle* (Oxystele sinensis). *This dark purple herbivorous snail occurs on rocky shores at the low-water mark and in tidal pools from the south-western Cape to Transkei.*

Octopus granulatus. *Occurs in pools and subtidally from Saldanha Bay to Natal, where it grows rapidly (as much as 30 cm a year) and can change colour for camouflage. The related cuttlefish* (Sepia officinalis) *is found in estuaries and sheltered bays.*

Cushion star (Patirella exigua). *One of the commonest starfish, occurring all around the coast, particularly in tidal pools; variable in colour.*

Brittle star (Ophiotrix fragilis). *Found from the subtidal to the low-water level under stones, from the west coast to East London; move by snakelike arm movements.*

Sea urchin (Parechinus angulosus). *Abundant in pools and subtidally from Namibia to KwaZulu. The spines of the live animals can easily become embedded in your flesh.*

Sea cucumber (Cucumaria sykion). *This black, sausage-shaped species occurs in rock crevices around the low-water mark from Cape Agulhas northwards; many other more colourful species occur.*

Redbait (Pyura stolonifera). *This filter-feeder, with siphons for sucking in and expelling water, is a favourite bait, found from the low tide mark down to a 10 m depth in wave-washed rocky areas.*

IDENTIFYING MARINE LIFE

Seaweeds and coastal plants

Kelp (Ecklonia maxima). *Found from Lüderitz to Cape Agulhas, this brown seaweed is the dominant kelp of the shallow subtidal region, forming the top canopy of the kelp bed. It reaches up to 12 m in length and has a buoyant, swollen area at the end which keeps the plant upright and the fronds floating at the surface. The epiphyte* Suhria vittata *(used for making jelly) is often attached to it.*

T HE FLORA AT THE SEASHORE is just as interesting as the fauna, and has to survive under the same difficult conditions. Trees such as mangroves have adapted to the salty estuarine environment, colonising glutinous mudbanks and creating a sheltered and detritus-rich area for creatures such as crabs and snails and a nursery for fish. Other plants, especially succulent creepers, stabilise sand dunes.

Perhaps most interesting of all are the algae, or seaweeds — although it may not seem so when they lie washed up and rotting on the beach. Underwater, however, they create a forest of fronds, shading from green to brown and red, and harbouring any number of marine creatures. Algae, the simplest of plant forms, constitute the basis of the marine food chain.

Unlike land plants, algae do not, as such, have roots, stems, leaves or seeds: they are anchored by a holdfast, rather than by nutrient-absorbing roots; the water and minerals needed for growth enter directly through the laminae (leaves) and stipe (stem), rather than being conducted through a network of vessels; and spores, not flowers or seeds, perpetuate life.

But like land plants, all algae contain chlorophyll, using the light energy absorbed by it to synthesise organic compounds from carbon dioxide and water. This green pigment may be masked by others, but it is always present and algae cannot grow at depths where no light penetrates for the chlorophyll to absorb. In general, the colour of the seaweed may be used as a rough indicator of where it grows, as the colour of light is filtered out at different depths (e.g., red is absorbed quickly, and cannot penetrate to the depths of blue light). Thus green algae, which readily absorb red light, thrive near the sunlit surface; brown algae grow low on the shore or in shallow water; and red algae, although also found growing low on the shore, may grow at depths of about 60 m, where they are able to absorb the remaining green and blue light.

Sea lettuce (Ulva). *A broad, flat plant and one of the most common green seaweeds right around the coast; it is generally found on the midshore but also in tidal pools.*

Hypnea spicifera. *One of the dominant seaweeds of the Natal coast where it forms dense dark green and maroon beds (it is a red alga) on rocky shores.*

Scaevola thunbergi. *Small, succulent-type plant that colonises and stabilises sand dunes along the east coast.*

ABOVE *Bietou* (Chrysanthemoides monilifera). *A small, robust shrub with bright yellow daisy flowers and clusters of black berries.*
RIGHT *White mangrove* (Avicennia marina). *Mangroves are the only trees adapted to living in salty tidal waters. Found from Transkei up the east coast, and characterised by pencil-shaped aerial roots that protrude from the mud.*

Gelidium pristoides. *Tufts of this chocolate brown-coloured seaweed (it is actually a red alga) characterise the midtidal region of rocky shores in the eastern Cape, Ciskei and Transkei.*

Plocamium corallorhiza. *A red seaweed found subtidally and low on the shore from Lambert's Bay to Mozambique.*

Eelgrass (Zostera capensis). *Estuarine plant with long, narrow leaves; occurs from Langebaan to Mozambique in beds that provide shelter for many invertebrates and fish.*

Salicornia. *A succulent creeper with jointed stems; occurs in salt marshes surrounding estuaries and lagoons.*

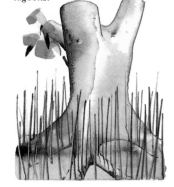

PART TWO

Exploring the coast

FROM THE KUNENE RIVER, around the tip of Africa and up to Kosi Bay, a coastline of spectacular contrasts stretches for some 4 600 km. We have divided the coast from west to east into five major geographic zones, made up of a total of 32 interleading regions. The easy-to-use maps of each region, with numbered places of interest described in vivid detail, help you to make the most of your seaside sojourn: how to reach the resort of your choice, what you can see and do there, what you might discover by exploring a little further afield....

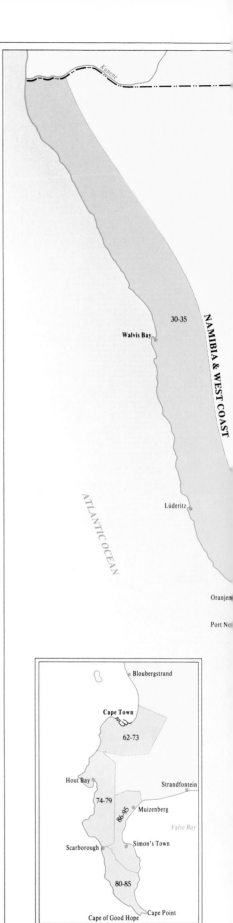

ZAMBIA

ZIMBABWE

MOZAMBIQUE

NAMIBIA

BOTSWANA

Windhoek

Keetmanshoop

Pietersburg

Nelspruit

Pretoria   Middelburg

Johannesburg

SWAZILAND

Kosi Bay

Potchefstroom

Vaal Dam

Pongola

264-269

256-263

Vaal

Newcastle

St Lucia

Kroonstad

248-255

Bethlehem

Richards Bay

Caledon

240-247

Upington

Kimberley

Pietermaritzburg

NATAL

228-239

Orange

Bloemfontein

LESOTHO

220-227

Durban
Amanzimtoti

36-41

214-219

206-213

Port Shepstone
Margate
Port Edward

*H F Verwoerd
Dam*

200-205

Umtata

Port St Johns

42-47

Queenstown

TRANSKEI

192-199

Lambert's Bay

Graaff-Reinet

CISKEI

CISKEL BORDER & TRANSKEI

186-191

Beaufort West

Sundays

Great Fish

Kei

180-185

Bisho

Saldanha

48-55

SOUTH-WESTERN CAPE

156-167

Grahamstown

174-179

East London

56-61

GARDEN ROUTE & EASTERN CAPE

168-173

Cape Town

102-109

Oudtshoorn

130-139

140-149

150-155

Port Elizabeth

122-129

96-101

110-115

Swellendam

116-121

Knysna

Plettenberg
Bay

Cape St Francis

Hermanus

Breede

Mossel Bay

Gourits

Cape Agulhas

INDIAN OCEAN

Where dawn fog lifts to bare scorched desert sands

Breakers echo the rounded Namib landscape.

THE COAST OF HELL, sailors named it, this strip of land between the stark dunes and plains of the ancient Namib Desert, and the icy waters of the Atlantic. The Skeleton Coast, it has become, strewn with the ribs of shipwrecked vessels that every night are shrouded in an eerie fog. The Namibian coast is a harsh and alien one, yet beneath its sands lies a brilliant wealth of diamonds and other minerals. Rare fortunes have been made here, but more often the dreams could not survive the hostile environment.

Today there is a new treasure trail to follow: a journey into an unspoilt land where you can marvel at the magnitude of nature. From the main road penetrating the country's central plateau leads a maze of rough and dusty ways, some of them dwindling into nothing, others winding finally to the lonely coastal road. Set off for adventure, but remember to respect the vast distances and scarcity of water and shelter. Above all, respect the land itself: leaving recognised roads means doing irreparable damage, for tracks remain on the gravel plains for up to fifty years.

1 From the Kunene to the Hoanib River

The Skeleton Coast Park stretches in about a 40 km-wide strip from the Kunene River on the Angolan border to the Ugab River, whose infrequent waters flow into the sea some 500 km to the south.

The northern and less developed of the two sections making up the park extends as far as the Hoanib River and is characterised by huge drifting dunes sculpted into surrealistic shapes, plains of gravel and apricot-coloured sands stretching into the far distance, and ancient canyons carved by water and wind.

This wild and desolate coast has earned its name time and again. Over the years countless ships — swamped by fog, caught in treacherous crosscurrents, hampered by heavy swells and unexpected sand bars reaching their fingers into the sea — have been thrust brutally onto rocky outcrops and banks. Their survivors have battled through cruel waves only to reach a shore unimaginably inhospitable and remote.

Remote it remains, with access to this wilderness area by air. Fly-in safaris operate from Windhoek, depositing visitors at the base camp at

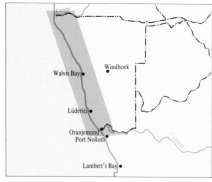

Sarusas, north of the Hoanib River. From here four-wheel-drive vehicles are used for guided tours to various places of interest.

One of the more northerly spots is Angra Fria, where the *Dunedin Star* ran aground in 1942. Here too are the remains of a research station, erected to explore the possibility of creating a harbour on this rocky coast. The only witnesses to the scene today are some 20 000 lustrous seals, basking in the sun. Even lonelier is Cape Fria, about 20 km south: enormous saltpans at the dried-up mouth of the Nadas River are surrounded by empty sands rising to black-topped hills.

Rocky Point, between the Khumib and Hoarusib rivers, is the site of the red-brick grave of Mathias Koraseb, yet another shipwreck victim who found no shelter. Washed up on the beach are the remains of the tug *Sir Charles Elliott*, stranded in a rescue attempt of the *Dunedin Star*.

The Hoarusib flows through a steep-walled inland canyon, a wonderland of creamy-layered 'castles' of sedimentary clay carried down over the ages by the waters. The river is a source of life for the game roaming the plains — elephants, springbok, gemsbok and others. South of the river mouth are the fascinating 'roaring dunes': granules of sand at their crest slip down the face, creating a rumbling boom that is intensified by the semicircular shape of the dunes.

Further south is Möwe Bay, a permanent camp for nature conservation personnel and the administrative centre of this wilderness section of the park. It started life as a diamond-mining venture, for geologically this area is a treasure chest. But, as in so many other instances, the enigmatic desert refused to yield its secrets and the venture failed. Note that permits from the Department of Nature Conservation are necessary to visit this and other sections of the park.

2 From the Hoanib to the Ugab River

After crossing the Hoanib, whose waters are absorbed by dunes before they can reach the coast, the road from Möwe Bay enters the southern section of the Skeleton Coast Park. This area, although wild, has more to offer the tourist in the

LEFT *Man's abandoned projects on the Skeleton Coast are colonised by sea birds.*

way of facilities but permits from the Department of Nature Conservation are still needed.

The most northerly resort is Terrace Bay, which lies about 40 km south of the Hoanib River. This popular angling spot and administrative centre for the park comprises buildings that once formed part of an ill-fated diamond-mining concern. Facilities include bungalows, a shop and a restaurant, and to stay here you must book through the department in Windhoek. No day visitors are allowed and there are no camp sites.

The resort is backed by a particularly attractive belt of sand dunes crisscrossed with deep red garnet crystals. Walks along the beach may unearth relics from ships or offer unexpected glimpses of animals, such as jackals and hyenas foraging for food among the rocks, and the occasional desert elephant wandering down to the water's edge. Tiny ghost crabs emerge from their sandy homes to scuttle towards the water, while

LEFT *Fog swoops low over the endless and empty Namib shoreline.*

THE LIVING DESERT

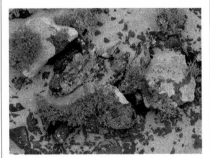

The subtle bloom of desert lichen.

The magnificent Namib, so hostile to human habitation with its endless gravel plains and arid ranks of dunes, in fact supports a host of life. The desert is blessed with an unusual source of water — fog, formed by the cold Benguela Current cooling the desert's warm air to the point of condensation.

A typical desert 'bloom' is lichen, its subtle patches of umber and dull orange making it easy to overlook. Lichen is a close association of fungi and algae: at night, the fungus absorbs moisture from the fog, and in the morning the alga reacts with the water and sunlight to create essential energy.

Adaptations of the insect world to fog are also interesting. To cope with the heat and aridity, most insects burrow into whatever level of the dunes the temperature best suits them, emerging when they sense fog in the air to 'drink' in the moisture. At the crest of a dune the fog-basking beetle, *Onymacris unguicularis,* turns head down, with its back to the fog. Droplets of water condense on the beetle and roll down its grooved back into its mouth. The dune beetle *Lepidochora discoidalis* shovels its way through soft sand to dig a long, thin trench edged by slight ridges. The trench collects droplets of water deposited by the fog on the ridges, and the beetle then crawls back through the trench, taking in the moisture.

This adaptability continues all along the line: the sidewinding adder (*Bitis peringueyi*) sucks droplets of condensed fog off its body, while jackals and other animals lick rock surfaces dampened by fog.

gulls and cormorants swoop through the air.

Continuing southwards you cross the Uniab River (after about 35 km), where the *Atlantic* was wrecked in 1977. The fertile river valley supports a prolific wildlife, including springbok, gemsbok and oryx, and birds flock around the river mouth. A further 12 km south lies the large camping and caravan resort of Torra Bay. It offers a shop and petrol station, but little else. It is, however, an angling paradise, with the added lure of finding semiprecious gems among the sand dunes.

Flanked by immense dunes that seem to threaten to swamp the road, the way continues south, passing Toscanini (an abandoned diamond-processing plant) after about 75 km, then crossing the Huab River and reaching the Ugab River and the southern border of the park after another 40 km. The entrance gate is about 15 km from the river mouth. The river comes down

in flood every few years, rushing down its banks lined with ana, wild fig and tamarisk trees. Springbok, gemsbok and, very rarely, the black rhinoceros may be seen around the waterholes. A three-day guided hiking trail in the area is conducted twice a month.

3 National West Coast Tourist Recreation Area

No permits are necessary to visit this 200 km stretch of protected coastline, with the Swakopmund-Möwe Bay coastal road tracing its length. It passes a string of popular fishing spots: Miles 110, 108, 105, 98 and 92, with Mile 108 the only caravan and camp site along this stretch, boasting its own airstrip and petrol station, and facilities such as ablution blocks and toilets.

About 60 km south of the Ugab River the road reaches Cape Cross, named for the cross erected by Portuguese explorer Diego Cao in 1486. Here more than 60 000 Cape fur seals make their home on the dark rocks, and 6 000 ha around the cape have been proclaimed a protected area. The reserve may be visited at certain times of year (check with the Department of Nature Conservation), but there are no overnight facilities.

Continuing southwards for about 15 km you reach Mile 72, another in the long line of fishing havens. The resort, equipped with a private airstrip, charges a small fee for use of its facilities (a caravan and camp site, a shop and petrol station, and ablution blocks and toilets). Then comes Mile 68, a fishing spot with no facilities.

The large and popular angling resort of Henties Bay, surrounded by flat gravel plains, lies some 50 km south of Cape Cross. Named after Major Hentie van der Merwe, who began the holiday settlement here in 1929, the resort has shops, a restaurant and hotel, and a number of holiday homes. Besides fishing, recreation includes swimming from the dark, sandy beach, and golf, with a dry riverbed serving as the course.

South of Henties Bay, through plains fringed in the distance by huge dunes hazy in the brilliant sunlight, lie the excellent angling spots of Solitude, Jakkalsputz (where there are camp and caravan sites, a shop and petrol station, and ablution blocks), Miles 30 and 26, Rock Bay, Wlotzkasbaken (mainly private holiday homes), Mile 14 (with the same facilities as Jakkalsputz) and Mile 8. About 12 km south of Mile 8 the coast road passes through shimmering white saltpans, before entering the busy town of Swakopmund.

4 Swakopmund

Not only is Swakopmund the centre of the National West Coast Tourist Recreation Area, it is also the major holiday resort on the Namibian coast. It began life in 1892 as a port-of-entry to the German colony, an alternative to the British-held Walvis Bay. This was no great success, and today the remaining metal pier serves only to provide a favourite vantage point for anglers.

RIGHT *A derelict diamond dredger, claimed by the rocky southern shores.*

The town lies at the generally dry mouth of the Swakop River, but receives sufficient supplies of fresh water to support the trees and shrubs that soften the desert landscape and add to the charm of the town. The pleasant climate throughout the year draws countless holiday-makers to fill the hotels, bungalows and camp sites. The fishing is rewarding, there are opportunities for sunbathing, surfing and swimming (a heated freshwater pool supplements the chilly sea), and sports facilities include a golf course. Running the length of the bathing beach is a palm-lined promenade, especially popular for strolls when the thick grey fog bank that blankets the desert every evening can

The pink blush of a flock of greater flamingos — typical along this coast — is in radiant contrast to the blue of Walvis Bay.

be seen looming on the horizon.

Setting Swakopmund apart from other resorts is the atmosphere created by the dignified German colonial architecture, reflecting the town's history. Standing proudly above the town is the old red-and-white lighthouse, built in 1902. Predating it by a year is the quaint railway station, topped by its 'witch's hat' turret. There is often marked contrast between the buildings, like the fortress-like barracks that once housed German troops, a few doors down from Woermann House (1905) with its delicate façade. Also tracing the town's history as well as the region's natural history is the Swakopmund Museum, housed in the old German customs post. To one side of the museum lies the attractive Namib Garden, featuring many typical desert plants. (Notable among these is the living fossil plant, *Welwitschia mirabilis*, a curious modified tree with a lifespan of at least a thousand years. A large stand of these plants can be seen some 30 km from Swakopmund on the gravel road to Windhoek.) Other local facilities include a public library and restaurants and shops.

South of Swakopmund, and stretching the rest of the length of the coast, is a long chain of rocky outcrops (and man-made wooden platforms), known to sailors as the Isles of Dead Ned because of their treacherous rocks. These serve as the breeding ground for millions of sea birds, including gannets, penguins and cormorants. The collection of guano (bird droppings) for commercial purposes — it is used as a fertiliser — is strictly controlled to protect the birds.

RESCUING THE RESCUERS

During the stormy war years, on the night of 29 November 1942, the British cargo liner *Dunedin Star* ran aground off the northern Skeleton Coast. The captain was able to put all 21 of his passengers and half his crew ashore, leaving 43 men on board.

By the time help (four vessels, including the tug *Sir Charles Elliott*) arrived three days later, it was clear that the members of the shore party were in real danger, for they had no shelter and their provisions were desperately low. The men were rescued from the wreck but all attempts to reach those on shore were frustrated by the boiling surf. The *Sir Charles Elliott* turned back for Walvis Bay to refuel, only to run aground itself some distance to the south. Real tragedy struck now, for one crew member was drowned and another — Mathias Koraseb — died of exhaustion after battling to shore.

The rescue bid had, in the meantime, taken a further development: while a police convoy set off overland from Windhoek, bombers were called in to drop supplies to the victims. On his way north the pilot of one of the bombers, a Captain Naude, spotted the stricken tug and radioed for help. His own mission of mercy came to an abrupt end when he was unable to take off after landing at his destination. Similarly, the police convoy was bogged down by sand and had to be rescued by a second convoy.

Eventually, it was a combination of all these rescue attempts — overland, by air and by sea — that saved the lives of the survivors of the *Dunedin Star* and *Sir Charles Elliott*, but it took a full month.

5 Walvis Bay

Golden dunes line the approximately 30 km-long coastal road that leads to the South African enclave of Walvis Bay. Bartholomeu Dias first encountered this natural harbour in 1487 and over subsequent centuries control passed from one European power to another, until in 1884 it was annexed to the Cape Colony. Today this thriving fishing centre and main entry port for Namibia is administered as part of the Cape Province.

The town, with its beautiful coastline, moderate climate and abundance of natural life, is a fine holiday resort. The bay is separated from the Atlantic by a hook of sand, guarded at its northern tip by the Pelican Point lighthouse. The deep water of the bay grows shallower towards the southern end and forms a lagoon, ideal for all watersports. Boardsailors, waterskiers and boaters should take care, however, to avoid the sandy ridges that lie beneath the surface of the water. The bay itself offers fine yachting and angling opportunities, while bathing from the main beach, Langstrand, is fairly safe. There is also a tidal pool here. Holiday accommodation is available in several hotels as well as the municipal caravan park.

This area is a food-rich haven for many bird species that nest along the coast. The lagoon itself, with sand dunes on one side and the Atlantic on the other, is a protected area for a host of greater and lesser flamingos and pelicans. Another sanctuary is Bird Paradise, between the dunes near the sewerage works, where pelicans and many species of waterfowl nest among the reeds.

Sunset bathes the scene at Diaz Point (near Lüderitz), named for the Portuguese navigator.

6 Sandwich Bay and the Namib-Naukluft Park

A four-wheel-drive track leads south of Walvis Bay for 42 km to Sandwich Bay (or Harbour) in the Namib-Naukluft Park. The bay is known for its excellent angling and prolific bird life. A lagoon formed here by the Kuiseb River, which flows below the sand dunes to re-emerge at the coast, supports a bird population that includes flocks of pink-feathered flamingos, squat pelicans and rowdy cormorants. These birds feed on the fish that find their way into the lagoon at high tide, and some lay their eggs on the reed-lined banks.

Sandwich Bay is fenced off from the rest of the park, and visitors, who need a permit from the Department of Nature Conservation, may enter only on foot. The coastal area south of Sandwich Bay, known as Diamond Area No 2 and previously the property of Consolidated Diamond Mines of SWA Ltd (a private diamond-mining concession), has recently been proclaimed part of the park but is not open to the public. (The coastline from Lüderitz south remains restricted.)

The dusty roads into the interior of the Namib-Naukluft Park, however, offer plenty of opportunities to explore further. Check with the Department of Nature Conservation and be sure to plan properly, taking sufficient fuel and provisions. Here you will find shimmering quartz plains, towering dunes and mountains of granite; there are waterholes where oryx, baboons, springbok, gemsbok and hyenas gather, and dolomite gorges and ridges where the protected mountain zebra can range in safety. Limited camping is available (book through the Department of Nature Conservation, Windhoek).

7 Lüderitz and Kolmanskop

The fine natural harbour at Lüderitz was christened Angra Pequena (little bay) by the Portuguese after Dias reached it in 1487, and in his memory, a cross has been erected on the cliff above the beach. The settlement of Lüderitz was established by German trader Adolf Lüderitz in 1883, and grew to a prosperous diamond, fishing and rock lobster centre, fortunately retaining many of its picturesque old buildings.

The coastline here, unlike the sandy or pebbly beaches further north, is characterised by steep jagged cliffs that jut menacingly into the sea. A few grey beaches lie between the rocks, and while swimming is fairly safe, the very cold water makes

---

THE DOUGHTY DAMARA TERN

The Damara tern (Sterna balaenarum).

An insignificant-looking little bird faces a fierce struggle for survival along the desolate Namibian coast. The Damara tern, the smallest of its kind, breeds almost exclusively here, with as much as seventy per cent of the world population limited to the coastal strip between Swakopmund and Terrace Bay.

As defence against the predators that prowl the shores, the tern builds its nest (a shallow scrape in the ground) as much as a kilometre inland. Its problems are not yet over, however. Its fine grey plumage stands out against the dull gravel plains, so the tern must make a solitary nest, rather than join the protection of a too-conspicuous colony. Then, because of the distance between the shore and its nest, the tern is able to carry enough food to feed only one chick, thus increasing the odds against its survival.

Sadly it is man who poses the most serious threat to the Damara tern. As soon as a breeding ground is disturbed, the bird must seek another. And the area that the tern favours and returns to breed each summer is becoming more and more popular with holiday-makers and fishermen, who unwittingly may jeopardise the continuation of the species.

---

angling a more popular pastime. Birdwatching is also rewarding, with a vast and varied bird life inhabiting the bay areas and nesting in pans between the rocky cliffs. The area is known too for its interesting 'dwarf' succulents.

Lüderitz, wedged between two restricted diamond areas, can be reached only by travelling west from Keetmanshoop through Goageb and Aus. No permit is necessary to visit the town, but the surrounding land has high security control. By contacting Consolidated Diamond Mines in Lüderitz, however, you may arrange to visit Kolmanskop, some 15 km to the south-east. Now a sand-engulfed ghost town, it was created as a centre for the thriving diamond industry, and in the early 1900s comfortably housed over 700 families. But as the diggings began to yield less and less, and with the discovery of rich diamond deposits at the mouth of the Orange, the people of Kolmanskop began to drift away, leaving shutters to bang hollowly in the desert wind and the sands to smother the empty homes. Elizabeth Bay and Pomona, further south, echo the deserted Kolmanskop, but no visitors are allowed.

8 Oranjemund and the diamond coast

The wide coastal belt of the southern Namib controlled by Consolidated Diamond Mines stretches south to Oranjemund on the border with South Africa. The strict security measures enforced have meant that most of this searing hot, dry wilderness has been left untouched by man, and animals are free to roam the plains.

Oranjemund, the centre of the restricted area, has all the amenities to keep its permanent population of company employees happy, and its moderate climate and plentiful supply of water from the Orange River compensate for the fact that the town is so cut off from civilisation. No visitors are allowed without permission.

BELOW *The loneliness of ghostly Kolmanskop.*

THINGS TO DO

Angling
For advice on local angling, contact sports shops or the Atlantis Sport Club in Walvis Bay. Boats can be hired from Namib Marine Services in Walvis Bay.

Beachcombing
Pebbly beaches offer exciting finds, like water-rounded agates, amethysts and carnelians. (Any diamonds must be handed to the police.) Few pickings remain from the Skeleton Coast's famous wrecks.

Birdwatching
The best areas are Rocky Point, the lagoon and Bird Paradise in Walvis Bay, and Sandwich Bay.

Boardsailing
Popular spots for boardsailing are Swakopmund, Walvis Bay's lagoon (a club is affiliated to the yacht club) and Lüderitz, where boards can be hired from the yacht club.

Boat trips
Trips to the jackass penguin colony on Halifax Island are organised by Lüderitz Safaris & Tours.

Bowls
Local municipalities have the details.

Camping and caravanning
There are camping and caravan sites at Torra Bay, Miles 108, 72 and 14, and Jakkalsputz; caravan parks at Swakopmund (some 500 sites), Walvis Bay and Lüderitz; and camp sites in the Namib-Naukluft Park. For details, contact the local municipalities or the Department of Nature Conservation (there is a booking office in Windhoek).

Angling — the most popular pastime on the Namibian coast.

Canoeing
The only really suitable venue is Walvis Bay's lagoon.

Diving
Rock lobsters, caught mainly at Lüderitz and Henties Bay, are the chief diving attraction.

Drives and viewsites
Driving to the coast entails long journeys from the main road through central Namibia, with the related problems of the isolation, lack of water and shelter, and road surfaces slippery with sand, but numerous spots inland are well worth exploring.

Making for the southern Skeleton Coast (via Outjo), visit the 200-million-year-old petrified forest near Khorixas and the 5 000-year-old rock engravings near Twyfelfontein. The route via Otjiwarongo passes Kalkfeld, near which there are fossilised dinosaur prints, estimated at 150-million years old. The mighty granite Brandberg range south-west of here preserves such famous rock paintings as the enigmatic 'White Lady' (probably depicting a Herero pastoralist).

To reach the coastal resort of Swakopmund from Windhoek, you pass the turn-off to the artesian springs and old Rhenish mission station — now converted into a modern spa resort — of Gross-Barmen. The Welwitschia Nature Drive, a three-hour self-guided trail from Swakopmund, introduces you to the main features of the seaward section of the Namib Desert. From Walvis Bay various trips can be taken into the Namib-Naukluft Park, including bus tours to view the game.

Golf
For details of courses at Henties Bay, Swakopmund, Walvis Bay and Lüderitz, contact the local municipalities.

Libraries
The public library at Walvis Bay also houses a small museum, and that at Swakopmund an art gallery (consult the municipalities for details). The Sam Cohen Memorial Library in Swakopmund preserves a fine collection of Namibiana.

Museums
LÜDERITZ MUSEUM, Dias Street, Lüderitz: Exhibits of the history of diamond prospecting.
SWAKOPMUND MUSEUM, Strand Street, Swakopmund: Displays of all aspects of the Namib, and of local history.

Powerboating
There is a launch ramp at Walvis Bay, where the lagoon also provides protected water for waterskiing.

Safaris
Details of guided tours, photographic safaris and hunting trips are available from local municipalities, publicity associations or the Department of Nature Conservation.

Shipwrecks
The two best-known wrecks to be seen (or what little remains of them) are: *Dunedin Star* (1942), a cargo liner that struck a shoal at Angra Fria; *Sir Charles Elliott* (1942), a rescue tug, stranded at Rocky Point.

Swimming
The icy sea is generally safer towards the south. Swakopmund has a heated indoor pool, and Langstrand at Walvis Bay a paddling pool.

Tennis and squash
Contact the municipalities at Swakopmund and Walvis Bay about courts.

Walks
The main hiking trail in the region is the three-day Ugab Trail, organised by the Department of Nature Conservation.

Yachting and dinghy sailing
Summer regattas are held at Swakopmund, and regular races between here and Walvis Bay. Both Walvis Bay and Lüderitz boast yacht clubs.

INFORMATION
- Consolidated Diamond Mines of SWA Ltd, Dias St, Lüderitz 9000. Tel 06331=2331
- Department of Agriculture and Nature Conservation, Tourist Office, Private Bag 5018, Swakopmund 9000. Tel 0641=2172
- Department of Nature Conservation and Recreation Resorts, Private Bag 13306, Windhoek 9000. Tel 061=226806
- Lüderitz Foundation, PO Box 233, Lüderitz 9000. Tel 06331=2532
- Namib Publicity and Tourism Association, PO Box 53, Swakopmund 9000. Tel 0641=2411
- National Sea Rescue Institute, Station 18, Walvis Bay. Tel 0642=8299
- NSRI, Swakopmund Jetty, Swakopmund. Tel 0641=2530 (office hours) or 0641=5574 (after hours)
- Walvis Bay Municipality, Private Bag 5017, Walvis Bay 9190. Tel 0642=5981

Nearest AA Office
- 15 Carl List Haus, Kaiser St, Windhoek 9001. Tel 061=224201

Fish type	Season	Best area	Best bait
Dassie	All year	Whole coastline	Mussels, musselworms, redbait, chokka, prawns, fishbait, shark flesh
Galjoen	Mar—Sept	Jakkalsputz, Miles 108 and 110, Terrace Bay	Chokka, crabs, mussels, musselworms, redbait
Kabeljou	Sept—May	Sandwich Bay, Swakopmund, Jakkalsputz, Solitude, Henties Bay, Miles 8, 72, 92, 98 and 105, Terrace Bay	Bloodworms, chokka, fishbait, prawns, spoons
Sharks	All year	Mile 8, Terrace Bay, Lüderitz	Fishbait, crabs, chokka, whale meat
Steenbras	Sept—Mar	In shallow water at Sandwich Bay, Swakopmund, Jakkalsputz, Henties Bay, Miles 72 and 105, Terrace Bay	Prawns, rock and white sand mussels
White stumpnose	Feb—Sept	Lüderitz	Mussels, redbait, prawns, shrimps,

The hidden treasures of a wild and lonely coast

I T WAS THE PROMISE OF UNTOLD RICHES that brought a tide of humanity to this dry, inhospitable land on the west coast. Fortune-seekers thrust deep into the heart of Namaqualand on a quest for copper, taming little pockets of land wherever they settled. Later it was the glitter of diamonds that sparked a wild rush of digging and delving for treasure all along the coast. But perhaps the real wealth of the west coast is a more subtle one: the sea, one of the world's richest fishing grounds. One day, when all the copper and diamond veins peter out, the sea — if harvested wisely — will remain a source of plenty.

To reach this rough and dusty stretch of coast, scored by only two perennial rivers (the Orange in the north and the Olifants in the south), follow the N7 running 50 km and more inland through countryside that every springtime bursts into radiant life with its show of wild flowers. Access to all but a few of the more popular spots is by lonely gravel roads of varying quality, so be sure you are prepared for the challenge, and always take along fresh water.

The sad hulls of wrecked fishing boats.

1 Alexander Bay

This small settlement, with its twin Oranjemund on the opposite bank of the Orange River, is the unlikely focus of South Africa's alluvial diamond industry, but it was the lure of copper that first brought development to the bay. Named after James Alexander, who in the first half of the 19th century pioneered the Richtersveld copper industry, the town experienced a brief flush of prosperity until the 1870s, when the copper rush was all but over. As the years passed, Alexander Bay became something of a ghost town, its spirit slowly eroded by the hot desert wind, until the discovery of diamonds there in 1926 gave it a new lease on life.

Today access to Alexander Bay, at the heart of the restricted diamond area, is limited to permit-holders, but the road beyond here and up the Orange River makes an excellent drive — the barren, gnarled Richtersveld contrasting with the fertile river valley. With permission from Ochta

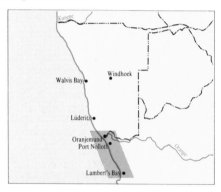

Mine, it is possible to cross the pont at Sendelingsdrif into Namibia and explore further.

2 Port Nolloth

The only holiday resort on the prohibited diamond coast is Port Nolloth, with its satellite settlement of McDougall's Bay. Protected by a series of

shallow reefs, it began life in the 1850s as a copper port, named after the man (Captain M S Nolloth) who first surveyed the bay. Ore was brought to Port Nolloth until well into the 20th century — first via tortuous wagon trails, and then narrow gauge railway — but the harbour, with its narrow, shallow entrance, never proved satisfactory, and the opening of a rail and road connection to Cape Town in 1942 eclipsed its importance.

Although it enjoyed a flurry of activity with the diamond rush of the 1920s and '30s, for the most part this frontier town languished until its emergence as a fishing port, with three rock lobster factories. Then, about a decade ago, a second diamond rush began, this time to scour the sea bed. With the advent of professional divers using undersea suction pipes, Port Nolloth has become the flourishing centre of small-scale marine diamond recovery.

Part of the attraction of Port Nolloth is its sense of adventure: young men, often straight from the navy, are drawn here by the prospect of diving for their fortune. For the holiday-maker there is shared excitement in strolling down the pier at sunrise to watch the diamond boats pull out of harbour to start the day's work.

Port Nolloth's other attractions include long stretches of beach and calm water within the protective reef. With sea temperatures chilled by the Benguela Current, however, the coast is more popular with anglers than with bathers. The northern point of the bay is guarded by the remains of an old fishing boat, protruding from the beach like the skeleton of a primeval creature that has succumbed to the ever-shifting coastal sands. To the south is McDougall's Bay's pretty cluster of seaside shacks and camping sites, as well as its newer houses for permanent residents.

3 Steinkopf and the Richtersveld

Port Nolloth is reached by a tarred road (R382) from Steinkopf on the N7. A Rhenish mission station, established by the Reverend Steinkopf at a place known by the local Nama people as *Tarakhois* (special woman), was the catalyst for

LEFT *The muddy mouth of the Orange River emptying into Alexander Bay.*

31

Sendelingsdrif
Ochta Mine

DIAMOND AREA NO 1

882
Vandersterrberg
RICHTERSVELD

Oranjemund

① Alexander Bay

1230

Noordoewer
Viooolsdrif

NAMIBIA

Orange River

Eksteenfontein
768
Kristalberge

Wreck Point

Lekkersing

Jackals Pit

Lochinvar

760
Kabib se Kop

Aggeneys

Anenous Pass
R382

PORT NOLLOTH ②

McDougall's Bay

735 Steinkopf ③

1064
Katkop

PROHIBITED AREA

R64

NABABEEP

Okiep

1033

Penguin Rock Grootmis

Spektakel Pass

⑤

Hester Malan
Nature Reserve

Kleinsee ④

SPRINGBOK

N A M A Q U A L A N D

Meskel pad

Buffels River

Gamoep

Arosa
Baratini

Swartlintjies River

C A P E   P R O V I N C E

1002

ATLANTIC OCEAN

Kamieskroon
Kamiesberg

R355

Hondeklip Bay ⑥
Aristea

Spoeg River

Garies

10 5 0   10   20 km

Spoegrivierbaai

R355

Groen River

R358

Nariep

Groenriviersmond ⑦

Kotzesrus

Bitterfontein
504

KNERSVLAKTE

Tietiesbaai

Nuwerus

HARDEVELD

N7

R27

Koekenaap

Lutzville Vanrhynsdorp

Gifberg Pass

Seal Island
Papendorp
Strandfontein ⑨

⑧

VREDENDAL

Klawer

Doring Bay
Doring Bay

Trawal

Heerenlogement

790

⑩

Lambert's Bay

Graafwater

SANDVELD

Clanwilliam

Elands Bay
Verlorevlei

Leipoldtville

43

DIAMOND DIVING: A NEW BOOM

Setting out at dawn for the diamond 'fields'.

About an hour before the sun rises over the distant mountains of the Richtersveld, spotlights go on around the small harbour at Port Nolloth and the day begins: diving suits are readied and decompression chambers and communications lines checked, as the suction pipes floating behind each boat slowly illuminate bright red and green against the oily blue swells. One by one the throbbing diesel engines are coaxed into life and the boats head out to sea.

Diving for diamonds is hard work. The divers work in water between 3 and 30 m deep (at this depth for a maximum of eighty minutes), in temperatures ranging from a bone-chilling 11° to 16°C. With visibility at between a few centimetres and a few metres, divers have to drag their commercial vacuum cleaners along the rough ocean bed, sucking up everything down to the bedrock. No boulder can be left unturned — not an easy task to perform in flippers and goggles.

Still, the rewards are high for finding the jewel of the sea. The source of the west coast's alluvial diamonds is undoubtedly the Orange River, but how the gems came to be scattered over hundreds of square kilometres has only recently been determined. Volcanic activity and other continental upheavals caused the Orange River on occasion to find its way to the coast along the present-day Buffels and Olifants river valleys, and maybe also the Kuiseb valley in Namibia. Throughout this time in geological history, the sea level fluctuated widely, and so left the diamonds spread out from Sandwich Bay in Namibia to Doring Bay in the south, and from the marine sands some 15 km inland to an equal distance out along the present sea bed . . . a treasure just waiting to be claimed.

the birth of this quaint village. Alongside the more modern iron huts you can still see the neat, domed *matjieshuisies* (mat huts) built to keep out Namaqualand's searing heat and stinging grit. The huts are traditionally made from reed mats over a wooden frame, but at Steinkopf sacking is now the preferred covering material.

From Steinkopf the road drops through the successive terraces of the Anenous Pass to make for the coast. About 20 km from Port Nolloth a turn-off to the right directs curious travellers to places such as Lekkersing and Eksteenfontein. Deep in the forbidding Richtersveld, these are hard-won prizes: the road is extremely bad and the chances of reaching the advertised destinations

without the aid of a four-wheel-drive vehicle are slight. The lonely mountains of the Richtersveld are rarely visited, but if plans to establish a conservation area here come to fruition, this remotest of areas in South Africa will become a place well worth visiting.

4 Kleinsee and Spektakel Pass

From Port Nolloth you can follow a good gravel road along the coastline to Kleinsee, at the mouth of the Buffels River, and the nearby settlement of Grootmis. All the land between the road and the sea is a prohibited diamond area, but the prospecting trenches can be seen from the car. Just past the small church that serves the people of

THE KELP COAST

Kelp, washed up by winter storms, lies thick on the beach at Hondeklip Bay.

After heavy winter storms, thick beds of kelp lie washed up on the beaches of the west coast, rotting under the hot sun well into summer. These rather offensive-smelling piles of kelp may seem like useless waste but they support a complex web of life, from bacteria to insects and the birds that feed on them.

Young kelp plants attach themselves to the rocky sea bed and immediately attract a thick coat of bacteria to them. As they grow, so a host of other creatures colonise the underwater forests of kelp stalks and fronds to feed there: sea urchins and cucumbers, mussels, redbait and sponges.

Once the kelp is washed up on the beaches, the decaying fronds are again set upon by bacteria, that in turn are consumed by a number of animals. The bacteria also help break down the kelp; this attracts scavengers, such as kelp flies and sand hoppers, which are preyed upon by beach carnivores, notably the plough snail. Squawking flocks of seagulls and terns settle in large flocks among the kelp, to roost and search for scraps, while smaller waders such as sanderlings and whitefronted plovers dart along the surf line or hop over the kelp, picking at the horde of small creatures that live there.

You need only roll over a piece of still wet, decaying kelp to get an idea of just how rich an animal life it supports, but now man has joined the food chain too. In recent years the harvesting of kelp has become a growing industry, with the plants being used mainly in the manufacture of health products.

Grootmis, a security guardhouse and boom bar entry to the modern town built here by the De Beers company to house the employees of its diamond-mining enclave.

Instead, head inland (on the R355) for the Copper Mountains over Spektakel Pass. Three centuries ago Cape governor Simon van der Stel explored the same area, making for the coast. Legend has it that when he crested the hills to look down into the hazy, pastel-shaded vista of the Buffels River valley below, he exclaimed, 'What a spectacle!', and inadvertently named the magnificent pass. The gravel road linking Kleinsee with the interior is, however, heavily corrugated in places and very dusty.

5 Okiep, Nababeep and Springbok

These three towns, situated in a rough triangle inland from Kleinsee, form the copper heart of Namaqualand. Okiep — a corruption of the Nama word *U-gieb* (large, brackish spring) — had only one shallow mine in 1856, but within a few years it had become the largest and richest in the world. A huge hole and slag heaps are all that remain of the mine, while the tall Cornish chimney stack and stone pumphouse are a reminder of the skilled Cornish miners who worked it.

Nababeep has since surpassed Okiep to become the country's premier copper town. Picturesquely surrounded by low hills, it is managed by the Okiep Mining Company and parts of it are out of bounds to the public. Guided tours are conducted through the mine's mill and smelter, and a museum depicts the town's mining history. Outside the museum stands *Clara*, a steam engine used to haul copper ore to Port Nolloth.

Along the N7 to Springbok are fortlike stone buildings and stone embankments and culverts running parallel to the road along the hillsides. These (again the heritage of Cornish miners) are the remnants of old water towers and the railway that ran from the copper mines to Port Nolloth.

Springbok, the administrative capital of Namaqualand, is close to the site of Van der Stel's original copper mine, now a national monument. The governor had led a copper expedition into the interior after being presented with copper goods worked by the local Nama Khoikhoi, and it was here that the first shafts sunk yielded their burnished ore. They could not be worked for a couple of centuries, however, for this was a strange and inhospitable landscape: curious kokerbooms or quiver trees (*Aloe dichotoma*) dotted mountains that glowed bronze in the sunrise and sunset, coloured by copper salts and bright lichens; there was a desperate lack of fresh water, and the tremendous distance from Cape Town meant insurmountable problems for the prospectors. But ultimately the potential was exploited and today Springbok is a modern town with all the amenities a visitor could want, including sports facilities and caravan and camp sites.

About 15 km north-east of Springbok is the Hester Malan Nature Reserve, which has reintroduced game such as mountain zebra, gemsbok and springbok to the area where the fleet-footed klipspringer has always been at home. Its main function, however, is to preserve the natural flora, and in springtime, with Springbok an ideal base from which to view Namaqualand's floral celebration, this reserve is a must.

6 Hondeklip Bay and surroundings

The small port of Hondeklip Bay, named for a dog-shaped rock, was originally used to export copper ore but fell into disuse in the 1870s. Today it is the base for complementary fishing and diamond diving enterprises. The small fishing fleet catches mainly snoek and rock lobsters but the strict quota system means it spends much of its time beached, so some of the boats double as diamond recovery vessels. A harbour factory processes the fish and also serves as the headquarters of the port's diamond industry.

As a seaside resort, Hondeklip Bay is patronised mainly by the local farming community and is popular for its angling. There is a camp site at the northern end of the village, set behind the shore dunes; a reed wall protects campers from the sea of shifting sand surrounding the entire settlement (and partly from the clouds of dust thrown up by the diamond excavations inland).

Hondeklip Bay can be reached from several points inland. From Springbok you could follow the Messelpad (masonry road) and proceed along the Swartlintjies valley, but the road twists sharply and is very narrow in places. Before the construction of the rail link to Port Nolloth, the road — braced by the stone embankments that gave it its name — was used to transport copper ore.

Another turn-off from the N7 to Hondeklip Bay is just beyond Kamieskroon, a town 'moved' from its original, unsuitable site to the present one at the foot of the Kamiesberg in 1924. The mountains here extend an unexpected island of fynbos into this semidesert area, for a single community of Namaqualand's only protea (*Protea sulphurea*) flourishes here. Further south, but before reaching the village of Garies (the Khoi word for the couch grass that softens the veld), is a third road leading to Hondeklip Bay. This bumpy road winds over the Killian and Grootvlei passes, past ancient granite hills pocked with kokerbooms and wild fig trees, and through tiny hamlets where winter-green wheat sways beneath the sun. For some way it follows the course of the Spoeg River, and here you can see a great variety of bird life: martial eagles and jackal buzzards hunting from telephone pole roosts, whitebacked vultures taking dips in farm reservoirs and Stanley bustards prowling the scrub for food.

A kokerboom near Springbok — the tree whose bark the San used to make arrow quivers.

7 Groenriviersmond

From Garies a gravel road follows the general course of the Groen River, undulating over rounded granite hills, to a shallow lagoon at the river mouth. A few diamond prospectors live in the brightly coloured shacks opposite the camp site, which has minimal facilities. (Note that no fresh water is available in the area.) The remoteness of the spot holds its own attractions for the more tenacious nature lovers: flamingos, like exotic pink junks, drift on the lagoon against a backdrop of shimmering coastal dunes; stilts wade along the shallow fringe of the water and blacksmith plovers utter their familiar tinkling call as they roam the shoreline for food.

From Nariep, on the river course, it is possible to follow several lesser farm roads south to Kotzesrus and from there to Waterval and Lepelfontein, both on the coast. The scenic drive along narrow, sandy roads, interrupted by many farm gates but not corrugated, is pleasant but there is nothing of note when you reach the coast — other than the satisfaction of having explored a seldom visited area.

8 Lutzville, Vredendal and Vanrhynsdorp

The link between Strandfontein on the coast and the main access route, the N7, is via these three towns. Lutzville on the perennial Olifants River is an island of green and golden vineyards in a sea of thorny grey bush — except when the first summer rains tap on the ground to waken a kaleidoscope of blooms that soften the veld's caked and scratchy surface. The 'vale of peace' of Vredendal is another such oasis, as well as the commercial and industrial centre of the region.

From here the road crosses the bleak Sandveld towards the comforting embrace of the Bokkeveld Mountains. It passes through Vanrhynsdorp, the gateway to Namaqualand and the ideal base for visitors to see the spring flower paradise. Beyond Vanrhynsdorp a steep gravel pass takes you into an unexpected gorge between the high ramparts of the Gifberg, past a waterfall and onto the

A fertile plateau of the Bokkeveld Mountains near Vanrhynsdorp, deep in the harsh Sandveld.

summit plateau where streams gurgle and lush farmlands are tucked into small, well-watered valleys. It was through this area that the famous Swedish botanist Carl Thunberg travelled in 1774, collecting and describing two new species of protea (*Protea laurifolia* and *P. repens*).

9 Strandfontein and Doring Bay

The aptly named Strandfontein is the holiday centre of the Sandveld, with a hotel and two camping and caravan parks (one set back from the beach in a natural amphitheatre protected from the wind, the other adjacent to the beach but less sheltered). Swimming is popular here (but there may be rip currents in the bay), as is surfing. The

best fishing is along the cliffs to the north of the town, especially at Third Point (or Deurspring), whose three rocky points are clearly visible from the town. A network of tracks leads to the excavations on the headland behind Third Point, and at low tide it is possible to scramble down to the beach and explore around the tall rock stacks, reminders of the sea's hunger to reclaim the land. You could also jog from Strandfontein to Third Point along the beach at low tide, or just go for a scenic ramble.

A longer excursion northwards is to follow the jeep track to the estuary of the Olifants River, where flamingos and other waders can be spotted in the summer. On the flood plain is Papendorp, a tiny cluster of buildings. In a lifestyle that goes back at least a century, the hamlet derives its living from collecting (in donkey carts) the natural salt from the pans here. A diamond recovery operation is underway on the northern bank of the river mouth, but visitors are not welcome.

Just south of Strandfontein an attractive, and rather unexpected, gorge-like valley leads to a rocky cove called Die Hel; this is a popular picnic spot but the swimming here is unsafe.

Further on, about 6 km south of the resort, is Doring Bay. This little coastal town has no holiday facilities to offer, but its good catches do attract anglers. Local enterprise includes a canning factory (fish, lobsters and vegetables), which also uses its boats for diamond recovery.

10 Heerenlogement

A dusty road leads south-east of Doring Bay (towards Graafwater), following a low line of hills whose essential importance is a freshwater spring that has lured travellers through this dry land for many centuries. On the west-facing band of rock topping the hills is a cave where many distinguished men have rested over the years: Heerenlogement (gentlemen's lodging), now a national monument.

The first known visitor to the cave was Oloff Bergh, who in 1682 was sent by Simon van der Stel to investigate the existence of copper deposits somewhere to the north. Bergh's guides showed him the cave, and he began the tradition of carving his name into the rock, to be followed by Van der Stel himself three years later. A host of noted personalities followed suit, including the artist, traveller and naturalist Francois le Vallaint (1783), the Swedish botanist Thunberg (1774) and the German K L Zeyher (1829), and the indefatigable builder, artist, writer and soldier Andrew Geddes Bain (1854). Other dignitaries such as the Rev John Campbell and Robert Moffat are known to have used the shelter, but did not inscribe their names on the cave wall.

Sit quietly in the cave looking towards the coast, and it is easy to imagine a line of wagons and a group of dusty travellers passing across the empty foreground. The wild fig (*Ficus cordata*) growing in a crack at the back of the cave is the same tree referred to in 1712 by Commander K J Slosbo . . . and it is still flourishing.

THE FLOWERS THAT PUT UP A SHOW

Springtime, and the bare landscape is flooded with colour.

After the winter rains the north-western Cape is transformed by a fabulously colourful carpet of wild flowers: rippling sheets of ochre and azure, clusters of mauve and clots of white blossom. This annual 'miracle' of nature draws thousands of people from across the land to witness it, but ironically it really stems from man's interference.

The true function of these brilliant flowering annuals is their role in so-called succession: when the flora of an area is damaged by farming practices or by natural erosion, these flowers move in as the first in a succession of plants attempting to re-establish the original vegetation — the grasses, bushes and trees. As long as grazing and other practices continue to frustrate the course of nature, the flowers will continue to flourish, year after year.

Several reserves have been established in Namaqualand to preserve the wild flower phenomenon, but what is likely to happen here is that with protection from grazing animals, the quality of the flower displays within their fences will eventually pall by comparison with the surrounding farmlands. But they will nonetheless still have provided a vital sanctuary for nature.

ABOVE *Tall sea stacks stand like sentinels on the shore north of Strandfontein.*
LEFT *History is carved in stone at Heerenlogement.*

THINGS TO DO

Angling
The west coast is renowned for the wealth of its fishing grounds. The most popular fish is galjoen (derived from the Dutch description of its fighting abilities), but its numbers, and those of several other species, have been seriously depleted by overfishing. Some of the rock and surf angling species are also taken from boats (e.g. hottentot, kabeljou, yellowtail and yellow rockcod), while snoek, the most common winter fish, is caught only out at sea. Sharks may be caught by handline but some are also hooked by shore anglers.

Beachcombing and shelling
The west coast is poor in shell species but littering the beaches are large piles of limpet, mussel and alikreukel shells, often pounded and ground by the surf to form interesting shapes. The many rock pools are worth exploring, with their limpets, starfish, sea urchins and sea anemones, sea cucumbers and many different seaweeds. Perlemoen shells can sometimes be found trapped in shallow pools or gullies.

Birdwatching
Waders and waterfowl are best viewed along the estuaries and lagoons at Groen and Olifants river mouths, while gulls, terns and cormorants are found in great numbers at all the fishing towns. Birds of prey, such as pale chanting goshawks, jackal buzzards, tawny eagles, martial eagles and whitebacked vultures, may be spotted along the dry riverbeds you follow between the N7 and the coast.

Boardsailing
The bays here all offer sheltered areas with varying surf. The winds are predominantly north-east and north-west in winter and south to south-east in summer. Boardsailors should avoid taking their boards out on the estuaries and lagoons, where they would disturb the bird life.

Camping and caravanning
There are caravan and camp sites at Strandfontein, Vanrhynsdorp, Garies (during school holidays only), Groenriviersmond, Hondeklip Bay and McDougall's Bay (Port Nolloth). Contact the local municipalities or publicity associations.

Canoeing
Two groups — Trailblazers (based in Johannesburg) and the Rivermen (based in Cape Town) — conduct canoeing trails down the Orange River. The more sheltered bays provide reasonable conditions for canoeing at sea, and here again canoeists should avoid estuaries and lagoons.

Cycling
The Johannesburg Trailblazers conduct a cycle tour of over a week through the Namaqualand flower regions, the semidesert coastal mountains and to some of the coastal fishing villages.

Diving
Vast kelp beds at all the resort areas offer good diving in calm weather. The major wrecks in the area are unfortunately all within restricted diamond areas but numerous lesser grounded vessels dot the various harbours and beaches.

A consolation is that rock lobsters abound; around Port Nolloth and McDougall's Bay there are many shallow, inshore reefs that offer endless opportunities for snorkelling and catching rock lobsters in summer.

Drives and viewsites
Drives throughout the area are most popular during the spring flower season, but other times of year have their own rewards. The Messelpad and Spektakel Pass offer fine views, but the roads are in poor condition. The drive from Garies along the Groen River is best for spotting wildlife and birds, and the area around Springbok, Okiep and Nababeep has excellent vistas of Namaqualand as well as of the Copper Mountains.

Golf
Port Nolloth, Springbok, Nababeep and Vredendal have golf courses; contact the local municipalities for further details.

Libraries
The municipal library in Springbok offers temporary membership.

Museums
NABABEEP MUSEUM, cnr White and Hotel Streets, Nababeep: Old and new sections of museum focus on items of geological history and a photographic history of the copper-mining industry; a narrow gauge steam engine and carriages stand outside.

VANRHYNSDORP MUSEUM, Van Riebeeck Street, Vanrhynsdorp: Local history exhibits, housed in the original jail.

Shipwrecks
While this coastline (boasting spots like Wreck Point) has a notorious disdain for ships and sailors, the main shipwrecks lie off the restricted diamond areas and cannot be seen. Many lesser boats lie wrecked on the reefs and beaches at all the villages along the coast.

Surfing
The best surf spots are Strandfontein, Groenriviersmond (pushing through thick kelp) and Port Nolloth (after a long paddle and scramble over the inner reefs to reach the shallow reefs way out beyond the harbour).

Swimming
The best swimming beach is at Strandfontein and stretches of beach nearby. Swimming is possible in any of the bays along the coast, but you should always be on the lookout for dangerous rip currents.

McDougall's Bay near Port Nolloth has a good swimming beach and shallow reefs that offer a degree of protection and safety; north of the harbour are long stretches of beach where you can stroll and swim in privacy.

Tennis
Courts are available at Port Nolloth and the other larger towns. Contact the local municipalities.

Walks
Several trails are laid out in the Hester Malan Nature Reserve near Springbok, while long hikes through the remote and lonely Richtersveld are conducted from the town.

The 80 km-long Namaqualand Coast Trail, between the Groen and Spoeg river mouths, is being planned by the National Parks Board.

Yachting and dinghy sailing
The bays in general (McDougall's, Hondeklip and Doring) offer fair opportunities for enthusiastic sailors but limited facilities.

Fish type	Season	Best area	Best bait
Elf	Sept—May	Shallow surf in the bays (McDougall's, Hondeklip, Doring)	Chokka, fishbait, artificial lures and spoons
Galjoen	Mar—Sept	Off rocky cliffs, especially at Strandfontein and Doring Bay	Chokka, crabs, redbait, mussels, musselworms
Hottentot	Mar—July	Shallow surf in the bays (McDougall's, Hondeklip, Doring)	Chokka, redbait, mussels, musselworms, fishbait, prawns
Kabeljou	Sept—May	Rocky beaches and points all along the coast	Bloodworms, chokka, fishbait, prawns
Leervis	Jan—April	Shallow surf in the bays (McDougall's, Hondeklip, Doring)	Live bait, chokka, spoons and plugs
Sea barbel	May—Sept	Near reefs and in estuaries (especially Groenriviersmond)	Crabs
White stumpnose	Feb—May, June—Sept	Shallow surf and estuaries all along the coast, especially at night	Worms, shrimps
West coast steenbras	May—Sept	Shallow surf in the bays (McDougall's, Hondeklip, Doring)	White and black mussels, prawns

INFORMATION
• Port Nolloth Municipality, Main Rd, Port Nolloth 8280. Tel 0255=8345
• SA Tourism Board, Piazza Level, Golden Acre, Cape Town 8001. Tel 021=216274
• Springbok Municipality, Namaqua St, Springbok 8240. Tel 0251=22071
• Springbok Tourist Information, Springbok Café, Voortrekker St, Springbok 8240. Tel 0251=21321
• Vanrhynsdorp Municipality, Church St, Vanrhynsdorp 8170. Tel 02727=91030
• Vredendal Municipality, 37 Church St, Vredendal 8160. Tel 0271=31045

Nearest AA Office
• AA House, 7 Martin Hammerschlag Way, Foreshore, Cape Town 8001. Tel 021=211550

Reaping the many pleasures of a bountiful sea

E VERY SPRINGTIME scores of people flock to the northern Sandveld to witness the wild flower spectacle there, while the earlier bursts of blooms that cloak the land from Lambert's Bay to Paternoster pass almost unnoticed. The quiet coastline here is characterised by low, rolling dunes and long, uninterrupted beaches, washed by the cold waters of the Benguela Current.

The icy sea supports massed concentrations of fish that are the lifeblood of most of the little coastal settlements here, and that draw keen anglers from all over the country. Rock lobsters — flourishing on the black mussels found in abundance on the rocky shelves and in the kelp beds — attract divers from near and far to what is often referred to as the *kreef* (lobster) coast. In the bays, when the wind is right, the sea is also irresistible to surfers who like to challenge the big, fast, hollow waves that are the stuff of surfing legend.

1 Lambert's Bay

Named after Sir Robert Lambert, the naval commander at the Cape in the 1820s, Lambert's Bay is the centre of South Africa's rock lobster industry, and thus the focus of the summertime tourist *kreef* route. A breakwater connects Bird Island to the mainland and this creates a sheltering harbour for the large fishing fleet that berths here. The brightly painted boats reflect in the dark water, amid kelp fronds that heave and sway in the pulsing sea swells.

Bird Island supports a second industry: for about a century it has been a valuable source of the phosphorus-rich guano used as a fertiliser, today yielding about 300 tons a year. The island is an important breeding place for the threatened Cape gannet and the few remaining jackass penguins, as well as a winter station for hordes of Cape cormorants and the occasional pelican. Birdwatchers can view the frenzied colony from close quarters.

Other attractions for visitors include a large tidal pool set among natural rock pools at the southern end of town, rewarding shelling along

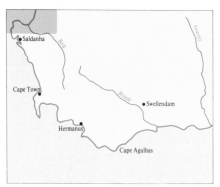

the adjacent beach, and — of course — the opportunity to dive for rock lobster. The sheltered waters of the harbour are ideal for waterskiing, and there is also a convenient slipway for yachts.

2 Inland via Clanwilliam

Between the sea and the Cederberg Mountains lies the flat scrubland of the Sandveld, dotted with isolated settlements that serve the local farming communities. Some 60 km east of Lambert's Bay, the road (R364) reaches Clanwilliam in the well-watered Jan Disselsrivier valley. The embracing mountains, often snow-tinted in winter, the green valleys, the town's quaint white church and traditional Cape houses all add to the considerable charm of the place.

There is much for the nature lover to enjoy here, from leisurely rambles at the two picnic spots of Boskloof and Kranskloof on the outskirts of town, to a visit to the 54 ha Ramskop Nature Reserve and wild flower garden on the eastern bank of the tranquil Clanwilliam Dam, and the fish-breeding station at the dam.

To explore further, follow the Pakhuis Pass east, engineered in 1887 by prolific roadbuilder and artist Thomas Bain. (After heavy rains the road can become a treacherous quagmire of churned-up clay.) The grave of poet C Louis Leipoldt, who spent his youth in the town, lies

LEFT *Brightly coloured rock lobster boats being hoisted at Elands Bay.*

Baboon Point juts into the sea at the south end of Elands Bay.

alongside the pass. From a picnic spot at the top you can walk through the rock mazes and mountain fynbos on either side of the road, with views of the weird, weathered rock formations for which the Cederberg is famous.

From Pakhuis the gravel road swings southwards, climbs a long hill and then enters the beautiful Biedouw valley, transformed in springtime by what may be the most spectacular spread of flowers to be seen anywhere in the Cape. The road winds on over the Koudeberg Pass, following a long kloof deep into the foothills of the Cederberg, to the hideaway village of Wuppertal (now best known for its tannery). Here, on the banks of the Tra-Tra River, the missionaries T von Wurmb and J G Leipoldt (grandfather of the poet) started the first Rhenish mission farm in South Africa in 1830. By 1834 attractive terrace houses and a gabled church had been built, and these can still be seen in the village. A short walk deeper into the kloof, starting from behind the church graveyard, brings you to a series of pools and rapids formed in a semicircle, like pearls threaded on a necklace, between sheer walls of rock.

3 Wadrifsoutpan and Leipoldtville

South of Lambert's Bay is the mouth of the Langvlei River, where backshore sand dunes have formed a barrier that dams the water to form a series of pans. The main pan, Wadrif, attracts a large population of flamingos, especially in winter when other permanent water bodies in the area are too deep for these waders to feed. Wadrifsoutpan is situated on the farm Krompoort, and on the neighbouring farm Wagendrift visitors may ask permission to see an antique wooden lock and key.

The road follows the Langvlei inland, reaching

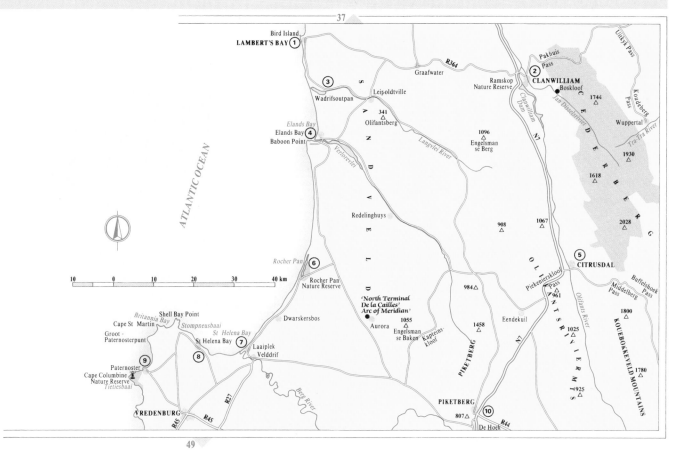

the little centre of Leipoldtville, founded by Louis Leipoldt's father, the Rev C F Leipoldt, in 1905.

4 Elands Bay and Velorevlei

This favourite weekend and holiday spot, with its tiny fishing harbour, combines the best of sea and river resort. Above all it is coveted by surfers for the legendary tubes that break here when the swell is big and the south-easter blows.

The town straddles Velorevlei mouth, the largest estuary on the west coast. The water is saline and poor for irrigation, but the estuary's importance is as a breeding and feeding ground for thousands of birds, including flamingos, pelicans, herons, egrets, gulls, terns, geese, ducks and coots, as well as lesser-known reed dwellers such as purple gallinules and moorhens. During the summer the vlei's population is swelled tenfold by the arrival of migratory waders from the northern hemisphere: turnstones, whimbrels, curlews, godwits and greenshanks, to name but a few. Because Velorevlei is a birdwatcher's paradise, all watersports are frowned upon by landowners, whose permission must be sought to venture along the banks of the vlei.

On the south side of Elands Bay the cliffs of Baboon Point project into the sea. A large shelter here (Bobbejaanberg Cave) is decorated with rock

art, and its vast shell midden is evidence of the long occupation of the cave. These deposits reflect fluctuations in climate and thus in the sea level at various times in geological history: when shellfish remains dominate, the sea would have been nearby, sometimes even lapping the cave entrance; when animal remains dominate, the sea would have been further out, perhaps even as much as 40 km from the present shoreline. Other domestic

waste found in the cave includes beads and tool shards, tortoise shells used as containers and various ornamental fragments.

5 Citrusdal

Inland from Elands Bay, about midway along the main road (N7) between Clanwilliam in the north and Piketberg in the south, is the little town of Citrusdal. Citrus groves carpet the farmlands in

RIGHT *The still beauty of Clanwilliam Dam, from Ramskop Nature Reserve.*

The Whales that Come Ashore to Die

One of the strangest and saddest mysteries of the seas is that of whale stranding, where these giants of the deep seem driven to beach themselves to die a slow and painful death. The west coast, and St Helena Bay in particular, has drawn the most numerous instances of whale stranding in South Africa. Generally, individual animals strand themselves, but in 1936 and again in 1981 two schools of false killer whales beached themselves on the shores of St Helena Bay ... most of them within the same 1 500 m stretch. In all, 123 whales died.

What drives the whales inshore is not yet understood. In the case of St Helena Bay it has been argued that the site of the strandings is a natural trap — a hook-shaped bay with a gently sloping beach, at the end of a submarine canyon — and that faulty navigation could have been responsible. What is quite inexplicable, however, is that the urge to beach themselves is so strong that whales resist attempts to refloat them.

Because the strandings often occur on remote beaches, they are rarely witnessed by scientists who could help to uncover the mystery. It is vital that no time is wasted in assisting stranded animals (by keeping them cool and damp) and notifying a scientific institution (such as a museum, the National Sea Rescue Institute or the Sea Fisheries Institute).

Fishing boats — a reflection of the enduring pattern of life at St Helena Bay.

the Olifants River valley, and during harvest-time the air is heavy with the scent of the fruit.

Citrusdal is reached via the Piekenierskloof Pass over the Olifants River Mountains, named for the party of pikemen who vainly pursued Khoi cattle rustlers through the mountains in the 17th century. It offers splendid views of the Swartland wheatlands and the Piketberg range in the west. The town also serves as a starting point for a drive further inland, over the spectacular Middelberg and Buffelshoek passes through the Kouebokkeveld Mountains, skirting the dramatic rock formations of the Cederberg.

6 Rocher Pan

The otherwise dry countryside between Elands Bay and the Berg River mouth is relieved in places by pans and vleis that act like oases in a desert. A series of lagoons called Die Vlei is found along this stretch, with a marine reserve of the same name along the coast. The last of these vleis comprises the Rocher Pan Nature Reserve, 12 km north of the little settlement of Dwarskersbos.

Rocher Pan is the northernmost location to see waterfowl such as the black crake and shy redchested flufftail. Ducks, teals, shovellers and geese compete with the ubiquitous coots on the water, while waders (notably flamingos) frequent the shoreline in varying numbers. To appreciate the bird life fully, take the ring road and stop off at either of the two observation platforms or the picnic site near the pan.

7 Velddrif-Laaiplek

Settlement along this reluctant coastline was slow but at Velddrif (the ford across the Berg River on the wagon route north from Cape Town) a store, a smithy and an inn were established. Late in the 19th century the Cape Town trader J C Stephan set up a base at Laaiplek, on the mouth of the Berg River. He began shipping wheat to Cape Town and snoek to Natal and Mauritius, and soon Laaiplek was a flourishing port, with several stores and a fish factory. In the course of the past half-century, the combined municipality of Velddrif-Laaiplek has risen to prominence by exploiting the bounty of the sea.

A graceful bridge now spans the Berg River at the site of the original ford, and this marks the finish line of the 280 km-long Berg River canoe marathon, which takes place each year when the river is swollen by winter floods. The race begins near Paarl where mountain streams form a churning chute of white water, and it takes three days for the leaders to reach the calm lower reaches of the river near Velddrif.

Midway between Laaiplek and Velddrif is the modern marina development of Port Owen, offering yachtsmen luxurious accommodation, mooring and access to the sea. During the week the yachts lie secured at their piers, all masts and rigging, their forms and colours shimmering in the dappled water. At the weekend sails are set and one by one the sleek boats glide out into the open.

8 St Helena Bay

This large, half-heart-shaped bay is dominated by fishing villages and fish factories, their chimneys belching out thick plumes of fish-tainted smoke.

LEFT *Port Owen, in the generous embrace of the Berg River.*

Stretching back from the shoreline an enormous patchwork of fields is laid over the hillsides: green wheatfields and pastures looking like crushed velvet, and the dark, ploughed Swartland soil like corduroy. In springtime, flowers fringe the land in a mosaic of yellow, white and orange.

St Helena Bay is the heart of South Africa's fishing industry, reaping the rich harvests of the cold Benguela Current. A dozen or more fish-processing factories perch along a 20 km-long shoreline; out to sea, rowing boats bob to a steady rhythm, or they are beached to laze like amphibians in the sun.

It was here that the Portuguese navigator Vasco da Gama landed with a small fleet on 7 November 1497 — St Helen's Day — after four months at sea, and stayed anchored for a week before continuing on his pioneering voyage to the East. A marble monument on the beach near

The pastoral air at Paternoster.

Stompneusbaai, at the western edge of the bay, commemorates Da Gama's arrival.

9 Paternoster to Tietiesbaai

From Britannia Bay, west of St Helena Bay, it is possible to follow a sandy track behind the beach all the way to Paternoster. The origin of the name Paternoster is uncertain, but it might refer to the prayer offered by shipwrecked sailors. Paternoster is perhaps the least commercialised and thus the most attractive of all the west coast fishing villages, with no smoking factories and no throbbing diesel engines in the bay.

Little has changed here over the years, except for the telephone and electricity lines that run between the rows of whitewashed cottages. Small rowing boats leave the bay at dawn each day, with their complement of three fishermen, a net, hand lines and bait, and a bottle of fresh water . . . just as fishermen have headed out to sea for thousands of years. Depending on what is running, the boats come back heaped with snoek or hottentot, rock lobster, sharks or the grotesque-looking (but quite harmless) elephantfish — a primitive type of shark with an ungainly snout.

To the south of Paternoster Cape Columbine's red-and-white lighthouse is visible, standing on a hill in the Cape Columbine Nature Reserve. Within the reserve there is a camp site at the sheltered cove of Tietiesbaai, where lichens paint the granite rocks brilliant shades of yellow and green, and daisies are sprinkled along the edge of the land, around the small vleis and right up to the lighthouse. Surf crashes against the rugged seascape here, which contrasts with the long stretches of open beaches and rippled dunes that typify the coast to the north.

Among this rocky coast's victims before the lighthouse was built in 1936, were the troopship *St Lawrence* and the *Lisboa*. When the latter ran

THE WELL OF LIFE

Holiday-makers on the west coast often find it curious that the sea is colder there in summer than in winter, perhaps plunging to a chilling 8°C, while at the same time temperatures out at sea are a lot more bearable. This strange situation arises in part because of the cold Benguela Current sweeping past our south-western coast, but it is heightened by the south-east wind. This wind blows parallel to the west coast, but the force of the earth's rotation pushes the surface water away from the coast.

Water currents move like winds, and deep down in the southern Atlantic there is a stream of dense, cold water that has sunk down in the Antarctic region and moves northwards off the south-west coast of Africa. It is this polar-chilled water that wells up to replace the surface water that the south-easter has blown away, and that shocks summer swimmers when they splash into the tempting waves.

It is also this upwelled water that supports the huge fish populations off our west coast. At sea, the remains of dead creatures decompose and filter downwards, collecting near the bottom. Heavy particles of nutrient salts also tend to collect at depths where there is no light and virtually no life to sustain. But when this water is upwelled (as it is off south-western Africa, Peru and California) to where there is enough light for plants and animals to live, the sea nourishes great shoals of pilchards (sardines), anchovies, maasbanker . . . the whole web of life that feeds billions of people around the world.

While the cold water supports a huge quantity of life, these same conditions severely limit the number of species. By contrast, warm-water coral reefs may have overwhelming numbers of different types of fish and plants, but their numbers will be only a tiny fraction of that of the colder, nutrient-rich waters.

THE TERRIBLE VOYAGE OF DE GOUDEN BUYS

In 1697 the Dutch East India Company ship *De Gouden Buys* dropped anchor in St Helena Bay after a long and arduous voyage. When it had set out from Europe, bound for Batavia, the captain and crew of nearly 200 had been confident of success, but their hopes were doomed almost from the outset.

In the vicinity of the equator *De Gouden Buys* parted company with the small fleet to which it belonged. Before it had followed its solo course for long, it was becalmed in the doldrums. As each long day faded into the next, the crew grew weaker and weaker. Without a supply of fresh food and its essential vitamin content, scurvy took its inevitable toll and one by one the men began to die.

Finally, a breeze sprang up to fill the sails . . . but then it gathered to gale force and snapped the main masts before the sails could be trimmed. With most of the crew so near death that they were unable to man the ship (the captain himself by this stage was so weak that he could issue orders only from his bed), *De Gouden Buys* floundered off the coast near the mouth of the Berg River.

Of the dozen men who had not yet succumbed to sickness, seven managed to row ashore to seek help, but the lack of fresh water and food in the Sandveld created further obstacles. For a month or more they roamed the harsh, sandy scrubland of the interior, eating berries and the occasional tortoise or hare. At one stage a group of Khoikhoi came to their rescue,

De Gouden Buys, *its course set for doom.*

but the sailors, believing themselves to be captured by cannibals, so infuriated their hosts with their hostility that they were once again abandoned to their awful fate.

Hunger, thirst and exhaustion weeded their number down to two, each wandering bewildered and alone. Finally, one man was found by a Khoi hunting party and word was taken to the Castle at the Cape; the other was rescued by one of the vessels sent to the aid of the stricken *De Gouden Buys*. Aboard this ghostly ship only one man still lived, but he died the day after being transferred to the vessel that had come to his rescue. Only two men had been able to survive the terrible last voyage of *De Gouden Buys*.

---

stronghold of both San and Khoikhoi, and in fact it was to check their cattle rustling that a military outpost (or picket) was first established here. Many of the caves in the surrounding hills are still marked by well-preserved rock paintings, typically done in red. In 1889 a spectacular pass was constructed to the summit of the Piketberg range, where orchards and fields were cultivated at a lonely mountain hamlet. Running through the middle of the range is Kapteinskloof, where wheat, oranges, vineyards, vegetables and fynbos grow beneath the heavily pleated sandstone crags. On the south-west side of the range a dirt road meanders up a long kloof, to emerge eventually in a cul-de-sac at Goedverwacht, a farming mission station started by Rhenish missionaries soon after the one at Wuppertal.

ABOVE *The low relief of farmlands inland from Paternoster.* BELOW *A field of west coast flowers, backed by blue sea and sky.*

---

aground in 1910, it was carrying a cargo of red wine that stained the surrounding sea crimson. Barrels of wine that were washed up intact were cause for great celebration once customs officials had left the area.

10 Inland via Piketberg

Directly inland from Paternoster is Piketberg, enfolded by mountains like so many other secluded hamlets and fertile farmlands. Off

the main road between Velddrif and Piketberg, near the village of Aurora, is a beacon referred to on maps as the 'North Terminal of De la Cailles' Arc of the Meridian'. At this spot in the mid-1700s the French astonomer De la Cailles ended his surveying of the lines of longitude. By a combination of astrological observations and surveying techniques, he attempted to determine the precise shape of the earth.

The mountains around Piketberg were long the

THINGS TO DO

Angling
The main angling fish along this coastline is the galjoen, which has a daily bag limit. Overfishing and damage to nursery grounds in estuaries have severely depleted the numbers of this and other angling fish. Both rocky beaches and points and sandy surf conditions are good for fishing, while snoek is taken mainly from boats.

Beachcombing and shelling
There are few places for good beachcombing along this coast, as either the areas are too rocky, or the beaches are strewn thick with kelp and black mussel shells. The practised eye can usually find a small bay that acts as a natural trap for shells, with one such place just south of the tidal pool at Lambert's Bay.

Birdwatching
There are many pans in the area where waterfowl and waders congregate, but Velorevlei is undoubtedly the best place to watch birds in the area. Flamingos will be found wherever there is shallow, brackish water and pelicans can usually be seen on the deeper stretches of permanent water. Most of the waders are summer migrants, and include some terns, curlews, plover species, godwits and greenshanks, most of which are seen at Velorevlei. Throughout the year you can see coots, herons and egrets, and various ducks and geese. The backwaters at Velddrif are also rich in bird life.

Boardsailing
Lambert's Bay and Elands Bay are the best places for boardsailing, while Britannia Bay is also a popular sailing spot. The long stretches of beach from Elands Bay to Laaiplek are not easily accessible and the landowners at Velorevlei do not encourage watersports in the area.

Boat trips
New Year cruises have become a custom at Lambert's Bay and they can be arranged through the museum or factory management. At Port Owen yachts, dinghies and canoes may be hired, and sunset cruises are also available here.

Camping and caravanning
There are two caravan and camp sites at Lambert's Bay, one at Elands Bay, two at Laaiplek and one at Tietiesbaai in the Cape Columbine Nature Reserve. Inland there are caravan and camp sites at Clanwilliam in the Ramskop Nature Reserve, at Citrusdal (and at the Baths, a hot spring on the Olifants River), a basic camp site at Wuppertal, and a camp and caravan site at Algeria in the

Fish type	Season	Best area	Best bait
Dassie	All year	Paternoster — Tietiesbaai in rocky gullies	Worms, shrimps, chokka, mussels, redbait
Elf	Sept — May	Shallow surf in large bays and along beach surf breaks	Squid, live bait, spoons and lures
Galjoen	April — Sept	Rocky cliffs and points throughout the area	White and black mussels, redbait, worms
Hottentot	All year	Deep or shallow water in bays	Redbait, shrimps, worms, mussels
Kabeljou	Sept — May	Rocky points and beaches	Sardines, squid, worms, prawns
Sharks	Sept — May	Open water behind breakers in bays	Large live bait, chokka, sardines
White steenbras	May — Sept	Shallow surf in bays (e.g. Elands Bay)	White and black mussels, prawns, worms

shadow of the Cederberg, where permits can be obtained to camp at Ribboksvlei on the Pakhuis Pass. Contact local municipalities or the Department of Environment Affairs for further information.

Canoeing
The Berg River is the obvious place to canoe, where paddlers can set out from Velddrif, or start further upstream and finish at the Velddrif bridge; paddling further downstream towards the river mouth is dangerous as a large fishing fleet berths there.

Diving
Rock lobster diving is one of the most popular activities among summer visitors here. The best spots are at Elands Bay in the kelp beds near the factory or at Baboon Point in good weather, at Paternoster around the rocky shore, and at Tietiesbaai. Note that there is a marine sanctuary in St Helena Bay from near the mouth of the Berg River to Shell Bay Point (which is situated towards the eastern edge of Brittania Bay).

Diving is restricted so check with the Department of Environment Affairs before taking to the water.

Drives and viewsites
Numerous drives offer the opportunity to explore the immediate area or far afield. The mountain drives are particularly interesting, and include the exciting gravel road from Algeria, past Krakadou Peaks to Clanwilliam; the Pakhuis Pass from Clanwilliam to Wuppertal (but beware of the clay surface after rains); the dizzy Middelberg and Buffelshoek passes from Citrusdal over the Kouebokkeveld Mountains; and the scenic Kapteinskloof road through the Piketberg range. Plan your trip well before setting out as these are isolated regions.

Golf
Clanwilliam and Lambert's Bay both have nine-hole golf courses. Contact the local municipalities for details.

Horseriding
There is a riding club for children at Lambert's Bay. Contact the museum for details.

Libraries
For information on the public library in Velddrif, contact the municipality.

Museums
SANDVELD MUSEUM. Church Street, Lambert's Bay: Exhibits include a fine collection of tools, weapons, clothes and furniture from the area; there is a splendid wild flower garden in front of the building.
PIKETBERG MUSEUM. High Street: A good collection of local historical exhibits.

Powerboating
Powerboats can be launched in Lambert's Bay where waterskiing is possible but the harbour area is small. Clanwilliam Dam has a boat club and slipway in the Ramskop Nature Reserve, situated next to the camp site.

Shipwrecks
Although there have been numerous wrecks along the rocky coastline of St Helena Bay and off Cape Columbine, nothing other than the remains of small fishing boats can be seen.

Surfing
Elands Bay is one of the best surf spots in the country but it works well only in a big swell with south-east wind. When conditions are right a large tube breaks between the hotel and fish factory, but onto a shallow ledge.

The rocky coastline from Stompneusbaai to Tietiesbaai has many point breaks that work under varying conditions: they may be very good or simply unrideable.

Swimming
Lambert's Bay's large tidal pool (south of the town) provides an excellent spot for swimming.

A small beach just north of the Berg mouth is sheltered and usually calm. Elands Bay, Britannia Bay and Tietiesbaai all have sheltered beaches with a wonderfully sheltered cove at Tietiesbaai.

Inland of this stretch of coast are several pleasant swimming spots. At Wuppertal there are fresh mountain pools in a kloof behind the town; there is a rock pool at Algeria in the Cederberg; and the Baths (Citrusdal) there is a hot spring.

Tennis
Use of the tennis courts at Lambert's Bay can be arranged through the municipality.

Walks
It is possible to stroll around all of the coastal towns and villages but Paternoster is perhaps the most picturesque of all.

There are also short walks throughout the mountain areas, but longer hikes should be well planned.

Yachting
Port Owen marina offers the best facilities for yachts and access to the favourite sailing area of St Helena Bay. Sailing on Clanwilliam Dam can be arranged through the boat club in the Ramskop Nature Reserve. It is also possible to launch yachts in the harbour at Lambert's Bay.

INFORMATION
- Citrusdal Municipality, PO Box 57, Citrusdal 7340. Tel 02662=81
- Clanwilliam Municipality, 2A Voortrekker St, Clanwilliam 8135. Tel 02682=215
- Lambert's Bay Municipality, Church St, Lambert's Bay 8130. Tel 026732=9
- National Sea Rescue Institute, Station 4, Saldanha Bay. Tel 02281=41726
- Sandveld Museum, Church St, Lambert's Bay 8130. Tel 026732=439
- SA Tourism Board, Piazza Level, Golden Acre, Cape Town 8001. Tel 021=216274
- Velddrif-Laaiplek Municipality, Voortrekker Rd, Velddrif 7365. Tel 022882=12

Nearest AA Office
- AA House, 7 Martin Hammerschlag Way, Foreshore, Cape Town 8001. Tel 021=211550

A saga of sea, sand and nature's splendour

BEHIND ITS MODEST FAÇADE of flat, windswept landscape, the Saldanha-Langebaan coastal area hides unimaginable riches for the modern-day voyager to discover. The perfect natural harbour of Saldanha Bay, where the ample harvests of the sea are landed, is channelled at its south end into the narrow length of Langebaan Lagoon. Left by retreating oceans of long ago, this is now home to countless sea birds of all descriptions. Along its shore a wilderness area has been reclaimed where wildlife might flourish undisturbed by the hand of man.

For the holiday-maker Saldanha-Langebaan offers sandy white beaches for sunbathing, clear warm water for swimming, sailing and sports, and long leisurely days in which to explore the area's rich natural history.

1 Jacobsbaai

Fishing is the main attraction at this pretty, secluded bay, where small rowing boats are moored in the shallow water. From the rocks on either side of the tiny harbour fishermen can cast into perfect breakers for their prey. The protected bay and its fishing village are reached by a gravel road which turns off the R45 between Saldanha and Vredenburg.

2 Danger Bay

The picturesque approach to Danger Bay is via the coastal route from Jacobsbaai, a fairly poor quality gravel road affording glimpses of beautiful, secluded beaches and rocky outcrops. At the higher spots old, dilapidated blockhouses can be seen. Danger Bay's long, white, sandy beach ends abruptly at its south end where a barbed wire fence demarcates South African Defence Force property.

3 Vredenburg-Saldanha

If you stand at Hoedjieskop above the town of Saldanha, it is easy to imagine a procession of tall-masted square-riggers, manned by the weary crews of long ago, entering the bay between the heads. To bring you back to the present, however, is the long finger of the iron ore jetty across the way, enclosing the beautiful Hoedjiesbaai on your left.

Saldanha Bay was named as the result of a misunderstanding. In 1503 the Castilian navigator Antonio de Saldanha entered the present Table Bay on his way to India, and named it Agoada de Saldanha (Saldanha's watering place). A century later the Dutchman Joris van Spilbergen mistakenly applied the name to the more northerly bay and gave Table Bay its present name.

Vredenburg, which shares a municipality with Saldanha, also earned its name in an interesting fashion. Originally this was the scene of a bitter quarrel between neighbours over their rights to a water source; when a church was built at the site in 1875, peace finally came to the settlement and it was named Vredenburg (town of peace).

The landscape surrounding Saldanha can appear flat and dull, but the seascape more than makes up for it. The climate too is pleasant, with

The distinctive markings of the Cape gannet, a voracious feeder along the west coast.

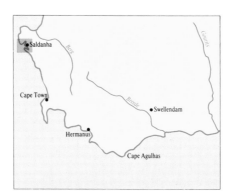

mild winters and temperate summers. Water-sports are a major attraction, with Hoedjiesbaai offering good, safe bathing and waterskiing, and Saldanha Bay ideal sailing conditions (an annual yachting regatta attracts hundreds of entries from all over the country).

A good quality gravel road leads 13 km from Saldanha past the iron ore jetty round to Langebaan, giving access to secluded beaches

BELOW *A view across the tranquil waters of the lagoon at Churchhaven.*

nestling among the rocks and perfect for sunbathing, fishing and strolling.

Saldanha, with its safe natural harbour, is in fact one of the great centres of the fishing industry, and a good place to land the rich and varied catches off the west coast. The main reason its early development as a major commercial harbour was hampered was the lack of fresh water, alleviated since the Second World War by piping water from the Berg River.

Today the area has factories for canning pilchards and anchovies, manufacturing fishmeal, preparing rock lobsters for export and processing seaweed for agar-agar. It also has a firm naval tradition, with a base for training recruits as well as a Military Academy (linked to Stellenbosch University) where graduates qualify with degrees in military science.

4 Langebaan

The resort of Langebaan has a holiday air, especially in spring when the landscape is carpeted in colourful wild flowers, especially the brilliant vygies, gazanias, buttercups and forget-me-nots. Separated by a strip of white sand from the blue of the lagoon, it lies at the head of the lagoon, at the point where it merges with Saldanha Bay. Opposite it are the islands of Meeu and Skaap,

partially blocking the channel.

Steady winds and sheltered waters make the lagoon a yachtsman's paradise. The beach, with its firm sand, is ideal for boat and dinghy launching and for anchoring small powerboats. On the lagoon side of Langebaan is the Langebaan Yacht Club where keel boats can moor in the lagoon estuary. It is strange to see yachts lying stern to the wind, or even broadside to the wind when the current is flowing with the tide. This current can often flow at up to five or six knots, in and out of the lagoon.

For many board and catamaran sailors Langebaan is a favourite launching place. Fresh winds from the south on most summer days guarantee thrills and spills for newcomers and the more experienced alike. Their bright sails and the white spume behind the high-speed catamarans add to the colourful picture.

The South African Naval Rescue Base SAS *Flamingo* is based at Langebaan and crash boats can be seen moored to the naval jetty.

The permanent population of Langebaan is small, connected mainly with the fishing and oyster-shell industries. The latter is based on deposits of some 30-million tons of oyster shells on the bed of the lagoon, in some places up to 7 m deep. The reason for the death of the oyster colonies many centuries ago remains a mystery (although it could possibly be attributed to a change in water temperature); however, the shells are now put to good use in the making of lime and poultry feed.

5 Langebaan National Park

The proclamation in 1985 of Langebaan Lagoon as a national park was the first major step in protecting the area's wealth of natural life. The plan is to acquire more land and extend the present area (some 6 000 ha, including the islands of Malgas, Jutten, Marcus and Skaap). The National Parks Board is charged with the delicate task of maintaining areas in the park for recreation (marked by buoys strung across the lagoon), while allowing nature to take its course unhindered by

AN OYSTER GRAVEYARD NO LONGER

Langebaan Lagoon guards a strange secret: it has long been the eerie graveyard of millions of oysters. Now, thanks to the ingenuity of one man, live oysters have been successfully reintroduced to adjacent Saldanha Bay, under conditions that simulate those of the lagoon.

Engineer Philip Steyn acquired a 35 ha area next to Saldanha's iron ore handling plant for aquaculture. The dam, with its sandy bottom (ideal for growing shellfish), is fed by a 2 m pipe that allows the water to flow in and out with the tide, keeping the shellfish fed by the nutrient-rich Benguela Current. The temperature is also kept at an optimum level because, even at its deepest point, the tidal dam reaches a mere 8 m.

As a natural progression from mussel-farming, oysters and clams were introduced to a different area of the dam. Although still in an experimental and research stage, it appears the species are flourishing.

The oysters are not an indigenous variety but were imported initially from the Channel Islands, off the north-western coast of France. These exotic oysters seem, however, to thrive in the local conditions.

Shellfish-farming is beset by a number of problems. Pollution has to be carefully monitored, especially with regard to red tides, which can cause the deaths of vast numbers of marine animals. This phenomenon occurs when red-pigmented phytoplankton (the tiniest plant form) bloom densely and colour the sea red. If ingested, they make mussels toxic, and these in turn attack, often fatally, the nervous system if eaten by humans. No trace of this has yet been found at Seafarm, but should there be any evidence of a red tide, the inlet can be shut off immediately.

Shellfish also require meticulous handling and as all the produce is sold fresh nationwide (although freezing and canning are being considered), packaging and dispatch calls for speed and care.

The work done at Seafarm is fascinating to expert and layman alike. Not only do the University of Cape Town and the Department of Environment Affairs maintain close links and monitor progress at the dam but visitors are also welcome.

Shellfish-farming at Saldanha thrives in the rich west coast waters.

man in the wilderness areas now associated with endangered fauna and flora.

The lagoon is 16 km long and 4,5 km wide, narrowing to a channel opposite Langebaan before joining Saldanha Bay, and edged by marshland, dunes and beaches. The peninsula of land formed separates the lagoon from the Atlantic Ocean in the west.

To the casual observer the shores of the lagoon appear quite empty but on closer inspection a myriad examples of life can be discovered. The mud, said to contain some 60-million bacteria in every cubic centimetre, is one of the world's most populous life-supporting areas: it oozes with countless molluscs, crustaceans and other mud-living organisms. What makes this possible is the

LEFT *Spring blooms brilliantly in the Postberg Nature Reserve.*

A strip of white-flecked blue sea separates the rocky shores of Malgaseiland from the gently sloped rise of the mainland.

fact that the lagoon is entirely marine, with little or no fresh water to change the salinity and disrupt the shore life. In turn this life forms the staple diet for innumerable wading birds, many of them migrants from Arctic breeding grounds, come to feed on this giant larder. The lagoon is thus one of the finest sites for birdwatching in the south-western Cape.

The islands of Marcus, Malgas, Jutten and Skaap are particularly rich in bird life: the first three are home to many thousands of jackass penguins and gannets, while Skaapeiland is the largest known breeding colony of kelp gulls in southern Africa. For some time the bird population of Marcus was threatened when the island was connected to the mainland by a wall, which offered protection to ships at anchor. This meant that rodents and other predators could simply follow the causeway to raid the island; finally, man stepped in and built a *muismuur* (mouse wall) to guard the island against invaders. Today the islands are wilderness areas that cannot be visited except by special arrangement with the Parks Board.

Fish life in the lagoon is not as prolific as the bird life, possibly because of the clarity of the water and the temperature. However, skates, rays and sand sharks can often be seen in shallow water. The latter have interesting feeding habits: they 'blow' sand prawns and worms out of the mud by flapping their 'wings'. Smaller fish such as gobies,

A SUNKEN TREASURE-TROVE

In the early 18th century a tragic shipwreck at Saldanha Bay deposited an elusive, and considerable cache of treasure beneath the turbulent sea which to this day still lures — and taunts — fortune-hunters and salvage experts.

It was 3 April 1702 when the Dutch East Indiaman *Meresteijn* sighted land. This was welcome indeed because after the long voyages the crew was suffering badly from scurvy, and the captain was thus keen to take on fresh water and food. Once he had positively identified the landfall as Saldanha, the captain decided to enter the bay.

With night approaching, lookouts were posted in the rigging and the forecastle. The wind came up and the course was set between Jutteneiland and South Head. Unfortunately, when the ship was to head up more into the wind to pass through the narrow channel, it did not respond properly and the captain panicked, ordering the anchor to be dropped. But the anchor did not hold in the strong wind. The chief mate, up in the rigging, shouted to cut the anchor and sail, as he felt sure that this way the ship could be brought under control.

While the captain hesitated, debating with his officers what to do, the ship drifted to the south-west of the island where the sea is at its most furious. Here the *Meresteijn* was pounded onto the rocks, its stern breaking away and the rest of the vessel being smashed apart within minutes.

Most of the crew, including the captain, perished in the icy waters, as did two women passengers and their five children. The few survivors were marooned on Jutteneiland, where they constructed a raft from the wreckage. Using this the boatswain and a sailor volunteer made a daring crossing to the mainland to go in search of help.

The Company, whose first concern was to salvage the sizeable fortune in the stern of the *Meresteijn*, dispatched a vessel to recover the treasure . . . and the castaways. Several attempts to recover the treasure failed; it had sunk where the surf was heaviest. Later another bid was made to retrieve it, this time by commissioning an English salvage expert, John Lethbridge, who had invented a diving bell — actually a wooden barrel! After six weeks and repeated efforts he too was forced to abandon the fruitless quest.

The treasure from the *Meresteijn* remained guarded by heavy seas until 1972 when two brothers, Reginald and William Dodds, with the aid of modern diving equipment, succeeded in recovering 1 300 silver coins, as well as chinaware and statuettes. Some of the coins form part of a display in the South African Cultural History Museum in Cape Town. A bronze cannon was recovered at a later date. It is believed this wreck will still yield more treasure.

A LAND OF PLENTY

There is little evidence in the bleak, windswept landscape around Saldanha and Langebaan today to suggest that this was once lush forest and grassland, teeming with wildlife and vibrant with the twitter of birds. However, the wealth of fossils excavated in the past few decades has led scientists to just this conclusion.

Some of the most important finds were made on the farm Elandsfontein, east of Langebaan. In 1944 a Dr J G Smit of Cape Town reported finding a few fossils here to eminent Cape Town palaeontologist Dr R Singer, who realised their full significance only seven years later. The finds from the extensive excavations that followed are now housed in the South African Museum in Cape Town.

Fossils collected represent over 200 vertebrate and invertebrate species living between 4- and 5-million years ago (Pliocene epoch). This gives remarkable insight into the once abundant wildlife in this area. The formation and subsequent melting of the Atlantic icecap resulted in a dramatic change in the level of the sea. It was substantially higher during the Pliocene, making islands of the high granite areas around Langebaanweg and Saldanha. Here, according to the fossil remains, were the breeding grounds of sea birds that today breed only on sub-Antarctic islands.

The mammalian fossils found belong to a later epoch, the Pleistocene (60 000-150 000 years ago), when the area enjoyed a warmer climate. These represent some fifty mammal species, about half of which are extinct, including a sabre-toothed cat (*Megantereon gracile*) and a short-necked giraffid (*Libytherium olduvaiense*). They indicate the presence of a large watering hole, or what might have been a series of vleis.

Associated with these fauna, but of even greater significance, was the find in 1953 of the remains of a human skull and jaw. Dubbed Saldanha man, he belonged to the Early Stone Age of southern Africa and represents the earliest recorded hominid remains to be found south of the Orange River. Saldanha man, with a thick-boned, heavy-browed skull, bears some resemblance to Europe's Neanderthal man. Stone artefacts found in and around the same area record the primitive cultural development of man in the Early Stone Age.

Man's arrival in the south-western Cape and his own development ironically accelerated the deterioration of the natural environment. Although initially he made little impact, later, with the discovery of fire, the local ecosystems underwent enormous changes. When Khoi herders arrived in the area some 2 000 years ago, veld burning coupled with overgrazing put further pressure on the environment.

But it is later man who proved to be the worst culprit of all, finally exterminating many of the indigenous mammals and, through carelessness and shortsightedness, contributing to the eradication of the earlier natural vegetation.

ABOVE RIGHT *A flotilla of yachts at rest on the still waters of Saldanha Bay, one of the most popular venues on the west coast for racing and cruising alike.*

'A CANOPY OF BIRDS'

'All of a sudden there arose from the whole surface of the island an impenetrable cloud, which formed ... an immense canopy, or rather a sky, composed of birds of every species and all colours...'

So wrote 18th-century French naturalist François le Vaillant of a visit to Malgaseiland (gannets island) in Saldanha Bay. Today the bird life remains extraordinarily rich and varied, thanks to the Saldanha-Langebaan area's high diversity of coastal habitats (salt marshes, open sand and mud flats, long dune-backed beaches and rocky shores), which support all manner of flora and fauna.

Jackass penguins put on a formal front on Malgaseiland.

formation, pursuing shoals of fish. The ordered control of the flight is disrupted when the shoal surfaces, each bird diving and darting underwater to gorge itself on the fish. Even after its successive spells of diving underwater, the cormorant remains capable of normal flight.

Gannets also hunt from the air, diving with astonishing speed as soon as a fish is spotted. With their creamy plumage edged in black, they make a beautiful sight against the summer sky. They, too, nest in great colonies on the islands.

The islands' jackass penguin population is gradually recovering after the onslaught of oil pollution in the last decade. This is not the first time these endearingly comical creatures, so clumsy on land but so at ease and graceful in water, have been threatened by man's activities. In the 1840s a brief guano rush stripped Malgaseiland of a 10 m-thick layer of guano, the bird droppings used as fertiliser. Without this layer, there were no convenient breeding burrows for the penguins and their numbers dropped drastically. The penguin population also suffered earlier this century when millions of their eggs, regarded at the time as a delicacy, were removed. Today, to protect the birds, the islands are closed to the public.

A few birds of prey, especially buzzards and kestrels, are also found around Saldanha and Langebaan. They can be seen hovering at great heights, or resting on posts by the roadside.

As many as 55 000 waders of more than twenty species frequent the area in summer, most of them from the Arctic north. These birds are reputed to consume 150 tons of shrimps, snails and worms annually. Among the countless waders and shore birds to congregate here are curlew sandpipers, terns, blacksmith plovers, turnstones, red-beaked black oystercatchers, sacred ibises, flamingos, herons, and, of course, gulls, those noisy scavengers common along the whole length of the western Cape coastline. A familiar sight is the large kelp, or southern blackbacked gull, swooping down on shell creatures exposed by the tide.

The five islands north of Langebaan Lagoon (Skaap, Meeu, Marcus, Malgas and Jutten) support large colonies of sea birds, totalling about a quarter of a million. Especially distinctive are the cormorants, which can be seen flying in vast 'V'

klipfish, silversides and pipefish are also found in the lagoon.

6 Postberg Nature Reserve

This nature reserve, which has recently been attached to the Langebaan National Park, is situated on the northernmost accessible part of the peninsula between the lagoon and the Atlantic Ocean; at the tip of the isthmus is Donkergat, a restricted South African Defence Force area. (From the sea near the mouth of the lagoon you can see all that remains of the once busy whaling station here − a jumble of rusting iron and abandoned buildings.) Throughout the reserve are beautiful views across the lagoon and to the west out to sea; but note that at the SADF security fence, cameras are prohibited.

Game can be spotted in the reserve, including antelope, zebra, wildebeest, ostriches, black-backed jackals, bat-eared foxes, Cape wildcats and many smaller animals, snakes and tortoises. Plans are afoot at the moment to reintroduce the indigenous Cape mountain zebra to this reserve. As a bonus for the birdwatchers, proud birds of prey perch casually on posts, quite undeterred by the occasional passing car.

The National Parks Board has laid out a trail, with an overnight camp, in the reserve. This is most popular in the spring when the whole area is a riot of colour, equal to Namaqualand's flower display far further up the west coast.

Of historic interest in the reserve is the old garrison of Oupos, which was once the scene of bitter fighting between French and Dutch for control of this spot, which was the site of a freshwater spring. (Today fresh water is piped under the lagoon to the military area.)

7 Kreeftebaai

About 2,5 km after entering Postberg Nature Reserve is a gate (unlocked) on your left, the unsignposted turn-off to Kreeftebaai. This is the only access to the sea by private vehicles for the entire peninsula. Travel with caution down this road as it is in very bad condition. You pass several private (locked) entrance gates, and at the end reach a small parking area right on the rocky beach. Just offshore is Vondelingeiland. Although the breakers pound in from the Atlantic the more intrepid divers can reap rich rewards of rock lobster and perlemoen from this area, hence the name Kreeftebaai.

8 Kraalbaai and Preekstoel

South of Postberg Nature Reserve is Kraalbaai, where in places the cliffs drop almost directly into the lagoon. This sheltered bay has mooring for keel boats from Langebaan Yacht Club and a limited number for visiting yachts, and is the perfect setting for boating and waterskiing. The less energetic can sunbathe and picnic, and occasionally cool off in the water.

The National Parks Board has demarcated a parking area (with toilets) and from here sturdy wooden steps lead down to the shore. Parks Board officials also have a small office in the bay and are planting bush to halt the soil erosion caused by landslides from the cliffs.

Preekstoel, just beyond Kraalbaai, offers the best of both worlds: shelter and wind. It is the latter that makes this a boardsailor's paradise; on sunny summer days the bright sails of the many boards can be seen reaching across the lagoon, driven by steady southerly winds.

The steps to the water's edge lead from a slightly smaller parking area than at Kraalbaai (also with toilets and rubbish bins).

9 Sestienmylstrand

This is a wild and beautiful stretch of coast, with the horizon always misty from the thundering surf. Aptly if prosaically named (sixteen-mile beach), it is ideal for walking and especially rewarding for beachcombers, as the rough sea deposits all manner of flotsam and jetsam, collected into piles by National Parks Board officials who patrol the beach. The sharp-eyed might spot an ancient coin but failing this, many other less 'precious' trophies are there for the taking. A kilometre or so along the beach is the wreck of the ill-fated *Pantelis A Limos*, which foundered on the shore in thick fog in 1978.

Sestienmylstrand is a little difficult to reach, having only one access point right next to the Postberg Nature Reserve entrance. It is best to leave your car at the Kraalbaai parking area (no

Kraalbaai, reached by a flight of wooden steps, is a favourite spot for watersports.

A PIRATE'S REVENGE

Saldanha Bay, with its safe and convenient harbour, has always been well used by mariners, either for emergency repairs or as refuge from the elements. In its more colourful days, among those who frequented the bay were pirates, although for them it did not necessarily provide a safe berth.

In May 1693 a strange ship, the *Amy*, arrived in the bay. Dutch suspicions were aroused by evidence that the ship had seen naval action. The *Amy*'s captain, George Drew, first denied this and then provided a rather unsatisfactory explanation — cause enough for the Dutch to seize the ship and its crew.

The *Amy* was retained as a prize while its crew were packed off to Holland to stand trial for piracy. For the Dutch this had rather embarrassing and expensive results: when the charge of piracy could not be proved, the men were freed and Drew sued successfully for damages.

However, this was not to be the end of the story. In 1699 word was received at the Cape that English pirates had taken control of Saldanha Bay. Even more disturbing was the news that the indomitable Captain Drew was one of their number. Anxious to vindicate themselves, the Dutch then hastily dispatched two ships to Saldanha, but it was already too late. The pirates had disappeared into the night, but not before they had stripped everything of value from a Dutch ship in the bay . . . the *Amy*.

vehicles are allowed on the beach as it is protected). If you walk along the fence towards the sea, the path will become evident as you go along. Allow about 25 minutes to reach the dunes. This walk takes you through unspoilt bush and, if you are lucky, you may glimpse buck, ostriches and other animals in the nature reserve on your right.

10 Churchhaven

This pretty little village consists of a cluster of cottages on the western shore of the lagoon. Although today the settlement seems isolated, in its graveyard, attached to St Peter's Church, many headstones bear the strange names of mariners who came here from distant lands.

A walk down from the church (which affords a beautiful view both up and down the lagoon) reveals a lovely private and sheltered beach, where the white sand contrasts strongly with the deep blue of the warm water. Here seagull sounds abound and sandpipers scuttle along the beach. The small fishing boats anchored offshore are testimony to a time-honoured lifestyle: by special government permission the Churchhaven fishing community may pursue its traditional livelihood even in this restricted part of the lagoon.

The three settlements of Stofbergsfontein, Churchhaven and Schrywershoek (named for Isaq Schrijver, a 17th-century explorer) flow into one another, the lagoon to their east.

BELOW *In springtime, the Langebaan landscape is flooded with colour as the wild flowers make their brief but spectacular annual showing.*

THINGS TO DO

Angling

For sea anglers there are a number of good spots at rocky outcrops along the shoreline, including Kreeftebaai in the Postberg Nature Reserve.

Organised deep-sea trips can be arranged by contacting the local municipality or the Sea Fisheries office at Saldanha. Much of the region around Saldanha is protected reserve area and restrictions are thus firmly enforced. Sports fishermen visiting the Langebaan National Park should contact the Parks Board office at Langebaan or Churchhaven for further details. Species that can be caught freely in the lagoon include kabeljou, mackerel, mullet, sharks and steentjie. Restricted species include elf, galjoen, geelbek, hottentot, leervis, white steenbras and white stumpnose.

Beachcombing and shelling

Sestienmylstrand is a beachcomber's goldmine, constantly fed by flotsam and jetsam carried onto the beach by the long Atlantic swells. Fishermen's baskets, nets, rope, buoys, and a variety of containers are commonplace. For the more discerning a large and varied shell collection is also there for the taking. Langebaan Lagoon, being sheltered, has little to offer beachcombers.

Birdwatching

Saldanha-Langebaan is exceptionally rich in bird life and as such one of the best birdwatching sites in the south-western Cape. Although the most densely populated areas — the islands of Skaap, Marcus, Malgas and Jutten — are restricted conservation areas, there is still much for the enthusiast to see. Contact the National Parks Board for details.

Boardsailing

Saldanha-Langebaan offers the best possible locations for beginners and experienced alike. Fresh breezes, shallow water, and the scant possibility for being blown offshore make the bay and lagoon a natural haven for boardsailors. There is a boardsailing club at Saldanha next to the caravan park, while at Hoedjiesbaai and Langebaan boards can be rented on the beach. The annual Western Province Dinghy and Sailboard Championships are held in April at Saldanha, with the large number of entries ensuring exciting racing. Contact the local municipality or the Western Province Sailing Association in Cape Town for details.

Boat trips

The *Big Bunny*, attached to the

Day's end on Langebaan Lagoon.

Panoramic Hotel at Langebaan, offers a cruise around the lagoon on Sunday mornings.

Bowls

The South African Transport Services Club at Spionkop welcomes visitors.

Camping and caravanning

Saldanha has a large municipal camp site right on the beach, where bungalows of various sizes can also be rented. It is advisable to book well in advance as this is a popular destination. Langebaan offers two camp sites and a holiday resort with rented accommodation. Contact the local municipalities for detailed information.

Diving

The Spionkop Underwater Club can advise on particulars and suitable locations.

Drives and viewsites

A leisurely drive around the lagoon from Saldanha to Postberg Nature Reserve is always enjoyable. Throughout the drive there are viewsites offering splendid vistas across the length and breadth of the lagoon.

Libraries

The small libraries at Saldanha, Vredenburg and Langebaan welcome temporary members. Contact the relevant municipality for details.

Powerboating

Powerboats can be launched from Saldanha Bay Yacht Club and from the beach at Langebaan. The National Parks Board controls the lagoon and a list of regulations applying to any motor-driven vessel is freely available. Staff patrol the lagoon areas and strictly enforce those regulations. Special attention is drawn to areas allocated by yellow buoys off the beach at Langebaan. These are set aside for swimmers, and no powerboats may enter, anchor or moor within their limits.

Vessels proceeding outside the Langebaan National Park should be equipped as required by the regulations regarding ships or small vessels used for sport or recreation.

Shipwrecks

Many vessels have met their end in the Saldanha-Langebaan area, but few of these are now visible. The remains of two trawlers can be seen at Hoedjiesbaai, as well as the wreck of the *Pantelis A Limos*, which foundered on the shore at Sestienmylstrand in thick fog in 1978.

Surfing

Experienced surfers can ride the breakers at Jacobsbaai, but they should be wary of the dangerous currents and undertows.

Swimming

The entire area of the Langebaan Lagoon is safe although the deeper channels of the lagoon, especially near the village of Langebaan, should be avoided because of the fast tidal currents flowing in and out of the lagoon. Close to the beach at Langebaan are areas especially demarcated for safe bathing.

Walks

The organised trail in the Postberg Nature Reserve is especially rewarding when the spring flowers are in bloom. Walkers are reminded that access to South African Defence Force property is strictly prohibited, and advised when planning a hike to take note of land ownership.

Yachting and dinghy sailing

Saldanha Bay Yacht Club and Langebaan Yacht Club have facilities for keelboat yachtsmen. Moorings are privately owned, and permission has to be obtained for overnight anchoring at the respective clubs. For dinghy and catamaran sailors the lagoon and Saldanha Bay offer superb stretches of flat water for racing and cruising alike. Dinghies can be launched from the beach for easy access to this yachting haven, with its sheltered bays and safe sandy landing spots. The Western Province Sailing Association, based in Cape Town, runs a very popular regatta here in April.

INFORMATION

- Langebaan Municipality, Bree St, Langebaan 7357.
  Tel 02287=2115
- National Parks Board, PO Box 25, Langebaan 7357.
  Tel 0020 ask for Churchhaven 15
- National Sea Rescue Institute, Saldanha Bay.
  Tel 02281=41813
- Vredenburg-Saldanha Municipality, Private Bag X12, Vredenburg 7380 or cnr Berg St and Saldanha Rd, Saldanha 7395.
  Tel 02281=41276

Nearest AA Office

- AA House, 7 Hammerschlag Way, Foreshore, Cape Town 8001.
  Tel 211550

Fish type	Season	Best area	Best bait
Galjoen	Mar-Sept	Saldanha coast	Chokka, crabs, mussels, limpets, redbait, musselworms
Hottentot	Mar-July	Saldanha coast	Redbait, mussels, musselworms, fishbait, chokka, prawns
Kabeljou	Sept-May	Langebaan Lagoon, Saldanha coast	Bloodworms, chokka, fishbait, prawns, octopus, spoons
Mackerel	Aug-June	Langebaan Lagoon, Saldanha coast	Fishbait, chokka, small spoons
Mullet	All year	Langebaan Lagoon	Fishbait, pilchards, worms, mussels
Sharks	All year	Langebaan Lagoon	Fishbait, crabs, chokka, whale or porpoise meat
Steentjie	Nov-Feb	Langebaan lagoon, Saldanha coast	Musselworms, shark meat, redbait, prawns, shrimps, vegetable matter

A chill coast charmed by summer's melting warmth

F OR A FLEETING SPELL in springtime, this stretch of Swartland coast is ablaze with flowers, a celebration of colour after the fog-wrapped days of winter. Then summer comes, and the long lonely beaches from Yzerfontein to Bloubergstrand, washed by the cold Atlantic, are flooded with fun-seekers under the hot sun.

This is a coastline that offers something for everyone: gently shelving beaches where children can splash about, great waves for the surfer and boardsailor to ride, the teeming life of countless rock pools to explore, and rocks from which generations of anglers have cast their bait into the rich waters of the Atlantic Ocean and not been disappointed.

The peace of a lonely west coast beach.

1 Yzerfontein

During the snoek run, Yzerfontein's tiny harbour throbs with life as busy boats come and go, while hundreds of gulls float patiently in the lee of the breakwater, waiting for the spoils. The harbour is overlooked by a craggy headland and just out to sea is guano-whitened Meeurots (gull rock).

Northwards, as far as the eye can see, smooth white beaches stretch, sheltered slightly from the south-easter by dunes but open to the west, and unshaded. The wide beach slopes gently to the water, with bathing safest just north of the rocks at the harbour end. Nearby, a thatched cottage overlooks a rocky bank with innumerable pools, and there are many more pools round the headland to the south, especially on the promontory called Skaapeiland. Black mussels abound, their shells littering the beaches.

Just south of Skaapeiland is Die Vleie, a sandy beach several hundred metres long, sloping rather steeply to the water. A scramble over the rocks brings you to the little inlets of Smoedbaai and De Goede se Baai. Like Die Vleie, these slope rather sharply and have a fairly powerful surf. From here, the beach runs south-east for some 18 km to a wide inlet formed by the mouth of the Modder.

Yzerfontein is a popular holiday destination. Its facilities include a caravan park, as well as toilets and drinking water.

2 The inland circuit

From Yzerfontein you can travel southwards on the coastal road (the R27), or follow the more scenic inland circuit, which takes in Darling and Mamre before rejoining the R27 just beyond Atlantis. The route is particularly attractive in spring, when the veld is carpeted with flowers.

Starting from Yzerfontein, the road passes between two old limekilns, now national monuments. Both are in excellent condition, and have been primed with shells and firewood to demonstrate the process of lime-burning. (The burnt lime was used as a plaster and also as a form of whitewash.) Continuing straight towards Darling (past the turn-off to the R27), vast, rolling wheatfields on the left contrast sharply with the natural vegetation as preserved in the Tienie Versveld Flora Reserve.

Darling itself is famed for its wild flower show held late each September, which is all the more spectacular for its extreme brevity (only a couple of days). On the outskirts of the town a gravel road on the left leads, after 8 km, to an Anglo-Boer War memorial. This is the site of the grave of Field-Cornet C B Hildebrand, killed in 1901 while fighting in General Manie Maritz's commando. Another memorial (a scaled-down replica of a British blockhouse) commemorates those of the district who have died in wars since 1914.

The road continues south through Darling, with its attractive old mission church and a number of important old homesteads, and passes close under Bobbejaanberg on the right before reaching the picturesque mission village of Mamre, with its white-walled, black-thatched cottages. Beyond this point is a long stretch of road, closely lined with trees. Some people experience discomfort or disorientation on this stretch as a flashing-light effect is produced by passing quickly and alternately through brightness and shade. The industrial and residential town of Atlantis is reached soon after this, before the road rejoins the coastal route.

3 Dasseneiland

On a piratical expedition to the Far East in 1605, the English adventurer Sir Edward Michelborne was stranded by rough seas for two days on this low-lying island off the west coast. (Apart from the modern lighthouse, the highest point is only some 10 m above sea level.) He named it for the many rock hyraxes (dassies) he saw there.

More than two centuries later, in 1876, the ship *Windsor Castle* ran onto Spout Rock, just west of Dasseneiland. The survivors were then transferred to the island to wait for help. Among the

BELOW *A scattering of houses behind the tiny harbour of Yzerfontein.*

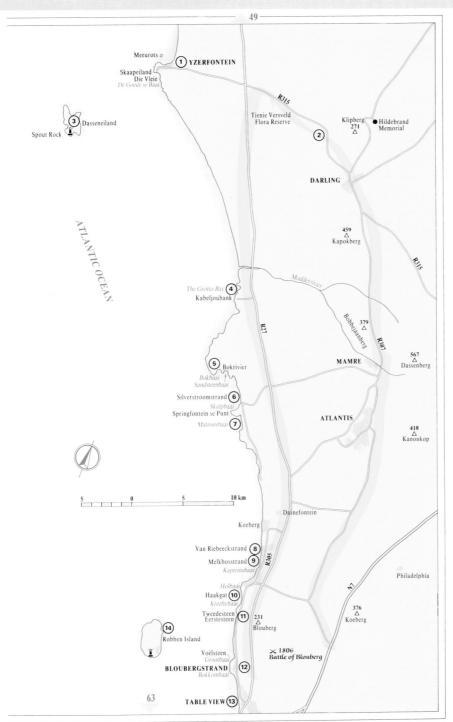

ROBBEN ISLAND CROSSING

Robben Island's historical lighthouse.

For some people, Robben Island seems tantalisingly close, and many have risen to the challenge of swimming through icy waters between the island and the mainland. On 6 December 1926, 13 people set out to swim from the island to Roggebaai on the mainland. The only one to succeed, with a time of 9 hrs 35 mins for the 13,6 km crossing, was 15-year-old Peggy Duncan. Peggy held her record for only a few days before Florrie Berndt reduced the time to 7 hrs 25 mins. Today the records for the 7 km swim between the island and Bloubergstrand have been cut to 2 hrs 20 mins for women (set by Coreen Swanepoel in 1977) and 1 hr 36 mins for men (set by Mark Edge in 1982).

The ambition of making a successful crossing to the mainland was for others — incarcerated on the island — far more pressing. There was seldom any shortage of raw materials for boatbuilding, with the island's shores often littered with debris from wrecks, but few successful escapes were made. At one point in the island's history a leper named Walsh had his boat seized by the island police who, for some reason, omitted to break it up. Walsh promptly stole it back and managed to reach the mainland, but was recognised and returned to the island. Another leper built a raft of empty barrels lashed together and successfully put to sea, but adverse currents washed him back to his launching point.

More successful was the chief of the Goringhaikona Khoikhoi, known to the authorities as Herrie, who was banished to the island in 1658, but the following year somehow managed to reach Saldanha Bay in a leaky boat. Decades later a Muslim holy man, Nureel Mobeen, was imprisoned on the island and he too made his escape — by miraculous means, according to vague legend.

passengers was Sir Theophilus Shepstone, of the Natal government, who, when asked what he did after the ship struck the rock, replied: 'I thought that I should like to die decent, and spent the time in hunting for my trousers.'

Today the island supports a large breeding population of sea birds, providing a good source of guano, used in the manufacture of fertiliser. Prominent species include Cape, bank, white-breasted and crowned cormorants, sacred ibises, kelp gulls and jackass penguins. This is also the only breeding ground in the Cape for the great white pelican. The island is administered by the Cape Provincial Administration and public access is thus restricted.

4 The Grotto Bay

A humpbacked dune, ending in a rocky 'finger', creates two sandy beaches in the bay, backed by scrubby sandhills. Often a boat or two can be seen drawn up on the sand, probably belonging to one of the few holiday cottages scattered here. Bathing in the sea is fairly safe, while north of the rocks, with their many tidal pools, is a stretch of gently shelving beach at the estuary of the usually dry Modderrivier. The course of the river is marked by a growth of indigenous, woody bush and Bokbaai vygies. Bird life, in addition to gulls and terns, includes Cape robins and guineafowl, while black mussels are plentiful along the shore.

Access to the Grotto Bay is via Kabeljoubank, a rather bleak, rocky promontory which nonetheless offers a varied carpet of shells and a

A WONDERLAND OF WILD FLOWERS

The bloom of spring in the Darling area.

In spring, the 20 ha Tienie Versveld Flora Reserve is awash with the multicoloured blooms of the reawakening land. Dedicated to the preservation of the region's natural vegetation (you will find no trees or large shrubs here), the site was donated by a local farmer, Martinus Versveld, and is administered by the National Botanic Gardens of South Africa.

About seventy species are represented here, including the predominantly blue *Babiana* species, with their strongly ribbed, slightly hairy leaves; the tiny *Lachenalia*, with their richly coloured and variegated flowers; and the creamy white or yellow spiked chincherinchees — perhaps so named for the sound made when the shiny flowerstalks rub together. Some of the species are well equipped to survive poor conditions: they have large bulbs that store so much nutriment that if the bulbs are removed from the ground at an early flowering time, the flowers will continue to open for several months. Another example of a well-adapted plant is the sundew (*Drosera*), which under normal circumstances obtains its supply of nitrogen from insects it traps and digests by a fluid secretion from the sticky tentacles on its leaves and stem. But even without this specialised source of food, it can continue to grow in soil so poor no other plant can survive.

The reserve lies along the road between Yzerfontein and Darling, and is entered by crossing one of two stiles across the roadside fence. From here a network of paths takes the visitor to all corners.

great number of rock pools to explore. To reach Kabeljoubank, take the gravel road from the R27 (opposite another road signposted for the farms Modderrivier and Pampoenvlei). From the car park walk north to the Grotto Bay.

5 Bokbaai and Sandsteenbaai

For close on two centuries, Bokbaai has been graced by a classic, gabled Cape Dutch dwelling standing on a shelf of rock almost within reach of the spray. This sheltered (but virtually unshaded), south-facing bay offers fairly safe bathing and outstanding views towards Table Mountain. Adjacent Sandsteenbaai, where the Bokrivier enters the sea (although it rarely flows), has a wider strip of beach between rocky little peninsulas, but is less deeply sheltered than Bokbaai and the beach shelves more sharply. Both bays can be reached by a jeep track from the R27, or by walking north from Silwerstroomstrand.

6 Silwerstroomstrand

This beach, with its wide, shimmering stretch of sand and inland dune curving away to the north and west, is ideal for long walks north to Sandsteenbaai and Bokbaai. To the south a track leads over the rocky point called Wintersteen, where there are numerous rock pools, to reach Skulpbaai (shell bay), which does indeed have a fair sprinkling of shells.

ABOVE RIGHT *The stern lines of Koeberg power station seen through the haze of sunset.*
BELOW *The timeless Cape Dutch home in perfect seclusion on the shores of Bokbaai.*

THE BATTLE OF BLOUBERG

In the early 19th century Melkbosstrand (or Losperdsbaai, as it was then known) was the scene of a dramatic turning point in South African history. Here the Battle of Blouberg was fought and its outcome resulted in the Cape reverting from Dutch to British control.

On 6 January 1806, watched over by the guns of Royal Navy battleships, British longboats loaded with soldiers rowed for the Cape shore. The Cape governor, Lieutenant-General J W Janssens, had a sorrowful force at his disposal — a motley pack of German mercenaries, Dutch regulars, French marines, as well as some civilians and slaves. These he drew up in line at the south end of Blouberg Hill and waited to be attacked. The British, outnumbering the defenders by about two to one, proceeded to fix bayonets and charge. The mercenaries were the first to break ranks and flee, followed closely by the Dutch regulars, with the others staying to fight it out at close quarters before they, too, were forced to retreat.

Janssens now withdrew to Rietvlei to reassemble his forces. From there he moved to Hottentots Holland, intending to cut off supplies from the interior, but on 10 January, the commander at the Castle, Count C von Prophalow, signed a deed of surrender at Papendorp (Woodstock) and Janssens, realising that further resistance would be futile, capitulated a few days later. The Cape was once again in British hands.

The seaside resort of Silwerstroomstrand is most popular with residents of nearby Mamre and Atlantis. Its facilities include a caravan park, camp sites, a restaurant, and — overlooking an artificial tidal pool for bathing and a toddlers' pool — lawned and shaded picnic areas. The safest area for sea bathing is at the resort end of the beach, but there is no shade and little shelter.

7 Matroosbaai

Just under 2 km of white, sandy beach are enfolded by the promontories of Springfontein se Punt to the north and Matroospunt to the south. A strong surf and backwash at most times make swimming inadvisable for all but the strongest swimmer, but the beach is an attractive setting for walks, and there are many interesting rock pools at both ends. A variety of shells can also be found, especially in the rock gullies, with black mussel predominating. Parts of the beach are backed by dunes bound by reeds and indigenous bush.

To reach Matroosbaai turn left onto a gravel road immediately after passing the entrance booms to Silwerstroomstrand resort. After about 3 km a track on your right leads towards the beach. The road continues to a quarry, and then on towards the Koeberg nuclear power station, but access to other beaches is difficult.

Koeberg itself is completely fenced off but the public may visit the information centre and viewing platform at the station. Attempts are being made to preserve the indigenous vegetation and even reintroduce animal species (like the bontebok) that once occurred here naturally. In addition, an aquarium at the station shows the typical west coast marine life and the effect on that life of the return of sea water warmed after cooling Koeberg's generators. (Local scientists also monitor these effects to ensure the protection of the marine environment.)

8 Van Riebeeckstrand

The solitude of this stretch of gently shelving beach contrasts oddly with the great grey bulk of the Koeberg power station that marks its northern limit. Smallish, scrub-covered dunes offer slight shelter from the wind, while inland at the northern end, a swampy zone supports a fine growth of bulrushes (*Typha latifolia*). For the rest, the dune vegetation consists principally of the alien rooikrans (*Acacia cyclops*).

The views from the beach are particularly fine. Above the line of dunes the roofs of the houses of Duinefontein peep out, and beyond them Blouberg Hill looms. More dramatic are the views of Table Mountain and the Twelve Apostles to the south, set beyond long lines of white breakers.

Bathing at Van Riebeeckstrand is reasonably safe. Otherwise, there is ample scope for long, long walks, a little casual shell-collecting (mostly black mussel with a sprinkling of white mussel) and some birdwatching (black oystercatchers, Hartlaub's gulls and blacksmith plovers.

There is a tarred parking area at the southern end of the beach, and toilets and tap water.

9 Melkbosstrand

A small but pretty inlet known as Kapteinsbaai lies just north of the main Melkbos beach and is bounded to the north by a rocky outcrop called Slabbert se Klippe, where there is a good variety of shells, with black mussel predominating. This and the main beach slope gently, with only small waves, so that bathing is fairly safe — if chilly, as it is along the entire west coast. The beach offers little shelter but at the southern end is a large lawned area, planted with shady trees and studded with braai sites and picnic tables. There are change-rooms and toilets nearby. In addition, Melkbosstrand has a caravan park, as well as a hotel, shops and restaurants.

This is a happy seaside resort, to be enjoyed to the full, which is precisely what happens every Tweede Nuwejaar (2 January) when devotees of *boeresport* pack the sandy beach for the now-traditional trials of strength and skill.

10 Holbaai, Haakgat and Kreeftebaai

These three adjoining beaches all have a delightfully secluded air. The first, Holbaai, is a

The classic view of Table Mountain across a foamy expanse from Bloubergstrand.

long curve of sand bounded by the rocky outcrops of Bontkop in the north and Haakgat in the south, both with interesting rock pools. The beach, tinged pink by shell fragments, is backed by a fair growth of indigenous coastal fynbos, but this unfortunately is being invaded by alien plants. It slopes very steeply (slightly less to the north) and the surf is fairly strong. There might be some shelter among the rows of low dunes, but there is no shade. Holbaai, which has a car park and braai sites, is little frequented and thus remarkably free of litter.

Haakgat is bounded on the sea side by rocks, where there are many tidal pools to investigate as well as large areas of shallows. Shells are reasonably diverse, and flotsam might include anything from shreds of fishing nets to water-worn pine cones and drifting wooden crates from passing ships on their way to Cape Town. The beach (reached from the car park above) has neither shade nor shelter, and offers no facilities.

At Kreeftebaai, the gently shelving beach is again barred from the sea by rocks, but there are a few entrance channels at the south end, marked by water swirling around stumps of rock. Bathing is reasonably safe but the water is often clouded.

Some slight shelter might be found in the bushy dunes, but there are no facilities or shade, and braai sites in the parking area are rather exposed.

11 Derdesteen, Tweedesteen and Eerstesteen

On clear days, Robben Island seems very close to Derdesteen, a somewhat bleak and exposed little beach sloping abruptly to the water, which is often clouded with sand particles. There are a few braai sites in the car park.

At adjacent Tweedesteen the braai sites are tucked away among the dunes, which provide slight shelter for this steeply shelving beach. Other facilities include toilets and water.

The beach at Eerstesteen slopes more gradually than the last two, and bathing is reasonably safe. The beach is well suited to long walks, used to advantage by the racehorses from nearby stables. Facilities include a lawned braai area with picnic tables, a large beachfront parking area, as well as toilets and drinking water.

12 Bloubergstrand

Lazy trails of black mussel shells mark successive tidelines on these flat, white sands lapped by gentle waves. From here the dramatic picture postcard

aspect of Table Mountain unfolds across the blue expanse of ocean.

Making up Bloubergstrand, the two beaches of Grootbaai and Kleinbaai are separated at low tide by a wide spit of sand that you can cross dry-shod to a large rocky area with many pools to explore. A little further out to sea a rock protrudes with a guano-whitened crown; this is Voëlsteen (bird stone), favoured by the birds as the other rocks tend to be covered when the tide rises. Across the rocks to the south of Kleinbaai lies shingly little Bokkombaai, where there are numerous rock pools in an extensive shelf of rock, making access to the sea difficult.

Grootbaai is the Cape Peninsula's premier venue for surfing and boardsailing contests, while at Kleinbaai only swimming is allowed. The beachfront area has restaurants and a hotel, and beach facilities include grassed picnic sites with tables and chairs, change-rooms and toilets. Members of the local lifesaving club are usually on duty at weekends.

13 Table View

This long and gently shelving white beach, which sweeps on southwards to link up with Milnerton, is backed by a sandbank that provides some shelter from the south-easter (but no shade). In addition, rows of cut branches have been placed in the sand to provide windbreaks, but their protection is minimal. Bathing is fairly safe along the entire length, and the beach is popular for sunbathing and for long walks. There are toilets and drinking water at several points.

14 Robben Island

One of the earliest attempts to colonise the Cape was made not on the mainland, but on Robben Island (seal island), which lies west of Bloubergstrand in Table Bay. In 1617 three condemned English convicts were to be set ashore there, but on seeing the island, they begged to be hanged immediately rather than left on its desolate shores. After this unpromising start, it became the practice for passing mariners to leave a few sheep, emaciated after the voyage from Europe, on the island. These would soon fatten and be taken by the next passer-by who, in turn, would leave his own quota of scrawny sheep.

The island has not had a happy history. Soon after the mainland was settled by the Dutch, it became a penal settlement, with prisoners ranging from Far Eastern nobility to errant employees of the Dutch East India Company. To these were added later the unwanted members of Cape society, including paupers, lepers, and the chronically sick and mentally disturbed. Shortly before the Second World War, control of the island passed to the Defence Force and in the 1960s to the Prison Service.

Robben Island excites a fair amount of interest on the grounds of its historical and natural heritage, and occasionally the Prison Service accedes to requests from specialist groups or individuals to visit the island.

MISSION OF PEACE

In 1808 the Earl of Caledon, governor of the Cape, requested the Moravian Mission Society to establish a mission station at what was then known as Groenekloof (green ravine). This mission would protect the surviving Khoikhoi. The name Mamre was given only in 1854, and referred to the upliftment of the people after they had been living miserable and despairing lives. (According to Genesis 13:18, Mamre is the place where Abram lived.)

The village has grown greatly in recent years, but many of the original, modest houses survive, some still retaining their thatch. They were built to comprise two rooms and a kitchen, and some have a small dormer gable above the front door.

At the heart of the village is the mission complex and watermill. The church is dated 1818, and was built on such an unusual scale that it has never needed to be enlarged. The gables were added within twenty years of the building's erection, and at one stage there was also a small bell tower on the roof. The parsonage is believed to have been a farmhouse predating the formation of the mission.

Behind the parsonage is a row of old buildings that probably served as storehouses, but are now used as dwellings. The centre one is contemporary with the parsonage, and the others were built slightly later. The watermill, which is combined with the miller's dwelling, has been restored to working order.

THINGS TO DO

Angling
This stretch of coast is exposed to the full fury of the north-west gales of winter, when the sea bottom is churned up and new gullies are scoured in the sand. These are ideal conditions for galjoen, and the Blouberg area has become justly famous for these tasty fish. Contact any of the larger sports shops or the Northern Areas Angling Club in Cape Town for further details.

Beachcombing and shelling
Fishing gear and nautical bits and pieces are most likely to be found after a good northerly or north-westerly blow, generally from Haakgat southwards, although items tossed overboard from passing ships may land up anywhere. Black mussel shells are the most common, forming dense carpets in places, but there are varied shells at Kabeljoubank, Skulpbaai, Matroosbaai and Melkbosstrand. There are numerous rock pools (though of varying degrees of liveliness), especially at Bloubergstrand, Haakgat, Holbaai, Matroosbaai, Wintersteen, the Grotto Bay and Kabeljoubank.

Birdwatching
Meeurots supports a breeding colony of bank cormorants, and is a roost for Cape cormorants. Kelp and Hartlaub's gulls are common along this stretch of coast, and black oystercatchers may be seen along Van Riebeeckstrand, together with blacksmith plovers and whitefronted plovers. Around the usually dry estuary of the Modderrivier you may see gulls, common terns, Cape robins, helmeted guineafowl and crowned plovers (kiewiets).

Boardsailing
Bloubergstrand is the most popular venue for boardsailing, although there is also some activity at Melkbosstrand. Be careful not to get blown out to sea in a south-easter.

Bowls
Contact the Western Province Bowling Association in Cape Town for details of clubs.

Camping and caravanning
Ou Skip Caravan Park in Melkbosstrand has all amenities, while there is a rather more basic caravan park and camp site at Yzerfontein. Silwerstroomstrand has a caravan park, camp sites and bungalows for hire. The last two sites are run by the Swartland Divisional Council.

Canoeing
You can canoe at Grootbaai, Bloubergstrand, but on good days there are lots of people exploiting the surf, making it rather tricky for canoeists. Melkbosstrand is fairly sheltered, with smallish waves.

Diving
Along much of the coast, suspended sand particles restrict visibility quite severely, sometimes to no more than a metre or so. There are interesting gullies off Skaapeiland at Yzerfontein, as well as the pools off the Grotto Bay and Kabeljoubank, where rock lobster may be taken. There is lots of life in the kelp off Sandsteenbaai, but the distance from the beach is perhaps too great for comfort. The promontories enclosing Matroosbaai offer possibilities for rock lobster and perlemoen in calm weather. The coast from Melkbospunt south is a rock lobster reserve.

Drives and viewsites
The Otto du Plessis Marine Drive follows the coast fairly closely until the vicinity of Koeberg, and from almost all parking areas there are outstanding views of the Table Mountain group. It is also possible to take a circular drive in this section of coast, following the R27 up the coast to Yzerfontein and then returning via Darling and Mamre. This is best done in spring, when the veld is festooned with flowers.

Libraries
Libraries run by the Regional Services Council at Atlantis, Bloubergstrand and Melkbosstrand welcome visitors.

Powerboating
Boats can be launched at Yzerfontein, from the inlet just north of Kabeljoubank, and from Silwerstroomstrand.

Surfing
In a light south-east or south-west wind, there is good surfing at Melkbosstrand, Bloubergstrand, Eerstesteen, Tweedesteen and Derdesteen. Haakgat is for the more experienced. Table View produces good surf in a north-east or north-west blow, but there is a strong rip current here, and surfers should be watched by someone ashore. Further afield, Yzerfontein is also good.

Tennis and squash
For details of clubs and courts, contact the Western Province Tennis Association and the Western Province Squash Racket Association, both in Cape Town.

Walks
Especially in spring, the paths through the Tienie Versveld Flora Reserve are well worth a stroll. For those interested in architecture or history, a walk around Mamre is rewarding. Van Riebeeckstrand and Table View offer long beach walks.

Yachting and dinghy sailing
Dinghies can be launched at Yzerfontein, Silwerstroomstrand and Melkbosstrand.

Fish type	Season	Best area	Best bait
Dassie	All year	Gullies throughout the area	Fresh redbait
Galjoen	All year; best in winter after a NW blow	Bloubergstrand and next to rocks throughout the area	Rotten redbait, wonderworms, bloodworms, white mussels, sand prawns
Hottentot	Mar-July	Wherever there are slight openings in the kelp	Fresh redbait, white mussels, chokka
Kabeljou (rare)	Sept-May	All rocky areas	Octopus, prawns, fishbait
White steenbras	Winter, with N or NW wind	Bloubergstrand; Kabeljoubank	Sand prawns, wonderworms, bloodworms
White stumpnose	All year; best in spring and autumn	Bloubergstrand; Kabeljoubank	Sand prawns, redbait, chokka
Wildeperd	All year	Gullies throughout the area	Fresh redbait

Bloubergstrand is a popular venue for competitive and recreational boardsailing.

The welcoming 'Tavern of the Seas'

The cable car, Cape Town's trademark, suspended over a sparkling sea.

CAPE TOWN, FOR CENTURIES known far and wide as the 'Tavern of the Seas', sprawls in the shadow of Table Mountain, a landmark for weary seafarers. Although the waterfront areas fringing Table Bay are less boisterous now than in the rollicking days of sailing ships, they retain much of their picturesque atmosphere.

In the streets of the mother city a long and colourful history rubs shoulders with the present: a gracious 18th-century dwelling may stand alongside a sleek skyscraper, or a traditional mosque beside a modern boutique. Squares alive with market stalls and music, buildings festooned with cast-iron tracery, beckon both the shopper and the sightseer. Edging further down the coastline, beyond Lion's Head, the Atlantic seaboard suburbs are strung along the narrow strip between icy sea and the steep-sided Twelve Apostles. For an incomparable overview of all this, of city and peninsula, bustling harbour and bikini beaches, there is the cableway to the summit of Table Mountain.

1 Rietvlei

This freshwater recreational area and bird sanctuary offers picnic and braai sites, and a series of small, sandy beaches along the southern shore (reached by gravel road). The water is safe for bathing, while other popular activities include yachting, powerboating and (except on Sundays) boardsailing. At weekends the skilfully made models of the the Cape Radio Fliers can be seen and heard above the marshes.

Rietvlei lies on the Diep River but historically this was the Salt River, forking around the original Paardeneiland (horses' island — where the Company's animals were kept) to enter the sea in two places. One of these is now the mouth of the Milnerton Lagoon but the second channel no longer reaches the sea, and is merely a series of stagnant pools between residential Brooklyn and the industrial area of Paardeneiland. The canalised Liesbeek River nearby is, however, often referred to as the Salt River, entering the sea near

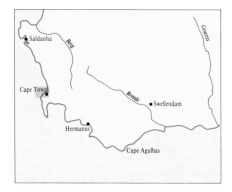

the original mouth.

To reach Rietvlei, turn inland from Otto du Plessis Marine Drive at the south end of Table View, then right into Pentz Drive and again into Sandpiper Crescent. An entry fee is payable.

2 Milnerton

The town of Milnerton is situated on the banks of a lagoon on the Diep River. Associated with it is a beach some 10 km long, a broad stretch of sand sloping gently to the water from high dunes dotted with dune grass, wattles and rooikrans (*Acacia cyclops*), with a few vygies on the seaward side. There are few intact shells on the beach (other than mussels), although quite large fragments of the translucent buff *Atrina squamifera* are found. Especially after a north-west blow, the tideline is littered with jetsam, while parts of the beach have a light stain of oil.

There is a strong backwash along most of the beach, making swimming safest at the southern end, where the Milnerton Lifesaving Club has its quarters. Another good spot is near the shallow mouth of the lagoon, which is rarely open to the sea. The stretch of lagoon from the mouth to the point where it is crossed by Otto du Plessis Marine Drive is also used by canoeists and boardsailors, but is out of bounds to powerboats. 'The island', a tongue of land between the lagoon and the sea, is the site of the Milnerton Golf Course; it is linked

Green Point's safe and sturdy lighthouse.

to the mainland by two bridges, although the old wooden one is closed to traffic.

Of historic interest are the much battered and barnacled remains of the *Winton*, a 4 388 ton freighter that went ashore in 1934, which may be seen in the surf; just inland, in the dunes, are the remains of a Second World War gun position, the circle of bolts for the base-mounting still protruding from the concrete. It was very close to here that the ship *Haarlem* was wrecked in 1647, an event that led directly to the establishment of the Dutch refreshment station at the Cape five years later.

South of the town the beach narrows towards Ben Schoeman Dock, which has covered Woodstock Beach, hailed in its heyday as the 'Brighton of South Africa'. Here tented bathing machines were hauled out into the surf where well-clad ladies emerged to take the waters, safe from prying eyes.

3 Table Bay Harbour

For more than two centuries Cape Town, for all its halfway house status on the route to the East, had no harbour. Ships anchored in the unprotected roadstead and goods and passengers were conveyed between ship and shore by small, single-masted cargo boats. A wooden jetty at the foot of Heerengracht, and another at the end of Bree Street, marked the sum total of harbour development. Inevitably, many ships and lives were lost, particularly during north-west gales. In 1860 a start was made with the breakwater, and by mid-1869 Alfred Basin was complete. (In the meantime, however, yet another 'Great Gale' had claimed some fifty vessels.)

Like the city it serves, the harbour is a happy blend of old and new. Starting at the Paardeneiland end, first is the Ben Schoeman Dock, with its up-to-date tanker and container facilities. Moving west, there is a laying-up berth for small vessels, as well as the extensive yacht basin with the headquarters of the Royal Cape Yacht Club — a venue for international competitions. Also at this end is the Sturrock dry dock, believed to be the biggest in the southern hemisphere. Duncan Dock, with an area of 117 ha, was completed during the Second World War and is used for general ocean-going traffic. Across the South Arm and connected to Alfred Basin is Victoria Basin, completed in 1895. The whole harbour is protected by the breakwater, which extends for some 1,5 km.

Throughout the older section of the harbour muzzle-loading cannon have been let into the jetties and used as mooring bollards. Among the many interesting buildings is the Clock Tower, on the South Quay in Alfred Basin. Built as the port captain's office in 1883, it is the local headquarters of the Ship Society of South Africa, and houses a varied collection of nautical relics, such as the original clock and tide-gauge. A fun way to reach the Clock Tower is by the short crossing from the Pier Head on the Penny Ferry (although the fare is no longer a mere penny). Also on the Pier Head is a popular restaurant in the former offices of the harbour engineer.

The National Sea Rescue Institute's Station 3 (Granger Bay) is situated on the East Pier, near the start of the breakwater. The bay is named for Robert Granger, a ship's chandler who in the mid-19th century single-handedly rescued the crews of several wrecked ships by rowing out to them in a small open boat.

The North Gate leads into Portswood Road where, on the left after a few hundred metres, are the grim walls of the old Breakwater Prison (now a hostel) where Cape convicts laboured on the rock piles. The treadmill for recalcitrant inmates is still in working order. Nearby Fort Wynyard Battery, named after Lieutenant-General R H Wynyard, twice acting-governor of the Cape in the 1860s, is being converted into a museum recording the history of South Africa's coastal defence, in which the fort played an important role during the Second World War.

4 Bokaap

Also known as the Malay Quarter, this residential area on the slopes of Signal Hill, long occupied by members of the Muslim faith, boasts numerous dwellings dating back well over a century. A guided tour (contact Captour for details) is the most rewarding means of visiting this charming area.

5 The Company's Garden

This green and tranquil haven in the centre of the city was the core of the Dutch settlement founded by Jan van Riebeeck in 1652. It began as a simple vegetable garden for provisioning passing ships of the Dutch East India Company but, within a few years, free burghers were producing more than enough grain and vegetables to meet the needs of the refreshment station, and the garden gradually became more of a botanical undertaking.

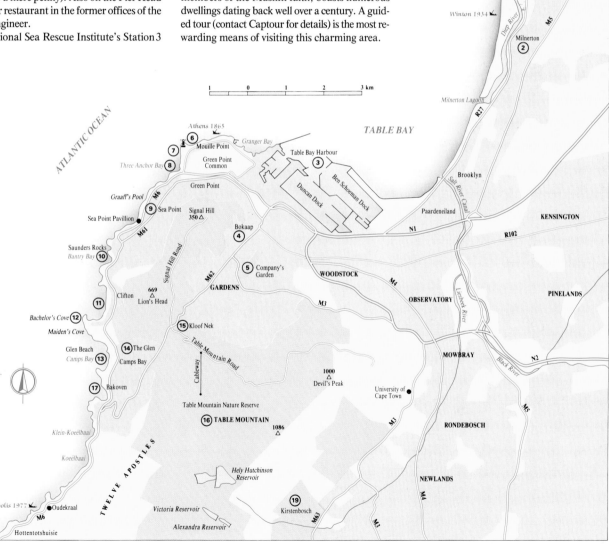

Now known as the Municipal Botanical Gardens, this is the ideal setting for a leisurely stroll or a light meal under the spreading trees, while the museums and galleries within the Gardens are well worth visiting. At the northern end of Government Avenue (the paved, oak-lined walk connecting the city with the suburb of Gardens) are the historic gateways to the former Company menageries; here is a collection of interesting old buildings that once formed the campus of the South African College. South Africa's oldest memorial sculpture, a statue of Cape governor Sir George Grey unveiled in 1864, stands in front of the South African Library.

6 Mouille Point

The mole or breakwater that gave its name to the suburb and stretch of beach can be seen only at very low tide. It was built under the direction of Hendrik Swellengrebel, first Cape-born governor of the Cape, in the 1740s. Farmers, bringing their produce to town, were obliged to transport a wagon-load of stone from the Strand Street quarry to the site of the new mole. When, as the story goes, a locust plague ruined their crops and they came to town only by cart, work on the mole (then about 100 m in length) ground to a halt. It is situated directly opposite the remains of the single-cylinder steam engine of the *Athens*, which protrudes from the breakers close to the shore.

The area from the harbour breakwater to its unsuccessful predecessor is known as Granger Bay, and includes a shipyard, the premises of the Oceana Power Boat Club and the General Botha Merchant Navy Academy. The remains of the foundation of the Mouille Point lighthouse can be seen in the grounds of the academy. This lighthouse functioned from 1842 to 1908, when the breakwater light rendered it unnecessary. To this day, however, many people refer to the Green Point lighthouse as the Mouille Point lighthouse.

The shore is rocky and unsuited to swimming, but offers interesting rock pools at low tide. Unfortunately, many of them are almost entirely covered with kelp at times, resulting in an unpleasant smell. There are few shells of note, although intact sea urchin shells may frequently be picked up beneath the retaining wall of the naval academy.

From the west end of Mouille Point a raised stone promenade extends all the way to Sea Point.

7 Green Point

This section is entirely covered by a lawned promenade. The lighthouse, the oldest on the South African coast, was erected in 1824. It was close to this lighthouse that the ships *George M Livanos* (1947) and SA *Seafarer* (1966) were wrecked.

Inland, Green Point Common (site of a Boer prisoner-of-war camp) was for long a favourite venue for sporting events. Today the modern Green Point Stadium maintains the old traditions. Near the lighthouse are a playground, a fun fair (in season) and a miniature steam train, while towards Three Anchor Bay is a Putt-Putt course.

TABLE MOUNTAIN – FACT AND FABLE

From the slopes of Signal Hill, the eye is drawn to the great bulk of Table Mountain.

Many stories, some highly coloured, have sprung up over the years in connection with Table Mountain, and in particular with Platteklip Gorge. The gorge is the gathering place for a variety of ghostly figures, including a leper boy and the mysterious Antje Somers — a man dressed in 19th-century women's clothing who is said to prey on passers-by.

About the middle of last century, Platteklip Gorge was the unlikely scene of a gold rush. Mark Salom, a colourful local auctioneer, claimed to have found easily recoverable gold on the mountain. Business in Cape Town came to a standstill as men swarmed up the gorge in the searing heat. Fortuitously, they were met by a wealth of food and drink, if not of gold. This was Salom's enterprise, and he laid on a feast ever higher up the mountain over the next five days, making a handsome profit while claiming he could no longer locate his fabulous 'strike'.

Table Mountain today has its 'bergies', vagrants who sleep on the slopes in old mines and other workings, but the original 'bergie' was probably Joshua Penny, an American seaman who had been press-ganged into the British Royal Navy. He arrived in 1799, aboard HMS *Sceptre*, and deserted at the first opportunity, making for Table Mountain, where he survived undetected for 14 months. He hunted by throwing stones, clothed himself in the skins of the buck he killed, and made his home in a sheltered cave beside a stream. When finally he came down and took refuge aboard a merchant ship he heard that, soon after he deserted, his ship had gone down with all hands during a gale in the bay. A slim book, describing his adventures, was published in 1815, but only in 1958 was it proved true beyond all doubt, when his cave, containing relics carefully recorded in his book, was rediscovered.

8 Three Anchor Bay

This tiny patch of beach at a bend in the promenade sports boathouses and a launch ramp, as well as an NSRI station, and is a popular power-boating venue. The beach, which has a change-room, is more suited to sunbathing than swimming, with the promenade offering shelter from the Cape's brisk south-easter. (The curious name is said to originate from the early defence of the bay, when chains strung across the water were held by three anchors.)

9 Sea Point

This golden strip is Cape Town's most sophisticated holiday playground, dense with restaurants, night clubs and up-market shops. The long promenade between Sea Point and Mouille Point is a favourite venue for strolling, jogging . . . or just being seen. There is a wide, grassed area for picnics (no fires), a trim-park, a children's playground, a measured kilometre for joggers to pace themselves, and the wide, smooth promenade itself, poised just above the sea.

The suburb was named in 1776 by one of Captain James Cook's commanders, who moved his men to safety there from Cape Town during a smallpox epidemic. In its early days it was linked to Cape Town by a privately owned railway, with most of the track following the scenic route along the shoreline.

Although much of the Sea Point beachfront is rockbound, there are several beaches and natural and artificial pools. First is Rocklands, a tiny beach, shelly rather than sandy. It is fairly well sheltered and, as it slopes gently, the water is shallow and safe for children.

Graaff's Pool, a natural rock pool, is reached via a concrete path leading seaward from the promenade, and is reserved for men. Nude bathing and sunbathing are permitted within certain limits — away from the public view. Next is Milton Pool, a shallow tidal pool suitable for children, with an adjacent wide beach.

The pools at Sea Point Pavilion are filled with sea water, usually a degree or so warmer than the sea itself. All tastes are catered for here, from a paddling pool for children to a deep pool with high diving boards. Alongside the Pavilion is a small patch of beach.

Sunset Beach, a sandy inlet with an artificial tidal pool, has toilets and change-rooms. Queens Beach is small and fairly rocky and more suited to sunbathing than swimming. The most northerly of the peninsula's west-facing beaches, where sunbathing can be enjoyed until late on a summer's evening, is Saunders Rocks, with its tiny pool and strip of beach. Here too a few surfers can usually be seen riding the swells.

10 Bantry Bay

This rocky inlet sees little swimming or watersports, but is surrounded by a variety of interesting architecture, from stately Bantrycourt (dating from the mid-1920s) to modern clusters closer to the tideline. The earlier name of Botany Bay (when ground was rented by a Dr Liesching to grow medicinal herbs) may have been changed to that of the Irish beauty spot because of unpleasant associations with Australia's convict station of Botany Bay. The rocks continue south, forming a protective headland for the Clifton beaches.

11 Clifton

Four sparkling white, sandy beaches, separated by great granite boulders, form the curve of Clifton Bay, where houses cling to precipitous slopes on either side of Victoria Road, the route from Sea Point round to Hout Bay. (Victoria Road, completed in the 1880s, was the last major work of Thomas Bain, the celebrated builder of so many of the Cape's roads and mountain passes.)

Sunbathing is the chief occupation at this sheltered spot, so much so that the name Clifton is synonymous with brief bikinis and bronzed bodies. Adding to the glamour and romance of the scene, yachts often moor off Fourth Beach over calm weekends.

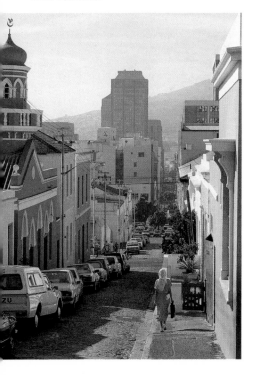

ABOVE *The shady sweep through the Glen links central Cape Town with the Atlantic seaboard.*
LEFT *The graceful lines of Bokaap buildings against the blur of the city below.*

The water, as along the entire Atlantic seaboard, is extremely cold but despite this, at least one fatal shark attack has been recorded — off Fourth Beach, in 1942. A lifesaving club, manned by volunteers, is based at Clifton, and there are change-rooms at the car park above Fourth Beach, as well as on the beach itself.

12 Bachelor's and Maiden's Coves

Bachelor's Cove, a small, sandy beach on the rocky promontory at the south end of the Clifton beaches, was formerly reserved for the use of men only. Large granite boulders provide shelter and a sense of seclusion.

Maiden's Cove, presumably named as a companion, has a small beach, a shallow tidal pool and a large, grassed area. To prevent overcrowding, the coves have been fenced and access is restricted.

13 Camps Bay

The northern end of Camps Bay Beach, separated from it by a large granite outcrop, is known as Glen Beach. Access is from the main beach, or via a concrete footpath from the car park. The beach is well sheltered from the south-easter, and is a popular surfing venue.

The long, white stretch of sand, rolling lawns dotted with palms, and the rugged backdrop of the peaks of the Twelve Apostles, make Camps Bay a most attractive beach. At the southern end there is a tidal pool, set in a grassed area with braai places. Towards the centre of the beach is a children's paddling pool. To add to the enjoyment of a day in the sun, beach umbrellas and deck chairs may be hired from a wooden kiosk nearby. The beach can be unpleasant, however, in a fairly strong south-easter.

The beach shelves steeply and there is a strong backwash, making bathing dangerous. As a precaution, swimming is restricted to areas demarcated by notice boards. Lifesavers are on duty generally only during the holiday season.

Camps Bay derives its name from the German Ernst von Kamptz, who in 1779 married the widow Koekemoer, owner of Ravenstein (now called Camps Bay House) in Kloof Nek Road. Both the house and bay were taken over by the Cape government, which erected fortifications, and the house served as an official residence for many years.

14 Camps Bay to Kloof Nek — the Glen

Just beyond the north end of Camps Bay Beach is an inland turn-off for 'Round House' and 'Kloof Nek'. From there turn sharp right into Kloof Road and right again at the fork to reach a narrow, somewhat bumpy road with magnificent views over the bay. This scenic drive passes between the Round House on your left, and a youth hostel on your right.

The Round House (now a restaurant) was built early last century, probably on the circular foundations of one of the small forts that guarded the Kloof Nek approach to Cape Town. It was used by Lord Charles Somerset as a shooting lodge, and a number of gun cupboards may still be seen inside. The present hostel was originally the outbuilding, and both are national monuments.

The Glen, a beautiful, wooded picnic site, is reached by turning right again after taking the fork in Kloof Road.

15 Over the Nek

Five roads converge at Kloof Nek, two of them — Camps Bay Drive and Kloof Road — providing a scenic route from Camps Bay. Kloof Nek Road descends steeply to Cape Town, while Table Mountain Road winds along the lower slopes of the mountain for several kilometres (past the lower cable station), offering a panorama of sea and city. Signal Hill Drive follows a contour just below the ridge of Signal Hill, giving sweeping views of the city and Table Mountain, passing a domed *kramat* (shrine) and reaching a parking and picnic area (no fires) overlooking the harbour and the Atlantic suburbs. The views are particularly spectacular at night, when the lights of the city lie spread beneath the hill.

16 Table Mountain

Dominating the northern end of the peninsula, this flat-topped massif — symbol of Cape Town — reaches a height of 1 086 m at Maclear's Beacon, above Newlands. Some 550-million years ago prehistoric seas deposited on an ancient base of granite a deep layer of silt known as Malmesbury slate. Then the sea level dropped and, for over a million years, it retreated ever further from our present coastline. But it returned, dramatically, around the beginning of the geological period known as the Devonian, which started about 400-million years ago. The seas rose higher, un-

THE NOON GUN

The firing of the noon gun, with its puff of white, recorded here in 1911.

Just a few seconds after noon each day, except on Sundays and public holidays, Cape Town's pigeons take to the air in brief alarm. They must be the only residents to be regularly startled by the boom of the noon gun from Signal Hill. The opening and closing of the Castle gates was announced by cannon-fire at sunrise and sunset in the 18th century, but the noon gun has been fired from Signal Hill only since 1903, when standard time was introduced in South Africa. A previous noon gun was fired from the (now demolished) Imhoff Battery in front of the Castle.

The gun itself is a muzzle-loading iron cannon that saw service at sea during the 18th century. Each firing day, well before noon, a soldier removes the muzzle-plug or tampion, and inserts a sponge-stave into the bore to ensure that it is dry. A bag containing a measured amount of old-fashioned black gunpowder is then rammed home, followed by a fibre wad. In clearing the touch-hole or vent, the soldier pricks the fabric of the bag, to expose some of the powder, and an electrical detonator is screwed into the vent. Precisely at noon, the detonator and, instantaneously, the main charge, are exploded by an electrical impulse generated from the SA Astronomical Observatory. Bag and wad disintegrate in the explosion, and it is the long flare of flame from the muzzle that announces the precise time, the boom taking several seconds to reach the centre of the city. On windless days, a great cloud of white smoke (a characteristic of black powder) hangs over Signal Hill for several seconds before dispersing.

til the entire peninsula, which may have been an island at that stage, lay deep beneath the waves. Once again layers of silt were deposited, but of a different kind, one that in time became known as Table Mountain Sandstone. Once again the sea receded, and breakers crashing on the flat summit produced the water-rolled pebbles that can still be seen there, especially in an area at the base of the rise on which Maclear's Beacon stands.

The faces of the mountain show dramatic cliffs and gorges, formed by erosion, while the summit is a plateau extending for several kilometres. This plateau is on two main levels: the small Front Table and the lower but larger Back Table. The north face overlooks Cape Town and, with Lion's Head to the west and Devil's Peak to the east, forms the 'city amphitheatre'. The west face is made up of the Twelve Apostles, a series of peaks to which Van Riebeeck gave the appropriate name of *gewelbergen* (gable mountains). The southwestern face overlooks Hout Bay, and the south face the southern suburbs.

ABOVE *Rocky inlets and high-rise buildings form a necklace around Green Point Common.*
LEFT *The grounds of Kirstenbosch clothed in their customary splendour.*

HEROES WHO BRAVED THE STORM

Wolraad Woltemade battles through the boiling seas.

Ageing Wolraad Woltemade's heroic deed in rescuing 14 men from the wreck of *De Jonge Thomas* at the Salt River in 1773, is well known. Seven times he spurred his horse into the raging surf, bringing back two seamen, clinging to his mount's tail. On the eighth attempt, he and the horse were dragged down and both drowned. Today a statue erected in his honour can be seen at Pinelands, while the home believed to have been his, Klein Zoar, still stands in Wemyss Road, Brooklyn — the sole survivor of the many fishermen's cottages that must have lined the now-vanished beach.

Unlike Woltemade, virtually unknown is Jochem Willemsz, whose acts of bravery took place in 1692. During a north-westerly gale in May that year, several ships grounded along Woodstock Beach, among them the *Hoogergeest*, which was in danger of breaking up as waves dashed over it. Willemsz, a seaman, proposed to rescue the crew by swimming to the wreck with a line, through water so rough that no small boat could survive.

With a light line tied around his body, Willemsz succeeded, after a long struggle, in boarding the *Hoogergeest*. A heavier line was then hauled across, and a raft was attached to this. Using the raft, the crew members were hauled ashore to safety, with Willemsz being one of the last to land.

All but forgotten is Francis Rose, who was just 17 years old when he set out on horseback to rescue sailors aboard the wrecked Danish ship, *Indian Packet*, in 1821. An unseasonal January north-westerly had blown it almost ashore near the old Salt River mouth. Francis succeeded in saving all on board, but was himself drowned, with his horse, on his last trip to the shore. The only commemoration of his brave deed is a plaque inside NSRI Station 3.

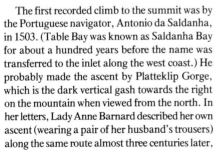

The first recorded climb to the summit was by the Portuguese navigator, Antonio da Saldanha, in 1503. (Table Bay was known as Saldanha Bay for about a hundred years before the name was transferred to the inlet along the west coast.) He probably made the ascent by Platteklip Gorge, which is the dark vertical gash towards the right on the mountain when viewed from the north. In her letters, Lady Anne Barnard described her own ascent (wearing a pair of her husband's trousers) along the same route almost three centuries later, but with slaves to carry 'two boxes of cold meats and bottles of port, Madeira and Cape'.

Today probably the most popular ascent is by the cableway, opened in 1929. The journey takes between five and seven minutes, and each car can hold 22 passengers, as well as the operator. The cableway carried its millionth passenger in 1957, its 2-millionth only 11 years later, and in December 1986, with the pace still accelerating, its 7-millionth. The view from the top is unsurpassed: on a clear day, visibility may be as much as 160 km. Facilities on the mountain include a restaurant at the summit, next to the upper cable station, and another near Rhodes Memorial, on the slopes of Devil's Peak.

The summer south-easter is responsible for Table Mountain's famous 'tablecloth', the flat cloud that drapes the summit and streams down over the edge to vanish before it reaches the city. This is formed by the cooling of moist air forced over the summit by the wind. According to legend, the cloud is formed by the re-enactment of a wager between an old pirate named Jan van Hunks and the devil himself. The two met on the mountain, and embarked on a smoking contest, so the appearance of the 'tablecloth' means that they have refilled their pipes yet again.

Table Mountain is the home of most of the 2 600 species of flora found on the peninsula, and among the most outstanding specimens are the silver tree (*Leucadendron argenteum*) and the red disa (*Disa grandiflora*), a member of the orchid family, also known as 'Pride of Table Mountain'. It flowers along streams and in cool ravines between January and March. Fauna include baboons (which may not be fed), dassies (rock hyraxes), porcupines, small predators and a number of indigenous and exotic larger antelope confined within paddocks. Tahrs, a Himalayan antelope, have multiplied greatly from the original pair introduced in 1937, and range freely over the mountain, causing great damage to the vegetation.

17 Bakoven

Essentially this is a residential area, with bungalows clustered about the rocky shore of the little bay. At the southern end, however, is a small, sandy beach, while the massed boulders are regarded by many as the perfect vantage point for a sunset picnic. The name Bakoven is said to be derived from a rock shaped like an old-fashioned baking oven, with a hole in it, but it is also possible that a limekiln may have been located here many years ago.

South of Bakoven are Klein-Koeëlbaai and Koeëlbaai, named for the small, rounded stones that make up their beaches. In the days of muzzle-loading firearms, the bullet (*koeël*) was cast in a

RIGHT *A jumble of rocks between Glen Beach and Camps Bay, with the Twelve Apostles behind.*

SAD FATE OF THE STEAMSHIP ATHENS

That sad lump of iron rearing from the sea at Mouille Point was once the pulsing heart of the Royal Mail Steamship *Athens*. Apart from shattered woodwork and the bodies of its crew, this was all that remained when the sun rose after the Great Gale of 1865. The single-cylinder steam engine, with an output of just 96 kW (less than many outboard motors today), turned a cast-iron propeller with a 3 m diameter to move the tiny 739 ton liner through the water. Naturally, it also carried sails, and the steam engine was no more than an auxiliary.

During the fierce north-westerly gale in May, *Athens* rode to its anchors, the tiny engine keeping it steaming into the wind to reduce the strain on its cables. Inevitably, though, they parted, and, at dusk, *Athens* struggled away from its berth off Woodstock Beach, and disappeared into the night. Although word was soon received that it was ashore almost at the base of the Mouille Point lighthouse, so rapidly did it break up that no life was saved nor anything salvaged intact. The captain, David Smith, had just been appointed to the command, and this was his only voyage in *Athens* as master. His confidence in the engine's ability to propel his ship through that wild sea led directly to disaster. Ironically, had *Athens* been just a sailing ship, Smith would have beached it — probably without loss of life — at Woodstock, when his last cable broke. Instead, he put his faith in modern technology, and lost.

Captain David Smith, master of the ill-fated Athens *on its final voyage.*

round shape, and to this day ordinary rifle ammunition is referred to as 'ball' ammunition, despite its pointed, cylindrical shape.

A short way up the slopes overlooking Koeëlbaai are two Muslim *kramats*, the graves of holy men. One of them was Nureel Mobeen, who was exiled to Robben Island from the East Indies in the late 17th century. Somehow he succeeded in escaping to the mainland, where he lived the remainder of his life as a refugee, probably tended by sympathetic slaves. His grave has become a place of local pilgrimage.

At the south of Koeëlbaai is a rocky promontory with a rock, named Geldkis (money chest), lying offshore. The name arose after the wreck of the East Indiaman, *Huis te Crayesteijn*, in 1698. According to Simon van der Stel's report, of the 19 money chests aboard, 16 were recovered, 'one was broken open and plundered by some wicked person', and two slid through the ports into the sea. Two large brass cannon were recovered from the site in 1870 but to date there has unfortunately been no sign of the missing money chests.

Close by and with bows hard against the shore, are the cut-down remains of the tanker *Antipolis* which, while being towed to a shipbreaker in the East, broke loose during a gale in 1977. The wreck is coated with black mussels.

18 Hottentotshuisie

Well sheltered from the south-easter, this small, partly shaded beach was once the gathering place of a group of Khoi Strandlopers (beachcombers) known to Van Riebeeck as Watermanns. The original Dutch name of Oudekraal still applies to the estate above the inlet. Fencing has been erected to restrict numbers, and a small entrance fee is charged to visitors.

Swimming is considered to be fairly safe along the sandy beaches, while further out, where the water is very deep, scuba diving can prove interesting. Note that this is part of a rock lobster reserve, and if you want to collect perlemoen, you must have a licence. Fresh water is available, and there are change-rooms and toilets.

19 Kirstenbosch

Open throughout the year during the daylight hours, Kirstenbosch Botanic Gardens cover some 528 ha on the eastern slopes of Table Mountain. Of this area, 60 ha have been cultivated and landscaped, while the balance of the land represents a natural reserve of beautiful indigenous flora.

Kirstenbosch, which was established early this century, today contains more than ten per cent of the 20 000 species of South African flora, as well as over forty per cent of the peninsula's floral species. The Compton Herbarium has over 250 000 species, dried and skilfully preserved as type specimens for reference. In addition, special features of Kirstenbosch include the Braille Trail and the Fragrance Garden, with labels marked with large print and in Braille. There is an information kiosk and book shop, as well as an indoor and outdoor restaurant.

BUILDING THE BAY

Fishing boats drawn up on the shores of the early Roggebaai.

Jan van Riebeeck made his landing in Table Bay in 1652 at about the point where his statue now stands, far from the sea. From this site, too, the Adderley Street Pier was built seawards in 1912, serving for almost three decades as a popular venue for concerts and public meetings, or romantic strolls. Just west of the pier was Roggebaai, where the intrepid Table Bay fishermen tied up their boats and volubly advertised their catch. (*Rogge* means skates — the fish — but the name could also be a corruption of the French *roche*, meaning rock.) Today the old tideline, traced with a bronze strip let into the floor, may be seen in the concourse level of the Golden Acre.

By the 1930s it was realised that a larger harbour was needed to serve the city, and towards the end of the decade a start was made with dredging. Bucket dredgers and large-bore reclamation pipes brought up ground from the sea bottom and deposited it closer to the existing shoreline, which was also extended by great masses of rock and rubble dumped from the landward side.

There can be no doubt that many ancient shipwrecks and, quite likely, a fair amount of sunken treasure, lie beneath Cape Town's Foreshore, never to be recovered. However, during December 1970 workers on the site of Cape Town's Civic Centre uncovered massive old timbers, and a great number of cannon balls. This was the ship *Nieuwe Rhoon*, which in 1776, after striking a rock near Robben Island, later sank at its moorings — but only after everything of value had been removed. To keep it firmly on the bottom in what was then a much-navigated part of the sea, the hulk was loaded with reject cannon balls and left to rot. Excavators, some two centuries later, noticed the strong smell of pepper about the timbers, a reminder of the spice trade with the East.

An aspect of the harbour today: a tranquil view from Alfred Basin.

ABOVE *A boardsailor skims across the calm curve of Clifton Bay, backed by Lion's Head.* BELOW *Sea Point promenade.*

A GEOLOGICAL RARITY

In 1836 Charles Darwin, controversial proponent of evolution, broke his round-the-world voyage at Cape Town to examine some exciting geological evidence. Today this piece of earth's history, inscribed in rock, can still be seen on the Sea Point beachfront. In the large car park between Queens Beach and Saunders Rocks, locate the plaque and plinth erected by the National Monuments Council on the seaward side. Looking over the sea wall here, you will see a rare exposed contact zone between an igneous and a sedimentary rock.

Some 500-million years ago, when the sea level was very much higher (at one time it covered Table Mountain), fine particles of wind-eroded rock set-

tled on the sea bed here. In time, these became compacted to form the rock known as Malmesbury slate. After a period of perhaps 50-million years, there was a fiery upthrust of molten granite, tilting the uniformly horizontal bedding planes of the slate, softening and even melting it as the granite forced its way along lines of weakness.

The contact area can be studied for about 100 m south of the plaque, with the fine network of granite veins producing an intimate mixture with the slate. The slate is the darker, sometimes spotted rock. The full extent of the contact area is not known, as there is another exposure at Platteklip Gorge, and the contact extends from at least that point seawards.

THINGS TO DO

Angling

Table Bay is essentially a winter fishing area for the angler, especially after a good north-west blow. To hire a boat for deep-sea fishing, inquire at Table Bay Harbour, at the small craft basin and Victoria Basin. This is not a noted angling area, but good catches may sometimes be made in the harbour or off the breakwater. To fish within the area of the harbour, you must be a member of a recognised angling club, and the holder of a permit issued by SA Transport Services (Railway Administration). Visitors who are not club members should inquire at the larger sports shops for the names of contacts at any one of several angling clubs in the area.

Art galleries

OLD TOWN HOUSE, Greenmarket Square: Michaelis collection of 17th-century Dutch and Flemish paintings.
RUST EN VREUGD, 78 Buitenkant: Part of William Fehr collection of paintings and antiques of SA interest. Balance of collection housed in the Castle.
SA NATIONAL GALLERY, Government Avenue, Company's Garden: SA and other works, Touch Gallery for the blind. Details of film shows and lectures obtainable from newspapers or Captour.

Beachcombing and shelling

The length of Milnerton Beach is littered with jetsam, especially after a north-west blow, as is the stretch from Granger Bay to the Green Point

Fish type	Season	Best area	Best bait
Hottentot	May—Sept	Oudekraal (the Ring), Hottentotshuisie, Table Bay Harbour	Redbait, mussels, chokka, prawns
Kabeljou	May—Sept	Table Bay Harbour	Chokka, fishbait, prawns, octopus, spoons
Maasbanker	May—Sept	Table Bay Harbour	Artificial lure, fishbait
Rockcod	May—Sept	Table Bay Harbour	Fishbait, octopus, redbait, crabs, chokka
Skate	May—Sept	Table Bay Harbour	Sardines, chokka, prawns
White stumpnose	May—Sept	Table Bay Harbour	Mussels, prawns, shrimps, limpets, chokka, fishbait

lighthouse. The area in general is not noted for shelling but see under individual beaches for more information. Rock pools at Green Point, Sea Point, Bantry Bay and Bakoven are worth exploring.

Birdwatching

Rietvlei is the largest breeding area for waterfowl in the Cape. About 150 species have been recorded there, including the fish eagle, pelican, flamingo, black backed gull, Egyptian goose and even the Arctic tern.
On the mountains you may see a great variety of birds, from lanner and peregrine falcon to the lovely voiced mountain chat.

Boardsailing

Inland, boardsailing takes place at Rietvlei, except on Sundays. Milnerton Beach is ideal most days, but risky for beginners in a high south-easter, which blows offshore; Saunders Rocks (Sea

Point) is fast but rocky; at Camps Bay Glen Beach is safe. Sailboards (usually beginners' boards only) can be hired from some specialised shops as well as from Sea Point Hire. Contact the Western Province Boardsailing Club.

Boat trips

Crest Cruises offer harbour tours and boat charter.

Bowls

For details of clubs, contact the Western Province Bowling Association.

Canoeing

The Milnerton Lagoon is reserved for canoeing and other nonpower sailing from the mouth to the Otto du Plessis bridge. The Milnerton Canoe Club can be contacted through the municipality.

Cycling

The Cape Peninsula, with its many hills and frequent high winds, is not ideal

country for the casual cyclist, but some fun cycling may be had along the beachfront from Sea Point to Mouille Point. Cycles may be hired from Sea Point Hire.

Diving

The entire area is a rock lobster sanctuary, but odds and ends from wrecks may be picked up among the rocks off Mouille Point (*Athens*) and the Green Point lighthouse (*Seafarer* and *George M Livanos*).
Hottentotshuisie offers the special attraction of two lost chests of gold coins. Several undertakings in the city and suburbs offer tuition and advice based on long local experience. The Atlantic Underwater Club is in Bay Road, Green Point.

Drives and viewsites

There are numerous drives along excellent roads with superb views, such as Table Mountain Road and Signal Hill Drive.
A round-the-peninsula drive, which offers many spectacular sea and mountain vistas, could begin in Victoria Road, leading to Hout Bay.

Golf

Clubs in this area are the Milnerton Golf Club, with its scenic and sometimes wind-lashed setting between sea and lagoon, and the Metropolitan Golf Club at Mouille Point. Both have 18-hole courses.

Horseriding

For rides in the area contact the Milnerton Riding Club and Gordon's School of Riding.

Libraries

Temporary membership can usually be arranged on payment of a small fee. Contact the local municipality.

Museums

STATE ARCHIVES, 62 Queen Victoria Street: Historical documents and pictures.
BERTRAM HOUSE, Government Avenue: Double-storeyed Georgian house furnished as an early 19th-century Cape-British dwelling.
BOKAAP MUSEUM, 71 Wale Street: 18th-century building depicting the home life of a 19th-century Muslim family.
CASTLE OF GOOD HOPE: Built from 1666, this is South Africa's oldest standing building.
CULTURAL HISTORY MUSEUM, Adderley Street: The original site of the slave lodge, later expanded and improved to house the Supreme Court and old Cape

A sail billows in Table Bay, against a background of cloud spilling over the mountains.

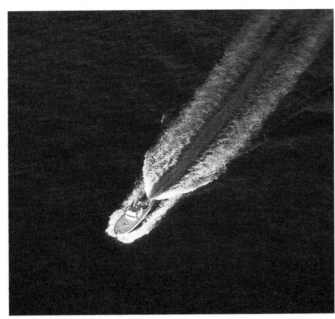

A luxury launch cleaves its way through the velvety sea.

Legislative Council. Exhibits cover the development in South Africa of weapons, postage, currency, domestic furniture and appliances, and so on.

IRMA STERN MUSEUM, Cecil Road, Mowbray: The late artist's home, housing some of her work, as well as antique furniture, art treasures and Congolese artefacts.

JEWISH MUSEUM, Company's Garden: The first synagogue built in South Africa (1863). Items of Jewish cultural and religious significance.

KOOPMANS DE WET HOUSE, 35 Strand Street: Perfect example of a late 18th-century townhouse, with collections of period silver, furniture and glass.

MOSTERT'S MILL, Rhodes Avenue, Mowbray: One of only two fully restored Dutch windmills at the Cape.

SENDINGGESTIG MUSEUM, 40 Long Street: Restored mission church first opened for services in 1802.

SA MUSEUM, Gardens: Natural history exhibits, including anthropology, archaeology and palaeontology. Recent extensions include a whale house.

Music and theatre
CAPE TOWN SYMPHONY ORCHESTRA: Concerts at the City Hall, Darling Street, Thursdays and Sundays.

BAXTER THEATRE, Main Road, Rondebosch.

LITTLE THEATRE and ARENA THEATRE, Orange Street: Part of the University of Cape Town.

NICO MALAN THEATRE CENTRE, DF Malan Avenue, Foreshore: Headquarters of Capab (Cape Performing Arts Board).

Powerboating
The freshwater recreational area of Rietvlei is the headquarters of the Milnerton Aquatic Club — contact the municipality for details. The Oceana Power Boat Club has premises on the Mouille Point side of Table Bay Harbour. There is a launch ramp at Three Anchor Bay.

Shipwrecks
Although many hundreds of ships have come to grief in Table Bay, little of them remains to be seen. Foreshore reclamation has covered many, while others were dynamited at the time of the Festival of Union in 1910. Those wrecks that are visible are:

Winton (1934), a few unrecognisable and battered fragments of which remain in the surf off Milnerton.

Daeyang Family (1986), a large ore-carrier that grounded on Whale Rock after dragging its anchors close to Robben Island.

Athens (1865), destroyed off Mouille Point in a north-west gale with 29 crew members. Still visible is the single cylinder of its steam engine.

Antipolis (1977), a derelict tanker that broke away from its tow and drove hard against the rocky beach at Oudekraal. It has been cut down to the tideline but is still visible.

Surfing
Radio Good Hope broadcasts a daily surf report at 07h15. Watch the local press for further details or contact any of the specialist shops.

Milnerton: Good in a big swell, with a south-easter.

Rocklands (Sea Point): Best when the wind is from the south or south-east with a good swell. (Not for beginners.)

Queens Beach (Sea Point): Best at high tide with a big swell, and a light wind from the south-east or north-east. The area is rocky, and a mistake could be dangerous. (Not for beginners.)

Clifton: Best under conditions of light wind. Surfing here is banned between December and February — the peak holiday season.

Glen Beach (Camps Bay): This famous spot with a challenging, hard-breaking wave, is best during a north-east or south-east blow.

Camps Bay: The corner nearest Glen Beach is often good in a light north-east or south-east wind.

Swimming
Suitable for children are Milton Pool between Sea Point and Three Anchor Bay, the pools at Sea Point Pavilion and those at nearby Sunset and Queens beaches, as well as the beaches at Rocklands (Sea Point) and Hottentotshuisie. Camps Bay has both a tidal and a paddling pool. There is calm, shallow water near the mouth of Milnerton Lagoon. Swimming is fairly safe at Bachelor's and Maiden's Cove. The backwash is fairly strong at Milnerton, Camps Bay and Clifton.

Tennis and squash
For details of clubs and courts, contact the Western Province Tennis Association and the Western Province Squash Racket Association.

Walks
There are many shady walks over gentle gradients along the network of paths in Newlands Forest above Union Avenue. From near the domed *kramat* next to Signal Hill Drive, a path leads around Lion's Head, and can be followed, with the aid of chains embedded in the rock, to the summit. The Contour Path leads from near the lower cable station all the way to Constantia Nek, but can be followed for shorter distances. For sea views, the Pipe Track can be followed from Kloof Nek beneath the Twelve Apostles.

For more information on walking tours and hikes, contact Captour. Before tackling any serious climbing, get a copy of the Table Mountain Guide and consult the Mountain Club of South Africa.

Yachting and dinghy sailing
The Royal Cape Yacht Club is based in Table Bay Harbour. Yachting also takes place at Rietvlei and Milnerton — contact the local municipality or the Western Province Sailing Association.

INFORMATION
• Captour, Strand Concourse, Adderley Street, Cape Town 8001. Tel 253320
• Cape Town Municipality, Civic Centre, Cape Town 8001. Tel 2103131
• Milnerton Municipality, Pienaar Rd, Milnerton 7405. Tel 522000
• Mountain Club of SA, 97 Hatfield St, Cape Town 8001. Tel 453412
• National Sea Rescue Institute, 4 Loop St, Cape Town 8001. Tel 215765; emergencies: 2183500
• SA Tourism Board, Piazza Level, Golden Acre, Cape Town 8001. Tel 216274

Nearest AA Office
• AA House, 7 Martin Hammerschlag Way, Foreshore, Cape Town 8001. Tel 211550

Hikers enjoy a ramble on the wooded slopes of Table Mountain.

Golden coast kissed by the sun's last rays

FROM THE TUMBLED BOULDERS of Llandudno, looping back around indomitable mountains to the heart of Hout Bay, then sweeping down the jagged sea-splashed coast to the wild expanse of Noordhoek and the hamlets of Kommetjie and finally Scarborough, this is the Cape Peninsula's westerly edge, the place of the setting sun.

Thousands make the summertime pilgrimage here each year . . . to soak up those last rays, to savour the charm of a fishing village just a step from the city's flurry, to sample the delights of the sea in all its rough splendour.

1 Llandudno

Viewed from above, Llandudno is a breathtaking curve of bright white sand backed by steep-sided slopes. It lies some 20 km from Cape Town, along Victoria Road — the magnificent marine drive skirting the peninsula's Atlantic seaboard. From here, a steep, narrow road, with fairly sharp bends, winds down to the beach past some fine architectural showpieces.

The beach is bounded at either end by great granite boulders, echoed offshore where the stern section of the tanker *Romelia* is firmly lodged, overlooked by the rather bare slopes of Klein-Leeukop (so-called because of its resemblance to Lion's Head).

Sunbathing is the main attraction, but there is little by way of shady relief and a dip in the sea is a chilling experience. Scantily clad bodies are often to be found sheltering from the south-easter among the rocks at the south end, or on the promontory at the north-east, the end also favoured by surfers. Beyond this lies Logie's Bay, a small (but hard to reach) inlet with interesting rock pools.

Facilities available at Llandudno include a small parking area, toilets, change-rooms, showers and drinking water.

2 Sandy Bay

This isolated beach, at the foot of the saddle between Klein-Leeukop and the Sentinel, has long been a haven for naturists — not necessarily one safe from the reach of the law, but dedicated sun-worshippers remain undeterred.

Access to Sandy Bay is by a footpath from the car park at the south end of Llandudno, overlooking the wreck of the *Romelia* off Sunset Rocks. The path, which crosses rock in places, rises and falls through indigenous fynbos, sprinkled with arum lilies and pelargoniums, although the area surrounding the bay is heavily

Seen from above, the path to Sandy Bay can be traced through the bush.

overgrown with the exotic rooikrans (*Acacia cyclops*). It also passes a large shell midden, historical evidence of long occupation by those Khoikhoi known as Strandlopers. Narrow paths lead off on both sides — seaward to favourite sunning sites among the rocks, and inland to high sand dunes. The walk, which takes about twenty minutes, is not difficult to negotiate but wear stout shoes, because there is a surprising amount of broken glass about.

Sandy Bay is the ideal beach for getting away from it all, and as such has no facilities at all. North of the beach itself is an immense rocky area with kelp-strewn pools worth investigating at low tide.

From Oude Schip, just beyond Sandy Bay, the rocky coast curves beneath Karbonkelberg (653 m), with the seal-covered Duikereiland a short distance offshore. Seen from the sea, the Sentinel (331 m) shows its small, inclined summit and then a sheer drop, the appearance that gave it its original name of Hangberg. The only access here is on foot.

3 Hout Bay

Shortly after his arrival, Jan van Riebeeck gave the apt name of *'t Houtbaaijen* (wood bay) to this sparkling bay, set in a green fold of mountains. Today this leafy seaside village is one of the most picturesque spots on the peninsula, especially when the fishing boats come in, trailing clamorous clouds of gulls and terns.

The beach stretches for over a kilometre between the harbour in the west and Flora Bay, at the start of Chapman's Peak Drive. Overlooking the scene, fairly benevolently, is a bronze leopard perched on a rock pinnacle between Flora Bay and the main beach. Erected in 1963, this was the work of sculptor Ivan Mitford Barberton, to commemorate the big cats that prowled Hout Bay's forests and mountains for centuries.

There is ample parking at both ends of the

LEFT *The curve of Hout Bay is shrouded in darkness against the setting sun.*

beach. Surfers tend to congregate at the east end of the beach (where there are also change-rooms and toilets), while boardsailors favour an area more to the west. Their colourful sails, and those of the many yachts that put out to sea here (the harbour has a yacht club, as well as a slipway), brighten any day. The swimming at Hout Bay is generally safe, and besides the sea there are shallow pools on the beach after high tides.

The estuary of the Hout Bay River forms winding shallows across the beach, but further upstream there are deep pools. The banks are lined with reeds and trees (many of them exotics), but there is a stand of milkwood on the east (later south) bank. Here pied kingfishers may sometimes be seen, and blacksmith plovers lower down in the vicinity of the estuary. Canoeing is possible on the

'A MOST DISASTROUS AND TERRIBLE SHIPPING CATASTROPHE'

So said the *Cape Argus* of 11 August 1909 . . . and it was no exaggeration. At midnight on 5 August, the steamship *Maori*, bound from Britain for Australia with 53 people on board, stuck fast on Duikerpunt, the most westerly point of the Cape Peninsula. Three lifeboats were put off, leaving 15 men behind. Two of the boats — and all on board — were never seen again. The third lifeboat attempted to come ashore on Noordhoek Beach, but capsized, losing six of its passengers. The surviving nine alerted the authorities to the fact that 15 of their shipmates were still aboard the wreck, and a tug was sent to investigate.

Tragically, after examining the wreck in the high sea and wind, the tug crew decided that nobody could still be alive in the stern section, almost the only portion of the *Maori* above the surface. The tug returned to port, leaving not only 14 frantic men in the sea-smashed stern, but one seaman, named Gladman, clinging to the foremast.

The desperate survivors were spotted by Hout Bay fishermen who, unable to put to sea in such weather, tied sinkers to light lines and threw these over the wreck. At last one fell over the stern, and a heavier rope was pulled across and made fast. Hand over hand, two men made their way to safety, but a third was torn away by the waves and drowned.

Those left on board decided to wait for the rocket brigade, which was, however, held up by having to move its apparatus over the difficult terrain from Simon's Town. After clinging to the mast for forty hours, Gladman could wait no longer, and he climbed hopelessly down the rigging and disappeared in the boiling surf. Only many hours later did the rocket brigade arrive, and rescue the remaining survivors.

To prevent a repetition of the tragic delay, a rocket station was built above Oude Schip (today in ruins).

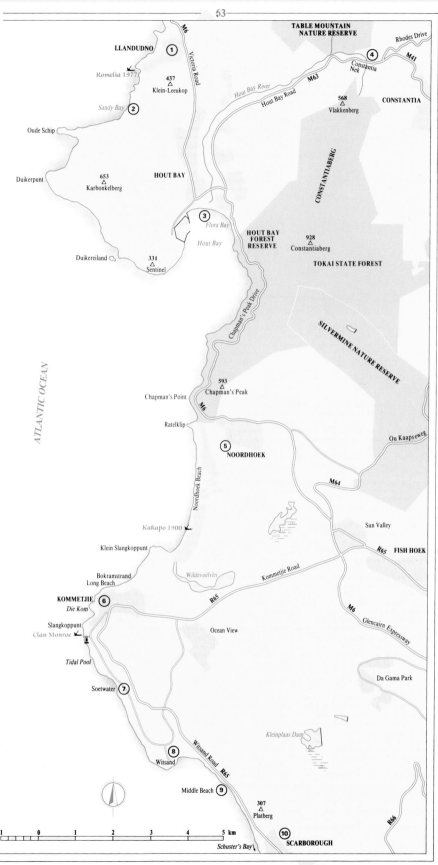

Hout Bay fishermen repair their nets.

A SLIVER OF ROAD BETWEEN SEA AND MOUNTAIN

Skirting Chapman's Peak, the 593 m southerly extension of Constantiaberg, is one of the most spectacular marine drives in the world. From Hout Bay Chapman's Peak Drive dips and soars above a rocky coastline broken briefly by the small, inaccessible beach of Koeëlbaai to turn inland just above the northern end of Noordhoek Beach. To appreciate the unfolding views fully, it should be driven in both directions.

The road was the idea of Sir Frederic de Waal, the first administrator of the Cape Province, after whom another roadway — De Waal Drive — is named. Work began in 1915, after engineers, geologists and surveyors had performed stupendous feats of mountaineering (often hanging from the cliffs by rope) to determine the best route. Their choice was an interesting one: for much of its course, it follows the soft band of shale between the mountain's granite base and the overlying sandstone. You can see this clearly if you look at the road from the vicinity of the harbour.

Shortly after leaving Hout Bay, the road passes the ruined stone barracks of the east fort, built by the British in 1795. The battery of cannons is still in position below the road. Near here, too, are the remains of a jetty from which manganese ore was shipped from mines on Constantiaberg.

A viewsite with guardrails has been constructed at the highest point of the road, offering spectacular views over Hout Bay. Rivalling this is the sighting of Chapman's Bay, with the long, white sands of Noordhoek Beach stretching away to a rocky headland, the distant Slangkop lighthouse rearing pencil-slim beyond.

river, but the water at times seems sluggish, choked by illegal dumping.

Hout Bay is rich in natural attractions, but besides these it offers hotels, restaurants and numerous shops, as well as a library, museum and children's playground.

4 Up to Constantia Nek
Hout Bay Road leads north out of the village, a narrow, winding road lined by oaks and pines. It passes the Cape Dutch homestead of Kronendal and also the detached wine cellar of Groot Moddergat, another very old farm. On the left is the lovely valley of the Hout Bay River, glimpsed through the trees. The road climbs easily to Constantia Nek, a gap in the mountains that run like a spine down the peninsula. From here, there are easy walks to the top of Table Mountain.

5 Noordhoek
The sudden glimpse of this vast sweep of untamed beach provides a dramatic highlight to the descent from Hout Bay via Chapman's Peak Drive. For some 8 km the band of white sand stretches between blue sea and green bush, ending at the rocky outcrop of Klein-Slangkoppunt. In the far distance is the dark mass of the steamer *Kakapo* that ran ashore in 1900 when its captain mistook Chapman's Peak for Cape Point.

There are small, shallow tidal lagoons at either end of the beach, the one at the south leading inland to the privately owned Wildevoëlvlei (wild bird lake). At the north end of the beach is a short, rocky promontory known as Ratelklip (honey badger stone), a popular fishing spot, especially for galjoen. Surfers also favour this end, as well as a spot near the *Kakapo*. (Tread carefully in the wreck area, as there are many sharp fragments of rusty metal, some only just beneath the surface of the sand.)

Swimming is reasonably safe — if cold — although the surf and backwash are fairly strong.

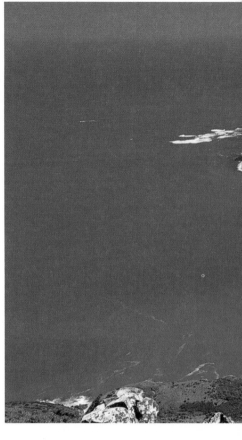

The beach has no shade, and is exposed to the south-easter throughout its length, but on calm days nothing can match it for a long, peaceful ramble or a canter on horseback.

Facilities include toilets and taps yielding drinking water at the north end of the beach.

6 Kommetjie
The name Kommetjie (little basin) is derived from the saucerlike tidal pool known as Die Kom, around which the hamlet clusters. After a high

Chapman's Peak Drive threads its way distinctly between the granite base and sandstone.

A bird's-eye view of Hout Bay's sickle beach ending in the sheltered harbour.

THE CALL OF THE SEA

Within the embracing curve of the mountains, Hout Bay's fishing fleet lies snugly at anchor behind the breakwater of the harbour. Alongside, yachts reflect their sleek hulls onto the still waters, mere playthings by comparison to the lumbering, diesel-powered trawlers.

Fishermen have been a permanent part of the Hout Bay scene for almost two centuries, since the first rough wooden shed was knocked together on the beach, and a batch of snoek was salted and dried. The western entrance to the harbour brings you to the 'working' section, where the trawler crews go about their business of unloading and weighing the catch, or readying the boats for the next trip to the fishing grounds.

There is always something going on. Today's nets may be made of nylon, instead of knotted strands of cotton soaked in ox blood for durability, but they still need to be repaired. Another chore of the deep-sea fisherman ashore is painting his boat, so that apart from a crisp coat of salt on return to harbour, the boats are generally immaculate in their bright colours.

Trek-fishing too is a traditional sight in Hout Bay. When the lookout spots a shoal of fish entering the bay, he signals to the team on the beach and they row out to sea in the direction he has indicated. One end of the 100 m-long net is firmly held ashore and the other in the boat as it

A glimpse of Hout Bay's fishing fleet.

circles the shoal, returning to the beach close to where it was launched. From the shore the ends of the net (kept buoyant by floats but weighted with lead to hang straight down) are hauled together, and the catch is slowly brought in. One trek in 1927 netted more than 3 300 kabeljou with an average individual mass of over 20 kg, but such a catch would be unlikely nowadays.

As a fishing harbour Hout Bay has a fascination all of its own, and of course it is the ideal place to buy fresh fish — or even the proverbial fish and chips, to eat on the nearby beach. For the visitor there is also a restaurant and souvenir shop, and the opportunity to book a boat trip to see the seals at Duikereiland.

tide, this makes a perfect swimming spot — especially as it is a couple of degrees warmer than sea temperature. On either side of Die Kom are sandy inlets, from which boats are launched, while the numerous rock pools in the vicinity can be fun to explore.

Associated with Kommetjie are two beaches to the north: Bokramstrand and Long Beach. Signs warn that bathing is dangerous, for there is a strong backwash. For spending a whole day on the beach, there is little shade or shelter from the south-easter, but facilities include change-rooms (at Long Beach), and toilets and a shower in nearby Van Imhoff Way.

Long Beach in particular is well known as a popular surfing venue, attracting fans even in the wet winter months, while conditions for boardsailing too can be good. The area also has its diving devotees: the kelp-grown rocky areas, especially off the lighthouse and at Slangkoppunt and Klein-Slangkoppunt, may yield good hauls of rock lobster. (The beaches themselves are often strewn with kelp, which grows luxuriantly along much of the Cape's west coast.)

Besides kelp, Kommetjie has large stands of indigenous white milkwood, with the distinctive bright green, leathery leaves. Today this tough wood, previously widely used for fencing posts, is a protected species.

Cormorants (including the whitebreasted cormorant) can often be seen 'drying out' with spread wings on the rocky shoreline, after diving for food at sea. To enable them to stay under water more easily, these birds swallow pebbles to

The view across to Noordhoek and Hout Bay from the white sands of Long Beach.

increase their mass — the same principle divers apply in wearing weight belts. Another frequent visitor to Kommetjie is the gull, which will swim quite unperturbed alongside its human counterparts, but be a little warier of the countless surfers and boardsailors.

7 Soetwater

Although it extends as a long coastal strip almost as far north as Kommetjie, the Soetwater resort and caravan park can be entered only from the south, by following the tarred turn-off from the main coast road. This attractive resort has all the amenities, and also provides areas for camping and picnicking. Most of the shore is rocky, with innumerable tidal pools, and heavy growths of kelp offshore. There are two large, artificial tidal pools for swimming, both of which receive large amounts of kelp at high tide.

8 Witsand

This charming, well-named bay is reached by a gravel turn-off from the road to Soetwater. The beach is backed by a large area of high dunes, with indigenous fynbos further inland. The sea here is fairly free of kelp, and swimming is pleasant and safe. There is, however, little shade and the bay is open to the south-easter. Many small boats are launched from the sheds near the beach, some of them supplying the rock lobster factory on the headland nearby.

9 Middle Beach

A sprinkling of cottages dusts the steep hillside on either side of the road above this beach (also known as Misty Cliffs), midway between Scarborough and Witsand.

The area in general is fairly rocky, with a number of small tidal pools and a beach that changes its size with the seasons. Much of the sand is washed away by winter gales, to be redeposited during the summer. Even in summer, however, the beach area is very small.

10 Scarborough

Most of this small seaside village lies at the foot of the Platberg on a fairly level plateau; beneath it is a long, wide beach ending, in the south, just beyond the Schuster's River lagoon. (The beach is reached via Camel Rock Road, so named for the roadside formation of Table Mountain Sandstone that closely resembles a camel.) Swimming in the open sea is dangerous, but the lagoon is shallow and safe for children, and the many interesting rock pools invite paddling. Milkwoods provide shade in some places, but the beach itself is exposed to the wind.

At the far end, the beach at Schuster's Kraal borders the Cape of Good Hope Nature Reserve, and is a favourite — but tricky — surfing spot. (The approach road to the beach should be taken slowly as there is an enormous and unheralded stormwater gully across it.) Both here and at Scarborough Beach there are picnic sites and toilets, while Schuster's Kraal also has a site for overnight camping a couple of hundred metres from the beach itself.

From Scarborough, a walk up the slopes of Platberg to the north provides wide and attractive views over the predominantly rock-girt coastline.

Angling

The Atlantic Boat Club, based at Hout Bay Harbour, is a game-fishing club.

Beachcombing and shelling

At Sandy Bay and Hout Bay you can sometimes pick up odds and ends from passing ships, especially trawlers, while Noordhoek may yield driftwood as well as trawl material. At most of the other beaches, dense kelp beds just offshore form a barrier against flotsam. There are interesting rock pools at Kommetjie, Soetwater, Scarborough and Schuster's Bay. Mussels, limpets and spirals can generally be found at Sandy Bay, Kommetjie and Soetwater, and a slightly greater variety at Scarborough.

The scarlet macaw and Knysna lourie can both be seen at the World of Birds.

Birdwatching

The thick bush on the way to Sandy Bay is particularly rich in bird life but aside from the occasional soaring black eagle or rock kestrel against the slopes of Klein-Leeukop or Suther Peak, the birds are generally heard, not seen. They include the cloud cisticola and malachite sunbird, while the whitefronted sandplover can be seen on the beaches at Llandudno and Sandy Bay. The World of Birds in Valley Road, Hout Bay, has large, walk-through aviaries housing over 3 500 birds of more than 300 species, both indigenous and exotic. This is an unexpected tropical paradise in which birds (and other animals) lead a free and fearless existence. Favourites with visitors are the colourful Australian lorikeet, the shy Knysna lourie in its gay plumage, as well as the hamerkop, ibis, spoonbill, egret, heron, blue crane and pelican. The swift tern and kelp gull frequent Hout Bay Harbour, with smaller numbers of Cape cormorant. The bank cormorant may be seen on Duikereiland and the whitebreasted cormorant at Kommetjie, where gulls are also plentiful.

THINGS TO DO

Boardsailing

Hout Bay, especially off the western part of the beach, is a popular boardsailing venue. Long Beach is good (and fast) in a south-west wind, while Middle Beach (for the experienced only) and Scarborough are good in a north-wester.

Boat trips

Several concerns run boat trips from Hout Bay Harbour, the most popular being an hour's excursion across the bay and to Duikereiland, where a seal colony supplies the entertainment. Two-hour sunset cruises (one way) are run to Table Bay Harbour during the holiday season. Boats are also available on private charter for special cruises.

Bowls

For details of clubs, contact the Western Province Bowling Association.

Camping and caravanning

Sites include the Imhoff Caravan Park, Kommetjie, and Soetwater Holiday Resort. At Scarborough there is an overnight camp site run by the Cape Divisional Council.

Canoeing

Hout Bay River offers about the only opportunity for canoeing, but the river is not always an attractive prospect.

Cycling

Chapman's Peak Drive is a part of the circuit for annual cycle races, but is recommended only for the very fit.

Diving

The wreck of the *Maori* off Duikerpunt may still yield the odd 'treasure'. In season rock lobster may be taken from among the rocks off Klein-Slangkoppunt, Slangkoppunt, off the Slangkop lighthouse, and around Scarborough. The entire area north of Beacon MB1, which is situated at Die Josie, south of Hout Bay, is a rock lobster sanctuary.

Fish type	Season	Best area	Best bait
Galjoen	May — Sept	Hout Bay, Chapman's Bay, Kommetjie, Slang-kop, Roussouwsbank, Witsands, Pegram's Rock, Scarborough	Rotten redbait, wonderworm, prawns, mussels, bloodworm
Hottentot	All year	Whole area, especially where there is kelp	Redbait, mussels, chokka, fishbait
White steenbras	May — Sept	See galjoen	Prawns, bloodworm, wonderworm
White stumpnose (rare)	May — Sept	See galjoen	Prawns, mussels, wonderworm, redbait, bloodworm

Drives and viewsites

Victoria Road, part of the round-the-peninsula drive, makes a dramatic entrance above the Hout Bay valley from Llandudno. The two main routes from Hout Bay are both picturesque: the narrow, treelined road to Constantia Nek, and the coastal Chapman's Peak Drive, leading to Noordhoek. From Noordhoek there is a link via Silvermine Road to the Ou Kaapseweg crossing to the east side of the peninsula.

Horseriding

At Hout Bay, horses may be hired from Glenellen Riding School, and in Noordhoek from the Sunbird Riding School.

Libraries

On payment of a fee, visitors may obtain temporary membership of the libraries in Hout Bay, Kommetjie and Ocean View.

Museums

HOUTBAAI MUSEUM, 4 Andrews Road: Exhibits cover local history (including that of the fishing industry) and prehistory.

Powerboating

There is a slipway in Hout Bay Harbour. For details, contact the harbour master.

Boats can also be launched at the inlets on either side of Die Kom, and at Witsand.

Shipwrecks

Those wrecks that are still visible along this coastline include:
Romelia (1977), the stern section of which can be seen at Sunset Rocks, Llandudno. With the *Antipolis* (which grounded at Oudekraal), this tanker broke loose from its tow while on the way to a ship-breaker in the East.
Kakapo (1900), the remains of which lie near the south end of Noordhoek Beach. This newly built ship was on its delivery trip from England to Australia when it ran aground here.

Surfing

Radio Good Hope broadcasts a daily surf report at 07h15. Watch the local press for further details or contact any of the specialist shops for information on favourite spots.
Sandy Bay: Fair in a south-easter, but it is a long hike with board.
Hout Bay: Suitable for beginners, in a north/north-west wind.
Noordhoek: Good in a south-easter.
Long Beach: A busy surf beach (especially in a south-wester) for the more experienced.
Kommetjie: Outer Kom, with its powerful waves, is for the very experienced only. Inner Kom is suitable for beginners.
Witsand: Best with the wind from north-east or north-west, and not for beginners.
Middle Beach: Rocky; for the experienced only.
Scarborough: Good in a south-easter, but there may be a dangerous rip current; suitable for the experienced.

Swimming

The water along this stretch of coast is cold — but refreshing.

Llandudno and Hout Bay have excellent beaches for bathing, while there are tidal pools at Kommetjie and Soetwater. Swimming is possible at the other beaches, but conditions are marred somewhat by

powerful surf and backwash, and strong rip currents.

Tennis and squash

For details, contact the Western Province Tennis Association and the Western Province Squash Racket Association.

Walks

The walk from the Llandudno car park to Sandy Bay is an attractive one, with small rocky inlets visible before the path enters the bush.

At the south end of Sandy Bay is the peninsula known as Oude Schip, and there is an interesting walk along the rocks to the point, and then up to the ruins of the old rocket lifesaving station. Along the way are two caves worth exploring. (The route is marked with blue paint from a point about 100 m beyond the large white cross painted as an aerial survey mark on a boulder.) There is a natural rock pool on the south side of the peninsula.

The workings of an old manganese mine can be reached by an easy climb from behind the east fort above Chapman's Peak Drive. You will need a torch, as the longest adit (shaft) extends for over 80 m. Avoid the walk during wet weather, as the shafts are slippery.

A walk along Noordhoek Beach is long but rewarding. If you cannot cover the whole distance, the more attractive end is at the south, from Kommetjie to the wreck of the *Kakapo*.

Yachting and dinghy sailing

Hout Bay in particular is a popular venue for sailing, with a slipway in the harbour. Contact the Hout Bay Yacht Club or the harbour master.

Gaily coloured sails are almost part of the landscape at Hout Bay.

The fairest Cape of all

HERE, AT THE TIP OF AFRICA, is what Sir Francis Drake, rounding the world in the 16th century, called 'a most stately thing and the fairest cape we saw in the whole circumference of the earth'. To safeguard its wonders, it now falls largely within the Cape of Good Hope Nature Reserve.

The dramatic coastline, stretching for some 40 km from Schuster's Kraal in the west to Smitswinkel Bay in the east, offers a series of wild and unspoilt beaches and magnificent coastal walks. But the fascination of the reserve is not limited to this: it lies also in the profusion and variety of its flora and fauna. Visitors may wander freely on foot throughout the reserve (access is barred only to sanctuary areas) or follow the tarred roads by car as they explore and enjoy the timeless Cape.

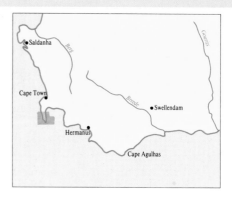

1 Olifantsbos

The first access to the coast on the western side of the nature reserve is at Olifantsbosbaai. North of this, from Menskoppunt up to Schuster's Kraal, is a sanctuary area — the rich breeding grounds of the black oystercatcher — which may not be visited by the public.

This is the site of a 2 km long lagoon formed by two rivers, the Klaasjagers and the Krom. The lagoon is separated from the sea by a narrow strip of perilous quicksand.

The name Italiaanse Kerkhof (Italian cemetery) seems appropriate along this lonely stretch of coast where the remains of ships lie shattered on the rocks or sink slowly beneath the sands. There is no longer any sign, however, of the graves of the Italian seamen who died when their ships, *Doge* and *Carlotta B*, were wrecked on Albatross Rock just offshore over a century ago.

Olifantsbosbaai has a small stretch of beach, but it consists mainly of slippery, kelp-strewn rocks, with pools visible when the tide is out.

Driftwood and a good variety of shells come ashore at the south end, among the rocks stained a bright orange with lichen. Amenities include picnic and braai sites, toilets, water, a large parking area and some shady trees and bushes. There is a smaller parking area further to the south, with less shelter from the gusty southeaster and no facilities.

The main attractions of Olifantsbos are the long walks that combine a sense of history with an air of space and unspoilt nature. South of the bay the coast is rocky, with dunes extending inland to ridges with a sparse growth of fynbos and grasses. You can proceed along the rocks, across the sand (which is deep and soft) or inland along a rough track that passes an old farmhouse now used as a field study centre.

The remains of the Liberty ship *Thomas T Tucker*, wrecked in 1942, lie on the rocks in three main sections, the stern being the most recognisable. (There are also numerous sharp, rusted bits and pieces just beneath the sand for some distance, so wear stout shoes.) One of the *Tucker*'s large boilers lies further south, near the hulk of the *Nolloth*, which went ashore in 1965 close to a tiny, sandy inlet. South of this, the coastal strip from Mast Bay to Hoek van Bobbejaan is a closed sanctuary area.

2 Gifkommetjie

Flat, low banks of rock line the shore here, forming countless pools to investigate at low tide. Named after a poisonous plant species, Gifkommetjie is reached by a number of footpaths from the car park on the low mound of Groot-Blouberg. It is the starting point for a short walk north to Hoek van Bobbejaan, where the wreck of the trawler *Phyllisia* lies in the surf and where a sanctuary area begins, or south to Platboom or Maclear Beach, or all the way to the Cape of Good Hope.

3 Platboombaai

The road to this secluded beach passes the cross-topped Dias Monument, commemorating the

Portuguese navigator's epic voyage around the Cape of Good Hope. At Platboombaai fine, sparkling white sand extends back to fynbos-covered dunes and rockier slopes. The long unspoilt beach features many interesting rock pools rich in small fish, starfish and sea anemones. Beachcombing is especially rewarding as you walk northwards across the rocks towards Gifkommetjie, with more varied shells available. Cuttlefish are common, while among the birds often seen here are the avocet, the brilliantly coloured sugarbird and the black oystercatcher.

There are picnic and braai sites, toilets, and fresh water at the car park. As at most car parks in the reserve, a resident troop of baboons appears

CAPE OF GOOD HOPE NATURE RESERVE

The Cape of Good Hope rears from a sea of blue.

With its combination of dramatic seascapes and soaring cliffs, as well as tremendously varied flora and fauna, this unique reserve (proclaimed in 1939) attracts as many visitors as the Kruger National Park. It differs from other reserves in that visitors are free to leave their cars and wander about most of its 7 750 ha, with only the sanctuary areas out of bounds.

Many of the original game species have been reintroduced to the reserve, including the rare mountain zebra and bontebok, while the animals most in evidence are the baboons. Because of the low nutritional value of the indigenous vegetation, high numbers of the larger mammals cannot be maintained, but the alert visitor is certain to see a

good variety, as well as some of the 150 species of birds found in the reserve.

The rich and varied indigenous flora is known as fynbos or Cape macchia, and includes the protea family. Characteristics are the hard, drought-resisting leathery leaves, and the woody stems and branches. The leaves are usually small, and many species are aromatic. The resin of most species is highly inflammable. Fynbos is remarkable for the restriction of different species to certain localities, often very small indeed, as a walk through the reserve will show. The bushy *Leucadendron macowanii*, for instance, grows wild only in one place in the reserve — and nowhere else in the world.

from the hillside to investigate new arrivals, so cars should be securely locked.

4 Maclear Beach
Descending to the coast, the road offers wonderful views of Platboombaai, before swinging left to run alongside Maclear Beach. This unsheltered beach seems to be most favoured by the reserve's ostriches, possibly because of the shingly consist-

ency of the sand; these great, ungainly birds are a surprising sight silhouetted against the background of blue sea. For the beachcomber prepared to sift through the periodic deposits of kelp, there is a good variety of shells and flotsam, as well as a number of rock pools. As in other kelp-strewn areas, the sea cockroach (*Ligia dilatata*) and the more nocturnal white sand hopper (*Talorchestia capensis*) are to be found feeding on

the decaying seaweed.

The remains of a forgotten wooden trawler can be seen at the north end of the beach.

5 Dias Beach
These two small inlets at the foot of towering cliffs make up the most southerly of the peninsula's beaches. The cliffs consist of neatly layered sandstone strata on a base of granite that has been

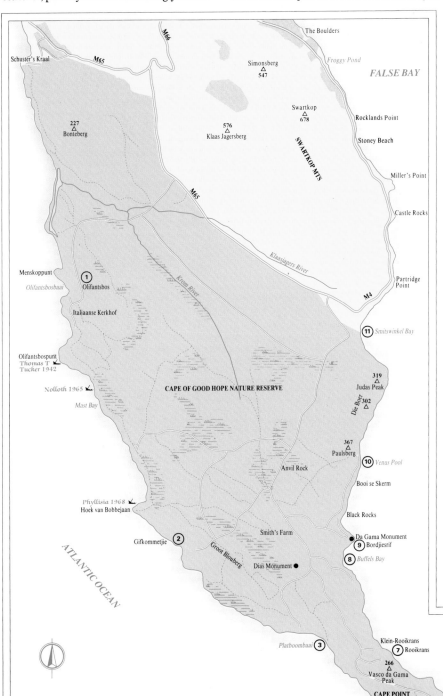

BEWARE OF THE BABOONS

A yawning chacma baboon.

Baboons are probably the most entertaining of the mammals found in the Cape of Good Hope Nature Reserve. These dog-faced chacma baboons (*Papio ursinus*) make up five resident troops, each led by a dominant male, and could be unique in that much of their diet comprises molluscs and sandhoppers gathered on the seashore.

Baboons are rarely aggressive towards people, although the troop that frequents the reserve's main car park has lost the shyness of the wild animal in the presence of humans. This is probably because visitors often feed them (despite the many signs warning that this is strictly prohibited). The baboons grow accustomed to this easy source of food, and show signs of anger when it is not forthcoming. Animals have had to be shot when they have shown a too-threatening attitude regarding food hand-outs.

Visitors should always keep their distance. Approaching a baboon in a friendly manner is no guarantee that the animal will understand your intentions; if young are about, the baboon may react by scratching or biting. Remember that a male may weigh as much as 80 kg, and have sharp, strong canines several centimetres long.

A PRIDE OF PROTEAS

The rare Mimetes fimbriifolius.

Among the most distinctive members of the group of plants known as fynbos are the proteas, although they appear in many and varied forms. In fact, the name protea stems from this: when Swedish taxonomist Linnaeus was sent a selection of species to identify, he named them after the Greek 'old man of the sea', Proteus, who was able to assume any form at will.

Proteas are concentrated in southern Africa and Australia. The Australian species are not readily recognisable as proteas (except for the waratah), and at least one example, the hakea, is regarded here as a weed and a threat to indigenous vegetation. There are more than 300 South African species, ranging from the king protea (*Protea cynaroides*) with its huge flowerhead (up to 300 mm in diameter) to the silver tree (*Leucadendron argentum*), which may reach a height of 10 m.

Proteas flower at various times of the year and there is almost certain to be a colourful display in the Cape of Good Hope Nature Reserve at most times. They might include the very common tolbos (*Leucadendron salignum*), found as far east as Port Elizabeth, and the much rarer *Mimetes fimbriifolius*, which is concentrated south of Smitswinkel Bay. South Africa's national flower, the sugarbush (*Protea repens*), is also found here. Early colonists made a syrup, known as *suikerbosstroop*, from the abundant nectar, and the botanist Thunberg gave it the appropriate name of *Protea mellifera* (honey-producing), not realising it had already been named.

An interesting association between the Cape sugarbird and proteas has been observed. When proteas are flowering, the sugarbird is often seen probing deep into the flowerhead to reach the sweet nectar. The pollen that adheres to the bird is then transferred to other flowers, promoting pollination. In addition, part of the sugarbird's diet consists of parasitic insects found on proteas.

battered and eroded by wave action. A large cave has been hollowed out at the east end, under Cape Point, but note that this can be reached only at low tide. The rather odd-looking wreck which is visible here is all that remains of the floating crane *Shir Yib*, which was wrecked after parting from its towing vessel in 1975.

Access to Dias Beach, one of Cape Town's most dramatically beautiful beaches, is by a very steep footpath from the upper car park, and the journey should be started at early low tide. There are no facilities and the beach is exposed to the south-easter... but the breathtaking scenery quite makes up for this.

6 Cape Point

The Cape of Good Hope, most southerly point of the Cape Peninsula, is traditionally taken as the meeting place of the cold Benguela and warm Agulhas currents. Oceanographers, however, say that the Agulhas Current, sweeping down from Mozambique, is deflected eastwards in the vicinity of Mossel Bay by the chilly Benguela Current moving northwards from the Antarctic. The true meeting place is somewhat further west, off Cape Agulhas, Africa's most southerly point, although there is some overspill in either direction. This accounts for the water in False Bay being warmer than that on the western side of the peninsula — the 'Atlantic seaboard'.

From the car park at the southern end of the reserve's main road (there is a refreshment kiosk here), a steep road (closed to private vehicles)

ABOVE *The distinctive cloak of fynbos that covers the nature reserve.*
BELOW *Waves lap the beached remains of a wreck off Cape Point.*

climbs towards the site of the original Cape Point lighthouse. A bus, named 'The Flying Dutchman' after the legendary ghost ship, takes the less energetic visitor up the road, from where a flight of steps leads upwards for some 10 m to all that is left of the lighthouse — its round iron base. There are outstanding views from here, looking down on the new (1914) lighthouse, with the Cape of Good Hope to the right and the impressive Cape Point (which may well be the cape over which Drake enthused) to the left.

7 Rooikrans

This 'red cliff' takes its name from the colour of the sandstone in the early morning sunlight. It is one of the most famous angling spots in South Africa and one of the few in the world where tunny can be caught from the shore. The rock ledges close to the sea are situated below Vasco da Gama Peak and are reached by a footpath from the signposted car park. The path is fairly rough and at times runs along the cliff edge before zigzagging down to the ledges. Views from the path are outstanding — down over the wreck of the trawler *Aggie*, across to Buffels Bay and beyond — but the walk is only for the steely-nerved.

8 Buffels Bay

The first beach on the False Bay coastline after Cape Point is Buffels Bay, in an attractive setting of indigenous milkwood thickets. Grassy picnic sites are situated alongside the gently sloping beach, which offers safe swimming, and a large tidal swimming pool adjoins a natural rock pool.

South of the bay, the rocky coast is lined for a distance by lawned picnic and braai sites. The rock pools here are well worth exploring, and the wreck of the *Tania*, a large, wooden trawler, can also be seen. Buffels Bay has fresh water and toilets, but only the milkwoods provide shade and shelter.

A footpath leads south from the car park and, after a short scramble over the rocks, continues along low cliffs to a spot known as Klein Rooi-krans. On the way, you pass a number of cavelike erosions in the rock, one of them called Antonies-gat, although the identity of Antonie has since been forgotten.

9 Bordjiesrif

From this sandy crescent of beach with adjoining tidal bathing pool there is an outstanding view of the peaks Paulsberg, Die Boer and Judas Peak, resembling great cowled figures with their backs turned to the southerly winds. There are interesting rock pools to the south, near a naval installation, and to the north at Black Rocks and Booi se Skerm.

Above Bordjiesrif is the Da Gama Monument, a large, stylised version of a Portuguese *padrao* (stone cross), honouring the man who discovered the sea route via the Cape to India. Such inscribed stone pillars, bearing the Portuguese coat of arms, were erected as landmarks by 15th- and 16th-century Portuguese explorers to proclaim sovereignty over the newly discovered land.

CURSE OF THE FLYING DUTCHMAN

The phantom ship, doomed to sail eternally.

Although the *Flying Dutchman* sailed from Amsterdam for Batavia in 1680, it still has not made port . . . or so the story goes.

Contrary winds frustrated all attempts to sail around Cape Point, and the captain, Vanderdecken, called out that if God would not help him to round the Cape, then he would do so with the help of the devil, even if it took until the Day of Judgement. Immediately, an angel appeared, and the blasphemous captain was condemned to battle vainly to round the Cape for as long as 'time itself shall last'. And so, over the centuries, the phantom ship has been sighted many times, often bringing misfortune to anyone unwise enough to hail it.

In 1857 it sailed right under the bows of the *Joseph Somers*, so close that Vanderdecken was seen clearly on his deck. A few days later the *Joseph Somers* caught fire and burnt to the waterline. Fortunately, the passengers and crew were rescued and brought to Table Bay — where more publicity was given to the ghost ship than to the destruction of the real one. In another incident, the future King George V of England, while sailing as a midshipman in HMS *Bacchante* in 1881, recorded that the *Flying Dutchman* crossed their bows: 'A strange red light as of a phantom ship all aglow.' The sailor who first reported the sighting was killed shortly afterwards in a fall from the rigging.

The fame of the *Flying Dutchman* has spread far and wide. It features in novels and in an opera, and at Cape Point it can even be seen . . . in the name of the bus running up to the viewsite.

From the Cape of Good Hope, trimmed with dazzling beaches, the eye is drawn across False Bay to the Hottentots Holland Mountains.

THE LIGHT THAT FAILED

Bartholomeu Dias is said to have named the great promontory Cabo Tormentoso — the Cape of Storms — in 1488, and planted a stone cross, dedicated to St Philip, somewhere on the western shore, possibly at Cape Maclear. The king of Portugal supposedly changed the name to Cape of Good Hope, although it is possible that Dias himself gave it this name, as he would certainly not have been able to land to plant a cross had the weather been bad.

Ironically, Dias and all his crew were to die in a storm while attempting to round the southern tip of Africa for the second time in 1500. It was to be another 360 years before the gleam of a lighthouse shone out from Cape Point to guide mariners through these stormy waters.

The lighthouse was built 268 m above sea level with the revolving beam visible 58 km out to sea . . . but only in clear weather. It was soon realised that the site had been badly chosen, because the beam was often obscured by cloud, even when conditions at sea level were clear. Reconstruction at a lower site was recommended in 1872, but was postponed until, as was inevitable, a big ship was wrecked on Bellows Rock, just 3 km from the lighthouse.

In 1911, the five-year-old Portuguese liner *Lusitania* was on a voyage from Lourenço Marques (Maputo) with some 800 people aboard. At 22h30 the light was sighted, and a course set to clear it by a safe margin. Soon afterwards, cloud obliterated the light. The *Lusitania* steamed on for an hour, when the cloud suddenly lifted and the light was sighted again, much too close for safety. The inshore set of the current had carried the *Lusitania* just into False Bay, and course was urgently changed to put back out to

The light that warns mariners away from the treacherous rocks of Cape Point.

sea. But the lookouts missed the foam that breaks permanently over Bellows Rock, and the *Lusitania* crashed into it bows on. A couple of days later it slid off the rock and sank.

Only three lives were lost but it was clear that a new lighthouse was now a matter of urgency. Construction began in 1914 at a height of only 87 m above sea level; when completed, the old light was dismantled. The base of the old lighthouse — an excellent viewsite — is all that remains of it, but of the *Lusitania*, there is nothing to be seen.

Bordjiesrif has large parking areas, with toilets and water, but very little shade.

10 Venus Pool

In calm conditions, lacelike spray drifts over the rocks to fill this natural fissure with water. During the course of the day, this becomes warmer than the sea itself and adds to the pleasure of a pool ideal for safe swimming. Venus Pool lies beneath Paulsberg, which from here presents a sheer, slab-sided aspect. Smaller, shallower pools run in line with the main pool, and the dark rock mass appears uptilted towards the sea, even obscuring it in places. Black zonure lizards may often be seen sunning themselves on the rocks.

There is a large old limekiln, though no longer readily recognisable as such, beside the road to Venus Pool. This is tarred but it is closed to vehicles; the walk, however, is rewarded by the sheer prettiness and tranquillity of the place.

11 Smitswinkel Bay

Steep, sheltering cliffs enfold this bay of white sand and gentle waves, lying partly within the Cape of Good Hope Nature Reserve. Few alien plants have established themselves among the coastal fynbos that extends from the edge of the beach up to the road, and bird life is plentiful.

There are a number of explanations for the name, one being that it was suggested by the proximity of Bellows and Anvil rocks. It could be translated as either 'Smit's shop' or 'smithy', and it is said that in days gone by, when there were many farms in what is now the nature reserve, a smithy was located next to the road above the bay.

There are several holiday cottages at Smitswinkel Bay, but no public facilities at all. The bay is reached by a very steep footpath.

THINGS TO DO

Angling
The entire west coast of the reserve, from Schuster's Kraal to Cape Point, has been declared a marine reserve, and fishing in this area is restricted. Inquire at the reserve itself or at any of the larger sports shops in Cape Town for further details.

Beachcombing and shelling
Most of the coastline, except Dias Beach, yields interesting flotsam but there are particularly substantial shipwrecks just south of Olifantsbospunt and at Hoek van Bobbejaan. Worth investigating are the fairly lively rock pools at Platboombaai, Olifantsbosbaai, Buffels Bay, Bordjiesrif and Maclear Beach. As far as shells are concerned, there is a wide variety to choose from, including barnacles, limpets, turban shells, lamp shells and perlemoen. Good sites are Olifantsbospunt, Maclear Beach and Buffels Bay.

Birdwatching
The Cape of Good Hope Nature Reserve boasts more than 150 bird species, including sporadic visitors such as the albatross, petrel and jackass penguin. Birds of prey include the fish eagle, black eagle, black-shouldered kite, kestrel, hawk, owl and the summer-visiting steppe buzzard. Among the marine birds are four species of cormorant, gulls, plovers and the black oystercatcher. Swifts, swallows, African hoopoes and paradise flycatchers are likely to be encountered almost anywhere.

Boardsailing
An additional fee must be paid on all boards brought into the reserve. The only really suitable beach is Platboombaai, especially when the south-easter is blowing, but even this is rather too rocky.

Cycling
The main road from the reserve gate to the upper parking area, and Circular Drive are attractive prospects on a bicycle, as they pass through much indigenous vegetation, and offer the chance of seeing birds and game close up. There are also fine views of sea and coast. The roads to the beaches, although tarred, are very steep.

Diving
Olifantsbospunt has interesting inlets for underwater life, but lies within a marine reserve. Divers may take the legal quota of rock lobster between Hoek van Bobbejaan and Cape Point. Good spots here include the kelp

growth north of Platboombaai, and off Maclear Beach — particularly the south end in good weather, when perlemoen and alikreukel may also be taken. Along the reef at Bordjiesrif there is abundant underwater life.

Drives and viewsites
Visitors to the reserve may drive only on the tarred roads, which offer fine sea views through the indigenous vegetation. If you leave your car unattended, make sure the doors are locked and the windows fully closed, as a protection against baboons.

Powerboating
A limited number of boats (ten per day) may be brought into the reserve and there is a launch ramp at Buffels Bay.

Shipwrecks
Among the wrecks still visible are:
Aggie (1950s): near Rooikrans.
Nolloth (1965): near Olifantsbospunt.
Shir Yib (1975): Dias Beach.

The Cape sugarbird is a familiar sight in the reserve.

Tania (1970): trawler, Buffels Bay.
Thomas T Tucker (1942): Olifantsbospunt.

Surfing
A fee is payable on all boards brought into the reserve. There are no great breaks but surfing is possible at Platboombaai and Buffels Bay.

Swimming
Venus Pool is the safest swimming spot, and there are artificial tidal pools at Bordjiesrif and Buffels Bay. Beach bathing is limited mainly to Buffels Bay and Smitswinkel Bay.

Walks
Walking is the ideal way of appreciating the wonders of the nature reserve and there are several options. The walk south from Olifantsbosbaai to Mast Bay (a sanctuary area) can be made along the beach in one direction, and along the dunes in the other. (Be sure to take water if tackling these.) From Groot-Blouberg, paths lead to the rocky coast, where you may go north as far as the sanctuary area that starts at Hoek van Bobbejaan, or take the long route south as far as the Cape of Good Hope. The first part of the path to Rooikrans, as far as the cliff edge, offers fine views of the sweep of False Bay and the mountainous coast of the southern peninsula. The walk south from Buffels Bay to Klein Rooikrans passes a number of sea-eroded caves.

Fish type	Season	Best area	Best bait
Elf	Sept — May	Rooikrans, Venus Pool, Bordjiesdrif	Sardines, spoons, mackerel
Geelbek	Sept — May	Rooikrans	Elf, mackerel, chokka, sardines, octopus
Hottentot	All year	Bordjiesrif	Prawns, white mussels, redbait
Katonkel	Feb — May	Rooikrans	Spoons
Red roman	All year	Bordjiesrif	Chokka, octopus
Red stumpnose	June — Sept	Rooikrans	Crabs, worms, chokka
Snoek	Aug — Oct	Rooikrans	Feather lures, spoons (use dull swivel)
Yellowtail	Sept — May	Rooikrans, Venus Pool	Feather lures, spoons
Yellowfin tunny	Nov — May	Rooikrans	Spoons

One of the rewards of diving: a handsome rock lobster.

INFORMATION
• W Cape Regional Services Council, 44 Wale St, Cape Town 8001. Tel 242200
• Cape of Good Hope Nature Reserve. Tel 801100
• Captour, Strand Concourse, Adderley Street, Cape Town 8001. Tel 253320
• Mountain Club of SA, 97 Hatfield St, Cape Town 8001. Tel 453412
• National Sea Rescue Institute, 4 Loop St, Cape Town 8001. Tel 215765; emergencies: 2183500
• SA Tourism Board, Piazza Level, Golden Acre, Cape Town 8001. Tel 216274

Nearest AA Office
• AA House, 7 Martin Hammerschlag Way, Foreshore, Cape Town 8001. Tel 211550

The coast that lures mariners and merrymakers

THIS LONG, LAZY CURVE OF COAST is the 'warm' side of the Cape Peninsula, where the influence of the Agulhas Current takes the chill off the waters. Its attractions are cosy, boulder-strewn hideaways juxtaposed with unbroken expanses of white sand and gently rolling surf.

Here it is possible to trace the whole length of the coast by car: from the wild approach to Miller's Point where the wind blows rainbow spray across the road, past sleek naval and rustic fishing harbours, through to the Victorian holiday jumble of Muizenberg and just inland to the lakes of the Cape Flats, vibrant with bird life. From the rugged heights of the mountains beyond, look down on all this and out over the great sweep of False Bay.

Guarding Roman Rock in Simon's Bay.

1 Miller's Point

The sea is not the only thing that sparkles at Miller's Point — the great granite boulders also glitter in the sunlight due to innumerable little intrusions of muscovite mica. This popular resort has a number of small, sandy beaches with scattered rocks, as well as an artificial tidal pool with a shallow area ideal for children. The pool is protected from the south-easter, while elsewhere boulders provide further shelter.

South of the point itself is kelp-strewn Koeëlbaai (bullet bay), named for its water-rounded stones that tumble noisily in the little inlet of Rumbly Bay. There is a lawned area here with a number of braai places. Alien rooikrans (*Acacia cyclops*) has taken over much of the vegetation, but further north, towards the caravan park, there is some indigenous fynbos with, in late summer, the scarlet bloom of the candelabra flower (*Brunsvigia*). The pleasant walk to the caravan park passes a launch ramp, and takes in two raised, rustic wooden bridges over the rocks. Along the way there are many interesting rock pools, as well as wide rocky areas that can be explored at low tide. Rock agama and black zonure lizards abound, and dassies (rock hyraxes) may also be seen, while the bird life includes Hartlaub's and kelp gulls, cormorants, terns and Cape rock thrushes.

Admission may be charged to the parking area, but usually only at weekends and during the holiday season. Miller's Point has a caravan park and camp site (with superb sea views), as well as a restaurant. Toilets and change-rooms have been erected at several places along the beaches. The headquarters of the Cape Boat and Skiboat Club are situated at Koeëlbaai, where there is another launch ramp.

North of Miller's Point and landward of a rocky zone lies Stoney Beach, a small, sandy beach which is fairly difficult to reach. The beach, which has no shade or shelter, is often covered at high tide, and the water is generally rather clouded with sand particles.

2 Oatland Point

The shore here, consisting of pockets of sand among the sheltering granite boulders, is divided into two beaches. The smaller, southern end is

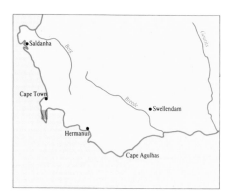

known as Beacon Beach, because it is the site of a pyramidical wooden navigational beacon; the larger is Fishermen's Beach, although few fishermen visit it now. (Just over the rocks to the north is a third, attractive little beach, well sheltered from the south-easter.) Beacon Beach, with its numerous rock pools, is favoured for bathing, although swimming at both beaches (if in rather murky water) is fairly safe. For beachcombers, there is a good variety of turban, limpet and lamp shells, as well as Venus ear and perlemoen. There are no facilities, and there is

also very little protection from the sun.

The name is derived from a small house built shortly after 1743 in the new 'Company's garden' that supplied shipping. It was enlarged and occupied later by the commandant of Simon's Town, Captain Henry Somerset (son of the Cape governor), who named the house after one of the family estates in England. Oatlands House was destroyed by fire in 1972.

Further north is Froggy Pond, a fairly large, sandy beach with the sea frontage rather limited by rocks (although these do offer slight shelter from the south-easter). The sand has covered an old Strandloper midden of shells of a variety no longer to be found here in any profusion. There is a small paddling pool for toddlers, and sea bathing is safe. The beach itself has no facilities. Across the road is Oatlands resort and caravan park, with its excellent facilities.

3 Windmill Beach

On the more northerly (and better sheltered) of these two sandy inlets, great granite boulders sprawl in the sun. This beach is separated from the sea by rock at low tide, which leaves numerous pools to explore. It also has a good sprinkling of

False Bay, viewed from above Smitswinkel Bay, is embraced by mountains.

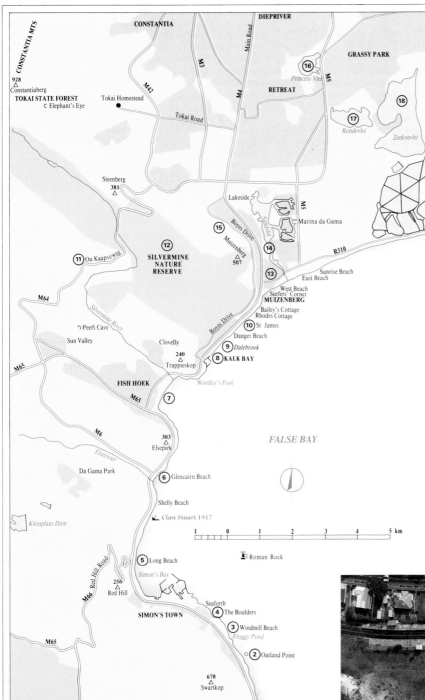

Rocky inlets at St James give way to sandy beach and a tidal pool.

tiny, colourful shells on the tideline. Bathing is safe, and more convenient off the south inlet, where there are several shaded picnic sites. Other amenities include toilets, change-rooms and a water tap, passed on the path from the car park.

The windmill that lent its name to this secluded beach has since vanished but its storage tank remains and still contains water, which could be a hazard for unwary children.

4 The Boulders and Seaforth

The massive granite boulders of the name shelter a succession of sandy inlets; here young children can splash happily in calm shallows, while the better swimmers can venture into deeper water. The most southerly beach (the first one you reach from the car park) is the most protected; from here, steps lead up to Willis Walk, which links the other inlets and can be followed all the way to Seaforth, through mixed exotic and indigenous vegetation harbouring some rather shy bird life. Alternatively, the other inlets can be reached by scrambling over the intervening boulders, picking up shells along the way.

At weekends and during the holiday season an admission fee may be charged on entry to the Boulders car park. On the road to the car park (Bellevue Road) you pass a rock with a small bronze plaque commemorating a Boer prisoner-of-war camp established at the turn of the century on the site of the present golf course. Amenities at the Boulders include toilets and drinking water.

Seaforth has large, well-shaded and lawned terraces sloping down to a sandy beach enclosed by granite boulders; a smaller, sheltered beach lies a short way to the south. A wooden raft moored off the main beach is within easy striking distance, and swimming here is safe. The flat Noah's Ark Rock about 700 m from the beach, beyond the group known as Hen and Chickens, lies within a naval security area, the SA Navy property forming the northern limit of Seaforth.

Seaforth has a restaurant, change-rooms and toilets, and drinking water is available. The beach is fairly well sheltered from the south-easter. An admission fee may be charged at the car park at weekends and during the holiday season, when the beach is likely to be very crowded.

5 Long Beach

On windless days this little-frequented beach offers scope for long walks with wide views of False Bay and the Hottentots Holland Mountains, as well as safe bathing. Beware, though, of tripping up in mole-holes, especially at the sandy, sparsely grassed southern end. Access is by a number of gaps in the brick wall alongside the Main Road and, about midway along the beach (opposite Hopkirk Way), by a flight of white-painted steps leading down from the road to an attractive beach with a small paddling pool. Several rocky areas are worth investigating at low tide.

The beach is exposed to the south-easter, and has neither shade nor shelter. Near the pool there are change-rooms and toilets, and a shower and freshwater tap. There are picnic sites near the southern end of the beach.

Offshore are the remains of the *Clan Stuart*, blown from its moorings during a south-easterly gale in 1917 and abandoned. By coincidence a sister ship, the *Clan Monroe*, was wrecked at Slangkoppunt, just a few kilometres away on the other side of the peninsula. With its cargo of dynamite and whisky, the *Clan Monroe* was in danger of breaking up in the heavy seas or blowing up. Fortunately all 82 people on board were rescued, and some of the dynamite was salved before the ship sank. But as for the whisky ... well, even though customs officials were stationed on the beach, it seems the locals, with their knowledge of the currents and inlets, were able to recover far more of the liquid gold than was declared.

At the north end of Long Beach lies tiny Shelly Beach, which does indeed yield a fair variety of shells (probably at its best for the collector after a south-east blow). The rock pools can be explored at low tide. The swimming is fairly safe, while the shallows of the adjoining tidal pool are perfect for paddling. Facilities include toilets.

Sunlight sparkles on a stretch of False Bay coast where rocks form a series of little pools.

A FATHER'S GRIEF CARVED IN MARBLE

The Anglican church of the Holy Trinity in Kalk Bay is an unspoilt example of mid-Victorian church architecture, and adding to its appeal is the moving story attached to its magnificent font.

On 7 January 1874 a wealthy Cape Town merchant, George Nicholls, took his three teenage daughters to Kalk Bay, at that stage the Cape's leading seaside resort. The bathing spot the girls selected was probably closer to the aptly named Danger Beach than to Kalk Bay itself, and soon after entering the water, they were in difficulty. The fierce backwash of the waves swept them out to sea, leaving their distraught father, unable to swim himself, helpless on the beach.

He begged local fishermen to go to the rescue, promising them a handsome reward if they could return his daughters. The men immediately set off and were able to bring all three ashore ... but alas, only one of the girls still lived.

George Nicholls was a man of his word, and he paid the fishermen their reward all the same. In memory of his lost daughters, Emma and Madeline, he also donated to the local church (then still being built) the font, carved in England from Carrara marble, and a teak choir screen.

The girls are buried in the churchyard of St Paul's, Rondebosch, where they are commemorated by other church fittings.

6 Glencairn Beach

This long curve of white beach lies below Elsepiek (sometimes known as Elsie's Peak) to the north, and is the end of the narrow Elserivier valley, with the river ending somewhat tardily several metres from the sea. There are interesting rock pools at the southern end, and the length of the beach is often littered with flotsam — usually odd bits of wood or pieces of fishing equipment and great quantities of black mussel shells. From the beach there are good views across the bay, as well as towards Simon's Town, where the buildings seem strewn across the hillsides.

There is no shade, and only slight shelter from the south-easter under the road and rail bridges. (On the road side of these are toilets.) Surf and backwash are brisk in some parts, but bathing at

A GOVERNOR'S LEGACY

Gracious Groot Constantia.

After his retirement as governor of the small Cape settlement in 1699, Simon van der Stel devoted himself to the development of his much-loved country estate, Constantia, where he had built a house several years earlier. Here, on the sheltered eastern slopes of Constantiaberg, he began producing the wines that would gain his cellar international recognition.

It was only after Van der Stel's death, when the property was subdivided and sold, that the site of the homestead became known as 'Groot' Constantia. The original house appears to have been double-storeyed, with three front gables, and forms the basis of the present classic Cape Dutch mansion, built for Hendrik Cloete around 1790. (This house, in fact, burnt down in 1925 but was subsequently restored to its former glory.) The alterations for Cloete are probably the work of architect Louis Thibault and sculptor Anton Anreith, as is the cellar or winery with its magnificently sculpted pediment.

Not only are the buildings themselves beautifully designed, but their layout too is in harmony with the natural environment. Thus, for instance, the jonkershuis (the house for the eldest son) is situated to the right of the approach to the main house. Traditional layout demands that the cellar be placed opposite the jonkershuis, but here it is behind the main house so as not to obstruct the fine view over the patchwork of vineyards to the blue of False Bay.

The main house now serves as a cultural history museum, portraying the gracious lifestyle at Constantia from the 17th century onwards, and the old cellar as a wine museum. Other attractions include restaurants and the noble Constantia wine on sale at the new cellar.

---

this often almost deserted beach is reasonably safe.

The overall impression of Glencairn is one of endless sand, which is why (sand being the principal ingredient of glass) a glass factory was established here early this century, making bottles for a brewery. It was the second such venture in this country but, like the first, did not last long. As a reminder, though, great lumps of molten glass can still be found among the bushes just inland.

7 Fish Hoek

The long expanse of Fish Hoek Beach lies at a break in the peninsula's chain of mountains, between Elsepiek and Trappieskop (steps hill) where, in the old days, the wagon road descended literally in steps. At the southern end, a picturesque pathway known as Jager's Walk has been constructed above the sea, and makes an attractive walk as well as a vantage point from which to view the activities on and off the beach. Along the way you pass numerous rock pools.

Most swimming takes place towards the southern end of the beach, and in general it is regarded as safe, with lifesavers sometimes on duty. Further to the north the beach provides a popular launching place for catamarans and sailboards, their colourful sails skipping across the bay in a cheerful display.

There is little shade or shelter at Fish Hoek, but facilities include change-rooms and toilets, fresh water and a restaurant on the beach. (Remember that Fish Hoek is 'dry': no liquor may be sold.)

At the far end of Fish Hoek is Clovelly. This beach can be reached by walking from Fish Hoek, but often access is from Clovelly railway station. Here the sea actually laps against the buildings, and steel girders have had to be erected to stabilise the railway track, and wooden sleepers embedded in the sand to prevent excessive sand drift. (A sign at the station prohibits angling from the platform!) The Silvermine River enters the sea at Clovelly, seeping into the sand where a notice warns of quicksands. A fair variety of shells comes ashore, including rather small cuttlefish, and kelp and flotsam frequently wash up at the station end. There are no facilities, and the beach is exposed to the full force of the south-easter.

A little further along is Woolley's Pool, an attractive artificial tidal pool with an adjacent smaller paddling pool and numerous rock pools on either side. It is reached through a gap in the roadside wall, and a subway, about midway between Clovelly and Kalk Bay. There are no facilities but this is a popular fishing spot, and

The little settlement of Kalk Bay, wedged between green hillside and harbour.

anglers can often be seen casting from the rocks while their children romp in the pool.

8 Kalk Bay

Two strong traditions prevail at Kalk Bay: it is both a fishing harbour and a popular resort. The name dates back to the 17th century, when servants of the Dutch East India Company gathered baskets of mussel and limpet shells for crushing and burning in their limekilns (*kalk* is Dutch for 'lime'). By the mid-19th century, the nucleus of a village had been established by trek fishermen. (The term refers to a fishing technique still practised, whereby a long trek-net — the ends secured on the shore — is used to encircle a shoal and haul the catch in.) The settlement swelled with the arrival of a number of Filipino immigrants, who made a great contribution to the fishing industry and whose descendants still live in Kalk Bay today.

Kalk Bay Harbour does not wear a pretty face to woo the tourist, but, down-to-earth and workmanlike, it has a fascination all of its own. Here the boats are generally smaller than those of Hout Bay, and made of wood, each with a tiny, shacklike wheelhouse. Above-deck space is divided into *laaitjies*, small compartments in which the fishermen sit and cast their lines, and also store their individual catches. Each man's catch is recorded, and the total haul may then be enthusiastically auctioned on the harbour wall.

A strip of beach lies within Kalk Bay Harbour, just beneath the railway embankment. This slopes gently to the water and paddling and bathing are quite safe, although at times the water may be somewhat polluted from the harbour activity. Several arches provide shade and shelter from the south-easter, which is not as fierce here as at some other beaches. The harbour has a refreshment kiosk, taps and toilets, while at Kalk Bay railway station there is a restaurant.

9 Dalebrook and Danger Beach

Three gaily painted wooden changing booths (known locally as bathing boxes) perch on a wedge of sandy beach next to Dalebrook Pool, a short distance north of Kalk Bay Harbour. The artificial tidal pool is shallowest at the railway side and around the central 'island', which can be reached by wading or by walking along the little stone peninsula connecting it to the shore. Turban, limpet and black mussel shells are common, and there are any number of rock pools to explore — but with care (a sign warns that no fishing is allowed, and that marine life may not be disturbed).

There are no facilities and no shade or shelter at Dalebrook, except in the subway which leads from the Main Road. (This subway and many others along this coast are interesting in that the sea end is of massive stone and vaulted brick construction. This is the section that was built when there was only a single set of railway tracks, the square-section subway being added later.) Almost directly opposite the subway entrance is a long, thatched dwelling (No 12). This was formerly known as Beaufort Villa and was the property of the Molteno family — Sir John Molteno, the first prime minister of the Cape Colony.

The sandy shore of nearby Danger Beach slopes gently to the sea at the southern end, while at the north it is fringed by rocks and bounded to the rear by the railway embankment. Sunbathers here have their favourite spots — some lie on the sand,

others on the rocks that close in the northern end. There are many rock pools between here and Dalebrook, but marine life may not be disturbed, and fishing is banned. Swimming is fairly safe, but try to spot the sunken rocks before you go into the water. Fresh water is available, but there are no other amenities, nor is there shade or shelter.

10 St James

A happy day spent at St James is a childhood memory of many Capetonians — sitting on the steps of one of the bright wooden bathing boxes, splashing in the pool, building sandcastles or exploring the rocks. The pool is safe for toddlers at the beach end, and slopes very gradually to become deep enough for modest dives from the wall at the seaward end. There are numerous rock pools on either side of the bathing pool, but marine life may not be disturbed — it is entertaining enough just to watch it. The beach is fairly well sheltered from the south-easter and has fresh water, toilets and change-rooms.

Two popular fishing spots (neither with any facilities) lie just north of St James. The first is directly opposite Rhodes Cottage (which Cecil John Rhodes bought in 1899 and where he died in 1902) and is reached by subway. The second, Bailey's Cottage (also reached by subway), is a tiny beach frequented mainly during the summer 'south-easter season' when good catches of kabeljou and steenbras may be made. The stone cottage here was built for Sir Abe Bailey, a colourful millionaire and politician, who also owned the mansion, Rust en Vrede (designed by Sir Herbert Baker in the style known as Cape Dutch Revival), just across the Main Road.

These homes are just one indication of the appeal a walk between St James and Muizenberg should hold for those interested in architecture. Along the way is the posthuys of 1673, a fine example of the simple Cape vernacular style, while Muizenberg railway station, opened in 1913, has been declared a national monument.

11 Ou Kaapseweg

From Fish Hoek there is a link inland to the romantically named Ou Kaapseweg (Old Cape Road). This scenic drive rises from Noordhoek on the western side of the peninsula, crosses the Steenberg plateau with its rocky outcrops and stands of indigenous flora, and descends by well-engineered bends to reach Westlake on the eastern side. Just below the entrance to the Silvermine Nature Reserve is a fine viewsite, looking out over Sandvlei and the Muizenberg beaches to the far side of the bay.

12 Silvermine Nature Reserve

This 2 151 ha reserve, which is reached by the Ou Kaapseweg, extends from above Kalk Bay in the east and across the peninsula to Noordhoek Peak. The dense indigenous vegetation on the mountain slopes of the reserve attracts colourful flocks of birds, including sugarbirds, sunbirds and Cape robins, while waterfowl can often be seen along the Silvermine River and at the reservoir. The many walks providing excellent views over the coastline on either side, as well as the picnic sites at picturesque spots — on the forested banks of the reservoir, near the tumbling waterfall — help to make this reserve a most attractive prospect.

Its name was derived from a nearby mining venture during the governorship of Simon van der Stel in the late 17th century. A so-called master miner persuaded the governor that payable silver existed in the rock, and secured himself a comfortable job for a number of years — until another 'master miner' denounced him as a fraud, resulting in his exile from the Cape to the Far East. Today the long tunnel, next to the Ou Kaapseweg, can still be seen.

13 Muizenberg

This colourful seaside resort has many reminders of its fashionable past, from the double row of colourful bathing boxes on the beach to the gracious examples of Victorian and Edwardian homes built long ago by wealthy families as seaside retreats. Today it remains one of the peninsula's most popular playgrounds, drawing visitors from far and wide.

Long rows of gentle breakers, one behind the other, sweep up to the white sands that extend

BELOW *A typical Cape scene: fishermen spreading their net are reflected in the wet and wintry sands of Fish Hoek.*

Sunbathers soak up the peace of the beach at St James with its characteristic bathing boxes — a Victorian legacy.

unbroken around the great curve of False Bay, creating a perfect beach for sunbathing, swimming and watersports. The westernmost part of the beach, nearest the railway, is known as Surfers' Corner (formerly Neptune's Corner), and the limits of the board-users' area are marked by signs on the beach. The shoreline at Muizenberg is divided into West Beach and East Beach, separated by the mouth of Sandvlei (often closed). Bathing along the entire beach is safe, as it slopes very gradually; at low tide, it is possible to wade out for a few hundred metres in many places.

The beachfront is dominated by the red-and-white striped pavilion, overlooking West Beach, with a number of restaurants where you can sit and savour the view. Beneath it large 'paddocks' for relatively wind-free sunbathing have been created by the erection of high, sheetmetal fences. These provide much of what shelter and shade there is on the beach. Entertainments on the beachfront include a miniature train, Putt-Putt, bathing and paddling pools, a playground and water slides. During the peak holiday season, it may be difficult to find parking near the beaches, and many people opt rather to travel by train. In the car park there are change-rooms and toilets.

There is no official dividing line between East Beach and Sunrise Beach, but it is probably around the mansion, Vergenoegd, built on the beach early this century for American mining engineer Gardner Williams. Although only about 2 km from the furthest end of Muizenberg, Sunrise Beach offers a better perspective of the peninsula mountains and unlike Muizenberg, the surrounding area is only very slightly developed.

The beach here too shelves gently in most places, making it possible to wade far out at low tide. Sunrise Beach, exposed as it is to the south-

THE SEAS THAT VANISHED

A sea strait once flooded the low land between Fish Hoek and Noordhoek.

The Cape Flats, the low plain that joins the Cape Peninsula to the African continent, once lay beneath the sea, creating an island of the prehistoric peninsula. This, in turn, was divided in two by another sea strait filling what is now the low-lying ground between Fish Hoek and Noordhoek.

This phenomenon was caused by changes in the sea level, brought about mainly by variations in the amount of water on earth. (Other factors affecting sea levels include vertical movements of the landmasses — Table Mountain, for example, was originally deposited as fine silt on the bed of a prehistoric sea, and later thrust upwards.) Shortly before the last ice age, the sea level was about 20 m higher than it is today, making islands of the 'peninsula'. Then, during the ice age, much of the water was 'bound up' in ice form and the oceans contained less water than they do now. This meant that the sea level dropped

to more than 100 m below what it is today and a greater area of the peninsula than now projected above the water.

The Cape Peninsula, roughly as we know it now, emerged after the end of the last ice age, some 11 000 years ago. The former sea strait retains its watery nature, with winter rains flooding the hollows between the sand dunes to form small lakes or vleis. The largest of these persist all year round and include Zeekoevlei, Sandvlei, Rondevlei and Princess Vlei. Old maps show that these lakes once covered a greater area, and were linked by natural channels which have since vanished. Governor Simon van der Stel considered emulating nature's example by cutting a navigable canal from Table Bay to False Bay, but in this he failed. Today, instead, the floodwaters are drained by a system of canals, in order to make the residential areas situated there stable.

An airy view of False Bay from Boyes Drive, showing the railway line edging the seaside.

THE FOOTSTEPS OF MAN

Sheltered from the north winds, Peers Cave on a ridge in the Fish Hoek valley has served as home to a variety of peoples for many thousand years. It is also known as Skildersgat (painters' cave), but the paintings on its rock walls — probably the work of San people in relatively recent times — have now been obliterated.

The cave is approximately 30 m wide and some 13,5 m deep. As time went by, the floor level rose as materials were simply discarded within the cave, and these form readily identifiable 'occupation layers'. Where the layers have been undisturbed, it generally follows that a skeleton found in the same layer as a particular implement is that of a user of that implement or, at least, comtemporary with it.

The importance of the cave lies in discoveries made by a father-and-son team of amateur archaeologists, Victor and Bertie Peers, in the late 1920s. Chief among these were three fossilised human skeletons, of unusually large brain capacity, identified as being ancestral to the San group of peoples.

Also found here were stone implements of various dates, from the Early Stone Age that began about half a million years ago to those of the more recent Still Bay Culture.

More evolved San skeletons were excavated closer to the surface of the same deposit, and the shells and fish bones found in the same layer indicate that they were of the Strandloper type, gathering their food on the nearby beaches. They ornamented themselves with beads of ostrich egg shells and seashells, and finely sharpened bone awls suggest that they made garments from skins, using the awls to puncture the skins before stitching them with sinews.

Peers Cave can still be visited, but it is a long, hot walk with little reward as most of the artefacts have been removed, and what remains cannot be touched.

easter, is a good beach for boardsailing, and areas have been allocated for this. In the well-signposted bathing area, the use of boards is restricted during the peak season. This beach is the headquarters of the False Bay Surf Lifesaving Club, and members are often on duty along the Muizenberg/Sunrise stretch, which is also patrolled by beach constables. There are toilets and change-rooms at the car park, and a refreshment kiosk which operates at weekends and during the holiday season.

14 Sandvlei
Seen from Boyes Drive or Ou Kaapseweg, Sandvlei is a glittering blue crystal, set in green lawns and crisscrossed by the bright, dragonfly dartings of multicoloured sails. It receives the waters of the Sandrivier (an extension of the Diep) and the Keysers and is sometimes open to the sea.

Watersports are the major attraction, but there are also facilities for other sports such as bowls and tennis. Powerboating is not permitted on Sandvlei, but provision is made for dinghy sailing (there is a resident sailing club), boardsailing and canoeing

(canoes can be hired at the restaurant). Paddling is perfect in the shallow water off the east bank of a peninsula near the parking area. Besides picnic and braai sites, there is also a well-equipped caravan park.

A portion of Sandvlei is a bird sanctuary and nature reserve, with well laid out paths, bridges and hides giving ideal opportunities for viewing. Permits to enter the reserve may be obtained from the Cape Town City Council's Department of Parks and Forests.

As well as the recreational possibilities at Sandvlei, an interesting housing development (Marina da Gama) has been laid out along its eastern and northern shores. Here artificial peninsulas and inlets have been constructed and sparkling white houses have been sited so that many of them have a water frontage, some with jetties and moorings.

15 Boyes Drive
This scenic, mountainside road can be entered from the Main Road in Lakeside as you travel south (a relatively new section of the road). Initially it offers wide, colourful views over Sandvlei and the coast towards Sunrise Beach, as well as the far side of False Bay. When the road narrows, becoming lined with pines, you have reached the old section, constructed in the 1920s.

From here you soon look down on Muizenberg railway station and the gentle rollers tumbling in to meet the long white beach. Then there are views of Kalk Bay Harbour, toylike on a calm day when the waves are not surging over the breakwater, and, even more distant, the house-dappled slopes of Simon's Bay. The road is tarred all the way, and has only one sharp bend — just before rejoining the Main Road almost opposite Kalk

Bay Harbour. There are roadside benches to enjoy the view at your leisure.

16 Princess Vlei
Many years ago (so the story goes), a beautiful Khoi princess who lived in the cave now known as Elephant's Eye in the Constantiaberg, was walking through the veld when she was captured by sailors off one of the early explorer's ships. Although she pleaded with them to release her, they refused, and she cried so bitterly and for so long that her tears formed the lake known as Princess Vlei. As Elephant's Eye was once known as Prinseskasteel (princess's castle), there may be some truth in the story, after all!

Often at this attractive lake, you can see horses standing in the water, their tails and manes blowing in the wind. There are shady picnic and braai sites on grassed areas, children's playgrounds, a launch ramp, toilets and drinking water. A licence must be obtained before fishing for the bass and carp in the lake.

17 Rondevlei
In this tranquil sanctuary, shady waterside paths, with conveniently sited benches, lead to hides and towers from which some of the more than 200 species of birds can be studied as they go about their business. Rondevlei was established in 1952 as the first sanctuary in South Africa for the protection of waterfowl. Alien vegetation — mainly acacia — is being progressively removed to allow the indigenous growth to re-establish itself around the shallow 50 ha lake.

The field museum contains well-mounted specimens of the birds likely to be seen, as well as some of the mammals and reptiles of the reserve. These include the genet, mongoose, otter, grysbok, steenbok, hippopotamus and various rodents. Hippopotamuses were introduced to Rondevlei in 1982, but hippo bones dug up in the sanctuary and estimated to be around 300 years old, confirm that the animals must once have occurred here naturally.

Among the more colourful resident bird species are the purple gallinule, black crake, Cape shoveller and great crested grebe, while visitors and migrant birds include the flamingo, fish eagle, hamerkop and hoopoe.

18 Zeekoevlei
Across the waters of this, the peninsula's largest lake, there are fine views of Table Mountain and its southward chain of followers. Zeekoevlei (hippopotamus lake) was named by Van Riebeeck, but the last hippo vanished many years ago, to be replaced by boating in almost all forms (there is a public launch ramp) — enthusiasts enjoy powerboating, dinghy sailing, rowing, boardsailing, canoeing and waterskiing.

There are picnic sites, toilets and fresh water at several places along the shores, and pleasant walks can be had through the well-shaded, grassy areas, rich in bird life.

The silver sliver of Sandvlei at Muizenberg.

THINGS TO DO

Angling
Angling books published earlier this century proclaim the fishing along this stretch of False Bay coast to be excellent. Today, unfortunately, much of the area is fished out, and other favourite fishing spots now fall in restricted naval areas. Still, especially in summer, there is good sport to be had. Contact any of the larger sports shops for more details, or the SA Marlin and Tuna Club in Simon's Town.

Beachcombing and shelling
Long Beach usually has odd bits of flotsam (mostly bits of fishing equipment), which also collect on Clovelly Beach, near the railway station. Much of the coast is fairly rocky, and there are interesting pools at Miller's Point, Oatland Point, Long Beach, along Jager's Walk at Fish Hoek, Dalebrook, Danger Beach and St James. This is not an area noted for shells, but small quantities of lamp, turban and limpet shells occur, as well as occasional Venus ear and perlemoen at Oatland Point. Windmill Beach sometimes has an assortment of small, colourful shells. Numerous black mussel shells can be found at Glencairn and around Bailey's Cottage.

'Beachcombing' with a difference takes place at Topstones gem factory in Simon's Town, the largest gem-tumbling plant in the world. Here children delight in sorting through the 'scratch patch' for brightly hued treasures.

Birdwatching
Rondevlei is a birdwatcher's paradise, where over 200 species have been recorded, about a third of them resident. Of these waterfowl predominate, but many other species can be also spotted from the conveniently sited lookout towers and benches and at the waterside hides. Along the coast, the most common birds are kelp and Hartlaub's gulls, and cormorants.

Boardsailing
Sunrise Beach and Surfers' Corner, Muizenberg, present a colourful spectacle, as they are often crowded with boards. Sandvlei benefits from both the north-wester and the south-easter for some exciting sailing, while Zeekoevlei is somewhat more sheltered but offers a larger expanse of water.

Boat trips
Make inquiries at Kalk Bay Harbour about hiring boats for deep-sea fishing trips.

Bowls
Contact the Western Province Bowling Association for details of clubs.

Camping and caravanning
The Cape Town Municipality runs camping and caravan sites at Sandvlei and Princess Vlei. Other established sites are at Miller's Point (on the water's edge), and Oatlands Holiday Village opposite the beach at Froggy Pond.

Canoeing
Canoes can be hired at Sandvlei, but Zeekoevlei and Princess Vlei are also suitable canoeing venues. There are rowing clubs at Sandvlei and Zeekoevlei.

Cycling
Pedalling about Constantia and Tokai to look at the old homesteads can be fun, but some of the roads in Constantia are rather narrow (although fairly shady and not too steep). The scenic Main Road to Simon's Town can be hazardous in summer traffic, as it is narrow for most of the way (and bumpy in patches). It is also unshaded.

Diving
This coastline has a number of attractive rocky areas with a richly varied marine life. The interesting underwater scenery at Miller's Point and Shelly Beach reaches fair depths, while the remains of the *Clan Stuart* off Long Beach form an artificial reef that is 'home' to a great assortment of sea creatures. Snorkel and flippers are all you need for exploring around the Boulders, Seaforth, along Jager's Walk at Fish Hoek, and at Danger Beach and St James. For more information about diving in the area, contact the False Bay Underwater Club.

Drives and viewsites
The coastal road south from Muizenberg is attractive, but the same scenery can be seen in more leisurely fashion from a train which, in any case, runs closer to the sea. Stopping at all stations, the train takes twenty minutes each way between Muizenberg and Simon's Town. The coastal road, however, continues from Simon's Town down to the boundaries of the Cape of Good Hope Nature Reserve, before swinging inland. Driving south on Boyes Drive gives excellent views over Sandvlei, Muizenberg, and of Simon's Town, as well as the sweep of False Bay and the Hottentots Holland Mountains. On the outskirts of Simon's Town is Red Hill Road, a steep, 4 km climb with a number of hairpin bends and outstanding views over Simon's Bay and across False Bay.

Going inland the Ou Kaapseweg winds through fine mountain scenery, passing Silvermine Nature Reserve. The drive inland to Constantia Nek is also very scenic. Starting from Wynberg's Main Road, Constantia Road leads towards a gap between Table Mountain and Constantiaberg, away from the suburban clutter, past double-storeyed Alphen homestead of around 1753 with its large, triangular pediment peeping out from among oaks and vines. The road narrows, and is lined by shady oaks as it passes the entrance to Groot Constantia, before looping its way up the hillside to reach Constantia Nek at about 200 m above sea level. (From here the road descends to Hout Bay, while Rhodes Drive leads north, passing Kirstenbosch Botanic Gardens, to Cape Town.) From the parking area at

Boardsailors strain to tame the wind at Sandvlei.

The naval tradition is remembered in Simon's Town's museum.

Fish type	Season	Best area	Best bait
Elf	Summer	Kalk Bay harbour wall	Fishbait
Kabeljou	Summer, especially in a south-easter; summer evenings	Bailey's Cottage	Bloodworms
Mackerel	Jan—Feb	Kalk Bay harbour wall	Artificial lures
White steenbras	Summer, especially in a south-easter	Bailey's Cottage	Bloodworms
White stumpnose	Summer	Kalk Bay harbour wall	White mussels, sand prawns, wonderworms

Constantia Nek there are easy walks to the flat top of Table Mountain.

Golf
Several clubs in the area welcome visitors, including Clovelly Country Club, Westlake Golf Club and Royal Cape Golf Club.

Libraries
Temporary membership can be obtained from the libraries at Kalk Bay, Muizenberg, Fish Hoek and Simon's Town. Contact the local municipalities for details.

Museums
MARTELLO TOWER, Simon's Town: SA Naval exhibits.

STEMPASTORIE MUSEUM FOR NATIONAL EMBLEMS, Church Street, Simon's Town: parsonage where the Rev M L de Villiers composed *Die Stem*, furnished

according to the times; other exhibits include heraldic designs.

SIMON'S TOWN HISTORICAL MUSEUM, Old Residency, Court Road, Simon's Town: the history of Simon's Town.

RHODES COTTAGE MUSEUM, Main Road, Muizenberg: modest house in which Cecil John Rhodes died in 1902; contains personal mementoes and a model of the Big Hole, Kimberley.

POSTHUYS, Main Road, Muizenberg: dating from 1673, the oldest European-built residence in the country (not open to the public at present).

GROOT CONSTANTIA, Constantia: classic Cape Dutch homestead with 17th- to 18th-century fittings and furnishings, and a wine museum.

Powerboating
The Cape Peninsula Aquatic Club has its headquarters at Zeekoevlei, where

there is a ski ramp and a public launch ramp. The headquarters of the Cape Boat and Skiboat Club are at Koeëlbaai, just south of Miller's Point where there is a public launch ramp. Powerboats are not allowed on Sandvlei.

Shipwrecks
Although many wrecks have occurred in False Bay, the remains of only one can be seen along this stretch of coast. This is the *Clan Stuart*, off Long Beach, which was blown hard onto the rocks in a south-east gale in 1917.

Surfing
Fish Hoek is ideal for beginners, especially in a south-wester or north-wester. In similar conditions, Clovelly has a bigger and more powerful break, and Kalk Bay reef is even larger and hollower (and definitely for the experienced only). Off Danger Beach and Bailey's Cottage there are good breaks during a north-wester with a good swell, but watch out for the rocks. Muizenberg and Sunrise beaches are best in a north wind, but the long, gentle rollers can be surfed at almost any time. Boards can be hired from The Corner Surfshop, Muizenberg.

Swimming
The waters of this section of the False Bay coast offer many safe, relatively warm bathing places, some marred only by the occasional inshore presence of sharks. It is known that very large specimens of the great white shark (*Carcharodon carcharias*) inhabit the deeper waters, but smaller specimens can swim in water that is only knee-deep to an adult.

Favourite and sheltered swimming spots are Miller's Point (tidal pool), the Boulders, Seaforth and St James (tidal pool). The other beaches tend to be more exposed to the prevailing south-east wind of the Cape summer.

Tennis and squash
Contact the Western Province Tennis Association and the Western Province Squash Racket Association for details of courts and clubs.

Theatre
The wooded grounds of Maynardville, in Wynberg, make an enchanting setting for annual Shakespearian productions. These are staged by Capab, the provincial performing arts company, early in each year.

Walks
For fans of architecture, a walk between Muizenberg and St James provides a number of highlights. Walks along the beaches and over the rocks on this coastline are pleasant, but care should be taken where there is only a narrow

strip of rock between the sea and the railway embankment. (Evidence of the power of the waves can be seen in the odd masses of concrete and bits of station wall lying about on the rocks.)

There are interesting and not too arduous walks in Silvermine Nature Reserve, but the more adventurous might prefer to explore the many caves in the mountains above Kalk Bay, caves with evocative names like Boomslang (it is long and tortuous) and Squeezer's Cave. Always make sure that someone in the party has some knowledge and experience of the caves; take a torch with you and never enter a cave alone.

A footpath leads to Elephant's Eye Cave in the Constantiaberg. To reach the start of the walk, take the Tokai Road turn-off from Main Road, Retreat, and follow it until at the beautiful, high-stoeped Tokai homestead. (Attributed to architect Thibault, this superb example of Cape Dutch architecture — a national monument but not open to the public — was built in about 1795.) Park to the left of the house, under one of the trees. The Department of Forestry has an information centre here, as well as an arboretum. From this point, take the track up to the cave, from where there are outstanding views over the southern peninsula and False Bay. Note that there is little shade and, once you have left the arboretum, no water.

Yachting and dinghy sailing
For deep-sea sailing, there is the False Bay Yacht Club, based in Simon's Town, and there are sailing clubs at Sandvlei and Zeekoevlei.

INFORMATION
• Western Cape Regional Services Council, 44 Wale St, Cape Town 8001. Tel 242200
• Cape Town Municipality, Civic Centre, Cape Town 8001. Tel 2103131
• Captour, Atlantic Road, Muizenberg 7945. Tel 881898
• Fish Hoek Municipality, Main Rd, Fish Hoek 7975. Tel 821112
• Mountain Club of SA, 97 Hatfield St, Cape Town 8001. Tel 453412
• National Sea Rescue Institute, 4 Loop St, Cape Town 8001. Tel 215765; emergencies 2183500
• Simon's Town Municipality, PO Box 31, Simon's Town 7995. Tel 861551
• SA Tourism Board, Piazza Level, Golden Acre, Cape Town 8001. Tel 216274
Nearest AA Office
• AA House, 7 Martin Hammerschlag Way, Foreshore, Cape Town 8001. Tel 211550

From sparkling seaside to vintage countryside

BRIGHT BURSTS OF COLOUR from exuberantly designed pavilions focus the fun along this stretch of the False Bay coast before it curves southward to the gently shelving beaches of the Strand and Gordon's Bay, drawing thousands of holiday-makers to their white sands and warm, shallow waters. Beyond Gordon's Bay great outcrops of rocks are a haven for anglers — but be warned, the sea here can be treacherous. As a backdrop to all this, the Boland mountains rear up, their slopes a mantle of vines and trees, graced by the timeless lines of Cape Dutch homes.

1 Sonwabe and Cemetery Beach

The long, sandy beaches that characterise this innermost curve of False Bay are virtually continuous, so that Sonwabe and Cemetery Beach seem to pick up where Muizenberg and Sunrise Beach left off.

At Sonwabe the beach slopes gradually, with shallow water extending far out and the waves breaking gently. Moving eastwards, however, the bottom shelves abruptly after the initial shallows, and there is a strong backwash. These conditions are echoed at Cemetery Beach, where the powerful backwash extends along the beach's considerable length and large waves break close to the shore, delighting — or dumping — surfers.

Sunbathing is fairly popular although neither beach (both rather gritty and sprinkled with black mussel shells) is shaded and dunes give only slight shelter from the south-easter. Both beaches have car parks, change-rooms and toilets, and Sonwabe has a refreshment kiosk.

2 Seal Island

South of Strandfontein lies the whitened lump of Seal Island, a bald granite rock with no sandy beach, shade or water. It is far from bare of life, however, serving as the breeding ground for countless seabirds and for the Cape fur seal (*Arctocephalus pusillus*).

These seals, found only along the south and west coast of southern Africa, have been hunted for

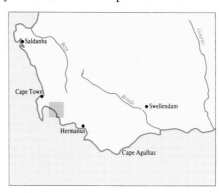

their fur since the early days of Dutch settlement. A certain amount of controversy surrounds their harvesting, perhaps because they yield fur only as pups of around seven to ten months old and because of the traditional method used (involving stunning and stabbing the seal). Pups have not been culled on Seal Island since 1982, but more recently an attempt was made to control their numbers (in response to complaints that they were depleting the fish harvest) by 'shooing' them away from the island during the breeding season. This was subsequently abandoned, but not before the birthrate was cut by more than half.

3 Strandfontein and Mnandi

Dominating Strandfontein is the large pavilion, rather like a geometric icing-sugar castle, which

The Steenbras Dam above Gordon's Bay echoes the blue of False Bay.

overlooks an enormous, beach-fringed tidal pool. On either side of the pool, long beaches slope away rather steeply, and there is a strong backwash. (Lifesavers are on duty during peak season.) Grassy, landscaped terraces make ideal picnic sites, sheltered from the wind by the pavilion. Adding to these attractions are a large waterslide and a reptile park. Facilities include a restaurant and refreshment kiosks, a large, tarred parking area and change-rooms and toilets.

On the sea side of the main coastal road, Baden Powell Drive, another tarred road links Strandfontein to Mnandi, with tarred, demarcated cycle tracks on either side and numerous side roads leading seawards. There are car parks and toilets at various points along the way (although the beaches shelve rather too steeply for comfortable swimming), as well as the Blue Waters Coastal Resort, with its camp and caravan sites and bungalows for hire, and amenities such as a shop, children's playgrounds and a roller-skating rink.

Mnandi Beach, with the group of rocks known as Kapteinsklip just offshore, is enlivened by a pavilion in bold primary colours. This affords some shelter to a vast, lawned picnic area and a large, sculpted pool set among plastic-fronded palm trees. Amenities include two long chutes for splash landings in the pool, a refreshment kiosk, parking areas, change-rooms and toilets.

Sea-bathing at Mnandi is popular and fairly safe, especially close to the pavilion, while to the east angling becomes the priority, with many favourite spots. A short road leads to Wolfgat, at

LEFT *A shimmering sheet of sea off the Strandfontein coast.*

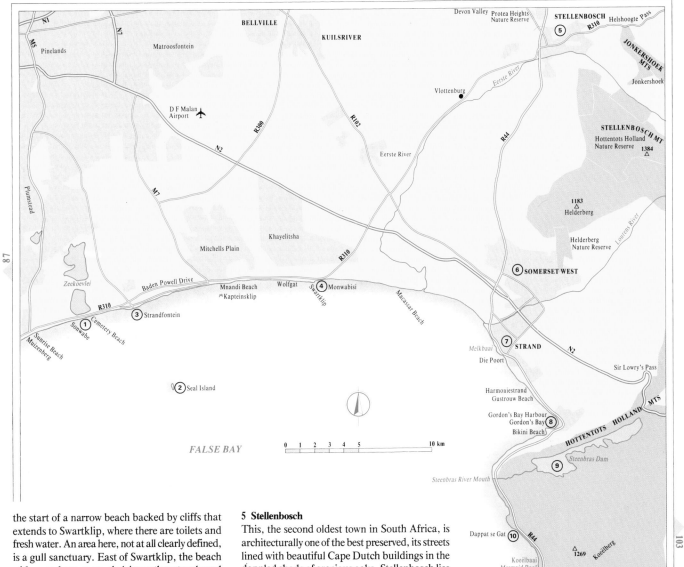

the start of a narrow beach backed by cliffs that extends to Swartklip, where there are toilets and fresh water. An area here, not at all clearly defined, is a gull sanctuary. East of Swartklip, the beach widens and curves on, shelving rather steeply and with no shade or shelter.

4 Monwabisi and Macassar Beach

A jutting arm of cliff provides good protection from the wind at Monwabisi. Here visitors relax at the gaily painted tables and chairs dotting the large, lawned area behind the pavilion, or cool off in the truly enormous tidal pool or the shallow pool for toddlers. Facilities include a refreshment kiosk, a parking area, change-rooms and toilets. Just west of Monwabisi are several rock pools, and a beach that slopes gradually, making bathing reasonably safe.

The long, white beach at Macassar, with little shade or shelter, is not really suited to swimming as it shelves very steeply, but there is ample scope for long walks towards Swartklip, with good views of the peninsula mountains. Macassar is also very popular for surf angling. Facilities at the beach include toilets and change-rooms, and a large car park with a shop on its landward side.

5 Stellenbosch

This, the second oldest town in South Africa, is architecturally one of the best preserved, its streets lined with beautiful Cape Dutch buildings in the dappled shade of gracious oaks. Stellenbosch lies in the fertile valley of the Eerste River, surrounded by vineyards and orchards and backed by mountains, and it has the dual character of a farming centre and a university town.

The heart of the town is the Braak, or town common, with an interesting variety of architectural styles, from the classic, gabled Burgerhuis (built in 1797) to the thatched and very English St Mary's Anglican Church (1852). The main thoroughfare, Dorp Street, is renowned for its old houses, Cape Dutch as well as classic Georgian and Victorian.

Perhaps the best reflection of this blend is the Stellenbosch Village Museum, a complex of houses of various periods, furnished in the appropriate styles, from the rustic Schreuderhuis (c. 1709) to the elegant Grosvenor House (c. 1803). Even the gardens have been planted according to

RIGHT *Green Boland farmlands in the shadow of the Helderberg.*

Follow the Helshoogte Pass into the Drakenstein Valley, where historical Boschendal lies.

the fashions of the times.

The outlying areas of Stellenbosch also have a great deal to offer. Devon Valley, to the north-west, is a picturesque enclave of vines and flowers, with the Protea Heights Nature Reserve the special preserve of indigenous plants like the rare painted lady (*Gladiolus blandus*) and the famous blushing bride (*Leucospermum* sp). The headwaters of the Eerste River are in Jonkershoek, to the south-east of Stellenbosch, a beautiful valley hemmed in by mountains. Recreation here includes walking and picnicking in the forestry reserve, or a visit to the fisheries research station and hatchery for trout and other freshwater species. (The Hottentots Holland Nature Reserve, with extensive hiking trails, stretches from here down to the Grabouw State Forest.)

6 Somerset West

Nestling in the basin of the Hottentots Holland chain is the charming town of Somerset West, which became 'independent' of the district of Stellenbosch early last century with the establishment of its own church (rebuilt in 1863 and still standing as the Dutch Reformed Mission Church). Surrounded as it is by farmlands, Somerset West has a peaceful rural quality, but at less than 50 km from Cape Town it also serves as a residential area for people commuting to work in the mother city.

Jutting out above the town is Helderberg (clear mountain), so-called because the 1 137m-high domelike summit is usually clear of the clouds that shroud its neighbouring peaks. This is the site of the 245 ha Helderberg Nature Reserve, a sanctuary for the indigenous flora of the region and deservedly famous for its variety of protea species and bird life.

7 Strand

The long, white beaches of the Strand, sloping very gently to the clear, warm water that rolls ashore in small, flat waves, have helped to make this a very popular holiday resort. The 3 km-long northerly beach, Melkbaai, is always the more crowded, and is separated from Die Poort by a rocky outcrop rich in tidal pools. At both beaches it is possible to wade out for over 100 m, especially at low tide. Unfortunately, the beaches are quite exposed to the south-easter, but some shelter can be found behind the bush-covered dunes near the north end of Melkbaai.

Facilities include a jetty and launch ramp (a sailing club also has its headquarters on the beach), as well as change-rooms and toilets at various points along the beach. In addition, there is the convenience of Beach Road, hugging the coast, with its numerous restaurants and cafés catering to the visitor's needs.

Between Die Poort and Harmoniestrand to the south is a rocky area with innumerable pools to explore. Harmoniestrand and adjacent Gustrouw, still further in the direction of Gordon's Bay, alternate short stretches of beach with more rock pools. There are no facilities here.

ON THE ROCKS

'Never turn your back on the sea' is an old axiom of the rock fisherman, and one that should always be remembered, particularly on the rocky stretch of coast beyond Gordon's Bay. Situated conveniently close to a large metropolitan area, the many apparently idyllic rock-angling spots are easy to reach from the coastal road. The sea is so close that neither fancy tackle nor superior casting ability is required, and the novice or the stranger is easily lured into potential danger.

A little caution can help to keep casualties down. Before going rock angling, note the weather forecast. On this coast, you can expect rough waters during or after a cold front from the west. Dangerously sudden higher seas are produced when, after the passage of the cold front, the wind swings from north-west to south-west or -east.

Never go rock angling alone, but take along as many fellow-enthusiasts as you can — after all, there really are plenty of fish in the sea. Wear stout, thick-soled boots to avoid slipping. Be sure to have your bait ready before you arrive, so that you do not have to lessen your concentration on the sea.

Before going down to the rocks, examine the nearest lifebuoy (these are placed at strategic intervals along the road) to make sure that everything is in

A rock angler challenging the sea.

order. Despite the penalties of doing so, vandals still tamper with vital safety apparatus.

When you spot a likely rock, watch it from a safe distance (and preferably, from above) for at least 15 minutes, checking the swells and the calms to see if the rock is dry even after the swells. Also note the direction of the currents so that if, despite your precautions, you are washed off the rock, you will not waste energy swimming against them. Swimming with or across a current should carry you to safety eventually — especially if you are wearing a life jacket.

As long as you maintain respect for the sea, it should provide you with many happy hours' fishing.

HARVEST OF BEAUTY

The cool, crisp fruit of the vine.

The Stellenbosch wine route, renowned as it is for providing the opportunity to sample and buy fine wines, is far more than just that. To travel it is to savour a countryside amply endowed with mountains, trees and streams, enhanced by man's hand in the row after row of vines, and the ageless beauty of gabled and thatched homesteads.

Within a 12 km radius of Stellenbosch, the wine route comprises a dozen or so private cellars, as well as a handful of co-operative wineries. The general features include wine tastings and sales, and cellar tours, sometimes rounded off by a meal. Each farm has some special quality, so take your time and follow the route of your choice.

For the winelover, one such fruitful tour could follow the R310 (off the N2 national road), which runs along the valley of the Eerste River. This passes the entrances to no fewer than four wine route farms (Welmoed Co-op, Spier, Eersteriviervalleise Co-op and Vlottenburg Co-op, as well as the Van Rijn Brandy Museum), some old, some new. Of these, Spier has the longest history, having been farmed since 1692. It has a selection of gracious, gabled buildings, some serving as restaurants, one showing works of South African artists.

A short detour from the R310 takes in the additional farms of Goedgeloof, Uiterwyk, Overgaauw and Neethlingshof. Uiterwyk was once the last farm within the bounds of the old district of Stellenbosch. Its gabled homestead, dating from 1791, retains its original yellowwood floors and ceilings, while behind the ornate façade of Neethlingshof (like Uiterwyk, a national monument) are a number of restaurants.

In Stellenbosch itself, large concerns such as Stellenbosch Farmers Winery and Bergkelder (its 'mountain cellars' tunnelled into the slopes of Papegaaiberg) offer tours and tastings, as well as audiovisual presentations.

From Stellenbosch the Strand road (R44) passes first gracious Blaauwklippen, where special attractions include a tour of the vineyards by horse-drawn carriage or a visit to the museum with its fine collection of old Cape furniture. Further on is Rust en Vrede, a historical old estate that produces red wines only. Last on this tour is Eikendal, on the slopes of the Helderberg. Its spacious cellar is an interesting blend of traditional Cape features and modern Californian architecture . . . much as the Stellenbosch wine route itself is a fine blend of the old and the new in a harmonious whole.

8 Gordon's Bay

On the hillside above the pretty resort of Gordon's Bay, whitewashed stones form an anchor between the letters 'G' and 'B'; this is a reminder of the days when the General Botha Merchant Navy Academy occupied the buildings now used by the SA Navy. Gordon's Bay also retains traces of its earlier character as a fishing community (it was originally known as Vischhoekbaai, but renamed after Colonel Robert Jacob Gordon, Dutch commander of the Cape garrison at the end of the 18th century). Today the tranquil waters of the harbour still reflect the sturdy lines of fishing boats, as well as the sleeker yachts and luxury cruisers.

The beach is a wide curve of white sand that slopes very gently, making it possible to wade out for great distances in the warm, usually calm, clear water. There is a grassed picnic area here. Once around the 'corner' of the bay there is a long stand of milkwood trees with a paved walkway and shady picnic sites (but no fires). The beach narrows here and slopes more sharply, giving way to a large rock outcrop after a number of rock pools. Besides the usual facilities (change-rooms and toilets), shops and restaurants are handily across the way.

Beyond the harbour, and connected to it by a wooden stile, is Bikini Beach, a small sparkle of sand. This slopes more sharply than the main beach, with short, dumpy waves, but it is fairly safe for swimming. It is better sheltered from the wind, with sunbathers opting to spread out against the breakwater, but there is no shade.

9 Steenbras Dam and river mouth

Just beyond Gordon's Bay a short but very scenic road leads up the mountainside to Steenbras Dam, surely one of the loveliest in the Cape. This vast lake with scattered islands fills the mountain valley, stretching into the far distance, its sandy shores fringed with massed pines. Recreational activities include fishing (from the banks only) and walking, especially along the sandstone footpaths threading their way through gardens of wild flowers in the ravine below the dam. A permit to enter the dam area must first be obtained from local municipal offices. Overnight accommodation in bungalows is available.

The river mouth is about 10 km from Gordon's Bay and just upstream is a tiny beach that comes and goes according to the tides. Here you can sunbathe, picnic or braai, or wander upstream.

10 Dappat se Gat and Koeëlbaai

From Gordon's Bay the road (first known as Faure Marine and then as Clarence Drive) is carved into the mountainside, overlooking the sea and offering spectacular views over the expanse of False Bay and back to the Cape Peninsula. The parking areas along the way are not necessarily viewsites but may serve merely as entry points to favourite angling spots. (Note that angling here can be dangerous, as is evident from the crosses and memorials commemorating anglers swept to their death from these rocks.)

The first beach reached is Dappat se Gat,

BELOW *Yachts crowd the small basin in Gordon's Bay Harbour, where birds guard the breakwater.*

consisting of three tiny, sandy inlets at the foot of the cliffs. Access is by a rough path winding through milkwood trees and crossing a small stream. At the first inlet, surging seas have created a sand hill against the cliff, and this is fully accessible only at low tide. There are caves at the second, smaller inlet, as well as one at the third; this lies above the tideline and is kept deliciously cool by a stream that enters the sea just here and percolates through the cave roof.

Just south of Dappat se Gat is the popular resort of Koeëlbaai, where a long stretch of lawn and beach is sheltered from the south-easter by fynbos-clad mountains. Bathing can be treacherous, as the beach shelves very steeply and the backwash is strong, with cross currents present. When lifeguards are on duty, flags are set up on the beach to indicate the safest bathing area. A sheltered, rocky inlet known as Klippetjies provides safer bathing, as well as numerous rock pools. Even more sheltered is Mermaid Pool, a similar inlet just south of the resort. Both pools are backed by shady, bush-covered dunes. Also near the south end, a stream and high tides combine to produce a pool safe enough for small children.

The resort, administered by Cape Town Municipality, offers picnic spots and sites for tents and caravans, all on smooth, shady lawns, as well as another caravan site on the landward side of the road. For the youngsters there is a play park, while a refreshment kiosk operates at weekends and during the holiday season. There are toilets and ablution blocks at various places throughout the resort (but no hot water or electricity). Firewood is on sale at the admisssion office, where entry permits must be obtained.

THE MAN WHO MOVED 'MECCA' SOUTH

At the end of the 17th century, a Muslim holy man died in exile near the lonely white sands of the Cape's Macassar Beach. That man, Sheik Yussuf, prince and brother of the sultan of the Indonesian port of Macassar, had opposed the monopolistic trading of the Dutch East India Company on the island of Bantam, and been exiled, first to Ceylon (Sri Lanka), and then to the Cape in 1694. Here he was kept in the Castle and later moved to the then remote farm of Zandvliet, near the mouth of the Eerste River in False Bay. During this time he is said to have founded the Muslim faith at the Cape.

Sheik Yussuf died in 1699, and in time, the site of his grave was forgotten. Years later, according to legend, it was discovered at Zandvliet by a young herdboy, who fell asleep and, on waking, realised that his sheep were lost. A stranger in a long green robe appeared, and offered to lead him to the sheep . . . found grazing peacefully at the long-lost grave . . .

The figure of Sheik Yussuf, clad in his green robe, is still said to appear in the area, where his grave has been marked by a *kramat* (shrine) with a prominent dome and four minarets. Four of his disciples are buried nearby. The *kramat* (the most important of the 'holy circle' of tombs surrounding and protecting Cape Town) is sometimes known as 'the Mecca of the south', and is visited by many pilgrims each year. In the East, however, it is claimed that the holy remains of Sheik Yussuf were returned to Macassar and reburied there. This site is held to be as holy as the *kramat* on the little hill that overlooks the winelands, and is within the sound of the surf.

Angling
The surf angling area that stretches from before Strandfontein ends beyond Gordon's Bay; from here, in place of sandy beaches and shallows, rocky cliffs drop sheer to deep water. Fish types thus vary tremendously, with this stretch of coast one of South Africa's finest for the angler.

Steenbras Dam, which is well stocked with brown and rainbow trout, is a popular freshwater angling spot. An angling permit can be obtained from any magistrate's office in the Cape, and a permit to enter the dam area from the Parks and Forests Branch, Cape Town Municipality.

Art galleries
REMBRANDT VAN RIJN ART MUSEUM, 31 Dorp St, Stellenbosch: Works by local and overseas artists.
OU KELDER, Spier Estate, Stellenbosch: Works by well-known contemporary South African artists.
UNIVERSITY OF STELLENBOSCH ART MUSEUM, Old Lutheran Church Building, Dorp St, Stellenbosch: Open only for specific exhibitions.

Beachcombing and shelling
This is a poor stretch of coast for shells and jetsam, but there are numerous rock pools, notably from the Strand to Gordon's Bay and south of Koeëlbaai.

Birdwatching
Good spots for birdwatching are Steenbras Dam (sightings include the giant kingfisher, Egyptian goose, yellow-billed duck and fish eagle) and Helderberg Nature Reserve (Cape sugarbird, malachite kingfisher, yellow-billed egret, orange-breasted sunbird, etc.). Along the beaches you can spot kelp and Hartlaub's gulls, Cape cormorants and terns, with a gull sanctuary near Swartklip.

Boardsailing
Melkbaai, the Strand, is a popular venue, with the headquarters of a local club on the beach.

Boat trips
The cruiser *Sandy Bay* operates daily from Gordon's Bay Harbour, following the coast in the direction of Koeëlbaai.

Bowls
Contact the Western Province Bowling Association in Cape Town for details.

Camping and caravanning
Blue Waters resort between Strandfontein and Mnandi beaches has camp and caravan sites and bungalows. It is run by the Cape Town Municipality, which also administers the resort (with similar bungalows) at

BELOW *Looking back in the direction of Gordon's Bay from the rough and rocky coast of Koeëlbaai.*

THINGS TO DO

Steenbras Dam, as well as Koeëlbaai resort, with its camp and caravan sites. The Strand and Gordon's Bay municipalities each administer resorts catering for campers and caravanners.

Canoeing
On calm days, Gordon's Bay is ideal. Note that no boating is allowed at Steenbras Dam.

Cycling
Hundreds of students make their way about Stellenbosch by bicycle, and this is a good way to see the lovely old town, and also to tour the wine route.

Diving
Only the rocks between the Strand and Gordon's Bay Harbour offer good diving possibilities.

Drives and viewsites
Aspects of the so-called Four Passes Drive (a great circle from Cape Town through rugged mountain country) can be followed. The Helshoogte Pass linking Stellenbosch to the Drakenstein Valley is a scenic gem with glimpses through the trees of enchanted valleys below. Despite the ominous name (heights of hell), the pass is an easy tarred gradient, passing the mission village of Pniel, as well as the exquisite Cape Dutch farmhouses of Rhône and Boschendal.

Connecting Somerset West with the hinterland is Sir Lowry's Pass, with a superb viewsite at the summit of the Hottentots Holland Mountains.

Faure Marine Drive and Clarence Drive beyond Gordon's Bay overlook the sea and offer panoramic views over False Bay to the Cape Peninsula. The Stellenbosch wine route makes a pleasant day's drive, as do the Franschhoek and Paarl wine routes.

Fish type	Season	Best area	Best bait
Dassie	All year	Strand, Gordon's Bay	Redbait, sand prawns
Elf	Sept — May	Strandfontein — Macassar Beach, Strand — Harmoniestrand	Fishbait
Galjoen	Mar — Sept	Swartklip, Macassar Beach, Strand — Harmoniestrand	Wonderworms, rotten redbait
Geelbek	Nov — May	Gordon's Bay — Koeëlbaai	Fishbait with chokka
Kabeljou	Sept — May	Strandfontein — Swartklip, Strand — Harmoniestrand	Fishbait, octopus, bloodworms
Sharks	Summer	Strandfontein — Macassar Beach	Fishbait with chokka
	Winter	Gordon's Bay — Koeëlbaai	Fishbait with chokka
White steenbras	Sept — May	Macassar Beach, Strand — Harmoniestrand	Sand prawns, wonderworms, bloodworms
White stumpnose	All year	Strandfontein, Strand — Harmoniestrand	Sand prawns, white mussels, redbait, chokka

Golf
Visitors are welcome at Somerset West Country Club and Strand Golf Club.

Libraries
There are libraries at the Strand, Gordon's Bay, Somerset West and Stellenbosch. Contact the local municipalities for details.

Museums
STELLENRYK WINE MUSEUM, 31 Dorp St, Stellenbosch: Exhibits include old Cape furniture, brassware and wine vats.
VAN RYN BRANDY CELLAR AND COOPERAGE, Vlottenburg: Demonstrations of the distillation of brandy, and the ancient art of the cooper in making barrels in which the brandy is matured.
VILLAGE MUSEUM, 18 Ryneveld St, Stellenbosch: Complex of four period houses and gardens, ranging from about 1709 to 1850.
VOC KRUITHUIS, the Braak, Stellenbosch: Houses a military museum, exhibiting cannon, edged weapons and firearms.

Music and theatre
There are theatres and a Conservatory of Music at the University of Stellenbosch, as well as the Oude Libertas open-air auditorium on the outskirts of the town.

Powerboating
Contact the Gordon's Bay Boat Angling Club for local information.

Surfing
Cemetery Beach is uncomfortably close to the sewage outfall but, like Strandfontein, is good in a northerly wind. Both places are reputed to be shark-haunted. The Strand is a good beginner's beach, especially in a light south-easter or north-wester. The north end of Koeëlbaai can provide a fine tube in a south-easter.

Swimming
The False Bay coastline is warmer than the Cape Peninsula's Atlantic seaboard but also has a greater incidence of sharks. There are pools at Strandfontein, Mnandi and Monwabisi, as well as the natural Mermaid Pool south of Koeëlbaai. The best swimming beaches are the Strand and Gordon's Bay.

Walks
Beach walks offer expansive views of False Bay and the mountains of the Cape Peninsula, and there are pleasant walks in the Helderberg Nature Reserve, the Steenbras Dam and the Jonkershoek area, as well as a historic urban trail through Stellenbosch. The Boland Hiking Trail (following the mountain spines through the Hottentots Holland Nature Reserve for more than 50 km) starts from the summit of Sir Lowry's Pass, and can be followed for a short distance to a turn-off on the left leading to the old Gantouw Pass. Here you can see deep ruts scored in the rocks by the drag-shoes of countless wagons, while nearby is the signalling cannon that warned of danger in the 17th and 18th centuries.

Yachting and dinghy sailing
Contact the Gordon's Bay Yacht Club for details.

INFORMATION
• Cape Town Municipality, Civic Centre, Cape Town 8001. Tel 021=2103131
• Captour, Strand Concourse, Adderley Street, Cape Town 8001. Tel 021=253320
• Gordon's Bay Municipality, School St, Gordon's Bay 7150. Tel 024=562135
• National Sea Rescue Institute, 4 Loop St, Cape Town 8001. Tel 021=215765; emergencies: 021=2183500
• NSRI Station 9, Gordon's Bay Harbour 7150. Tel 024=561992
• Somerset West Municipality, cnr Victoria & Andries Pretorius Sts, Somerset West 7130. Tel 024=22421
• SA Tourism Board, Piazza Level, Golden Acre, Cape Town 8001. Tel 216274
• Stellenbosch Municipality, Plein St, Stellenbosch 7600. Tel 02231=2111
• Stellenbosch Information Bureau, Plein St, Stellenbosch 7600. Tel 02231=3584
• Strand Municipality, Main Road, Strand 7140. Tel 024=31333

Nearest AA Office
• AA House, 7 Martin Hammerschlag Way, Foreshore, Cape Town 8001. Tel 021=211550

The textured slopes of the Helderberg, a haven for hikers.

Where wild flowers carpet the craggy coast

ALONG THE RAGGED COAST between Rooiels and Hermanus the picturesque mountains of the south-western Cape tumble headlong into a clear blue sea. Mighty waves, rolling slowly in from the southern ocean, crash against broken cliffs of warm red and golden rock with a deep-voiced roar and a shower of crystal spray. Where streams have cut through the mountains the great waves curl gracefully into little bays and break with translucent beauty onto gentle white sands. From the water's edge, footpaths lead directly into the moody quiet of the mountains, whose steep slopes and shady kloofs are home to a magical realm of heaths and wild flowers, the richest concentration of flowering plants in the world.

1 Rooiels

Rooielsrivier, named after the rooiels (red alder) trees that early explorers found growing along its banks, has cut a rugged gorge through the coastal mountains and created a small, pretty bay at the point where it finally spills into the sea. On both sides of the river mouth the coastline consists of jagged, wave-smashed rocks and violently twisted cliffs, but in the bay there is a quiet beach of fine, soft sand — a pocket of gentleness amid wild surroundings.

The south-east wind sometimes blows strongly here in summer, but on wind-free days the shallow lagoon at the river mouth makes a perfect swimming place for young children. It is also possible to swim in the sea. Although the main beach may have a strong backwash when the tide is high, there are several short stretches of sandy beach tucked away among the rocks to the west of the river mouth where swimming in the shallow water is regarded by local residents as quite safe.

Rooiels village consists of a cluster of holiday homes (and a shop but no petrol station) stretching along the coast west and south of the river mouth. The houses here offer easy access to a very attractive coastline: clear blue waters splash restlessly against honey-coloured rocks, and the coastal fynbos, particularly rich in wild flowers and watered by small perennial streams, reaches down almost to the water's edge. The rocky coast to the south of the village has long been popular with fishermen and has become a favourite locale for scuba divers.

Both the bay and the village are dominated by the towering cliffs of Klein-Hangklip, reaching a height of over 300 m. A line of mountains then stretches almost due south from Klein-Hangklip, ending in the twin peaks known as Twee Susters. The main road south runs along the inland side of these mountains, but there is also a narrow stony track that leads between the mountains and the sea, emerging eventually at Pringle Bay.

2 Pringle Bay

This beautiful bay at the mouth of the Buffelsrivier was named after Rear-Admiral Thomas Pringle, a naval commander during the first British occupation of the Cape late in the 18th century. As

soon as the British had taken possession of the Cape they set to work surveying their newly acquired territory, and the surveyor, a Lieutenant-Colonel Collins, recommended that Pringle Bay be developed as a port. This would mean that farm produce from the interior could be shipped across False Bay to Simon's Town or Cape Town, thereby avoiding the difficult haul over the Hottentots Holland Mountains. His advice was not heeded, with the result that Pringle Bay remains a somewhat sleepy, one-shop village, whose

Soft light bathes the coastline at Pringle Bay.

residents and holiday visitors feel deeply grateful that history passed them by.

A wide, white sand beach runs the length of the bay and slopes gently into the sea. Local residents rate it as one of the safest swimming beaches along this stretch of coast. A small lagoon at the river mouth offers more protected swimming for children, and canoes can be paddled inland along the winding river for roughly a kilometre before the water becomes too shallow.

3 Cape Hangklip

As the name indicates, Hangklip (overhanging rock) is an impressive geological formation — an

BELOW *View across the mouth of the Rooiels to a scattering of holiday homes.*

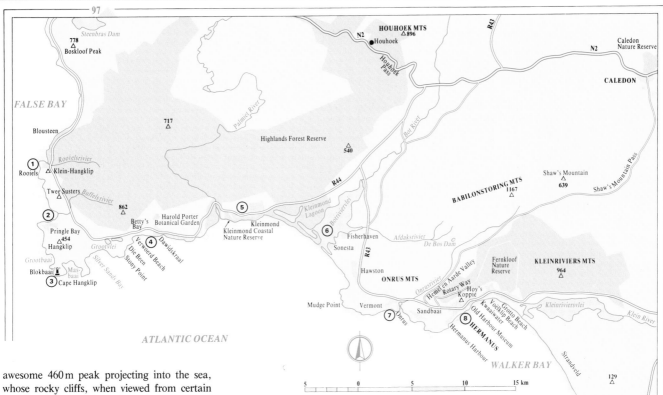

awesome 460 m peak projecting into the sea, whose rocky cliffs, when viewed from certain angles, appear to overhang the narrow strip of land lying hundreds of metres below.

Cape Hangklip marks the eastern limit of False Bay, while the Cape of Good Hope marks the western limit. The two capes are geologically similar, and Cape Hangklip was known to the early Portuguese navigators as Cabo Falso (false cape) because it was so often mistaken for the navigationally more important Cape of Good Hope. Sailors making their way down the east coast would spy the sharp peak rising up out of the sea mist and would turn into False Bay, mistakenly thinking that the promontory they had rounded was the Cape of Good Hope.

The broken shoreline around Cape Hangklip offers a succession of rocky points and more or less sheltered beaches, each with its own distinct character. Travelling around the coast from Pringle Bay, the principal beaches are to be found at Grootbaai, Blokbaai (also called Moonshine Bay), Masbaai (mast bay) and Silver Sands — all four of which are regarded as reasonably safe for swimming in fair weather conditions.

Summer's prevailing south-easter blows offshore at Grootbaai and Blokbaai, which are both on the eastern side of the cape. This keeps the water clear and produces a kind of breaker that sculpts generously rounded beaches. Blokbaai is smaller and more secluded than Grootbaai, and has large kelp beds offshore. The sheltered stretch of clear water that lies immediately next to the little beach, because it is completely surrounded by thick beds of kelp, is a particularly safe and pleasant place for swimming.

Masbaai, so named because a ship's mast was washed ashore here, is large and shallow, and is well protected by the rocky points that reach out and around it. There is less in the way of sandy beach along its shore, but its enclosed situation makes it a favourite launching spot for fishing boats, and there is an easily accessible slipway here. The Cape Hangklip lighthouse stands out prominently from amid the dunes that separate Masbaai from Blokbaai.

Silver Sands, running along the eastern shore of the cape, is a good deal more exposed to the south-easter, but is still considered a safe swimming beach by local residents. It is certainly a beautiful beach, with a wild, romantic character. As its name suggests, the sand here is a brilliant white, and in the course of thousands of years the south-easter has swept great quantities of this 'silver' sand up the mountainside behind the beach, forming enormous dunes that can be seen clearly from the slopes above Hawston and Onrus.

BELOW *A commemorative cross to a victim of the sea near rocky Cape Hangklip.*

The steep walls enclosing Leopard's Gorge.

In 1938, when much of the world was gearing up for war, a wealthy Johannesburg businessman who frequently visited Betty's Bay and who loved its unspoilt simplicity, bought a large tract of land in the mountains immediately behind the little village. His name was Harold Porter. He had no desire to develop the land in any way, nor to derive any profit from it, but he wished merely to preserve its extraordinary beauty and charm for future generations to enjoy.

He called this little wild flower reserve 'Shangri-la',

and on his death he bequeathed it to the National Botanic Gardens. The administrative authorities promptly renamed the reserve in his honour, hence it is now the Harold Porter Botanic Garden.

At the foot of the mountains there are several hectares of lawns and cultivated garden with a pretty stream running through from pool to pool along a narrow, pebbly bed. From this central garden footpaths lead into completely unspoilt surroundings. One path leads through the forested Leopard's Gorge to a tall waterfall. The leopards that gave the gorge this name are still common in the area, but they are largely nocturnal and are seldom seen. A second path leads along another gorge, known as Disa Kloof, to yet another waterfall with a deep pool at its foot. Overlooking the pool is a steep, shady, constantly moist cliff where numerous red disas (*Disa uniflora*) can be seen flowering on inaccessible ledges.

Between these two gorges is a zigzag path that leads high up into the mountains, and turning off from the walk into Disa Kloof is still another path, known as the Rod Smitheman Trail, that winds along the mountainside to the western end of Betty's Bay. All four of these paths lead through attractive scenery and an astonishing variety of plants. In terms of number-of-species, the coastal fynbos that covers these mountainsides and the small forests that fill the shady kloofs constitute the richest vegetation type in the world . . . so Harold Porter's dream is indeed one that is well worth preserving.

anyone seeking a get-away-from-it-all holiday the attractions of this coastal spot are certainly hard to beat. Three small lakelets lie a short distance inland from the coast: Grootvlei, Kleinvlei and Bass Lake. Bass Lake in particular is a popular place for swimming, canoeing and boardsailing. Nature-lovers have at their disposal the Harold Porter Botanical Garden, the prettiest botanical garden imaginable, set in a sheltered hook of the mountains where two rocky kloofs join, almost at the water's edge. Finally, residents have a selection of beaches on their doorstep, some fairly safe for swimming, all of them beautiful.

The stretch of coast immediately adjacent to the village is now incorporated in the H F Verwoerd Coastal Reserve. The main beach within the reserve, known as Verwoerd Beach, is one of the very few along this coast where paper nautilus shells are washed ashore in the winter months. A smaller beach set between the rocks at the eastern end of the reserve is known as Dawidskraal, after a herdsman who formerly lived at this spot. An area of open water here, surrounded by kelp beds, offers fairly safe swimming.

Among the rocks near the southern end of the reserve the remains of an old whaling station can still be seen, with the skeletal wreck of an old whaling boat, the *Una*, protruding from the shallow water. The southern limit of the reserve is the low-lying Stony Point, where a small colony of penguins can be seen nesting on the rocks — one of the rare mainland colonies in South Africa.

5 Kleinmond

The holiday town of Kleinmond owes its name to the fact that it grew up alongside a minor mouth of the Bot River. This, the largest settlement between Gordon's Bay and Hermanus (and with

Late in the 18th century the wild countryside around Hangklip, which was of little use to farmers, served as a refuge for bands of deserters and outlaws of every kind. A group that became known as the Hangklip Drosters (deserters) regularly preyed on the farmers living in the Overberg region. They stole cattle and other livestock, and brought these back to their base camp, a large cave in the vicinity of the mountain. The authorities finally acted when these outlaws became so bold that they murdered a party of herdsmen in the Hottentots Holland Mountains and kidnapped several children. They were then tracked to their remote hideaway, where 43 of their number were killed and the children were rescued.

Today the cape serves as a more peaceful refuge for fishermen, scuba divers, and escapees from the city who like the rustic and easy-going lifestyle. Facilities include camp and caravan sites and a hotel (with a petrol pump), but the nearest shops are several kilometres away at Pringle Bay and Betty's Bay.

4 Betty's Bay

To aficionados, many belonging to old Cape families who have been holidaying here for generations, the several hundred scattered cottages that make up the village of Betty's Bay lie at the very heart of this holiday coast. Repeated attempts to introduce electricity have been resisted by a community that is prepared to put up with considerable inconvenience to preserve a simple

lifestyle. (Betty's Bay does, however, have the convenience of a couple of handy shops as well as petrol pumps.)

The village was named after Betty Youlden, the daughter of a former property developer, and to

BELOW *A creamy variant of the king protea* (Protea cynaroides) *in Fernkloof, Hermanus.*

all the necessary amenities), is reputed by residents and regular visitors to be sited on one of the most wind-free stretches of this coast, sheltered perhaps by the high mountains that tower to over 600 m immediately behind it.

The Kleinmond Lagoon, at the small mouth of the river from which the town took its name, is a safe and popular place for swimming and canoeing. The magnificent beach that runs along the coast from here slopes steeply into the sea and is not safe for swimming, but it is a favourite spot for surf angling. The coast immediately adjacent to the town is rocky and aesthetically attractive. It too is popular with fishermen, and is broken at one point by a tiny natural harbour with a slipway.

To the west of the town lies the Kleinmond Coastal Nature Reserve, surrounding the very beautiful lagoon of the Palmiet River and reaching

FRAGILE TREASURES FROM THE SEA

The delicate tracery of the paper nautilus.

In the stormy winter months, from mid-May to early September, when certain conditions of tide and current coincide, the seas deposit onto one or two of the beaches along the southern coast a rare and fragile treasure — perfect specimens of the paper nautilus shell. Seagulls smash the fragile shell to get to the tasty creature inside, but if keen collectors reach the beach with the first grey light of dawn, they may still make the find of a lifetime.

The animal that makes and lives in the paper nautilus shell is a member of the octopus family, but while its octopus relatives live their lives out on the sea bed among rocky crevices, the paper nautilus (known to scientists as *Argonauta argo*) has launched out into the open sea.

The fragile shell of the paper nautilus is unlike any other seashell. The octopus family discarded their shells millions of years ago, but the paper nautilus reinvented a new kind of shell that would give it buoyancy, and thus enable it to live a free-floating life in the oceans. The shells of other molluscs are produced by the mantle (the outer layer of cells), but the paper nautilus shell is created by two weblike arms growing from the animal's sides.

The paper nautilus differs from the common run in another interesting way. The males of the species are far smaller than the females, and it is only the larger female that produces a shell. The male attaches himself to the female and leads what is virtually a parasitic life. He lives inside the female's shell, sometimes even right inside her mantle cavity, where he feeds off scraps of her food.

ABOVE *From the air, the settlement of Kleinmond lies wedged between green mountain and blue sea.*
BELOW *Vegetation blurs the rocky shores at Kleinmond.*

Gently sloping stone steps lead down to the Old Harbour in Hermanus, with the central fish-drying stands etched against Walker Bay.

high into the mountains. Although the lagoon lies in the heart of a nature reserve, swimming, boardsailing, canoeing and powerboating are all permitted. At the head of the lagoon, where the road bridge crosses the river, are several attractive natural swimming pools.

A particular feature of Kleinmond is the extensive network of footpaths leading through the fynbos-covered mountains, both in the nature reserve and in the adjacent Highlands Forest Reserve. The region is famous for its extraordinary variety of plant life (roughly a thousand species), and walkers have fine views from the mountain slopes over the coastal strip and the sea.

6 Botriviervlei

The Bot River meanders through one of the most fertile regions in the southern Cape. The Khoikhoi who pastured their cattle here called the river the *Couga*, which can be translated as 'rich in fat', or 'lots of butter'. Early European settlers at the Cape journeyed here to barter for barrels of butter, and they adopted the Khoi name for the river, calling it first the Botter, then later the Bot.

The river flows into a large, lazy lagoon before finally reaching the sea, and this great expanse of shallow water has become an increasingly popular holiday playground — ideal for swimming, boardsailing, canoeing, yachting, powerboating and waterskiing.

There is an inlet halfway along the lagoon's eastern shore where the small Afdaksrivier runs in from the nearby Babilonstoring and Onrus

by the Cape Provincial Administration as an exclusive resort, this is a completely self-contained holiday village with manicured lawns and a wide range of facilities, including accommodation in furnished rondavels and luxury bungalows, an attractive caravan park, a swimming pool, tennis courts, a restaurant, a well-stocked shop, and a yacht-launching slipway at the edge of the lagoon.

South of Sonesta, a short distance along the coast, the small town of Hawston serves both as a holiday resort and as an outlying residential suburb of Hermanus. There is easy access to the sea here, and a wide, white sand beach. Immediately adjacent to the beach is a green-lawned camping and caravan park.

7 Onrus

The name of this little village, originally spelt Onrust, means 'restless' and presumably refers to the tireless thundering of the waves on the steep little beach and the rocky shores that flank it. This has been a wild, get-away-from-it-all holiday refuge for many generations. When Lady Anne Barnard passed through the area two centuries ago, there was already a small inn alongside the river mouth.

Onrusrivier is only a few kilometres long, drawing its water from the attractive Hemel en Aarde Valley, then cutting through the Onrus Mountains at a sharp angle and emptying into a pretty little reed-fringed lagoon before entering the sea. The lagoon offers fairly safe swimming and canoeing for children. The beach is less safe for swimming as it slopes steeply into the sea and has a strong backwash at high tide, but it remains popular with sunbathers.

In recent years the community at Onrus has expanded rapidly, overflowing into the adjacent holiday settlements of Vermont to the west and Sandbaai to the south-east. Locals claim that Sandbaai is one of the least windy spots along this coast, due to some lucky feature of the coastal topography. Serving the large holiday population are several caravan and camp sites in the vicinity, as well as shops and at least one restaurant.

Despite rapid growth, Onrus retains something of its character as an artists' colony (over the years it has been the sometime home of such leading writers as Uys Krige, Elsa Joubert, Jan Rabie and Jack Cope, and painters Marjorie Wallace, Gregoire Boonzaaier and Cecil Higgs). A physical expression of this can be found in a small Greek chapel recently erected on a rocky outcrop by two members of the local art school. The chapel is so tiny that it can accommodate only eight persons, but it is a fully consecrated church, and so perfectly constructed that it merits a visit. (To reach it, turn left from Beach Road into Erica Road, then right into Riverside Drive.)

8 Hermanus

The resort town of Hermanus took its name from Hermanus Pieters, an itinerant teacher and sheep farmer. Pieters came to the Cape from the Netherlands early last century and settled in the

mountains. Along the southern bank of this sheltered stretch of water a sprawl of cottages and holiday homes comprises Fisherhaven. Near the houses, at the water's edge, there is a club for yachts and powerboats, while a small establishment at the head of the inlet rents out sailboards and offers instruction in the art of sailing them.

Closer to the sea, also on the eastern shore of the lagoon, the luxury resort of Sonesta has been established on a low-lying spit of land that offers easy access to both the lagoon and the beach. Built

Caledon district. There he served as a roving schoolteacher to the children of local farmers, and he took up sheep farming as a sideline. Each summer he brought his sheep to the coast here for the valuable grazing. In his wake came fishermen, then parties of holiday-makers from the Cape.

As recently as 1902 the little village was still known as Hermanus Pietersfontein, but for convenience this was abbreviated to Hermanus. The original village has now grown into a substantial town with several hotels, numerous shops, many restaurants, and a full complement

Haemanthus coccineus — a flare of colour on the Hermanus cliff walk.

FRIENDLY LEVIATHANS OF WALKER BAY

As the warmth of late summer days gives way to the first cold spells, the residents and holiday-makers of Hermanus keep a lookout over Walker Bay for a regular winter visitor — the southern right whale.

For the whales, who live for most of the year in the frigid waters of the Southern Ocean, the water along South Africa's southern coast, even in winter, remains pleasantly warm. Females come to calve here in the shallow bays and inlets, and they are often accompanied and protected by other individuals from the schools to which they belong. Walker Bay is one of several coastal spots the whales seem to favour, and they frequently swim close inshore. To see several of these giant guests sporting in the clear blue water is a memorable experience.

The southern right whale grows to a length of 15 m and may weigh as much as 55 tons. Until the early decades of this century it was hunted mercilessly for its oil and it came perilously close to extinction, largely because it is a particularly docile creature that scarcely threatened its hunters, and also because it moves surprisingly slowly, with a top speed of only a little over six knots. An additional factor that was of importance to the whalers who hunted it was that, once dead, it floated on the surface. Some species of whale sink, making it difficult for the whalers to haul in their 'catch'.

Since 1935 all species of right whale have been protected by international charter, and gradually regional populations have grown. It is estimated that there are now some 5000 southern right whales all told, with the South African regional population numbering as much as 500.

Further protection was granted to these 'South African' whales in 1980 when the South African government made it a criminal offence to disturb or harass any whale during the winter breeding season. Powerboats, yachts and aircraft are prohibited from approaching closer than 300 m. In the event of a whale surfacing near a boat, the person in charge of the boat is bound by law to move away to a distance of at least 300 m.

of banks and petrol stations. There are also a number of caravan parks and camping grounds in the vicinity.

Along the coast there are several beaches, each with its own individual character. Grotto Beach is considered the safest for swimming, and both Grotto and Voëlklip beaches are popular with surfers. (There is also fairly safe swimming in two tidal pools set among the rocks.) For shell collecting the best spot is Kwaaiwater.

An attractive feature of the Hermanus coastline is the popular cliff walk, a series of paths leading along the coast for many kilometres. The paths wind past interesting coastal rock formations, pretty half-hidden beaches, and through little glens filled with wild flowers, all contributing to a delightful half-day excursion.

Inland lies Fernkloof Nature Reserve. Here there are walks ranging from twenty minutes to seven hours. The reserve is famous for the immense variety of indigenous plants it contains, and it is crisscrossed by some 40 km of footpaths, some reaching high into the mountains. From the higher slopes there are magnificent views over the coast, and the reserve itself is always attractive as the local fynbos has no dormant season — there is something in flower every day of the year. Close to the entrance to the reserve the visitors' centre provides maps, leaflets and free walking sticks.

It is possible to reach the upper slopes of the Fernkloof Reserve by car. To do this you drive out of town in what seems to be the opposite direction — as if driving to Cape Town. On the outskirts of the town you turn right, following the signs onto the Rotary Way. This is a tarred 4 km scenic drive that leads up and along the crest of the mountains, providing wide views over Hermanus and Walker Bay, and joining up with several tracks.

Looking down on Hermanus from the Rotary Way you can see the small reserve that surrounds Hoy's Koppie. This low outcrop of rock in the midst of the town is hardly noticeable at ground level. It was named after Sir William Hoy, one-time general manager of the railways who is said to have prevented the railway from reaching Hermanus because he felt that such accessibility would spoil the town's holiday character. Paths wind up to the top of the koppie, one of them leading past an old Strandlopers' cave.

Lying to the east of the town, and ranking as one of its principal attractions, is Hermanus's beautiful lagoon — strictly speaking, Kleinriviers-vlei, the estuary or coastal lake at the river mouth. A great expanse of white sand, the clear water of the lagoon, and the picturesque mountain backdrop combine to make this an extremely popular place with holiday-makers. Separate sections of the lagoon are reserved for power-boating and sailing. The shallows near the mouth of the lagoon are the favoured place for swimming and canoeing.

From its earliest days Hermanus has been famed as a fisherman's paradise and many who come here have fishing uppermost in their minds. There is excellent fishing in the lagoon, and sea angling all along the coast. One spot that might perhaps be singled out as particularly good is Kwaaiwater. Hermanus is unusual among coastal resorts in that it also caters for the freshwater fisherman; there is fine trout fishing to be enjoyed in the De Bos Dam, just a few kilometres inland in the Hemel en Aarde Valley.

LEFT *Rowing is popular in the still shallows of the lagoon of Hermanus.*

THINGS TO DO

Angling
The fisherman can take his pick here from rocky headlands, sandy beaches and shallow stretches of coast with extensive kelp beds. Galjoen and white steenbras are the popular quarries in winter, kabeljou and geelbek in the summer months. The lagoons at river mouths offer fine leervis, elf and kabeljou, while anglers who wish to fish the deeper waters offshore can hire launches at Hermanus Harbour. Hermanus also offers trout fishing in De Bos Dam, situated just outside the town.

Beachcombing and shelling
At Rooiels fine shells can be found washed up on the smaller beaches west of the main beach. Silver Sands and Verwoerd Beach at Betty's Bay are famous for the paper nautilus shells washed ashore under certain conditions during the winter months.

Along the coastal stretch at Hermanus, the little beach at Kwaaiwater is good for shells as well as attractive water-worn pebbles.

Birdwatching
Fernkloof Nature Reserve in Hermanus is known for its wide variety of bird life, as are the mountain slopes behind Kleinmond. A particularly striking bird to watch for in the fynbos is the malachite sunbird, and high in the mountains you will often be able to spot black eagles.

Botriviervlei is home to a great number of waterbirds and waders, including greater flamingos, pelicans and spoonbills.

A surprising diversity of waterfowl can also be seen in the reed beds of the small lagoon at Onrus.

Boardsailing
This has become a popular pastime on the three large lagoons of the region — the estuaries of the Palmiet, Bot and Klein rivers. Although Bass Lake at Betty's Bay is relatively small, it is easily accessible and here too boardsailors are a common sight.

The best places for boardsailing in the sea would be at Pringle Bay and Masbaai at Cape Hangklip. Sailboards can be hired at Hermanus from Lagoon Boat Hire and at Fisherhaven on the Botriviervlei.

Boat trips
During the summer and Easter holiday seasons launches make short excursions into Walker Bay from the New Harbour at Hermanus; for further details of these boat trips contact Hermanus Publicity Association.

Fish type	Season	Best area	Best bait
Elf	Oct — April	Hangklip area, Kleinmond and Hermanus lagoons	Strips of sardine or mullet, spinners
Galjoen	All year, especially April — Aug	Rooiels, Hangklip area, Kleinmond, Onrus, Hermanus	Rotten redbait, bloodworms, white mussels, sand prawns
Geelbek	Oct — April	Rooiels, Hangklip area, Hermanus	Sardines, mullet, mackerel, chokka
Hottentot	All year, especially Mar — July	Throughout the area in rocky gullies and near kelp	White mussels, fresh redbait, chokka, sardines
Kabeljou	Oct — April	Hangklip area, Dawidskraal, Kleinmond Lagoon, Hermanus	Sardines, mullet, mackerel, chokka, sand prawns, bloodworms, spinners
Leervis	Jan — April	Kleinmond and Hermanus lagoons	Live bait, mullet, mackerel, chokka
Roman	All year	All rocky parts of the coast	Strips of mullet or sardine, chokka
White steenbras	All year, especially July — Nov	Hangklip area, Kleinmond, Hermanus	Sand prawns, wonderworms, bloodworms

It is also possible to hire a variety of small craft for use on the Hermanus lagoon from Lagoon Boat Hire.

Bowls
For details of bowling greens at Hermanus, contact the local publicity association. Kleinmond has three greens in a beautiful setting; the local municipality has the details.

Camping and caravanning
Contact Hermanus Publicity Association for details of the several large camping and caravan parks in the Onrus-Hermanus area. Other sites exist at Hangklip, Betty's Bay, Kleinmond, Hawston and Sonesta. Contact the local municipalities.

Canoeing
Canoes may be used on all the coastal lagoons in the region, and also on Bass Lake at Betty's Bay. In the holiday season you can usually hire canoes at Kleinmond and Hermanus.

Diving
All the rocky parts of this coast offer good diving, with favourite spots along the coast south of Rooiels, around Cape Hangklip, and between the two harbours at Hermanus.

Drives and viewsites
The 4 km Rotary Way along the crest of the mountains at Hermanus makes a delightful short jaunt.

There are also two longer drives inland, one leading from either Hermanus or Kleinmond up the valley of the Bot River (R43) and over the well-wooded slopes of the Houhoek Pass (N2 to Cape Town). The other leads from Hermanus through Hemel en Aarde Valley and rises to Shaw's Mountain Pass, with fine views of the pretty farming valley below. The road continues to the small town of Caledon, which is renowned for its spring wild flower show.

Golf
Hermanus has an attractive golf course; contact the publicity association.

Horseriding
Contact Hermanus Publicity Association for information.

Libraries
There are good public libraries at both Kleinmond and Hermanus; inquire at the local municipalities.

Museums
OLD HARBOUR MUSEUM, Hermanus: A national monument and tribute to Hermanus's fishing past.

Powerboating
This is permitted on the lagoon at Hermanus (restricted), and also on the lagoons at the mouths of the Bot and Palmiet rivers. Craft can be hired during the holiday seasons at Hermanus; contact Lagoon Boat Hire.

Shipwrecks
The only visible wreck on this stretch of coast, the whaling boat *Una*, lies near the southern end of the H F Verwoerd Coastal Reserve, Betty's Bay.

Surfing
The most popular surfing beaches in this region are Verwoerd Beach at Betty's Bay, Kleinmond Beach (east of the town), and Grotto and Voëlklip beaches at Hermanus. It is best to check conditions with the locals.

Swimming
There is relatively safe swimming all along this coast, notably at the lagoons at Rooiels, Pringle Bay, Kleinmond, Onrus and Hermanus.

Swimming is also good at the beach at Pringle Bay, at Blokbaai and Silver Sands (Cape Hangklip), at Dawidskraal (Betty's Bay), and at Grotto Beach (Hermanus).

Tennis and squash
There are courts for both games at Hermanus (contact Hermanus Publicity Association for details), and there is a private tennis club at Kleinmond (contact the municipality).

Walks
At Hermanus there are fine walks along the coast, collectively known as the cliff walk, and 40 km of footpaths among the mountains in the scenic Fernkloof Nature Reserve.

Other paths can be explored in the Harold Porter Botanical Garden at Betty's Bay and in the Kleinmond Coastal Nature Reserve. At Rooiels there is an easy walk, lasting a couple of hours, over the shoulder of Klein-Hangklip.

Yachting and dinghy sailing
Sailing is permitted at the lagoon in Hermanus and at the lagoons on the mouths of the Bot and the Palmiet. It is not at present possible to hire yachts or dinghies, although sailboards are available.

INFORMATION
- Kleinmond Municipality, Main Rd, Kleinmond 7195. Tel 02823 = 3030
- Hermanus Municipality, Magnolia St, Hermanus 7200. Tel 02831 = 21122
- Hermanus Publicity Association, Main Rd, Hermanus 7200. Tel 02831 = 22629
- National Sea Rescue Institute, Station 17, New Harbour, Hermanus 7200. Tel 02831 = 23180

Nearest AA Office
- AA House, 7 Martin Hammerschlag Way, Cape Town 8001. Tel 021 = 211550

Where endless hills dip down to Africa's southernmost shores

T HIS MOST SOUTHERLY PART of the continent presents a strangely gentle landscape of softly rolling hills, painted a brilliant emerald green each year by the winter rains, then turning warm and golden in the summer sun. Eventually the land peters out into the sea at Cape Agulhas, turning point for the early voyagers rounding Africa on their way to the East. Most of the low-lying sandy coast is wild and unspoilt, serenely beautiful for days on end, but occasionally transformed into a scene of operatic violence by the dreaded storms that destroyed so many of those ancient ships.

1 Stanford

In the mid-19th century, the British government made the controversial decision to establish a penal colony at the Cape. Feelings on the matter were running high when HMS *Neptune* docked in Cape Town in 1849 with the first batch of convicts on board.

The Cape burghers banded together and refused to supply food for the convicts, but one farmer, Captain Robert Stanford, broke ranks and supplied provisions from his lands — thus doing his duty as he saw it to the British crown. Stanford was ostracised by his fellow farmers but he was awarded a knighthood by the highly appreciative British authorities and the village established on his farm Klein River (on the banks of that river) was named in his honour.

This peaceful little country town, overlooked by the darkly shaded slopes of the moody Klein River Mountains, is spread along the southern bank of the river just before it widens out to form a coastal lagoon. A feature of this principal farming and commercial centre for the fertile valley of the Klein, is the charming 'Engelse kerk', a tiny sandstone building topped by a neat black thatch roof — a church that would not look out of place in some faraway English village.

2 Salmonsdam Nature Reserve

A few kilometres east of Stanford the three peaks of Perdeberg, Akkedisberg and Tafelberg rise

majestically from the low rolling hills of the southern Cape, and at the feet of the three peaks a sparkling mountain stream runs through the Keeromskloof. The Salmonsdam Nature Reserve encompasses this whole valley and the mountain slopes that surround it.

In the midst of the reserve there is a camping and caravan site, with a couple of small cottages for hire. From here footpaths lead up the Keeromskloof on both sides of the stream, and a path into a side valley brings you to a series of pretty waterfalls tumbling through a rocky gorge. On the eastern side of the stream there is a gravel track that enables you to drive up the mountain slopes to a viewsite overlooking the valley.

The reserve is best known for its rich fynbos flora — including some fifty protea species and

Silver-grey seas caress the curves of Struisbaai.

more than 150 erica species — but there is also a variety of animal life: bontebok, klipspringer, grysbok, caracal, baboon, genet, porcupine, and many other smaller mammals.

3 Die Kelders and Gansbaai

One of the most unusual geological features of this southern coast is a series of underground pools beneath the cliffs at the eastern end of Walker Bay. Long known as Die Drup Kelder (the drip cellar) but now simply called Die Kelders, these are small natural caves, with a few stalactites and stalagmites, and a number of crystal clear pools set in the floor with water that is pleasantly cool and perfectly comfortable for swimming. On the cliff-top immediately above the caves is a hotel, and the rocky shore on both sides is renowned for the fine angling it offers.

Just a couple of kilometres south of Die Kelders lies the fishing harbour of Gansbaai. To all but the dedicated angler this appears to be a rather uninspiring stretch of coast, backed as it is by bare mountains and exposed to a fair amount of wind. But here at Gansbaai there are two well-sheltered harbours in the small bay, and there are also beautiful views to enjoy across the bay to the mountains overlooking Hermanus.

At the northern end of the little town there is a tidal swimming pool set amid the rocks, and about a kilometre further north there is a tiny beach in the sheltered inlet known as Stanford's Cove (again named after Sir Robert Stanford). Next to the beach there are toilets and braai places.

LEFT *Gansbaai's harbour, providing the focal point of the community.*

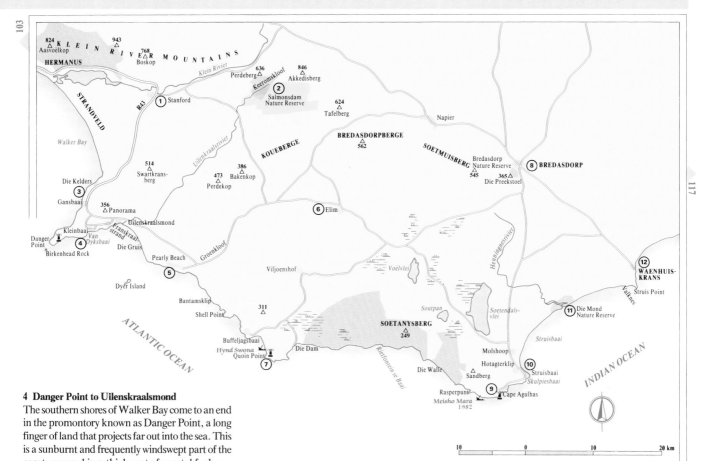

A cluster of holiday houses at Franskraalstrand, where sunshine softens a jagged coast.

4 Danger Point to Uilenskraalsmond

The southern shores of Walker Bay come to an end in the promontory known as Danger Point, a long finger of land that projects far out into the sea. This is a sunburnt and frequently windswept part of the coast, covered in a thick mat of coastal fynbos.

As its name implies, this has long been one of the most dangerous spots for coastal shipping. Not only is the land very low-lying and difficult to see in poor weather, but the sea remains shallow for some distance offshore and there are deadly pinnacles of jagged rock waiting just beneath the waves for unwary mariners.

The most famous wreck here was that of HMS *Birkenhead*, and the treacherous rocky islet on which it came to grief is still known today as Birkenhead Rock. Since then a lighthouse has been built on a small hill behind the point to warn ships away. A fisherman's track leads across private land to the point.

The coast immediately to the east of Danger Point is particularly wild, with just one or two primitive wooden shacks tucked away in the coastal bush, until you reach the small inlet known as Kleinbaai. This and adjacent Van Dyksbaai make up a virtual single community of holiday homes, occupying a particularly pretty spot. The little bay is relatively protected from the wind and there is an attractive tidal swimming pool here as well as a sheltered launch ramp for powerboats.

A few kilometres further along the shore brings you to the slightly larger holiday resort of Franskraalstrand. The houses here run alongside a rocky stretch of coast with many rock pools to explore at low tide. At the eastern end of Franskraalstrand you come to Uilenskraalsmond (owl

farm), the mouth of the Uilenskraalsrivier. Here, after gathering its waters from the low-lying mountain ranges of the immediate interior, the Uilenskraal forms an attractive blue lagoon at the point where it reaches the sea.

In a small forest of milkwoods on the west bank of the river mouth there is an extensive and well-shaded caravan park, with a number of holiday bungalows for hire. The adjacent lagoon is ideal

for canoeing and offers fairly safe swimming, but the area next to the mouth should be avoided during the outflowing tide as the current becomes extremely strong and dangerous.

5 Pearly Beach

Approaching Pearly Beach from Elim along an undulating gravel track, you traverse a range of what at first appear to be low coastal hills, separating the sea from the green and fertile valley of the Boesmansrivier.

As you drive over the crest of the hills you find you are higher than expected, and you have a fine view down through Groenkloof to the great sand dunes that line the shore and to the blue ocean behind them. The hillsides to your left and right are blanketed in fynbos and rich in wild flowers — notably ericas, proteas and the extraordinary everlastings (*Helichrysum*).

You reach Pearly Beach after descending through Groenkloof and crossing the new coastal highway. There is a large caravan park here, set amid lawns and immediately alongside the beach, and running westward from the caravan park is a considerable township of holiday homes. The shoreline to the east of the caravan park consists of a fine wild sandy beach; to the west, in front of the line of holiday houses, there is a stretch of jagged rocks which is then followed by another slightly smaller sandy beach.

The traditional whitewashed thatched homes of Elim in the still heart of the country.

THE BIRTH OF A LEGEND

HMS *Birkenhead* was one of a new breed of ships. Its hull was built of iron rather than wood and it was equipped with steam-powered paddle wheels in addition to the usual complement of sails.

On 25 February 1852 it sailed from Simon's Town with 638 passengers and crew, 476 of these being soldiers heading for the eastern Cape where the Eighth Frontier War was raging. Tragically, within hours of crossing False Bay, it hit a rock off Danger Point — and so began one of the most heroic shipwreck sagas in the lengthy annals of Britain's maritime history.

Of the eight lifeboats carried on board, only three could be released and lowered into the water. These were quickly filled with the handful of women and children who were among the passengers, then the captain called out to the soldiers and crew to jump overboard and head for the shore. But at this point the commanding officer of the military contingent, a Lieutenant-Colonel Seton, ordered his men to 'stand fast'. He realised that the men would make for the boats and that their numbers would be a burden that would almost certainly result in the drowning of the women and children.

Dutifully the men lined up on deck and refrained from attempting to save their own lives at the expense of the women and children. As they stood there the raging sea threw the ship over onto its side and cast several hundred brave men to their deaths — including both Seton and the captain. But with their deaths they gave birth to a legend, and a tradition of heroism at sea that is still referred to as the 'Birkenhead Drill'.

A more mercenary legend holds that the *Birkenhead* also went down with a fortune of gold on board, funds that had been intended for use in financing the frontier war. Attempts to salvage this treasure trove have frequently been made, but without any evident success.

6 Elim

Coming from the west, the east or the south, you arrive without warning in the little village of Elim. But if you come from the north, travelling over the hills from Napier, your first glimpse of this tiny mission settlement with its fairy-tale character is a distant glistening cluster of whitewashed houses huddled at the eastern end of a huge low hill and tightly bounded on all sides by rich farmlands.

The village dates back to 1824 when Bishop Hallbeck of the Moravian Brothers bought the farm Vogelstruiskraal and established a mission around the old farmhouse. The little mission station was renamed Elim after the biblical town of that name, and gradually a village grew up around the church and the mission buildings. The church, beautiful in its simplicity, remains the lively heart of the small community. A few metres up the hill from its front doors a whitewashed monument commemorates the freeing of slaves on 1 December 1838, and behind the church is a watermill dating back to 1828.

The Moravian missionaries were justly renowned for the fact that they taught practical skills as well as religious beliefs, and the skilled craftsmen of Elim — particularly the thatchers — are noted far and wide for the quality of their work, which is reflected in their pretty homes.

7 Quoin Point

A quoin is a wedge of wood that was used to raise and lower the barrels of ships' cannons. This particular shape of wedge, so familiar to the seafarers of earlier centuries, gave its name to Quoin Point. The point itself is simply a low-lying promontory, but a short distance offshore lies a rock with the distinctive quoin shape.

Like so many of the low rocky promontories along this coast, Quoin Point has claimed its fair share of ships, with the 18th-century wrecking of a Danish East Indiaman, the *Nicobar*, being especially poignant.

After a disastrous voyage to the Cape, during which many of the crew died from injuries or scurvy, the captain made up his complement by taking on several Indian sailors (as well as two young Indian women passengers) who had been wrecked on the *Grosvenor*.

The *Nicobar* now continued hopefully on its way to India but after just a solitary day's sailing it was wrecked on the rocks of Quoin Point and most of the crew were drowned. Miraculously, one of the Indian women survived and eventually voyaged safely home.

Just to the west of Quoin Point a gravel road leads to a handful of fishermen's cottages at Buffeljagsbaai (buffalo hunt bay), and a dilapidated jeep track branches off from this road and winds through the dunes to a position very close to the point. Buffeljagsbaai itself is a tiny inlet with a sandy beach that offers sheltered swimming in calm weather.

To the east of the point another track leads to a caravan park at Die Dam, set amid the dunes and alongside a beautiful curving white sand beach, with a view across the bay to the low hills that overlook Cape Agulhas.

8 Bredasdorp

The southern Cape presents the visitor with a quiet world of sheep farms and wheat fields, spreading away endlessly over long ranks of gentle hills. In the midst of this peaceful landscape lies Bredasdorp, founded in 1838 and named after the man whom many regard as the father of South Africa's merino sheep industry, Michiel van Breda. The rivalry between Van Breda and his neighbour, P V van der Byl, led to the establishment of two separate churches on their farms, and eventually two separate towns grew up around them (Bredasdorp and Napier).

The grand old church and the new municipal offices nearby remain the heart of modern Bredasdorp, but from a present-day tourist's point of view the heart of the town is its excellent museum complex, just a few paces downhill from the towering church. The restored Rectory is furnished in styles typical of several eras, and is particularly interesting because of the extensive use of furniture salvaged from numerous shipwrecks. The neighbouring shipwreck museum has a range of exhibits from the skull of some unfortunate seaman to brass telescopes, finely made navigational instruments, exotic coins and superb china and ceramic ware. A third building in the complex is the Waenhuis (wagon house, or cart shed), with a variety of old vehicles from the days of true horsepower and various primitive farming implements.

Immediately south of the town is the Bredasdorp range, with the 80 ha Bredasdorp Nature Reserve on its northern slopes. Several footpaths lead through the reserve's largely unspoilt fynbos, and from the summit of the mountain there are splendid views in all directions.

9 Cape Agulhas

The fact that Cape Agulhas (or Cape L'Agulhas, as it is also known) is the southernmost point of land on the African continent is common knowledge, but how it came by its name (cape of needles) is a mystery. One theory holds that the early Portuguese navigators gave it this name because at this point the needles in their compasses

LADY ANNE'S ADVENTURE

Lady Anne Barnard.

The British had been in control of the Cape for scarcely two years when, in the year 1798, the intrepid Lady Anne Barnard journeyed into the interior with a handful of companions to see what this strange new African land might offer.

As the party travelled eastward along the coast they heard of the underground caves now known as Die Kelders, '. . . a curious cave for petrifactions, at five or six hours' distance'. They decided to take a look. They traversed 'bushy mountains' and 'sandy holes' and 'stupendous hills of white sand', to arrive eventually at the coastal cliff wherein lay the cavern, and after a perilous climb reached their destination.

As Lady Anne recorded the event in her diary: 'We had fortunately brought a tinder-box, and the gloom of the recess was soon illuminated with a set of wax candles, which had been packed up after my last party in Berkeley Square; they little thought, when their tops had the honour of shining upon some of their Royal Highnesses . . . that their bottoms would next illuminate the Drup Kelder at the Cape of Good Hope.'

Fortunately the candles 'did not refuse to shew us the curiosities of the place. The pointed *drup-stones* descended from the roof in great numbers, and sometimes met with others which had risen from the ground to meet them.'

---

pointed true north without any magnetic deviation. Another possibility is that it was named after the jagged and slanting rocks that project from the surf offshore, like a thousand needles waiting to pierce the hull of any stray ship.

East of the cape a sprinkling of holiday homes and two caravan parks lie behind the shore at the foot of a low-lying coastal hill — a surprisingly modest mound covered in coastal scrub and fynbos, rather an anticlimactic finale to the continent's geological grandeur. The coast here is shallow and rocky, and not especially spectacular, but for holiday-makers there are several tidal swimming pools set amid the rocks.

Just a few hundred metres from the cape stands the old lighthouse, dating back to 1849 and designed to appear like a fortress when viewed from the sea. During the present century the

LEFT *Cape Agulhas — the end of Africa — drenched in light from a moody sky.*

An early start to the day's fishing from Struisbaai's rock-tumbled shores.

strength of the light was increased, but it was replaced by a more modern light in 1962 and the old building then fell into disrepair. Recently it has been restored and is now being developed as an extension of the Bredasdorp Museum.

Immediately to the west of the cape you can still see the substantial remains of the *Meisho Maru*, which was wrecked on the rocks here in 1982, one of the latest in a long line of maritime casualties.

10 Struisbaai

Struisbaai, together with its neighbouring communities of Hotagterklip (left rear stone) and Molshoop (mole hill), makes up a sizeable collection of holiday homes spread along the beautiful sandy shore north-east of Cape Agulhas.

There is some debate as to the origin of the name. Some authorities argue that it means 'straw bay' and that it earned this soubriquet by virtue of the fact that the fishermen's cottages here were originally built of straw. Others claim that it is derived from the Dutch *vogelstruijs* or 'ostrich'. The low scrub-covered land lying behind the shore is certainly ostrich country and you will still see a good number sharing the terrain with dairy cattle and merino sheep.

There is a picturesque fishing harbour here, and moored in the shallows just off the sandy beach is a collection of very small fishing boats, looking particularly vulnerable in relation to the wildness and violence of the southern ocean on some of its stormier days. Next to this little harbour a magnificent broad beach of gently sloping white sand curves gracefully north and east as far as the eye can see. On a clear day the sea is translucent and calm, and this is a popular swimming beach in the summer. (There are change-rooms alongside the beach, with showers and toilets.)

11 Die Mond Nature Reserve

Between the holiday resorts of Struisbaai and Waenhuiskrans the Heuningnesrivier lazes its

The simple architecture of a Cape fishing village gives Waenhuiskrans its painterly air.

THE SHEEP WITH THE LUCKY TALE

The magnificent woolly merino so familiar in the southern Cape originally came from Spain. Late in the 18th century the king of Spain, as part of a political exercise, presented several fine animals to the royal family of Holland. Holland's moist climate did not favour the sheep, so in 1789 six animals — two rams and four ewes — were sent to the Cape.

Here they were entrusted to the care of the military commander, Colonel Robert Gordon. Gordon kept the small flock at Groenekloof where the town of Mamre now stands. When the Spanish heard that the sheep had been sent to the Cape they objected to the Dutch that they had not wished the sheep to be sent out of Europe, and the Dutch obligingly ordered Gordon to send the animals back. Gordon obeyed the order to the letter and sent back the full complement of six sheep. However, by this time the original animals had produced a number of offspring; these Gordon kept, and they became the ancestors of the many millions of merino sheep to be seen throughout South Africa today.

In South Africa the process of breeding continued, steadily producing improvements in the strain. Foremost of the breeders was the farmer Michiel van Breda, who founded Bredasdorp and after whom the town is named. The climate and soils of the southern Cape are particularly well suited to sheep farming and Van Breda worked for many years at his farm Zoetendalsvlei, systematically improving the breed.

way to the sea through a low, gently undulating landscape, a sunbaked expanse of long-established dunes covered in coastal fynbos, and richly carpeted with wild flowers throughout the spring and summer. When the river reaches the coast it spreads out into a beautiful tidal lagoon. The clear, shallow water, running over clean white sand, presents all shades of blue.

This peaceful spot — the whole of the lagoon and much of the surrounding land — is now preserved in the 301 ha Die Mond Nature Reserve. At the head of the lagoon, roughly a kilometre from the mouth, a long wooden footbridge spans the widening river and from here you can walk along either bank of the lagoon to the mouth, where the river finally spills out into the sea over a wide beach that stretches away into the distance.

12 Waenhuiskrans

The coast east of Cape Agulhas consists of a succession of shallow, sweeping bays, lined by broad sandy beaches. Struisbaai is the first of these great bays, and it comes to an end in the stony promontory known as Struis Point. A few hundred metres east of this point there are several low sandstone headlands jutting out into the sea, and in the first of these a huge cavern has been gouged out of the rock by long ages of wave action.

The migrant farmers who explored this great cave were struck by its resemblance to a giant wagon house, the kind of dome-roofed tent they constructed to shelter their wagons and carts when not in use. The analogy stuck, and in time the rocky headland that contains the cave came to be known as Waenhuiskrans (wagon house cliff).

In the spring of 1815 a tragedy occurred here that stirred people to such an extent that the area acquired a new name. The British transport ship HMS *Arniston*, on its way to England from Sri Lanka, ran aground here in stormy weather and 372 lives were lost, including 25 children. Only six men made it to the beach alive.

A small fishing village subsequently grew up here, little more than a tiny huddle of whitewashed cottages, exposed to the weather but able to take advantage of the rich fishing offshore. For a long time the village was known as Arniston after the memorable wreck, and to many local people this remains its name, but recently the village was subject to an official name-change and reverted to the older name of Waenhuiskrans.

At the same time the tiny settlement has become a fashionable holiday resort. The fishermen's cottages have been joined by chicly renovated or newly built holiday homes, at least some of which preserve the original style with whitewashed walls and dark thatched roofs. Set amid these is a small-scale caravan and camping area, and overlooking the beach is a luxurious hotel, all adding up to a charming miniature coastal refuge.

Close to the village several gently sloping beaches offer fairly safe swimming. Alongside the main beach there is a slipway for fishing boats, and a few metres from here, overlooking the main beach from its opposite end, there stands a simple memorial to several of those who died so tragically in the *Arniston* disaster.

Along the coast to the south of the village are numerous rock pools that can be explored at low tide, and after walking along the shore for roughly 2 km you reach the headland that contains the 'waenhuis' cavern. At high tide there is no way to enter the great cave, but for an hour or two at low tide it is possible to clamber in through a hole at the back where the waves have broken through the thin wall separating the large cave from a smaller one on its northern side.

BELOW *The vast cave gouged from rock which has earned Waenhuiskrans its name.*

THINGS TO DO

Angling
Powerboat rather than shore angling is favoured here, with numerous launch ramps or convenient beaches providing access to the sea. Spearfishing is also popular along the rocky sections of the coast. For details of restrictions on angling, contact the magistrate's office in Bredasdorp.

Beachcombing and shelling
The best place for shell collecting is the small Skulpiesbaai Beach between Cape Agulhas and Struisbaai. Another good area is the relatively inaccessible stretch between Pearly Beach and Buffeljagsbaai, but note that quicksands have sometimes been reported here.

Birdwatching
The several inland vleis lying just a few kilometres from the coast are thickly populated with waterfowl and waders of every kind, with popular sightings including flamingos, wild geese, sacred ibises and blue cranes.

Boardsailing
Two popular and less exposed spots are Struisbaai and Waenhuiskrans.

Boat trips
Small boats can sometimes be hired for the day at Struisbaai. Inquire at the offices of Suidkus Eiendom in the main road through the village.

Bowls
Visitors are welcome at the bowling club in Bredasdorp; contact the local publicity office for details.

Camping and caravanning
There are many camping and caravan parks all along this coast, notably at

Fish type	Season	Best area	Best bait
Elf	Dec—Aug	Uilenskraalsmond, Pearly Beach, Waenhuiskrans	Sardines, freshly cut fish fillets, spinners
Galjoen	Mar—Oct	Die Kelders, Gansbaai, Agulhas	Musselworms, rotten redbait, white mussels
Hottentot	All year	Rocky parts of Waenhuiskrans coast	Worms, redbait, white mussels
Kabeljou	Nov—April, especially March	Die Kelders—Uilenskraalsmond, Pearly Beach, Buffelsjagsbaai—Die Dam, Cape Agulhas, Struisbaai, Waenhuiskrans	Sardines, chokka, freshly cut mackerel fillets
Leervis	Nov—April	Waenhuiskrans	Live bait, mullet
Mussel-cracker	All year, especially August	All rocky part of coast in foamy water	Venus ears, chitons, alikreukel, fresh redbait
Red stumpnose	Oct—April, especially March	Die Kelders, Gansbaai, Kleinbaai, Buffelsjagsbaai—Die Dam, Waenhuiskrans	Octopus, chokka, redbait, worms
White steenbras	Mar—July	Die Kelders—Uilenskraalsmond, Pearly Beach, Buffelsjagsbaai, Heuningnes mouth	Wonderworms, bloodworms, sardines

Gansbaai, Uilenskraalsmond, Pearly Beach, Die Dam, Cape Agulhas, Struisbaai and Waenhuiskrans. Contact the local municipality or the Bredasdorp Publicity Office for more detailed information.

Canoeing
The sea is generally too rough for canoeing but the lagoon of the Uilenskraalsrivier is ideal, except for the area near the mouth where currents can be very strong.

Diving
This section of the coast is popular with scuba divers, partly for the fishing but mainly because of the many shipwrecks. For details of the underwater diving club in Bredasdorp, contact the publicity office.

Drives and viewsites
All the country roads in this area make attractive drives, particularly in spring and summer when wild flowers fill the fields. There are also 'Wool Route' excursions organised by the Bredasdorp Publicity Office, visiting historical farms in the area and featuring demonstrations of sheep-shearing and sheepdog work.

Golf
Contact the local publicity office about play at Bredasdorp's fine nine-hole golf course.

Libraries
There are two libraries in Bredasdorp and one each in Stanford, Gansbaai and Napier. Contact the local municipality.

Museums
BREDASDORP MUSEUM, Independent Street: An excellent complex covering the region's history, with special emphasis on the coastline's many fascinating shipwrecks.

Powerboating
Struisbaai is the only place along this coast suitable for waterskiing, the rest being too rough as a rule. There are, however, a number of launch ramps and suitable launching beaches for powerboat fishermen (including Gansbaai, Kleinbaai, Buffeljagsbaai, Die Dam, Struisbaai and Waenhuiskrans).

Shipwrecks
Few stretches of coastline in the world can have claimed so many ships, with the *Birkenhead* and the *Arniston* the best-known victims. The remains soon disappear from view after being broken up by storms, but divers are continually discovering wrecks offshore — and occasionally treasure troves.

Surfing
The best surfing spots in this region are at Uilenskraalsmond, Struisbaai and Waenhuiskrans.

Swimming
The most popular swimming spots are the beaches at Struisbaai and Waenhuiskrans, the two coastal lagoons, and the tidal swimming pools set in the rocks at Gansbaai, Kleinbaai and Cape Agulhas.

Tennis and squash
There are courts for both games at Bredasdorp and visitors are welcome; contact the Bredasdorp Publicity Office. There are also tennis courts at the resort of Struisbaai.

Walks
The entire coastline offers magnificent walks along unspoilt beaches and rocky shores. Inland there are attractive walks in the Salmonsdam and Bredasdorp nature reserves.

Yachting and dinghy sailing
Struisbaai is virtually the only suitable venue, with the rest of the coast generally too rough.

The Waenhuiskrans slipway gives easy access to a rich fishing ground.

INFORMATION
- Bredasdorp Publicity Office, Municipal Building, Dirkie Uys St, Bredasdorp 7280. Tel 0284=42584
- Gansbaai Municipality, 42 Church St, Gansbaai 7220. Tel 02834=40111
- Nature Conservator, Salmonsdam Nature Reserve, PO Box 5, Stanford 7210. Tel 02833=789

Nearest AA Office
- AA House, 7 Martin Hammerschlag Way, Cape Town 8001. Tel 021=211550

A seaside still life slumbering in soft sunshine

N ARC OF SHIMMERING WHITE SAND and rocky cliff curls around a jagged headland at Cape Infanta and into St Sebastian Bay. From here, with the peaks of the Langeberg piercing the northern skyline, the sickle-like contours of the southern Cape coast continue towards Mossel Bay, embracing a hinterland of gently sloping hills carpeted with coastal fynbos and golden fields of wheat. Here, in this place of peace where sun-bronzed sand dunes guard a sparkling kingdom of fish, you can soak up the splendour of unspoilt nature.

1 De Hoop Nature Reserve

Between the rustling grainlands of the Overberg and the gentle curves of the southern Cape coast, lies one of the most biologically diverse sanctuaries in the world: De Hoop. Recently extended to more than 40 000 ha (including the entire coastline north-east of Skipskop to Cape Infanta), the reserve today ranks as one of the great floral wonderlands of the subcontinent, with a premier calving and mating ground for the southern right whale offshore.

To reach the reserve you can travel either from Bredasdorp in the west or from Swellendam in the north. (Permits are issued at the gate with the reserve open from 07h00 to 18h00.) On the western approach, the gravel road tumbles down into a vast, green plain covered by fynbos and rich, riverine bush. On the near side of this plain the shimmering waters of a huge, landlocked vlei, some 15 km long, reach southwards to giant sand dunes that stretch a further 2,5 km to the sea.

The vlei is the lifeblood of the reserve, its waters providing sustenance for one of the country's richest concentrations of bird life. More than 200 bird species, from coots, ducks and grebes to small waders, herons and egrets, bring a vibrant world of colour and sound to the vlei, while thousands of bats cling to the dark corridors of limestone caves at its northern end.

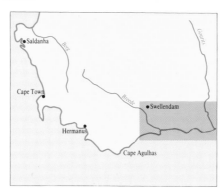

Occupying a special place at De Hoop are the endangered Cape vulture, which nests among the rocky ledges of Potberg Mountain in the north-eastern part of the reserve, and the bontebok and Cape mountain zebra, which roam the area in the company of eland, grey duiker, grysbok, steenbok, grey rhebuck and klipspringer. Other less conspicuous mammals to look out for are caracal, Cape fox, water mongoose, striped polecat and various species of rats, mice and gerbils. Reptiles and amphibians are also well represented (in summer you might see the puffadder, boomslang and cobra); watch out for tortoises on the road.

Drives around the reserve (about 20 km of good gravel road are open to the public) traverse a floral

Golden wheat under a bruised sky.

kingdom of some 1 500 plant species, including a wide spectrum of ericas and proteas, notably leucadendrons and pincushions. Picturesque trails include the Vlei Trail (6 km), the Potberg Trail (4 km) to the summit of Potberg Mountain, and a coastal hike, which takes you along the fringes of translucent intertidal pools inhabited by octopuses, sea anemones and black mussels.

Facilities at the reserve include a couple of rondavels on the rims of the vlei, with kitchen facilities, ablution blocks, toilets and fireplaces. There are also sites for camping. The Potberg Environmental Centre in the eastern part of the reserve is not open to the public, but organised groups may apply for courses in conservation, and educational trails.

2 Swellendam

The town of Swellendam basks in sunshine at the foot of the Langeberg, its fringes touching the banks of the Koornlandsrivier. Here, behind avenues of ancient oak trees, stately, whitewashed homesteads dating back more than 200 years stand as monuments to the pioneering spirit of the earliest European settlers in the Cape.

The Dutch East India Company, pushing the frontiers of the Cape further and further inland, saw the tranquil valley of the Breede River as an ideal setting for an administrative centre. This, in 1747, became Swellendam, after the Dutch governor Hendrik Swellengrebel and his wife Helena ten Damme.

One of the first buildings erected was the Drostdy, whose original rafters and floorboards were hewn from the yellowwood forests of the Langeberg in 1746. Lying east of the Koornlandsrivier, the Drostdy faces Swellengrebel Street, once part of the original 'Cape Wagon Road'. Today the Drostdy, converted into a cultural history museum in 1943, houses furniture and other priceless memorabilia from the early days of Swellendam. (Part of the museum complex is a Victorian house with a charming period garden.) Diagonally across from it is the second oldest building — the Old Gaol — where wayward inmates were flogged or put into stocks for their

LEFT *A solitary bontebok surveys the scene at De Hoop Nature Reserve.*

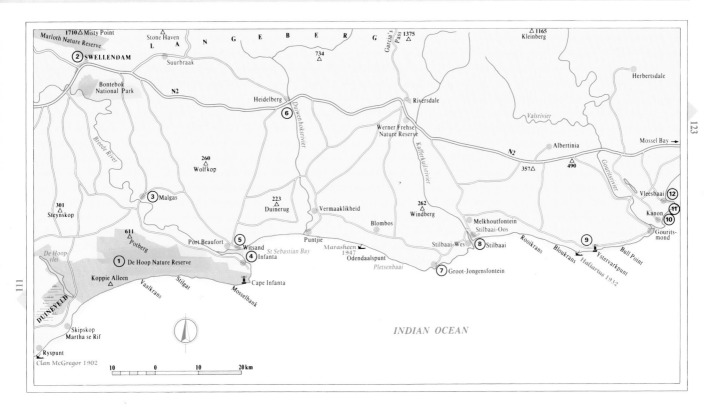

misdeeds. Next door is a thatched house known as the Old Post Office but which formerly served as the residence of the jailer.

Other beautiful and historical buildings in the town include the Old Boys' School (1825), a gabled residence converted into a school in 1870; the Oefeningshuis (1838), built as a place of worship and also an education centre for freed slaves; Heemraden House (1839), the former home of Joseph Barry, head of the commercial empire of Barry and Nephews; and the Dutch Reformed church (1910), with its brilliant white walls, domed arches and spires, erected on the site of a church more than a century older.

Swellendam, with its attractive municipal caravan park, is within an easy drive of two enchanting nature reserves, the Bontebok National Park (7 km to the south-east), and the beautiful Marloth Nature Reserve. The latter sprawls across the lofty peaks and verdant valleys of the Langeberg, forming the heart of protea country, a huge, natural garden-in-the-sky dominated by spectacular forests of stinkwood and yellowwood, towering above flowering trees such as wild gardenia and almond.

This is the domain of leopard and baboon, of a rich variety of bird life (from sugarbirds and sunbirds to eagles and falcons); of various antelope roaming the 11 300 ha reserve, and of a number of reptiles and amphibians, including the rare ghost frog. Slashed by icy mountain streams and waterfalls, encircled by the Swellendam Hiking Trail, this panoramic reserve offers a picnic site and huts for overnight hikers, but no other facilities. Permits are obtainable from the Swellendam State Forest Station.

SAVING THE BONTEBOK

The bontebok (*Damaliscus dorcas*), with its coat of 'many colours' — rich browns glossed with purple and patches of white — was staring extinction in the face earlier this century. In the 1920s, only a score remained; in the 1930s a small sanctuary was established for them south of Bredasdorp but this was not entirely suitable for their needs and their numbers struggled upwards.

Then in 1960 the 2 786 ha Bontebok National Park was proclaimed near Swellendam and 61 bontebok were transferred there. On this land, flanked by the broad waters of the Breede River and overlooked by the magnificent peaks of the Langeberg, the bontebok have thrived, their numbers swelling to more than 400 and surplus animals even being sent to other reserves or game farms.

Today they share their undulating grasslands with springbok, grey rhebok, Cape grysbok, steenbok, duiker and bushbuck. The bird and plant life is also prolific: 184 bird species (including secretary birds, spurwinged geese, fish eagles and guinea fowl) dart about a colourful environment harbouring more than 470 plant species.

Visitors to the park (reached off the N2 just east of Swellendam) can enjoy all this by following the tour roads or foot trails through the park. Other attractions include fishing and swimming, picnicking or camping.

3 Malgas

Slumbering on the west bank of the Breede River, just off the gravel road between Swellendam and Infanta, is the tiny settlement of Malgas, the place of South Africa's only river pont.

During the 1850s, the commercial firm of Barry

BELOW *The isolated shores near Skipskop.*

Graceful old architecture and soaring mountain scenery typify the Swellendam area.

and Nephews, which dominated trading activities in the Overberg, decided to establish a riverside port far up the Breede to serve as a crucial trading link between Swellendam and Cape Town. They chose Mallegaskraal (Malgas), a farm 35 km upstream from the river mouth as the ideal site, and Joseph Barry immediately commissioned shipbuilders in Glasgow to build the coaster *Kadie* to navigate the river.

At Malgas, the Barrys built warehouses, a hotel, a wool store, a bottlestore and a pont to carry traffic across the river. The good ship *Kadie* steamed between the Breede River and Cape Town for six years, laden with sheep, grain and wool for the Cape and returning each time with consumer goods for the Overberg. Finally, in 1865, it hit the rocks on the west bank of the Breede and broke up, bringing to an end not only its own important role in the region, but also relegating Malgas to the backwaters. Today, however, the hand-pulled pont still serves as a vital link between the coastal communities east and west of the Breede.

4 Infanta

South of Malgas, the Breede River writhes through a countryside of aloe- and acacia-covered hills, bypassing isolated clusters of milkwood and dense fringes of sugarbush proteas. Eventually, with the sea in sight, it broadens out into a massive estuary, its tumbling waters colliding with the rolling breakers of St Sebastian Bay. Here, on the western side, framed by a rocky headland, lies the small holiday resort and fishing hamlet of Infanta, named after Joao Infante, commander of the second caravel under Dias.

Access to Infanta is along a roller-coasting gravel road that turns off the N2 just west of Swellendam. The large caravan and camp site between milkwood and rooikrans trees is within walking distance of the river and the sea, and provides easy access for anglers and surfers.

St Sebastian Bay and the surrounding hills cloaked in fynbos, are a nature lover's and fisherman's delight. There is a slipway for launching powerboats at Infanta, and a rocky shoreline with good diving and angling spots.

5 Witsand and Port Beaufort

Named after the shimmering, sun-bleached sands on its doorstep, Witsand is a charming seaside resort perched on hills that roll down to the eastern bank of the Breede River and the blue waters of St Sebastian Bay. A flat, rocky terrace hugs the coast as it sweeps eastwards, providing rock pools alive with tiny marine organisms. Fishing in the bay, river and sea is outstanding, and there are launch ramps for powerboats.

The Breede River estuary is a breeding ground for oysters — and sharks are known to dwell here too. In spring calving southern right whales cruise up and down the coastline, close to shore. (Between May and December, boats should be wary of colliding with whales.)

A large caravan park, on grass under trees some 500 m from the beach, offers sites for tents and caravans (some with electricity), as well as luxury chalets and rondavels.

Port Beaufort, lying slightly upriver from Witsand, was named by Lord Charles Somerset in 1817 and was later used by Barry and Nephews as a busy harbour serving the Overberg districts. Today this small resort still retains some historical

landmarks, including the Barry Church, built in 1849 by Thomas Barry, and an old inn that used to be a customs house.

The most popular ways of reaching Witsand and Port Beaufort are either via the Malgas pont, or from Heidelberg.

6 Heidelberg-Vermaaklikheid-Puntjie-Blombos

The soaring peaks of the Langeberg form a magnificent backdrop north of the N2 between Swellendam and Riversdale. At Heidelberg, midway between these two towns, the Duiwenhoksrivier snakes down to the sea, growing in volume and size as it passes Vermaaklikheid near the coast to merge with the Indian Ocean at the tiny settlement of Puntjie.

To reach this remote corner of the coast from the N2, take the Vermaaklikheid turn-off east of Heidelberg. From Port Beaufort take the tarred road north-east to Heidelberg, turning right after 12 km. This gravel road leads you through an open, rustic countryside peppered with old, isolated farmsteads, eventually descending into the valley of the Duiwenhoks where Vermaaklikheid nestles between hills. There is a shop, a church and a small post office, but no camp site in this 200-year-old little settlement. You can, however, picnic on the banks of the Duiwenhoks, you can fish or even launch a boat to take you on a beautiful trip between the hills and sand dunes to the sea at Puntjie.

Just 10 km south of Vermaaklikheid, on bush-covered hills overlooking the sea and the swirling waters of the Duiwenhoksrivier, are the unique, thatched roofs of Puntjie's *kapstyl* (truss-style) houses. These strange dwellings consist of a roof supported by a series of trusses reaching down to the ground, and are modelled on the first houses of the trekboers. Puntjie is privately owned, and barred by a locked gate. However, there is access near Puntjie to the banks of the Duiwenhoks where there are some lovely picnic spots.

East of Puntjie, not far from the spot where the *Marasheen* was wrecked in 1947, huge sand dunes slide down to an isolated beach, known by fishermen as Blombos. There are only two or three privately owned cottages at Blombos and you can get there only on foot, after driving over a bumpy and unpredictable road for 3,5 km.

7 Groot-Jongensfontein

In spring the coastal terrace between Puntjie and Jongensfontein is ablaze with the reds, yellows and lilacs of late-flowering proteas, pincushions and other wild flowers. Along this lonely part of the coastline sugarbirds and sunbirds abound in a crisp, clear environment of milkwood trees and gentle hills that slope towards tawny sand dunes and the sea.

At Jongensfontein, the hills fall away more sharply to reveal the fishing shacks and houses of a tidy holiday resort perched on the fringes of a promenade of jagged rock. Just off a small, sandy beach in the centre of Jongensfontein is a caravan park with a dozen or more rondavels. There is

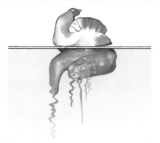

BATTLING BLUEBOTTLES

The bluebottle, or Portuguese man o'war.

Bluebottles pose a real hazard to bathers (especially children) along the coastline between Stilbaai and Vleesbaai, where they may sometimes be washed up in their thousands after strong onshore winds.

Aimlessly drifting at the whim of the wind and the currents, the bluebottle is not a single organism, but an amazing colony of interdependent animals, each with a separate function to perform in order to ensure the others' survival. These organisms are kept afloat by a nitrogen- and carbon monoxide-filled bubble (itself an organism), below which hangs a cluster of thin tentacles, some as long as 10 m. Along the length of these are lidded stinging cells that burst open on contact, sending out hollow, barbed spears containing poison. Injected into the prey, this poison causes paralysis, and the tentacles can then seize the prey and contract (sometimes to as little as 10 cm long) to pull the prey up to the feeding organisms below the bubble.

This sting can be extremely painful to man. It should be treated by applying a meat tenderiser, methylated spirits or alcohol, or the stricken area should be immersed in hot water. Remember that even when bluebottles are high and dry on the beach, their tentacles can still give a nasty sting.

High up on the hills above the river's east bank, the wild flowers of the Pauline Bohnen Nature Reserve rustle in the wind above the sunburnt sweep of coastline that arcs 3 km eastwards towards a popular fishing spot known as Die Preekstoel. This sandy stretch of coast culminates further on in a hump-backed headland that plunges far out to sea.

A bridge across the Kafferkuilsrivier takes you to the west bank and a quaint harbour and breakwater. A drive past the harbour runs parallel to a rocky coastline and stops at Skulpiesbaai where you can fish, swim or collect shells. Stilbaai has another attraction in the massive freshwater eels that frequent its streams. Weighing up to 8 kg, some are so tame you can feed them by hand.

Access to Stilbaai is either via the gravel coastal road from Puntjie, or along a tar road that turns off the N2 12 km east of Riversdale, an attractive little farming centre favoured as an overnight stop by travellers heading for the Garden Route and beyond. (The nearby Werner Frehse Nature Reserve, featuring several antelope species, is also popular with visitors.) Just north of Stilbaai is the small village of Melkhoutfontein, conspicuous for its quaint cottages and small churchyard containing graves adorned with shells.

9 The coast to Gouritsmond
The contours of the coastline between Stilbaai and Gouritsmond are irregular, with wide expanses of sand giving way to rocky terraces and small coves. This region is undeveloped and largely un-inhabited and even Ystervarkpunt, with its lighthouse and seaside fishing shacks, has been closed to the public.

But the coastal drive eastwards through a countryside of leucadendrons, pincushions and proteas, backdropped by the shimmering blue sea,

is rewarding, bringing you eventually to the broad valley of the Gouritsrivier. On the west bank, where the river meets the sea, and set 100 m back from the shoreline, is the hamlet of Gouritsmond, with its camping ground and single hotel. This is an excellent fishing spot, but bathing at the river mouth is dangerous, because of the presence of treacherous currents.

Access to Gouritsmond from the N2 is along a tar road that branches off the N2 just past the Gouritsrivier bridge east of Albertinia.

10 Kanon
Aloe-scarred hills descend gently towards the cluster of holiday homes that stands metres from the boulder-strewn shore at Kanon. The settlement braces itself against the windswept sea on the fringes of a rocky promontory some 3 km east of the Gouritsrivier mouth, and faces a gentle sweep of bay. Confronting you as you enter this tiny huddle of homes are three ancient cannons, mounted in front of one of the houses. They were salvaged from the French man o'war *Le Fortune*, which was wrecked at nearby Fonteintjies, just west of Fransmanshoek, in 1763.

The little settlement at Kanon is private property, but a gravel road bypassing it leads you westward past piles of driftwood and lizards sunbathing on lichen-coloured rocks to the mouth of the Gourits and some excellent fishing spots on the way. There is a slipway for launching powerboats nearby. Just north of Kanon another gravel road leads you down to the rocky terrace fringing the bay, where huge shell middens between the dunes testify to large communities of Khoikhoi that once lived here.

Access to Kanon from the west bank of the Gourits is via a gravel road that branches right 10 km from the mouth and crosses the river to

fairly safe swimming here and tidal pools for children. A gravel road along the rocky terrace to the west leads to some good angling spots, while east of the hamlet, a long, sandy beach is good for walking and shell collecting.

8 Stilbaai
Known by the locals as 'the bay of sleeping beauty', Stilbaai is one of the most popular of the southern Cape's resorts, with excellent boating, fishing and swimming. Here, ramshackle fishing cottages mounted on stilts, thatched-roof houses and stately granite homes peer down from the east and west banks across the waters of the Kaffer-kuilsrivier and the tranquil blue bay that gave the town its name. For most of the year, these homes remain locked and shuttered, but during the festive season holiday-makers converge on Stilbaai, turning it into a vibrant, bustling resort. They easily fill the very large caravan park on the east bank, within walking distance of the river and a fine swimming beach.

RIGHT *The hand-hauled pont across the Breede River at Malgas.*

A translucent sea smooths lonely sands backed by green-glossed dunes between Rooikrans and Bloukrans, beyond Stilbaai.

rejoin the tar. After a further 2 km a turn-off leads to Kanon.

11 Fransmanshoek

Pale beaches dominated by a mighty phalanx of copper-coloured dunes curve east of Kanon towards a mushroom-shaped peninsula of jagged rock known as Fransmanshoek, an allusion to the 440 Frenchmen who put ashore from the *Le Fortune* after it was wrecked. This peninsula protects a small, sandy bay on its eastern side where the swimming is regarded as fairly safe and shells abound.

Fransmanshoek is the nucleus of one of the finest fishing areas in southern Africa. It also affords spectacular views over Vleesbaai and what is colloquially known as the Sleeping Beauty of the Outeniquas — a profile in rock of what appears to be a young woman sleeping.

12 Vleesbaai

Between Fransmanshoek and Boggomsbaai, perched on hills overlooking the aquamarine expanse of Visbaai, lies the little hamlet of Vleesbaai. The early Portuguese navigators called this Cabo Vacca (Cape of the Cows) after the cattle the Khoikhoi bartered with them along the sandy beaches. Later, in 1601, two Dutch ships sailed into the bay. The crew of the first, the *Hop van Holland*, called the bay Visbaai because of the abundance of fish they caught there; the crew of the second ship, *Vereenigde Lande*, called it Vleesbaai for the cattle they bartered there.

There are magnificent views from Vleesbaai; the locals say that the sunsets here are so spectacular that the sea blushes like an innocent bride when the sun casts its crimson hue across it. The settlement of a hundred or so houses tucked into the western corner of the bay is privately owned, but you can park near the beach where there are interesting rock pools and plenty of shells. Swimming here is fairly safe, and a twenty-minute walk eastwards along the beach will bring you to the small fishing settlement of Boggomsbaai.

Vleesbaai (reached via the road from Gouritsmond or from the N2 west of Mossel Bay) has a shop and a petrol pump, but no public accommodation. However, a caravan park on the Fransmanshoek peninsula — a terraced camp site set among milkwoods and rooikrans overlooking the glittering waters of Visbaai — will give you unsurpassed views of the bay stretching eastwards towards Cape St Blaize and the headland that shelters Mossel Bay. Much of this coastline is inaccessible, with the next resort — Danabaai — virtually on the outskirts of Mossel Bay and offering mainly unspoilt beaches and a number of good angling spots.

LEFT *Ancient fish traps at Stilbaai took advantage of the tides to harvest the sea.*

THINGS TO DO

Angling

The coastline between Cape Infanta and Mossel Bay is one of the finest angling areas in southern Africa — not only for the numbers of fish caught, but also for their enormous sizes. Powerboating is also very popular, particularly because of the easy access to the rivers at Infanta and Witsand, Stilbaai and Gouritsmond.

Beachcombing and shelling

The small, sandy beaches between the rocks at Groot-Jongensfontein and Skulpiesbaai west of Stilbaai are particularly good shelling places; so too are the beaches near Kanon, Fransmanshoek and Vleesbaai, while the coastline beyond Gouritsmond is good for beachcombing.

Important Stone Age sites were found west of Stilbaai early this century, leading to the identification of what archaeologists call the Still Bay Culture. These sites and the huge Strandloper middens along the coastline, particularly in the Gouritsmond, Kanon and Vleesbaai areas, may be seen by adventurous hikers, usually in and around the coastal dunes.

Also to be seen along the Stilbaai coastline are rocky fish traps, known as *vywers* and built by early man to trap fish on the outgoing tide.

Birdwatching

The Bontebok National Park offers some excellent birdwatching, but in this region De Hoop Nature Reserve is the real drawcard, with as many as 228 species to be seen (more than sixty per cent of the total number of species in the south-western Cape).

Fish type	Season	Best area	Best bait
Kabeljou	Oct — April	St Sebastian Bay, Gouritsmond, Fransmanshoek	Octopus, mackerel, mullet
Elf	Sept — April	Stilbaai, Gouritsmond, Fransmanshoek, Vleesbaai	Mackerel, mullet, chokka, lures and spoons
Galjoen	Mar — Sept	Gouritsmond	White mussels, redbait, chokka
Mussel-cracker	Sept — Mar	Gouritsmond, Fransmanshoek	Redbait, chokka, crabs, mussels
White steenbras	All year	St Sebastian Bay, Stilbaai	White mussels, shrimps, prawns, bloodworms

Boardsailing

St Sebastian Bay and the Breede River are used by boardsailors on both sides of the river. Further up the coast, at Stilbaai, the Kafferkuilsrivier provides relatively safe and scenic boardsailing, and at Vleesbaai the experienced ride in the open sea.

Boat trips

Powerboats for fishing trips up the Breede River can be hired from the riverside botel at Witsand.

Bowls

Greens are available at Swellendam, Heidelberg, Witsand, Riversdale, Albertinia and Stilbaai; contact the local municipalities.

Camping and caravanning

There are well-equipped camp sites at De Hoop Nature Reserve, Swellendam, Heidelberg, Infanta, Witsand, Riversdale, Stilbaai, Groot-Jongensfontein, Albertinia, Gouritsmond and Vleesbaai. Contact local municipalities or the parks.

Canoeing

The Breede, Duiwenhoks and Kafferkuils are ideal for short or long paddles by canoeists, but enthusiasts should stay well clear of the strong tidal currents at the river mouths.

Diving

Scuba diving and snorkelling are popular on the western fringe of St Sebastian Bay, where big fish can be speared. Stilbaai is also a good spot.

Drives and viewsites

A pleasant diversion on the N2 between Swellendam and Heidelberg is the road that branches off to the north along the foot of the Langeberg to the rustic town of Suurbraak. East of Suurbraak, a beautiful drive takes you through the leucadendron-coloured Tradouw Pass, which slashes through the Langeberg. Another scenic gateway to the Little Karoo is Garcia's Pass, north of Riversdale. The gravel roads running parallel to the coastline between Puntjie and Vleesbaai provide innumerable viewsites of the rolling hills and the sea, carpeted in spring by flowers.

Golf

There are golf courses at Swellendam, Heidelberg, Albertinia and Stilbaai; contact the municipalities for details.

Libraries

Swellendam's public library has a large collection of books dealing with the history of the southern Cape; there are also municipal libraries in Heidelberg, Riversdale, Albertinia and Stilbaai.

Museums

DROSTDY MUSEUM, Swellengrebel Street, Swellendam: Houses valuable relics of the early days of the town.

Powerboating

The Breede River as far as Malgas and the Kafferkuilsrivier at Stilbaai are both excellent for powerboating and upriver fishing trips. If you are powerboating on the Duiwenhoksrivier between Vermaaklikheid and Puntjie, watch out for shallow water and sandbanks.

Shipwrecks

The wrecked *Marasheen*, near Blombos in 1947, and the *Haliartus*, which broke up near Ystervarkpunt in 1932, are both inaccessible.

Surfing

The surf's up most of the time in St Sebastian Bay, Groot-Jongensfontein, Stilbaai and Vleesbaai.

Swimming

Swimming at the confluence of rivers and the sea is usually dangerous. There are fine swimming spots, however, at Infanta, Witsand, Stilbaai and Vleesbaai.

Tennis and squash

There are tennis and squash courts at Swellendam; and tennis courts at Riversdale, Albertinia, Heidelberg and Stilbaai. Contact the municipalities.

Walks

One of the major scenic attractions of the Swellendam area is the 81 km Swellendam Hiking Trail, tracing a six-day circuit across the tumbling slopes of the Langeberg, with quiet, forested kloofs and rolling terraces of fynbos. Entry is by permit, available at the Swellendam State Forest Station next to the reserve.

The other nature reserves in the area also offer interesting trails, and there are charming coastal walks between Groot-Jongensfontein and Stilbaai and between Vleesbaai and Boggomsbaai.

Yachting and dinghy sailing

The Breede River at Witsand and the Kafferkuilsrivier at Stilbaai are suitable for these sports, with Stilbaai and Vleesbaai providing reasonably sheltered waters.

Southern right whales just beyond the breakers off the Infanta coast.

INFORMATION
• De Hoop Nature Reserve Officer-in-Charge, Private Bag X16, Bredasdorp 7280. Tel 02922=782
• Heidelberg Municipality, Private Bag X2, Heidelberg 6760. Tel 02962=11
• Riversdale Municipality, Van den Bergh St, Riversdale 6770. Tel 02932=32418
• Stilbaai Municipality, Main Road-West, Stilbaai 6785. Tel 02934=41230
• Swellendam Municipality, Voortrek St, Swellendam 6740. Tel 0291=41100
Nearest AA Office
• Millwood Building, cnr York and Victoria Sts, George 6530. Tel 0441=742090

Voyage's end at an ancient, evergreen land

THE SOUTHERN COAST, after several hundred kilometres of low-lying sandy shores, reaches Cape St Blaize and curls into a gentle blue bay. The golden sand continues around the bay, punctuated by sleepy river lagoons, but now a high range of mountains comes into view and the sands give way to a gigantic coastal shelf that juts out into the sea.

The mountains are the Outeniquas, and they bring year-round rains to the land at their feet, keeping it constantly emerald green. Where the coastal shelf meets the sea, waves have ground it away into high cliffs of orange-red rock, and here and there have carved coves and inlets. Many a ship has come to grief on this violent shore, and legend has it that a chest of treasure lies caught here in the rocks amid the foaming surf.

1 Mossel Bay

Giant waves relentlessly punish the awesome, towering cliffs that line the southern shore of Cape St Blaize, baring the rock strata and gouging out huge caverns. And yet, just 3km along the coastline, tucked away around the corner of the cape, the water in the sheltered little cove known as Munro's Bay is as calm and gentle as an inland lake ... which is why this spot was the first landing place of Bartholomeu Dias and his men. Today the calmness of the water in the bay, one of the most sheltered stretches of open sea along the entire southern African coast, attracts thousands of holiday-makers and watersport enthusiasts.

All along the Mossel Bay shore there are beaches sprinkled among the rocks. Even at the very point of Cape St Blaize there is a sandy channel set between two rocky ridges that has long been treated by locals as the town swimming pool — known to all as the 'Poort'. Travelling around the great bay from here the first major inlet is the harbour, then comes Munro's Bay, Santos Beach, a string of little beaches separated by rocky ridges and known collectively as Die Bakke, then Pansy Beach and the long golden stretch of Dias Beach. At all these beaches the water is calm, but it is especially so at Munro's Bay and Santos Beach,

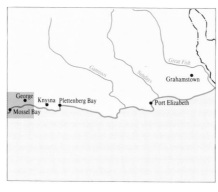

which in summer become the vibrant heart of the holiday town. The coast immediately behind the shore is kept tidy and attractive with green lawns and a succession of neat camping grounds and caravan sites, interspersed with clusters of luxurious holiday chalets.

Anyone tiring of the lovely beaches will find the town itself has much to offer. Its history is well presented in a new museum complex near the old Post Office Tree where Pedro d'Ataide posted South Africa's first 'letter' in 1500. A section of the museum is devoted to maritime history, another to a shell collection with fine specimens gathered

Seal Island, basking in the sun off Mossel Bay.

from various seashores all over the world.

Also interesting is a drive or walk past the harbour to the Point at Cape St Blaize. You will pass a large number of sturdy stone houses: there are at least 200 of these, many of them built during the last century by immigrant Cornish stonemasons. The majority of the houses in the town are built in ranks that climb up the hillside, with the result that most residents wake in the morning and retire at night to magnificent views out over the little harbour and across the bay to the jagged blue-grey line of the Outeniqua Mountains in the distance. At the Point, directly above the sandy Poort, you will see a cave in the cliff face beneath the Cape St Blaize lighthouse; this was long the home of so-called Strandlopers. From the south side of the cave a narrow footpath zigzags up towards the base of the lighthouse then leads east for several kilometres along the clifftops, offering grand vistas down over the majestic cliffs.

Mossel Bay offers a variety of holiday accommodation and recreational activities. Especially popular is the range of opportunities for the angler, produced by the varied character of the shoreline and the extreme differences in sea conditions; Mossel Bay is also one of South Africa's leading centres for powerboat fishing.

Recently the development of offshore oil wells in the region has begun to transform what was once a slightly sleepy coastal town into a bustling growth centre, but this is unlikely to mar the appeal of the place for holiday-makers. The town will remain blessed with an attractive blue-sky climate (the rainfall here is roughly a third that of George, only a few kilometres away), and there are so many beautiful beaches along the shore that they can absorb huge numbers of holiday-makers without being spoilt.

LEFT *Viewed from the harbour, the town of Mossel Bay sprawls against the hillside.*

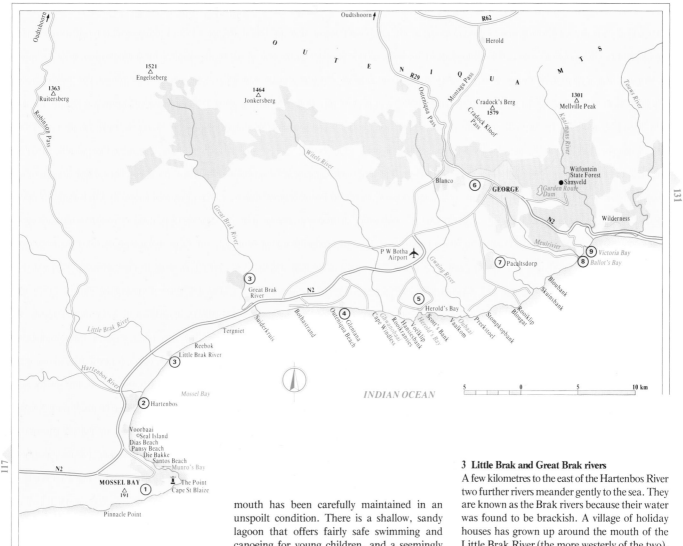

2 Hartenbos

The settlement and the river of Hartenbos owe their name to a shipwreck that occurred close offshore early in the 18th century. A local farmer, Esaias Meyer, assisted the shipwrecked mariners and for his efforts was rewarded by the Dutch East India Company with a grant of land, which he named Hert en Bos (deer and wood).

Most of the area was later bought by the Afrikaanse Taal en Kultuurvereniging and turned into a major holiday resort. A large open-air stadium, seating 10 000, is used for cultural festivals, church services and sporting events. A short distance from the stadium is the Voortrekker Museum. Among the several full-size wagons displayed are two that were used in the 1938 commemorative trek to Voortrekkerhoogte.

Although Hartenbos has now grown into a substantial town, the area adjacent to the river

RIGHT *The holiday settlement of Hartenbos, between river and sea.*

mouth has been carefully maintained in an unspoilt condition. There is a shallow, sandy lagoon that offers fairly safe swimming and canoeing for young children, and a seemingly endless expanse of golden beach for walkers and surf anglers. Sea bathing is good but the surf can be rough.

3 Little Brak and Great Brak rivers

A few kilometres to the east of the Hartenbos River two further rivers meander gently to the sea. They are known as the Brak rivers because their water was found to be brackish. A village of holiday houses has grown up around the mouth of the Little Brak River (the more westerly of the two), and to the east are the coastal settlements of Reebok and Tergniet. The three adjacent communities add up to a fair-sized holiday resort.

The still and sandy mouth of the Little Brak, with Mossel Bay in the distance.

Where it reaches the sea the Little Brak forms a pretty lagoon that offers fairly safe swimming and canoeing for children, and at low tide a cluster of interesting rock pools to be explored. The beach on both sides of the river mouth is popular with surf anglers, and leervis are caught in the lagoon.

East of Tergniet is the large, green-lawned Souwesia caravan park, then a string of seashore holiday homes comprising the resort of Suiderkruis (southern cross). Lying at the eastern end of Suiderkruis is the beautiful mouth of the Great Brak River — a particularly restful and unspoilt retreat. The lagoon at the mouth is divided into two sandy channels with a small island between them. The island, with its charming holiday homes, is reached from the mainland by a narrow wooden bridge. Short lanes lead between the houses down to the sandy beach alongside the lagoon — an extremely pretty spot sheltered by a low bluff lying to the east of the river mouth. On the west bank of the lagoon is a shaded picnic site at the water's edge, and a short walk from here is a camping and caravan park. Scarcely a kilometre upriver brings you to the tiny village of Great Brak River, where yet another attractive caravan park is situated.

The village dates back to 1859, the year in which a toll-bridge was built over the river, and one Charles Searle appointed as toll-keeper. Searle and later his family gradually built up a succession of local industries, until eventually a whole village came into being with virtually all its inhabitants employed in one or another of the Searle enterprises. Today at the heart of the village stands the beautiful little Searle Memorial Church. Almost next door is a small museum whose charming exhibits offer an insight into the lifestyles of last century.

From both Little Brak River and Great Brak River there are several gravel-surfaced country roads that lead inland. These can be dusty at times, but they offer an assortment of interesting excursions into the farming country at the foot of the Outeniqua Mountains.

4 Glentana

East of the Great Brak River the coast is edged by a string of seaside holiday-house developments: Hersham Beach, Bothastrand, SAOU Strand (owned by a teachers' union) and Outeniqua Beach. The line ends in the little holiday village of Glentana, where the long golden beach meets the first rocky bluffs of the Outeniqua coastal terrace, and where rank upon rank of attractive homes perch on a steep hillside.

Quiet little Glentana hit the headlines in 1902 when a giant floating dock, being towed from England to Durban, broke its tow ropes and was driven onto the rocky shore about 1,5 km to the east of the small settlement. It is possible to reach the wreck on foot, and this makes an attractive coastal walk. The cliffs here are composed of the orange-red rock characteristic of the region, clothed in rich evergreen coastal vegetation and studded with caves and small inlets. At low tide you can walk along the sandy beach, broken by picturesque rocky outcrops; at high tide you can reach the wreck by means of a rough path that runs along the foot of the cliffs.

The beach at Glentana slopes fairly steeply, but it is a popular venue for surfers and surf anglers. The small village has a shop, picnic and braai areas on a stretch of lawn overlooking the beach, and nearby an attractive caravan park is situated in a sheltered position behind low dunes.

RIGHT *The beach at Glentana, framed by the wreck of a floating dock.*

5 Herold's Bay

Several kilometres south of George's P W Botha Airport a narrow country road winds down from the grassy hilltops through a valley blanketed in indigenous forest to arrive eventually at an attractive cove in the coastal cliffs. This is Herold's Bay, named after the Rev Tobias Herold, first minister to the George congregation of the Dutch Reformed Church.

Deep in the cove there is a pretty beach of golden sand, flanked by rugged russet-coloured headlands. In addition to the beach, two tidal pools offer reasonably safe swimming, and a picnic area overlooks the beach, equipped with braai sites and fresh water.

Over the years a great many regular visitors have erected holiday homes here, and these now line the rocky base of the western headland and climb high up the eastern hillsides. There is also a hotel here, a shop, and an attractive little caravan park, and chalets can be hired from the resort high up on the slope.

One of the main drawcards of Herold's Bay is the fishing from the wave-pounded rocky outcrops, reached by walking along the shore. A somewhat worn fisherman's path leads along the eastern headland above the thundering surf, while a more defined path leads along the western headland at a higher level, ending at a viewsite perched atop the Voëlklip promontory. From this site there are fine views along the coast in both directions, and you can look down into large caverns that over the years the waves have carved into the cliffs beneath you.

6 George

Although Dias had landed at what is now Mossel Bay in 1488, and although during the years that followed many mariners had stopped to refresh and re-equip themselves there, they did not explore the countryside behind the coastal strip for they were only passing by this land on their way to and from the East Indies. It was only in 1688 that

ONLY HERE FOR THE BEER

Hops, the special ingredient of beer.

Beer would not be beer were it not for the hop plant. While you can make a beer without hops (the word 'ale' is thought originally to have meant exactly that), it is the hops that give to beer the distinctive flavour that most drinkers would probably consider to be the essence of the brew. These are the soft green cones of the plant *Humulus lupulus*. Only the female plant produces cones, and the magic ingredients that the brewer seeks are found only in tiny glands at the base of each leaflike bract within the cone.

The hops contribute to the making of beer in several ways, notably the addition of taste and smell. Bittering hops give the brew its characteristic bitter taste, while aroma hops give it its beery scent. Hops also act as a natural preservative, help to clarify the beer and to form and fix the frothy head.

Until the early decades of this century all the hops used in South Africa's brewing industry had to be imported, but in the 1920s the brewers began to wonder if it would not be possible to grow their hops at home. The conditions for the plant's growth, however, were stringent: a minimum number of daylight hours in summer, a six- to eight-week dormant period in winter when it needs to be chilled, and a plentiful water supply throughout the growing season. Only one small part of the country met these conditions: the rich farmlands around George, and one or two well-watered valleys in the Outeniqua Mountains. Today 480 ha are cultivated, enough for half of South Africa's needs.

A visitor cannot miss the hop fields in summer. The plant is a fast-growing climber that shoots up in spring, the specially erected trellises towering as much as 4 m above the ground so that the fields look like giant vineyards. The rate of growth is so remarkable — up to 20 cm a day — that some farmers (the older ones, who have had time to sit down and study such things) insist that the patient visitor will actually see a plant growing taller before his eyes.

Ensign Hieronymus Cruse explored the immediate interior, and then only in the hope of finding meat and fresh water.

To the Khoi people living there, the region was known as Outeniqua, and the first European explorers thus referred to it as Outeniqualand. Literally translated, it means 'man laden with honey' — perhaps because the people living there collected honey from the flower-filled mountain slopes to trade, and became known as 'the men laden with honey'. It might also be that the Khoi

Craggy arms reach down to the foaming sea near Herold's Bay.

language was more poetic and metaphorical than the Europeans realised, and that the name means, in effect, 'land of milk and honey'. The Khoikhoi must have been all too well aware that this was a particularly rich and fertile land, lush and green, a paradise in comparison with the far drier stretches of countryside nearby.

A settlement was proclaimed here in 1811 and named George Town, in honour of the reigning king of England, George III. This was to be the administrative centre of the lands around Mossel Bay and Outeniqualand. To help the little place to grow, plots were granted to six families, all woodcutters, on condition they supplied timber for the several public buildings that were needed. Gradually the little hamlet grew into a town, a refreshment station on the road along the coast and a commercial centre for the developing forestry industry. But it has always been a peaceful, easy-going place, quietly enjoying its extraordinarily beautiful natural setting. The author Anthony Trollope, visiting George in the latter half of the last century, declared it 'the prettiest village in the world'.

Peaceful as these years were, they cannot have been as ideal as we might like to imagine, for one of the town's most famous landmarks is the 'slave oak'. Slaves were certainly bought and sold in the town in the early days, and legend has it that the slave market was held under the spreading boughs of this old oak tree. The oak still stands outside the old library building in York Street, and you can still see, embedded in its trunk, a length of very old iron chain, with the remains of a hefty lock attached. A 100 m walk from here brings you to the old Drostdy building at the head of York

RIGHT *Even the urban outline of George cannot dim the green of the countryside.*

Street, now the town museum. The first thing you see on entering the museum is a huge cross-section of a yellowwood tree trunk, believed to date back to about 1220 and a fitting exhibit for this capital of forestry. Of particular interest are exhibits of stone-age tools and other archaeological finds from the area, in strong contrast with the museum's most famous collection of old gramophones and music boxes.

From a practical point of view George is a convenient place for the holiday-maker. This is the largest town on the Garden Route and has all the necessary amenities, including two theatres, and beautiful buildings like the Dutch Reformed church with a stinkwood pulpit and yellowwood domed ceiling. Other attractions are a small crocodile farm on the outskirts of the town, a

The pretty, peaceful beach at Herold's Bay is well guarded by its headlands.

ONE DAY UPON THIS GOLDEN SHORE

About half a thousand years ago, on a summer's day when small waves lapped gently on golden beaches, a meeting occurred here that was of singular historical importance: the exploring mind and adventurous spirit of Europe encountered the wildness and grandeur of southern Africa.

For many years the Portuguese had been venturing down the western coast of Africa, hoping at every moment that they would see the land to the east of them fall away, opening up a sea route around the African continent to the spice-rich lands of the East. The man finally to do this was Bartholomeu Dias, although he rounded the Cape of Good Hope without knowing it, for he had sailed away from the coast and when eventually he turned east, he found no coast. Guessing, however, that he had rounded the tip of Africa, he turned north and finally spotted land.

The tiny caravel (a wooden sailing ship) drew close to the mouth of the river we now know as the Gourits but did not attempt to land, because of the rough waves. Instead Dias sailed east, and on 3 February 1488 he rounded a rocky headland and found himself in a sheltered bay where he could land. This day was the day of Sao Bras (St Blaize), so Dias named the headland Cabo de Sao Bras.

Nine years later Vasco da Gama called here, following Dias's directions. Then in 1500 Pedro d'Ataide, returning from the East, left a message here describing a terrible storm he had passed through and details of his Indian trade. He placed the message in a seaman's boot and hung the boot from the branches of a milkwood tree alongside a little spring, where it would undoubtedly be spotted by any other seamen making a landing. It is claimed that the great old milkwood that still stands on this spot is the original tree, the Post Office Tree.

Over the years this gentle bay was given many other names, including Hog Bay. A century after D'Ataide left his message in the boot, a Dutch visitor, Paulus van Caerden, reported that he had found the place 'a lovely land, without many trees, but with deer and elephants'. However, he also complained that, except for the fresh water they obtained, they found nothing else of value but mussels — and this inspired him to rechristen the place Mosselbaai.

Although the modern town of Mossel Bay covers the whole promontory of Cape St Blaize, and much of the neighbouring land, the visitor can still stand in the shade of the old Post Office Tree and look out over the gentle welcoming cove. The bay, the sandy beach, the distant mountains . . . they all remain just as they were 500 years ago.

beautiful lake — the Garden Route Dam — a short distance to the east, and several kilometres beyond this the forestry school of Saasveld, in a lovely setting well worth viewing. A special feature of this region is the Outeniqua Choo-choo, huffing and puffing between George and Knysna and stopping at all the quaint little country stations.

7 Pacaltsdorp

When George Town came into being in 1811, the Outeniqua Khoikhoi were living nearby at Hoogekraal. At the request of the community, the London Missionary Society sent Charles Pacalt, a German by birth, to minister there. He worked at Hoogekraal until his death in 1818, after which the settlement was renamed in his honour. In 1825 a small stone church was built, and it still stands today at the heart of the growing town.

The coast south of Pacaltsdorp is particularly rugged and majestic, and there are two roads leading down to it. Continuing on the main road through Pacaltsdorp, you reach a junction some 2 km after the tar surface gives way to gravel: the road to the right takes you to the mouth of the Gwaing River; the road straight ahead takes you to Rooiklip (red rock). The mouth of the Gwaing is scenically one of the most impressive spots along

SIX WAYS TO CROSS THE MOUNTAINS

Montagu Pass — like a snail trail through rich mountainside.

All along the southern edge of the continent a wall of mountains bars the traveller from venturing inland beyond the coastal strip. The section visible from Mossel Bay and George is the Outeniqua range and over the centuries, six different road passes have been built over these high, fynbos-covered mountains.

The first was opened up by Ensign Isaq Schrijver as early as 1689. Schrijver and his men followed an ancient elephant path through a winding defile that emerged eventually onto the stony plains of the Little Karoo. Named the Attaquas Kloof Pass, after the Khoikhoi living in the area, it is the most westerly of the six routes through the mountains and can still be followed on foot.

The second pass, built far away to the east, wound up the green slopes of a peak called Duiwelskop (devil's peak) and led into the great valley known as the Langkloof. It too is now closed to vehicles but can be followed on foot. A third pass was constructed directly behind the settlement of George in 1812, when the Cape was under the governorship of Sir John Cradock. The towering peak up whose slopes it climbed was named Cradock's Berg and this new route was known as the Cradock Kloof Pass. No one would dare undertake this extremely steep and difficult pass in a vehicle today, but the route can be walked and the most southerly stretch is one of the starting sections in the Outeniqua Hiking Trail.

The fourth route blazed over the mountains was the Montagu Pass, opened in 1847 by the colonial secretary of the day, Sir John Montagu. The Montagu Pass follows a route very close to the old Cradock

Kloof Pass, but the engineer who built it, Henry Fancourt White, decided to spend more time winding around the lower slopes of Cradock's Berg, thereby keeping to a far more manageable gradient, and he finally crossed the watershed at a lower point. The pass has a fairly good gravel surface and can still be travelled by car. It makes an attractive drive, leading you into an older, slower-moving world, where the rushing sound of a peaty-coloured mountain stream can be heard as it tumbles over the rocks far below.

Cutting grandly across the face of the mountain directly opposite the Montagu Pass is the most modern of the routes, the Outeniqua Pass. A drive over the Outeniqua Pass in a southerly direction, from the Little Karoo to the coast, offers magnificent views across a huge green valley to the golden brown ribbon of the Montagu Pass and to a line of white beacons marking the Cradock Kloof Pass, then out over the green coastal shelf to the azure sea.

The last — and highest — of the six is the Robinson Pass, which carries the main road between Mossel Bay and Oudtshoorn and crosses the mountains just a few kilometres to the east of the old Attaquas Kloof. At the 860 m summit you can feel the cool high-mountain air brushing against your face, and looking to the west you have an Olympian view over a succession of soaring mountaintops. South of the summit you drive through the attractive Ruitersbos Forest Reserve, and after gliding serenely down for 9,7 km you reach the Eight Bells Mountain Inn, where teas and lunches are served in a beautifully peaceful setting.

---

this entire coast. The access road zigzags steeply down into a deep gorge through which the river sweeps forcefully into the sea. After rains the strongly flowing river clashes chaotically with the incoming tide and surf — a grand battling of the elements, beneath an enormous weathered cliff of orange-red rock. A short scramble over the rocks to the east of the river mouth opens up views of an extremely rugged, wave-battered stretch of coast, and when the tide is very low a tiny, beautiful beach appears. Where the road ends there are several attractive braai sites set on the hillside overlooking the turbulent surf, and nearby there are change-rooms, toilets, and a tap with fresh water.

Continuing straight from the junction, you drive through hilltop farms to arrive eventually on the crest of a high, windswept bluff overlooking the sea. From here a walk down through the fynbos to the Rooiklip promontory offers magnificent views.

8 Ballot's Bay

In the year 1879, a sailing ship, the *Mabel Young*, broke up in a storm several kilometres south of Ballot's Bay. Twelve people managed to escape from the sinking ship in a small boat, and one of them, the Baron Josef Wilhelm von Mollendorf, brought with him an iron chest — said to contain a large part of the family's treasure. As the little boat approached the shore it overturned in the

violent surf, and both the baron and the chest disappeared. Legend has it that the chest became wedged between the rocks, just visible at very low tide. Although many attempts have been made to find it, all have failed and as far as is known the ancient chest remains there to this day. The only record we now have of the event is a gravestone kept in the George Museum. It commemorates one Charles E Shaw, aged 26 years, 'passenger from the barque *Mabel Young* who was drowned whilst landing at Ballots Bay'.

Ballot's Bay, named after Simeon Ballot, an early minister to the George congregation, is almost inaccessible. Anyone venturing there will appreciate how easy it must have been for a small boat to come to grief in the raging surf. The access road is scenically attractive and winds along the hilltops, then plunges steeply into the deep gorge of the Meulrivier. Although there are some short stretches of concrete paving at the steep corners in the road, the condition of the surface is often suitable only for four-wheel drive.

The inlet is the smallest of all the accessible coves along this coast. There is only a tiny pebbly beach sandwiched between the cliffs, and there are no facilities whatsoever. Visitors do make their way here, however, seeking not only the treasure chest of legend, but also the handsome fish that are caught from the rocks along the shore.

9 Victoria Bay

A few kilometres east of George a short but very scenic tarred road branches off from the N2 towards the coast, winds gracefully down among the rich green coastal hills, and comes to an end at the head of a beautiful bay where golden sands are gently caressed and swept smooth by the last ripples of the breaking waves. Flanking the small beach are two great headlands and along the shore to the west are numerous rock pools, incessantly splashed and refilled by the surf.

This pretty cove was known to the early settlers as Gunter Bay, but the name was changed in 1847 to Victoria Bay in honour of England's young queen. Behind the beach there is a delightful, lawned picnic area with thatched umbrellas, braai sites and a freshwater tap, and nearby change-rooms and toilets. Behind the rock pools along the western shore are some quaint holiday cottages, some of them now old and dilapidated, but radiating the spirit of barefoot, carefree holidays by the sea. In front of them there is a tidal swimming pool, but bathing from the gently sloping beach is regarded by locals and regular visitors as safe. The bay is something of a surfers' paradise, while the rocky shore to the west is highly rated by surf anglers. Two attractive caravan parks set a short distance up the adjacent hillsides give lovely views over the bay.

BELOW *The emerald brilliance of the well-watered land near George.*

THE TIMBER TRUSTEES

The explorers of the 17th and 18th centuries who journeyed eastwards from Cape Town came to a halt at the foot of the Outeniqua Mountains. Here the towering peaks closed in towards the sea, and the narrow coastal shelf that lay between the mountains and the sea was deeply gashed by a succession of river gorges, making it virtually impossible for wagons to travel any further. Pampoenskraal, the farm established on the last piece of accessible land, was a lush, thickly forested tract.

This attracted many of the famous explorer-naturalists of the late 18th century, who stopped to study the wealth of wild flowers and indigenous trees. No fewer than 135 different species of tree filled the forests, including magnificent specimens of valuable yellowwood and stinkwood. Along with the naturalists came woodcutters, to fell these great trees for the growing settlements in the west.

In the middle of the last century Pampoenskraal was acquired by the Baroness Gesina van Rheede van Oudtshoorn, who renamed it Saasveld after her ancestral home in Holland. Almost a century later, in 1932, South Africa's first small forestry school was moved here from Tokai in the Cape Peninsula, to become an important educational institution.

Only a tiny portion of South Africa is covered by indigenous forest — roughly half of one per cent. The close-canopied indigenous forests total only 300 000 ha, and almost all of this forest is found in a narrow strip of land running along the southern and eastern coasts, then extending north along the Drakensberg escarpment. The forestry industry has preserved what remains of this indigenous forest, and has introduced vast new forests of valuable exotics, mostly pines and eucalyptus, to supply all South Africa's needs for timber and paper-making. For the preserving and skilful husbanding of these forests we rely largely on graduates from Saasveld.

Angling
The coast is very varied in this region, ranging from scenes where tremendous waves crash violently against giant cliffs to bays and lagoons so gentle that they might be inland lakes. As a result the angler has a wide range of choices, but note that the rocky coast between Glentana and Victoria Bay is dangerous: massive waves occasionally throw floods of water high up the cliff faces, reaching spots that might have appeared quite safe. Also worth noting is the fact that Mossel Bay is one of South Africa's leading bases for powerboat fishing, with an annual competition in March attracting enthusiasts from all over the country.

The steep challenge of the Outeniqua trail.

Beachcombing and shelling
Only one area here may prove rewarding: the stretch between Tergniet and the mouth of the Great Brak, where fine shells are sometimes found among the rocks at low tide.

Boardsailing
The lagoons along this coast are rather small for boardsailing, but the sport has become very popular on the sheltered waters off Mossel Bay's Santos Beach (sailboards can be hired here) and Munro's Bay.

Boat trips
During holiday seasons a motor launch operates out of Mossel Bay Harbour, taking visitors along the coast past the Post Office Tree and Munro's Bay, then Santos and Die Bakke beaches, and eventually visiting Seal Island, a few hundred metres off Dias Beach, where a colony of roughly 2 000 seals can be studied at close quarters.

Bowls
Contact the George Bowling Club about greens and fixtures. For information on Mossel Bay's facilities, contact the publicity association.

THINGS TO DO

Camping and caravanning

Even to count the number of caravan parks and camping grounds along this stretch of the coast would be a difficult task. They are sprinkled all along the shore from the Point at Cape St Blaize to Victoria Bay, and inland at George and Great Brak River. Contact the relevant municipalities for details of the caravan parks and camping grounds in each area, or the SA Tourism Board's office in George.

Canoeing

Canoes may be used on the three small lagoons in this region: at the mouths of the Hartenbos, Little Brak and Great Brak rivers. As a general rule the sea at Munro's Bay and Santos Beach is also calm enough for canoeing, but should not be treated as safe for young children to use.

Diving

The entire stretch of rocky coast from Glentana to Victoria Bay is generally looked upon as too rough and dangerous for diving, but the relatively calm waters off Mossel Bay are very popular with enthusiasts. Scuba equipment (and lessons on how to use it) can be hired at Santos Beach.

Drives and viewsites

The three negotiable passes over the Outeniqua Mountains — Robinson, Outeniqua and Montagu — all offer splendid scenic drives, while the many small country roads between Little Brak River and George take the explorer through delightful stretches of farming country at the foot of the mountains. Most of the drives down to the coast in the George area are scenically attractive, winding over grassy hilltops until the blue sea comes into view, then plunging dramatically to the shore.

Golf

George is famous far and wide for its magnificent golf course, laid out on the edge of the town in a beautiful setting. Mossel Bay Golf Course is also attractive, set high on the crest of Cape St Blaize with grand views eastwards over Vleesbaai.

Horseriding

The forested lands surrounding George make fine riding country. Contact the George Riding Club or the George Publicity Association.

Libraries

There are excellent public libraries at both Mossel Bay and George, and a small modern library at Pacaltsdorp. For details, contact the relevant municipalities.

Museums

GEORGE MUSEUM, York Street: Exhibits include old gramophones and music boxes, cameras, typewriters and sewing machines; fine old pieces of furniture made out of indigenous woods from the surrounding forests; and various early weapons and firearms.

GREAT BRAK RIVER MUSEUM, Amy Searle Street: All kinds of bric-a-brac from the past century.

POST OFFICE TREE PROVINCIAL MUSEUM, Market Street, Mossel Bay: A complex

A plaque commemorating Mossel Bay's roots.

comprising a maritime history museum, a local history museum, a superb shell museum and a reception centre in the old granary.

VOORTREKKER MUSEUM, Majuba Avenue, Hartenbos: Features eight dioramas of the days of the Great Trek and exhibits of wooden farm implements, kitchen utensils and firearms.

Music and theatre

The people of George are rightly proud of the fact that they have two theatres, one run by the English and the other by the Afrikaans amateur dramatic society. For details, contact the publicity association.

Powerboating

The lagoons and few inland bodies of water in the area are all too small for powerboating, but the calm waters off Mossel Bay's beaches are a popular place for powerboats and waterskiing. There is a launch ramp at the Mossel Bay Yacht and Boat Club in Munro's Bay, and a municipal launch ramp alongside it.

Shipwrecks

A short walk eastwards from Glentana brings you to the wreck of the floating dock that was driven aground there in 1902. The superstructure has long disappeared and today little remains of the dock. A small wreck off Santos Beach dates from 1920 and is still visible at low tide.

Surfing

In the Mossel Bay area the most popular surfing spots are at Cape St Blaize and Die Bakke. Further east there is often good surfing at Glentana, but by far the most famous surfing spot is at Victoria Bay where the angles of the rocky shore and the incoming waves breaking from west to east often combine to provide unusually long rides.

Swimming

The lagoons at the mouths of the Hartenbos, Little Brak and Great Brak rivers all offer sheltered swimming. For swimming in the sea, the beaches along the Mossel Bay coast (especially Munro's Bay and Santos Beach) are renowned for their calm waters and relatively safe conditions. Further east, the beaches at Herold's Bay and Victoria Bay have a gentle slope and are regarded as fairly safe, and both also have tidal pools.

Tennis and squash

There are courts for both games at Mossel Bay and at George. For details contact the local publicity associations.

Walks

On the slopes leading up to the summit of Robinson Pass there are several walks in the Ruitersbos Forest Reserve, for which the nearby Eight Bells Inn serves as your 'check in' point. There is an attractive walk along the rugged southern face of Cape St Blaize and another rather similar but much shorter walk along the western headland at Herold's Bay. Both offer impressive views of great cliffs, pounded by the surf. Saasveld Forestry School, just a few kilometres east of George, serves as one of the starting points for the Outeniqua Hiking Trail and as both the start and finish of the Groeneweide Forest Walk.

Yachting and dinghy sailing

The lagoons are a little on the small side for sailing, and the sea along the Outeniqua coastal shelf is far too rough, but the waters off Mossel Bay are ideal for yachting and catamarans can be hired at Santos Beach. The Mossel Bay Yacht and Boat Club has its headquarters and launch ramp at Munro's Bay.

INFORMATION

- George Municipality and Publicity Association, Courtenay Street, George 6530.
  Tel 0441=742271
- Mossel Bay Municipality and Publicity Association, 101 Marsh Street, Mossel Bay 6500.
  Tel 04441=2065
- National Sea Rescue Institute, PO Box 734, Mossel Bay 6500.
  Tel (emergencies) 04441=3015
- Pacaltsdorp Municipality, Mission St, Pacaltsdorp 6534.
  Tel 0441=82400
- SA Tourism Board, Old Library Building, York St, George 6530.
  Tel 0441=5228

Nearest AA Office

- Millwood Building, cnr York and Victoria Sts, George 6530.
  Tel 0441=742090

Fish type	Season	Best area	Best bait
Black musselcracker	Mainly winter	Glentana — Victoria Bay	Fish fillet, strepie
Elf	Mainly summer	Dias Beach, best near rocks	Sardines, fish fillet
Galjoen	Winter	Rough water with rocky bottom	Musselworms, redbait, white mussels
Hottentot	Mainly summer	All rocky parts of coast	Musselworms, redbait, white mussels
Kabeljou	Mainly summer	Sandy gullies from Great Brak to Glentana	Chokka, sardines, small live bait, strepie
Leervis	Summer	Little Brak lagoon at outgoing and low tide; off rocky ledges at Herold's Bay and Victoria Bay	Mullet
Spotted grunter	Summer	Rough surf at Dias and Santos beaches; Little Brak and Great Brak river mouths	Prawns
White musselcracker	Oct — Dec	Cape St Blaize	Red rock crabs, Venus ear
White steenbras	Winter	Clear river mouths, shallow sandy gullies	White mussels, prawns

Striking it rich in a land of lakes and primeval forests

T HE HEART OF THE GARDEN ROUTE must be somewhere here among the lakes of Wilderness, hidden in the emerald green of the Goukamma valley or lurking in the waters of the lazy Knysna Lagoon. This is South Africa's most popular holiday refuge, where pleasurable pursuits include paddling up the Touws River, treading softly through the Knysna forests in search of elephants, cruising serenely across the lagoon to the Knysna Heads, exploring the forest streams where gold was panned — and where gold may still be found.

1 Kaaimans River

The name of this river, translated literally, would mean 'cayman' or 'alligator', suggesting that the river was once home to many crocodiles. The name is, however, more likely to be a corruption of Keeroms (turn around river). Three rivers join here, within just a few hundred metres of the coast — the Kaaimans, the Swart and one of its small tributaries — and each of the three runs through a steep-sided ravine. In the old days farmers and traders travelling by ox-wagon found it extremely difficult to cross the rivers, the Kaaimans in particular, and the track they followed twisted and turned around on itself many times — perhaps the origin of the unusual name.

Before reaching the sea the rivers form a small, romantic lagoon, notable for its unusually dark water and for the picturesque rocky walls of the narrow gorge that has formed where the Swart River twists away westwards from the Kaaimans. On the steep western bank of the lagoon there are

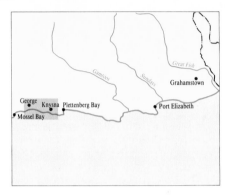

Adrift on the placid waters of Knysna Lagoon.

several quaint holiday homes dating from the turn of the century, whose occupants still have to row across the water to reach their front doorsteps.

At the seaward end of the lagoon the opposing forces of outflowing river water and inflowing tides have formed an attractive sandy beach (scarcely visible as you drive past on the N2), and at the mouth there is a raised rail bridge, mounted on tall pylons, which carries the famed Outeniqua Choochoo across the water twice a day on its round trip between George and Knysna. A short distance upstream there remains an old causeway, accessible from the N2, which crosses the Kaaimans just above the point where the Kaaimans and the Swart join. This leads to a small spit of land between the two rivers where members of the George Skiboat Club maintain a launch ramp under shady trees.

As you travel eastwards on the N2 you cross the Kaaimans on a broad, curving bridge, then you climb the coastal headland that forms the eastern bank of the lagoon. As you round the headland there are two parking areas alongside good viewsites. Looking westwards from here you have a fine view down over the lagoon mouth and the rail bridge. Looking eastwards you are treated to a splendid vista: the holiday refuge of Wilderness, the Wilderness lakes in the distance, and along the coast as far as Walker Point.

2 Wilderness

There are several theories as to how the village of Wilderness got its name, but by far the most romantic holds that a young Cape Town man won

LEFT *The N2 sweeps over the Kaaimans, and melds into the coastal hillside.*

the hand of his sweetheart only on the strict condition that he would take her to live in the wilderness as soon as they were married. He fulfilled his promise by buying a farm here at the mouth of the pretty Touws River, and by naming his purchase 'Wilderness'.

Although it is relatively small, Wilderness has been an enormously popular get-away-from-it-all holiday resort for many decades. Early in the century it acquired a reputation as the perfect place for honeymooners, and the natural attractions that made it so remain unaltered and unspoilt today: the tiny village is cupped between green coastal hills, with the serenely beautiful Touws River lagoon on one side and a magnificent sweep of golden beach on the other.

Anyone visiting Wilderness should make a point of driving along the narrow gravel track known as White's Road. This winds up the hillsides immediately behind the village, and from a point roughly two-thirds of the way to the top you have a splendid view eastwards over the lakes. As you climb still higher you turn inland and there is a fine view on your right over the Touws River valley. Eventually you reach a T-junction with the tarred road that leads inland — turn right here onto the tar, and almost immediately afterwards turn left onto another gravel track, signposted Map of Africa. This second track leads eventually to a viewsite overlooking a big bend in the Kaaimans River. It is known as the Map of Africa viewsite because the form of the land enclosed in the bend of the river, together with the pattern of the vegetation, strongly resembles the map of Africa as viewed from the south.

The splendid wild beach that stretches east from Wilderness for as far as the eye can see is not safe for swimming, but it offers invigorating walks on the golden sand, as sea mist rolls in from the long lines of breaking waves offshore. For swimming, and also for canoeing and paddleboating, holiday-makers have the pretty

Touws River lagoon. Canoes, rowing boats and paddleboats can be hired from the Wilderness Rest Camp run by the National Parks Board, and also from several of the private resorts on the river banks. Powerboating and waterskiing are allowed on only a section of the lagoon, but canoes and rowing boats can be taken far up the Touws River into a completely unspoilt forest world.

The whole of the Touws River estuary and the small Ebb and Flow Nature Reserve that was sited upstream have now been incorporated in the Wilderness National Lake Area, and the staff of the National Parks Board have created the circular Kingfisher Hiking Trail to explore the estuarine environment. The trail consists of a system of paths: you can spend an hour or two walking one section or take a day to complete the full circuit. From Wilderness village the trail begins with a boardwalk that leads through the reed beds on the northern bank of the lagoon. Later you cross the Touws River and the Serpentine — the waterway that links the Touws River lagoon to Island Lake — then meander back through the Touws River's floodplain and along the beach to the river mouth.

The trail takes its name from the fact that five of South Africa's ten kingfisher species are seen here — the giant, pied, halfcollared, malachite and brownhooded kingfishers.

3 The Lakes

South Africa can offer the traveller few vistas so serene and gentle as the view down from the coastal hills to the perfectly calm waters of Swartvlei, backed by rolling hills smothered in

The endless stretch of surf-scalloped beach at Wilderness invites long, romantic strolls.

dark green pine forests, and with line after line of ever-higher hilltops stretching away into the hazy distance until the eye settles on the jagged blue-grey outline of the Outeniqua Mountains.

Swartvlei is the largest of a string of six lakes stretching for over 40 km along the southern coast from Wilderness in the west to the Goukamma River valley in the east. From west to east they are the Touws River lagoon at Wilderness, Island Lake (also known as Lower Langvlei), Langvlei, Rondevlei, Swartvlei and finally Groenvlei.

The lakes have existed in their present form only for some 2 000 years, but they are a result of several million years of geological vacillation, as the world swung back and forth between ice ages and interglacial warm spells. Each successive ice age saw a massive increase in the size of the polar ice-caps, and as the water froze the level of the world's oceans dropped dramatically. When the weather became warmer the ice melted and the level of the oceans rose again. Each movement of the sea built up a line of dunes along this stretch of coast, and the lakes were formed by various low-lying areas of land being blocked from the sea by the dunes. Langvlei, for example, is simply an inundated area caught between the dunes. Swartvlei is a drowned

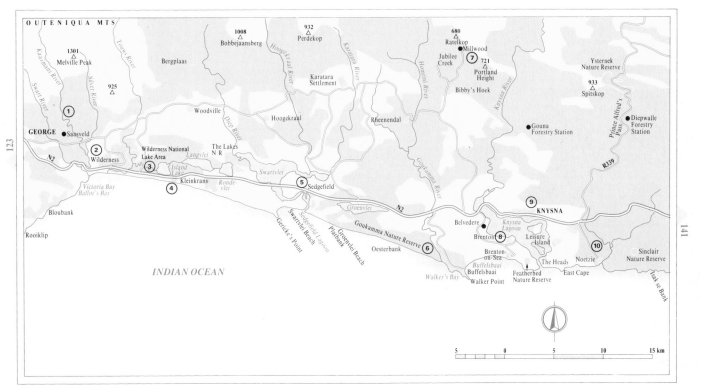

The green-tinted waters of Swartvlei — the largest of the lakes — provide a rich feeding ground for countless birds, including these spoonbills.

river valley. Rondevlei is thought to have been a shallow pan excavated by wind, which has gradually filled with water.

The lakes and the area surrounding them are now incorporated in the Wilderness National Lake Area, and the aim of the National Parks Board has been to zone the entire area in such a way that the goals of conservation and of holiday recreation are both adequately catered for, appealing not only to the nature lover and the conservationist but also to the angler, the boardsailor and the yachtsman.

The Touws River lagoon and Island Lake have been set aside for predominantly recreational use. Langvlei and Rondevlei are zoned for wildlife conservation and together form the 'conservation heart' of the lake region. They offer an unspoilt world where coastal fynbos mixes with semi-aquatic reeds, sedges, rushes and water grasses, and they constitute one of the richest refuges for waterfowl in the whole of South Africa: of the 95 species recorded throughout the country, 75 can be seen in this relatively tiny area. (This is also one of the few places in the southern African region where both the marsh harrier and the grass owl are known to breed.)

Swartvlei is not only the largest of the lakes but also the deepest — and many would judge it the most beautiful, having a distinctive grandeur of its own. Although the reed beds that fill the floodplain at its eastern end are zoned as a conservation area, the main body of the lake has been set aside for recreational use.

In some ways the most interesting of the lakes is Groenvlei. Several thousand years ago Groenvlei was linked to Swartvlei but the two were eventually separated by windblown sand. Groenvlei then converted gradually to a freshwater lake, the only one in the region. Algae growing in the freshwater environment give the lake a greenish tint — hence its name. (It was formerly known also as Lake Pleasant.) Another consequence of its being fresh water is that it has become home to a large population of the North American black bass, the prized quarry of local and visiting anglers.

At the western end of Groenvlei there is a stylish old hotel and a large holiday resort, both of which retain the old name of Lake Pleasant. Immediately behind the hotel you will find a gravel track that leads south over the coastal hills and that brings you after 4 km to a small parking area overlooking a wild stretch of beach at Platbank (also known locally as Groenvlei Beach). Wooden steps lead down to the beach, which is especially popular with surf anglers.

The N2 runs along the crest of the huge dunes that separate most of the lakes from the sea, and it offers splendid views. But it is also possible to explore the region more intimately by following any of a network of mostly gravel roads leading among the lakes then climbing the forested hills behind them.

4 Kleinkrans

Between Wilderness and Sedgefield a sign pointing to Kleinkrans leads south from the N2 on a road down to the beach. The road levels out into a lawned parking and picnic area overlooking a wild stretch of sandy shore, generally too rough for safe swimming, but magnificent simply to look at and to walk along in the salty haze. Set back from the parking area there are change-rooms, showers and toilets.

Just half a kilometre east of here lies the small village of holiday houses known as Kleinkrans. At several points near the houses attractive wooden steps and walkways lead down the grass-covered dunes to a similar stretch of unspoilt beach.

5 Sedgefield and Gericke's Point

The beautiful dark waters of Swartvlei form a huge S-bend as they laze their way to the sea. This lower, meandering portion of the vlei is known locally as Sedgefield Lagoon — Sedgefield being the name of the sprawling holiday town that has grown up on its eastern banks. To many who have chosen to live here, or who regularly holiday here, Sedgefield has a restful charm that is not quite equalled by any of the other resorts in the region.

The lagoon is a paradise for waterfowl, and offers fairly safe swimming and canoeing for children. East of the lagoon's attractive sandy mouth there is a low-lying bluff that offers a fine view along the shore to Gericke's Point, with the Outeniquas in the distance. Archaeological investigations have revealed that this coastal bluff, conveniently situated between sea and lagoon, was used as a regular camp site by so-called Strandlopers.

On the west bank of the lagoon a road signposted Swartvlei leads off the N2 towards the coast, ending in a parking area above Swartvlei Beach that is roughly halfway between the lagoon mouth and Gericke's Point. You can walk westwards from here, or from the lagoon mouth, first along the sandy beach then across low platforms of flat sandstone, to arrive eventually at Gericke's Point. This is a great mound of sandstone that projects into the sea, easy to walk

THE OLD ROAD THROUGH THE PASSES

Before the modern highway was built along the coast, anyone wishing to travel between George and Knysna had to take the old inland road that led through almost impenetrable forests and had to negotiate no fewer than seven difficult river-valley passes. This old road can still be used and it offers modern explorers a way to see the back country — a rural world of farms and forests, where life is lived at a far slower pace.

To get onto this old road you drive out of George on the N2 for Knysna and almost immediately turn left for Saasveld. After a few kilometres you pass the Saasveld Forestry School on your left, then you drive through the first two passes, crossing the Kaaimans and Silver rivers. The turn-of-the-century stone bridges over the rivers are national monuments (as are the passes themselves). After crossing the Silver River you continue straight onto gravel for Knysna, then cross the Touws River on an iron-girder bridge and come to a T-junction with a tarred road, where you turn left for Knysna.

After about 3 km a gravel track on the left leads to the Big Tree picnic site (with the convenience of braai places, picnic tables and toilets) and from here a short path crosses a wooden footbridge over a forest stream to bring you to the Woodville Big Tree — a massive Outeniqua yellowwood estimated to be roughly 800 years old. A short forest walk starts at the Big Tree and will take you through an attractive area of indigenous woodland.

Back on the main road, you continue your journey on tar for a few kilometres and immediately this ends you cross the Diep River, and thereafter the Hoogekraal, passing through a valley richly blanketed in forest. After crossing the Karatara River and then the Homtini you reach the bottom of yet another deep valley covered in a great expanse of indigenous forest. Shortly afterwards the road surface reverts to tar. (A turn-off here to Bibby's Hoek leads to the Millwood goldfields of last century and makes a fascinating excursion, both in the historical sense and in that you are taken deep into the heart of typical Knysna forest.) Soon after passing through the little country village of Rheenendal you catch your first glimpses of the Knysna Lagoon and the Knysna Heads and then reach a T-junction with the N2, where you turn left to wind down from the hills into the valley of the Knysna River. (The more adventurous can reach Knysna via the steep Phantom Pass.)

bank of the pretty lagoon has been developed as an attractively lawned picnic area (with stone tables and seats, braai places, drinking water and toilets). From the northern (inland) end of this picnic area you can walk across a long suspension footbridge over the dark water of the river, then take any of a variety of footpaths leading through the western section of the reserve. The principal hiking trail through the reserve leads to a stretch of coast known as Oesterbank: an area of surf-battered rocks that is home to the indigenous oyster *Crassostrea margaritacea*.

The reserve contains a wild region of scrub-covered sand dunes, the whole of Groenvlei, and many kilometres of unspoilt coastline. It is noted particularly for the variety of bird species that can be spotted here — roughly 150, including the African fish eagle and the marsh harrier.

7 Millwood

In the late 1870s alluvial gold was found in the forest streams west of the Knysna River. It took a while to assess the value of the find but by 1887 the rush was on. Where once there had stood only a small water-powered sawmill in the forests, suddenly there appeared a town with six hotels, three competing newspapers, over twenty shops and banks, and a population estimated at more than 700 fortune-seekers.

There was gold, both alluvial and reef gold, but not very much of it. After a few exciting years the mines began to close, the diggers moved on to the Witwatersrand and the site of the short-lived boom town returned to nature. Today it is almost impossible to believe that a town once existed here. What was once its main street is just another track through the forest.

To explore the old goldfields, take the Rheenendal road (off the N2 from George to Knysna) and immediately after passing through

to at low tide but risky to get back from once the tide begins to rise. Near the point are several picturesque wooden sheds where local fishermen house their boats.

6 Goukamma Nature Reserve and Buffelsbaai

The new tarred access road to Buffelsbaai undulates for several kilometres through the brilliant green valley of the Goukamma River, crosses several lines of scrub-covered sand dunes, then runs in a south-easterly direction along the coast past two beautiful golden strands. The first is the long beach at the mouth of the Goukamma, the second is the attractively curved and gently sloping beach of Walker's Bay. Eventually you reach the little village of Buffelsbaai, a tight cluster of holiday homes set on the narrow promontory of Walker Point.

Here visitors enjoy a surfeit of fine sandy beaches. In addition to those at Walker's Bay and the Goukamma, a lovely beach sweeps eastwards from Walker Point along the entire coast to Brenton-on-Sea and the back of Knysna's western head. This is a popular beach for both swimmers and surfers, and is particularly scenic also, forming a great curving ribbon of gold, backed by the green hills of Brenton.

Walker Point itself is rocky, with numerous fascinating rock pools to be explored at low tide. On its eastern side, where the Buffelsbaai beach meets the first stretch of stony shore, there is a particularly gentle bay and a slipway for powerboat fishermen. On its western side ridges of rock run roughly parallel to the shore, creating

deep-water gullies and offering many vantage points to anglers fishing from the rocks. Several hundred metres to the west, from the smaller rocky promontory that forms the western limit of Walker's Bay, there is a striking view along the coast past Gericke's Point to the distant bulk of the Outeniqua Mountains.

Buffelsbaai village abuts directly on the eastern end of the Goukamma Nature Reserve, which incorporates the lagoon at the mouth of the Goukamma River and the entire coastal strip stretching westwards to Groenvlei. The eastern

RIGHT The moody Swartvlei curves into the lazy lagoon at Sedgefield.

the village turn right onto a gravel road signposted Bibby's Hoek. This brings you to the shady picnic site of Krisjan-se-nek in the heart of the indigenous forest. Driving on from here, keep left where the road divides, and at the second fork go left again. This road leads down into Jubilee Creek, an attractive picnic and braai area and one of the streams where alluvial gold was found. A footpath leads upstream along the right bank, bringing you eventually to several old mine openings and a small pool at the foot of a waterfall.

When you drive back from Jubilee Creek turn left at the first fork. After about 4 km you reach the site of Millwood, passing on your right a road to the old town cemetery, and then reaching a fork. The road leading left here, merely a forest track now, was once Millwood's main street. If you take the road leading right, and at the next fork go right again, you will eventually reach the boiler of an old steam engine in a clearing on your left; this was the site of the stamp battery for the old Bendigo mine.

A sign here points downhill to the opening of the main Bendigo tunnel, which you can reach most easily by driving back the way you came and taking the first turn to your left. The tunnel reaches 200 m into the hillside but is too dangerous to explore.

8 Belvedere and Brenton

An attractive drive along the western bank of Knysna's lagoon, winding down the hillside, brings you to the charming little Holy Trinity Church at Belvedere, a perfect example in miniature of the Norman churches built in England during the 11th and 12th centuries. The church was erected here in the mid-19th century by Thomas Henry Duthie.

Duthie, a captain in the 72nd Highland Regiment, was stationed at the Cape and went on a hunting trip to the Knysna area, where he met his future wife Caroline, the daughter of George Rex. After living for a while in England they returned to Knysna and Duthie bought from his father-in-law the estate of Belvedere (beautiful to behold) — a splendid tract of land here on the western banks of the lagoon. With the help of his neighbours he then set about building this little church. The work took five years, and a great many difficulties and obstacles had to be overcome. (The bell that now hangs above the main door was cast in England and was lost overboard in the lagoon, being recovered only several months later.)

Continuing coastwards, the road climbs steadily, offering grand vistas over the lagoon, and after cresting the hills and passing a side road to the lagoon again at Brenton, drops to the resort of Brenton-on-Sea, an assortment of smart holiday houses sprinkled over the coastal hillsides. The road ends at a small hotel, where a short path will take you down to a wide stretch of golden beach reaching away to Walker Point in the distance. About a kilometre east of here is another beach, more gently sloping and preferred as a bathing beach by locals and regular visitors, but getting to and from it involves a considerable hike.

A WALK THROUGH THE LEAFY WILDERNESS

The delicately hued bloom of Knysna's chestnut trees.

'In some places you see hill rising behind hill, like billows on the sea, each fainter in the distance, and each clothed with dark, glossy evergreen woods. In others, you have glens where lofty trees of giant growth, heavy with lichens, support their living roof of leaf-clad branches high overhead, whilst a tangled wilderness of underwood, itself composed of trees and tree-like creepers, fills the space between. . . .'

So did the Duke of Edinburgh describe the Knysna forest during his visit to the region in 1867. Large tracts of this forest still exist within a few kilometres of Knysna, remaining virtually untouched by man. To walk through the depths of this forest is to all but lose yourself in a still, dark, grey-green world, the home of the last few Knysna elephants and of a wide assortment of birds, whose striking calls occasionally rupture the almost tangible silence.

To experience the forest at first hand, follow the 20 km Elephant Walk from the Diepwalle Forestry Station (reached from the R339 towards Uniondale).

The full walk is divided into three great loops, each of more or less the same length, so you may, if you wish, undertake only one third of the full distance. The route leads past the giant King Edward VII Tree, a massive Outeniqua yellowwood, and takes in several picnic sites. Along the way you can appreciate the rich variety of species the forest contains — Cape beech, knobwood, blackwood, white pear, bladdernut, white stinkwood and tree fuchsia. Although the odds against seeing an elephant are high, walkers have glimpsed them along this route.

A second, shorter trail, known as the Terblans Walk, leads through the Gouna forest several kilometres west of Diepwalle (reached by driving from Diepwalle along the sideroad known as Kom-se-pad). The walk, with a natural swimming pool en route, is circular and only 6,5 km long, but you could take a whole day to enjoy the forest at your leisure — and you are more likely to spot an elephant in this remoter part of the woods.

9 Knysna

One of the most striking geological features along the entire southern African coastline is the pair of huge, brightly coloured cliffs known as the Knysna Heads. They flank a deep but potentially treacherous channel through which the sea pours in to flood the wide and breathtakingly pretty lagoon at the mouth of the Knysna River.

The name Knysna is a Khoi word and scholars are uncertain as to its exact meaning. It could mean 'place of wood', or it could mean simply 'fern leaves', but its most probable meaning is 'straight down' — an obvious reference to these immense perpendicular cliffs whose ruggedness and beauty leave a lasting impression.

Several European stock farmers and woodcutters had already established themselves in the Knysna district by the end of the 18th century but the colourful part of Knysna's history began in the year 1804, the year that saw the arrival of an extraordinary character known as George Rex.

Legend insists that George Rex was an illegitimate son of England's King George III, but historical research has failed to provide even the smallest scrap of evidence to support this belief. What is known is that he held an official position at the Cape during the first British occupation, and after the British relinquished the Cape he moved to Knysna and purchased the farm Melkhoutkraal on the eastern banks of the lagoon. Here he produced a large family and gradually acquired a huge tract of land, including both sides of the lagoon and the heads.

While Rex laboured to establish the Knysna River as a harbour, the little hamlet of Melville grew into being on the northern shore of the lagoon. Eventually Melville and two neighbouring settlements merged to form a town, and the town was officially given the name of Knysna. Farming, woodcutting and furniture-making, and a certain amount of coastal trading — these remained the principal industries of the region for well over a century, but more recently the town has emerged as one of South Africa's leading tourist resorts.

The centre of the town is now a chic collection of restaurants, souvenir shops, and outlets for the local furniture industry which produces splendid pieces using such indigenous timbers as the Outeniqua yellowwood and stinkwood. But there are still a few places where the atmosphere of the past lingers on. One of these is the little graveyard where the remains of George Rex lie interred.

ABOVE *Looking back towards Buffelsbaai along the green slopes of the Brenton coast.* BELOW *Time has stood still at Belvedere's peace-shrouded little church.*

There are no signs directing the way, but you can reach the site by driving out of town on the N2 towards Port Elizabeth, passing George Rex Drive on your right (which leads to the heads), then taking the second turn right. Almost immediately you then turn left onto a gravel road, and after a few metres reach a cluster of trees, with the tiny stone-walled graveyard on your left.

Another place to seek out if you wish to recapture the past is Millwood House. This small wooden home was originally erected in the heart of the goldrush town of Millwood during the 1880s. When the gold ran out the house was dismantled and brought to Knysna, where it now serves as a small but fascinating museum. It houses an interesting collection of last century's everyday furniture and domestic bric-a-brac, early photographs of Knysna and of the many shipwrecks that have occurred here over the years, and most interesting of all, several photographs of the old gold diggings at Millwood.

Only a few paces away from Millwood House is Thesen House, named after another of Knysna's influential families. Thesen House is now home to Bitou Crafts, a nonprofit community programme

KNYSNA'S MOUTHWATERING HARVEST

To some people the mention of Knysna Lagoon recalls long days of lazy living aboard a houseboat or cabin cruiser. To others the name conjures up a picture of the curious little sea horse, living gracefully and unobtrusively amid the watery reed beds. But to gourmets far and wide the words Knysna Lagoon signify the salty succulence of fresh oysters.

Oyster farming has been carried on in the lagoon for two decades, and some 20 ha of the lagoon are now crisscrossed by 'oyster beds' — the wooden racks and mesh bags that hold the young oysters while they grow into mouthwatering delicacies.

The coast at Knysna is a natural home to *Crassostrea margaritacea*, our common coastal rock oyster, and the Knysna oyster companies have limited concessions to harvest a few of these when the tides are especially low. But these indigenous oysters do not live in the lagoon, and for farming purposes thousands of tiny Pacific oysters, *C. gigas*, are imported from Europe and Japan. This is the most common species cultivated throughout the world, and it is favoured in part because it grows to an edible size so quickly. Provided it is held where the tides bring it a regular and rich store of food — plankton and other microscopic forms of sea life — it will grow to a succulent size within just two years.

Knysna is famous for the serenely green and shady forests that blanket the region.

that has become deservedly famous for its pottery and woven fabrics, and that welcomes visitors and browsers. Over the years Knysna has become something of an artists' colony and many of the shops in the town stock the paintings, pottery and craftwork of local artists, vying with the curios and furniture wrought by local craftsmen.

No visit to Knysna would be complete without a trip to the heads. To get there, drive seawards on George Rex Drive, which runs along the eastern shore of the lagoon. As you approach the eastern head, take the road leading left where a sign indicates a viewpoint. This road climbs steadily until you reach a parking area on the crest of the head. A few metres downhill from the parking area there is a fine viewsite. If you now drive back down the hill, then follow the lower road, you arrive eventually at a second parking area alongside a restaurant. A footpath behind the restaurant leads around the base of the eastern head into a rocky fantasy world of mysterious caves and turbulent seas. A few paces from the parking area there is a small aquarium run by the National Sea Rescue Institute, where you can see several Knysna sea horses (*Hippocampus capensis*).

While the eastern head is now encrusted with smart houses, the western head remains undeveloped and is completely enclosed in the privately owned Featherbed Nature Reserve. Members of the public are allowed to walk

through the reserve, but access is only by boat from across the lagoon. From the pretty sandy landing place a narrow footpath leads up the slopes of the western head through a mixture of fynbos and lush coastal forest to several spectacular viewsites. On the way you can peer into great caverns, and walk under and over a huge natural arch where the towering cliff has been undercut by waves.

The heart of Knysna is the lagoon itself, home of the extraordinary sea horses and at least 200 other species of fish. Today the lagoon is administered by the National Parks Board under the official title of Knysna National Lake Area. The lagoon has been zoned: certain parts are maintained as nature reserves and others set aside for powerboating, waterskiing and sailing.

At least two establishments on the banks of the lagoon hire out pleasure craft, ranging from cabin cruisers to sailboards and paddleskis. A speciality of the region is the chance to spend your holiday afloat on one of the several live-aboard cruisers that can be hired. Once you have embarked on one of these you can meander about where you please and can choose each evening from any of four or five overnight anchorages.

10 Noetzie

The Noetzie River is all but inaccessible, its several tributaries winding tightly through the dense indigenous forest that lines the coast east of Knysna. The name Noetzie means 'black' and refers to the extreme darkness of the river's water, coloured by the humic acids leached from the carpet of leaves that cover the forest floor.

Where the river eventually meets the sea it has formed an exquisitely pretty lagoon, then it flows

out over a small and equally beautiful sandy beach, flanked on both sides by awesome rocks of red-orange sandstone. To reach the river mouth you drive out of Knysna on the N2 in the direction of Plettenberg Bay, turn right at the crossroads (where the R339 leads left to Uniondale) and follow a gravel track that meanders over the hilltops towards the coast. You have fine views to your right over the Knysna Lagoon, and you pass through stretches of tall, cool eucalyptus forest. Finally the road leads over the crest of a fynbos-covered hill and you look down on a ruggedly attractive coast marked by great outcrops of rock,

OPPOSITE *The Knysna Heads hold majestic sway over the lagoon.*

RIGHT *Knysna, with its boat-dappled lagoon reaching down to the sea through the heads.*

already an orange colour naturally, and painted more brilliantly so by flourishing lichens.

The road ends in a small parking area. Walk down the concrete strip road that starts at the bottom of the parking area, pass the wooden gates and keep right where the strip road forks. Lower down, just before you reach the end of the road, take the stone steps leading down to your left.

The steps bring you out onto the lovely beach, and by walking a few metres to your left you reach the little lagoon, clasped between forest-smothered hillsides. The lagoon is safe for swimming, but the beach slopes too steeply to be treated as safe.

Noetzie is almost as famous for its 'castles' as it is for its pristine charm. The castles are in fact stone holiday homes complete with battlements and parapets. Several legends have grown up around them, one holding that they were built by Portuguese seafarers some centuries ago, another that one was built by an 18th-century Italian duke who imprisoned his wife here to punish her for some infidelity. In fact they are relatively modern constructions built within the past sixty years.

When the level of the river is low it is easy to wade across. The attractive indigenous coastal forest that covers the hills on the eastern side of the river forms part of the Sinclair Nature Reserve. A footpath leads into the reserve and gives access to a magnificently wild stretch of coast, but a permit from the Department of Environment Affairs (forestry branch) is needed to enter the area.

LAST RETREAT OF NATURE'S SHY GIANTS

The deep forests north and east of Knysna, especially those in the Diepwalle and Gouna reserves, are the last home of the immensely shy Knysna elephants. These giants of the forest are so seldom sighted that for a while it was thought they had died out entirely, but in recent years they have on occasion been seen and photographed.

The Knysna elephants are the same in every respect as the elephants found elsewhere in southern Africa: the subspecies *Loxodonta africana africana*. Their shyness and their near-extinction (only three are known to survive) are both due in large part to the callousness with which they were hunted in years gone by. Old records relate horrifying tales of slaughter.

Recent research has shown, however, that it is not only the hunter who is to blame for their diminishing numbers. Before the arrival of European settlers the elephants roamed far more widely than they do today. Their home territory included not only the deep forest but also fynbos-covered hillsides, grasslands, and swampy river estuaries, and it appears that the elephants needed the varied vegetation that these differing habitats provided. All but the deep forest have since been fenced in and claimed by man, so the elephants now have to survive on the diet that the forest alone provides, and this, according to scientific reports, is not enough to keep them healthy.

Angling
The waters off the Knysna Heads and Walker Point are popular with powerboat fishermen. Many use the slipway at Buffelsbaai (the Walker Point end of beach), others launch in Knysna Lagoon and motor out through the heads. Knysna Lagoon is itself a popular fishing ground, offering spotted grunter, steenbras, kabeljou, leervis and elf.

Beachcombing and shelling
This part of the coast is not particularly noted for its seashells but one place where fine shells may sometimes be found is the great sweep of golden sand that fringes Buffelsbaai, from the stony headland of Walker Point to the first stretch of rocks at Brenton-on-Sea. You will occasionally find pansy shells here. There are also several small beaches set among the rocks immediately west of Knysna's western head. These are slightly better for shell-collecting but they are difficult to get to. The easiest access is from Brenton-on-Sea.

Birdwatching
The Wilderness National Lake Area is one of South Africa's foremost sanctuaries for waterfowl. Of the 95 species recorded in South Africa, 75 can be seen in the Langvlei-Rondevlei area. Sedgefield Lagoon, the Goukamma Nature Reserve and the Knysna Lagoon also have rich bird life.

Boardsailing
Swartvlei is the most popular boardsailing venue along this stretch of coast, but sailboards are almost as common a sight on Island Lake and the Bollards Bay area of Knysna Lagoon. Sailboards can be hired in Knysna from the Southern Seas Charter Company and from Lightley's Holiday Cruisers.

Boat trips
Scenic cruises on the Knysna Lagoon are offered all year round by the Southern Seas Charter Company and Lightley's Holiday Cruisers. A popular outing is a cruise to the heads, then to the Featherbed Nature Reserve on the western head where you can explore the reserve and the caves in the cliff, before boarding the cruiser once again for the return trip.

Bowls
Knysna's two bowling clubs — one in the town and one on Leisure Island — are both set in attractive surroundings. Contact the publicity association or the local municipality.

Camping and caravanning
There are camping grounds and caravan parks throughout the region,

An enchanting holiday 'castle', backed by a fortress of green, shimmers in the sands at Noetzie.

THINGS TO DO

notably at Wilderness, Island Lake, Swartvlei, Sedgefield, Groenvlei (Lake Pleasant), Brenton-on-Sea, and all around the Knysna Lagoon. Contact the Knysna Publicity Association and the National Parks Rest Camp at Wilderness.

Canoeing
Canoeing is a popular pastime on the Touws River at Wilderness, on Island Lake, Swartvlei, Groenvlei and Knysna Lagoon (but note that it is dangerous to approach the heads during high or outgoing tides). Canoes can be hired from the National Parks Rest Camp at Wilderness and from several other resorts in the area, from the Lake Pleasant Holiday Resort at Groenvlei, and in Knysna from the Southern Seas Charter Company and Lightley's Holiday Cruisers.

Cycling
Knysna has an active cycling club that welcomes visitors. Cycles can be hired in the town from Cycle and General.

Diving
The most popular spot along this coast for scuba diving is at the Knysna Heads, on the seaward side. For local information contact the Knysna Angling Club on the lagoon-front near the railway station.

Drives and viewsites
The old road through the passes between George and Knysna, and the route to Jubilee Creek and Millwood are two of the most interesting drives in the area. Also recommended are the short drive along the western side of Knysna

Following the sinuous curves of the boardwalk at Wilderness.

Lagoon to Belvedere and Brenton-on-Sea, the drive up White's Road at Wilderness, and for the more adventurous the drive inland over Prince Alfred's Pass. Fine views can be enjoyed from the crest of Knysna's eastern head and from the hills overlooking Brenton. A particularly grand view can be obtained from the summit of Spitskop, inland from the Diepwalle Forestry Station.

Golf
Knysna Golf Club, with a small but scenic course, welcomes visitors.

Horseriding
Much of this region is fine riding country. Horses can be hired from Cherie's Riding School at Sedgefield.

Libraries
Knysna has a newly renovated library in the heart of the town (Memorial Square) and another modern library in the suburb of Hornlee. Contact the municipality for details.

Museums
MILLWOOD HOUSE MUSEUM, Queens Street, Knysna: Originally erected at the Millwood goldfield, then dismantled and brought to Knysna when the gold dwindled, the house is filled with interesting relics and collections of old photographs.

Powerboating
This is permitted within demarcated areas on the Touws River, Island Lake, Swartvlei and Knysna Lagoon. Cabin cruisers can be hired for personal use on the Knysna Lagoon from the two Knysna companies: Southern Seas Charter Company and Lightley's Holiday Cruisers.

Shipwrecks
Although the Knysna Heads have claimed many ships, no wrecks remain to be explored. The shipwreck history of Knysna is well documented in photographs on display at the Millwood House Museum.

Surfing
The outstanding surfing spot in this region is Buffelsbaai, especially the Walker Point end.

Swimming
Only one spot along this stretch of coast can really be recommended as a fairly safe place for swimming in the sea: the Walker Point end of Buffelsbaai beach (at the slipway used by powerboats). Two other good beaches are Walker's Bay, and the 'eastern' beach at

Brenton-on-Sea, but note that this last involves a considerable hike.

Tennis and squash
There are tennis courts and four squash courts at Knysna's Loerie Park Sports Grounds, and visitors are welcome.

Walks
There are many attractive walks in the area, including the Kingfisher Hiking Trail at Wilderness, the several footpaths that lead through the Goukamma Nature Reserve, and the Terblans and Elephant walks in the Gouna and Diepwalle forests.

Best of all is the heady Outeniqua Hiking Trail that takes eight days to complete and leads from Witfontein at George to Diepwalle in the forests just north of Knysna.

It ranks as one of the most strenuous walks in the country, involving steep gradients and long distances between overnight huts, but while it is possible to walk smaller sections of the trail, the rare emotional and mental experience of the full hike in this magnificent stretch of wild landscape makes it worth the effort.

Yachting and dinghy sailing
There is an attractive yacht club at Knysna with a clubhouse overlooking the lagoon, and it is occasionally possible to hire yachts or sailing dinghies. Contact the Southern Seas Charter Company or Lightley's Holiday Cruisers for information.

INFORMATION
• Department of Environment Affairs, Main Road, Knysna 6570. Tel 0445=23037
• Goukamma Nature Reserve, Sedgefield. Tel 04455=939
• The Lakes Nature Conservation Station, Sedgefield. Tel 04455=302
• Knysna Municipality, PO Box 21 Knysna 6570. Tel 0445=22133
• Knysna Publicity Association, Main Road, Knysna 6570. Tel 0445=21610
• National Sea Rescue Institute, Station 12, Knysna. Tel 0445=22675
• National Sea Rescue Institute, Station 23, Wilderness. Tel 0441=71112 or 0441=5944
• Sedgefield Municipality, PO Box 3, Sedgefield 6573. Tel 04455=640

Nearest AA Office
• Millwood Building, cnr York and Victoria Sts, George 6530. Tel 0441=742090

Fish type	Season	Best area	Best bait
Elf	All year	Platbank, Buffelsbaai, Knysna Heads, Noetzie	Freshly cut fillets of fish, spoons
Galjoen	Winter	Platbank, Buffelsbaai, Brenton-on-Sea, Noetzie	Redbait, bloodworms white mussels
Kabeljou	Sept — April	Swartvlei, Buffelsbaai, Knysna Heads and lagoon	Pilchards, freshly cut fillets of fish
Leervis	Nov — April	Swartvlei, Knysna Heads and lagoon, Noetzie	Live bait, spoons
Mussel-cracker	Oct — Mar	Brenton-on-Sea, Knysna Heads, Noetzie	Venus ear, redbait
Spotted grunter	All year	Swartvlei, Knysna Lagoon	Prawns, bloodworms
White steenbras	All year, especially winter	Swartvlei, Buffelsbaai, Brenton-on-Sea, Knysna	Prawns, bloodworms, pilchards, white mussels
White stumpnose	All year	All along the coast, Swartvlei and Knysna Lagoon	Prawns, bloodworms, white mussels, freshly cut fillets of fish

Where nature's palette paints a perfect picture

THE BRILLIANT COLOURS and the clear light of the Garden Route seem to reach a peak here in the vicinity of Plettenberg Bay: the deep blue of the sea washes against the sunburnt cliffs of Robberg, an endless lace of snow-white surf caresses the golden sands of the *bahia formosa* (beautiful bay), and the translucent turquoise lagoon at the mouth of the Keurbooms and Bitou rivers contrasts against the rich greens of the Tsitsikamma forest. Here, all in one small area, the holiday-maker can choose between the still pleasures of an untouched wilderness on the one hand and the elegant sophistication of fun-filled Plettenberg Bay on the other.

1 Bracken Hill Falls, Garden of Eden and Kranshoek
Approaching Plettenberg Bay on the N2 there are several spots that invite the traveller to linger, to picnic or to stroll through beautiful natural surroundings.

About 20 km from Plettenberg Bay is a turn-off seawards to Bracken Hill Waterfalls. After passing a small cluster of particularly tall eucalyptus trees, including a karri gum that was planted in 1922 and now towers 67 m, you reach an attractive lawned area alongside the falls. Here a lovely forest stream, the Witels (white alder), tumbles through several dark pools then over a high rocky ledge into

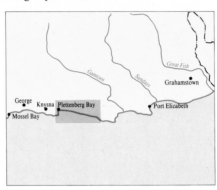

The sea-misted Tsitsikamma coastline.

a deep gorge thick with primeval forest. There are picnic tables and toilets nearby.

Some 5 km closer to Plettenberg Bay, a turn-off left from the N2 brings you to the Garden of Eden, a reserve protecting a small patch of indigenous forest, so sorely depleted in the region. Leading off from the picnic site here (with braai places and toilets) is a short circular walk through the forest covering a distance of roughly a kilometre. The footpath winds along a murmuring, fern-lined forest stream, passing fine specimens of Cape ash, white alder, stinkwood, Outeniqua yellowwood and Cape holly — their ancient trunks thickly covered in mosses and lichens. The animals of the forest are seldom seen, but among the inhabitants you might spot are the bushbuck, duiker, caracal, honey badger, baboon, vervet monkey, porcupine, bushpig and genet.

Even closer to Plettenberg Bay is a gravel turn-off to Harkerville (then turn left after a kilometre and right after 500 m). The road leads through dense indigenous forest to a pair of picnic sites on the crest of the coastal escarpment. From the first of the picnic sites a short footpath leads to a point from where you can view the small Kranshoek River cascading over a sheer rock face. (The path is not completely fenced and children must be held.) From the second picnic site, 800 m further along the road, you have a tremendous view westwards along the coast below. There are toilets at both picnic sites, but only the first has the added convenience of braai places.

The first of the picnic sites, alongside the waterfall, also serves as the starting point for

LEFT *Rugged Robberg, cloaked in green, thrusts into the sea.*

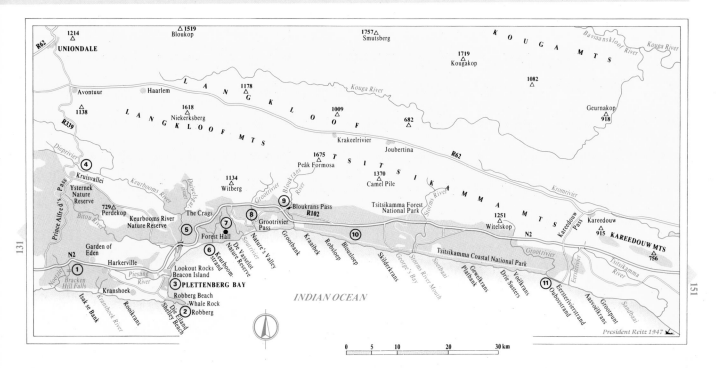

the Kranshoek Walk. This leads through thick forest down into the Kranshoek River gorge, hugs the rugged coast for roughly 2 km, then climbs the coastal escarpment again and returns to the starting point through forest plantations. The full distance is only 9 km, but this includes some strenuous climbing. Besides the magnificent scenery, there are several swimming places along the route.

2 Robberg

At the south-western end of Plettenberg Bay the land has thrust out into the blue Indian Ocean a massive arm of sunburnt rock. Its walls are sculpted into mighty cliffs of russet, orange and sandy coloured stone. Around its perimeter are lesser promontories that catch the breaking waves, and countless hidden beaches that are seldom stepped upon by human feet. To all who live in the region this awesome peninsula is a constant presence, its moods changing through the day as the sun swings slowly overhead, constantly adjusting the complex pattern of shadows that etch its rocky faces.

This is Robberg, known originally to the Dutch navigators as Robbe Berg (seal mountain). In those early days large numbers of seals basked on the inaccessible ledges around its shores. The explorer Thunberg reported seeing them in the latter part of the 18th century. No longer are these wave-splashed ledges home to such large colonies, but there are usually one or two seals, or small clusters, to be seen in the vicinity.

The whole of the Robberg peninsula is now a

RIGHT *Man is dwarfed by the giant yellowwoods in the Tsitsikamma park.*

nature reserve, roughly 240 ha in extent. The reserve is noted for its variety of bird species, its especially rich intertidal life and its varied coastal vegetation. Fishing is permitted within the boundaries of the reserve and the whole peninsula is crisscrossed by fishermen's paths, making it possible to reach almost every vantage point along the shore.

There are several large caves to be seen on the southern side of the peninsula, and one of these, the Nelson Bay Cave, has proved a rich archaeological site. Numerous artefacts have been excavated here, showing that this was for a long time the home of prehistoric man.

3 Plettenberg Bay

In the year 1576 a Portuguese navigator and cartographer, Mesquitada Perestrelo, named the great bay at the mouth of the Keurbooms and Bitou rivers *Bahia Formosa* (beautiful bay). It is easy to see why: a great expanse of clear blue water is captured by the rugged Robberg peninsula and a curving beach of golden sand that stretches away to the east for 20 km. A slowly advancing necklace of frothy white surf constantly adorns this giant sweep of gold, and behind the beach lies the clear turquoise lagoon of the Keurbooms and Bitou rivers. Fringing the lagoon, fresh green hills stretch away to the interior, to be stopped only by the soaring blue-grey summits of the mighty Tsitsikamma Mountains.

This bay was the scene of the first European settlement on South African soil, albeit by accident rather than by design. In the year 1630 a large Portuguese vessel, the *Sao Gonzales*, returning to Lisbon from Goa, anchored in the bay for two months to effect repairs after a storm out at sea. While lying at anchor it was caught once again by a violent storm and driven onto the shore, with the loss of over a hundred lives. The remaining hundred or so survivors, who were lucky enough to have been ashore at the time, lived here for several months in the lee of the peninsula and built themselves two boats. When eventually they set sail, one headed east and reached the Portuguese settlement at Mozambique; the other was picked up by the homeward-bound *St Ignatius Loyola*, which was tragically wrecked within sight of the Portuguese capital of Lisbon.

In 1778 the 'beautiful bay' suffered a name-change. The governor of the Dutch East India Company's settlement at the Cape, Baron Joachim

THE PANSIES OF PLETTENBERG BAY

The perfect pansy to pick.

The unofficial emblem of Plettenberg Bay is the pansy shell, so named because it has a form reminiscent of the pansy and a perfect five-petal flowerlike design 'carved' on its upper surface. The pattern is actually made up by many holes perforating the shell.

The pansy shell (*Echinodiscus bisperforatus*) is closely related to the sea urchin, but differs in that it has a definite front and back and will always move forwards. When alive it has a purple colour and is covered with short, thin spines that give it a furry appearance. By moving these spines it burrows just under the surface of the sand, collecting microscopic food particles. When the animal dies the spines fall off and the shell is soon bleached white by sun and salt water — to produce the 'pansies' that are then washed onto the beach by the tides.

A fair amount has been discovered about the pansy shell through patient study by marine biologists. At the centre of the petal pattern is a little star, and at four of the star's five points there are holes. It is through these holes that the eggs and sperm are released at breeding time. Fertilisation takes place in the water and larvae result; these are washed eventually onto the sandy shore, where they develop into tiny pansy shells, thus continuing the cycle.

The pansy shell is concentrated along the shores of the southern Cape and is a prized collector's piece. A closely related species is found along the coast of California but this has a more rounded shape, earning it the name 'sand dollar'.

The smooth sands of Plettenberg Bay stretch away towards the landmark Beacon Island.

van Plettenberg, had mounted an expedition deep into the interior, venturing as far as the modern-day town of Colesberg. The party then returned to the Cape by travelling along the coast, and Van Plettenberg was so taken with the beauty of the bay that he decided to name it after himself. While he toured the area on horseback he had his men erect a beacon on one of the hills that overlooked the central stretch of the bay, effectively taking possession of the territory.

Another of the consequences of Van Plettenberg's expedition was the discovery that the forests of this region were rich in usable timber, and in due course a woodcutter's post was established here. In 1788 a large stone timber store was built just a few metres below the spot where Van Plettenberg had set up his beacon — and the

modern town of Plettenberg Bay thus had its humble beginning.

Today the town is a chic assembly of holiday accommodation, luxurious homes, and stylish restaurants and shops, but there are still a few places of historical interest that are well worth a visit, including the site of Van Plettenberg's beacon. The original beacon has been taken to the South African Cultural History Museum in Cape Town for safekeeping, but an excellent replica has

been erected in its place. It consists of two hefty slate slabs, held together with lead, carrying the monogram of the Dutch East India Company and Van Plettenberg's own arms. Although the beacon is presently surrounded by bush, you can appreciate the excellent view that would originally have been obtained from this rocky lookout on top of which it was erected. Directly below Van Plettenberg's beacon stand the nostalgic ruins of the old Timber Store, now partially restored. (This

is reached from the car park in the middle of Central Beach.)

The prominent Beacon Island that stands out from the beach at the mouth of the Piesang River takes its name from the fact that a navigational beacon was erected here back in 1772. Today Beacon Island is the site of a hotel notable for its bold architectural design, but a replica of the navigational beacon can still be seen in the grounds, standing on the original site. Also in the grounds are an old cast-iron blubber pot and a

harpoon gun, reminders of the island's occupation early this century by Norwegian whalers.

Rich as this region is in history, its principal attraction remains its outstanding physical beauty. A fine viewpoint to head for in order to appreciate this beauty is the small patch of green lawn on the crest of Signal Hill. Looking down from here you can see the complete string of beaches that line the bay. To your right (south), between Beacon Island and Robberg, stretches Robberg Beach, popular with walkers and surfers. Immediately

below you lies the smaller Central Beach, stretching from Beacon Island to the small promontory known as Lookout Rocks; this beach is best for swimmers, boardsailors and catamarans. To your left (north-east) you can see Lookout Beach stretching from the Lookout Rocks to the mouth of the Keurbooms-Bitou lagoon, a more spacious beach for swimming and surfing. Beyond the mouth of the lagoon the sandy beach continues to Keurboomstrand. This most distant stretch is not safe for swimming but it does offer wonderful walks.

The ideal time to look out over the blue sea from here is during the late winter months; that is when the whales arrive to calve in the shallow waters of the bay, and you may be lucky enough to see several of these amiable giants spouting and diving just a few metres offshore.

4 Over Prince Alfred's Pass

An interesting excursion from Plettenberg Bay is the drive over the mountains to Avontuur, using the gravel Prince Alfred's Pass constructed by Thomas Bain more than 120 years ago. You drive out of Plettenberg Bay on the N2 in the direction of Port Elizabeth, but after just a few kilometres turn left (after crossing the bridge over the Bitou River but before crossing the bridge over the Keurbooms River).

The road now winds inland along the northern bank of the Bitou, then begins to climb the fynbos-covered hills. Eventually it climbs to a considerable height, running just below the crest of the 729 m Perdekop. From here you have magnificent views over wild valleys to the still blue peaks of the Langkloof Mountains.

Shortly after this you reach the forestry settlement at Kruisvallei where a road enters from your left. (This is the R339 from Knysna and is an optional route if you wish to begin your journey by driving through the Knysna forests.) After Kruisvallei you descend into the valley of the Dieprivier, and as you cross the river there is a green-lawned picnic area on your left. There are protected braai places here, and a cairn commemorating builder Thomas Bain.

Then you begin climbing through changing vegetation as you wind your way among ever-drier mountainsides and kloofs. Eventually you crest the mountains and find yourself in the Langkloof, an eastern extension of the Little Karoo.

At Avontuur you join the main road running east-west through the Langkloof and you can pick from several return routes. You can drive east and return to Plettenberg Bay via the short but attractive Kareedouw Pass. Alternatively you can drive west and return to Plettenberg Bay via George and Knysna — which means recrossing the mountains either by means of the spectacular Outeniqua Pass or by using the quaint old Montagu Pass.

A MARINE WORLD IN MINIATURE

Wave-tumbled rocks on the Tsitsikamma shore.

The fascination of tidal rock pools is the glimpse they provide of the secret life under the sea. The Tsitsikamma coastline is particularly rich in pools where you can stop and stare for hours . . . but be sure that you do nothing to disturb the delicate balance of life there.

One of the most familiar rock creatures is the sea anemone, a little animal that rather resembles a beautiful flower, with tentacles coloured from white to yellow and orange, or even as deep as purple. The sting in these tentacles paralyses the prey, which is then crushed into the central mouth. Also familiar are starfish, their five spiny arms tapering from a central disc. These are used to prise open the shells of prey such as mussels or oysters.

Another creature with a spiny or bumpy skin is the sea cucumber. At one end of its cylindrical body is the mouth, surrounded by tentacles. These are extended to capture food particles and then folded into the mouth for feeding. The sea cucumber generally has numerous flexible 'feet', which it uses to creep forward, or to anchor itself to rocks by sunction.

The sea slug, despite its unappealing name, is one of the loveliest inhabitants of rock pools. It is a mollusc whose dainty body may be frilled and brightly hued — from clear white, pink and red, to gay yellow or sombre black. The colour is its camouflage, just as the lack of colour is the camouflage of its drab mollusc 'relative', the chiton, so you might have to look quite closely before spotting either.

5 Keurbooms River

The large lagoon to the east of the town of Plettenberg Bay is the estuary of the Keurbooms River, supplemented by the waters of the Bitou River which flow in from the west.

The N2 crosses the Keurbooms River at the head of the lagoon, and the forested hills on the landward side of the bridge, on both sides of the river, are incorporated in the Keurbooms River Nature Reserve. This 760 ha tract of delightfully unspoilt terrain is covered for the most part in dense forest. Among the many indigenous trees that grow here is the sublimely scented keurboom — hence the name of the river.

On the western bank of the river, immediately downstream from the N2 bridge, the Plettenberg Bay Angling Club has its headquarters and clubhouse, with a small marina. Powerboats, rowing boats and canoes can be hired here, and these may be used to explore far up the river. The upper reaches are flanked by wild jungle and there are small sandy beaches along the banks where

LEFT *The mouth of the Keurbooms River: a symphony of sea and sand.*

THE TREES THAT BUILD THE FOREST CANOPY

The lush vegetation in the Tsitsikamma Forest National Park weaves a green and secret wonderworld.

'High forest' is the term used to describe the woodlands of the Tsitsikamma region. The 'high' does not refer to the altitude at which this kind of forest grows, but to the fact that the forest canopy of leafy branches is carried high above the ground. To the inexperienced eye the many mossy and lichen-covered tree trunks that hold this canopy up to the sky look fairly similar to one another, but in fact the forest contains a surprising variety of tree species.

A typical patch of forest, measuring a hectare or so, may easily contain fifty or sixty different species of tree. The largest and the best known is the rough-barked Outeniqua yellowwood (*Podocarpus falcatus*), reaching up to 60 m in height. Growing only half as tall is the most valuable species, stinkwood (*Ocotea bullata*), whose fine-grained, dark-hearted timber is always in great demand by furniture manufacturers. In earlier days one of the most useful of the forest trees was ironwood (*Olea capensis*), whose timber proved immensely strong although it was difficult to work. Ironwood, its small white flowers starred against glossy green leaves, is the most common species in the Tsitsikamma forests, accounting for nearly a third of all the trees, but today its chief use is as firewood.

Apart from the gigantic and the commercially valuable, there are many others that have attractive features. The Cape chestnut (*Calodendrum capense*) is a large tree with a spreading crown, which looks beautiful in summer when it bursts into mauve flower. The keurboom (*Virgilia oroboides*) is regarded with the greatest affection by many who are familiar with the forest. It is not a large tree but in spring it produces a great mass of pink to violet flowers that are reminiscent of sweetpeas, spreading a wonderful scent through large tracts of forest.

you can disembark and picnic.

There are several caravan parks and camping sites on the eastern bank of the lagoon, with some offering chalet accommodation. Above the N2 bridge, on the western bank of the river, the Cape Provincial Administration has established a public resort with caravan and camping sites. This is a particularly attractive place to spend a holiday, with many shady trees and a lovely green lawn that leads directly down to the river.

LEFT *The majestic frame of Cathedral Rock, at Keurboomstrand.*

6 Keurboomstrand

The resort village of Keurboomstrand comprises a cluster of holiday homes at the eastern end of the long sandy beach that stretches east from the Keurbooms River mouth. Here the green coastal hills are set back several hundred metres from the shore. At the end of the access road there is a small hotel and a tea room, and also a caravan and camping ground that is almost entirely concealed by the indigenous forest in which it is set.

Starting from the caravan park there is a beautiful walk east along the coast, especially worthwhile when the tide is low. The shoreline here consists of a jumbled collection of great rocky outcrops, interspersed with golden beaches and patches of fascinating rock pools to explore. The rugged hills behind the beach are smothered in rich subtropical vegetation and this gives a romantic scent to the velvety sea-mist air that you find yourself walking through.

At one point a narrow passage through colourful sandstone rocks veined with glistening quartzite leads onto a pristine, secluded beach at the mouth of the Matjies River. On your right, immediately after you emerge from the passage, you can inspect an 'arch rock' formation worn into the stone by the waves. Some metres above the river mouth an ancient cave is concealed by the dense bush; archaeological investigations have turned up many Stone Age implements here, showing that this small paradise-like setting was the home of man long ago.

A few metres east of the river mouth you come to a spectacular, far larger 'arch rock' formation (known as Cathedral Rock), a giant outcrop of sandstone through the base of which the sea has cut a channel. Continuing still further east from here a rudimentary path leads along a most picturesque stretch of the coast, passing numerous formations where wave action has created natural rock shelters, caves and arches.

7 Forest Hall and The Crags

In the middle of last century W H Newdigate, having established himself as one of the most prosperous landowners of the district, set about building himself a grand manor house on the coastal hills a short distance to the east of the Keurbooms River. Stonemasons and carpenters were imported from England and eventually a magnificent gentleman's residence arose amid the fields and forests. Newdigate named his impressive new home Forest Hall. Today this same manor house serves as an inn with accommodation in the original bedrooms, and day visitors are catered for with tea on the front porch.

A special attraction of this charming old estate

DIARY OF THE PAST

Captain John Fisher Sewell was the harbour master at Plettenberg Bay from 1875 to 1897, at a time when the population of the little settlement was no more than 700. His wife Maria was the younger daughter of Knysna's George Rex. He considered himself 'half a doctor', virtually appointed himself the local apothecary, and on occasion conducted funeral services. He built a house close to the sea on land rented from the church for £3 a year, and since his job 'was as onerous as that of those sleeping in their graves in the churchyard', he filled his time by recording day-to-day events in his diary. The diary came to light again thanks to local publisher Clare Storrar, and a handful of entries convey the character and pace of life in that earlier, slower-moving age.

1875:

June 25, Friday: Wind SW and fair weather. The post did not arrive till 9 pm. 14 hours overdue.

July 21, Wednesday: Saw Mr Jones at the meeting who told me that he had taken Annie Newdigate's baby which she had been delivered of, to take care of it. And that he did not care if Newdigate was cross or not.

October 18, Monday: Went up to the sale of the wreck (*Louis Alfred*) which commenced on the beach, with the hull fetching £16.

December 25, Saturday: I went to Church and spent the day at the Parsonage . . . Dick came round to Jan and they got hold of some wine and Dick got drunk and was going about with an axe, so I gave him a quilting.

1887:

October 6, Thursday: After breakfast Maria wanted to try the new Automatic Washing Machine so I told her to make a good fire up in the kitchen and to tell me when it was ready. So at 11 am she came and told me and, as I had no boiler large enough, I took my bath, and Fred coming, I made him fill it with water and make a good fire under it. And when it began to boil I put my Machine in and Maria brought her dirty clothes she had worn while away — some of them very much soiled — and I put them into the bath and in a short time it began to act. And in 15 minutes the clothes were perfectly clean and Maria took them out, rinsed them and hung them out to dry and in 2 hours they were ready to be mangled or ironed. And they smell so sweet and no one ever put a hand to them till they were washed and ready for rinsing out. It is certainly a wonderful invention and this is the first ever to come to this colony.

October 28, Friday: . . . Maria in her tantrums again and very annoying. I wish I could have a little peace. She is slovenly herself and won't allow me to have things tidy. But I will!

October 31, Monday: This is my birthday; but I really don't know how old I am. I think 61 . . . Maria had a sumptuous dinner, a fine turkey, pig's cheek, stew etc etc, no end of vegetables, and afterwards a large cake with good pontac and sherry and ginger beer to wash it down.

---

is a fairly easy thirty-minute walk that leads down the coastal hillsides through forest and fynbos to a beautiful and secluded beach. The coast here consists of short stretches of golden sand interrupted and partially protected by colourful rocky outcrops and promontories. A short walk eastwards along the coast towards the promontory called Grootbank will bring you to a beach that is known for the fine shells that can be found washed ashore at low tide. For a longer and even more interesting walk there is a second path that leads westwards along the crest of the coastal hills then descends to the shore at Cathedral Rock, bringing you out eventually at Keurboomstrand.

Just a few kilometres inland from Forest Hall there is a particularly attractive waterfall and pool in the course of the Duiwelsgatrivier (devil's hole river), which is well worth visiting if you are in the area. To get there, drive along the N2 to the small settlement known as The Crags, then turn north-west onto a gravel road following the sign to the Keurbooms Forestry Station. This road winds through farming country and forested hills, and you pass the forestry station where you must stop momentarily to obtain a permit to enter the Keurbooms Reserve. Eventually the road crosses the small Duiwelsgatrivier and turns around on itself to bring you to a pretty pool downstream. From this a short footpath leads along the river bank still further downstream to a very impressive waterfall, set in a steep valley of bright green ferns and with a large dark pool at its base.

8 Grootrivierpas and Nature's Valley

The mighty gorge of the Grootrivier, densely overgrown with indigenous forest, posed a major obstacle for the roadmakers whose job it was to blaze a highway along the coast between the districts of George and Humansdorp. Their answer was a spectacular winding pass that hairpinned its way down to the river and up the other side. Today a magnificent bridge speeds traffic over the gorge in a matter of seconds, but the old road through the pass remains the better route to take if you have time to enjoy the scenery.

At its mouth the river forms an attractive dark-water lagoon, which then spills out into the sea over a wide sandy beach. The hillsides overlooking the lagoon are thickly covered with forest, now incorporated in the 2 560 ha De Vasselot Nature Reserve, and the shores both east and west of the sandy river mouth are rocky and ruggedly photogenic. The whole composition has a wild beauty that has deservedly earned it the name Nature's Valley.

Among the sprinkling of holiday homes on the western bank of the river are many attractive wooden chalets mounted on stilts. From this small settlement footpaths lead to the beach, and others wind into the forested hills. One path that merits a special mention leads west from Nature's Valley along the coast, crossing the fine sandy beach, then leading along a rocky coastal shelf, and finally climbing the hillside at an angle through indigenous coastal forest.

After some thirty minutes you emerge at the pretty mouth of the little Soutrivier, surely one of the wildest and most tucked-away spots along the South African coastline. The sea breaks through the front line of coastal rocks to form a small cove, and once it has penetrated the land it fans out onto a gentle, perfectly curved sandy beach. From here

BELOW *A tiny pocket of the Tsitsikamma coast is tamed at this secluded rest camp.*

Finely etched against an awesome seascape, holiday-makers cross the suspension footbridge strung between the rocky banks of the Storms River.

you can walk up the bed of the little river until it loses itself amid hills drenched in dense jungle — the haunt of fish eagles, wild boar, troops of monkeys and the occasional leopard.

After walking inland for one curve of the river a further path branches up the forested hillside to the east, climbing to a point that offers a grand view back over Nature's Valley.

9 Bloukrans

The gracefully arched bridge over the immense gorge of the Bloukrans River ranks among the world's most inspiring examples of modern architecture, comparing favourably with the finest 'pieces' of roadbuilding technology in Italy's network of autostrada or Germany's autobahns. To stop halfway across the bridge in order to look down into the gorge is prohibited by law, but there is a spacious rest area on the eastern side of the gorge, which costs nothing to enter, and which has a well-designed viewing platform as well as a small museum covering the bridge's construction.

Looking down into the gorge you can see the river far below making its way to the blue sea in the distance. The steep walls of the gorge are ruggedly picturesque, and particularly beautiful in summer when the Cape chestnut trees are in bloom, bathing the whole scene in a magical lilac light.

Before this bridge was built the traveller had to negotiate a twisting road pass through the river valley, a full 7 km of hairpin bends through moss-shrouded indigenous forest. As is so often the case with such older roads, this (the R102) is the more attractive route to take if you have the time to appreciate the scenery. From the bottom of the old pass there is a superb view of the new bridge, soaring overhead in the blue sky, so high and distant as to seem quite surreal.

Another short drive is also well worth taking. On the western side of the Bloukrans Pass, exactly as the old road reaches the plateau at the top of its climb and begins to level out, there is a gravel track leading south (towards the sea) to the offices of the Bloukrans Forestry Station. Ask at the forestry station for directions, and for the key to the initial gate that needs to be opened, then follow this gravel route over the forested plateau towards the sea. You cross the toll road on a narrow bridge, and arrive eventually on an old track that runs along the crest of a high coastal bluff with Olympian views down over the rugged coast. On a clear day there is a fine view west to the Robberg peninsula, and a short walk eastward through the fynbos will bring you to a point on the down-curving hilltop from where you have an eagle's-eye view over the lower reaches of the Bloukrans River.

10 The Tsitsikamma National Parks

The Tsitsikamma (perhaps meaning 'sparkling water') Mountains reach steeply to the sky just a few kilometres inland from the southern coast. They catch the moisture-laden breezes from the sea, bundle them into cotton-wool clouds, then squeeze the rain out onto the narrow coastal plateau at their feet. This year-round supply of rain has nurtured a belt of dense forest running along the coast between the sea and the mountains, and the runoff from the mountain slopes, channelled into a series of rushing streams, has gashed the coastal plateau with deep river gorges.

Much of this rich forest wonderland is now enclosed in two national parks: the Tsitsikamma Coastal National Park and the Tsitsikamma Forest National Park. The coastal park stretches eastwards along the coast from the Grootrivier mouth at Nature's Valley for nearly 75 km. It encompasses a particularly wild strip of land, largely covered in dense, all but impenetrable forest, and made still more inaccessible by the many steep-sided ravines that cut through it, like jagged wounds through its velvety green skin.

The access road into the coastal park turns southwards off the N2 and is well signposted. It leads through extensive pine and eucalyptus plantations, then winds down the coastal hills through a grey-green jungle of indigenous forest to arrive at the park's administrative centre, just a few hundred metres from the mouth of the Storms River. There is a restaurant here, and a dusting of attractive wooden chalets set back from the shore in a neatly lawned setting (the chalets may be hired from the National Parks Board).

From the administrative offices and the restaurant there are several paths leading into the reserve. A particularly interesting one that takes roughly an hour and a half to complete leads along the shore and through the coastal forest to the mouth of the Storms River. There is a suspension footbridge across the river mouth from which you have fine views of the river's gorge, and just a few metres from the bridge, on the western bank, there is a small cave that is known to have been the home of prehistoric man.

At the western end of the cluster of chalets you will find another footpath winding away westwards along the rocky coast. This is the start of the famed Otter Trail, a five-day hike along the shore to Nature's Valley. The Cape clawless otter (*Aonyx capensis*) from which the trail takes its name is a secretive creature and is seldom seen, but you are likely to see some evidence of animals such as the bushbuck, blue duiker, rock hyrax, vervet monkey, baboon, porcupine, bushpig and even the leopard, as well as schools of dolphins out to sea. Roughly 3 km along the Otter Trail path there is a scenic waterfall, and you are able to walk this far without obtaining an Otter Trail permit.

A special feature of the coastal national park is that its boundaries reach three nautical miles (5,6 km) out to sea, enclosing a varied world of marine life. To enable visitors to appreciate what a rich realm this is, an Underwater Trail has been established for divers.

Thick coastal bush clings to the steep slopes shielding Oubosstrand from the public gaze.

The Tsitsikamma Forest National Park lies a few kilometres inland from the coastal park and encloses 478 ha of indigenous forest on the western bank of the Storms River. The principal entrance to the reserve is at the Paul Sauer Bridge, where you will find a restaurant and a petrol station.

There are three short walks through the forest reserve: the 15-minute Big Tree Trail, which starts a short distance to the west along the N2 and leads to a giant Outeniqua yellowwood tree; the one-hour Tree Fern Trail that starts and ends at the restaurant; and the Bushpig Trail linking the other two. All three give an excellent introduction to the world of the high forest. A major trail, the Tsitsikamma Trail, entails a 61 km hike inland through mountain fynbos and forests. (This is beyond the bounds of the park.)

Before the Paul Sauer Bridge was built, anyone wishing to travel along this coast had to cross the Storms River by means of the old road pass, a few kilometres south of the N2. This pass was built more than a century ago by Thomas Bain, and it is still possible to drive through it by car, although it is more usually treated today as a walk. The track crosses the river on an old causeway, known as Oubrug, and there is a small shaded picnic area here set in the heart of the forest.

The land on the eastern bank of the river forms part of the Blueliliesbush State Forest and you need a permit from the forestry office to enter. Armed with this, you can make your way along the eastern bank of the river to arrive eventually at a fine viewpoint overlooking Storms River Mouth.

11 Oubosstrand and Eersterivierstrand
The Tsitsikamma Coastal National Park extends along the coast between two river mouths — with both rivers, quite by coincidence, having the same

name: Grootrivier, meaning simply 'big river'. The rivers draw their water from the adjacent mountains and they are not big rivers in the sense that the Orange or the Tugela are big rivers, but they were 'big' in the eyes of the early settlers who had to cross them somehow when they came this way in their wagons.

From the mouth of the Grootrivier at the eastern end of the park a string of holiday shacks and modern coastal villas stretches eastwards to the smaller mouth of the Eersterivier. There is scarcely any noticeable break in the line of buildings but the settlement is divided into Oubosstrand (the western end next to the Grootrivier mouth) and Eersterivierstrand (the eastern end near the Eersterivier mouth).

The access road to this far-flung holiday community meanders coastwards through peaceful cattle ranches and over the crests of grassy hills. Eventually it dips down to the shore and runs along the coast between the shacks and houses, many of them set back in thick coastal bush. The coast itself is a strikingly rugged assemblage of wave-battered rocks and small beaches, with many deep gullies between outlying reefs of rock that run parallel to the shore.

From the point at which the road ends a short walk along the beach brings you to the mouth of the Grootrivier, a particularly beautiful spot. A jagged gorge, whose rocky walls are covered in brilliant orange lichen, encloses a golden, sandy riverbed. A small but strong river rushes across the sand into the sea, its water dark brown from the mountain vegetation. Unfortunately this extremely scenic place is not open to the general public. The land has remained in private hands and access is strictly limited to the owners of holiday homes and their guests.

Angling
As along so much of the Cape coast, the fishing in the Plettenberg Bay area is not nearly so rich as it was twenty or thirty years ago. Nevertheless, this area can still offer the angler a great deal of variety — surf fishing, rock angling, fine lagoon fishing in the Keurbooms-Bitou estuary, as well as deep-sea fishing from powerboats.

Art galleries
GALLERY OF THE PLETTENBERG BAY ARTS ASSOCIATION, Florina Place, Main Street, Plettenberg Bay: The varied work of some of the many South African artists who either live in Plettenberg Bay or holiday here on a regular basis can be viewed here. Not only the graphic arts are well represented but also ceramic work, weaving, jewellery making, beadwork and woodwork.

Beachcombing and shelling
The closest 'collectors' beach to Plettenberg Bay is the aptly named Shelly Beach between Kranshoek and the Robberg peninsula. Another good place to go is the Grootbank area, a short stretch of coast near Forest Hall. If you are searching specifically for pansy shells, try Robberg Beach or Lookout Beach at low tide. The best rock pools to explore are found along the Tsitsikamma coastline.

Birdwatching
The Keurbooms-Bitou lagoon and the marshy lower reaches of the Bitou River are good places for spotting waterfowl of every kind. The Robberg Nature Reserve is also noted for its great variety of bird species, including rock kestrels and sugarbirds as well as such sea birds as gannets and terns. Birdwatching in the dense forests can be a peculiarly frustrating task, but there are various species that are only found in a forest environment, among them the narina trogon and the Knysna lourie.

Boardsailing
A section of Plettenberg Bay's Central Beach has been demarcated for use by boardsailors and the Keurbooms-Bitou lagoon offers a splendid sheet of sheltered water. It is sometimes possible to hire sailboards in the town, as well as at Central Beach during the holiday season.

Boat trips
It is usually possible to take a launch trip around the bay and along the shores of the Robberg peninsula; inquire at the 'leisure desk' in the foyer of the Beacon Island Hotel. You can also hire powerboats at the Plettenberg

THINGS TO DO

Bay Angling Club on the western bank of the Keurbooms River, giving you the choice of cruising around the lagoon or exploring far upriver.

Bowls
Plettenberg Bay has a bowling club that welcomes visitors, and there are two attractive bowling clubs at Knysna, equally well disposed to visitors and less than a thirty-minute drive away.

Camping and caravanning
There are several camping grounds and caravan parks in this region. Contact the Plettenberg Bay Business and Publicity Association in the first instance. For facilities in the Tsitsikamma parks contact the offices of the National Parks Board.

Canoeing
Canoes and paddleboats can be hired at Central Beach for use on the Piesang River and off the beach itself. You can also hire canoes from the Plettenberg Bay Angling Club on the western bank of the Keurbooms River for use on the Keurbooms-Bitou lagoon as well as on the 'inland' stretch of the Keurbooms River.

Diving
The Underwater Trail in the Tsitsikamma Coastal National Park provides one of the most pleasurable and informative introductions to this stretch of coastline. Another popular venue for scuba divers is Plettenberg Bay. There is an underwater reef off Beacon Island that is kept free of all fishing and the fish here are now so tame that the diver might almost be in a 'natural' aquarium. Other popular diving spots in the area are Whale Rock, Grootbank and Die Eiland. A wide range of underwater diving

A cairn along the Otter Trail.

Fish type	Season	Best area	Best bait
Elf	All year	Beacon Island rocks, Nature's Valley	Sardines, spoons
Galjoen	Winter	Robberg, Oubosstrand	Rotten redbait, white mussels, prawns
Geelbek	Summer	Oubosstrand	Chokka, mackerel
Hottentot	All year	Oubosstrand	Musselworms, prawns, rotten redbait
Kabeljou	Summer	Keurbooms-Bitou Lagoon, Keurboom-strand, Oubosstrand	Chokka, sardines, bloodworms
Leervis	Summer	Robberg Point, Keurbooms-Bitou Lagoon	Live bait, spoons
Red steenbras	Summer	Oubosstrand	Octopus, sardines
Spotted grunter	All year	Keurbooms-Bitou Lagoon	Prawns, bloodworms, pencil bait
White musselcracker	Nov — Mar	Kranshoek — Robberg, Keurboomstrand	Crabs, Venus ear, redbait
White steenbras	Winter	Robberg Beach, Keurboomstrand	Bloodworms, pink prawns, white mussels

equipment can be hired at the Beacon Island Hotel, and instruction in its use is also provided.

Drives and viewsites
The most notable of the scenic drives in this region are the short excursion through the Harkerville Forest to Kranshoek; the longer drive over Prince Alfred's Pass (perhaps including the road through the Knysna Forest at Diepwalle); and the drive on the old R102 through the Grootrivier and Bloukrans passes. Shorter drives in the eastern section of the region are the road to the coast from the Bloukrans Forestry Office and the old Storms River Pass to Oubrug. A recommended viewsite is the parking area at the beginning of the Robberg peninsula — short walks of just a few metres give you fine views to the north over the bay and to the south along the coast.

Golf
There is a golf course at the Plettenberg Bay Country Club, which you reach by driving inland along the Piesang Valley road. Contact the Plettenberg Bay Business and Publicity Association for further details.

Horseriding
Horses may be stabled at the Brookfield Equestrian Centre in Harkerville. Horses can also be hired here and riding classes are held. The Kurland Hunt and Polo Club at The Crags also offers stabling facilities, and sometimes there are horses to be hired.

Libraries
Plettenberg Bay has a small modern library (with a beautiful view from its verandah); contact the municipality for further details.

Powerboating
A section of Plettenberg Bay's Central Beach has been demarcated as a launching area for powerboats, and powerboating and waterskiing are allowed on the Keurbooms River. Small boats with 2,5 hp engines can be hired at the Plettenberg Bay Angling Club on the western bank of the river.

Shipwrecks
Although there have been many wrecks along this stretch of coast, notably the *Sao Gonzales*, the only wreck still visible is that of the *Athena* which went aground in the bay near the base of the Robberg peninsula. It can be seen from above as a dark shape under the water, and scuba divers often visit it.

Surfing
This is not known as a particularly good stretch of coast for surfing. The most popular areas are the 'sanctuary' section of Robberg Beach and a break at the mouth of the Keurbooms-Bitou lagoon (situated at the eastern end of Lookout Beach).

Swimming
Both Central Beach and Lookout Beach are considered fairly safe for swimming, and you can swim in the Piesang and the Keurbooms-Bitou lagoons, but avoid the strong currents at the mouth of the latter. Plettenberg Bay also has a municipal swimming pool. Elsewhere along the coast there is good swimming in the lagoon at Nature's Valley, and in two small inlets alongside the restaurant at Storms River Mouth.

Tennis and squash
There are courts for both games at Plettenberg Bay; contact the

Plettenberg Bay Business and Publicity Association for details.

Walks
In the heart of Plettenberg Bay is the recently created Signal Hill Nature Trail, starting at Signal Hill, then leading through the Piesang Valley and along the beach past the old Timber Store. There is also a magnificent coastal hike at Kranshoek, and a whole network of footpaths crisscrossing the Robberg peninsula.

Two of the country's most popular hikes (and many shorter walks) are associated with the Tsitsikamma National Parks: the five-day Otter and Tsitsikamma trails. The Otter Trail begins at Storms River Mouth and ends 48 km later at Nature's Valley in the west. The short daily distances allow you time to enjoy to the full the succession of headlands and river mouths, the cresting bluffs and coastal vistas. The Tsitsikamma Trail is the Otter Trail's inland twin (but administered by the Directorate of Forestry), and is walked from west to east between the same two points. It meanders through the forests that lie between the coast and the mountains, and climbs the foothills of the mountains through rich fynbos.

Yachting and dinghy sailing
A section of Plettenberg Bay's Central Beach has been specially set aside as a launching area for catamarans and small sailing boats. The surf elsewhere is generally too rough. The Keurbooms-Bitou lagoon is rather shallow for any vessel with a keel.

Where wild white waves wash fragile sea treasures ashore

FROM THE RICH AND RUGGED Garden Route, the coastline pares down to the scrub-bound beaches and dunelands typical of the eastern Cape. The river valleys become shallower and sea cliffs give way to rolling coastal pastures, where the air is tainted with the acrid scent of heath. At the generous sweep of St Francis Bay, the long rows of folded mountains that have followed the shore for nearly 1 000 km seem finally to sink into the ocean and legions of sand dunes stand between land and sea.

These seas of sands are the essence of this holiday mecca. Names such as Cape St Francis and Jeffreys Bay have a special magic, conjuring up visions of long, carefree days sifting through the wealth of shells spread on the sands, tussling to wrest a sparkling host of fish from the waters, and best of all, rising to the challenge of riding what has been called the world's most perfect wave.

1 Tsitsikamma River to Oesterbaai

The first section of this region is generally inaccessible, unless you have four-wheel drive, but it is an angler's paradise. Huisklip, alongside the river mouth, is a combination of rocky and sandy beach that takes its name from a large boulder with a deep groove, as big as a house. It is reached by sandy farm tracks climbing over high stabilised dunes and dropping steeply down again. The sea is usually rough and the swell treacherous.

Access to the river mouth itself is not possible as this is via private property, but from Huisklip avid fishermen are used to footslogging along the shore where cows and sheep, and the occasional ostrich, graze among the grey slangbos, and in spring the bloom of vivid yellow *Moraea*, mauve and yellow daisies and glossy white arum lilies softens an otherwise drab landscape. The low hills inland appear blue-grey in the haze, usually shrouded in low mist.

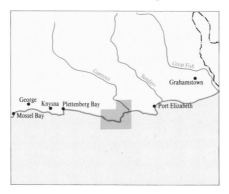

The first really accessible holiday spot along this coastline is Oesterbaai, with its wide beach partly sheltered from the westerly storms. This small holiday outpost has a cosy camp and caravan site, and such attractions as good fishing (especially west of the resort) and fairly safe bathing, although

Swirling foam at the base of Cape St Francis.

the waves do not always break cleanly. When an onshore wind produces *wynwater* (wine water), masses of plankton make the sea seem like a foamy soup and large shoals of fish are drawn to the food source. A favourite fishing spot here is Hendersen's Point, on the western edge of the bay.

A good day's outing can be had by packing a picnic basket and heading east along the rocky shore towards Cape St Francis. The path edges a private nature reserve and then crosses a number of sandy coves where you can swim. The rocky areas, splashed with bright vygies and rust-coloured lichen, offer hours of pleasure in exploring the numerous gullies and pools. No less fascinating is the 15 km-long 'Sand River' that cuts across Cape St Francis from Oesterbaai to St Francis Bay. This natural corridor of moving sand is the source of much of the beach in St Francis Bay, dumped by the sea at Oesterbaai and moved across by the strong westerly winds. This tiny false desert at times comes alive with small animals and birds attracted by the seasonal shallow, reed-fringed pans. Commonly seen here is the black oystercatcher, considered to be an endangered species in South Africa. Fewer than 5 000 of these black birds with their bright red legs and beaks remain on the coast, their existence threatened by such disturbances as seaside resort developments and the use of beach vehicles.

2 Cape St Francis, St Francis Bay and the Kromrivier

The rocky cape of St Francis protects a hooked bay that was named after the patron saint of sailors by the navigator Manuel Perestrello in 1575. He described how the mountain ranges, 'tacked onto one another from the Cape of Good Hope', finally peter out in line with Cape St Francis. Where the mountains end, so do the lush forests of the Garden Route, for the rain clouds are no longer trapped here. The westerly winds that churn up the Tsitsikamma seas are blocked by the aspect of the bay and a golden arc of sand sweeps around

LEFT *The mouth of the Tsitsikamma River, shrouded in sea mist and stillness.*

to the north-east, giving shelter to one of the most exclusive holiday resorts in the country.

On Seal Point, the westernmost extremity of Cape St Francis, is a cylindrical lighthouse, built in 1873 and now a national monument. This marks what local anglers would claim is the best fishing spot in the land. For yellowtail, at least, few people would contest the title and large shoals can still be encountered during the summer.

Cape St Francis is a typical modern holiday development, with a hotchpotch of houses, old and new, and camping and caravanning facilities. Seal Bay, between the two rocky capes, is a good spot for shell collecting and for swimming, but powerful rip currents sometimes form in the surf.

A major attraction is the surf break known locally as 'Seal's' — from the lighthouse to Seal Bay — which is one of the spots that has put this area on the international surfing map. (But it is 'Bruce's', a wave that sweeps down the eastern side of Cape St Francis, that is an orchestration of form and motion to surfers.)

Surfers flocked here from the mid-1960s, and before long the dusty track from Humansdorp to a lonely group of fishing shacks was carrying a throng of holiday-makers to bask in the glorious summers. Fortunately the township developer here set strict aesthetic standards for houses in what was first called Cape St Francis, then Sea Vista and now correctly St Francis Bay. This

holiday resort forms a harmonious whole, the whitewashed, thatched houses blending pleasingly with the dunes and general seascape.

From the bay towards the cape, along the rocky shore where Bruce's waves break, is a spot known as Second Bush. This is the favourite fishing, diving and picnicking spot of the bay, but the track through Santareme Bay township can be very bad. At the end of the track you reach the Cape St Francis Nature Reserve where the natural dune habitat and coastal fynbos are protected. It is possible to walk here from either Cape St Francis or St Francis Bay townships.

Between the mouth of the Kromrivier and the sailing area upriver, where there is a launching

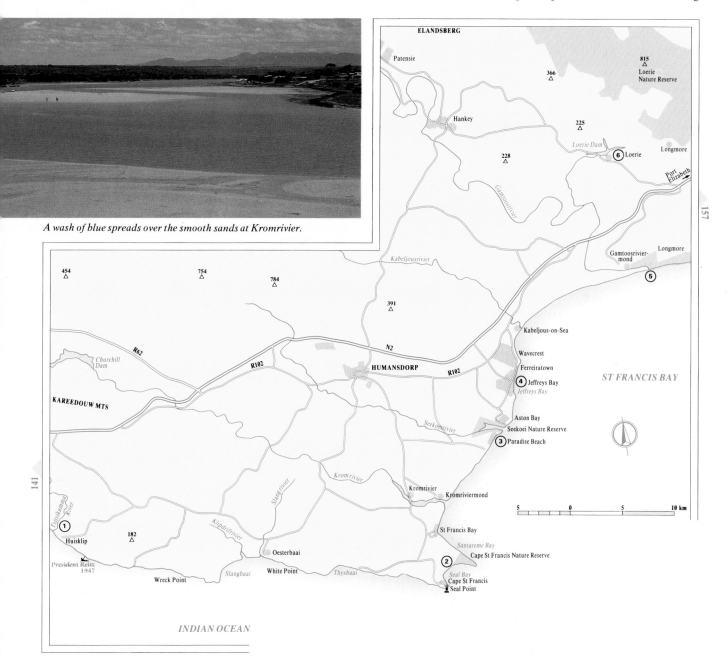

A wash of blue spreads over the smooth sands at Kromrivier.

ramp, lies the first marina resort to be developed in South Africa. The style here is a continuation of the St Francis Bay theme, and residents can cruise the canals and ride out the river mouth to the sea. When not too many powerboats are out, it is pleasant to canoe through the network of canals, past green lawns and jetties and under bridges and then either further upriver or out to sea on the right tide.

In winter aloes brighten the banks of the river, while in spring otherwise dull erica plants burst to life, with their tiny bell-shaped flowers creating a symphony of colour, accompanied by the more brassy tone of trumpet-shaped arum lilies. There are two holiday settlements on the eastern bank of the river, one (Kromriviermond) near the mouth opposite the marina, and the other (Kromrivier) further upriver.

3 Paradise Beach, Seekoeiriviermond and Aston Bay

When the ship *Cape Recife* was wrecked off Cape St Francis in 1929, a crew member managed to release a pair of swans, confined to a crate while being transported on board. They flew to the shore and settled initially on the Kromrivier, but today the few wild swans living in the area congregate around the Seekoeirivier estuary, a nature reserve and bird sanctuary just east of the Kromrivier mouth. On the eastern bank of the river you enter the Seekoei Nature Reserve, where a hide on stilts beside the water makes observation of the swans, cormorants, flamingos and other birds easy.

On the northern side of the river is Aston Bay township, with a swimming pool and public facilities. Paradise Beach holiday resort occupies the southern bank of the river. The private homes — set among the dunes to give protection and good views of the sea and estuary — create a pleasing texture of modern architecture blending into the natural environment. The camping and caravan parks at Aston Bay and Paradise Beach are well laid out, set back from the exposed waterfronts and cut into the natural bush so that each site is

fairly secluded, with nature coming right up to your doorstep. There is good swimming at both Paradise Beach and Aston Bay.

A causeway across the lagoon connects Paradise Beach and Aston Bay, a good place for bait collecting. Between the sandy areas of the beach, the several rocky platforms make fine fishing spots. At low tide you are likely to catch small reef fish, while at high tide the bays between the reefs become a source for some very large surf fish. When the sea is rough the beach east of Aston Bay is excellent for reef fish.

4 Jeffreys Bay, Kabeljous-on-Sea and Humansdorp

In the last century, before the construction of railway lines, the little communities in this part of the country were served by coasters that docked in the bay. To channel the goods a store was started here in 1849 by two partners named Jeffrey and Glendinning. Long after the store vanished, the settlement that grew around it retained the name of one of its founders.

Twenty or more years ago, Jeffreys Bay was a quiet fishing village where local fishermen launched their small craft into the bay each dawn and life was slow and generally hard. During the 1960s, however, holiday-makers discovered the excellent swimming beaches here, where each high tide deposited a glowing treasure of shells... cowries, harp and helmet shells, comb and cone shells, paper nautiluses and pansy shells.

In time Jeffreys Bay grew to be the most important holiday centre of St Francis Bay, situated between the already established centres of Algoa and Plettenberg bays. (On closer examination, these half-heart-shaped bays follow an ever-tightening spiral from the long arcs of sweeping beaches to their rocky points. Look on a map and you will see the same pattern repeated right around the South African coastline; the waves approaching the coast erode the windward side of the points and deposit sand on the leeward side, creating these mathematically precise shapes,

ABOVE *A moment of unparalleled peace and privacy at Jeffreys Bay.*

just like that seen in the perlemoen shells that litter the beaches. If you continued the curve of each bay inward, the arc would form a concentric spiral.)

While avid fishermen and shell collectors returned summer after summer to Jeffreys Bay, their children were becoming part of a new surfing culture that was growing around the world. Before long they realised that Jeffreys Bay was among the most ideal places to surf, with a tubing wave not quite as good as Bruce's but far more consistent. Surfers who found it hard to leave such an idyllic spot have turned Jeffreys Bay into a year-round fun place to be, making their living there by handcrafting clothes, jewellery and leatherware for the summer holiday trade, and exporting their craft to the commercial centres of the country.

LEFT *A composite of lichen and bright flowers in Cape St Francis Nature Reserve.*

enjoyment of nature. The osprey, that migratory fishing eagle with its white and brown plumage and 'mask', can be seen resting on the shores of the lagoon or soaring over the water. When it sees a fish it hovers directly above and then plunges feet first into the water, rises, shakes its wings dry and then takes off with its prey grasped in its talons. Redbilled teal and yellowbilled ducks glide along the backwaters but take strongly to the air when approached; redknobbed coots bob around the reed fringes where stark white egrets probe the mud for frogs and crabs. Purple herons stride through the reed beds and short grass and when they take off, are all neck and dangling legs as they hover and glide short distances ahead of any danger. The blue lagoon is fringed by silvery-

'DEM'S BIG WAVES!'

Riding the waves at Cape St Francis.

In 1961 two American surfers embarked on a world surfing and filming safari. One scene from the film they subsequently made of their adventures shows them on a sandy track leading to a lonely, wintery eastern Cape beach. They ask a local fisherman if there are any waves in the area and he replies, pointing towards St Francis Bay: 'Oh yes, dem's big waves dere.' As luck would have it, Bruce Brown and his companion arrived here on one of the few days each year when 'the world's most perfect wave' thunders down the bay.

The film *Endless Summer* immortalised the wave that breaks down the inside western arm of the bay and it has henceforth been known simply as Bruce's. The wave works only in a north-westerly wind at low tide, directly after an easterly wind has whipped up a big ground swell in the bay; then these large waves peel along the rocky shore, throwing out 4 m-high barrels of water for one of the longest rides possible.

Later surfers, always in search of a more perfect wave, found that in nearby Jeffreys Bay there was a break that, while not quite matching the force and beauty of Bruce's, was far more consistent and worked all year round. This dangerous but exhilarating wave — Super Tubes — sweeps steeply along and in towards the rocks, throwing out churning white water in what among surfers is termed a tube. To ride inside a large tube is considered to be the ultimate surfing experience, but only a truly proficient surfer can manage this breathtaking ride, catching the wave at its breaking lip and then cutting back to sit inside the thundering, whirling vortex of translucent sea water.

Moving eastwards up the coastline, you reach the adjoining holiday townships of Wavecrest and Kabeljous-on-Sea, between the deep turquoise of the Kabeljous lagoon, the golden ribbons of beach and the emerald green of lucerne fields. Following the course of the river you find an unusual type of veld (known as valley bushveld) where succulents and thorn trees abound. The salt-spray aroma of the small, inconspicuous herb *Agathosma* spikes the air, inspiring a flood of seaside memories. On the river's edge fish eagles perch on the tall succulents, issuing their spine-chilling call. Among the cabbage trees and bitter aloes the bush is alive with smaller birds, and while weavers and sunbirds prefer the nectar of aloe blooms, doves and starlings — and children — love the astringent fruit of the cat-thorn.

Inland from this string of holiday settlements (linked by the R102 to Jeffreys Bay) is Humansdorp, on the grassy plain where the folded mountains end. Along with the burgeoning

development of the coast, this town has also grown from an insignificant railway village into an important commercial and agricultural centre. Three hotels, a motel and a caravan park here make up for the rather scant facilities at the St Francis Bay resorts. The town is on the narrow gauge Apple Express line that runs between Port Elizabeth and Avontuur.

5 Gamtoosriviermond
Lying midway in the wide sweep of beach and dunes of St Francis Bay, this river mouth creates a rich lagoon wetland with more bird life than anywhere else in the area. The entire mouth area and massed surrounding dunes are a forestry reserve but a camp site and picnic spots are found here. Upstream of the mouth is the convenience of a second caravan park and just beyond the national road is a hotel at the site of the original ferry crossing of the river.

Gamtoosriviermond is a place for the quiet

THE LIVING SAND

Forms sculpted in sea sand.

When summer finds you dreaming on the sizzling beach at St Francis Bay, try to imagine the sand beneath you as a living organism, for it moves and, in a sense, eats and breathes too.

Winter storm waves devour large sections of these beaches, but year after year, the sand is replenished. Between St Francis Bay and Oesterbaai is what is known as the Sand River, a constant stream of sand moved by the westerly winds to replenish the beaches on the sheltered side of the bay. This happens all around the coastline, so that while beaches themselves appear to be permanent, the actual sand that makes

them is constantly on the move, driven like conveyor belts by ocean currents and winds.

Each square metre of beach sand is packed with tiny animals making up a mass of about 1,5 kg, so that this is one of the richest natural systems in the world. These tiny organisms can be likened to the digestive system, the kidneys and the lungs of this sand creature. Every day, 10-million ℓ of sea water are flushed through each kilometre of beach. This water brings decaying material from the sea, which is then broken down (or 'digested') and returned to the sea as pure nutrients of the food chain. At the same time, the water is cleansed of any pollution. And while this is happening, the wave action on the beach oxygenates the water.

Man has not been content to leave nature to its own devices, and with constantly shifting seas of sand creating headaches for township developers, many of the dunes have been stabilised by planting exotics, like rooikrans and Port Jackson willow (*Acacia cyclops* and *A. saligna*), where nothing else would grow. These, in turn, have choked natural bush, and the upshot is that these legendary beaches in their splendid settings will never again be quite as magnificent as nature intended.

kingfishers perch jewel-like on branches, reflecting in the water among the water lilies; rednecked francolins foraging in the grass under the yellowwoods scatter in a whir of wings at your approach; in the aloe gardens bright yellow weavers, metallic sunbirds and starlings flit brazenly around the camp sites.

Between Hankey and Patensie the road again descends into the Gamtoos valley, winding along the field edges where boulder hills have been sliced through by river and road; in springtime yellow and white daisies, soft mauve geraniums and blue irises line the road and cling to the lower slopes.

At Patensie, a busy little agricultural centre, you will be faced with three choices. The first — making a full day's outing — is to carry on straight, up the long gravel road through the Baviaanskloof and all the way to Willowmore, a drive on gravel for nearly 200 km through spectacular scenery. The second choice is to turn right after Patensie to ascend the Elandsberg range and look across a crinkled brown and green landscape to the prominent Cockscomb peaks. The third choice is to do an about turn where the tarred road ends some way out of Patensie and head back the way you came, or south via Humansdorp and back to the coast.

topped reeds and surrounded by massive golden sand dunes. Far beyond to the north-east, the Cockscomb stretches out as a blue-grey silhouette.

6 Inland via Loerie, Hankey and Patensie

From the mouth of the Gamtoos, take a leisurely drive inland and explore the quiet countryside. Across the N2 to Port Elizabeth, the main road to Loerie leads into a valley spilling out over a wide fertile floodplain that is a ribbon of intense irrigated agriculture sandwiched between hills of dry bushveld. In the thick tangled bush alongside the road vervet monkeys play, just waiting for a chance to raid the fields. After reaching a T-junction, the road leads to the small town of Loerie. Above it lies the Loerie Dam, and still beyond this, in a hidden valley, the small but developing Loerie Nature Reserve. Here you can go hiking or canoe amid scenic mountains. The puffing Apple Express passes through the town on its way up the Langkloof.

From Loerie, named after the bird found in the forests around here, the road climbs the rank of hills that line the Gamtoos valley to reach the attractive town of Hankey, which was founded as a Khoi mission station in 1822 and named after a treasurer of the London Missionary Society. As the road enters the town, a sign on your left says 'Enjoy View': a viewsite here gives excellent vistas of the richly textured and lush valley below, and the surrounding natural bush is alive with bird life.

The little town itself does not take long to explore, and continuing onwards you reach Yellowwoods, a camping site where these massive trees stand in a copse alongside a stream and create huge spreading canopies, uncharacteristic of the usually towering forest giants. Malachite

SHELLS: SCULPTED JEWELS OF THE OCEANS

Along the southern African seashore, few places are more plentifully supplied with seashells than Jeffreys Bay. Some very rare shells are found here, especially the beautiful cowries that are so highly prized.

Few people who casually collect shells along the beaches here during their holidays realise that these wave-worn sculptural marvels are really the skeletons of living creatures often far more beautiful than their exterior casings. The life story of each mollusc will be reflected in the shape of its shell, which grows along with its inhabitant. The creature's mantle (folded fleshy tissue) excretes a solution of lime that hardens

in a matrix of crystal rings around it to form the shell. In this way the shape of the mantle will determine the sculptural elements of its shell. Ornamental features of the shell, like spines or nodules, are determined by the degree of frilling of the mantle edge. The sometimes brilliant colours of the mantle may be determined by dyes in the food eaten, which are transferred to the shell to camouflage the white lime.

Jeffreys Bay is a good locality for shells because of the pocket bays that form between rocky gullies, where the shells are trapped unbroken — to form the basis of an important 'industry' here.

BELOW *The green valley of the Gamtoos, with the shadowy silhouette of Cockscomb in the distance.*

THINGS TO DO

Angling
Excellent fishing can be had along this coastline, with Seal Point probably being a front runner in popularity.

Beachcombing and shelling
Jeffreys Bay is generally considered the best spot along the whole southern African coast for shelling. Near St Francis Bay the Second Bush area has many tidal pools teeming with both shells and sea life, while the nature reserve beach is good for combing. On the opposite side of the point is Seal Bay, which along with Oesterbaai and its nearby rocky gullies can also be rewarding.

Birdwatching
The lagoon on the Gamtoos is the best place to observe sea and land birds, with ospreys and fish eagles often seen here, as well as ducks and waders. The Krom, Seekoei and Kabeljous are all good places to see birds; the further upriver you go, the fewer marine birds and more terrestial birds and raptors you will see. Oystercatchers and beach waders, especially the summer migrants, abound around the river mouths, while land waders such as flamingos, as well as wild swans and fish eagles may be seen on any of the four major rivers in the area.

Boardsailing
Upstream of the marina on the Krom is a special boardsailing lagoon, but the Seekoei and Kabeljous lagoons are also good spots. When conditions are right, boardsailors take to the sea from Hobby Beach in St Francis Bay.

Bowls
The Jeffreys Bay and Humansdorp country clubs have many sporting facilities, including bowling greens.

Camping and caravanning
There is a small but attractive camp and caravan site at Oesterbaai. Humansdorp, Cape St Francis (not St Francis Bay), Paradise Bay, Jeffreys Bay, Kabeljous-on-Sea and Gamtoosriviermond (and inland) all have caravan parks with camping facilities; Hankey has a camp site and Patensie has a municipal caravan park.

Canoeing
The Kromrivier and the associated marina are possibly the most popular canoeing areas, but the Seekoei, Kabeljous and Gamtoos are all tranquil spots for a quiet paddle.

Diving
The best places to dive are on either side of Cape St Francis proper (also known as Far Point). Second Bush on

the St Francis Bay side is most sheltered but when conditions are right the Seal Bay side is more challenging.

Drives and viewsites
The best drive is from Gamtoosriviermond following the river to Loerie, then up to Hankey and Patensie and either on up Baviaanskloof or east over the Elandsberg. Note that beyond Patensie the roads are gravel and generally quite poor.

Golf
There are full golf courses at both St Francis Bay and the Jeffreys Bay Country Club. A golf course is also run by the Hankey Country Club.

Horseriding
Horseriding is possible only at St Francis Bay, and inquiries can be made through the hotel.

Libraries
Humansdorp and Jeffreys Bay have libraries, and the latter houses the Charlotte Kritzinger shell collection.

Powerboating
It is possible to powerboat and waterski on the Krom, upstream of the marina

area where yachting holds priority, but licence holders can launch powerboats from the river or marina out the mouth. The Kabeljous lagoon is also a popular spot for powerboating but care should be taken not to disturb the prolific wildlife here.

Shipwrecks
As is the case along most of the coast, while many ships have been wrecked off the rocky points, little remains to be seen and often that can be approached only through private land. A well-known shipwreck along this stretch is that of the *President Reitz* (off Huisklip near the Tsitsikamma in 1947). In 1929 the *Cape Recife* was wrecked off Cape St Francis, leading to the release of the swans now well established in the area.

Surfing
For surfing there are few places in the world that compare with St Francis Bay, with seldom a time when good surf cannot be found somewhere in the area. While Bruce's is considered the best (breaking along the Second Bush area of the main bay), it works only once or twice a year. Super Tubes at Jeffreys Bay, east of the main swimming beach,

produces an awesome and consistent tube that has now become the prime surf spot of the area. Seal Point, Seal Bay and St Francis Bay all have variable beach and point breaks, depending on the swell and wind.

Swimming
All the resorts in the area have excellent swimming beaches but for the all-round best conditions St Francis Bay cannot be beaten. Oesterbaai is generally a little rougher than the beaches lying further east.

Tennis and squash
The Jeffreys Bay Country Club offers tennis and squash, as well as badminton. Tennis courts are also available at the Humansdorp Country Club, Kabeljous caravan park, Cape St Francis and St Francis Bay.

Walks
Short walks can be taken from Oesterbaai eastwards towards Seal Point, around the Gamtoos lagoon and the St Francis Bay and Seekoei River nature reserves. Just outside Hankey a viewsite is reached at the natural stone arch called the Bergvenster, up a steep slope. Slightly longer walks are possible in the Loerie Nature Reserve, while the Cockscomb peaks in the Groot-Winterhoekberge offer true wilderness conditions where only experienced hikers should venture.

Yachting and dinghy sailing
Once again St Francis Bay offers the best sailing facilities with the Kromrivier marina having been developed especially as a refuge for ocean-going yachts. Hobby Beach (St Francis Bay) and Jeffreys Bay are launching sites for smaller boats.

Fish type	Season	Best area	Best bait
Baardman	All year	Huisklip (Tsitsikamma), Oesterbaai, St Francis Bay	Wonderworms, sand prawns, white mussels
Bronze bream	All year	Huisklip, Paradise Beach, Aston Bay	Wonderworms, prawns
Elf	Summer	Huisklip, Henderson's Point (Oesterbaai), Seal Point, Paradise Beach, Aston Bay	Sardines, strepie
Galjoen	July—Aug	Huisklip, Henderson's Point	Worms, redbait, mussels
Kabeljou	Summer	Huisklip, Oesterbaai, Seal Point, Paradise Beach, Aston Bay, Kabeljous-on-Sea to Gamtoosriviermond	Live mullet, sardines, mackerel, spinners
Leervis	Summer	Oesterbaai, Seal Point, Gamtoosriviermond	Mullet, lures
Mussel-cracker	All year	Huisklip, Aston Bay to Jeffreys Bay	Venus ear, prawns
Red steenbras	All year	Huisklip, Seal Point	Live bait, mackerel, chokka
Sharks and skates	All year	Cape St Francis, Paradise Beach, Kabeljous and Gamtoos mouths	Fish heads (sharks), sardines, chokka (skates)
White steenbras	All year	Oesterbaai, Seal Point, Gamtoosriviermond	Prawns, worms, crabs
Yellowtail	Summer	Seal Point	Spinners

INFORMATION
- Algoa Regional Services Council, PO Box 318, Port Elizabeth 6000. Tel 041=561000
- Humansdorp Municipality, PO Box 26, Humansdorp 6300. Tel 04231=51111
- Jeffreys Bay Municipality, PO Box 21, Jeffreys Bay 6330. Tel 04231=31111
- St Francis/Kromme River Trust, 9 George St, St Francis Bay 6312.
- National Sea Rescue Institute, Kromrivier Marina, PO St Francis Bay 6312. Tel 04231=4545/4231
  Nearest AA Office
- AA House, 2 Granville Rd, Greenacres, Port Elizabeth 6001. Tel 041=341313

Feast in the fun of a friendly port of call

I N YEARS GONE BY, the site of present-day Port Elizabeth was referred to on navigational charts only as a 'landing place with fresh water' — but even so, it was not a very attractive one, with open Algoa Bay often swept by harsh winds. It was the development of the 'Friendly City' that changed the bay's inhospitable reputation. Here it was that the 1820 Settlers were welcomed to their new land, and here they built their graceful period homes that today help to soften the silhouette of a modern, busy city.

Port Elizabeth sprawls comfortably in all directions, its smooth sweeps of beach thronged by thousands basking in the sun and fun of the seaside. Strung like so many pearls around the bay and linked by scenic coastal drives are satellite holiday resorts, all offering something special to the visitor: great waves to ride, a thrust of prime angling rocks, a breath of African wildlife....

The sinuous line of the harbour breakwater creating sheltered waters.

1 Van Stadensmond

Dwarfed by massive sand dunes and with the Van Staden's River gently lapping at its edges, this resort, the first in the run-up to Port Elizabeth, nestles in a sheltered amphitheatre. The turn-off from the N2 takes you through undulating wooded country before a steep descent to the river, closed to the sea most of the year and navigable for some distance inland.

Kilometres of unspoilt beach entice the jogger and walker, and also offer good surf angling. Currents make the sea itself dangerous for swimming, but the lagoon is a pleasant alternative. Paddleboats and canoes can be hired for use in the lagoon, which also makes good, if a little tame, boardsailing water; for the adventurous, sandskis are available to tackle the dunes. Facilities at the resort include thatched rondavels and camp sites sandwiched between indigenous bush and pounding surf, as well as a small café, table tennis under cover and a playpark for the youngsters.

2 Van Staden's Gorge and reserve

The pass to the bottom of this 125 m-deep gorge is a pleasant, winding drive that, like many of the original passes in South Africa, has now been by-passed by more direct, quicker routes. But this longer deviation along the 'old Cape Road' through wooded slopes is well worth it: with the hum of traffic from the modern bridge high overhead, you can relax in the cool calm of the Van Staden's rock pools, wander along the banks of the river and braai in shady spots immediately below the gorge rockface.

Standing on a destroyed causeway and with the old bridge in front of you, there is time to admire an engineering feat: one of the longest concrete arch bridges in southern Africa (350 m), spanning the gorge. The arch was built simultaneously from opposite banks and opened in 1971.

Another view of the bridge can be had from the Van Staden's Wild Flower Reserve along the eastern banks of the gorge. The reserve comprises

RIGHT *The still expanse of Van Stadensmond cast in silvery light.*

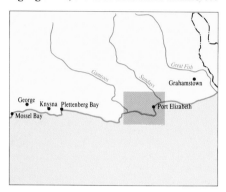

southern wooded slopes and northern river banks but is largely a plateau that in ox-wagon days was an outspan on the road to the Gamtoos valley, the Langkloof, and Cape Town. The reserve protects a wide range of flowering plants, particularly the naturally occurring erica and protea fynbos, but many other plants have also been introduced.

Although there are good gravel roads throughout, this is a 'walkabout' reserve and signs encourage you to leave your car. Besides the many strolls, there are two longer walks in the reserve:

the River Walk, which begins opposite the main picnic area and follows a contour between the Van Staden's River and the plateau, eventually descending to river level; and the Forest Walk, which descends through fynbos to a shady kloof before entering a forest.

The reserve also offers a specimen house (on the left as your enter), where you can also obtain drinking water, dams with waterfowl, some swimmable river pools and shady picnic sites (but no overnight camping).

3 Maitland River Mouth

This river, rather marred by two elevated pipelines across its mouth, has a large camping and caravan site along the east bank, just a short wade away from the huge sand dune on the opposite bank. Facilities include braai places, ablution blocks and taps. The main attraction of the resort is angling, with local enthusiasts recommending this as the best spot for galjoen.

Above the river mouth is the Maitland Mines Nature Reserve, named after a 19th-century lead mine in the area. Entrance to the reserve is through

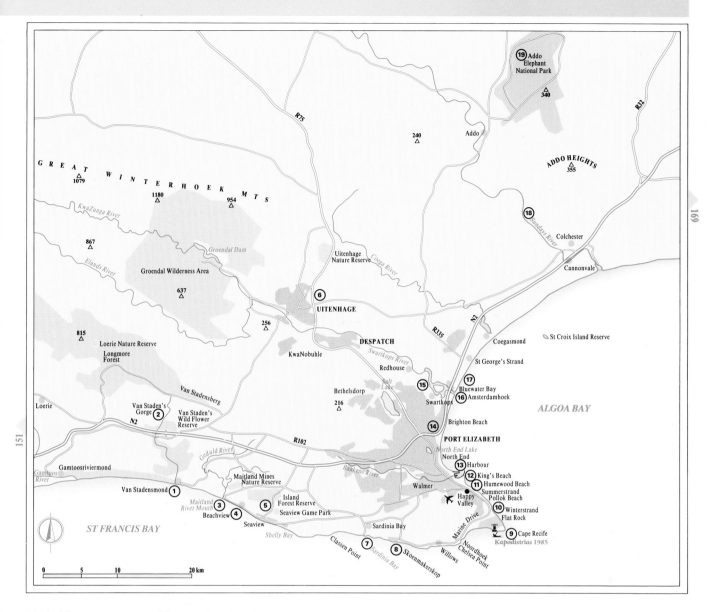

a locked farm-type gate west of the coastal road. An undulating path, in part along an old wagon trail, passes through virgin forest where an abundance of bird life can be seen; and if you are lucky you might spot bushbuck, blue duiker, aardvark and porcupine. To add to your appreciation of the reserve, conservation literature is provided in boxes along the route. A free entrance permit (and the key to the gate!) is obtainable from nearby Beachview resort.

4 Beachview and Seaview
The terraced Beachview holiday resort above this rocky coast is primarily a caravanner's park, but there are chalets and tent sites sheltered by natural windbreaks, and day visitors are welcome.

Here you can braai on a grassy area just above the rocks while watching dolphins playing in the surf; you can potter about on the small beach among the rock pools or swim in the tidal pool; or

you can enjoy some fine rock angling. Resort features include a restaurant, café, tennis court and a playpark, and it is handily near the Maitland Mines Nature Reserve and Seaview Game Park.

One of the most pleasant aspects of Seaview is the drive there, taking you over gently rolling hills past homesteads tucked cosily away behind towering bluegums.

Seaview itself is a small cluster of homes centred around a hotel. For swimming there is a large, weather-beaten tidal pool as well as a children's pool. There is no beach as such but low tide reveals large gullies and pools among the rocks. For the energetic, the coastal walk to Maitland River Mouth past Beachview offers fine views.

5 Island Forest Reserve and Seaview Game Park
Just off the Seaview-Maitland River Mouth coastal drive is the Island Forest Reserve, offering self-guided walks down forestry roads, alongside pine

plantations and through indigenous bush and forest. Known collectively as the Bushbuck Walk there are several circuit trails, varying in length from a 1,5 km stroll around the forester's home and office to a 16 km hike right around the reserve.

All the trails are over easy terrain, although the longer ones might prove to be tiring in hot weather. They also provide some excellent viewsites (from a beacon that can be scaled using an iron ladder, or from a fire lookout tower over the entire forest and stretching as far afield as Jeffreys Bay and Cape St Francis).

Marked on a map obtainable from the forester are several trees of special interest: a fine hard pear tree, white Cape beech, Cape teak, Cape chestnut, Outeniqua yellowwood, and a veld fig growing around a bush boer-bean. More than eighty different birds have been spotted in the reserve and vervet monkey, bushpig and small antelope, including the rare blue duiker, might be also seen.

There is a picnic and braai site (with water) near the entrance, but there are no facilities for overnight camping.

Seaview Game Park, just 2,5 km from Seaview resort, transports you from the roar of the surf to that of Africa. This private park features rhinoceros, lion, cheetah, giraffe, nyala, warthog, lynx, wildebeest, monkey and a variety of antelope. You can enjoy the park in a number of ways. From the wide wooden verandah of the tearoom, above the park, you have a panoramic view of the surrounding hills. You can walk through the large aviary with its many indigenous species or follow a catwalk into the heart of the cheetah enclosure. Conducted tours are also available, and if you get there at the right time, you can watch the cheetahs or lions being fed.

The park has a caravan and camping site with toilet facilities and (cold) showers.

6 Uitenhage

There was a time in Uitenhage when not to own (and be able to ride) a horse was considered a disgrace as frequent calls were made upon citizens to rally to the call to arms as a mounted commando. Nowadays Uitenhage, situated on the banks of the Swartkops River at the foot of the Winterhoek, is a peaceful, shady, industrial town barely thirty minutes from Port Elizabeth on the freeway.

The 'senior' town of the eastern Cape (it was a thriving village when Port Elizabeth consisted of only a fort and farmhouse), Uitenhage has retained many links with its past, including, in its main thoroughfare Caledon Street, the old Drostdy (1806), which now houses the Africana Museum, the ornate Victoria Tower (1899) and the Dutch Reformed Church (1843).

Just out of town on the Port Elizabeth road is Cuyler Manor, one-time home of General Jacob Cuyler, landdrost of the district. With the aid of a sketch drawn in 1827 the building has been restored to reflect the style of those pioneer days

and has an adjacent watermill. (A mohair farm situated here offers visitors demonstrations of spinning and weaving and further related attractions are also being planned.)

Two other national monuments in Uitenhage, Blenheim House in Baird Street, with its metre-thick clay and straw walls, and the Railway Museum in Market Street, are particularly well worth visiting, as is the monument on the site of the former Boer War concentration camp at Pannel's Mill.

Other attractions include Magennis Park (off Church Street), a popular park with an aviary, fountains and flowerbeds; the Willows Dam where the small working steam engine *Little Bess* is a must for children; and the Cannon Hill cactus garden with its fine view of the town.

The resort and nature reserve known locally as the Springs, situated 8 km out of town on the Graaff-Reinet road, is named for the artesian springs bubbling millions of litres of crystal-clear water up from the ground.

The resort offers visitors facilities such as chalets, rondavels, a caravan park and camp sites, swimming pools, tennis courts and a restaurant, and has horses and ponies for hire. The reserve has four walks, varying in duration from thirty minutes to five hours and offering superb views as far as Algoa Bay and the chance to admire the more than 300 plant and tree species.

Further afield is the Groendal wilderness area, protecting Uitenhage's main water supply (Groendal Dam) and believed to have been the last refuge of the San between the Gamtoos and Kei rivers. The vegetation is valley, bushveld and false fynbos; various buck may be seen as well as baboons and wild pigs; and forest birds — especially the Knysna lourie, with its distinctive green plumage — are plentiful.

Blindekloof (16 km) is the best-known walk, approached from the forest station where details of other walks can be obtained. These vary in difficulty but remember that the remoteness,

combined with the danger of heat exhaustion in summer, has inherent dangers. Permits are obtainable from the Groendal forester.

7 Sardinia Bay

Surrounded by a marine and beach reserve, Sardinia Bay is a popular spot for long walks along an unspoilt shore. The area is known for its potentially unstable dunes, and extensive efforts have been made by conservation authorities to protect them. The marine reserve serves not only to protect marine organisms but is used as a reference area to study dune movement.

Sardinia Bay is also a popular swimming spot, but the dangerous undercurrents mean that great care should be exercised at all times. Stick to the demarcated swimming area where lifeguards are on duty during peak times. A large boardwalk

LEFT *Sandy dunes stretch between Van Stadens-mond and Maitland River Mouth.*

runs from the parking area and ablution block across the dunes to the beach. Because the beach forms part of a reserve, no fishing is allowed but you may launch powerboats from the beach. The coastal walk through the reserve from Sardinia Bay to Skoenmakerskop is very popular, and in springtime offers the particularly striking sight of thousands of pink forest lilies growing on a hillside of stunted knee-high milkwoods.

8 Skoenmakerskop and Willows
The hamlet of Skoenmakerskop with its single tearoom and handful of houses (whose most famous one-time resident was playwright Athol Fugard) overlooks the rocky coastline where the Portuguese galleon *Sacramento* was smashed to pieces. In the plentiful gullies and rock pools to explore, you may even pick up centuries-old ebony from the wreck. About a kilometre from Skoenmakerskop is a high, man-made dune placed to cut off a gulchway along which drifting sand once moved to threaten the suburbs of Walmer, South End and Humewood.

Moving towards Willows you reach Mangold's Pool, a caravan site almost on the beach with a magnificent tidal pool taking full advantage of the natural gullies in the area. The Willows holiday resort itself offers superb caravan, tent, cottage and bungalow accommodation, with picnic spots, two tidal pools, a tennis court, shop and restaurant. Fishermen rate the rock angling here along with the finest in the world, and the Noordehoek powerboat angling club is situated handily nearby.

9 Cape Recife
The lighthouse at Cape Recife is the third oldest in the country and is still manned to warn mariners of the dangers of Thunderbolt Reef and Recife Point. This area is the graveyard of many vessels, including the *Paris Maru* (1901) and the *Pati* (1976), both of which have since disappeared, as well as of the more recent *Kapodistrias* (1985).

A favourite area for anglers, fishing is by permit only to allow the area — a reserve — time to recover from overexploitation of bait and damage by off-road vehicles. The sewage settling ponds in the reserve combine with the coastline and scrub of the cape to attract vast numbers of birds, especially waders. You can expect to see, among others, flamingo, teal, gannet, cormorant, tern, duck, bulbul, robin and shrike. You can walk the attractive circuit of the reserve, or stroll for short distances at a time. Entrance for beachwalkers to the reserve is free, but if you intend to drive in you must first obtain a permit (from the manager's office at Happy Valley, Humewood).

10 Winterstrand, Pollok Beach and Summerstrand
Next to the Cape Recife Reserve is Winterstrand, a favourite braai spot with sites tucked in next to the dunes that line Marine Drive. The beach itself

RIGHT *The lonely lighthouse guarding a deceptively peaceful Cape Recife.*

The rocky coastline embracing a little pocket of clean white sand and green bush at Skoenmakerskop.

is rocky. Next-door Pollok Beach, popular among surfers for its hard-running breakers, is a mainly sandy beach with a rocky outcrop at one end creating a sheltered area for children and an excellent angling spot.

Summerstrand is famous for sailing, and weekends see a colourful spectacle at the aptly named Hobie Beach. There is a launch ramp here but no lifesavers are on duty, so take extra care.

A very pleasant path runs along Summerstrand, ideal — with its conveniently placed benches — for that lazy stroll. A monument here to renowned Voortrekker leader Piet Retief commemorates the fact that Summerstrand was originally part of his farm Strandfontein.

11 Humewood Beach and Happy Valley
Of all Port Elizabeth's beaches, Humewood is the best known. Protected all day by municipal

lifeguards, it is sheltered by the promenade above, where the change-rooms are situated.

From the beach there is direct access through a subway beneath Marine Drive to Happy Valley, an area of level lawns with a path running alongside a stream and lily ponds. During the summer months it is illuminated with a display of colourful lights and nursery rhyme figures. More fun can be had by playing on the giant chessboard here (the pieces are available from the beach manager's office). Other facilities include the McArthur swimming pool beyond Humewood, with its freshwater and tidal swimming pools and two supervised water slides for young children.

About 200 000 visitors a year visit the Port Elizabeth museum complex opposite Humewood Beach. The complex, unique in southern Africa, embraces natural and cultural history museums as well as an oceanarium, snake park, tropical house and children's museum.

The museum is the third oldest in South Africa and has marine and bird halls, a historical and costume hall, a curiosity corner, as well as many natural science, archaeological and geological exhibitions. The 'touch' museum introduces young children to the animal world.

The snake park houses about 150 indigenous and exotic snakes, crocodiles, alligators and pythons (measuring nearly 5 m!). Leading from it is the tropical house, a large free-flight aviary in which the beauty of more than forty species of birds is enhanced by a setting of waterfalls and bridges among lush tropical vegetation. In addition, there is a night house in which nocturnal animals may be observed.

The oceanarium was established in 1960 and has large fish tanks, penguin and seal pools and a dolphin lake. Devil firefish, angelfish, rays, sharks and sea turtles, among others, can all be seen, and at the underwater observatory you can watch the grace of the dolphins.

Humewood Beach, nudging the city, is the focus of seaside fun in Port Elizabeth.

12 King's Beach

So named because the British royal family swam here in 1947, King's Beach offers excellent swimming and surfing, with no backwash and municipal lifesavers on duty at all times. The 1,6 km-long beach is lined with change-rooms, children's paddling pools and water slides, as well as an open-air amphitheatre, the Sea Breeze Express miniature train (operating daily in season), miniature golf and trampolines. During the summer a regular beach, entertainment programme in the amphitheatre is organised by the municipality.

13 Port Elizabeth Harbour

Although explorers suggested as far back as the 18th century that a harbour in Algoa Bay would open up the surrounding areas to trade and commerce, it was not until 1933 that Port Elizabeth finally saw the opening of the docks. In the interim many ships were sunk or driven ashore by the south-east gales that often swept the bay.

A good place to start any exploration of the harbour is at the Campanile next to the railway station. A stiff climb up a narrow spiral staircase (204 steps) ends on a viewing platform with a commanding view of the city and harbour. This 52 m-high brick structure was completed in 1923 and commemorates the landing of the 1820 Settlers just south of the tower on what was then a beach. From the tower the relationship between Market Square and the harbour, once joined by Jetty Street, is clear and it is easy to imagine townfolk wandering down to the North Jetty to greet incoming ships. Unfortunately the harbour has now been divorced from the city by a flyover.

A tranquil glimpse of the normally bustling harbour in Algoa Bay.

At the King's Beach end of the harbour the manganese ore jetty, the fishing trawlers and the Algoa Bay Yacht Club moorings lie within close proximity of one another, and here, too, are the headquarters of the National Sea Rescue Institute and the Port Elizabeth Deep Sea Angling Club. Flanking the yacht club is the tug quay gate, and these spic-and-span workhorses of the sea are well worth a visit. It is from here that the tug *Blue Jay* leaves to take visitors on trips around the bay.

Walking back towards the Campanile you pass the citizen force naval unit, SAS Donkin, before reaching No 2 and No 3 quays. This is literally the

---

THE MYTH THAT LAUNCHED A THOUSAND SHIPS

While Port Elizabeth's Horse Memorial is justly famous as one of possibly only two memorials to the horse in the world, an equally unusual but lesser-known monument stands opposite the Post Office in Market Square. This is the monument to a man who never lived — the mythical king-priest Prester John who, during the Middle Ages, was thought to rule over a realm of 'the three Indies' somewhere in the region of Ethiopia.

Although he may never have existed, Prester John was partly responsible for Europeans reaching southern Africa for it was his mysterious reputation that for many centuries helped drive explorers on their search for the sea route to India. In 1165 a letter allegedly written by Prester John was sent to the Byzantine emperor, Manuel I, and to the Holy Roman emperor, Frederick Barbarossa. It described Prester John's realm as 'a land of natural riches, marvels, peace and justice, administered by a court of archbishops, priors and kings'. When John II of Portugal, continuing the work of Prince Henry the Navigator, sent out expeditions to find the route to India, he instructed the leaders to seek the kingdom of Prester John.

Although Portuguese explorers did finally reach Ethiopia in the 15th century, the legend died only in the 18th century when Scottish explorer James Bruce penetrated that land during his search for the source of the Nile.

Port Elizabeth's monument is described by sculptor Phil Kolbe as 'born of both legend and history' and is dedicated to the memory of the Portuguese seafarers and their quest for Prester John. In the form of an Ethiopian Coptic cross, the sculpture (unveiled in 1986) shows Prester John and a Portuguese mariner.

end of the line for much of South Africa's citrus for it is here that the Apple Express finally delivers the fruit of the Gamtoos valley. Vast cooling sheds dominate the quay and tons of citrus and apples are stored here before being shipped overseas.

The Charl Malan Quay on the northern side of the harbour stands on the spot of the old iron pile North Jetty. The iron jetty was buried by reclamation work in 1976. The Charl Malan Quay usually looks like an office parking lot with rows of brand new cars lined up ready for the ro-ro (roll on/roll off) vessel that transports them.

Two further buildings complete a tour of the docks. The White House, used for seventy years for harbour administration, is regarded as one of the best examples of art nouveau architecture in South Africa. The railway station, north of the Campanile, was constructed in 1875 and its restored cast-iron structure is typical of that era.

14 City of Port Elizabeth

When the 4 000 1820 Settlers disembarked near the mouth of the Baakens River on their way to the frontier, they would have seen only a small, nameless group of houses huddled along the shoreline protected by Fort Frederick atop the plateau. Today Port Elizabeth (named in 1820 by Sir Rufane Donkin after his wife Elizabeth) has developed to become South Africa's fifth largest city. It was originally built on a narrow raised beach between the sea and the plateau behind, but it did not take the early settlers long before they expanded up and over the escarpment.

The city is fortunate in having three open spaces near its centre, the oldest of which is the Donkin Reserve. This was the spot chosen by Donkin, then acting governor of the Cape, for the pyramid-shaped memorial to his wife, who had died in India in 1818. The lighthouse alongside the memorial was built in 1861 and is no longer in use although it still acts as a beacon for ships in the bay. A hard climb gets you to the light platform — a fine site from which to view the city. A military museum is housed in the buildings alongside, and across the park are the Donkin Street houses, a

The green heart of Port Elizabeth — Donkin Reserve, its far edge trimmed by a picturesque terrace of Victorian houses.

much-photographed terrace of Victorian houses, each stepped lower than its neighbour.

The oldest park in the country, St George's Park, lies at the top of Pearson Street (behind the pyramid). St George's is the site of several South African sporting firsts: it was here that the country's first cricket and bowling clubs were formed and here, too, that the first cricket and rugby tests were played. The park, with the King George VI Art Museum flanking its entrance, has a botanical garden, a large swimming pool with steam baths, a tearoom, large play areas, and, on the first Sunday of every month, Art in the Park, an open-air exhibition and market for local crafts.

Although it forms a large open space (it is 2 km long) in the heart of the city, Settlers Park is practically invisible from nearby roads as it lies in the Baakens River valley. The valley, which cuts central Port Elizabeth in half, is today a place of peace and quiet only five minutes from the City Hall. You can follow any number of walks here, crossing the river by stepping stones. Besides its spacious lawns, graced by plants and trees, the park is also known for the many beautiful birds that inhabit it, making this a popular choice for the Port Elizabeth Bird Club.

Fortunately for the visitor much of the city's historical legacy has survived its rapid development and many buildings within walking distance of historic Market Square (where farmers, sailors and locals once met to trade) reveal elements of the past. The City Hall in the square was destroyed by fire in 1977 and many valuable paintings of early Port Elizabeth were lost. A national monument, it was reopened in 1981. In front of the building stands a replica of the Dias cross erected by the Portuguese navigator at Kwaaihoek in 1488.

Enter the Library Building facing the square across Main Street and you are immediately transported back to the beginning of this century. Stained-glass ceilings, gleaming brass and ornate iron and wood surround you at every turn, setting the mood for a historical stroll. The building is an excellent example of Victorian gothic architecture and its stucco façade was made in England and sent to Port Elizabeth in numbered pieces.

Immediately behind the library (in Whites Road) is the Victorian building that houses the oldest functioning opera house in the country. One block from the library (in Baakens Street) is the Feathermarket Hall where, as the name suggests, ostrich feathers and other goods used to be auctioned. The steep road alongside the hall leads to the oldest house in the city, Parsonage House, built in 1830 by the Rev Francis McCleland.

Completely refurnished to present a picture of 19th-century life, it houses a collection of furniture and domestic objects that reflect a thriving mid-Victorian household. A small toy museum, packed with Victorian and Edwardian toys, fills an outside room.

Across the road from this domestic museum are the Sterley Cottages, one of which was owned by the city's first policeman, Thomas Sterley, appointed in 1822. Off Belmont Terrace at the top of Castle Hill Fort Frederick, named after Frederick, Duke of York, still watches over the city although its eight 12-pounder guns no longer guard the ramparts.

15 North End Lake, Swartkops and Redhouse

Surrounded by industrial sites and the suburb of North End, the small stretch of water known as North End Lake is the home of the Eastern Province Power Boat Club. There is a private jetty, slipway, ski-ramp and clubhouse. The lake is edged by a narrow grass strip.

The suburb of Swartkops, with its built-up river bank, is the site of the Zwartkops Yacht Club and a popular area for anglers. The road alongside the river, known as The Strand, has ample parking space and offers a fine view of the many craft out on the water on weekends. You can hire rowing boats and buy bait from the Swartkops Rod Club.

Upriver from Swartkops, Redhouse boasts the oldest rowing club in the country: the Zwartkops Rowing Club, founded in 1873. A beautiful towpath allows you to watch the weekly yacht races held here in summer. There is a launch ramp for powerboats but no waterskiing is allowed within the Redhouse area. You can beach your boat at sandy places along the river, and choose a grassy slope for picnicking.

16 Amsterdamhoek

Although sometimes thought to be named after the Dutch appearance of the houses and jetties lining the Swartkops River, this is more likely to get its name from the Dutch man o'war *Amsterdam* that had to be run ashore close to the mouth of the river in 1817. Amsterdamhoek is instantly recognisable to the passing motorist not only for the single row of houses built along the water's edge but also for the Second World War blockhouse situated atop the rise immediately above the suburb.

The area cannot be reached from the beach as the narrow road is barred at the point where it crosses under Settlers Bridge. From the N2, turn inland and follow the signs to Amsterdamhoek, passing the Tippers Creek Aloe Reserve on your right. In July this Addo-type bushveld is a blaze of red and the path skirts the escarpment above the river, presenting long views of the sea, the city and the mountains beyond Uitenhage.

Although most of the jetties and slipways of Amsterdamhoek are private, there is a public

THE APPLE OF THEIR EYE

Once a year Port Elizabeth hosts one of the most unusual road relay races in South Africa: the Great Train Race.

Staged between Humewood Station, just outside the city centre, and the little village of Loerie 68 km distant, the race pits thousands of runners against one of the narrow gauge locomotives known collectively as the Apple Express. The train is considered to have the edge in this tough race, but its popularity illustrates the special place the Apple Express has in the hearts of Port Elizabethans.

When not racing humans the trains' major purpose is the transport of fruit from the Gamtoos valley orchards to the coast. The track is one of the few narrow gauge railway lines left in the world and the diminutive steam engines have been puffing their steady way along it since 1906.

From June to January, an apple-green locomotive carries passengers through residential areas of the city before reaching delightful mountain and forest scenery. This is rugged country covered by thick bush interspersed with splashes of aloes. The train crosses the Van Staden's Gorge over a 77,1 m-high steel girder bridge — the highest of its kind.

The train then steams through rolling countryside of hills and forests presided over by the Groot-Winterhoek range with the impressive Cockscomb rising to nearly 2 200 m. Then it puffs its way through a steep pass into the Gamtoos valley before reaching Loerie. From here, the track continues across the Gamtoos to Humansdorp and the Langkloof, while a branch goes up the valley to Hankey and Patensie.

slipway at the end of the road near the bridge. You can find bait in the river, but must adhere to the local restrictions.

There are no lifesavers on the beach at the river mouth and swimming is at your own risk in the river near the bridge because of dangerous currents. Popular with boardsailors is nearby Dufour Park, with its braai sites, picnic amenities and launching facilities.

During spring and at low tide a detailed exploration of the Swartkops floodplain can be absorbing, with plants ranging from sea lavender, succulents and grasses adapted to living in brine, to a host of flowering bulbs, pelargoniums and sages. Winter also has its highlights, easy to follow by taking the Zwartkops Trust winter walk.

17 Northern beaches, Bluewater Bay and St George's Strand

For some kilometres immediately north of the city the beaches are buried under railway lines and freeway. The stretch of coast is popular with anglers, however, and it is possible to drive along behind the breakwater for some distance. At Brighton Beach you reach the first beach facilities again, with change-rooms and a playpark for the youngsters.

An energetic walk from Bluewater Bay to Coegasmond offers placid seascapes in which the islands of St Croix Island Reserve beckon tantalisingly. The Coega estuary is occupied by vast salt recovery pans, usually inhabited by hundreds of flamingos. The beach has a panoramic view of the city to the right and the

BELOW *The shallow, sandy Swartkops, just a step from the city centre, is the perfect place for idling away a lovely summer's afternoon.*

Huge sand dunes — much loved by a new breed of fun 'skiers' — loom over a sparkling stretch of the Sundays River.

island reserve to the left. Lifesavers are on duty during peak times, and there is an ablution block.

A couple of kilometres from Bluewater Bay is St George's Strand, a wide-open beach lined by sand dunes. A tarred road leads to parking, picnic and camping areas (caravans and tents) with an ablution block. Fishing is popular here, especially from the rocks further up the beach. Swimming is considered fairly safe and lifesavers are on duty during peak times.

18 Sundays River

A left turn off the N2 at St George's Strand past Settlers Bridge over the Swartkops River takes you to the irrigated citrus-growing Sundays River valley (which now also enjoys diverted Orange River water).

The main attractions here are the Addo Elephant Park, the grave of Sir Percy Fitzpatrick (well-known author of *Jock of the Bushveld*) and in spring, the sight of hundreds of blue-flowering jacarandas and fresh green oaks and the heavy sweet scent of orange blossom.

Fossilised tree trunks can be seen at the drift at Drunbrody and at Sunland there is a turn-off to The Lookout, a national monument and site of the grave of citrus pioneer Fitzpatrick. The tower affords magnificent views of the luxuriant valley and winding river that has its source in the Sneeuberg range in the Great Karoo. This may seem a placid valley but it has known its share of floods and war: in 1819 the entire area was plundered by raiding bands of Xhosa and in 1901, the main centre of the valley, Kirkwood, was looted by Boer general Jan Smuts during his eastern Cape campaign.

At its mouth the Sundays River broadens to a wide, calm stretch of water providing opportunities for waterskiing, powerboating, boardsailing, canoeing and fishing. To reach the mouth turn right off the N2 at Colchester (40 km

MONKEY BUSINESS

The memorable signalman Jack.

For many years the old Uitenhage Railway Station was famous for the activities of one of its 'signalmen': Jack, the working baboon. Jack, who was trained by signalman James Wide to change the signals at his command, was known throughout the land for his prowess and, for many years, the highlight of any train journey was to shower the appreciative 'signalman' with fruit at the end of the trip.

Wide had lost both his legs while constructing the line from Uitenhage to Graaff-Reinet. Given a position as signalman at Uitenhage, he bought Jack at the town market and trained the baboon to operate the points at his command. Jack soon learnt that one blast of a train whistle meant he should operate the Port Elizabeth/Uitenhage points and he would stand gravely by, watching the safe passage of the train. Thus he worked at the station for many years, eventually dying of overstrain in 1890.

Photographs of Jack and his master can be seen in the inspector's office of the Old Railway Museum in Market Street. The museum is, in fact, the old Uitenhage Railway Station, the end point of the first railway line in the eastern Cape, reaching the town from Port Elizabeth in 1875.

from Port Elizabeth) and drive along the gravel road through the privately owned holiday resort of Pearson Park. The road runs out at the Woody Cape Nature Reserve and you have to walk to the mouth itself.

The area is well loved by surf, rock and river anglers, but another sport is to hire sandskis for an exciting ride on the biggest expanse of coastal dunes on the Cape coast. There are five jetties on the river and launch ramps. The resort (comprising two caravan parks, a tent site and bungalows) is open all day long to allow night fishing. A café, garage and general dealer are situated conveniently nearby.

From the beach you can see the St Croix Island Reserve, proclaimed in 1981 to protect its flora and fauna, notably the endangered jackass penguin. A diving trail in the reserve is a special treat: the rocky bed of pinnacles and valleys is rich in marine life and good visibility gives glimpses of fish (and other divers) up to 10 m away.

19 Addo Elephant National Park

Situated 72 km north-east of Port Elizabeth, the Addo Elephant National Park is well within the range of a day trip from the coast. It is open throughout the year, there is an observation point for birdwatchers at a dam, chalets and rondavels are available for hire and there is a caravan park, a restaurant and pleasant picnic spots.

The old saying that good fences make good neighbours could be applied aptly to the establishment of the Addo Elephant National Park. The park's story is essentially that of a fence, and of a conservation triumph that was very nearly an irreversible environmental disaster — the near extinction of the Addo elephant (*Loxodonta africana africana*) in the 1920s.

As the area surrounding the impenetrable Addo bush was gradually 'colonised' and cultivated by farmers in the first decades of this century, clashes between the elephants and their new neighbours increased.

Crop damage and night raids had become something of an Addo elephant speciality when the administrator of the Cape, Sir Frederic de Waal, engaged Major Jan Pretorius in 1919 to exterminate the herd. Pretorius was spectacularly successful and in a year managed to shoot about 120 of the lumbering beasts. Fortunately public outcry brought the slaughter to an end and in 1931 the park was proclaimed.

But the elephants continued to make night raids on adjoining farms, causing great damage and sometimes even loss of life. Electrified fencing failed to contain the elephants who soon learnt that they could push down the standards supporting the wires with impunity. It was only with the erection of a fence made from old lift cables and tram lines in 1954 that the elephants were finally protected from man and vice versa.

Beside the present population of 130 elephants, the 8 590 ha park is also home to the Cape buffalo, antelope, eland, red hartebeest, black rhinoceros and hippopotamus.

A mighty Addo elephant, safe within the sanctuary specially created for it.

WHEN 'STRONG MEN SHOOK AND WOMEN WEPT'

'Never before in its history has this port suffered under overwhelming disaster such as we record today,' wrote the local *Eastern Province Herald* on 2 September 1902 of the Great Gale that wrecked 21 ships and 22 lighters in a single night when a relentless hurricane swept unprotected Algoa Bay. Describing the 'hopeless horror' of the event, the reporter wrote how 'body after body' was washed ashore on the morning after the storm.

In all, 41 people drowned that dreadful night when the Italian, German, British, Norwegian and Swedish ships dragged their anchors and were pounded to pieces along the unyielding shoreline. Of the dead, six were courageous would-be rescuers who drowned 'in the blackest tragedy of the day' after being washed away while using a lifeline in an attempt to reach a floundering sailor.

The *Herald*'s report of a disaster — hopefully, one never to be repeated — makes compelling, if pathetic, reading.

'One after another of the maritime fleet temporarily occupying the almost singular inhospitability of our storm swept bay were driven upon its treacherous seas. In many cases help was beyond human means. The ships came on to their doom with relentless tread across the troublesome main. The pitiless forces of the storm defied the best seamanship and laid at naught the wiles and nautical lore and art. . . . Soon the North End beach from the gasworks to the Jarawar was one panorama of derelict shipping. Huge four-masted ships and stately barques alike shared in the dreadful confusion.'

The report continues: 'During the morning one of the most pitiful sights was the crew of a large ship huddled on the bowsprit awaiting the succour which never came. The efforts of the (rescue) brigade to reach the doomed crew were unavailing, and after holding on with that pertinacity of purpose which the struggle for life alone creates, after a brave struggle with the elements for unnumbered hours, were swept from their fancied security, while those ashore stood aghast with chill suspense, filled with the fear that congeals the blood.

'In that fell swoop, the captain, his wife and their children, who happily associated in life, in death were not divided. In the presence of such tragedy strong men shook with emotion and women wept the tears that could not be withheld.'

A simple monument to the dead now stands in South End cemetery.

THINGS TO DO

Angling

With the area boasting some of the finest fishing grounds in southern Africa, this sport is highly organised at Port Elizabeth. There are 26 angling clubs in and around the city, and the Eastern Province Rock and Surf Angling Association publishes the *Anglers' Guide and Yearbook* with tips on the best spots, what fish can be caught and what restrictions apply. Note that Port Elizabeth Harbour is closed to fishing.

Art galleries

KING GEORGE VI ART GALLERY, St George's Park, Port Elizabeth: Housing 19th- and 20th-century British art and a South African collection.

Beachcombing and shelling

Ebony used in packing the guns of the *Sacramento* can be found on the beach between Skoenmakerskop and Sardinia Bay. Algoa Bay is not a good area for shelling but Kini Bay on the road to Seaview, Amsterdamhoek, Hougham Park opposite St Croix Island and Flat Rock just before Cape Recife are the best bets.

Birdwatching

Settlers Park in the heart of Port Elizabeth is a haven for many birds, including the dramatic Knysna lourie, the secretive Burchell's coucal, the

Fish type	Season	Best area	Best bait
Elf	Winter	Maitland River Mouth	Spinners, fillets, live bait, chokka
Galjoen	June — Sept	Maitland River Mouth	Mussels, redbait, worms, prawns
Hottentot	Oct — Mar	Cape Recife	Prawns, mussels, worms, redbait
Kob (kabeljou)	All year	All along the coast	Pilchards, chokka, fish fillets, live bait, worms
Leervis	Mar — May, Sept — Nov	Bluewater Bay, surf at Sundays River	Live bait, mullet, spinners
Mussel-cracker	Aug — Nov	All rocky areas, Cape Recife	Perlemoen, crabs, redbait, mussels
White steenbras	May — July	All surf areas, especially Van Stadensmond, Maitland River Mouth, Brighton Beach	Prawns, worms, mussels
Zebra (wildeperd)	All year	Sundays River surf, Brighton Beach surf	Redbait, worms, mussels, prawns, fish fillets, chokka

hoopoe, and kingfishers, nightjars and hadedas. Habitats for birds range from offshore waters and beaches through estuaries and dune scrub to forested kloofs. Favourite watching spots are Settlers Park, Island Forest Reserve, Van Stadens Wild Flower Reserve, Maitland Mines Nature Reserve and Cape Recife. The Eastern Cape Wild Bird Society organises regular outings.

Boardsailing

The whole of Algoa Bay is great boardsailing water, and an annual Bay Crossing Race attracts international competition. Dufour Park in the Swartkops estuary is ideal practice water for beginners: shallow, sandy-bottomed and rarely without a steady breeze. When the south-westerly is blowing, the best areas are Noordhoek,

just south of Cape Recife, and the Swartkops River mouth.

Boat trips

During the holiday season, the South African Transport Services tug *Blue Jay* takes trippers out of the harbour, along the beachfront to the wreck of the *Kapodistrias* off Cape Recife.

Bowls

Port Elizabeth's 16 clubs welcome visitors (contact the publicity association for details).

Camping and caravanning

There are camping and caravan sites at Van Stadensmond, Maitland River Mouth, Beachview, Seaview Game Park, Willows, St George's Strand, Sundays River and the Addo Elephant National Park, as well as several other sites in Port Elizabeth itself. Contact the publicity association or local municipality for details.

Canoeing

Two resorts, one on the Van Staden's River and the other on the Sundays, hire canoes for paddling on these placid stretches of water. Rowing boats can be hired from the Swartkops Rod Club.

Cycling

The Marine Drive circle along the seafront for 24 km to Skoenmakerskop then inland around Driftsand Forest

The working harbour of Port Elizabeth has a light-hearted side too: it also shelters the pleasure craft of countless boating enthusiasts.

The wreck of the Kapodistrias *is a stark reminder of the dangers of the Algoa Bay coast.*

and back through the suburbs of Walmer and Humewood is the most popular run. The Port Elizabeth Pedal Power Association organises fun runs twice a month (contact any cycle shop for details). Two-person tricycles can be hired on the beachfront during the holiday season.

Diving
The Dolphin Underwater Club has a clubhouse at Humewood and has scuba, snorkel, training and underwater hockey sections. Some favourite diving spots are the old slipway pillars at Humewood, Willows, Sardinia Bay and Cape Recife. Contact the Department of Nature and Environmental Conservation for details of the underwater diving trail at St Croix Island.

Drives and viewsites
The most popular short drives are to Skoenmakerskop by either the Marine Drive or Driftsands routes, and to Cape Recife (off Marine Drive) to see the lighthouse, seascapes and wreck of the *Kapodistrias*. Good viewsites include Fort Frederick, Donkin Lighthouse, Amsterdamhoek and the Seaview-Maitland River road.

An unusual alternative is a day trip on the Apple Express (take along a picnic basket). Contact the publicity association or the station for details.

Golf
Humewood Golf Links is the best known, with other major courses including Port Elizabeth, Wedgewood and Walmer country clubs.

Horseriding
Port Elizabeth has two riding schools (Rothman Place and Greenhaven), while horses and ponies can be hired at the Springs near Uitenhage.

Libraries
The dozen or so municipal libraries offer temporary membership.

Museums
CHILDREN'S MUSEUM, Beachfront, Humewood, Port Elizabeth: A touch museum that introduces children to the animal world in an imaginative way.
CUYLER MANOR, Uitenhage: Restored home reflecting pioneering days.
DONKIN LIGHTHOUSE, Donkin Reserve, Port Elizabeth: A military/naval museum with access to the light platform as a viewsite.
DROSTDY, Caledon Street, Uitenhage: Houses the Africana Museum.
FORT FREDERICK, Belmont Terrace, Port Elizabeth: Overlooks the mouth of the Baakens River, landing place of the 1820 Settlers.

OLD RAILWAY MUSEUM, Market Street, Uitenhage: Memorabilia from the past century, including a station shop with shelves of goods from a bygone era, and two steam locomotives with gleaming brass and rich wooden interiors.
PARSONAGE HOUSE, 7 Castle Hill, Port Elizabeth: Displays mid-19th century household goods, including jewellery, clothing, kitchen implements, furniture, as well as period toys.
PORT ELIZABETH MUSEUM/OCEANARIUM, Beachfront, Humewood: Complex of modern museum, oceanarium, snake park and tropical house.

Music and theatre
FEATHERMARKET HALL, Military Road, Port Elizabeth: Used as a concert hall.
FORD LITTLE THEATRE, Belmont Terrace, Port Elizabeth: Leased for productions by the Port Elizabeth Musical and Dramatic Society.
OPERA HOUSE, Whites Road, Port Elizabeth: Refurbished Victorian theatre, and headquarters of Capab (Cape Performing Arts Board) in the eastern Cape.
MANNVILLE, St George's Park, Port Elizabeth: Open-air theatre, home of the annual Shakespearean Festival.

Other large auditoriums are found at the Technikon and the University of Port Elizabeth.

Powerboating
Powerboats may be launched from ramps at Humewood (Hobie Beach); the harbour; Zwartkops Yacht Club; Redhouse Yacht Club; North End Lake; Noordehoek Skiboat Club, Pearson Park. Boats can also be launched from the beach at King's Beach and Sardinia Bay (no ramps).

Shipwrecks
The exposure of Algoa Bay to south-east gales made it a deathtrap for shipping before the harbour was finally constructed early this century. Although many ships sank in the bay, the only visible wreck is that of the *Kapodistrias* (1985), on Thunderbolt Reef off Cape Recife. Some remains of the *Western Knight* (1929) can be seen opposite the old Port Elizabeth Club building in Marine Drive.

Surfing
Radio Algoa broadcasts a daily surf report for the area at 06h50, with an update at 15h55. The Pipe in Summerstrand has a shallow reef with a beach break; the Fence up against the harbour wall at King's Beach has a left-breaking peak; Avalanche at the beginning of Pollok Beach during low tide has a right-hander break; Millars Point just before Bird Rock has a long, slow right-hand breaking wave (this is suitable for beginners.) Contact any specialist shop for further advice.

Swimming
The safest swimming for children is at King's Beach, Humewood and McArthur Pool as municipal lifeguards are on duty every day.

Tennis and squash
For details of tennis clubs and courts contact the Eastern Province Tennis Association, while the Port Elizabeth Publicity Association has a contact number if you wish to play squash at any of the private clubs.

Walks
The Donkin Heritage Trail links 37 historical monuments in a walking tour of Port Elizabeth (a detailed booklet is available from the publicity association). For an easy stroll Happy Valley, Settlers Park and St George's Park all offer shady paths and peaceful areas. The publicity association has prepared a pack of comprehensive information about twenty walks ranging in duration from less than an hour to all day in areas surrounding the city.

Yachting and dinghy sailing
Seagoing yacht clubs are Algoa Bay Yacht Club based in the harbour and Port Elizabeth Beach Yacht Club (mainly catamarans). River sailing takes place at Zwartkops Yacht Club and Redhouse.

INFORMATION
- National Sea Rescue Institute, Station 6, Port Elizabeth Harbour. Tel 041=5202716
- Port Elizabeth Publicity Association, Library Building, Market Square, Port Elizabeth 6001. Tel 041=521315
- SA Tourism Board, 310 Mutual Building, 64 Main St, Port Elizabeth 6001. Tel 041=27761
- Uitenhage Municipality (Library), PO 45, Uitenhage 6230. Tel 0422=26011

Nearest AA Office
- AA House, 2 Granville Rd, Greenacres, Port Elizabeth 6001. Tel 041=341313

Sweeps of sandy shore where serenity has settled

THIS IS SETTLER COUNTRY, but as the 1820 Settlers discovered all too soon after their arrival here, it was the promised land of milk and honey only if you brought your own cows and bees. There is a certain harsh quality to this meeting place of climatic zones and vegetation belts, and historically of cultures.

For the holiday-maker, though, it has much to offer. Here the coast alternates between long windswept beaches and dunefields, rocky points and platforms, and small coves and river mouths. Sleepy resorts laze on the river estuaries and lagoons, and even the important fishing port of Port Alfred on the Kowie River is a tranquil getaway. English villages set in African bushveld lend a quaint, translocated character to a land chock-a-block with monuments and places of interest.

Port Alfred's weathered wooden piers provide a berth for birds.

1 The Alexandria coastline

Between the mouths of the Sundays and the Boesmans is a vast and lonely dunefield, with only a few isolated spots accessible along dusty tracks from the Alexandria-Port Alfred road. The town of Alexandria is a centre for the chicory and pineapple lands in the area, and offers some tourist accommodation, including a caravan park.

Between here and the sea is a southern extension of the subtropical coastal forests found in Natal and Transkei. Preserved as the Alexandria State Forest, it features sneezewood, yellowwood and ironwood trees, white pears, wild plums and figs, white milkwood and forest olives. A hiking trail traverses the forest and crosses the dunefields near Woody Cape (you need a permit from the forestry station), reaching a hut on the beach. Angling is a major drawcard — the water here is generally shallow with flat reefs and sandy gullies — but access is difficult. Cape Padrone further along is a lonely and barren place seldom visited by anyone other than the odd angler, as access is by foot over kilometres of sand dunes. The

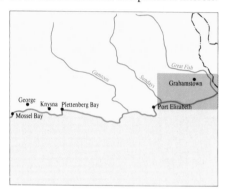

road running inland of both capes links Cannon Rocks with Alexandria.

In the region of Alexandria there are two historical landmarks. The first is a monument to Voortrekker Karel Landman and the people he led from this area into an unknown future. The other is the grave of Nongqawuse, a young Xhosa girl who in the 1850s foretold that if her people destroyed all their cattle and crops, they would —

on a specified day — be freed from white domination. When that day dawned and the prophecy was not fulfilled, a nation faced starvation and thousands subsequently died.

2 Cannon Rocks and Boknes

A small resort lies on the Boknes lagoon, with a few streets of private cottages and a caravan park. Along with Cannon Rocks to the west of the lagoon (so named for the two cannons and anchor erected near the beach), this is a popular angling spot. Cannon Rocks itself is actually quite a way along the beach from Boknes and you need a beach vehicle to reach it, but first obtain a permit from the Alexandria forestry station. The long and narrow sandy beach in front of the Boknes lagoon offers fairly safe sea bathing.

3 Kwaaihoek and the Dias Cross Memorial

The Dutch called this place Kwaaihoek (angry corner), because seldom a day went by without the wind howling and the sea smashing into the cliffs. It was here, in 1488, that Bartholomeu Dias erected a cross after his historic rounding of the Cape. It was only this century that the crumbling fragments of that forgotten cross were unearthed. Today a replica marks the furthest spot east where Dias stepped ashore.

To reach Kwaaihoek you take the Boknes turn-off from the R72 and then a signposted farm track through three farm gates to a fence behind the forested dunes. A path leads through the forest and to the crest of a high dune, where you look down and across about a kilometre of windswept dunes to the commemorative cross.

4 Boesmansriviermond, Kenton on Sea and Kasouga

About 8 km east of Boknes you reach the first resort along the coastal road from Alexandria; this is Boesmansriviermond, lying on the river's western bank at the edge of the Alexandria forest

LEFT *The majestic beauty of the lonely dunes near Woody Cape.*

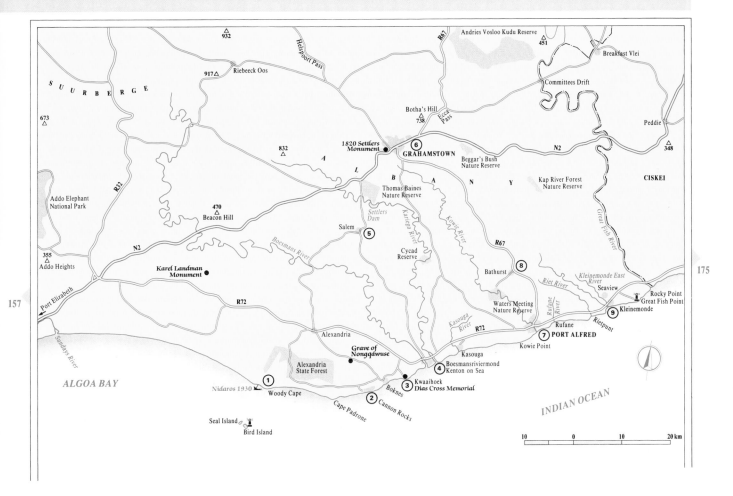

reserve. The cottages nestling among the indigenous coastal bush belong to local farmers and Grahamstown families making the most of the coast's pleasant climate. A caravan park is set in a splendid garden of natural trees and flowers, landscaped in terraces with large fig, milkwood, coral and other trees sheltering each site.

Kenton on Sea is one of the most picturesque resorts in the country and the jewel of this stretch of coastline; it lies between the mouths of the Boesmans and the Kariega, hedged on three sides by river and sea. Both rivers are navigable by small boats for several kilometres upstream. Lazy and wide, they twist tightly in and out of the wooded hills, in places forming near oxbow lakes. Anyone canoeing upstream in the early morning or at dusk will be delighted by the variety of birds.

The Boesmans estuary is a popular spot for powerboating, while the river and sandy beach also offer good prospects for angling and bathing. The Kariega estuary forms a lagoon where in the summertime the colourful sails of dinghies and sailboards dash across the water like jousting pennants. The two mouths are separated by 2 km of mixed rocky and sandy beaches that offer fairly

safe and secluded bathing as well as excellent beachcombing opportunities. This short stretch condenses the best of the whole coastline: take a walk along sandy beaches, past rock arches and tall eroded pedestals, over rocky platforms pocked with clear pools and long gullies, and over headlands to secret coves enclosed by cliffs with small beaches and caves.

RIGHT *Sunlight sparkles on the steely waters of the Kariega, locked between wooded banks.*

THE CROSS THAT DIAS BORE

The commemorative Kwaaihoek cross.

On 12 March 1488 the navigator Bartholomeu Dias planted a limestone cross (*padrao*) on the Kwaaihoek headland, where waves smash into the 30 m-high cliffs and plumes of stinging sand blow off the lips of the surrounding dunes. The cross was to mark the point at which he was forced (mainly by his unhappy crew) to abandon his pioneering voyage eastwards and return home. Not only did he leave his cross, dedicated to St Gregory, behind on that lonely headland, he left his hopes too.

That was not the only cross Dias planted on the southern African shore; he marked his return voyage also with crosses near Cape Point and Lüderitz Bay — desolate places all that must have given those early sailors a grim view of the 'dark continent'. But the Kwaaihoek cross was special. For about 150 years it served as a navigational point but thereafter no further mention of it was made.

Then, more than three centuries later — and almost five since it was planted there — historian Eric Axelson began a concerted search for the cross. In 1938 he discovered fragments buried by dune sands some 14 km east of where it had been thought to lie. From this and other fragments found at the base of the wave- and wind-lashed cliffs of Kwaaihoek, the 2 m-high cross could be reconstructed. Several replicas were made at the same time: one for Portugal, one for Lourenço Marques (Maputo), one each for a number of South African cities, and finally one for Kwaaihoek. The original cross, the oldest relic of European culture in southern Africa, is housed at the University of the Witwatersrand, where it was reconstructed.

The beach east of the Kariega estuary is less accessible, with only a few old fishing shacks on the river, but it has excellent surf conditions for swimming, snorkelling and spearfishing. At low tide the weird formations of the so-called High Rocks area project as alien shapes on the beach, while at high tide they are partly submerged to form an underwater amusement park. Low tide is a good time for looking for shells here, but nowhere are they plentiful.

It is a long but pleasant beach walk from the Kariega to the next little private resort of Kasouga.

RIGHT *The simple lines of a restored settler house in rustic Salem.*

named for the Khoi word referring to the leopards that once roamed the valley. The lagoon offers fairly safe bathing, and it is also wide enough for boardsailing, but the beach is quite exposed.

5 Salem

Inland from Kenton on Sea the view over gentle countryside fades from deep green to dull brown, as the land becomes drier and less fertile towards the village of Salem. Here a party of 1820 Settlers, under the leadership of Hesekiah Sephton, put down their roots. Early letters home talk of grasslands 'like an English park', but the dry aloes and sweet-thorns surrounding settler cottages speak rather of years of overgrazing.

The settlers of Salem (taken from Psalm 76 and meaning peace) built their first church in 1822; ten years later this building, now restored as a national monument, was replaced by a larger stone church and it was here that the people of the district sought refuge during the Sixth Frontier War in 1835. Heartily tired of the continual conflict adding to the hardship of their lives, one of their number, Quaker Richard Gush, dropped his gun and strode from the church. Confronting the Xhosa war party, he asked what their grievance was, and on hearing that their people were hungry, he returned to the church and came back laden with supplies — much to the annoyance of his fellow settlers. He achieved his aim, however, for the Xhosa then left them in peace.

A plaque in front of the original church commemorates Gush's stand, and his memory lives on as his descendants still occupy his original home. Many of the cottages in the villages have been renovated and preserved by other descendants of the men and women who were sent to tame this wild frontier. They have not forgotten their links with the past and in true English tradition, every summer Sunday afternoon the Salem cricketers take to the village green.

6 Grahamstown

Surrounded on all sides by low hills, this is the City of Saints, nicknamed for the forty-odd churches whose steeples pierce the skyline here. In 1812 its founder, Colonel John Graham, chose a spot in this well-watered basin as a military outpost. A fort with a semaphore tower was later built on Gunfire Hill to serve as the nerve centre for the network of signal towers built across the eastern frontier.

The outpost acted for some years as a trading station but it did not rate as a town until the arrival of the 1820 Settlers, when some parties were allocated land in the fort's protective shadow. By 1861 it had grown substantially and acquired both municipal and city status.

Grahamstown's history and character are reflected in its many beautiful buildings and a stroll in almost any direction will acquaint you with aspects of the city. Drostdy Gateway, leading now to the campus of Rhodes University, was completed in 1842; the original drostdy (which no longer stands) was built in part by Piet Retief, destined to be one of the most influential leaders of the Great Trek.

Rhodes (designed by the famous Sir Herbert Baker) is not the only institution upholding Grahamstown's strong reputation as a centre for learning: from the first school built there in 1814 for soldiers' children, there are now a number of renowned schools, including St Andrew's, Kingswood and Graeme colleges, and the Diocesan and Victoria schools for girls.

From Drostdy Gateway, High Street runs down to the Anglican Cathedral of St Michael and St George (1824), which dominates the town and houses many memorial tablets and other commemorative objects from the past. The cathedral is surrounded by many fine historical buildings of as many styles as there were periods.

Among the other interesting features of Grahamstown — from an almost endless list — is Grocott's Building in High Street, where *Grocott's Mail* is published: the oldest newspaper in the country still being published under the same name and from the same premises. Around the corner, in Bathurst Street, is the newly renovated Observatory Museum, originally the home of jeweller Henry Galpin and now extremely popular

ABOVE *Close of day on the Kowie River.* BELOW *A moody view down Grahamstown's rain-rinsed High Street to the cathedral.*

for the camera obscura Galpin built into the roof.

The cultural heartbeat of Grahamstown is provided by the 1820 Foundation hosting the annual national arts festival in the monument next to Fort Selwyn on Gunfire Hill. Since its inception more than a decade ago, this week-long event has grown from a cosy gathering of artists to a feast of the country's best theatre, dance, music, art and crafts, and film and video.

Surrounding the monument is the 61 ha 1820 Settlers Wild Flower Garden, displaying the indigenous flora of the areas where the immigrants settled. Among the other places of interest to nature lovers is the 975 ha Thomas Baines Nature

Reserve south of the city with typical valley bushveld vegetation, prolific bird life and such animals as eland, bontebok and white rhino. Settlers Dam here has no facilities (other than toilets), but is a good spot for canoeing, boardsailing and dinghy sailing. This reserve also administers the largest known colony of the endangered cycad *Encephalartos caffer*, a national monument. These palmlike cycads are a link with the first nonflowering plants to appear on earth almost 200-million years ago.

Further afield (to the north-east of the city, off the R67) is the Andries Vosloo Kudu Reserve, covering some 6 493 ha and featuring (besides the

THE MEETING PLACE

Where waters meet ... reflective Horseshoe Bend on the Kowie River.

The Waters Meeting Nature Reserve situated near Bathurst is well named for this Border area is indeed a meeting place, not only of the tidal and fresh waters in the river itself, but also of climatic regions and hence of floral types.

The area between Bathurst and Grahamstown is hard to define because here four weather zones and four veld types meet, each capable of showing a different face or blending together into a unique potpourri of colour and scent. Here you will find Cape fynbos plants, such as proteas, heaths, gladioli and watsonias, in abundance, while the Karoo is represented by succulents such as crassulas, euphorbias, aloes and vygies (Mesembryanthemum). Subtropical flowers too make a show: speartipped blue and orange crane flowers, delicate blue plumbago, shocks of scarlet flowers draped heavily in coral trees. Finally, in the sour grasslands, there are the sprinklings of lilies and amaryllis flowers that once wove dense carpets across an uncultivated land.

THE HARBOUR THE SEA RECLAIMED

For the 1820 Settlers, the journey overland to Bathurst from Algoa Bay was rough going, and it was decided that the establishment of a closer port would be most welcome. Henry Norse was sent to investigate what the possibilities were further east, and with him travelled Benjamin Moodie, who at the time was developing Port Beaufort on the Breede River as a trading harbour. They decided on the mouth of the Kowie River as suitable, and Moodie was given the initial responsibility for developing the harbour.

The first ship to cross the bar at the river mouth was the *Elizabeth*, specially built to serve the port, but on its very next voyage to Port Elizabeth it was wrecked on Cape Recife. Other coasters soon replaced the *Elizabeth*, negotiating the sand bars, strong currents and billowing winds with varying success, a number running aground in the process. The struggling harbour received a boost in 1825 when the Cape governor, Lord Charles Somerset, visited it and appointed a magistrate here, at the same time renaming it Port Frances in honour of his daughter-

in-law. For a while trading took place between here and Port Beaufort but the vagaries of the river proved too great and by 1831 it had fallen into disuse.

Then in 1836 the settler William Cock changed the course of the river and opened a new harbour on the river's west bank. Within a few years a large fleet was carrying wool and beef to Mauritius and St Helena, and large mailships also called regularly at the port that was again renamed in 1860 to honour the visit of Prince Alfred. But the expense of maintaining the harbour was great and when a railway link was established to Grahamstown in 1882, it again fell into disuse and the mouth that had been regularly dredged began to silt up.

In the 1930s another attempt was made to develop the port into a major harbour but the onset of the Second World War put a final stop to this. Today Port Alfred is simply a peaceful coastal resort where small fishing boats and pleasure craft berth and sea birds perch on the wooden piers braiding the river banks through the town.

landdrost, to survey their new homes. In 1968 a toposcope was built around the stone survey beacon there, with 57 bronze plaques giving details of each party. Many South Africans visit this spot to trace their roots in Africa.

Bathurst lies on a luxuriant slope, its roads lined with the brilliant scarlet flowers of coral trees and huge wild fig and oak trees, planted by the settlers to remind them of the land they had left behind. After initial attempts at farming, many of the settlers turned rather to other enterprises and opened mills, smithies and inns, some of which still stand as testimony to the past. In 1821 Thomas Hartley opened a forge and an inn (the Pig and Whistle), which survived fires and lootings to earn its place as a favourite stopover and local watering hole. In the same year Samuel Bradshaw built a mill on a stream just out of town, used initially for wool and later converted into a grain mill. Today it has been fully restored, and the original grindstone can still be seen.

From Bathurst a gravel road leads westwards to the Waters Meeting Nature Reserve, with a viewsite near the entrance overlooking the classic horseshoe canyon on the Kowie River before the road descends to a picnic site on the river banks.

kudu) red hartebeest, springbok, blue duiker, steenbok and bushbuck. Several guided hiking trails are conducted here.

7 Port Alfred

Straddling the Kowie River, this town is an important fishing port and the major holiday resort along this stretch of coast. Its origins date back to the arrival of the 1820 Settlers, who hoped to use the river mouth as a means of landing supplies from Algoa Bay, thereby avoiding the tedious trip overland. But ships had great difficulty in negotiating the mouth, so for only short periods did it ever serve as a major trading port.

Today Port Alfred is a quiet and quaint holiday town with excellent fishing and swimming beaches

and other holiday attractions. The river mouth is the main fishing spot, especially for sharks and tigerfish. From the pier across the mouth are consistent breaks that for most of the year have no one to ride them — something that suits the few local surfers down to the ground! Beachcombing is also rewarding with the beaches in the area having yielded as many as 1 800 different varieties of shells, including cowries, perlemoen and alikreukel shells, as well as the flimsy paper nautiluses that seldom survive intact.

The wide river is the mooring site for many small craft, which either break out to sea through the mouth or travel upstream for as much as 20 km. The river is also the setting for one of Port Alfred's more recent attractions: the two-day Kowie River Canoe Trail, with a 40 km-long return paddle and a 12 km hike. Canoeists use the tides to negotiate the river's course as far as Waters Meeting Nature Reserve near Bathurst, where they hike through forests famous for sheltering barred owls. These tiny birds were first described in the eastern Cape in 1834 but were not seen here again until a single dead bird was washed up at Kenton on Sea in 1980 and then some years later a pair was spotted in the thick forest of this reserve.

8 Bathurst

From Port Alfred the road inland rises through a small gorge covered by succulents before reaching a gently rolling plain with low hills in the distance. At the foot of these hills stands the village of Bathurst that served as the regional centre to the 1820 Settlers before Grahamstown rose to prominence as capital of the eastern Cape. On a hill above the town the leaders of several parties of settlers met Colonel Jacob Cuyler, Uitenhage's

LEFT *The original workings of the early 19th-century mill at Bathurst.*

9 Rufane, Riet and Kleinemonde river resorts

Eastwards from Port Alfred as far as the Ciskei border at the Great Fish River, small holiday villages cluster around the main river mouths, which are generally blind, forming lagoons behind the coastal dunes where the beaches are wide and the sea wild. The main attraction all along here is angling. Bathing in the sea can be dangerous but you can always dip in the rivers.

The first little coastal resort is a camp site below towering dunes, beside where the Rufane River dissipates into shallow pools on the beach. There are no cottages here, and cultivated fields run right down to the dunes, separated from one another by clumps of sweet-thorn trees, with their dense nests of long white thorns. Next is the small cluster of private cottages on the lagoon of the Riet. Oystercatchers stand at the surf's jagged edge, trotting away at your approach; cormorants line the lagoon like Egyptian friezes, their wings spread to dry; malachite and halfcollared kingfishers sway on the long reed stems arching over the river. This is an utterly beautiful and peaceful spot, where the dunes and cottages reflect in the lagoon's surface, fringed in emerald by milkwood thickets.

The beach stretches on in a wide band of golden sand, flanked by a moody blue-grey sea and silver dunes. At Kleinemonde the river of the same name splits to form two shallow lagoons. The west mouth is lined with colourful old fishing shacks (some on wooden stilts), which have belonged to local farming and town families for many generations. Above the eastern mouth, also lined with cottages, is the new Seaview development with modern houses rather then cottages.

The coastal road veers inland here, heading for the border crossing and bypassing the Great Fish Point lighthouse guarding this lonely coast.

THINGS TO DO

Angling

This is a favourite coastline with anglers but access is often difficult; note that vehicles are not allowed in dune areas.

Art galleries

Temporary art exhibitions are often held in the 1820 Settlers Monument and at Rhodes University in Grahamstown.

Beachcombing and shelling

The beaches and coves of Kenton on Sea and east of the Kowie River mouth are the most rewarding areas.

Birdwatching

Waters Meeting Nature Reserve, Bathurst, has a real gem in the only known barred owls in the eastern Cape, as well as fish eagles and kingfishers and numerous forest birds. All the major rivers and their mouths provide a fair share of delights for birdwatchers, with the Great Fish River estuary, bordering Ciskei, best for sea birds and waders, especially the summer migrants. Bird Island off Woody Cape has a large gannet colony as well as penguins and cormorants.

Boardsailing

Settlers Dam (Thomas Baines Nature Reserve) outside Grahamstown, Kenton on Sea and the Kowie River estuary are the best and safest places to boardsail.

Boat trips

Port Alfred has a boat club and private arrangements to hire can generally be made with local owners of fishing boats. A launch also operates from here.

Bowls

Greens are available at Kenton on Sea, Port Alfred and Grahamstown.

Camping and caravanning

There are caravan parks at Alexandria, Boknes, Boesmansriviermond, Kenton on Sea, Port Alfred, Bathurst and Grahamstown. Contact the local municipalities or publicity associations.

Canoeing

The Kowie River Canoe Trail is a popular two-day paddle, while for casual canoeing the Boesmans and Kariega are navigable for about 30 km each from their mouths and the river at Settlers Dam outside Grahamstown provides a pleasant but shorter stretch.

Cycling

Cycling is one of the better ways to see this area, with good roads from Port Elizabeth to Alexandria, and then along the coast from Kenton on Sea to the Great Fish River. From Grahamstown through Bathurst to Port Alfred is a strenuous but interesting

Fish type	Season	Best area	Best bait
Bronze bream	All year	Gullies at Woody Cape, Port Alfred, Kowie River mouth, Rietpunt	Prawns, wonderworms
Elf	Summer	Woody Cape, river mouths	Strepies, cutbait
Kabeljou	All year	Gullies, Boesmansriviermond, Kasouga, Port Alfred eastwards	Sardines, mackerel, spinners
Leervis	Summer	Gullies and sandbanks near Woody Cape, Kasouga, Kowie River	Live mullet, lure
Mussel-cracker	All year	Woody Cape	Prawns
Sharks	All year	Surf areas, Kowie	Fish heads, mackerel
Skipjack	Summer	Most beaches and open rivers	Any flesh bait
Spotted grunter	Summer	Kowie River, shallow surf areas	Worms, sand prawns
White steenbras	All year	Gullies, Woody Cape, Port Alfred	Prawns, worms, crabs

ride; the road from Grahamstown through Salem to Kenton on Sea is less interesting as a ride but the going is much easier.

Diving

It is possible to snorkel in shallow pools and gullies between the mouths of the Boesmans and the Kariega (Kenton on Sea) when the sea is not angry, but otherwise the diving off Port Alfred's east beach and other reef areas is for the experienced only. This is a good spearfishing area. Contact the Kowie Underwater Club for details.

Drives and viewsites

Again, as for cycling, the best drives are along the coast from Kenton on Sea to the Great Fish, and inland from Port Alfred to Grahamstown. The toposcope above the town of Bathurst provides an excellent view of the surrounding country, with echoes of the past.

Golf

Grahamstown and Port Alfred both have good golf courses.

Horseriding

There are stables outside of Port Alfred and Grahamstown; contact the publicity associations for details.

Libraries

Grahamstown has a library in Hill Street, and the headquarters of the South African Library for the Blind in High Street. Port Alfred also has a library.

Museums

ALBANY NATURAL HISTORY MUSEUM, Somerset Street, Grahamstown:

Exhibits include natural history, fossil history and prehistory; a children's wildlife touch gallery; and the Tracey Gallery of African Music (sub-Saharan instruments and taped examples of music). Also attached to the museum are the Old Provost, an early 19th-century military prison, and Fort Selwyn on Gunfire Hill.

J L B SMITH INSTITUTE OF ICHTHYOLOGY, Rhodes University, Grahamstown: Marine fish displays, notably the coelacanth (discovered by Smith).

KOWIE MUSEUM, Post Office Building, Port Alfred: The history of the settlement since 1820 (including an index system popular with genealogists), featuring some fine paintings by Thomas Baines.

RHODES MUSEUM OF CLASSICAL ANTIQUITIES, Rhodes University, Grahamstown: Collection includes Greek and Roman vases and coins.

1820 SETTLERS MEMORIAL MUSEUM, Somerset Street, Grahamstown: Includes a Settlers Gallery, Military Gallery, Costume Gallery and an Early Grahamstown Gallery, and houses a Thomas Baines collection.

Music and theatre

The 1820 Settlers Monument in Grahamstown hosts an annual national arts festival and is used for other musical and drama productions. The university also puts on productions.

Powerboating

The Boesmans, Kariega and Kowie river estuaries are all popular powerboating spots. There is a powerboating club in Port Alfred.

Surfing

The most suitable spot for surfing is in the vicinity of the pier at Port Alfred, but beaches to the east and west of the river mouth are also popular.

Swimming

There are good bathing beaches at Boknes, Boesmansriviermond, Kenton on Sea, Kasouga, Port Alfred, Rietpunt and Kleinemonde, with possibly the safest and most attractive spots in the coves along the Kenton coastline.

Tennis and squash

Grahamstown and Port Alfred have tennis and squash facilities while Kenton and Boknes have tennis courts. Contact the local municipalities.

Walks

The two-day Alexandria Trail is the focus of hiking in this area, but shorter walks include across the dunefields to Dias Cross, in the forests of the Waters Meeting Nature Reserve (Bathurst), through the 1820 Settlers Wild Flower Garden in Grahamstown and the Thomas Baines Nature Reserve and Andries Vosloo Kudu Reserve outside the city. Grahamstown itself is the ideal city to explore on foot.

Yachting and dinghy sailing

The boat club on the Kowie River estuary is the only berth for yachts in this area, but dinghies can sail on Settlers Dam and the smaller Boesmans and Kariega estuaries.

INFORMATION

- Alexandria State Forest, PO Box 50, Alexandria 6185. Tel 04652=1103
- Algoa Regional Services Council, PO Box 318, Port Elizabeth 6000. Tel 041=561000
- Grahamstown Municipality, PO Box 176, Grahamstown 6140. Tel 0461=22043
- Grahamstown Publicity Association and Information Bureau, 63 High St, Grahamstown 6140. Tel 0461=23241
- Kenton on Sea Municipality, PO Box 5, Kenton on Sea 6191. Tel 04682=26
- Port Alfred Municipality, PO Box 13, Port Alfred 6170. Tel 0464=41140
- Port Alfred Publicity Association, PO Box 63, Port Alfred 6170. Tel 0464=41235

Nearest AA Office

- AA House, 2 Granville Rd, Greenacres, Port Elizabeth 6001. Tel 041=341313

Bathe in the sunshine of an untamed shoreline

EXPLORE AN UNSPOILT COASTAL WILDERNESS at your leisure. Here, for the sprawling length of the Ciskeian coastline and then beyond to Kidd's Beach, you are free to wander along sparkling beaches wet by the spray of the warm Indian Ocean, to cast a line from a ragged reef and reel in the sea's glistening treasures, to steal through dune forests and catch a glimpse of their shy inhabitants. You can reach this secluded coast by leaving the main southern route (R72) and winding down quiet country tracks to tiny seaside villages; or, even better, you can leave your car behind and instead follow the whole shoreline on foot . . . in as little as three days, or as long as you like, while you soak in the peace of a landscape unmarred by man.

The typical Ciskei coastline, with sand barring a sparkling river from the sea.

1 Great Fish River

This river marks the southern boundary of Ciskei, but there are no border formalities. Two bridges span the river, the more modern one built after devastating floods in the 1970s. (If necessary, the old bridge — lying rusting peacefully in the sun — can be used to cross the river; wading across the river should not under any circumstances be attempted as this can be very dangerous.)

The Great Fish was initially chosen as the site for a port, but had to be abandoned as it silts up badly. Today this spot, with its wide beach, shelving shallowly, is favoured for beachcombing and fishing. On either side of the mouth are rocky points: the one on the right (facing the sea) is known as Granville's Gully and is good for shelling; the one on the left, a headland of sea-eroded caves, blowholes and raw cliffs, is good for fishing. This is also the scenic site of a planned casino complex.

On the southern bank of the river is a wide floodplain, teeming with bird life, including Cape teal and Egyptian and spurwing geese. Near the mouth is a camp site, and tucked in among the forested dunes, out of the wind, are privately owned cottages and shacks.

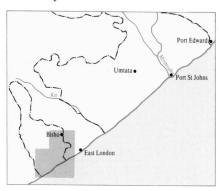

2 Waterloo Bay

Immediately east of the headland at the mouth of the Great Fish River is Waterloo Bay, named during the frontier wars. Here soldiers and supplies were offloaded for Fort Peddie in the interior. The headland itself was the site of the port captain's headquarters, and at one time as many as 63 sailing ships lay at anchor in the roadstead.

About 2 km beyond the Fish River bridge a dirt road leads down to picnic and braai sites tucked into the trees at the blind mouth of the Old Woman's River. (Fort Albert was built near here

to protect offloading operations.) A great sweep of unspoilt beach, backed by coastal forest and passing Stalwart Point — where the steamship *Stalwart* was wrecked in 1866 — at the eastern edge of the bay, leads after 12 km to Mpekweni (with a caravan and chalet complex on the southern bank, just off the coastal road). Along the way there is prolific bird life to enjoy, such as the fish eagle, water dikkop, white fronted plover and whitebreasted cormorant.

3 Mpekweni, Mtati and Mgwalana rivers

The coastal road (R72) runs only a kilometre or so from this stretch of shoreline, with its wide beaches, high forested dunes and lovely blind river lagoons. Access to the pretty lagoon of Mpekweni is via a long downhill run, flanked by the dunes that divide road from sea. The sophisticated Mpekweni Marine Resort occupies the northern side of the beach approach, offering residents such facilities as tennis and squash, a swimming pool and sailboard hire.

By contrast, the nearby Mtati Lagoon is quite isolated, and access may be barred by a locked farm gate. Perhaps this is why the beach remains wholly unspoilt.

Where the road crosses the Mgwalana River there are good views of the lagoon to both left and right. About half a kilometre to the north is a farm gate with a track leading down to private holiday shacks overlooking the river mouth and towering green-clothed dunes. (Four-wheel drive would probably be necessary in rainy weather.)

4 Begha Mouth

Unlike many of the rivers along this coast, the Bira or Begha flows into the sea. Begha Mouth is one

LEFT *The broad expanse of the Great Fish River forms a formidable barrier.*

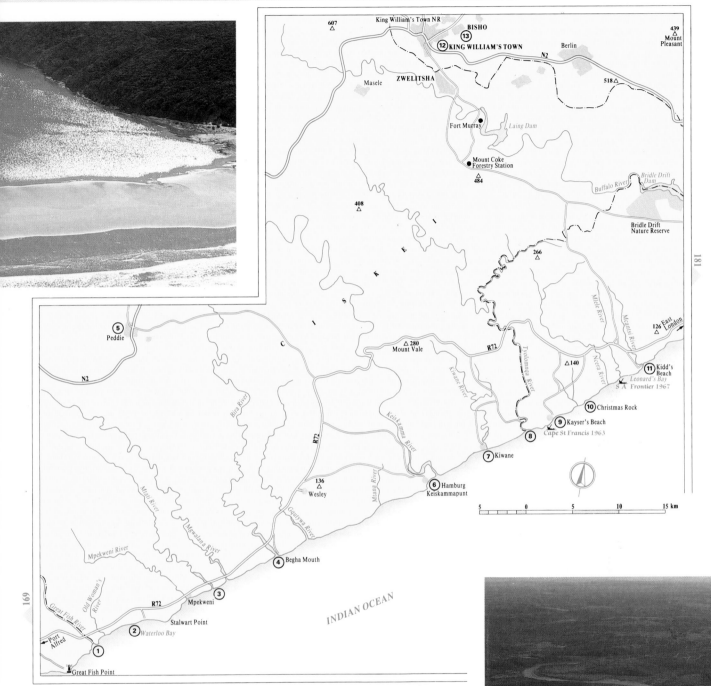

of Ciskei's prettiest coastal sites, but at present it is still pleasantly out of the way, reached by a track that falls steeply down to the peaceful river and sea. (The north bank is not open to the public.)

From the south bank (where a nature conservation officer mans a shack) a rocky reef, which is exposed at low tide, stretches far into the sea. The beach it shields is excellent for shell collecting and for spotting birds, especially migratory waders. The typical high forested dunes backing the beach are also home to the shy duiker, bushbuck, genet and mongoose.

As part of a development plan for the area, the Ciskei Tourist and Holiday Trust has built a parking lot and sea wall, but the attractive thatched white rondavels, clustered on immaculate lawns on the north bank of the river, are privately owned.

From a hill north of the settlement, you have an excellent view of the ridge of rocks known as Madagascar Reef since the steamer *Madagascar*

RIGHT *The Mtati River flows through sculpted land forms to the sea.*

THE MYSTERY OF THE RIETBOK

On a misty night in March 1967, the South African Airways Viscount *Rietbok* with 25 people on board disappeared on the short flight from Port Elizabeth to East London, apparently crashing into the sea in the vicinity of Kayser's Beach.

At the time, this was the worst air disaster in South African history, and it was made more poignant by the fact that all attempts to locate the wreck and the bodies of the victims failed. Even today the loss of the *Rietbok* remains a mystery.

The *Rietbok* disappeared without a sound — no signal was sent, no radio contact was made with airport control. What could have happened to prevent the crew from somehow alerting the authorities to their plight? At the official inquiry into the disaster, several possible causes of the accident were ruled out. These included poor visibility and turbulence; engine, electrical or structural failure; collision with birds; sabotage; even incapacitation of both pilot and copilot by noxious gas or explosion.

What the inquiry could not rule out was that the pilot, Captain Gordon Benjamin Lipawsky, had had a sudden heart attack. Lipawsky, a decorated veteran of the Second World War and as a model pilot, had six months earlier complained of not feeling well, but after medical examination and treatment had been declared fit for duty. What now seems possible is that the 48-year-old Lipawsky, gripped by pain, stood up and then fell forward between the seat and control columns. The copilot would simply not have had time to try to regain control of the aircraft and also to reach for the radio microphone to call for help.

All this is speculation, and it seems it will always remain so. The only concrete testimony is in the simple plaques on Kayser's Beach in memory of some of the victims of the *Rietbok* tragedy.

Jutting from the sands at Kayser's Beach is all that remains of the trawler Cape St Francis.

was wrecked here in 1858. Even before then, however, the reef had claimed a victim in the sailing ship *Elizabeth*, wrecked in 1839.

Just north of Begha the R72 loops away from the coast and heads inland, but it is possible to walk the 20 km along the shore to the village of Hamburg on the Keiskamma River. (Note that between the mouths of the Gqutywa and Mtana rivers along the way, there is a restricted military area above the high-water mark; take care not to trespass.) If following the road to Hamburg, linger at the little mission village of Wesley, named after Methodist father John Wesley. Both the village church and Kei Carpets, unique in southern Africa as a hand-knotted carpet factory, are well worth a visit.

5 Peddie

The town of Peddie lies on the N2, the main inland route through Ciskei, between Grahamstown and King William's Town, at the point where you would turn off for the little coastal settlement of Hamburg.

Cradled by hills, this forgotten town — with its tin-roofed hotel, paint-peeling church, country supermarket and herbalist — is rich in military history. It was named after Lieutenant-Colonel John Peddie of the 72nd Highlanders, commander of the British troops and responsible for the building of an eight-pointed, star-shaped fort there in 1835. Peddie played an important role in the defence of the eastern frontier, notably in the hostilities between the Xhosa and the Mfengu. The fort itself has not survived, but a double-storey watchtower (a national momument) on a ridge above the town is a reminder of the past.

6 Hamburg

The Keiskamma is a large river, flowing down to the sea in a great loop of water fringed with reed grass and marshy floodplain. The Khoi translation for Keiskamma is 'sweet' or 'shining waters', and the sunlit lagoon against its backdrop of green hills is just that.

The substantial holiday settlement of Hamburg is situated about 3 km from the mouth of the river and boasts among its amenities a hotel, chalets and a caravan park, as well as a petrol station and postal agency. Its name is a reminder of its origins, as it was established by a party of German settlers in 1857.

Once legendary as an angler's paradise, the main recreation at the resort is still angling (a few fishing boats can be hired from the hotel), but all forms of watersport — boardsailing, waterskiing, powerboating, sailing — are very popular, and the area is also frequented by hikers and birdwatchers. (The local nature conservation officer, whose office is high on a hill overlooking the village and the endless coast, is a good source of information on the environment.) A spacious, crescent moon-shaped swimming beach leads to Keiskamma-punt, where the rocks and reef make ideal angling spots, and a tarred road leads down to a boat launching site.

7 Kiwane

Of all the rivers along this coast, the lagoon at Kiwane (fig tree) is possibly the loveliest, rather like a Scottish loch with its expanse of soft water and rise of high mountains. When the evening shadows lengthen, it becomes a composite of pale pinks and blues, pierced by bird calls.

The gravel road from the R72 is an easy one, passing small villages with the occasional scatter of geese or hens as your car drops gently down towards the sea. Kiwane offers plenty of caravan sites and chalets for the visitor, but provides only fresh water and rudimentary shelter so is perhaps better suited to boy scout outings than family holidays. For even the most sophisticated tastes, however, there is the irresistible cocoon of silence and beauty, as the sea laps a smooth beach backed by desertlike sand dunes.

8 Tyolomnqa River

The mouth of the Tyolomnqa (or Chalumna) River is less than 5 km from the Kiwane, but to reach it by road can be tricky, demanding four-wheel drive to wind through the rural hills, dusted with acacias and grazing cattle. The effort is worthwhile, though, as the river mouth amid high hills is very beautiful. Note that the mouth is very deep (it is never sealed by sand) and dangerous, so do not attempt to cross it except by boat.

The rocky area south of the river is known for its shells, especially large black mussels, and this mainly rocky stretch, interrupted occasionally by small sandy bays, continues north of the river as far as Kayser's Beach.

The Tyolomnqa may seem an insignificant mark on the map but it gained international recognition in 1938 when the first coelacanth (*Latimeria chalumnae*) — a fish long thought extinct — was netted in the sea off the river mouth.

9 Kayser's Beach

This popular little resort draws visitors mainly from King William's Town in the interior, and it is particularly favoured by anglers. There are several caravan sites, and holiday homes reach almost down to the beach, with its green lawn and informal parking area. The dunes edging the shore are covered with state-protected coastal forests.

The boulder-strewn beach crunches underfoot with thousands of tiny shells — an endless playground for children, but the sea itself has a powerful backwash. The rusting hulk of the trawler *Cape St Francis*, wrecked in 1963, provides a handy backrest for sunbathers, while the reef on which it ran aground provides good surf.

An intriguing rock carving at Kayser's Beach has long been a source of speculation. Some have claimed that it is a message left by a sailor of long ago, others that this is a clue to buried treasure ... which despite all efforts, no one has been able to find. Still, there is reward enough for everyone in the sun-splashed seascape.

10 Christmas Rock

This large, squared rock is surrounded by water except at low tide. The name derives from the nearby farm Christmas Vale, so-called because of the many farming families who camped on the

THE COURAGE OF THE CRANE

A graceful bird on land and in flight.

The graceful blue crane (*Anthropoides paradisea*), spotted generally inland rather than on the Ciskei coastline, is a symbol of that nation and has been incorporated in its heraldry, appearing on the flag and coat of arms, as well as in the logo of the Ciskei Department of Tourism and Aviation.

To the Xhosa the blue crane is known as *iNdwe* and it is deeply rooted in their culture. Traditionally, when someone had distinguished himself by great bravery, his chief would decorate him with a headdress made from the crane's tail feathers. The use of the blue crane in the flag thus symbolises the determination of the people to be brave and steadfast, and to work diligently for a better future.

Blue cranes (incidentally also the national bird of South Africa) are generally found in pairs, and may be highly gregarious, gathering in flocks of several hundred and showing off their excellent flying skills. They favour open countryside near water, and may even be seen sleeping while standing upright in water.

Long-legged and long-necked, blue cranes bear a fair resemblance to storks, but unlike the usually silent storks, they utter a bold, guttural croak. The plumage that earned them their name deepens from a very pale blue-grey to slate grey, and they are distinguished by the long black ornamental feathers that curve to the ground.

beach over the Christmas holiday. Its sandy beach, interspersed with numerous reefs, attracts beachcombers and anglers (there is a good spot for launching powerboats). Besides the main caravan park and resort, with a number of holiday houses, there is a second little resort further along the road, in the lee of the dunes alongside Lilyvale Creek.

Thanks to the protected state forest above the high-water mark, the bird and other wildlife is particularly good.

11 Kidd's Beach

Favoured by King William's Town residents, this resort, with its long main street, lies alongside the Mcantsi River and its lagoon. The river is heavily treed and the gravel road fringing the rocky reefed

BELOW *Even the popular resort of Hamburg, a mecca for tourists on the Ciskei coastline, has not cast off its timeless rural trappings.*

Kidd's Beach on the banks of the Mcantsi, where an inviting tidal pool is set among ragged rocks.

shore looks over lovely green lawn. At the foot of the main road into the town is a tidal pool. Kidd's Beach is very popular with anglers, but boardsailors and surfers also enjoy its excellent surf, and boaters opt for the lagoon.

Besides Kidd's Beach's facilities (which include a hotel and two caravan parks), accommodation is available at Palm Springs (named for the wild palms growing along the Mlele River) about 3 km to the south through rolling farmland. Here a charming lagoon between high cliffs leads down to the beach at Leonard's Bay.

12 King William's Town
There is a good road link between Kidd's Beach, the last of the resorts before the start of what can be considered the East London coastline, and

King William's Town on the upper reaches of the Buffalo River. Named in 1835 after William IV of England, it was established on the site of an earlier mission station and grew to be the main military and administrative centre of the volatile eastern Cape frontier region.

The town is steeped in history and perhaps the best way to absorb the atmosphere is to wander through its streets, guided by the walking tour pamphlets issued by the Kaffrarian Museum. Historical buildings to look out for include the Holy Trinity Church (1850), erected originally as a military chapel; the South African Missionary Museum, housed in a former Methodist church building (1855); Grey Hospital (1859), with its imposing bell tower; the Town Hall (1867), with the borough arms in relief on the gable; the neoclassical lines of the Victoria Drill Hall (1897); and the Natural History Museum (1898).

The well-known Kaffrarian Museum (1884) demands a longer visit to enjoy its many varied exhibits: military displays; cultural history exhibits focusing on, for instance, the 19th-century German settlers; a recently created Xhosa Gallery tracing social change among the Xhosa-speaking peoples of the Ciskei; and an extensive natural history section, with about a thousand display specimens. (The internationally known research collection of some 35 000 mammal specimens is separately housed and on view only to scientists.) Best-loved here is certainly Huberta the hippo, whose long trek south from Zululand in the late 1920s earned her a place in the heart of a nation. Sadly she was shot at the Keiskamma River but the museum staff ensured that she would not be forgotten, and today she even serves as the distinc-

LEFT *Gracious Grey Hospital, King William's Town, framed by greenery.*

tive logo of the museum.

In addition to the 68 ha nature reserve within the town's boundaries, where valley bushveld is preserved (including the sweet thorn, cabbage tree, euphorbia and camphor bush), King William's Town is handily near the Pirie Forest (with its trout hatchery dating back to 1896) and the Amatola Mountains, which means several nature trails are accessible to visitors.

13 Bisho
The capital of Ciskei, Bisho lies dreamlike at the end of a long hill-climb from King William's Town. Picture the fairy-tale confectionary house from *Hansel and Gretel* and you have some idea of this pastel extravaganza, perhaps based on a traditional Xhosa village. Multistoreyed buildings in pink, green and biscuit face the brooding slopes of the Amatola (Mathole) Mountains. Besides the collection of administrative buildings, Bisho boasts a broadcasting centre, a large sports stadium and a luxury hotel and casino complex.

THINGS TO DO

Angling
This is a popular coastline for angling, although some fishermen complain that flooding has reduced catches in recent years. In favourable conditions powerboat anglers still make good catches of geelbek, rockcod, red steenbras and seventyfour, among others. Fishing boats can be hired at Hamburg (through the hotel).

Check with the Division of Nature Conservation in King William's Town about any restrictions applying to angling. Also, contact the King William's Town Municipality about trout fishing at the Maden and Rooikrans dams (located off the Stutterheim road).

Beachcombing and shelling
This coastline is renowned for its shipwrecks and there is a fair amount of flotsam and jetsam to draw beachcombers. Shards of blue-and-white porcelain have been found along the coast between the Mtana and Keiskamma mouths. The numerous money cowries (small, blue-black shells used as currency in early trading days) to be found at the Mtana mouth probably came off a wreck.

Areas particularly good for shelling include Kayser's Beach, Begha Mouth and the shoreline south of the Tyolomnqa, but as much of the coast is rocky with reef outcrops, practically anywhere can be rewarding.

Birdwatching
The Fish River mouth with its marshy floodplain offers a particularly rewarding variety of birds, including geese, teal and other ducks, stilts and smaller migratory waders. In general, bird life is rich along the often empty beaches, in the forested high dunes and at the blind river estuaries.

The hiking booklet produced by the Ciskei Department of Tourism and

Fish type	Season	Best area	Best bait
Bronze bream	All year	Waterloo Bay, Mtati River mouth, Begha Mouth	Prawns, redbait, mussels, chokka
Galjoen	Mar — Sept	Kidd's Beach	Chokka, crabs, mussels, redbait
Garrick (leervis)	Mar — Oct	Fish River mouth, Kayser's Beach	Live bait, chokka, strips of mackerel, spoons, plugs
Kob (kabeljou)	All year	Fish River mouth, Hamburg, Kayser's Beach, Christmas Rock	Sardines, squid, bloodworms, chokka
White steenbras	May — Aug	Tyolomnqa River — Ncera Point	Prawns, bloodworms, mussels

Aviation has a very useful checklist of well over 200 birds likely to be spotted all along the coast.

Boardsailing
Any of the larger river estuaries and many of the beaches are suitable for boardsailing, but particularly popular are Mpekweni (where boards can be hired), Hamburg and Kidd's Beach (suitable for beginners).

Bowls
Greens are available at Mpekweni (contact the resort) and King William's Town (contact the municipality).

Camping and caravanning
There are caravan and/or camp sites at Fish River mouth, Hamburg, Kiwane, Kayser's Beach, Christmas Rock and Kidd's Beach. For a small fee, you are allowed to camp anywhere on the beach, except in the military zone between the Gqutywa and Mtana rivers. Contact the resort of your choice or the Department of Tourism for details.

Canoeing
The river estuaries in general are excellent for canoeing and some of the many rivers are navigable upstream.

Diving
The numerous reefs make for good diving, rich as they are in life.

Drives and viewsites
The Ciskei Department of Tourism issues several brochures on motoring trails, including one on the coastal circuit. The route covers the coast from Kidd's Beach to the Fish River, and goes inland as far as Bisho and Peddie. The easiest lap is the dune-hugging stretch between the Fish and Begha Mouth, at which point the main road heads inland.

Golf
Contact the municipality at King William's Town about golf courses.

Libraries
A library operates at Kidd's Beach twice a week. The municipal library in King William's Town also houses a valuable collection of Africana.

Museums
KAFFRARIAN MUSEUM, Alexandra Road, King William's Town: The museum complex includes the Thomas Daines Wing (previously the public library), the Xhosa Gallery and the excellent Natural History Museum.
SOUTH AFRICAN MISSIONARY MUSEUM, Berkeley Street, King William's Town: Unique in the country, this museum features displays of the Moravian, London, Glascow, Wesleyan and Baptist missionary societies. The press that printed the first Xhosa Bible in 1859 is housed here.

Powerboating
The main powerboating spots are Mpekweni and Hamburg, with boat launching sites on the beach at Hamburg and Christmas Rock. Laing Dam (via Fort Murray off the King William's Town road) is the launch site of the Ciskei Powerboat Club.

Shipwrecks
The coast is littered with wrecks, so much so that the Ciskei Department of Tourism has named its coastal hiking trail the Shipwreck Trail. This names some 18 wrecks, but do not expect to see much: it takes the sea and sand only a short while to bury a ship. The remains of the trawler *Cape St Francis*, wrecked in 1963, can be seen at Kayser's Beach and those of the coaster *Frontier* (1957) at the Ncera River.

Surfing
Hamburg offers quite a good beach break, and Kayser's Beach and Kidd's Beach are also popular with surfers.

Swimming
There is excellent swimming along the length of the coast but avoid swimming across river mouths and at high tides because of the shark hazard. There is a sparkling swimming pool and a paddling pool at Mpekweni and a tidal pool at Kidd's Beach.

Tennis and squash
Both sports are available at Mpekweni and at King William's Town.

Walks
The main organised walk in the area is the approximately 65 km, three-day Shipwreck Hiking Trail, from the Great Fish River up to the Ciskei border or beyond to Kidd's Beach. Make sure you have a copy of the Ciskei Department of Tourism's trail booklet, which describes the route in detail and gives a checklist of birds, fish and vegetation you might expect to see. You can decide how much or how little of the trail to do, but always remember to provide protection from the sun, to take along a water bottle (fresh water is available only at resorts) and to carry a tide table so that you cross river estuaries only at low tide.

The Great Fish River, a camp site of unruffled serenity.

INFORMATION
• Ciskei Department of Tourism and Aviation, Private Bag X0026, Bisho, Ciskei. Tel 0401=91131
• Division of Nature Conservation, Private Bag X501, Zwelitsha, Ciskei. Tel 0401=42011
• King William's Town Municipality, PO Box 33, King William's Town 5600. Tel 0433=23450
• SA Tourism Board, NBS Building, Terminus Street, East London 5201. Tel 0431=26410
Nearest AA Office
• AA House, 27 Fleet Street, East London 5201. Tel 0431=21271

The warm heartland of the Buffalo

THE BALMY HOLIDAY PLAYGROUND of East London, on the Buffalo River, started life on a much more serious note. Initially it was a port and a place to land military supplies for the troubled frontier region, and it also served as a fort, one of nine between the endlessly green, sand-duned coast and the stronghold of King William's Town in the interior. This was a restless and turbulent land that somehow could not accommodate what seemed to be mutually incomprehensible cultures, but it was also an achingly beautiful land, one with many rivers, rolling downs and silent shores.

It is this beauty that draws visitors to East London all year round. Here the equable climate lets you relax and enjoy the warm waters, surf swells and angling shores at beaches within strolling distance from town.

The Buffalo, at the heart of the city.

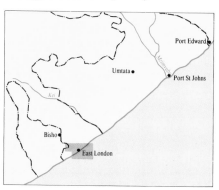

The sturdy bulk of Cove Rock rears from a blue sea against the backdrop of a paler sky.

1 Cove Rock

Travelling along the main coastal road from Port Elizabeth (R72), this perfect natural fortress is the first landmark on the East London coast. (Before you reach it, at the mouths of both the Gxulu and Goda rivers, are small resorts with caravan and camp sites, and opportunities for angling, boating and swimming.) Cove Rock is a spectacular knuckle of green shrub-covered rock projecting from the ocean, with pounding surf on three sides and on the fourth, waves of yellow sand dunes stretching back 500 m to the coastal forest. From the pottery shards and black mussel and limpet shells found, it seems early hunter-gatherers may have lingered here from time to time.

The name Cove Rock is a corruption of the earlier Coffin Rock or Doodkist, as Dutch seafarers referred to it. In Xhosa it is known as Gompo, perhaps because of the sound of waves thundering into the gap or cove, a sort of amphitheatre carved out by the sea.

Gravel roads lead to Cove Rock's eastern and western shoulders, the former to the official Cove Rock Park and picnic area and the latter to Rockclyffe-on-Sea holiday resort on the blind mouth of the Hlozi River. From both approaches

there is a kilometre walk to the rock, well rewarded by the sight of perhaps the widest variety of waders and sea birds on this stretch of coast, including sanderlings and turnstones (migrants from Europe), terns, gulls and Cape wagtails and dikkops. Rock pigeons and redwinged starlings breed on Cove Rock, and black oystercatchers in the area between here and the Hlozi.

It is best to avoid Cove Rock when the wind is blowing, for this thin peninsula is very exposed. Swimmers should take note of the backwash, and anglers should watch out for rogue waves.

2 West Bank resorts

A scenic drive skirts the coastline between Leach Bay and West Bank, taking in several small resorts. From the R72 the road heads for the coast, crossing Hickman's River. On a bend of this river, just back from its mouth and set in a wooded valley, is a small resort on an attractive lagoon.

From here several popular resort areas merge into one another, offering wide beaches backed by impressive dunes and sprinkled with interesting rock pools. The road runs very close to the sea so access for beach-goers is easy and drivers can stop at almost any point and enjoy the view. The first

resort reached is Leach Bay, where the main attraction is the swimming pool. Between here and Fuller's Bay a caravan park is pleasantly situated on gently rising grassy downs. The next stretch of beach is rockier and draws mainly anglers but a vast artificial tidal pool is also found here.

At this point the road loops inwards on a circuit of the original South African Grand Prix racetrack, inaugurated in 1934 but overtaken in the late '60s by Kyalami. Linking it to the R72 is Potter's Pass, trailing through hills and windy grasslands which in spring and early summer are flooded with colour by the bloom of harebells, watsonias, fire lilies, gladioli and everlastings. In all, some seventy species of wild flowers are protected in the Potter's Pass reserve.

Back on the coastal route, grassy picnic sites overlook the surf and the rocky shore of Shelly Beach, where you can sift through the sands for innumerable shells bleached by wave and sun. From nearby Hood Point lighthouse, the road veers inland again to West Bank, the site of the original Fort Glamorgan, of which only the powder magazine remains.

3 Berlin

The village of Berlin, about 40 km inland from East London on the N2, is one of several settlements in the Border area that owe their existence to German immigration. Some 5 000 Germans came to South Africa in the mid-19th century, about half of them soldiers of the German Legion, recruited by Britain during the Crimean

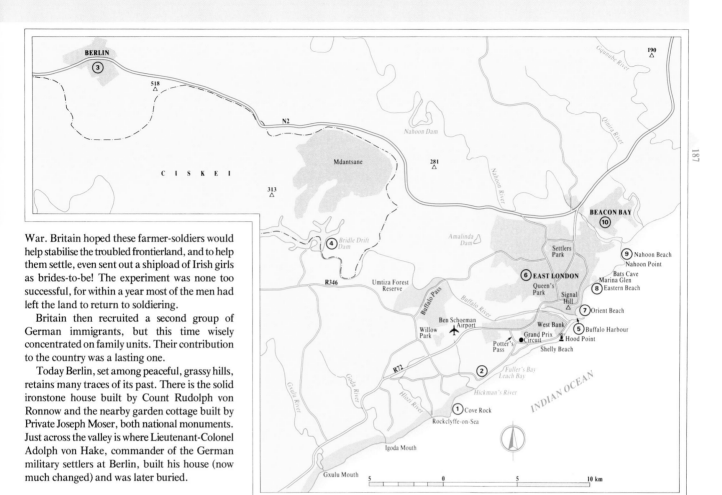

War. Britain hoped these farmer-soldiers would help stabilise the troubled frontierland, and to help them settle, even sent out a shipload of Irish girls as brides-to-be! The experiment was none too successful, for within a year most of the men had left the land to return to soldiering.

Britain then recruited a second group of German immigrants, but this time wisely concentrated on family units. Their contribution to the country was a lasting one.

Today Berlin, set among peaceful, grassy hills, retains many traces of its past. There is the solid ironstone house built by Count Rudolph von Ronnow and the nearby garden cottage built by Private Joseph Moser, both national monuments. Just across the valley is where Lieutenant-Colonel Adolph von Hake, commander of the German military settlers at Berlin, built his house (now much changed) and was later buried.

4 Bridle Drift Dam and Buffalo Pass

Approaching East London via the R346, or Mount Coke road, you pass several places of interest. About 25 km from the city, a little way off the main road, lies the extensive Bridle Drift Dam, filling several rugged, high valleys of the Buffalo River. This popular recreational spot is home to a sailing and a powerboat club, and areas for both activities are clearly demarcated. To protect the dam's particularly rich bird life, no boating or fishing is allowed in the area set aside as a sanctuary. A tongue of land juts out into the water with peaceful picnic spots beneath shady trees.

Further along the Mount Coke road towards East London is Reptile World, a crocodile breeding and research station that welcomes visitors and offers tours around the crocodile, snake and other exotic reptile cages. The setting is spectacular as the station looks directly down into the Bridle Drift Dam valley.

About 9 km from Reptile World is the Agricultural Research Station, specialising in the pineapple industry and featuring an agricultural museum. (To visit the station, contact the Department of Agriculture in East London.) Just beyond here is Buffalo Pass, a steep-sided and

RIGHT *Ambling, angling or just paddling are all popular at Eastern Beach.*

heavily wooded road constructed during the Second World War as a precaution against the severing of the bridge over the Buffalo, the only link between the two sides of the river. Flanking the river is the Umtiza Forest, 560 ha of valley bushveld vegetation protecting a rich wildlife —

birds such as narina trogons, forest weavers and crowned eagles, as well as shy blue duikers and bushbuck and blue samango and vervet monkeys. The many trees include the Buffalo thorn (*Umtiza listerana*), endemic to the area. Several hiking trails and picnic spots can be found in the reserve,

but permission must first be obtained from the Department of Environment Affairs.

5 Buffalo Harbour

From his eyrie on Signal Hill, the port captain of East London's harbour looks down on Buffalo River and the busy dockland that has mushroomed on both banks since that day in November 1836 when George Rex's brig, the *Knysna*, anchored off the sandbar. Its arrival at the river the Khoikhoi called the 'place of buffaloes' and early Dutch seafarers called the Eerste, was to supplement military supplies for the colonial forces in the volatile eastern Cape frontier zone. More importantly it signalled the beginning of the development of the area, which subsequently became known as Port Rex. In 1848 this was annexed by the colourful Cape governor Sir Harry Smith, who renamed it East London. Yet another piece of Africa had been added to Queen Victoria's far-flung empire.

East London grew to the extent that today its sophisticated port — the only river port of any commercial significance in South Africa — has six wharves on its east bank and seven on its west and handles export cargoes of pineapples, wool, citrus, copper and maize. The grain elevator on the western bank has a voracious capacity of 70 000 tons and can load a ship at the rate of 1 600 tons an hour. There is a dry dock for ship repairs just below the two bridges over the Buffalo.

Container ships seem to squeeze past the long, dolos-reinforced arm of south breakwater and the shorter east breakwater (Orient Pier) to enter the harbour and its roomy turning basin before berthing at one of the wharves. Before the completion of the turning basin in 1937, larger ships had to anchor at sea and send their cargo into harbour by lighter. The unfortunate passengers coming ashore were 'offloaded' into wicker baskets first and these were transferred to lighters. Nowadays, the harbour can accommodate substantial ocean-going vessels.

DAMMING THE SEA WITH THE DOLOS

The indomitable dolos.

It used to be said that some shipowners, anxious to claim handsome insurance payouts, would send their vessels to East London to be wrecked. The coast east and west of the Buffalo, and the river mouth itself with its notorious sand bar, indeed proved extremely hazardous and almost a hundred ships were lost here.

Extensive improvements to the harbour had to be made over the years, but still it seemed nothing could hold back the relentless sea. After the original breakwater was breached by fierce storms in 1944, a seemingly impenetrable wall of 41-ton concrete blocks was erected to protect the moored ships. But a scant twenty years later this massive barrier had all but succumbed to the ocean.

East London harbour engineer Eric Merrifield thought long and hard about the problem and began experimenting with irregularly shaped armour blocks that would be less susceptible to wave action. Eventually he came up with the dolos, so-called because the shape was reminiscent of an ox knucklebone. This 18-ton unit is shaped rather like an H with one of the uprights twisted through ninety degrees to interlock with the next unit. The principle involved is that the dolos does not resist the force of wave action but rather breaks it up, dissipating its energy and at the same time absorbing the shock. Its anchorlike ability to interlock gives it enormous strength and stability.

Merrifield's great contribution to harbour engineering has been recognised internationally and today the dolos can be found protecting not only local harbours (for instance in the 2 km-long wall guarding Port Elizabeth's shoreline), but also ports scattered all around the globe.

Buffalo Harbour is home to the city's yacht club and the National Sea Rescue Institute station. Upriver, past all the railway shunting and the quarry, are the powerboat and rowing clubs.

The main entrance to the harbour is off Hely Hutchinson Road, where there are four customs gates. To reach the western bank of the harbour, follow the yellow lines from the main entrance.

6 City of East London

The mixed ancestry of East London is well reflected in the heart of the city. Oxford Street, running from the harbour to suburban Belgravia, has elegant church spires not unlike its university namesake and, as in that other London, is a long and busy shopping street. Other hints of England are found in this green and pleasant city and its up-and-down suburbs like Cambridge and Chiselhurst. The atmosphere is spiced with Indian and Chinese touches, and there are traces too of the German lineage, introduced by the settlers of the previous century. But this city, roughly halfway between the coastal borders of Ciskei and Transkei, remains quintessentially African, with the urban sprawl of Mdantsane 20 km from downtown Fleet Street.

Features of this modern city include some fine historical buildings: the railway station (built in 1877), the City Hall in Oxford Street (1897) and the Drill Hall in Fleet Street (1906). Best of all is gracious Gately House at the bottom of Caxton Street, home of the first mayor of East London and preserved in its Victorian glory as a national monument. Some of the excellent facilities include the East London Museum (Oxford Street), world-renowned for its exhibits of the prehistoric coelacanth and an egg of the extinct dodo; the Ann Bryant Art Gallery (Oxford Street), with contemporary and older works; as well as the intimate Guild Theatre (Dawson Road) and a well-stocked library (Buxton Street).

Providing breathing space in the city is Queen's Park, a 34 ha botanical garden sloping between the city centre and the Buffalo River. Besides preserving indigenous vegetation, the park also contains a zoo with more than fifty mammal species and half that number of reptile species, as well as about 150 different birds. On the opposite side of town (in Union Avenue, the extension of

LEFT *The long south breakwater guarding the vulnerable entrance to Buffalo Harbour.*

ABOVE *Nahoon River, a lazy drift of dappled blue water solidly flanked by densely forested banks.* BELOW *The stone memorial to the German settlers.*

Oxford Street) is Settlers Park, an indigenous garden serving as a memorial to the British settlers. (The German settlers are commemorated in a sculpture by Lippy Lipschitz near the aquarium on the seafront.) A little further afield, in the north-western suburb of Amalinda, is the small, century-old Amalinda Dam, enclosed by a 134 ha nature reserve. The dam and the numerous smaller ponds provide water and swamp habitats to support a refreshing variety of bird life, which can be enjoyed from the several shady picnic and braai sites. The fisheries station here breeds fish for stocking dams.

7 Orient Beach

East London's beachfront, a mere five minutes from the City Hall, begins at Orient Pier, the older and shorter of the two harbour breakwaters. The name comes from the Russian sail-rigged steamship *Orient*, which was wrecked here in the winter of 1907 while approaching the harbour.

Most of the ship lies buried beneath the pier today, but part of its rusting hull can be seen at low tide.

Orient Beach is tucked into the lee of the pier, safe from the ceaseless rollers a few hundred metres away. Popular with swimmers and surfers, it has everything the holiday-maker could want: a children's playground and paddling pool, toilets and change-rooms, umbrellas for hire, a restaurant and a Putt-Putt course. Orient Bath is a sea-water pool.

The beachfront continues from here as a sea-wall road (the Esplanade) overlooking a smidgeon of sand and black rock reef whose jagged edge is lullabyed day and night by the compassionate ocean.

8 Eastern Beach

About halfway between Orient and the next beach, Eastern, is the aquarium, which is well worth visiting, especially to view the entertaining Cape fur seals. The original seals were rescued as pups

Neat little Orient Beach, tucked between its namesake harbour pier and green-verged pools.

from the stormy seas and hand reared. Besides their outdoor tank, which is lapped by the sea, indoor tanks hold a wide collection of marine and freshwater fish, including some of the favourite angling species found along this coast.

Eastern Beach, softened by its legion of forested dunes, is one of East London's most popular spots, especially with surfers (who may enjoy their sport even in the evening when the beach is floodlit). Its facilities, and those of the adjoining parklike Marina Glen, vie with those at Orient Beach and include a small nature park, a children's miniature railway that operates at weekends, a restaurant, change-rooms and toilets. Camp and caravan sites are also situated here.

9 Nahoon Beach
Dividing Eastern Beach from Nahoon Point is the landmark known as Bats Cave, part of a giant chunk of wave-weathered, scrub-topped rock jutting out into the surf. The coastal vegetation on either side of it forms a delicate and widely variegated botanic garden.

The beach between the point and Nahoon River is a long wash of white sand backed by huge forested dunes. (This thicket creeps inland to the first suburbs and around the local golf course, forming a vital green lung in the urban environment.) The beach is a favourite with swimmers and anglers, while the reef at Nahoon Point is a major draw for surfers and the setting for several surfing contests.

The mudflats at the Nahoon estuary, with what must be the most southerly community of mangroves, are the frail refuge for a variety of wetland grasses and birds such as sandpipers, pied kingfishers and reed cormorants. Upriver the small Nahoon Dam provides excellent recreational opportunities for fishing, boating and dinghy sailing, and there are also several attractive picnic and braai sites.

10 Beacon Bay
Between the Nahoon and Qinira rivers lies Beacon Bay, seemingly a suburb of East London but in fact autonomous. Previously, the rugby-pitch wide stretch of beach leading off the pretty lagoon at the blind mouth of the Qinira was known as Bonza Bay, but after union with Beaconhurst farm the area became the municipality of Beacon Bay.

Today it boasts a shopping complex, holiday resort and hotel, a country club, an attractive coastal forest off the beach (the beach is reached by a paved walk from the parking area), and two nature reserves. In honour of its riverine location, Beacon Bay street names include a mix of the trees, flowers and birds found here.

THINGS TO DO

Angling

For advice on local conditions or on boat charter for deep-sea fishing trips, contact any of the larger sports shops. Note that to fish in the harbour vicinity you must be a member of a club (temporary membership can be organised through sports shops), and permits are then obtainable from the Harbour Revenue Office in Gasson Centre. A similar arrangement must be made for fishing (catches include blue bream, bass and carp) at Amalinda: you must have a Cape Provincial freshwater angling licence and a permit from the officer-in-charge (PO Box 3084, Cambridge 5206).

In general, the fishing is good but it is worth noting that for several weeks after the annual sardine run (usually in late June), prospects are very poor.

Art galleries

ANN BRYANT ART GALLERY, Oxford Street: Stately Victorian house with works by mainly South African artists, but also British 19th-century artists.

Beachcombing and shelling

Wherever there is a rocky beach (like Shelly Beach), you will find shells, which the East London Museum will willingly identify for you. Inshore reefs prevail on many of the beaches along this section of coast and beachcombing is consequently good, particularly in tidal rock pools. Try the reefs at low tide in front of the Esplanade, Fuller's Bay and Leach Bay, and for flotsam comb the beaches at Cove Rock.

Birdwatching

The best areas for birdwatching are Cove Rock (e.g. waders, black oystercatchers), the Nahoon estuary (kelp gulls, terns, cormorants, kingfishers), Potter's Pass (black-winged plovers, longtailed widows, Cape longclaws), and Amalinda Dam (bulbuls, glossy starlings, canaries, waterfowl, flycatchers).

Boardsailing

Good spots include the Nahoon River and Beacon Bay, and the Bridle Drift Dam inland on the Buffalo River. Note that Nahoon Reef is excellent in a south-wester but strictly for the experts. Contact any of the major sports shops to get in touch with the Border Surfsailing Association and the Border Windsurfer Class Association.

Boat trips

Contact major sports shops for information on deep-sea fishing charters and the publicity association for details of jaunts.

Fish type	Season	Best area	Best bait
Bronze bream	Mar — Aug	Beacon Bay, Cove Rock	Chokka, mussels, musselworms, prawns, fishbait, redbait
Galjoen	Mar — Sept	Rocky areas all along the coast	Chokka, crabs, mussels, musselworms, redbait
Kob (kabeljou)	All year	Esplanade/aquarium area, Nahoon Reef, Bats Cave, Cove Rock	Bloodworms, fishbait, prawns, sardines, squid
Leervis	Mar — Oct	Cove Rock, harbour wall	Chokka, spoons and plugs
Shad (elf)	Dec — April	Harbour wall, Esplanade/aquarium area	Artificial lures and spoons, chokka, fishbait
Stumpnose	All year	Rocky areas all along the coast	Fishbait, prawns, shrimps
White steenbras	May — Aug	Harbour wall, Eastern Beach	Bloodworms, mussels, prawns, redbait, fishbait

Bowls

There are more than a dozen bowling greens in the area. Contact the publicity association or the East London Bowling Club for more information.

Camping and caravanning

Camp and caravan sites can be found at the Gxulu and Goda mouths, and at Hickman's River, Fuller's Bay, Eastern Beach, Nahoon and Beacon Bay. Contact the municipality or publicity association for further information.

Canoeing

Bridle Drift Dam and the Nahoon River are particularly suitable for canoeing. Local sports shops can help you get in touch with the Buffalo and Leander rowing clubs.

Diving

Contact local diving shops for information on organised diving trips and hire of equipment. Nahoon Reef is popular for spearfishing and Orient Beach (headquarters of the Border Undersea Club) for shipwreck divers.

Drives and viewsites

One of the most attractive coastal drives is that along to West Bank, while the Esplanade is popular for parking and watching the ships entering and leaving the harbour. A good drive inland follows the N2 to the small settlement of Berlin, steeped in history from the German settler period.

The municipality runs several trails in and around East London, including the Milk Run to a dairy and milking parlour. Best known is the Pineapple Trail, covering some of the city's older buildings, the coast beyond West Bank to Cove Rock and a pineapple research station in this vicinity, and returning via Reptile World, the Umtiza Forest Reserve and Buffalo Pass. Other drives

planned by the Automobile Association are published in the handout 'East London Driveabouts'.

Golf

Visitors are welcome at the East London and West Bank golf clubs, and at Alexander Country Club. There is a Mashie golf course (with short holes) at Cambridge Sports Club.

Horseriding

Beginners and the more experienced are catered for at Welcome Stables, Igoda Mouth.

Libraries

There are municipal libraries in Beacon Bay and East London, the latter (with nine branches) issuing a monthly newsletter on its many activities.

Museums

EAST LONDON MUSEUM, Oxford Street: A comprehensive natural history collection that includes the first coelacanth to be caught and the only known dodo's egg.

GATELY HOUSE MUSEUM, Caxton Street: Elegant 19th-century townhouse, preserving many rich furnishings.

Music and theatre

GUILD THEATRE, Dawson Street: Regular dramatic performances.

ORIENT THEATRE, Orient Beach: Seating 1 000, it features musical evenings, particularly symphony concerts.

Powerboating

The East London Skiboat Club is on the Buffalo River, a little way upriver from the harbour, as is the Border Boat Club. The Border Aquatic Club operates from Bridle Drift Dam, which is the venue for waterskiing at weekends. There are launching places on the Buffalo River, Bridle Drift Dam, and at Nahoon and Beacon Bay.

Shipwrecks

About 150 ships have been wrecked since 1847 within a 5 km radius of the Buffalo Harbour, but the only visible wreck is the *Orient* (1907), part of which can be seen at low tide from the beach named after it.

Surfing

East London is renowned for its surfing, with Nahoon suitable for beginners and the reef at Nahoon Point superb for the experienced. Daily surfing reports are broadcast on Capital Radio at 06h40 and 15h40. Contact Border Surfriders Association for further information.

Swimming

Orient, Eastern and Nahoon are the city's three main swimming beaches with Beacon Bay not far away. The East London Surf Lifesaving Association is based at Nahoon. Lagoons popular for fairly safe, secluded bathing include Qinira, Nahoon and Hickman's. The tidal pool at Fuller's Bay is a favourite family bathing spot.

Tennis and squash

The East London and District Tennis Association or any of the larger sports shops can help with details of courts.

Walks

The Esplanade linking Orient and Eastern beaches is the choice city walk, with breathtaking beach views. Nature walks further afield include Amalinda Dam, Potter's Pass, Cove Rock and Umtiza Forest. Or take a stroll through the zoo, set in the 34 ha of Queen's Park.

Yachting and dinghy sailing

There is sailing from the East London Yacht Club in the harbour and from Bridle Drift Sailing Club.

INFORMATION

- Border Tourism Association, Civic Centre, Sherwood Ave, Beacon Bay 5205. Tel 472400
- Greater East London Publicity Association, City Hall, Oxford Street, East London 5201. Tel 26015
- National Sea Rescue Institute, Station 7, Buffalo Harbour, East London 5201. Tel 22555; emergencies 442142
- SA Tourism Board, NBS Building, Terminus Street, East London 5201. Tel 26410

Nearest AA Office
- AA House, 27 Fleet Street, East London 5201. Tel 21271

A secluded coast where bird cries pierce the green peace

THIS COAST OF HIGH KRANTZES and green forested dunes, brooding over still lagoons, sea-misted beaches and turbulent reefs lashed by waves, stretches beyond East London to the border of Transkei's Wild Coast.

The approach to the coast is through the wide pastures of sheep and cattle farms and the contrasting prickly parade of pineapple plantations. A necklace of holiday resorts is strung along the coast, almost all lying at river mouths where the luxuriant greenery shelters a wealth of bird life. Here visitors can opt for the thrill of rock angling off the reefs or casting a line from a shady river bank, for skipping along the water on a sailboard or slicing silently through it in a canoe, for lazing on the wide white beaches or sifting the sea's treasures from the sand. The whole length of the coast — from Kei Mouth to East London — can be walked: for three days follow the Strandloper Trail, retracing the footprints of the early inhabitants of this coast and those of the many castaways of days gone by.

Dolphins speckle the aquamarine seas.

1 Gateway to Transkei

Access routes to the coastal resorts beyond East London all lead — directly or indirectly — off the main road (N2) to Transkei, which heads in a north-easterly direction, reaching further and further inland as it approaches the border. The drive of some 70 km sweeps through rich green valleys, scored by rivers and sprinkled with sweet-smelling acacias, euphorbias and aloes.

Just before it descends into the great valley of the Kei, it is joined by the inland route from King William's Town, via the little town of Komga. Here you can walk down the main street at night and the only sounds to disturb the peace are the chirping of crickets and the mournful wail of a train. Links with the town's past are commemorated in its historical buildings, like St Paul's Anglican Church, a national monument reminiscent of an English country church. A plaque says the church, built in 1866, was used to shelter women and children during the frontier war of 1877-8.

To reach the Transkei border, where the formidable Kei is bridged, the N2 drops 330 m in less than 10 km.

2 Gonubie

Off the N2 just outside East London is Gonubie, lying at the mouth of the Gqunube River (named for the wild bramble berries growing on its banks). Gonubie has all the charm of a small village, with the main road taking you past municipal offices and the town's shopping centre before heading for the beach, where it becomes a 4 km seafront-hugging drive.

There are, in fact, two beaches: Gonubie Beach at the river mouth and German Bay further south. The wide sandy beach at the mouth stretches south for a kilometre before encountering the reefs that line the rest of the Gonubie shoreline. The river reaches the sea in a grand loop of water flanked on one side by a bank dotted with homes and on the other by a bluff, deep green with vegetation. Swimming here is reasonably safe but for the

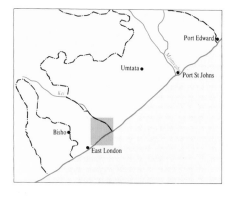

children there is also a tidal paddling pool.

There are countless pleasures to pursue at Gonubie: the river is navigable for up to 4 km upstream and it is popular with fishermen (note that no skiing is permitted and powerboats must keep to the speed limit); rock angling offers a variety of options, with heavy tackle required at the

river mouth; there is a pretty riverside picnic area as well as a choice of invigorating seafront walks. With two hotels and caravan parks, there are also facilities such as a bowling green, tennis and squash courts and a golf course.

The 8 ha Gonubie Nature Reserve, comprising two vleis and marshland alongside a coastal dune and residential area, is of special interest to bird lovers. More than a hundred species have been noted here, including jaçanas, dabchicks, moorhens and coots. They can be studied from the observation stands and hides overlooking the vleis where, amid the cries of the birds, the thunder of surf is always present. Also of interest in the reserve is a herbalist's garden of medicinal plants.

3 Rainbow Valley and Sunrise on Sea

North of the N2 turn-off to Gonubie, a loop road leads off to take you to a series of resorts along the

BELOW *Paddleskiing in the water at Gonubie.*

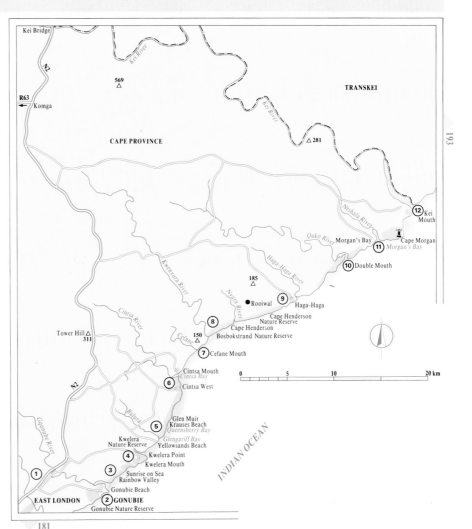

east coast. About 20 km from East London is the picturesque resort of Rainbow Valley, nestling among trees and sand dunes. Access to the Gqunube River, just over the hill, is on foot. This secluded spot, with its attractive beach and good angling reefs, is more suited to canoeing than powerboating, and its quiet charms draw holiday-makers back year after year. Amenities include chalets and caravan sites, a swimming pool and tennis court, and a small shop.

Adjacent Sunrise on Sea consists of a clutch of mainly holiday cottages, sheltering behind sand dunes with a small stream running in their lee. The township, with road names like Neptune and Shelly, was first developed in 1931 but has remained secluded, not even boasting a shop. The beach is rocky in the main with reefs and offers some good fishing opportunities.

4 Kwelera Mouth

A popular holiday destination for early farmers making the trip from the interior to the coast by wagon, was Kwelera, and what is now known as the Kwelera Nature Reserve. This coastal forest reserve lies between the Kwelera tidal river and the Gqunube (Rainbow Valley and Sunrise on Sea thus fall within it), and consists of heavily wooded sand dunes running parallel to the sea and reaching a maximum height of more than 250 m above sea level. Night poaching is something of a problem in this reserve, with its small buck, monkeys and rich bird life.

The settlement of Kwelera has only a handful of houses and no shop. A beautiful circular marine drive (passing the concrete launch ramp at Kwelera Point) provides dramatic views over the river mouth. Even 2 km upstream the river, which is open all year round, is still some 50 m wide. There are two resorts and caravan parks on the eastern side of the river. From the lower, at the mouth behind a forested dune ridge, little paths lead to the Yellowsands Beach through the

RIGHT *The indented coastline from Glengariff back to distant East London.*

A DEED OF VALOUR

The unparalleled Victoria Cross.

In 1856, shortly after the end of the hard-fought Crimean War, Queen Victoria instituted the Victoria Cross, the highest British decoration for gallantry in the face of the enemy. This award was first made on South African soil in 1877, during the ninth and last frontier war. The man who earned it was Brevet-Major Hans Garrett Moore of the Connaught Rangers, attached to the Frontier Armed and Mounted Police in the eastern Cape.

On 29 December 1877, Moore rode out on patrol. At a place called Draaibosch about 11 km from the village of Komga, one of his scouts, Trooper Giese, was surrounded and attacked by the enemy Gaika. Moore and two of his men, Sergeant D Harber and Corporal J Court, immediately went to his rescue but they were unable to save him from his fate and Moore himself was wounded.

For his actions he was awarded the Victoria Cross. This bronze medal in the shape of a Maltese cross was struck from the metal of two Russian cannons captured at Sebastopol during the Crimean War. (This source of metal ran out in 1942.) It has the lion and crown of the British royal crest and a maroon ribbon, with a scroll reading 'for valour'.

In addition, a monument was erected on the site at Draaibosch to commemorate Moore's bravery. This 2,5 m high monument with its cold, cobbled façade is no work of art but it lends an air of distinction to a pleasant roadside picnic spot, with a windy view over the long, rolling, green hills.

Paddling and casting a hopeful line in the still shallows of the lagoon at Cefane Mouth.

rocky western point facing the wide Krauses Beach. There are some good rock angling spots (fishing rods can be hired), and mussels and cockles can be gathered on a restricted basis.

About 10 km from Glengariff Bay, the roads from Rainbow Valley onwards converge and several stores are located here, with such supplies as food, cooking gas and fishing tackle and bait.

Several resorts are situated along the alternating stretches of rocky coast and beach that mark the roughly 5 km between the Bulura and Cintsa rivers. First is Glen Eden (with caravan sites and chalets), overlooking the broad, rocky mouth of the Bulura River. You can drive right down to the expansive Krauses Beach where lagoon, beach and reef meet. The river itself is not particularly good for fishing (rock angling is more popular) but it is ideal for boardsailing. It deepens with the summer rains, making powerboating upriver possible. The estuary and heavily forested dunes are a birdwatcher's delight.

Glen Navor (with cottages and caravan sites) is well protected from the wind by the sheltering dunes and trees. It shares an attractive beach, which is fairly safe for swimming, with Queensberry Bay. The emblem of the latter resort and caravan park is the flame lily, which flourishes wild along the Border coast in November and December with the settling in of the rains.

The coastline of this region is mainly rocky, with tidal pools rich in marine life and good fishing, and excellent surfing off the beach reefs. Other recreational attractions here include sports like tennis and Putt-Putt.

The last of these resorts is Glen Muir, where again rock angling and shell collecting are the chief pastimes. (Kob can be caught off the rocks when the water has been churned up.) This is fertile ground for beachcombers but the reefs make this whole stretch of coast rather too rugged for swimming, although good for snorkelling. All the resorts look to Bulura River for freshwater sports and to Krauses and Glen Navor for swimming.

6 Cintsa

Between Cintsa West and Cape Henderson, four major rivers reach the dunes, if not always the sea, of Cintsa Bay. The bird life at the estuaries of these rivers (the Cintsa, Cefane, Kwenxura and Nyara) and in the Cape Henderson Nature Reserve here is particularly rich and rewarding, and invites some careful study with a pair of binoculars and a bird identification book. Among the many species that can be spotted are the sacred ibis, ringed plover, little egret, greenshank, black stork, kelp gull and several species of tern; there are also various European migrant waders in the summer and the droves of gannets that follow the sardine shoals north to Natal in the winter.

Cintsa itself is divided into two areas: Cintsa West and Cintsa Mouth or East. The first is a giddy spot to the right of the river with two resorts offering wall-to-wall holiday activity, from a restaurant to an artificial tidal pool. Cintsa Mouth on the opposite bank, reached by a 12 km detour, has a good beach, chalet and caravan facilities, a store with petrol and a postal agency.

Popular pastimes at the resorts include sea angling, fishing on the river, boardsailing on the large lagoon and swimming with reasonable safety at Cintsa Mouth and the two smaller beaches of Cintsa West. The casual rambler is also rewarded by some spectacular views: on a clear evening, the distant Cape Morgan lighthouse can even be seen from a hill overlooking the lagoon.

7 Cefane Mouth

Facing a pyramid of mountain and fringed by coastal forest, a lovely tranquil lagoon marks Cefane Mouth. Beyond the blind river mouth is the beach and the huge scimitar of Cintsa Bay, stretching far into the floating sea mist to north and south. It was near here that the Portuguese ship, *Nossa Senhora da Atalaia* (Our Lady of Atalaia), was wrecked on 7 July 1647. About 200 survivors of the wreck set out to walk from here to Mozambique's Maputo, a journey that took five

forest where hadedas nag and fret. The other, on a loop of the river, faces high cliffs covered with honey and river euphorbia trees. Besides accommodation, facilities provided include a playground and water slide, as well as canoes and horses for hire.

5 East coast resorts

Glengariff Bay, the first of a number of 'glens' among the east coast resorts, is at the mouth of the Bulura River with a hotel and rustic chalets on the months and claimed the lives of 55 of their number. A cannon from the wreck is preserved in the East London Museum.

The holiday resort of Kefani, with its thatched rondawels and caravan sites, offers such recreation as tennis but nothing disturbs the peaceful atmosphere, enriched by the wealth of bird life. There is a good swimming beach and the gentle, sedged banks of the lagoon make it an ideal spot for youngsters.

The areas from Cefane Mouth northwards become progressively more like the Transkei coast in their ruggedness.

8 Bosbokstrand

This private nature reserve and holiday resort lies in the secluded valley of the Nyara River, its accommodation facing the lagoon with its reed banks and abundant bird life (to date more than seventy species have been identified). Two game trails penetrate the rich vegetation of the valley that rises steeply behind the resort, and here you may spot eland, zebra, bushbuck, impala, and even a tame lynx. The beautiful, wild beach at Cape Henderson is a mere five-minute walk away, while Bosbokstrand itself stretches in a lazy sweep 5 km south to Cefane Mouth. This is the ideal place for quiet rambles through unspoilt nature.

9 Haga-Haga

This coastal village is reached via a direct turn-off from the N2 some 40 km from East London, rather than by the loop road off the N2 that has served the preceding resorts. Haga-Haga is said to derive its name either from the Xhosa word for wild pig (*hagu*) or from the noise of the constant pounding of the surf. The river mouth separates the village (and hotel) from the holiday houses of Marshstrand, 10 km away by road.

Haga-Haga River is normally very shallow but you can boardsail and paddleski in the sea. The beach at the mouth is a sandy bay with access for powerboats from both wings of the village. (Note that vehicles are not allowed on the beach other than to launch boats, a rule that applies to the whole coast from Cape Morgan to south of East London.) In the main, Haga-Haga's coast is rocky and best suited to angling and beachcombing, and especially exploring the many rock pools. The area also offers some good walks: the gently sloping approach to the village provides a panoramic view of the coast, while a rocky 8 km coastal walk will take you past Rooiwal to Cape Henderson and the Bosbokstrand holiday resort.

Other facilities include a provincial library (open a few days a week), Putt-Putt, a golf course and tennis court, an airstrip 6 km from the village, and a petrol station.

10 Double Mouth

Double Mouth is so named because the Quko and the much smaller kuMqotwane (river of wild figs)

RIGHT *The rock-tumbled shoreline at Haga-Haga, rinsed by the sea.*

A FURRED, FOUR-LEGGED FISHERMAN

The Cape clawless otter makes a meal of fish.

The eastern Cape coast is known for its good fishing, and one of its firmest fans is the Cape clawless otter (*Aonyx capensis*). As the name implies, this otter — one of two species in South Africa — does not have claws and only its hind feet are partly webbed. It is the larger of South Africa's two otter species, reaching a length of 1,5 m and weighing in at up to 18 kg. This short-legged, thick-necked creature, with a sparkling sheen to its dark brown, white-bibbed fur, is predominantly aquatic but happy enough to hunt on land. (Its diet may include fish, octopus, crabs, frogs and even birds and insects.)

Its preference, however, is for marine areas near vertical rock faces and just below the surface of the water. When hunting fish, the otter swims under water until it spots its prey. Once caught, it will often play with the fish, swimming to the surface with it and tossing it into the air, then diving to recapture it. With smaller fish the otter might tread water while eating it, but return to shore with a larger fish — where it will frequently dunk the fish in the water as if it were a tasty sauce! Once the meal has been finished, the otter will go through a meticulous process of cleaning its face and paws.

Otters use their tails for propulsion in water and can move very quickly. They can also be like children, playing tag with each other and indulging in bouts of mock fighting. They are, however, generally solitary, and on the rare occasions they are spotted on shore, will mostly be bounding along alone.

The smooth, wave-washed sands of Morgan's Bay lie in the lee of a green bluff.

meet in a lazy lagoon that overlooks a shell-strewn beach and a small caravan park. Access is through two farm gates over the cliffs from Morgan's Bay, 4 km distant. The rocky cove in which the caravan park nestles is a mother lode for shell collectors, while at 'treasure' or 'bead' beach, 1,5 km to the south, carnelian necklace or rosary beads and fragments of 16th-century Ming dynasty china can occasionally be found washed ashore, possibly from one of the East Indiamen wrecked off this coast centuries ago.

11 Morgan's Bay

Access to both Morgan's Bay and Kei Mouth is via a turn-off from the N2 close on 60 km from East London. A good gravel road leads through grazing lands with clusters of pastel-coloured Xhosa huts and then pineapple plantations. Some 15 km along the road to the coast you pass the Ocean View Guest Farm, which offers a quiet birdwatching holiday. Several trails through the indigenous forest valleys present the opportunity to view some of the 180 bird species recorded there,

including blue cranes, sunbirds, hornbills and perhaps a crowned eagle, a deep forest predator so strong that it can take off vertically with a full talon-load, like a monkey.

The road forks for Morgan's Bay and its twin village, Kei Mouth. By road the two are a distance of about 16 km apart, but a coastal walk of only an hour or so separates them. The walk passes a secluded coastal forest, sheltering blue duiker and bushbuck, as well as the workings of an abandoned titanium mine.

Morgan's Bay (and Cape Morgan, with its automatic lighthouse) takes its name from A F Morgan, sailing master of the *Barracouta* in which Captain W F Owen surveyed this coastline in 1822. Despite its rather prosaic name, it has some of the most dramatic high sea-cliff scenery anywhere south of Transkei's Wild Coast. Here successive waves explode against the rock face, hurling spray 30 m up to drench the white-breasted cormorants that nest on the cliffs. The bird life is prodigious, with about 200 species recorded in the area, while the flora includes a fine banyan tree, a specimen noted for the aerial roots that grow down into the soil to form additional trunks.

The tiny village is essentially a handful of holiday homes, a hotel and a caravan park on the south bank of the Ntshala River. The pretty lagoon formed by the river is popular with bathers (the beach is also suitable for swimming), canoeists, waterskiers and boardsailors.

Fishing is, however, probably the favourite pastime. Bait is plentiful and good catches can be made in the river and along the coast at spots like Cracker Bay, Puffadder, Breakwater and Leonard's Gulley. One rather sad 'catch' recorded was a 60 ton sperm whale, washed ashore during the high winds and floods of winter 1970. A harpoon tip removed from this sea giant is on display in the East London Museum.

12 Kei Mouth

In days gone by the great Kei River, being up to 200 m wide and one of the few rivers that actually

LEFT The mighty mouth of the Kei River.

flows into the Indian Ocean, was a disheartening barrier to shipwreck survivors trudging the beaches south to Cape Town or north to Maputo. Now the midpoint of the river serves to mark the boundary between South Africa and Transkei.

As a resort, with hotels, bungalows and caravan sites, Kei Mouth has much to offer. There is good swimming in warm waters, rewarding beach-combing and birdwatching (especially in the coastal forest), river boating and other watersports, and exciting deep-sea or rock angling. The village itself boasts a monthly newsletter, a post office, a supermarket, butchery and garage, a library, and — best of all — the Hazel Jeffries Shell Museum, with more than 2 500 specimens from all over the world.

A trip across the river to Transkei is available on weatherworn outboard ferries like the *Masakane* (pull together), with free passage to customers of the local trading stores. A passport or identity document is advisable but there is no immigration post on either side.

THINGS TO DO

Angling
Fishing is good just about anywhere on this coast, but for advice on local conditions, ask at the resorts or the larger sports shops serving the area. Note that Bulura Point (Glengariff Bay) and Cintsa West, and stretches of the cliff coast between Haga-Haga and Morgan Bay are deep-water areas and can be very dangerous.

Beachcombing and shelling
There are many rock pools to explore and shelling is good where reef and sand meet, in small coves, and particularly between the Bulura and Cintsa rivers. The East London Museum will identify any finds, but live shells should not be disturbed.

Birdwatching
Particularly rewarding spots for birdwatching are Gonubie Nature Reserve, Cape Henderson Nature Reserve (between the Kwenxura and Nyara rivers), as well as the river estuaries in general.

Boardsailing
Nearly all the lagoons at river mouths are good for boardsailing. On the sea, the warm winds blow from the north-east from January to March, and the cold south-westers for the rest of the year, peaking in the winter months of July and August.

Boat trips
Some of the resorts offer powerboat trips out to sea or upriver, and there is a ferry service across the Kei.

Bowls
There are greens at Gonubie, Cintsa West, Morgan's Bay and Kei Mouth.

Camping and caravanning
Nearly all the resorts along this coastline have caravan sites, usually situated close to both river and beach. Contact either the resorts themselves, the local municipalities or the Border Tourism Association for further details.

Canoeing
River canoeing is a popular pastime here and many places have canoes for hire, including Rainbow Valley (Gonubie), Areena (on the Kwelera), Morgan Bay Hotel and the camp at Double Mouth.

Diving
In general, diving is good wherever there is a reef, but be wary of deep-water cliff spots. To find out about hiring scuba gear, contact any of the major sports shops.

Fish type	Season	Best area	Best bait
Bronze bream	All year	Especially reefs near Haga-Haga	Prawns (sand or pink)
Garrick (leervis)	All year	All along coast, especially Gonubie Point	Largish spoons, reeled in fast
Kob (kabeljou)	All year	Off rocky points into sandy area, especially where sand is churning (Cintsa and Kei mouths)	Sardines, white squid (and in combination)
Shad (elf)	Sept–Nov	Bulura Point (Glengariff Bay)	Fishbait or spinners
Spotted grunter	All year	In or near river mouths (Kei Mouth)	Sand prawns

Drives and viewsites
Besides short drives around the coastal resorts, a full day's excursion inland could follow the route from Gonubie (N2) to Kei Mouth (R349) and back via Komga, Kei Road and King William's Town, with an optional extra drive down the twisting road to Kei Bridge and the border post. Particularly spectacular coastal views can be had from the high cliffs at Morgan Bay and the lagoon at Cefane.

Golf
There are nine-hole golf courses at Gonubie, Kei Mouth and Haga-Haga.

Scaling the cliffs at Morgan's Bay — only for the experienced.

Horseriding
Horses can be hired from resorts at Kwelera River, Queensberry Bay and Cintsa West.

Libraries
Gonubie, Haga-Haga and Kei Mouth all have public libraries.

Museums
HAZEL JEFFRIES SHELL MUSEUM, Main Rd, Kei Mouth: Displays about 2 500 shells from all over the world.

Powerboating
Powerboating is popular offshore (especially at Glengariff Bay) and waterskiing on some of the rivers and lagoons (notably Kei Mouth). Among the several powerboat clubs is the Gonubie Marine Club.

Shipwrecks
Nothing is visible of the shipwrecks off this coast, but you might still sift from the sands (particularly at Double Mouth) some reminder of them, like beads or pottery shards.

Surfing
Good spots include Kwelera Point and Queensberry Bay (for the more experienced) and the beaches at Gonubie and Yellowsands (for beginners). Capital Radio broadcasts surfing reports daily at 06h40 and 15h40.

Swimming
Lovely stretches of beach include those at Kwelera Mouth, Glengariff, Krauses Beach, Glen Navor, Cintsa, Cefane, Bosbokstrand, Morgan Bay and Kei Mouth. Check locally about backwash and menaces like jellyfish and sharks (open river mouths can be tricky).

Tennis and squash
There are tennis courts at Gonubie, Rainbow Valley, Glengariff Bay, Glen Eden, Glen Navor, Buccaneers Retreat, Cintsa West, Cefane, Bosbokstrand, Haga-Haga, Morgan's Bay and Kei Mouth; Gonubie and Cintsa West also have squash courts.

Walks
There is a wide range of walks in this area, from long hikes to gentle beachfront strolls. Highlight is the three-day, 65 km-long Strandloper Trail, organised by the Wildlife Society and the Greater East London Publicity Association, which traces the shoreline from Kei Mouth to East London. It varies considerably, with tramps through coastal forests, over cliff tops with the wave-lashed reefs below, and along wide white sandy beaches interspersed with rocky shores. The signposted trails in Bosbokstrand Nature Reserve are also popular, as is the more dramatic walk over the cliffs from Morgan's Bay to Double Mouth.

Yachting and dinghy sailing
The larger rivers, such as the Gqunube, Kwelera and Kei, are the best for dinghy sailing but all the rivers when full will take smaller boats.

INFORMATION
• Border Tourism Association, Sherwood Avenue, Beacon Bay 5205. Tel 0431=472400
• Gonubie Municipality, PO Box 20, Gonubie 5256. Tel 0431=404000
• Greater East London Publicity Association, City Hall, Oxford St, East London 5201. Tel 0431=26015
• Kei Mouth Municipality, PO Box 1, Kei Mouth 5260. Tel Kei Mouth 4
• National Sea Rescue Institute, Station 7, East London 5201. Tel 0431=451022; emergencies 0431=22555
• SA Tourism Board, NBS Building, Terminus, East London 5201. Tel 0431=26410

Nearest AA Office
• AA House, 27 Fleet Street, East London 5201. Tel 0431=21271

Beat a retreat to the quiet of a coastal wilderness

THEY CALLED IT THE WILD COAST, because of the harsh conditions early shipwreck survivors encountered there, and 'wild' it remains, unspoilt by overdevelopment. This southern section of the Transkei coast is one of low hills, sprinkled with traditional huts, rolling down to a shoreline where wide rivers meander into tranquil lagoons fringed by forests.

For a get-away-from-it-all holiday, there are many fine family resorts here, casual and comfortable, all offering a lovely mild climate, seas neither too warm nor too cold, and — best of all — prime fishing. To reach the resorts at their remote river mouths usually means taking the N2, which runs parallel to the coast and about 50 to 70 km inland, and then branching off along a network of lesser roads in varying condition. Often to get from one resort to another, only a few kilometres apart, involves a 100 km loop inland, so plan your journey carefully.

1 Butterworth and Kentani

Known as the gateway to Transkei, because it is the first town you approach from the south, Butterworth developed around the Wesleyan mission station built on the banks of the Gcuwa River in 1827. Named after Joseph Butterworth, treasurer of the Wesleyan Missionary Station at the time, this — the oldest town in Transkei — is today the industrial capital of the country and a fast-expanding commercial centre.

Outside the town on the Gcuwa River are cascades that tumble some 90 m, while nearby on a tributary are the Bawa Falls, otherwise known as the High Executioner, where the force of the 100 m-high torrent bellows its power.

Butterworth is also the gateway to the southernmost resorts of the Wild Coast, leading first to the village of Kentani, as though stepping down gradually from developed to rural environments. This was originally a British army outpost, established in the mid-19th century. In 1878 the final frontier war was fought here: a 5 000-strong combined army attacked the earthen fort, to be sprayed by heavy gunfire and then to fall to a cavalry charge — a crushing defeat for once-mighty chiefs.

This otherwise sleepy settlement has developed into a regional administrative centre, complete

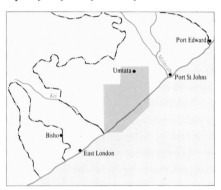

with quaint country hotel and a main thoroughfare more potholed and corrugated than the roads leading out of the town to the Qolora and Nxaxo river resorts.

2 Qolora Mouth

The Qolora River derives its name from the steep gorge cut into the coastal terraces before it reaches the gentle coastal hills. Here thatched round huts form small villages amid cultivated fields and sweet grasses where cattle graze serenely. Behind the bushlined dunes where the river dissipates its energies into a tranquil lagoon, are two hotels, both renowned for their hospitality and their range

White-spumed waves wash the Wild Coast in the vicinity of Dwesa.

of good sporting facilities.

Families come here to relax in verdant luxury and to enjoy the good swimming. There is excellent surf and rock angling, but the Qolora estuary is more often than not closed to the sea. This does, however, offer holiday-makers an excellent venue for more tranquil watersports such as canoeing, boardsailing and swimming.

The area also offers several pleasant walks, including the 4 km stroll inland along a rough track to the Pool of Nongqawuse on the Gxara River. It was here more than a century ago that the young Xhosa girl gazed deep into the pool's languid waters and 'saw' how, if her people destroyed all their cattle and crops, they would be freed of white domination: a vision with tragic consequences.

The wide beaches on either side of the Qolora also offer good rambles: towards the Kei River and its prolific bird life several kilometres to the south, or towards the wreck of the *Jacaranda* about 4 km to the north near the Kobonqaba River mouth. When this Greek coaster ran aground in 1971, its holds were empty so the ship was tossed right up to the beach and became firmly wedged in a narrow gully. Here it still lies, slowly rusting and succumbing to the sea, while sea birds keep watch from their roosts on the peeling masts.

At Kobonqaba there is a cluster of small private holiday cottages typical of all the smaller resorts set at river mouths along this coastline. You may obtain a permit to camp (from the nearest forester or in any of the major centres), but there are no facilities. Remember that whenever camping on the Wild Coast it is essential to carry sufficient drinking water.

3 Nxaxo Mouth

The iNxaxo and Ngqusi rivers meet in a maze of meandering channels and islands and then run into a wide estuary that is permanently open to the

LEFT *Following a typical sandy Transkei track down to the sea at Qolora.*

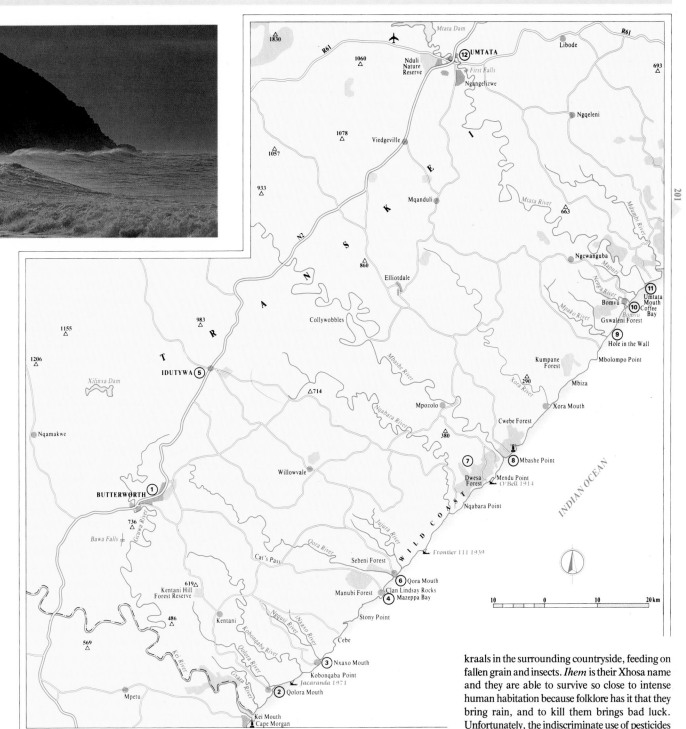

Map labels:

1830
R61
1060
R61
Libode
693
Mtata Dam
Nduli Nature Reserve
UMTATA ⑫
First Falls
Ngangelizwe
R61
1078
Viedgeville
Ngqeleni
1057
K I E
933
Mtata River
Mqanduli
663
860
Ngcwanguba
Elliotdale
Negra River
Mazunyi River
Umtata Mouth Coffee Bay ⑪
Bomvu ⑩
Collywobbles
Mpako River
Mbashe River
Gxwaleni Forest
⑨
Hole in the Wall
Kumpane Forest
Mbolompo Point
983
1155
T R I
Xora River
290
Mbiza
1206
IDUTYWA ⑤
△714
Mpozolo
Xora Mouth
Xilinxa Dam
Cwebe Forest
Ngabara River
380
Nqamakwe
⑦
⑧ Mbashe Point
Willowvale
Dwesa Forest
Mendu Point
O'Bell 1914
INDIAN OCEAN
BUTTERWORTH ①
Nqabara Point
736
Bawa Falls
Jujura River
Kentani Hill Forest Reserve
619△
Qora River
Cat's Pass
Sebeni Forest
Frontier 111 1939
⑥ Qora Mouth
Manubi Forest
Clan Lindsay Rocks
④ Mazeppa Bay
486
Kentani
Stony Point
Gcuwa River
Kobonqaba River
Nxaxo River
Negusi River
569
Cebe
③ Nxaxo Mouth
Kei River
Kobonqaba Point
Qolora River
Jacaranda 1971
Mpetu
Oxara River
② Qolora Mouth
Kei Mouth
Cape Morgan

10 0 10 20 km

sea. On the northern bank of the estuary is a high ridge of dunes that, over the years, has squeezed the river mouth up towards the rock and pebble beach on the southern bank. In the tall trees that cover the dunes fish eagles nest, swooping low over the water to hunt and scattering egrets and cormorants in terror. Equally unmistakeable inhabitants are the trumpeter hornbills, with their enormous bills, black-and-white plumage, and clumsy, dipping flight.

The silty islands at the rivers' junction are fringed by mangrove swamps. Lying forward of these is a small island of beach sand: Ihem Island, a nesting and breeding colony of the beautiful and stately crested crane. These large birds with their regal plumage stroll through nearby fields and kraals in the surrounding countryside, feeding on fallen grain and insects. *Ihem* is their Xhosa name and they are able to survive so close to intense human habitation because folklore has it that they bring rain, and to kill them brings bad luck. Unfortunately, the indiscriminate use of pesticides has, in fact, killed large numbers of these birds.

The Wild Coast does not host many sea birds or waders, but here whimbrels and plovers forage along the intertidal flats in search of the snails and crabs that live in the glutinous mangrove mud. The river is heavily colonised by giant mud crabs (*Scylla serrata*), which have a carapace of up to 10 cm across.

Holiday-makers are drawn to this hotel resort not only by the natural charms of the area, but also

A scene of sheer serenity: late sunlight lightly touches the wide waters of the Qora, sheltered by the river's folded banks.

by the good fishing (especially the giant shad, or elf, caught in the estuary) and the watersports. When conditions are right, there is a reasonable surf break, and canoes and sailboards for riding the river are available at the hotel. About 10 km to the north of the resort is the fishing spot of Cebe, reached by an inland detour. The few shacks here are private, but you can get a camping permit from the forestry office in Butterworth.

4 Mazeppa Bay

The name of this resort derives from a schooner that used the bay as a trading port in the 1830s, reputedly for gunrunning. This ship played a fascinating role in events of the time, including being captured by the Voortrekkers besieging Durban in 1842 but successfully escaping to rescue the families of the British garrison.

The natural surroundings of Mazeppa Bay make it a very attractive resort. Dense groves of wild date palms fringe the beaches, their fronds gleaming like scimitars in the rising sun. (This is also a practical palm: the sap is tapped to make a strong alcoholic drink, the fruit is eaten by both people and animals, the shredded fronds are used for making mats, and the strong midribs are made into brooms.) All along the surf line on the beaches, flocks of sanderlings race up and down, ploughing their bills through the wet sand for any titbit they can find.

Accommodation at Mazeppa Bay includes a hotel, a large cottage resort and a camp site (with no facilities). The main attraction is fishing, particularly on The Island, a favourite spot for deep-water angling and hooking sharks. The Island is connected to the mainland by a suspension bridge, which — after storm batterings — can still be used, but not by the faint-hearted. Other excellent fishing spots include Shark Point (best fished in an east wind) and the Boiling Pot (best in a west wind).

Sheltered between The Island and Clan Lindsay Rocks, named after a ship wrecked there in 1898, is First Beach, the best place for swimming and relaxing. It is guarded by rocky points and high dunes behind, where gnarled milkwood trees provide shade along the grassy fringe between dunes and beach. Second and Shelley beaches are found to the south of the hotel, heading towards the small river that forms an estuary there. These are delightful places for swimming and picnicking. The surf along the coast here is often good, making this one of the few popular Wild Coast surfing venues — despite the presence of sharks.

From Mazeppa Bay there is a 6 km walk along a wide beach and past the highest dunes of this coastline to the resort at Qora Mouth; by road the drive — looping inland — is more than 100 km.

'A BOY IS BUT A DOG'

To reach maturity Xhosa males are traditionally required to undergo initiation. Even youths living in distant cities may return home to participate in the ritual, for there is a saying that 'a boy is but a dog'.

In May, the married women of each village build grass huts in a remote spot, where the youths will spend much of the next few weeks in seclusion. A respected elder acts as their guide, instructing them in the ways and traditions of their community. This elder may also act as surgeon for the circumcision.

Until their wounds heal the youths are treated as virtual outcasts, not being seen and living a frugal existence. When they do emerge from their isolation they disguise themselves by painting their bodies and faces with white clay and clothing themselves in specially patterned blankets. When the time is right, they don heavy grass or palm skirts and tall masks, and move from hut to hut in their own village to show their skills in the *Abakhwetha* dances.

To mark the end of their initiation, the young men wash themselves clean in a nearby river. All their possessions from the initiation period are placed in the grass hut and set alight — symbolising the end of their childhood. That done, they file back home to enjoy the village feast and be presented with a new set of clothes in which to step into the world as men.

5 Idutywa and Willowvale

While Butterworth is the gateway to the southernmost part of the Wild Coast, Idutywa serves as the jumping-off point from the N2 for the coast from Mazeppa Bay northwards for about 40 km to the Mbashe River mouth. The town is an important commercial centre, but it lacks the modern facilities of Butterworth or Umtata. The name of the town means 'place of disorder', and refers to a tumultuous time when it was attacked by Zulu invaders.

Idutywa has long been a venue for *Abakhwetha* dances — part of the initiation ritual of young Xhosa men who, painted and disguised by masks, dance for the local people.

From Idutywa a good road leads to Willowvale, a picturesque village halfway to the coast and the traditional seat of the Gcaleka paramount chief. The town is named after the wild willow trees that once grew along the river valleys here, but the light wood was much favoured for a variety of uses and so, in time, all the trees disappeared. In 1839 a mission station was built at nearby Beecham Wood, but after the tragic starvation of the 1850s following the Xhosa cattle killing, the area was deserted. In 1876, with resettlement here, the Malan Mission was built at Willowvale.

6 Qora Mouth

The road from Willowvale to the coast follows a narrow ridge for some way, with grand views of the Qora and Jujura rivers and their tributaries on either side. At the wide Qora River mouth is a popular resort, with fishing again the main

SHIPWRECKED ON THE WILD COAST

From the time the Portuguese ship the *Sao Bento* left Cochin in February 1554, things had not gone well. After the heavily laden ship sprang a leak at sea and lost its rudder, it approached the African coastline like a wounded bird. The sight of land caused great excitement among the weary crew, but soon this turned to apprehension as the coast revealed itself as wild and rocky.

Inevitably, the caravel struck an offshore reef, with the force of the impact splitting the ship in two. In the ensuing pandemonium some people tried to swim or float ashore on the bobbing flotsam, but most of these drowned or were dashed against the rocks; ironically those who could not swim and clung to the superstructure were carried safely to shore on the tide.

By evening there were 99 Portuguese and 224 slaves alive on a beach near the Mtata River mouth; another 150 shipwreck victims had perished in the surf. Washed up on the shore around the survivors was a fortune in perfumes and luxury materials, but little of practical use in a hostile land. Their knowledge of the territory was hopelessly limited, but haunted by the memory of a shipwreck party being massacred on their trek to the Cape, they turned their attentions to Delagoa Bay.

For many days and then weeks they laboured over the wooded hills, having to construct rafts to cross the numerous rivers they encountered. One by one the sick or wounded and the elderly lagged behind and were left to the mercy of the wilds. Near Port St Johns they passed the remains of the *Sao Joao*, wrecked two years previously, and were unpleasantly reminded that only a score or so survivors of that ship were found after a year making for Delagoa Bay.

When they could, they kept to the coast to forage for mussels and oysters, but they were constantly harried by the local peoples who picked off the stragglers and sometimes threatened the main party. They met other survivors of the *Sao Joao* who had thrown in their lot with the local peoples, and two of their number joined the *Sao Bento* party. In Zululand the now desperate and depleted party was forced far inland and the party members began squabbling.

Finally, after 72 days of constant marching, 56 Portuguese and six slaves reached the banks of the Maputo River. They were cordially received but had to continue to fend for themselves until a ship arrived to take them back to Portugal. When it did five months later, only twenty Portuguese and four slaves remained alive. It was their account, and that of other shipwreck victims, that earned the south-east coast of Africa the name the Wild Coast.

feature. The best way to exploit the fishing is by powerboat, because of the number of shallow offshore reefs where giant 60 kg kob (kabeljou) can be hooked as they pass this way in winter from the cooler Cape waters. The river mouth has the added attraction of a large oyster bed yielding generously sized oysters and white mussels.

Besides the angling opportunities, walkers can take the rowboat ferry across the river for a coastal stroll, while watersports on the estuary are catered

BELOW *Angling in the swirling surf at Dwesa is a popular sport, but to conserve resources, it is strictly controlled by the reserve authorities.*

for by the hotel (where Gcaleka women also sell their attractive bead and shell handcrafted jewellery). The beach yawns northwards for avid hikers, but the next accessible coastal resort is at distant Mbashe Point.

7 Dwesa

Together with Cwebe over the Mbashe River, Dwesa (formerly known as Beecham Wood) forms the oldest forest reserve in the country. Because of this the flora here is preserved in its natural state. Game has been reintroduced into the reserve and north of the forest camp, on grassy hills, you can see rhinoceros, buffalo, zebra, eland, blesbok and hartebeest. Smaller antelope inhabit the forests and it is not unusual to see duiker on the beaches early in the morning. Self-contained wooden bungalows are set deep in the forest where white stinkwood and yellowwood trees are some of the more impressive species. You may also camp on a grassy enclave between two arms of the forest where the bungalows hide. A short walk from the camp along a stream and then over low dunes through dune forest emerges at one of the loveliest beaches on this coast.

Rocky points punctuate wide golden sands where polished driftwood trunks stand like abstract sculptures and ghost crabs — their eyes like balloons on stalks — scuttle across the sand and disappear down holes. At low tide the sea exposes all the wondrous life forms of the intertidal rock pools: feathery-fingered anemones, suckerlike carpets of zoanthids, and the brilliantly coloured, many-pleated sea slugs called nudibranchs. The remains of giant *Charonia* or pink lady shells litter the beach (large specimens are often trapped in these pools), along with elaborate cones, cowries and volutes. When the sea is calm this is the perfect place for snorkelling and exploring the reefs beyond the limits of otherwise land-bound humans.

Angling and spearfishing are strictly controlled in the reserve so ask the warden for details. All supplies and sufficient drinking water must be brought with you.

8 Mbashe Point

It is possible to reach the Mbashe River mouth from Dwesa by following a seldom-used inland road that crosses a number of rivers and winds in and out of their valleys — a spectacular but rough route. A direct route from the N2 passes through Elliotdale with the nearby Collywobbles on the Mbashe River. Here you have amazing views down into the serpentine valley as the river writhes through uncountable twists and doublebacks that have been cut deep into the land. (In 1859 regional magistrate George Colley, while surveying the area, looked down into the convoluted valley and is said to have exclaimed: 'My, how it wobbles', whereupon one of his men replied: 'Yes, sir, it Colley Wobbles' — and so the name stuck.) In springtime the scene is enriched by the flowering coral trees that splash the hillsides with their brilliant scarlet blooms.

From here to the coast there are many fine views of the hills and valleys, with forested gorges and ploughed slopes, where round huts — half white, half ochre — cling to the hills like barnacles to the shore. Traditionally these huts face east to receive the warming morning sun; the sunny side is painted white to reflect the sun's direct rays, while the shady side is kept the natural earth colour to absorb as much heat as possible. With a thatched roof these huts keep a near constant temperature. With the emergence of Western-influenced iron-roofed square homes, the Xhosa are losing this natural air-conditioning system.

The Mbashe (sometimes spelt Bashee) River reaches the sea in a wide estuary, its rocky mouth flanked by fine beaches. On the southern bank, on a hill overlooking the river, there are private cottages, while on the northern bank a hotel is set within the Cwebe Forest Reserve. The river itself is the traditional boundary between the southern Xhosa and the northern Thembu. Like a sentinel to these once-troubled lands and frequently wild seas, a steel lighthouse stands on top of the line of coastal dunes.

There is excellent reef fishing from 1st, 2nd and 3rd Krantzes, as well as Mendu Point and The Island, and there is also good angling up to 14 km upriver (mainly for pike congers). The beaches here are among the best for swimming, and while the area is not noted for its shell yields, it is always pleasant combing them for common species. It is possible to camp in the Cwebe reserve and walking here is a fine alternative to fishing.

9 Hole in the Wall

On the road to the next coastal resort, Coffee Bay, you find a turn-off to Hole in the Wall, one of the most enchanting spots anywhere on the southern African coast. The place was so named in 1823 by the crew of the British survey ship *Barracouta*, because of the portal carved through an island rock castle with sheer dolerite walls. The Portuguese had called the rock *Penido das Fontes* (rock of fountains), while the rock's Xhosa name is *esiKhaleni* or 'the place of sound', from the gushing waves that continuously crash through the great hole.

The hole lies directly in the path of the Mpako River and it is this, rather than the surf, that has eroded the hole. By climbing to the top of the cliffs that overlook the Hole in the Wall, it is possible to make out how the dolerite once formed a con-

tinuous cliffline across the river's present course.

But while the river has eroded the hole itself, the angry surf that crashes against these rocks has played its own part in eroding the coastline and in adding an element of danger to the site. There are tales of people being pounded to death by surf pulsing unexpectedly through the cavern while they were collecting mussels at low tide; of at least one foolhardy swimmer perishing while attempting to breach the gap; and of those who have had to be rescued from the cliffs of the island fortress after failing to scale them. The treacherous cliffs here and the shallow reefs that lie off them have also claimed a number of ships.

LEFT *Hole in the Wall, viewed from close up.*
BELOW *The truly awesome spectacle of Hole in the Wall can be fully appreciated from the air.*

The milkwood forest that looks out towards the hole was once the most enchanting camp site imaginable, with lush grass carpeting the ground under the giant spreading trees, the sea sounding through the hole and washing up the pebble beach and sheer dolerite cliffs on the left. Now, however, all the coastal milkwood forests on the Wild Coast have been fenced off to preserve their fragile beauty: generations of campers have left their mark, while cattle grazed the herb understorey making a soft grass floor but undermining the forests' natural richness.

Where the road from Ngcwanguba store reaches the sea, there is a long, narrow beach with two rocky arms projecting far out to sea, creating a perfectly sheltered bay where you can float in the easy swell for hours. When you tire of this, you can lie under the milkwoods on the banks of a small

stream that trickles out across the beach sand. A new bungalow-style hotel has been built opposite this beach and on the hillslope behind the hotel are private cottages — some new, some old and dilapidated from the days when this was a truly wild and remote spot.

Recreation at Hole in the Wall includes some very good angling, while it also offers a greater variety in short walks than most places, with gentle beaches and rugged cliffs, a warbling river and crashing surf, dense forests and grassy hills dusted with huts.

Although there is no craft market as such, you can still purchase or barter for authentic ornaments and beadworked clothing superior to that found in many other places.

10 Coffee Bay

Some time in the past, a ship returning to Europe from the East is said to have been wrecked off the Wild Coast, where its cargo of coffee beans was washed up onto the beach. Apparently some of the seeds germinated there and for a time coffee trees took root and gave their name to the attractive bay between the Nenga and Bomvu rivers.

Coffee Bay offers considerable comfort: the road all the way from the N2 is tarred, and the small village has two hotels and a well-run camp site (situated in a wood on a bank of the Nenga). A kilometre-long beach offers fairly safe swimming, while the breakers off the bay's southern point provide one of the few consistent surfing waves on the Wild Coast.

Above the cliffs that guard the bay's northern shore is a windswept but exciting nine-hole golf course, while the Nenga River is familiar with the throb of outboard motors of the powerboats that berth there during many a fishing contest. Because of its popularity with powerboat owners, there was a plan to establish a more secure berthing venue on the Mapuzi River just north of Coffee Bay, but this has not yet been developed.

The beach at Coffee Bay is a promising one for shell collecting, especially at the rocky points where shells tend to heap up in pockets at the low-tide mark. Some tropical species wash up here, carried south by the current, and some of the rarest cowries — those most desirable shells to collectors — have been found in the stomachs of musselcrackers, which swallow the molluscs whole.

The harvest of the shores represents a great treat as well as an important source of protein for the local inhabitants. At low tide women appear with dishes and flat irons to scrape black mussels off the rocks, where they live in dense colonies. The women walk barefoot over the razor-sharp shells, often buffeted by unexpectedly large swells, to reach the choicest specimens, and as they gather them, they happily eat their fill. (If you should be offered any shellfish for sale, be sure that you are aware of all the relevant regulations restricting size, quotas and seasons, or you could land in hot water yourself. Transkei is conservation conscious, and the days of camping wherever your fancy took you and reaping as much shellfish as you chose are

A tiny huddle of homes, dwarfed by cliff, on the rocky shores of Umtata Mouth.

a thing of the past.)

To reach the next resort of Umtata Mouth, you could take a fascinating day's outing north from Coffee Bay along the coast, past Mapuzi Point to the mangrove swamps on the Mtata estuary.

11 Umtata Mouth

Turning north a few kilometres inland of Coffee Bay, you climb up and over into the wide, fertile Mtata River valley, through cultivated fields that mark the boundary between Thembu and Mpondo territories. The road is passable if taken with care, but the low causeway over the river is vulnerable during heavy rains.

Snuggling between the Mtata and Mdumbi rivers are a hotel and holiday shacks, which attract mainly fishermen to favourite angling spots on the rivers and from the rocky shore.

The Mtata estuary has the added attraction of extensive white and black mangrove forests. These are home to hordes of fiddler crabs that scuttle over the mud in search of food, diving down holes at the slightest alarm. With a permit it is possible to camp on the river bank near the mangroves, and this offers excellent opportunities to see the wonders of this unusual half-world of land and river, and the strange creatures that live here.

This wild coast must have seemed particularly alien to the shipwreck victims cast ashore here. In 1554 and 1593 respectively, the Portuguese caravels *Sao Bento* and *Santo Alberto* were wrecked in the region of the Mtata River mouth, and surviving parties from both ships set out on foot for Delagoa Bay (Maputo), some 2 000 km to the north. The hardships they experienced lie buried in the distant past as you stand dreamily

with fishing rod in hand, or loll in the warm waters of the glorious swimming beaches.

12 Umtata

Inland of Umtata Mouth and lying on the same river is Umtata, capital of Transkei. Both settlements and the river were named for the once-abundant sneezewood (*umtati*) trees, famous for their handsome wood and excellent medicinal properties.

Umtata was laid out in 1879 after the British annexation of the area. The earliest buildings included a church, school and hospital and growth was so rapid that by 1882 Umtata was proclaimed a municipality. The city retains many fine old buildings in the neoclassical style that was popular in colonial times, and also has many modern administrative and shopping centres, office blocks and hotels. On the outskirts of town you can see the ultramodern university buildings opposite the plush homes in the ministerial township. Although the nature of the city is strongly tied to its status as an important political and commercial centre, Umtata is also a centre for handicrafts and here you can buy a variety of goods such as pottery, cane work, woven mohair products, batiks, beadwork and other jewellery and ornaments.

Situated at the junction of Transkei's arterial roads, Umtata has eight hotels and a camping and caravan site in pleasant surroundings. Recreational facilities include bowling greens and a golf course; Mtata and Mabeleni dams offer boating, skiing and picnicking opportunities; and the Nduli Reserve a few kilometres outside of the city is the nucleus of the country's wild breeding herds, source of the stock for the other reserves.

THINGS TO DO

Angling
It is fishing more than anything else that draws holiday-makers to the Transkei coast, and it was the fishermen who first built the cottages and shacks at remote points and estuaries. During summer catches include huge reef fish such as musselcracker, and in autumn the annual sardine run brings with it fighting game fish.

Beachcombing and shelling
This entire coast is excellent for beachcombing and bits and pieces from old shipwrecks are still found along the water's edge. Most sandy beaches will reveal cowries, cones and murex shells, among others, and it is a good idea always to look in the nooks between beaches and rocky points. The rock pools at low tide offer a rich world of marine life. The best beaches for shell gathering are at the Qolora, Qora and Mtata mouths, at Coffee Bay, and especially at Dwesa.

Birdwatching
Sea bird watching along this stretch of coast is disappointing, but the coastal forests host many colourful and exotic species such as paradise flycatchers, trumpeter hornbills and narina trogons. The rare mangrove kingfisher is a shy resident of the mangrove swamps, while four other kingfishers are common waterside birds in the area. Fish eagles are a delight on many of the riverways, while the regal crested cranes can best be seen at Ihem Island where they roost and breed.

Boardsailing
This coast is not really for those who like wave jumping, but for gentle lagoon rides there is no shortage of venues and most of the hotels have boards for use free of charge to residents. For beginners, there is nothing to beat sailing gently up the wild river courses.

Boat trips
Again, most hotels have boats for use or hire, while local entrepreneurs operate ferry services across most deep rivers.

Bowls
There are greens at Qolora, Mbashe and Coffee Bay resorts, as well as in Umtata and Butterworth.

Camping and caravanning
There are official camp sites with no facilities at Qolora Mouth, Nxaxo Mouth, Mazeppa Bay, Qora Mouth and Mbashe Point, as well as the more remote spots of Cebe and Xora Mouth, for which permits must be obtained from the forestry offices in Umtata or Butterworth; at Dwesa, Coffee Bay and in Umtata you buy a permit at the camp site (where there are some facilities). Wherever you intend camping or caravanning, it is essential to carry your own drinking water. (Contact individual resorts for further information regarding available accommodation.)

Canoeing
The many rivers are superb venues for canoeing, with wild and often convoluted courses that are often navigable upriver for 10 km or more. Most hotels have canoes for free use by residents but these are not always sleek, speedy models so if you intend doing any serious rowing, you should bring your own boat or make inquiries before you arrive.

Diving
When the water is calm and clear, which is most likely from January to May, the diving on the Wild Coast is indeed wild and prolific. Rocky outcrops and shallow reefs (such as those found at Dwesa, Hole in the Wall and Coffee Bay) are the best for snorkelling. Never venture into the open sea when it is anything but clear as the presence of sharks will almost certainly be a problem.

Drives and viewsites
From the N2 to each spot on the coast is in itself a worthwhile drive with breathtaking viewsites and exquisite scenery, but the roads are not always kind to cars. The best sign of a passable road is one that leads most directly to a well-known resort. Features include picturesque Cat's Pass, roughly between Kentani and Mazeppa Bay; and Collywobbles, one of the finest views in southern Africa (approached from Elliotdale), where the Mbashe River twists its way through many tortuous bends in the valley far below. The more adventurous driver may use a 1:50 000 surveys map to plan a route more or less parallel to the coast through rural landscapes and wild river valleys — an exciting and spectacular trip.

Golf
There are golf courses at Idutywa and Umtata, while at Qolora Mouth there is an 11-hole course, at Coffee Bay an elevated nine-hole course, and at Butterworth and Mbashe there are nine-hole courses.

Libraries
Umtata has two public libraries.

Powerboating
Mtata Dam is a pleasant powerboating and skiing venue, while Coffee Bay on the coast offers the most convenient launching site for powerboats.

Shipwrecks
The Wild Coast has claimed more than its fair share of shipwrecks over the centuries, but very little of these remains to be seen. The *Jacaranda*, a light coaster wrecked off the Kobonqaba mouth in 1971, is the only wreck that remains virtually intact and it is a popular destination for hikers from the Qolora resort area.

Surfing
Only in recent years has this coast begun to be explored for its surfing possibilities. There are many beach breaks that work when swells and winds are right, but it is the river mouths that promise the most consistent and exciting breaks. Coffee Bay is perhaps the most frequently surfed area, but Nxaxo also has a fairly consistent pointlike break. Sharks may prove to be a problem to surfers in murky water around river mouths.

Swimming
There are excellent swimming beaches at all the resorts and in fact you can swim virtually anywhere along the coast. The water is usually cool to warm and clear, but you should never swim in dirty water around the river mouths after floods.

Tennis and squash
There are tennis and squash clubs in Umtata and Butterworth, and only the smaller, more remote resorts such as those on the Nxaxo and Mtata mouths do not offer visitors fine all-weather tennis courts.

Walks
The resorts here are set in the most wonderful natural environments with yawning stretches of river and sea frontage, and hills, forests and picturesque villages to the landward side. Many hotels offer organised outings or will prepare picnic lunches for those going out on self-guided trails. There are also official hiking trails along much of the coast, for which you must book and stay in the overnight huts provided (contact the nearest forestry office).

Yachting and dinghy sailing
Mtata Dam offers the only proper sailing venue in this area.

Fish type	Season	Best area	Best bait
Blacktail (dassie)	Winter, spring	Kobonqaba, Coffee Bay, Mtata mouth	Redbait, shrimps
Galjoen	All year, best in April – June	Mazeppa Bay, Mbashe mouth – Coffee Bay	Redbait, mussels
Garrick (leervis)	All year, best in winter	All open estuaries, especially Nxaxo, Qora and Mtata rivers	Mullet, sardines, artificial lures
Kob (kabeljou)	Autumn – spring	All along coast, especially Qora Mouth	Artificial lures and most other baits
Mussel-cracker	All year, best in Sept – Mar	All along coast, best in deep water, offshore reefs	Redbait, crabs, mussels
Pike congers	Mainly summer	Mbashe River	Mullet, prawns
Shad (elf)	Autumn – spring	Kobonqaba, Hole in the Wall, Coffee Bay, Mtata mouth	Sardines
Sharks	All year	Mazeppa Bay	Live bait
Skipjack	Summer	Qora Mouth	Sardines, shrimps
Yellowtail	Winter	Mazeppa Bay	Spinners

INFORMATION
• Department of Agriculture and Forestry, Private Bag X5002, Umtata. Tel 0471 = 24322
• Department of Commerce, Industry and Tourism, Private Bag X5029, Umtata. Tel 0471 = 25191
• Transkei Airways, PO Box 773, Umtata. Tel 0471 = 24636/7/8
• Wild Coast Holiday Hotels, Central Booking Office, Private Bag X5028, Umtata. Tel 0471 = 25344/5/6

Nearest AA Office
• AA House, 27 Fleet St, East London 5201. Tel 0431 = 21271

Where sea cliffs dive to the dance of spindrift

THE GENTLE HILLS AND SPRAWLING SANDS of the southern Transkei coast are barred to the north by sheer cliffs, reducing the beaches to little coves around river mouths, easily washed away by periodic floods. Inland crags and interlocking spurs frame meandering valleys of old, wide rivers such as the Mzimvubu and Msikaba, which form wide estuaries where they mingle slowly with the sea. But when the land steps down in terraces to the coast, and young rivers such as the Mfihlelo find their way blocked by awesome cliffs, their urgency is so great they simply leap over the sheer edge into the surging surf below.

The coast is appropriately wild here: deep gorges shield their secrets with impenetrable forests, languid in the subtropical heat; groves of rare palms or primeval mangrove swamps seep down to the water's edge; tall sea stacks stand like strange sentinels on the sand; and out to sea, the primitive force of freak waves, which can swallow ships whole, remains untamed.

The green-gold coast north of Port St Johns.

1 Hluleka and Mpande

To reach the resorts of this region, you proceed from Umtata towards Port St Johns (the central resort of the area), and then on to Lusikisiki and Bizana, the quality of the road varying with the season. On the R61 to Port St Johns, just past Libode (where you can buy beadwork at a weekly market), there is a turn-off to Hluleka Nature Reserve — a road for the most part in good repair.

At Hluleka wooden chalets on stilts, surrounded by protected forest, overlook the sea on one side and a small estuary on the landward side, while bungalows stand in the bush nearer to the beach. This reserve was originally called Strachan's Grant, after being presented to William Strachan last century. Later, a magnificent stone mansion was built here and gardens planted among the forest trees, creating a wonderful holiday hideaway. When the 772 ha tract of land was bequeathed to the government — on condition that it be retained as a reserve — the homestead became the administrative offices. The

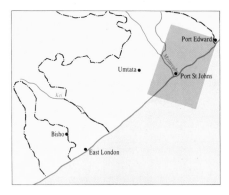

reserve is stocked with a variety of game, from eland to impala, and birds are prolific in the forests and along the streams, while the forest fringes attract a mass of butterflies.

A short walk from the chalets brings you to a picnic spot on the verge of the forest, and then to a semicircular beach enclosed by rocky points and walled in by thick wild banana pickets. The shale arms that embrace the main swimming beach form narrow gullies and pools and crumbling cliffs, where fishermen clamber; yellow daisies grow on the low ledges and highlight the lichen colouring the rocks. Shells are tossed up on the beach and collect in the pools, where you can snorkel when tide and swell permit.

By following a succession of lesser gravel roads north of Hluleka, you come within easy walking distance of the beautiful beach of Mpande Bay, formed where two small rivers reach the sea. This is the spot for those wanting to leave behind all traces of civilisation, with the main attractions being rock angling and harvesting mussels, oysters and rock lobsters. There are no facilities but camping permits are available (from the nearest forestry office).

2 Mngazana and Mngazi river mouths

Taking the Port St Johns road for the next coastal resort leads you through the Mlengana cutting where the Mngazi River has carved an impressive valley, lined by ordered ranks of crags and with a fertile, heavily cultivated floor. Although the road here is tortuous and poor, the scenery is captivating: it is easy to see why the dominant feature of the cutting, the *mlengana* or 'hanging' rock, was corrupted in English to the 'rock of execution'. The road begins high up above the valley and slowly descends to cross it after about 30 km just downstream of the Amphitheatre. It was here last century that a fierce battle gave the river its name — 'the place of blood'.

Shortly after crossing the river a turn-off leads to a hotel on the Mngazi River, resting on the banks of a dune-engulfed lagoon. As the moon rises over the dunes opposite the hotel, the water takes on the sheen of mercury, a vast sheet ringed by the polished silver of the dunes.

More than 130 bird species have been recorded in the vicinity of the hotel: on the sandbank at the river mouth, kelp gulls roost among vast colonies of terns, which take to the air in a swirling mass of white wings that seems to fill the sky. A wide range of recreational activities is offered, including organised hikes and boating trips up the river. For fishing there is the permanently open river and the

LEFT *A sliver of sand between sea and bushed land runs north from Mngazana.*

sea to choose from, with a number of rocky points in easy walking distance from the hotel. There is a pleasant day hike from the hotel to Port St Johns, passing the wreck of the *Horizon* where the ribs of the ship's hull can be seen at low tide, and taking in the spouting Blowhole and the precarious Crack rock formations.

Undoubtedly the best walk is to the mangrove swamps on the Mngazana River estuary, 4 km south of Mngazi. There is a rowboat 'ferry' service across the river mouth to the most extensive mangrove swamp forest on the Wild Coast, and the only one where red, white and black mangrove tree species are found together in large communities. To appreciate fully the fascinating life cycle of these strange but bountiful swamps, try to spend at least six hours between the tides, waiting and watching.

3 Port St Johns

Since its inception in 1878, Port St Johns has been a frontier town with a blend of African wilderness and colonial order. Its setting is perhaps the most dramatic in the country — here the mighty Mzimvubu River has cut a great gorge to the sea, two mountain bastions overlook the river and sea, forests cloak the mountainsides and flowers and creepers trail a profusion of colours. The town and its surroundings offer the natural attractions of forest and mountain, river and sea, with the focus on the Mzimvubu gorge and a nature reserve, as well as numerous amenities.

The origin of the town's name is the subject of some dispute, but most reliable sources put it down to the Portuguese caravel, the *Sao Joao*, wrecked near the mouth of the Mzimvubu River in 1552. The Mpondo call the deep river that cuts a magnificent gorge through to the sea 'the home of the hippopotamus', for until the colonial trade in ivory and skins tamed this corner of Africa, the river and surrounding forests and kloofs teemed with game, the river with hippos and crocodiles.

The river mouth was for some time known as Rosebud Bay after the *Rosebud* became the first ship to cross the large sand bar at the mouth in 1846. After that the estuary proved to be a convenient venue for trading — and smuggling. In 1878, the British government decided that the river was an important strategic harbour, and by arrangement with the local chief, the harbour area was ceded to Britain. Six years later Britain annexed the area (with a population of about 300) to the Cape.

A town grew rapidly around the garrison but the sand bar across the mouth was always a problem for ships. They had to wait until spring high tide to breach the bar, and if conditions were against them, they simply sailed on to Durban or East London. The wagon riders who were commissioned to load and unload produce at the harbour thus earned a precarious living, leading in some cases to legendary drinking parties under the canopied wild fig trees along the river. (The bell of the *Clan Gordon* outside the town hall was, for instance, lost by its captain in a wager.)

Today the approach to the town passes between Mount Thesinger and Mount Sullivan, which form the imposing Gates of Saint John. Along the wide river beneath the gates, stalls offer bead, batik and cane crafts, and the luscious fruits — pawpaws, mangos, avocados and bananas — that thrive in the subtropical warmth. The atmosphere of Port St Johns is one of lazy charm, belying the efficiency with which facilities such as accommodation, the golf course and the natural history museum are run.

An unhurried ferry operates between First Beach and the beginning of Agate Terrace, which forms a satellite resort to the town. First Beach is overlooked by a hotel and is the favourite fishing spot in Port St Johns, but swimming here could lead to a close encounter with a shark. From the beach there is a popular walk to the lighthouse, and along this whole stretch fishing is excellent. Another walk, a good day's outing, leads from the ferry's docking point through the indigenous forest

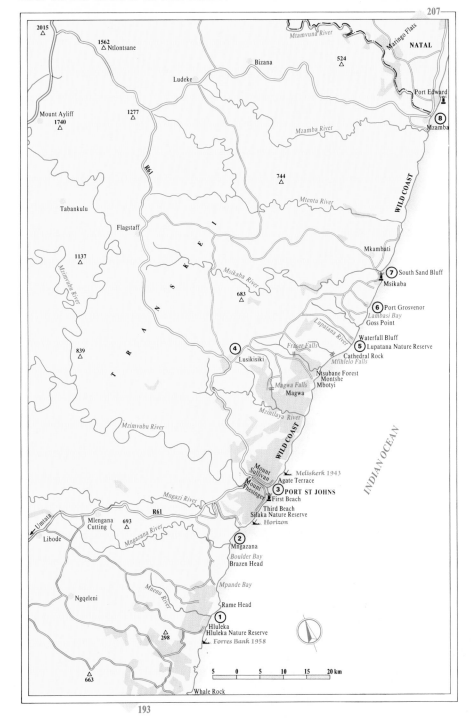

to the summit of Mount Sullivan and down to the Lusikisiki road.

Second Beach, situated on the south side of Mount Thesinger, has an informal air, with a marvellous swimming and surfing beach, open-air cafés and markets and the lifestyle of a tropical island. Bungalows as well as camping facilities are available here, drawing mainly young people to laze away the long summer days and nights, and snap up the various attractive crafts made by the local residents.

South of Second Beach the road winds steeply uphill to the gate of the Silaka Nature Reserve, and then drops steeply down again to Third Beach. Kingfishers — giant, pied, malachite and brownhooded — perch on branches and reeds above the stream while cormorants nest on Bird Island off the pebble beach. Iron-hard dolerite and softer shale chunks have been pounded by the restless sea into a mass of rounded, glistening stones. There are bungalows for rent in the reserve, just the kind of place that children cherish as a holiday paradise.

4 Lusikisiki to Mbotyi

Leaving Port St Johns on the main road north you cross the bridge over the Mzimvubu River and enter a lush world with spectacular views of the Gates of Saint John, before winding up and over the next valley. White-walled huts dot green fields, with the Drakensberg's foothills in the far distance. The sound of the wind through the reeds along the rivers here is said to be the root of the name Lusikisiki, a dusty trading, transport and labour-recruiting centre of the region. Men here wear their tribal blankets and mine helmets as a sign of manhood, much as they once wore the symbolic leopard skins.

A turn-off to Magwa leads through the tea estate of that name and then on to the small resorts on the wildest section of the Wild Coast, but camping is permitted only at three spots, and of these only Msikaba has any facilities. The fishing here is so good, however, that little else matters. Make a short detour to the Magwa Falls by bearing right all the way through the tea estate.

THE MARVELS OF MANGROVE SWAMPS

The swirl of murky waters forming the mangrove swamps at Mngazana.

The mangrove swamp forests that grow along the braided channels of the Mngazana River estuary are the largest and healthiest of these fragile but fertile communities on the Wild Coast. Three of the main mangrove tree species — the red, black and white — grow at Mngazana.

Mangroves have specialised 'breathing' roots that project above the surface of the oxygen-poor mudflats in which they grow, to enable them to absorb as much oxygen as possible. The red mangrove (*Rhizophora mucronata*) produces high stilt roots equal in length to the distance between tides (sometimes up to 2 m). This means that at high tide, the tree appears to float on the water, while at low tide its spreading root structure is exposed. The black mangrove (*Bruguiera gymnorrhiza*) produces short prop rather than stilt roots, as well as elbow-angled breathing roots. The white mangrove (*Avicennia marina*) has an extensive underground root system and thrusts up masses of pencil-like breathing roots, up to 40 cm long.

Seed germination of the mangroves also has to be specialised to survive under these tidal conditions.

The red and black mangroves produce seedlings that germinate on the tree and then drop off as cigar-shaped fruits, which begin to put down roots within hours of landing on the mud. The seedlings of the white mangroves are, however, round and are often carried away by the water before washing up on a distant beach to take root and pioneer a new mangrove community.

Among the creatures that opt to live in the glutinous mud of a mangrove swamp are mangrove snails, which keep just above the water level (and out of reach of predators) by migrating up and down the tree trunks with the tides; the shy black-and-red fiddler crabs, which dart about at low tide scooping up blobs of mud or detritus to feed; and the giant river crabs, whose menacingly large nippers are generally confined to catching tiny molluscs. Besides sheltering these and other inhabitants, the swamps provide a rich natural food chain that supports any number of organisms from bacteria to mangrove kingfishers and fish. Measures to conserve the vital 'nursery' of Mngazana are now being rigorously applied.

These magnificent, 140 m-high falls with their hanging forests resemble a miniature Victoria Falls when in flood, complete with rainbows, gushing white plumes and roaring 'smoke' — all overlaid by an eerie silence.

The first coastal spot of real interest is Mbotyi and to reach this pretty beach resort with private cottages and a store, the road snakes its way into the twilight world of the Ntsubane Forest, vast and teeming with birds such as louries, paradise flycatchers with their cinnamon streamers, broad-winged crowned eagles (the only forest-dwelling eagle), bush shrikes and cuckoos, as well as small antelope and wild pigs.

The way to the sea through the forest is steep

LEFT *A band of ice blue hedged by the steep-sided Mzimvubu gorge.*

Inland, on the route between Lusikisiki and Bizana, the landscape broadens into a peaceful pastoral scene, studded with rustic huts.

and slippery, and access can be cut off by heavy rains. A small river emerges from the forest and forms a shallow lagoon behind the kind of beach dreams are made of. There are not many beaches along this stretch of coast, but the cliffs that reach out from here are spectacular. Climb the ridges behind the beach and you enter villages almost forgotten by time, where animal skins and horns adorn the dusky insides of the huts. If you intend camping (you need a permit, obtainable from the forestry office in Lusikisiki), check in with the local headman as a courtesy and to protect your own interests as pilfering is rife.

5 Lupatana

From Lusikisiki the road to Mkambati deteriorates progressively, but shortly after the Mboyti turn-off, a better road leads to the Lupatana Nature Reserve where a camp site is situated between the milkwood forest and a ring of large boulders. A group of shacks cling like barnacles to the grassy bank of the Lupatana River, for the waves that pound the rocky shelves here send up monstrous sprays that rival anything the stormy Tsitsikamma coast can stir up.

The main attraction of Lupatana is that it is the closest kick-off point for a walk to Waterfall Bluff, Cathedral Rock and the Mfihlelo Falls. An obvious path crosses the river and skirts the pounding surf, then heads above the first cliffs and diagonally down to a viewsite at the base of Waterfall Bluff, with the main fall over 100 m high. Retrace your steps and head around the back of the falls to Mamba Pools and another viewsite on the opposite bluff. Red-hot poker blooms in summer and aloe minarets in winter enliven a landscape where jackal buzzards and ravens glide over pools tumbling one into the next in a long procession of laughing waters.

THE ELUSIVE TREASURE OF THE GROSVENOR

Rusting dreams at the site of the wreck.

A century after the wreck of the English ship the *Grosvenor* off the Transkei coast, rumours began to circulate of the indescribable wealth that had been lost with the ship. The ship's bills of ladings showed a cargo of bullion, and it was whispered that unlisted were incomparable treasures looted by adventurers — including the Peacock Throne of Persia.

In 1882 a Lieutenant Beddoes and Sidney Turner found about 150 gold and silver coins washed up on the beach at Lambasi Bay. The excitement this created led a year later to a group of spiritualists employing a medium named Andy to locate the riches. The boy's guiding ghost turned out to be a sham and the expedition hastened home, bankrupt and shamefaced.

The salvage attempts now became more concrete. Around the turn of the century, local trader Alexander Lindsay blasted the sea bed where the ship was thought to lie and succeeded in recovering 240 coins. He also brought a steam crane to the site by ox-wagon but his money ran out and the crane was abandoned to the ravages of rust. In 1907 another salvage attempt was launched by the Grosvernor Treasure Recovery Company (again involving Lindsay): the idea was to use a dredger to remove sand from the wreck and send divers down to loot the treasure, but the rough seas aborted the plan and cost a diver his life and the venture was scuttled.

In 1921 two men, both named Webster, formed the Grosvenor Bullion Syndicate and began tunnelling under the sea bed to where they thought the wreck lay. Within six months the tunnel was about 80 m long, but the men could not entice further financing and the tunnel was left to collapse. Another attempt at tunnelling in the late 1920s ended the same unsatisfactory way, with the tunnel entrance left as a monument to credulity.

In 1938 the Van Delden brothers began an envisaged 400 m-long breakwater that would engulf the wreck, allowing the area to be drained to form a dry dock around the wreck. The eruption of the Second World War halted construction and the untamed sea washed away their work. The next plan, to use a giant grab crane to drag up the wreck, also came to naught when money ran out, stranding the crane in Durban's harbour.

Finally, in 1952, a diver operating off a boat found the 'Grosvenor Gully' to be barren, but eight cannons were recovered nearby and they reside in various museums around the country. Ironically the richest haul from the *Grosvenor* was probably the ballast iron, recovered by the ship's blacksmith who settled in the area with two Mpondo wives and found a ready market for his wares and skills.

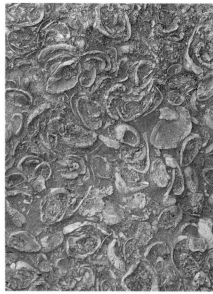

Marine fossils embedded in rock.

By skirting around another wooded gorge the path leads to the edge of an escarpment that drops directly into the sea. Here you look down the deep clefts to formations that have been carved out of the cliffs to form the Cathedral Rock. Two towering sea stacks have had tunnels gouged right through them, and then adorned with rock bridges that seem to have been built like the flying buttresses of gothic cathedrals to support the towers. Just south of this oceanic cathedral are the 160 m-high Mfihlelo Falls, dropping straight to the sea with a grandeur almost impossible to appreciate fully from above.

6 Port Grosvenor

The next turn-off, to Port Grosvenor on the Lambasi River, is worse than the previous one but not as bad as the final approach to Msikaba at the end of this road. The settlement was named after the ill-fated *Grosvenor*, which sank off Lambasi Bay in 1782 after 'colliding' with the continent on a stormy night. Rumours that it was carrying a great wealth in bullion and the looted Peacock

Throne of Persia precipitated a rush of futile efforts to regain these prizes from the hungry sea. As you stroll along the bay, you will stumble across rusting boilers, the decaying base of a crane, a tunnel leading under the sea and other signs of the great enterprise undertaken here which has since succumbed to the forces of nature.

The story of the *Grosvenor* castaways is a tragic one, for they set off southwards on foot, believing that Cape Town was nearby. Six months after beginning their trek, only six of the original 138 survivors reached distant Algoa Bay. Expeditions sent out to search for the others eventually rounded up 12 more stragglers but the rest perished from weakness, sickness or starvation, or gave up hope and settled with the local peoples.

There are no public facilities at Lambasi Bay, but history and romance continue to attract visitors to this lonely spot.

7 Mkambati: South Sand Bluff to the Mtentu River
Between the Msikaba and Mtentu rivers the largest nature reserve in Transkei is being devel-

oped, but as yet camping facilities and a solitary bungalow exist only on the southern bank of the Msikaba River, at South Sand Bluff. The river mouth is particularly attractive and typical of the Wild Coast's wide estuaries, where thick indigenous forest comes right down to the water's edge. An automatic steel lighthouse stands on the bluff and the fishing here and at both river mouths (including Msikaba Island and Danger Point), yields great fighting fish. There are many walks in the reserve, including a section of the coastal hike between the Mtamvuna River in the north and Port St Johns in the south that takes in Waterfall Bluff and Cathedral Rock.

The route to the northern bank is a long, roundabout one, but for naturalists it is a worthwhile one for there grow groves of the rare Pondo coconut (*Jubaeopsis caffra*). This species of palm does not have the tall trunks of most other palms and its fruit is hard and fibrous, sometimes holding milk.

8 Mzamba
The final resort on the Wild Coast is Mzamba. The road from Bizana (R61) to Port Edward, across the Transkei border, passes behind a casino complex. The complex is located on a prime spot in an elbow between the Mtamvuna River mouth and the sea, and the focus here is wholly sophisticated. Just south of the complex are the holiday shacks at the Mzamba River mouth and Mzamba Beach. At low tide it is possible to walk along the rocky intertidal zone of the beach to see the Mzamba Cretaceous Deposits — shell fossils embedded in the rocks just north of the river mouth, reminders of sea creatures that lived about 100-million years ago. Most of the fossils are the spiral shells of a squidlike creature, but the deposits also contain shells of prehistoric sea urchins and clams.

LEFT *The secluded little beach at Mzamba provides the quiet climax to the Wild Coast.*

THINGS TO DO

Angling

This entire coastline is a fisherman's dream, the meeting place of temperate and tropical species, but with the exception of Port St Johns, there are few facilities and access is difficult. Most of the coast is rocky with high cliffs falling into deep water and only small sandy coves situated near the river mouths.

Beachcombing and shelling

This is not a good area for shelling as the shells are ground up by the heavy swells and rocky shore, but for beachcombers there is the chance of finding relics from many shipwrecks: finds of coins, bits of metal and pottery are fairly common.

Birdwatching

Mngazi and Mngazana rivers have prolific bird life, including terns and the rare mangrove kingfisher. Port St Johns has probably the most varied bird life (notably forest species) because of the varied habitats. The best places for birdwatching are invariably the larger estuaries where sea, land and forest species congregate and the majestic fish eagles nest.

Boardsailing

There are no really suitable spots for serious boardsailing but estuaries such as at Mngazi and Mbotyi offer sheltered venues for gentle sailing.

Boat trips

There are morning and sunset boat trips up the Mngazi River.

Camping and caravanning

Port St Johns has two fully developed camping and caravanning sites, while at

Fish type	Season	Best area	Best bait
Bronze bream	Winter — spring	Mngazi, Port St Johns	Mussels, redbait
Garrick (leervis)	All year, best in winter	Mngazana, Mngazi, Port St Johns, Mkambati, Mtamvuna	Artificial lure, live bait
Kingfish	Summer	Mkambati	Live bait
Kob (kabeljou)	Winter — spring	Mngazana, Mngazi, Port St Johns, Mkambati	Sardines, anchovies
Mackerel	Autumn — winter	Msikaba	Artificial lure
Mussel-cracker	Summer	Port St Johns — Port Grosvenor	Crabs, redbait, mussels
Shad (elf)	All year	Open river mouths	Sardines, anchovies
Sharks	All year	Port St Johns	Live bait

Mkambati there is a camp site with an ablution block in the reserve. At Lupatana and Mbotyi the camp sites have no facilities. The roads are generally poor, so it is not practical to tow caravans anywhere but to Port St Johns. (Contact individual resorts for further information regarding accommodation.)

Canoeing

The Wild Coast rivers are beyond compare for paddling and can be navigated for many kilometres upstream, but bring your own canoe. The casino complex and the hotel on the Mngazi River have canoes for residents, while the Rivermen organisation (based in Durban) offers rafting trips down the Mzimvubu River.

Diving

The waters of this region are not generally suited to diving, being too rough and turbid. Snorkelling is, however, often possible around the rocky points at places like Mbotyi and Lambasi Bay.

Drives and viewsites

The Msikaba River valley, on the way to the Mkambati reserve, is a forested gorge where the Mateku tributary plunges 120 m to the main valley floor. It is a short walk from the road to a number of viewsites. On the main road to Port St Johns, you traverse the dramatic Mlengana cutting above the Mngazi River valley, while the north and south entrances to Port St Johns are quite stunning.

Golf

Port St Johns has a small but pleasant and very green nine-hole course.

Museums

The small natural history museum in Port St Johns has interesting displays of fauna and molluscs, a section devoted to tribal customs and costumes, as well as some mythical oddities like the weird creature that is known simply as 'it eats rock rabbits'.

Powerboating

Mngazana estuary has private berthing facilities for powerboats, and boats can be launched at Port St Johns (but the conditions are tricky).

Shipwrecks

Although not actually visible, the site of the *Grosvenor* wreck is probably the most intriguing of all: relics of past salvaging exploits are nearly as interesting as the wreck itself. The ribs of the *Horizon*, just north of Mngazi, are visible at low tide. Otherwise it is the saga-filled histories of the castaways from wrecks such as the *Sao Joao* and other sailing ships that are of the most lasting interest.

Surfing

Only Second Beach at Port St Johns has any surfing potential, but the wave here is inconsistent.

Swimming

Once again, Second Beach at Port St Johns has by far the best swimming environment of this region, but smaller beaches at Mbotyi, Lambasi Bay, Mkambati (South Sand Bluff) and Mzamba are considered fairly safe when the sea is calm.

Tennis

The hotel at Mngazi River has all-weather courts, while there is a club in Port St Johns.

Walks

Nothing beats the Wild Coast for walking: you can take short walks from the resorts through silent, primeval mangrove swamp forests, explore the high yellowwood forests, climb mountains above dramatic gorges or amble along the golden beaches. For the more energetic, take day outings from any of the resorts, or book one of the national hiking trails for a five-day adventure that will take you through some of the wildest and most beautiful coastal scenery in the world.

Trailblazers and Drifters, both based in Johannesburg, offer Wild Coast hikes as part of their itineraries, whereas Wild Side Ventures, based in Port St Johns, offers day outings from there and Mngazi, five-day hikes, or a month-long expedition covering the entire Wild Coast. It is also possible to obtain a permit from the Department of Agriculture and Forestry to hike any of the unofficial coastal trail sections (including the Mtamvuna mouth to Port St Johns) on your own.

Cathedral Rock, an awesome highlight of a coastal hike in Transkei.

INFORMATION

- Department of Agriculture and Forestry, Private Bag X5002, Umtata. Tel 0471 = 24322
- Department of Commerce, Industry and Tourism, Private Bag X5029, Umtata. Tel 0471 = 25191
- Transkei Airways, PO Box 773, Umtata. Tel 0471 = 24636/7/8
- Wild Coast Holiday Hotels, Central Booking Office, PO Box 103, Umtata. Tel 0471 = 25344/5/6
- Wild Side Ventures, c/o Nature Ventures, PO Box 18981, Hillbrow 2038. Tel 011 = 7255726

Nearest AA Office
- 35a Wooley Street, Port Shepstone 4240. Tel 0391 = 22503

Where jewel-like resorts are strung along a glittering shore

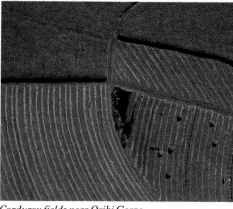

Corduroy fields near Oribi Gorge.

THE COAST OF DREAMS.... OF the entire Natal seaboard, the gilded sands, calm lagoons and velvety surf that link Port Edward to Port Shepstone perhaps most deserve such a title. From humble beginnings (when annexed to Natal in 1866 it was referred to as No Man's Land), this 50 km of coast has filled out to a busy canvas of fun in the sun, where seaside resorts nudge one another. Huge growth is predicted for a region where slick recreation units already overshadow cosy cottages and family hotels, and where life in the fast lane has been brought to once sleepy villages by the magnet of a casino a short drive away.

Yet, in the cooling breezes off the Indian Ocean, with fishing rod in hand and not a blot on the horizon, the magic remains undimmed. Somehow the pulsing holiday playground seems to step back a bit, clearing a space where you can still dream.

1 Mtamvuna River valley

Entering Natal at its southernmost point is delightfully scenic. The boundary between Transkei and South Africa is the Mtamvuna River with its dramatic, forested krantzes and the elegantly soaring Mitchell Bridge — an award-winning design. From here the river mouth and beach are clearly visible, while waterskiers sport on the wide, deep waters below and pleasure boats churn upstream.

Today the river is a sight to gladden the holiday-maker's eye, but for early travellers, crossing the river was a turbulent business. You went either on horseback or, from 1935, in a small boat operated by the Banner's Rest storekeeper. The first pont was built in 1943, about 1,6 km inland, and later moved to the current site of the Old Pont Caravan Park, where its remains can still be seen. The pont, powered by two men pulling a rope, was swept away in the 1959 floods, then rebuilt, but finally bowed out to modern engineering.

The Old Pont Road is reached by heading inland at the Port Edward intersection until you reach the river's edge in a caravan park that caters for picnickers and boaters. A pottery and a tea-garden are situated close by.

2 Umtamvuna Nature Reserve

The southern entrance to the Umtamvuna Nature Reserve is near the gates of the Old Pont Caravan

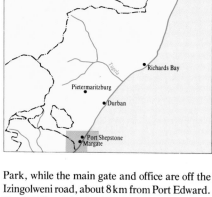

Park, while the main gate and office are off the Izingolweni road, about 8 km from Port Edward. The 3 257 ha of riverine forest and steep gorges are very popular with bird and plant lovers. More than forty pairs of the protected Cape vulture breed on a cliff known as Iron Crown, and Umtamvuna shelters more endemic plants — including a number of rare woody plants — than any other Natal reserve. Even the antelope colony is special as, in addition to grey and blue duiker, reedbuck and ordinary bushbuck, the reserve has an albino bushbuck: white with pinkish horns and hooves.

Several walks of varying toughness are laid out, and a herbarium of 1 300 plants can be visited by appointment. Entrance fees must be paid to the ranger who will supply maps and trail details.

3 Port Edward

Named during the 1920s after the Prince of Wales (who was later to abdicate from the British throne as Edward VIII), Port Edward's beach — with sandy widths, 'supertube' and lawns — is dominated by the shadow of history in the form of Tragedy Hill. Named Isandlundlu in Zulu (because of its hutlike shape), its placid, bush-covered slopes were rumoured to have been the site of a massacre. In 1831, soldiers of Dingane allegedly caught and killed a party of settlers thought to be fleeing with royal cattle, but only fossil, not human, remains have been found here.

Rumour also had treasure buried on North Sand Bluff, a spur of the hill overlooking the Sandlundlu River, while shipwrecks of past centuries left many a tide-borne legacy on the Port Edward sands. Phoenician trading beads made from red agate (carnelians) were thought to have been lost from Arab dhows, while the *Ivy*, wrecked nearby, was responsible for fragments of blue-and-white china that may still occasionally be picked up from the beach.

Port Edward boasts another rarity. Due to an error in an early survey map, the Sandlundlu Lagoon and adjacent beach were for a long time the only privately owned piece of coast in Natal, now enjoyed by visitors to the attractive caravan park laid out on the shores.

For many years, the focus of Port Edward's holiday activity was the SAP Holiday Resort, built in 1948. Today, the good swimming and surfing at Silver Beach (the main beach), the terrace of excellent fishing rocks, and the proximity of the casino complex on Transkei's Wild Coast have turned Port Edward into a pulsing beach resort. Restaurants and shops, a hotel, cottages and ranks of apartments add to the attractions.

4 Munster

The township of Munster, occupying a narrow, 6 km strip of coast between the Boboyi and Kandanhlovu rivers, came into being in its present

LEFT *The placid waters of the Mtamvuna flowing between Transkei and Natal.*

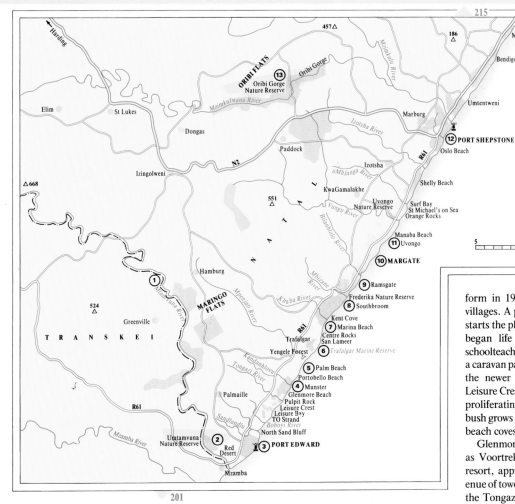

form in 1967 with the amalgamation of four villages. A pleasant beach known as TO Strand starts the pleasure ball rolling from the south. It began life as a closed resort for Transvaal schoolteachers, but is now open to the public with a caravan park and swimming beach. Next up are the newer developments of Leisure Bay and Leisure Crest, with their stylish beach homes and proliferating duplex apartments. Thick coastal bush grows right to the sands of a series of inviting beach coves with rewarding fishing.

Glenmore Beach — with its post office known as Voortrekkerstrand — is the main Munster resort, approached from the R61 along an avenue of towering eucalyptus trees on the banks of the Tongazi River. The hotel-turned-timeshare complex has a perfect site overlooking the

BELOW *The sun lightly gilds a splendid symphony of sea and sand at Leisure Bay.*

This lagoon at Southbroom, separated from the sea by a ribbon of sand, is ideal for boardsailing.

sheltered lagoon and bathing beach, and from its balconies, the remains of the *Nightingale* can be seen on the rocks north of the river, with Pulpit Rock to the south the best-known fishing perch. Cottages and holiday flats are scattered throughout a cool and largely wooded Glenmore.

Munster's oldest established segment is Portobello Beach, registered in 1934 on the farm of Walter von Baumbach. He came from a family of German missionaries and it was he and an Irish surveyor who gave Munster its name. A sports club, caravan park, lots of shady trees, shark-netted beach and popular fishing nooks fill in the holiday picture of this modest, cottagey spot.

5 Palm Beach

Feathery ilala palms, competing with aloes and wild bananas for dune space, are responsible for naming this still tranquil beach settlement. Cottages are dotted along roads with quaint street signs, and a holiday/caravan camp and shop are located near the main beach with its tidal pool. The sands here, with their tossing of multihued rocks, are ideal for pleasant strolls.

The Mpenjati River (with its broad lagoon popular with boardsailors) serves as the northern boundary for Palm Beach, and it is here that the Mpenjati Resort is being developed by the Natal Parks Board. On the north bank of the river is the Yengele Forest, a stretch of protected coastal forest that is to be included in the Mpenjati Resort. Close by, on private Trafalgar property, is the enigmatic 'black lake', so named for its peat-stained water.

6 Trafalgar Marine Reserve and San Lameer

From just south of the Mpenjati River in Palm Beach, to Centre Rocks, 5 km north, the beach has been proclaimed a marine reserve in order to protect what remains of the only marine fossil beds in South Africa. The fossilised forest at Mzamba,

just south of the Mtamvuna River, now falls under Transkei jurisdiction so the Trafalgar beds are of extreme archaeological importance.

Extending from the high-water mark to 500 m out to sea, Trafalgar Marine Reserve permits swimming and rod and line angling, but bait-collecting and shellfishing are prohibited. The petrified forest, situated in the intertidal zone, can be seen at low tide south of the Trafalagar pool, seeming rather like a low outcrop of rock.

The reserve is backed by coastal forest and the beach along here is largely untamed, although the

development area of Trafalgar is steadily filling with holiday homes. Situated on the beach side of the R61, past farm stalls and sugar and banana plantantions, Trafalgar has taken on a distinctly nautical theme: from streets named after admirals and naval battles to a pair of small cannons outside the Victory tearoom!

The public beach offers picnic tables, toilets and a small pool among the dunes, as well as a tidal pool and shark nets.

Falling within the reserve is the beach fronting San Lameer, a holiday complex run as an exclusive, self-contained estate since 1977. Only guests are allowed entry into the landscaped grounds with their 300-plus terracotta villas, hotel rooms, sport facilities, shop and restaurants.

7 Marina Beach

Named after a British princess who toured South Africa during the 1930s, Marina Beach is a tiny holiday-cum-residential township between San Lameer and the Khaba River. It prides itself on the lush natural vegetation within its boundaries, and the exotic pines that crept in over the years have had to make way for reintroduced indigenous trees.

Caravan parks and a sprinkling of shops lie off Marina Drive, and a family hotel is situated on a breezy headland site. From here you have a splendid view south over a crescent-shaped bay of green dunes and sandy beach, which, at Centre Rocks, becomes Trafalgar Marine Reserve. Swimming at Marina Beach, with shark nets, is at the foot of the headland where a tidal pool and parking, toilet facilities and a café are situated. North of the headland are several small, rocky coves and the swimming surf of Kent Cove at the lagoon before Southbroom.

HISTORY CARVED IN ROCK

Packed into 50 km of coast between the Mtamvuna and Mzimkulu rivers is a veritable history of rock, with some granites over 1 000-million years old alongside youngsters a mere 60-million years old.

Well-known stars on this geological stage of shore and river gorge are the Orange Rocks ranged along the beach between Uvongo and St Michael's on Sea. They are actually Table Mountain Sandstone containing small grains of iron oxides which, on weathering, take on a distinctive orange-yellow tint. Just north of the Uvongo tidal pool, the sandstone layers are seamed with reddish veins prompted by a secondary iron oxide. Also discernible from the cross-bedding of the thick layers of sandstone is the direction from which the currents flowed which carried and laid down the original sand: north-east, or where the sea is again during our time.

The oldest rocks of the region are marbles and limestone in the area known as Marble Delta, inland from Port Shepstone, and strips of granulite that fishermen and beach-walkers encounter as rocky outcrops between Port Edward and Manaba Beach, often studded with reddish garnets.

During the geological period known as Carbon-iferous, when the northern hemisphere tropical forests flourished and later became coal, much of the southern hemisphere was one vast sheet of ice. When this melted, it left a layer of debris called Dwyka Tillite, a clay matrix holding huge fragments of rock and boulder now weathered to a yellowish-brown colour. To geologists, the tillite exposures between Shelly Beach and the Izotsha River are a thing of immeasurable beauty.

A sideshow freak among this geological cast is the so-called Red Desert, west of the main road outside Port Edward. Scientists have been unable to agree as to the cause of this surreal landscape of terracotta-tinted sand and half-hearted, scrublike plants. Covering only a few hectares, the fine sand is resculpted every time the wind blows. One theory maintains that the sand is merely rock reduced to ruddy powder by natural agents such as wind and water, but another apportions some blame to human imprint. Dig deep enough, and white sea sand emerges, a legacy from the period of a higher sea level. It could be that the phenomenon is merely the result of fine sea sand slowly oxidising to its present photogenic shade of red.

8 Southbroom

On the map, Southbroom is at the tail of what appears to be solid coastal development all the way to Shelly Beach, 18 km north. But this hardly does justice to a resort known as the Houghton of the south coast! Lying between the Khaba and Mbizane rivers, dozens of sumptuous homes have turned the narrow roads around Southbroom's handsome golf club and village centre into a prestige area.

The shore between the rivers is a string of small, rocky bays set against unspoilt dunes stippled with aloes. The privately established Frederika Nature Reserve here (over 7 ha of natural forest between beach and golf course) has been handed over to the care of the local authority. Caravan parks, holiday flats and sports facilities cater for holiday-makers, as do Southbroom's two lagoons. The pretty, reed-rimmed Khaba River mouth offers boating and boardsailing from the parking and tearoom area, and shares glowing beach sands with Kent Cove. To the north, in another picturesque setting, the Mbizane Lagoon boasts a tidal pool, tearoom, parking and toilet facilities, as well as shark-netted bathing from the beach. From the northern side, the lagoon is identified as Big Tree Bay and is ideal for boardsailing, but powerboating is prohibited.

A short way upstream is River Bend Crocodile Farm. Established in 1981, its several pools and crocodile information centre are supplemented by a plant nursery, art gallery, curio and fresh produce shop. The complex stands at the side of the main road (R61), immediately before you reach the Mbizane bridge.

9 Ramsgate

A farm, at the mouth of the bubbling Bilanhlolo River, was where artist and violin-maker Paul Buck settled in 1922, naming the spot Blue Lagoon. The town now blurs into the beach metropolis of Margate, but something of Buck's Bohemian lifestyle seems to have stamped its character on Ramsgate. Although the main road (R61) is the town's central street busy with shops, two hotels, offices and holiday flats, Ramsgate retains a quaint, almost lazy, charm. Antique shops and art galleries are refreshingly as much a feature of local commerce as suntan lotion and fishing tackle.

Blue Lagoon still lives on in the name of an ornamental tea house situated at the river's edge, predictably colourful with its jade vines, red oriental bridge and adjoining art gallery — where a tree grows through the roof. Guests in the hotel on the opposite bank can fish from the wall outside their bedroom windows, and pedal boats wind about a kilometre upriver.

The main beach of sheltered sands and tree-covered braai sites is beside the lagoon, and features include lifesavers, a tidal pool and offshore shark nets. The nets extend south to protect bathers at Ski Boat Bay, where local

RIGHT The Vungu River squeezes between rocky walls to reach the sea at Uvongo.

A SAFE ROOST FOR THE MASTER OF THE SKIES

To the human eye, the grey cliff face of Iron Crown, high over the Mtamvuna River, appears uncompromisingly bleak and chill, but to the Cape vulture, whose numbers have been declining, it is a haven of hope. Here, in the Umtamvuna Nature Reserve, more than forty pairs of these majestic birds are maintaining a vital nesting colony.

Found only in southern Africa, *Gyps coprotheres* is the second largest vulture on the continent, with a wingspan of 3 m. Although it nests on cliffs and soars at altitudes of 500 m when scanning the ground for food, this scavenger is vulnerable around people. Few nature reserves have suitable breeding habitats, so these birds rely more and more on private land, where their behaviour is often unappreciated by farmers and numerous have been killed.

Increasing their vulnerability is the fact that each pair produces only one egg a year, with both parents incubating and feeding the chick. When old enough, the immature vulture leaves the colony, often flying great distances to join other young birds at a nursery area with plentiful food. When sexually mature — at five or six years — the vulture is able to breed, often returning to its home colony to do so.

The Umtamvuna colony is unusual in that the Cape vulture population is concentrated in the Transvaal mountains and the Transkei/Lesotho highlands. Their hosts here (the Natal Parks Board and local farmers) are thus doing everything possible

The imposing Cape vulture (Gyps coprotheres).

to nurture these fierce-looking birds. A supply of food left on a remote, open hillside, where the birds can land and take off easily, is often the vultures' only source of food. Their eating habits are awesome — with a group of fifty or so able to strip a buck or sheep carcass in twenty minutes — but at the same time, they help to stop the spread of disease and also to keep the veld clean.

commercial fishermen launch their craft, and at Big Tree Bay.

Ramsgate's famous landmark, The Crayfish Inn, was started as a humble hostelry in the 1940s by a Mrs Noel Quarry. The inn's nautical theme evolved after the Second World War, prompted partly by the number of wrecks that have occurred off Natal's southern coast. With items salvaged from shipwrecks and marine scrapyards all over the world, Mrs Quarry created a popular corner that was both an atmospheric eating place and informal maritime museum.

10 Margate

The beach means business in Margate and, if you want it that way, your fun in the sun can be

PLUCKY HERO OF THE NARROW GAUGE RAILWAY LINE

The sturdy steam engine that pulls the Banana Express.

Take a trip into the past aboard the Banana Express . . . not that distant a past, mind you, but one almost wiped out by modern technology.

The Banana Express is the tourist face of the Alfred County Railway, a narrow gauge operation that puffed along 122 km of line between Port Shepstone and Izingolweni for over 75 years. The little trains provided a goods service as a branch line of the South African Railways. Pulled by Garratt locomotives, which were specially designed to coax loaded carriages up the steep gradients from the Natal south coast, the railway emerged as something of a rarity. Not only were the toylike Garratts the most powerful steam locomotives in the world to run on 610 mm gauge (thus attracting international attention from train buffs), but by the beginning of 1986 the Apple Express at Port Elizabeth was the only other narrow gauge line left in South Africa.

By then, thousands of holiday-makers, young and old, had puffed along in what they knew as the Banana Express — in fact just a handful of passenger coaches added to the working train. Then, in October 1986, the blow fell. The transport authorities declared the line uneconomical, and closed it down. To them, the steam era had had its day. Over two dozen

locomotives and 400 wagons threatened to turn Port Shepstone station into a train graveyard.

But no one had counted on the initiative and determination of a group of people who established the Alfred County Railway Committee. Their objective: to save the Banana Express. Local farmers, business people and community leaders wanted the train reinstated for goods use. Professional trainlovers wanted it for tourism.

Petitions were signed and special Save the Train seasons operated during school holidays. The committee asked to take over the line as the first privatised railway service in South Africa. This can only be finalised by parliament but, in the meantime, the Banana Express keeps on tracking!

Setting off from Port Shepstone, the train jolts and sways along the beach before curving inland, its whistle blowing and soot flying furiously from the smokestack. Day trips go as far as Paddock, whose tiny station has been declared a national monument, while half-day outings travel to Izotsha. With motorists stopping to stare and wave, the line winds through oceans of strelitzia and sugar, with a stop for tea and scones at Shelly Beach on the way home.

Roll on, the 20th-century railway barons!

organised to the last splash. The town's holiday hub is a wide curve of pale sand and safe surf rimmed with flats, shops, hotels, cafés, ice-cream parlours and sun terraces. A supertube, swimming pool, paddling ponds and seasonal entertainment add to the attractions, with the result that young people are never bored.

A leisurely meander south from the beach along Panorama Parade (which links again with Marine Drive after a kilometre or so) provides sea breezes, a fishing pier and tidal pool. Across the river to the north, another tidal pool lies off Manaba Beach, where dune forest has been cleared to make way

for holiday flats and chalets.

A farm that turned township in the early 1920s, Margate grabbed the headlines in 1924 when an unidentified 'sea monster' washed up on its beach. Its beach offerings are a lot more glamorous nowadays, with the Hibiscus Queen competition having launched many into international beauty stakes. The town is the centre of the most developed section of the south coast, with retirement villages, shopping malls, a country club and airport in addition to its generous holiday facilities.

The well-run office of the South Coast Publicity Association stands under the slender, sway-

backed palms of Margate Beach, and is a useful starting point for local and more distant outings. Away from the beach are sports clubs, a small bird park and, inland, a game and snake park.

11 Uvongo, St Michael's on Sea and Shelly Beach
Clusters of small shops and a variety of holiday accommodation greet the traveller through this trio of resorts. Boasting good bathing, camping, fishing and surfing, each has a handful of caravan parks and a tidal pool, while Uvongo and St Michael's also have shark-netted beaches.

At Uvongo, the most striking feature is the

The wide sweep of beach at Margate, where holiday pleasures are crowded into the perfect seaside setting.

Vungu River, which narrows into a rocky gorge as it nears the sea and spills 23 m over a waterfall just below the main road bridge. A multimillion-rand luxury holiday complex is planned for the site overlooking the estuary, to incorporate the waterfall, lagoon and adjacent beach.

Running on either side of the river for about a kilometre is the Uvongo Nature Reserve, a tranquil picnic and strolling spot with a concentrated kaleidoscope of local flora and fauna.

From just north of the lagoon to St Michael's, it is possible to stroll or cycle along Saints Walk.

This is a grassy promenade laid out along the shore between the frontline of flats and cottages and the distinctive Orange Rocks with their excellent angling and kite-fishing.

The beach at St Michael's is at the mouth of the uMhlanga River, with the sands on the opposite bank known as Surf Bay. Lifesavers keep an eye on bathers, and beach facilities include a café, change-rooms, lawns and parking. Small boats can be hired from in front of the modern cabanas of the timeshare hotel, and a nine-hole golf course curves along the river, inland of the main road.

Shelly Beach has a sloping, rocky beach where most of the action is provided by boats taking off through the surf. They launch beside the tidal pool from one of the busiest powerboat bases on the south coast. A National Sea Rescue Institute base operates from beside the boat club, while a drive-in cinema and enormous modern shopping centre punctuate the business area.

12 Port Shepstone
One of Natal's grand rivers, the Mzimkulu, hits the coast at a latitude of 30° south, and if its

211

MARGATE'S MYSTERIOUS MONSTER FROM THE DEEP

Many pages of history have turned since late 1924 when a 'sea monster' was seen on the beach near Margate. That it appeared, there is no doubt. But just what it was remains a mystery.

It was on Saturday 25 October that a Mr W White and Mr F Strachan visited the beach known then as Baven-on-Sea. They had heard from the local Zulu that a deep-sea monster had been washed ashore, and they wanted to see for themselves. To support their find, they sketched and measured the creature, White drawing in his notepad what he called a 'record octopod' — a creature with eight tentacles (which he thought had been bitten short by sharks) and two thick 'front feelers' (also truncated). He measured the white-coloured body as almost 3 m in diameter, and over 9 m in length (including tentacles). Its skin was so tough that no knife could hack through it.

Inviting those interested in sea monsters to call on Strachan, on whose farm the beach stood, White estimated that the creature would be approachable for at least a week. Whether the curious took up his offer is not known, but a Port Shepstone newspaper correspondent wrote subsequently of a weird monster that had washed up again on the coast and, quite dead, had stuck fast on the rocks. Was this the same one sighted near Margate, only to have been carried out to sea and dropped ashore again by spring tides?

The description had changed somewhat. The already rotting beast looked like a well-soaked sheepskin, its body covered with long slimy hair. But there was no clear shape to the 2 m-wide body, no eyes, mouth or fins. The only feature was a 'hollow' that ran the length of the body (estimated at 5 m).

Was this the creature photographed by one A C Jones, whose pictures were published in the *Rand Daily Mail*? And the creature described by local farmer H Ballance? He wrote of a fight between what he thought were two whales and some sea monster, about 1 200 m from shore. The latter resembled a polar bear of mammoth size. 'This creature I observed to rear out of the water for fully twenty feet (6 m) and strike repeatedly with what I took to be its tail at the two whales, but with seemingly no effect.'

After three hours, the whales swam off, leaving their antagonist floating on the water. When washed up on the shore, it measured 14 m long, 3 m wide and 1,5 m high. It had a trunk at one end, and a 13 m-long tail at the other. Its apparently bloodless body was covered in snow-white hair. The monster was too heavy for a span of 32 oxen to budge — but after ten days it vanished, thanks no doubt to the spring tide.

No matter what the discrepancies in the descriptions, the Margate monster was enough to put this now popular seaside resort on the map.

---

estuary were not so unreliably navigable, Port Shepstone might have been a major harbour.

From 1880, when William Bazley began working on the harbour mouth, Port Shepstone served as a port for 26 years. It became a full fiscal port in 1893, able to import cargo directly through its own customs house. Shallow-draught coasters such as the *Somtseu*, *Pioneer* and *Sobantu* were able to sail upriver to Batstone's Drift, loading local sugar, tea, lime, fruit and coffee.

But, like Natal Bay, the Mzimkulu mouth kept silting up, and once the railway crossed the river in 1907, sea transport was swopped expediently for rail. Harbour aspirations flared anew during the 1950s, but the 1959 siting of the main bridge across the river mouth put paid to such hopes. Remains of harbour walls can be seen along the river bank, and the cast-iron lighthouse, which was transferred here in 1905 from the Aliwal Shoal, still beams to passing ships.

From such salty origins, Port Shepstone settled down to become the region's administrative centre, bristling with schools, shops, churches, offices and, lately, industry. The railway line from Durban ends here, at the start of the narrow gauge line used by the Banana Express to steam inland to Izotsha and Paddock. A memorial on the corner of Wooley and Dick King streets is a reminder of another trip: King's mercy dash to Grahamstown to save the besieged British force in Durban.

Three hotels accommodate visitors, and the beach, although equipped with tidal pool and change-rooms, is more a fishing than swimming haunt. Port Shepstone Beach extends south past the residences and cottages of Oslo Beach, with the sands north of the Mbango River providing a mellow walk. The Mzimkulu River, with a fully fledged country club on its north bank, is used increasingly by waterskiers and boardsailors, and for powerboat launching.

Bordering on Port Shepstone is the township of Marburg, which was founded in the 1870s as a German mission station.

13 Oribi Gorge

Magnificent river gorge scenery, walking trails, riverside picnic spots and excellent birdwatching beckon the nature-lover at this scenic landmark, less than a 30 km drive from the coast. Driving inland from Port Shepstone on the Harding road, it is possible to loop through the Oribi Gorge, which, named after the small antelope, is a 24 km-long chasm etched through sandstone strata 300-million years ago by the Mzimkulwana and Mzimkulu rivers.

Sheer cliffs echo with bird calls while water snakes at least 400 m below: such dizzying views can be had from several vantage points. Driving the route anticlockwise, the first 'official' viewsites are in the vicinity of the Oribi Gorge Hotel on Fairacres Estate. The drive to the hotel passes through busy KwaZulu settlements before dropping into the stony Mzimkulwana valley and passing limestone works on the climb to the comparatively bland plateau named Oribi Flats. From the hotel, an entrance fee buys a map to lookouts such as Baboon's Castle, Horseshoe Bend, Camel Rock, Lover's Leap, Lehr Falls, Sphinx and the famous Hanging Rock.

Back on the road, the Mzimkulu valley lies off to the right before turning left towards Oribi Gorge Nature Reserve. A public road cuts through this peaceful 1 809 ha reserve, and several walking trails of varying length are signposted from road lay-bys. A picnic site at the Mzimkulwana River presents a different gorge face, but beware of swimming or paddling in the river as bilharzia lurks. The Natal Parks Board hutted camp, close to the Paddock/Harding road, provides overnight accommodation (and trail maps). From the reserve entrance, there is a 21 km drive back to Port Shepstone.

LEFT *Camel Rock, perched above Horseshoe Bend in deep green Oribi Gorge.*

THINGS TO DO

Angling
Almost the entire coastline of southern Natal offers good fishing. Locals pick out their favourite rocks and gullies, but visiting anglers may be sure of ample rewards from any of the following places: Port Edward, Munster, Trafalagar, Margate, Uvongo, Orange Rocks and Port Shepstone.

Art galleries
Several galleries displaying and selling work by local and nationally acclaimed landscape painters are situated in and around Ramsgate and Margate. The Emithini Pottery near the site of the old Mtamvuna pont (Port Edward) has on show a huge selection of ceramics from its own studio.

Beachcombing and shelling
Despite the name, Shelly Beach does not deliver the goods for shell collectors the way it used to, although small specimens can sometimes still be found. Beaches to concentrate on are Port Edward (look out for ancient carnelians and china fragments), Leisure Bay, and the unspoilt beach along the length of Southbroom.

Birdwatching
The nesting grounds of the Cape vultures of Umtamvuna Nature Reserve are not easily seen, unless on a bird club outing, but the birds can be spotted, as can rare birds such as the purple heron, black oystercatcher and green twinspot in the Uvongo Nature Reserve.

Oribi Gorge is also rewarding for birdwatchers, with a bird list available from the Natal Parks Board office situated in the nature reserve camp.

Boardsailing
The number of estuaries along this stretch of coast means good boardsailing as far south as the Mtamvuna River. Sailors set out from the Old Pont camp site, although the high valley walls sometimes cause erratic wind conditions. The Mzimkulu River at Port Shepstone is similarly at the mercy of the wind, but does prove a pleasant spot when the wind is from the north-east.

The small lagoon at St Michael's on Sea is suitable for beginners, although the river mouth often opens in summer, leaving little water to exploit. The most popular — and prettiest — spot is Southbroom, on the Mbizane Lagoon (also known as Big Tree Bay). At Palm Beach (the Mpenjati Resort) the sailing conditions are best when the south-wester comes up.

Bowls
Visitors are welcome at the Port Edward, Southbroom, Munster,

Fish type	Season	Best area	Best bait
Bronze bream	Sept – Jan	Port Edward, Glenmore Beach, Trafalgar, Margate	Prawns
Garrick (leervis)	June – Oct	Palm Beach, Uvongo lagoon, Margate pier, Port Shepstone	Live bait, squid, spoons
Galjoen	Aug – Jan	Port Edward, Glenmore Beach, Trafalgar, Margate	Squid, prawns
Kob (kabeljou)	June – Nov	Munster, Ramsgate, Boboyi River mouth, Port Shepstone	Sardines, live bait, squid
Shad (elf)	Dec – Aug	Marina Beach, Margate pier, Shelly Beach, Mzimkulu River mouth	Sardines, fish fillets
Sharks	All year	All along coast, but mainly Port Edward	Sardines

Ramsgate, Margate and Uvongo bowling clubs and the greens of the Port Shepstone Country Clubs.

Camping and caravanning
Almost every holiday centre has a clutch of caravan resorts, with municipal facilities at Port Edward (on the Mtamvuna River).

Canoeing
Canoes can be hired and enjoyed on the Mtamvuna River and Southbroom's Khaba Lagoon, as well as at St Michael's on Sea and Uvongo.

Diving
Attractive reefs off the Margate pier, Uvongo and Shelly Beach keep scuba divers busy.

Drives and viewsites
A comfortable drive with spectacular views is the circuit through Oribi Gorge from Port Shepstone. This short loop can be extended further inland, passing through the small farming centre of Paddock and continuing to climb, via Wilson's Cutting, to Izingolweni (the route taken by the sturdy narrow gauge engines of the Banana Express). From the 2 000 m heights of Izingolweni, take the Port Edward turn-off, descending steadily through rugged KwaZulu territory. Nearing the coast, the landscape smooths out and returns to farm cultivation, with the green of sugar, timber and fruit trees setting off the blue of the sea.

Golf
Guests are welcome to play 18 holes at Southbroom, Margate and Port Shepstone, and there are nine-hole courses at Port Edward and St Michael's on Sea.

Libraries
This stretch of coast seems as well supplied with books as beaches. Small libraries are found in villages such as Munster and Marina Beach, with larger, well-stocked libraries at Port Edward, Margate and Port Shepstone.

Museums
The municipality of Port Shepstone has the nucleus of a first-rate local history museum waiting for a home. For information on existing exhibits, contact the town clerk's office in the Civic Centre, Connor Street.

Powerboating
Powerboats launch from the banks of the Mtamvuna River, especially for waterskiing, and Shelly Beach has the largest powerboat base on the lower south coast. Boats are also launched from the banks of the Mzimkulu River at Port Shepstone.

Shipwrecks
In 1878 the British barque *Ivy* came ashore unexpectedly just north of Port Edward — with a cargo of liquor. The salvaged cargo was auctioned off at a very festive sale, with the purchaser of the wreck claiming he was going to build a church with the timbers. The anchor of the *Ivy* is displayed on the lawn in front of the children's home in Glenmore Beach.

In 1933 the fishing trawler *Nightingale* was wrecked at Glenmore Beach. No lives were lost, and the boiler of the ship remains lodged in the rocks just north of the lagoon.

Surfing
The lower south coast boasts some of the most consistent wave-breaking beaches, with St Michael's famous among international surfers for its

right-hand point break. But Uvongo is not far behind, nor are Southbroom and Trafalgar. Margate is surfed off the Point and, in a north-easter, the north end of the beach.

Swimming
Good swimming is part of the holiday attraction of this coast, with shark nets at Port Edward, Leisure Bay, Glenmore Beach, Trafalgar, San Lameer, Marina Beach, Southbroom, Ramsgate, Margate, Uvongo and St Michael's on Sea. There are tidal pools at Marina Beach, two at Southbroom, Ramsgate, two at Margate, Manaba Beach (north of Margate), Uvongo, St Michael's and Shelly Beach. On a coast of so many small coves, there is usually a natural rock pool around somewhere for cooling off.

Tennis and squash
There are tennis courts at Munster, Southbroom, Uvongo, and Port Shepstone, while squash courts are found at Port Edward and Port Shepstone country clubs and Uvongo and Munster Sports Club.

Walks
Six scenic trails are laid out in the Oribi Gorge Nature Reserve and can be enjoyed by day visitors as well as camp residents. Trail maps are available from the ranger, as they are from the office at Umtamvuna Nature Reserve. Walks range from very demanding ravine hikes to a half-hour Granny Stroll. The Uvongo Nature Reserve has two comfortable riverside walks that take in an old wagon track and a San cave.

Saints Walk provides a refreshing, sea-level stroll between the lagoon at Uvongo and St Michael's on Sea, while at most points, the beach has endless possibilities. (Try Trafalgar Marine Reserve, setting out from San Lameer and ending at Mpenjati.)

INFORMATION
- Natal Parks Board, PO Box 680, Umtentweni 4235. Tel 0391 = 51068
- National Sea Rescue Institute, Station 20, Shelly Beach. Tel 0391 = 21916
- Port Shepstone Municipality, Connor St, Port Shepstone 4240. Tel 0391 = 21100
- South Coast Publicity Association, PO Box 25, Margate 4275. Tel 03931 = 22322

Nearest AA Office
- 35a Wooley Street, Port Shepstone 4240. Tel 0391 = 22503

A pocket of peace on a prized holiday coastline

W ITH PARKLIKE SCENERY, intimate resorts, mirrorlike lagoons and invitingly empty beaches, the middle Natal south coast offers a tranquil breathing space between the fast-paced development of its neighbours. This 50 km shoreline remains comparatively untouched, recalling childhood memories of dreamy seaside holidays. Fishing from rock and beach is the stuff that angling tales are made of, and children wander barefoot onto the sand from a rainbow of holiday camps, cottages and caravanning spots.

The tarred road dips through the ubiquitous Natal canelands, and occasional timber and fruit plantations, and KwaZulu settlements rub shoulders with narrow strips of beach resort. Travelling close to the shore at times, dazzling seascapes surprise you around many a curve in the road, while you cross rivers with names like musical tongue twisters.

1 Umtentweni

With the Mzimkulu River between them, Umtentweni is something of a northern suburb to Port Shepstone. Yet Umtentweni, with its business centre and homes screened from national road traffic by tall, dense trees, looks and feels very different from its more exposed, southerly neighbour. In addition to its residential and retirement side, Umtentweni has holiday flats, hotels, caravan park and sports facilities ranged along a pretty, 4 km-long beach. The main bathing area is approached via terraced parking with the sandy expanse of Evans Bay to the north. Beachgoers enjoy the small tidal pool and rock pools, inviting walks in both directions, and, just north of the Mzimkulu, the excellent local fishing spot of Sharks Rocks.

The Mtentweni River (named for the spiky grass growing on its banks) forms the resort's boundary to the north. As much natural flora as possible between the two rivers has been preserved, making for pleasant rambles through the remaining coastal forest.

The Old St Faiths Road undulates inland from Umtentweni, travelling some of the way close to the north bank of the powerful Mzimkulu River

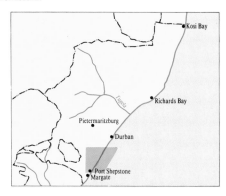

before cutting north-west to Highflats. The road — single lane, and somewhat crudely tarred before changing to gravel — provides some scenic valley and sea views before reaching St Faiths. Old mission stations, country trading stores and granite ridges accent the landscape, and the drive continues inland through hillside KwaZulu settlements and schools.

2 Bendigo

This is the name of the farm that once spread over this 6 km length of coast, and when, in 1967, four

A glittering jewel: the emerald south coast.

seaside villages amalgamated under a single town board, they took on the farm's name as an umbrella identity. Each resort has retained its own railway station and coterie of cottages and caravan parks. There is hardly a highrise in sight and the only 'industry' is beachgoing and fishing ... which is how the locals and regulars like it.

First up is Sea Park with wide, clean sands geared more for fishermen and beachcombers than bathers. The route to the beach is not signposted, so from the clutch of shops on the beach side of the main road, head seawards and park wherever a path through the dune bush presents itself.

Crossing the Mhlangamkulu River lands you in Southport. This is the beach ace in the Bendigo pack, and is far more geared to visitor needs. Roomy parking grounds at the main beach sport a popular restaurant and spreading milkwood trees. The beach itself is quite narrow, its dunes crowded with aloes and strelitzia, and with a pretty tidal pool cupped among a chain of rocky outcrops. Shark nets, ablution facilities and summer lifesavers add to holiday comforts, and Bendigo's only hotel is on the main road as it streaks through Southport.

The 4,5 ha Bendigo Nature Reserve is reached by turning inland at Valley Road. The local authority has laid out paths through the bush and

LEFT *Sea Park's tangled setting, tamed by sweeping roads.*

THE BANANA BEACHES

The indigenous wild banana.

Part of the charm of the south coast landscape is the profusion of indigenous flora still to be seen, with one plant standing out above all others: the wild banana or *Strelitzia nicolai*. Growing sometimes to an impressive 9 m in height, these plants crowd in dense groups around the many lagoons and between beach and highway.

The young leaves of the wild banana are a shiny, pale emerald, unfurling to become oblong expanses of dark green as much as 1,8 m long, the edges torn by wind to give a tattered effect. The plant flowers throughout the year, its spiky blue-and-white flowers emerging from a narrow, purplish sheath. Once this splits, a column of flowerheads results, producing so much nectar you can see it spilling down the outside of the blooms.

This is what attracts the birds that pollinate the plants — and the flower is formed so as to give the pollen carriers as much help as possible. The sheath surrounding the flowers acts as a platform on which the birds can perch. The blue petals form a channel containing the stamen and style, and their arrowlike arrangement is such that, when the bird thrusts its beak into the flower for nectar, the petal channel opens and pollen is rubbed off onto the bird's breast feathers, ready for transferral to the next flower.

Cousin to the wild banana is the bird-of-paradise or crane flower (*Strelitzia reginae*), a popular garden species with its equally striking flowers of orange (or yellow) and blue.

---

bird life is good. The offices of the Bendigo Town Board are in Southport, and visitor information is available from their staff.

Before you know it, Anerley comes up next with its church holiday camps and caravan parks. A network of gravel roads laces between the main road and the beach with its tidal pool.

Sunwich Port is situated beyond the Domba River, and the beach here is reached by crossing the railway line at the Saame holiday complex. Large rocks at Domba Bay attract anglers, while a tidal pool and good surf keep bathers happy. Shark nets are laid offshore.

3 Melville

Bendigo blurs into Banana Beach, a family favourite with its tidal pool, shark nets, lagoon paddling and surfing. Crammed with accommodation, Banana Beach is aptly named for the profusion of strelitzia still evident in the bush, and it comes under the control of the Development Services Board of Melville. This, in its turn, is signposted off the main road after crossing the Koshwana River, with dozens of holiday chalets and rondavels tucked between beach and railway line. The sea is reached from several casual paths through the bush, and

Cracker Bay attracts many rock anglers. A tidal pool and toilet block are situated on Melville's beach as well as at ePhumula, which also falls under the Melville banner. Near ePhumula, the Capuchin Convent of the Franciscan order is something of a hilltop landmark on the inland side of the main road, and the sisters have become known for their exquisite embroidery.

Fishing and shark-meshing boats launch from the mouth of the iNtshambili River (which forms Melville's northern boundary), and it is here that the remains of the whaler *Novonia* can be seen. Wrecked at this spot in 1934, a few sheets of iron can still be seen by those prepared to clamber over the rocks from beneath the bridge. A gun, which had been covertly cut from the damaged vessel by former residents, is now in the keeping of the Port Shepstone municipality.

4 uMzumbe

About a kilometre past the iNtshambili River, with the landscape fanning out into cane cultivation, you enter the tiny resort of uMzumbe. American missionaries arrived in 1860 to build a church station about 10 km up the Mzumbe River. The peoples that they ministered to were said to descend from cannibals who preyed on all comers,

and their kraal was known as *Umuziumubi* (the bad homestead) — suggesting the origin of the village name.

A-frame chalets crouch like a colony of upright rabbits on the hillslope overlooking the village, while a caravan park, secluded cottages and popular hotel make up the resort between main

It was on 3 August 1868 that George Parsons thought he had struck it rich. After months of panning rivers south of Durban, he found in the Mtwalume River what he had been seeking so anxiously: gold. Just a fortnight later, one of his prospecting partners, Walter Compton, pounced on a gleam of gold in the nearby Mhlungwa River.

The south coast gold rush was on.

While Natal seethed with excitement and men from every corner of the young colony converged on the crystal waters of the Mtwalume, Parsons visited Pietermaritzburg with his haul. It was a humble one — actually, a single fleck of gold. But on the strength of it, government officials granted him funds (the equivalent of R160) for two months' more mining.

In November that year, gold seekers were deflected temporarily from the coast by a find on the Tugela River, much further north. But the south coast continued to trail its gilded petticoats. The energetic Parsons claimed to be 'finding colour' in every river from the Mzumbe to the Mpambanyoni (where Scottburgh now lies), and George Sides reported a gold find in the Fafa River. But the most promising traces of gold appeared in the Little Mgeni, a tributary of the Mtwalume.

It was a chill, deep pool near the junction of the two waterways that beckoned like Aladdin's cave. Its banks, lined with acacia trees, grew trampled and muddy as dozens of hopefuls set up camp and got to work. Most proficient among these was Parsons, who (backed by more government cash) began to drain the flats, presumably to expose all the gold just waiting to be found.

But the warning signs were already there. A party of English diggers, led by Captain Augustus Lindley, noted: 'In many places we succeeded in obtaining the colour in very minute particles, but so trifling in quantity as to be quite unworthy of further attention.' A group of Australians who prospected as far south as the Mzimkulu gave up in disgust after finding only ten ounces of gold. Parsons, after months of sluicing the Little Mgeni, picked out only 12 grains. By November 1869, just nine men remained, with calloused hands and fast-fading dreams. Finally, two years of prospecting by about a hundred diggers yielded a mere twenty ounces of gold....

Stripped of holiday crowds, the coast at Hibberdene shows a wild and lovely face.

was consecrated in 1947, were laid by Italian prisoners of war.

5 Hibberdene
With the residential suburb of Woodgrange-on-Sea to the south and a children's home at its northern lip, Hibberdene is a bustling holiday destination boasting its own civic centre and substantial shopping and accommodation facilities. The main beach inclines rather steeply from tree-covered dunes behind the railway station, with plenty of parking, a large tidal pool and deep water tailormade for anglers. The beach fun is supplemented by an amusement complex on the north bank of the lagoon and boating on the Mzimayi River. South of the river, the Simpson landing strip is used by visitors with private aircraft, and for microlite training.

Two hotels stand on the beachfront, and with its holiday rondavels, caravan camps and, more recently, retirement villages, Hibberdene swells visibly with seasonal influxes of holiday-makers.

6 Mtwalume
Some 2 km north of Hibberdene, at the Mhlungwa River, the single-lane N2 forks into a double-lane highway that hugs the shore, and the old south coast road tagged as the R102. Crossing the Mfazazana River, the highway passes Kajim Rocks, where the *St George* fishing boat was wrecked, then parallels an enormous reef that runs for about 2 km close to the shore. This is a good local fishing spot, particularly Reef End (opposite Mfazazana rail halt) and Kings Rock at Turton.

The R102 is an optional and less busy route, travelling slightly further inland for about 22 km,

and intersecting the N2 shortly before Sezela. Like the favoured main road, it cuts alternately across sugar estates and KwaZulu smallholdings, with a hotel located at the junction of the R102 and a link road to the beach.

Two holiday and caravan camps stand on either side of this link road, with a postcard view of the Mtwalume bridge and lagoon from the hilltop above Long Beach camp. Mtwalume — named for an indigenous tree, whose bark has been used by herbalists as a dysentery treatment — is a tranquil and unspoilt cottage resort. A small station and handful of shops overlook the main swimming beach with its huge tidal pool, picnic lawns and tables, toilet and parking facilities. Clean sands stretching south from here are ideal for walking and beachcombing.

road and beach. Commerce offers little more than a shop, post office and rail halt, so well-greened uMzumbe is ideal for quiet holidays and is also a popular fishing haunt. With sands sloping from dunes to the waterline, the beach focus is south of the hotel at Stiebel Rocks. This is an excellent spot for kite fishing as the rocks protrude further into the sea than any other outcrop along this limb of coast. A parking lot, tidal pool and toilets are provided, and a pleasant walk to the Mzumbe River mouth is possible.

The turn-off to the village is opposite the Dominican convent of St Elmo's, which was founded in 1918 as a resthouse for nuns from other convents. It has since developed into a convent school, and the foundations for its church, which

RIGHT *From the air, the little beach resort of Mtwalume seems almost toylike.*

Bazley Beach, its wide golden sands sheltered by the bulk of a grey-green headland, fulfils the dream of every fisherman.

7 Ifafa Beach

Here are all the ingredients for a delightful seaside resort: a beautiful lagoon, wide sandy beaches for strolling and fishing, and a pair of caravan parks on either side of the Fafa River. Yet with its tiny hotel, petrol station, a shop or two, and straggle of cottages, there is an almost forgotten air to this village. Its literal high point is a headland (at the end of Leuchars Road), with breezy views out over the lagoon and the original farm settlement of Bazley to the north.

A suburb named Elysium sports a growing number of holiday and retirement homes, with the main buzz of holiday activity upriver at the Club Marina. On a curve of the river where it passes through a slight gorge, caravans and mobile homes settle comfortably into well-managed grounds with all the mod cons adding to the scenic attractions. Guests make the most of boating, fishing and waterskiing on sparkling, clear water — the water that gave its name to the place, for

THE DANCER THAT DELIGHTS ANGLERS

The scientific name of the shad or elf, *Pomatomus saltatrix*, means 'the one who dances' — a glorious description of this sleek, silvery-blue wave dancer that baits anglers right around the southern African coastline, but particularly in Natal.

Since the turn of the century, shad — out of more than 150 species of Natal angling fish — has dominated sporting and commercial catches here. It seemed for a time that there were almost limitless stocks of this fierce marine predator, but with the harvest being shared by more and more fishermen, catches in the 1960s and early '70s decreased by as much as sixty per cent.

Migrating each winter from the Cape to Natal, where it spawns in spring before returning south, the shad capitalises on currents, water temperature and the handy sardine run menu. But during the months

when it is most plentiful along the Natal shores, shoaling in shallow bays — and therefore keeping anglers busiest — the fish is at its most vulnerable, being most likely to be tempted by angler's bait when preparing to breed. Clearly controls were needed.

The regulations (including an initial ban) were extremely unpopular, and anglers went to astonishing lengths to beat them. But as the conservation measures began to be appreciated, catches again picked up and the restrictions could be somewhat relaxed. Today fishermen can once more land their first shad in twenty minutes, unlike previously when they might have waited four hours.

With its human predators under control, the shad has only one other worry: the garrick (leervis), a large, leathery-skinned and highly aggressive fish with a definite taste for shad.

TREASURES FROM THE SEA

Two examples of the sea's bounty: Haliotis spadicea, *the true Venus ear with its characteristic pearly interior; and* Cypraea tigris, *the sought-after brown-spotted tiger cowrie.*

Shell collecting has become such big business that overzealous gathering of these ocean beauties — with international prices quoted in dollars — has meant the disappearance of many specimens from our shores. To guard against this in the future, there are now restrictions as to the number of live shells that may be taken a year.

To most people, however, shell collecting simply means a browse along the waterline when the tide begins to go out, and they are free to gather to their heart's content the dead shells sprinkled on the sand. Often, because of the pounding seas, only shell fragments are washed ashore — making the find of a whole shell all the more exciting.

The best known collector's items, although not found so often these days, are the cowrie shells. One reason for their popularity is the glossiness of their shells. As a defence against predators, cowries often camouflage their shells under a fleshy mantle rather resembling seaweed. This gives the rounded cowrie a beautiful, unweathered appearance.

Cowries vary hugely in pattern and colour, with one of them — *Cypraea leucodon* — being considered the rarest of shells. There are hardly more than a dozen such specimens in the world, found mostly in the South Seas and the Philippines. Slightly less rare is the prince cowrie (*C. valentia*), while the orange cowrie (*C. aurantium*) is thought to be the most beautiful of shells. Tiger cowries (*C. tigris*) are very well known, and all-time favourites.

South coast beaches deliver a variety of shells, including Venus ears, with their pretty mother-of-pearl interiors, the delicate bubble shells and the exquisitely shaped and shaded cone shells.

---

the Zulu *iFafa* may be translated as 'light glittering on the surface of the river'.

8 Sezela

The formal estate gates and landscaped village of Sezela belie the hair-raising legend which is attributed to its name. Zulu tradition recalls that, in the early 19th century, a man-eating crocodile made its home in the river, and was known as *iSezela* because of its habit of 'smelling out' the trails of its victims. It made life miserable for the Malangeni who lived in the region — until King Shaka, travelling south on a military raid with his soldiers, decided he wanted the crocodile's skin. He dispatched his men into the river, and there they remained until they had hunted down the reptile with their spears.

Maybe such legendary echoes inspired famous poet Roy Campbell to write some of his most acclaimed verse while holidaying at Sezela. But now, the place named from the river beast is all sweetness. With the smell of molasses heavy on the sea air, Sezela is centred around a large sugar mill built in 1914. Along with the railway halt and a dusty hotel, the mill stands almost within splashing distance of the surf.

Sezela is reached from the R102, shortly after its intersection with the N2.

9 Umdoni Park and Pennington

These once formed a single estate, owned by a pioneer farmer killed on the coast by a leopard. Sugar baron Sir Frank Reynolds subsequently bought the southern section of parklike land, naming it after the profusion of water myrtle (*mdoni*) trees growing there. Here he built a seaside mansion to honour South Africa's first prime minister, General Louis Botha. Standing on about 400 ha of forested land known as Umdoni Park Trust, the secluded Botha House has official state president's holiday residence status, and its red-and-white roof can be glimpsed from the beach, protruding above the trees.

Access to Umdoni Park beach and golf club is through a toll gate on trust grounds. Now something of a small game sanctuary with a wealth of indigenous flora, the park holds one of the biggest spider populations in the country, as well as unusual moths and orchids.

The beach with its natural rock swimming pool and surf fishing can also be reached by strolling from the bathing and leisure sands of Pennington, a short way to the north. With its tidal pool, picnic lawns and toilet facilities, Pennington beach fronts a host of holiday cottages, chalets and caravan parks. Most of the accommodation is tucked into lush coastal bush, giving the place an air of privacy. A tea garden is located left of the road from the R102 into the village, and the RDLI Memorial, commemorating lives lost during the Second World War, stands in shady grounds above the main beach.

LEFT *The romantic Fafa River, in the cool embrace of verdant vegetation.*

THINGS TO DO

Angling

Numerous small bays and close inshore reefs make virtually every resort beach a potentially good fishing spot. Rock and surf favourites vary from year to year as channels and tides change, while the fruits of deep-sea fishing from powerboats remain more consistent. One of the fishing highlights is the annual sardine run, and competitions are launched from ePhumula.

Beachcombing and shelling

Plenty of shells are washed up along this stretch of coast, but tides and pounding seas sometimes frustrate the amateur collector. Southport and Anerley are recommended by locals — especially at neap tide — and there is promising beachcombing at the quieter lagoon spots such as uMzumbe and Mtwalume.

The shiny, delicate Venus ear shell (*Haliotis queketti*) is localised in this area, and worth looking out for.

Birdwatching

Pelagic birds such as the Cape cormorant, sandwich tern, Cape gannet and whitechinned petrel can be spotted accompanying the sardine run in winter. The most common birds seen on the beaches include the whitefronted plover, sanderling, whimbrel, kelp gull and greyheaded gull.

Boardsailing

The really experienced boardsailors take to the ocean wave from many of

Fish type	Season	Best area	Best bait
Bronze bream	June – Nov	Umtentweni – Hibberdene, Bazley	Chokka, redbait, mussels
Garrick (leervis)	May – Nov	ePhumula, uMzumbe, Mtwalume, Sezela	Live bait
Rockcod	All year	Umtentweni – Mtwalume	Fish fillets, sardines
Shad (elf)	August	uMzumbe, Hibberdene, Turton, Ifafa Beach, Sezela	Fish fillets

the regular swimming beaches. Otherwise the Mzimkulu River is a regular spot, especially when the water is flowing deep and fast. You must, however, look out for sharks then, because such conditions usually follow heavy rain, and that means dirty water.

Bowls

Visitors are welcome on the bowling greens at Umtentweni, Southport and Hibberdene.

Camping and caravanning

Every resort, no matter how small, has at least one camping and caravan park (easy to spot because of the vivid notices festooning the roadside).

Canoeing

Pleasure boats can be hired on the Mzimayi lagoon at Hibberdene.

Diving

A shallow scattered reef lies quite close inshore along much of this coast, and

spearfishing is popular at Sea Park, Banana Beach, ePhumula and Hibberdene. Unstable weather and dirty water tend to limit the diving season, however, and many of the locals travel further north to Aliwal Shoal. Panorama Diving at Umtentweni hires out diving gear and advises on local conditions.

Drives and viewsites

Take a circular drive of about 200 km inland to Highflats — and pack your picnic basket. Travelling clockwise, you start from Umtenweni, taking in St Faiths, and returning to the coast via uMzinto and Park Rynie. The road climbs among endless Natal hills, some of them ruggedly scenic. For a shorter outing, nip along the Mzimkulu valley, past Batstone's Drift from Umtenweni as far as Mehlomnyama, turning back (before hitting a gravel road) for postcard views of the sea.

Golf

Golfers can choose between the facilities of Umtentweni Country Club (Port Shepstone), which is situated on the banks of the Mzimkulu River; the Umdoni Park Trust Golf Club, which almost rubs shoulders with one of the presidential holiday homes; and the attractively landscaped fairways of Selborne Park Golf Club near Pennington.

Powerboating

Powerboats launch from Hibberdene, where the local club has its headquarters, and from ePhumula on the iNtshambili River.

Shipwrecks

Some remains of the *Novonia* can be seen at ePhumula at the mouth of the iNtshambili River. The rocks north of the mouth of the Mhlungwa River (outside Hidderdene) were responsible for the loss of the Durban-based fishing boat *St George*, which ran aground in 1961 with the loss of one life.

Surfing

Good wave action is found at Umtentweni, at Anerley's Saame Park, and Banana Beach.

Swimming

Protected swimming is a major ingredient of the south coast's holiday magnetism, and where there are no shark nets or lifesavers, there are invariably tidal pools and natural rock pools. The Natal Sharks Board maintains nets at Umtentweni, Southport, Sunwich Port, Banana Beach, uMzumbe, Hibberdene, Mtwalume and Ifafa Beach.

Tennis and squash

Courts are available for visitors at Umtentweni club and Hibberdene.

Walks

No formal trails or hikes have been laid out in this area, but the beach is a never-ending supply of walking possibilities. Try the beach between Umdoni Park and Pennington, Stiebel Rocks to the Mzumbe River mouth, and the Bendigo shore.

INFORMATION

• South Coast Publicity Association, PO Box 25, Margate 4275. Tel 03931 = 22322
• Bendigo Town Board, Bendigo Road, Southport 4230. Tel 0391 = 3257/8
Nearest AA Office
• 35a Wooley Street, Port Shepstone 4240. Tel 0391 = 22503

Powerboat angling yields excellent rewards along this coast. Here, a boat is launched into the surf at Bazley.

Lazing the days away on a lush and lovely coast

T HE INTOXICATINGLY LUSH AND SUBTROPICAL COASTLINE between Kelso and Isipingo looks just the way a holiday coast should. Its waters — never too chilly — teem with marine jewels. Around almost every headland there is a calm, heaven-reflecting lagoon, rimmed with reeds and mangroves. The beaches are a broad ribbon of pale sand, running like a hem along the skirt of coastal forest rich with colour and texture. Palm fronds wave beside the bright red berries of the amatungulu, lilies flame between the exotic hibiscus and bougainvillea, and the wild banana (*Strelitzia nicolai*) thrusts distinctively from every clump of dune forest, earning this the name Strelitzia Coast.

It is no wonder so many popular resorts have blossomed here, all within easy reach of one another, of the sea, and of Durban. You can reach them via the multilaned N2, set a little inland; the quieter R102 or old south coast road, gliding closer to the sea; or the main railway line from Durban, hugging the contours of the shore.

1 Kelso Beach and Park Rynie

Once an estate whose owners named it after their Scottish family home, much of Kelso Beach — with its growing residential area and handful of shops — remains secluded and bush-covered. It is a small haven for caravanners and campers, and day visitors can picnic close to the beach in the bush clearings of Ocean View Farm. A large caravan storage park provides a useful between-holidays service. The beach is simple: sloping sands, no official bathing, and a discreet toilet or two along the access paths.

The beach focus at nearby Park Rynie lies south of the town centre, where the turn-off to Rocky Bay Caravan Park bumps across the ever-present railway line to the remains of the old whaling station. Built before the First World War, a weathered stone jetty is about all that is left of the station, but it provides a backdrop to a pretty and sheltered beach. The local powerboat club

Access to the Natal south coast via the swift and scenic N2 through country hills.

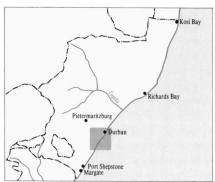

launches from here, and paddleskiers, divers and bathers favour the spot, although it has no shark nets. A small lagoon adds to the appeal, and many a fisherman takes his stand on an outcrop of rocks that are almost the colour of smoked salmon.

Park Rynie, which was named after Renetta 'Rynie' Hoffman (wife of the man on whose farm the town now stands), is largely residential with its northern boundary blurring into Scottburgh South. The business centre includes hotels, holiday cottages and three caravan parks.

2 uMzinto and the Vernon Crookes Nature Reserve

About 8 km inland from Park Rynie is uMzinto, sharing the sweet roots of many a Natal coastal town. The hilly terrain around the Mzinto River was considered excellent for growing cane, and the planters and millers got busy from 1857. A year later Natal's first public sugar company started up at uMzinto, but it was plagued with problems, finally going bankrupt after the mill was struck by lightning in 1864. This did not, however, prevent the area from becoming the pivot of the south coast sugar fraternity, a busy town with a fetching combination of colonial and Indian architecture and weekend relaxation that includes traditional country cricket on an attractive oval.

West of uMzinto is a delightful expanse of valley

LEFT *Paddling in the warm, clear waters at peaceful Park Rynie.*

and grassland with picnic sites and magnificent views. About 3 km along the road to Ixopo is the turn-off to the Vernon Crookes Nature Reserve, which is run by the Natal Parks Board and stocked with game and bird life. The reserve is enjoyed mainly by day visitors although a small camp of rustic huts is available. You can follow a bumpy, narrow road through a hilltop corner of the 2 198 ha reserve with two designated picnic spots en route. Small dams attract the occasional freshwater angler, and wildlife includes zebra, nyala, eland, blue wildebeest, several varieties of mongoose, and hordes of vervet monkeys.

3 Inland to Ixopo

uMzinto is the first call on a leisurely drive that sets out from Park Rynie on the R612, heading inland for Highflats and Ixopo, with the option of making for Durban via Richmond or tracing your route back to the south coast. The striking scenery switches from sugar estates with stately roadside entrances to rugged valleys, timber forests and hillsides scarred by erosion. One of Natal's few narrow gauge railway tracks appears first on one side of the road, then the other, as it climbs from uMzinto to Highflats.

Worth a call along the way is the Ndonyane Weaving Centre at St Michael's Mission, reached by a turn-off some 37 km from uMzinto. An extremely rough road jolts down to the centre, where the weavers work (Mondays to Saturdays) from a stone building behind the pair of churches. Back on the R612, about 17 km on, a small stone church stands off the left-hand side of the road. The St James Anglican Church, with a number of 19th-century settler graves in its churchyard, edges on a steep, rocky ravine that, when the Mtwalume River is in full spate, boasts a lively waterfall. A couple of kilometres later you reach the farming centre of Highflats, with some of its lovely old buildings (dating back to its founding in 1863) still intact. The last 20 km-odd lap to Ixopo, at an altitude of over 700 m and climbing, is real timber country. The town itself has the style of a pretty, old-time village, featuring two hotels with mock Tudor exteriors.

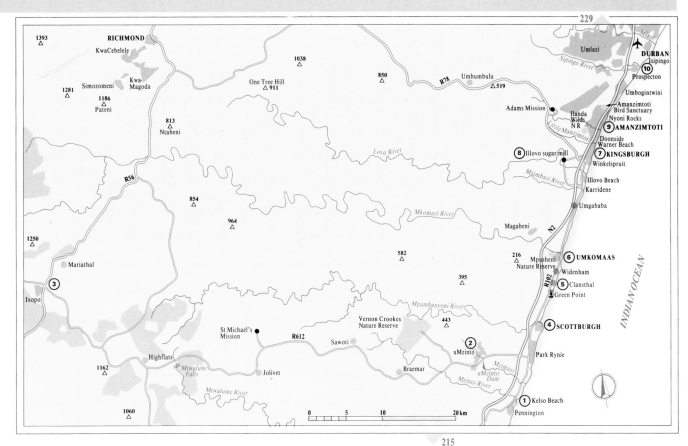

215

From Ixopo you can make for Durban (on the R56) through forested hill-country. You reach Richmond beyond the Mkomazi valley, after corkscrewing down its dramatic depths and rising again between bush-marked, creased hillsides. These are the lower foothills of the Drakensberg, and it was here around 1870 that Cecil John Rhodes made a half-hearted attempt to farm. Richmond village, studded with old homes, has a quaint air, and its pioneering days are recalled in the Richmond, Byrne and District Museum. Beyond Richmond and its citrus orchards, the road continues to Umlaas Road and the link-up with the N3 to Durban.

4 Scottburgh

One of the most attractive and popular resorts on the Natal south coast, Scottburgh's big appeal lies in its sheltered bathing beach — known as Scott Bay — and expanses of terraced lawn that provide sand-free sunbathing.

Situated at the mouth of the Mpambanyoni River (one of the few along the coast with a lagoon north of a headland or promontory), Scottburgh was the first town to be laid out south of Durban. At the turn of the century, a fleet of fishing boats was based where surfers and swimmers now frolic. And the shallow bay was, for a time, a promising 19th-century harbour — much to the

RIGHT Drive inland from Park Rynie through lushly quilted countryside.

excitement of local sugar pioneers eager to transport their harvest to Durban. They named the bay Devonport, but although it was used by a few shallow-draught coasters, the railway line thrusting south eventually proved more practical.

The beach is geared for holiday fun, with the miniature railway, inviting tidal pool and supertube adding to the natural attractions of

protected bathing and rock and surf angling. The town boasts several good hotels, holiday flats, sporting facilities and a caravan park as close as possible to the beach.

5 Clansthal

Heading north towards Clansthal, the R102 almost parallels the Aliwal Shoal about 4 km from

221

A MODEST HERO

The simple white memorial to Dick King in Isipingo.

'A man of action rather than of learning' is how Dick King's son described the man whose legendary ride from Durban to Grahamstown not only saved lives but affected the course of history in Natal.

King was eight years old when he came to South Africa with the 1820 Settlers, and his was destined to be an adventurous life. But the name the Zulu gave this trader and hunter was that of peacemaker or Mlamulankunzi — lyrically translated as 'the man who parts the fighting bulls'.

King was able to prove his mettle early on, racing a warning to save Voortrekker lives after Piet Retief's party was killed by Dingane, fighting in the savage Battle of Tugela a few weeks later, even surviving being mauled by a lion! (A photograph of the small dagger he used to stab the beast is preserved in the Durban Museum.)

The deed for which he is remembered, however, occurred in 1842, with a British garrison besieged by Voortrekkers in what is now Durban's Old Fort. It was 29-year-old King who crossed Natal Bay under cover of darkness on 25 May to fetch help from Grahamstown, 1 000 km away. King, who may have been accompanied for part of the journey by a retainer called Ndongeni, took ten days to cover the distance, with two of those days spent recovering from illness. All he would later say of this marathon trip, involving crossing nearly 200 rivers, was: 'I did no more than any Englishman would do. I said I would get the message through, and I did it, and that's all there is to say.' Reinforcements arrived in Durban from Port Elizabeth, and the siege ended 32 days after King had set out.

Rewarded with money and farm land at Isipingo, King now embarked on a more settled life, but his sense of adventure remained untamed. In 1868, three years before his death, floods in the area stranded a number of families on a hill. And the man who built and paddled a raft with provisions across the raging waters? Dick King.

the shore. This shoal is rich in marine life but rises treacherously close to the surface of the water. Almost a kilometre wide in places, it is a favourite dive for scuba enthusiasts and spearfishermen but disastrous to shipping, as several unfortunate vessels have discovered in the past century. The most recent victim was the *Amy Lykes*, which ran aground on the reef one balmy morning in 1970 while sailing to Durban. It was pulled off by two tugs, but only after having dumped almost all of its cargo.

The Green Point lighthouse, erected in 1905, beams out a powerful warning to passing ships, and can be seen on its hilltop perch on the inland side of the road at a point called Blamey's Bay. Just before the lighthouse is the entrance to Crocworld, a large, hillside park specialising in displays of Nile crocodiles. Other reptiles (including alligators and turtles) and birds are also on view, and rabbits can be fed by hand in the Bunny Park. A resource centre, short walking trails, and a Zulu kraal and curio shop ensure that visitors are kept entertained, while the timbered restaurant at the entrance commands a sweeping, not-to-be-missed view of the sea.

Clansthal, with its collection of private cottages and untamed beach, lies between the R102 and the sea, about 4 km south of Umkomaas. Named by a German farmer after one of his homeland towns, Clansthal is surrounded by so much coastal bush as to be almost obscured from the eyes of passing motorists. Access to the beach is on foot from one of several small parking spots. The sand shelves steeply into the sea, and with no shark nets for protection, beachgoers confine themselves to walking, shelling and sunning, although local surfers are constantly tempted by challenging waves. Clansthal has a caravan park and a railway halt (confusingly spelt Claustal).

6 Umkomaas

Originally known as South Barrow, Umkomaas — like Scottburgh — was envisaged by its early settlers as a potential harbour. But although a few small vessels managed to sail some distance upriver and take on sugar cargo, tricky currents and the typical Natal coast sand bar at the entrance to the lagoon eventually put paid to shipping possibilities.

With the building of the south coast railway line in 1897, the desultory settlement flared into life, but it was only in 1924 that it took on the name Umkomaas. Mkomazi is Zulu for 'the river of the cow whales' and, according to local folklore, the name stuck after Shaka spotted several whales at the mouth with their calves. The river flows from the foothills of the Drakensberg and its once crocodile-ridden waters are frequently used for gruelling canoe marathons. Saiccor, a large cellulose mill, is situated immediately inland of Umkomaas and it is effluent from this factory that occasionally discolours the lagoon and surf.

Umkomaas itself perches on the crest of a headland with delightful seaward views from above the railway line and the R102. Dotted with

Splash-down at Scottburgh's popular supertube: a whirl of fun for everyone.

trees and well-kept gardens, this attractive town is served by several hotels and restaurants. Many of the residents are retired, and much of the resort activity revolves around the Widenham caravan park. The beach is narrow and rocky with parking areas, a café and change-rooms. Swimming is restricted to a tidal pool just south of the lagoon, and anglers usually congregate along the water's edge for rock and surf sport. A highly rated golf course almost encircles the town, and the small Mpusheni Nature Reserve is located south of the river off the Saiccor road.

A swamp on the banks of the river has for some years been a source of controversy, and of great interest to aviation enthusiasts. It was here, in March 1944, that a Kittyhawk crashed and sank after a simulated dogfight with another of these now-rare fighter planes. Several efforts have been launched to locate and excavate the aircraft, buried with its pilot under at least 5 m of mud. If ever successful, the plane would be one of the last two known to exist in the world, and could take pride of place in the SA Air Force Museum.

Between Umkomaas and the holiday resort of Umgababa are two clusters of roadside curio and fruit stalls. After passing Ilfracombe Station and the Mnini Holiday Camp, the line of Iminwe stalls is situated on the left-hand side of the R102. A short distance north is the turn-off on the right-hand side to the larger, red-and-white roofed Umgababa Curio Centre. Both have similar wares and are extremely popular with visitors. Baskets and grass mats abound among the beadwork and

The Mkomazi River curves down to meet the surf-edged sea.

clay pots, with most items the handiwork of local Zulu. Seasonal fruits — such as bananas, pineapples, avocado pears, litchis and mangos — are also a drawcard.

7 Kingsburgh

Named in honour of Dick King, whose 1842 ride took him through this coastal turf, Kingsburgh is the umbrella name given to a municipality that incorporates several beach resorts. From Karridene to Doonside, one resort flows into the next, and it is easy to see why their 8 km of coast is packed with caravan parks, holiday camps and flats. The beaches link into a wide ribbon of soft, blonde sand, stabbed here and there with rocky pools and a couple of modest lagoons. Up till Warner Beach, the shops, cottages and commuter homes (Durban is a freeway sprint or quick train ride away) nestle among vegetation bristling with aloes and strelitzia, while north of this point, highrise blocks crowd against the dunes.

The first resort area is Karridene and Illovo Beach. Between the Msimbazi and Lovu rivers, the beach is open, little developed and a delight to beachcombers as well as four-wheel drivers. Access to the beach is generally on foot via a myriad bush paths across the railway line. These are not always signposted, but following your nose in the direction of the sea invariably gets you to your destination.

This is not a built-up resort area but caravanners' terrain, and a string of parks lies edge-to-edge along the beach. The Illovo Beach

SARDINE FEVER

Everyone takes to the water during the annual sardine run.

A winter highlight along Natal's south coast is a fishy phenomenon known as the sardine run, which has as fascinating an effect on human beings as it has impact on marine life!

Every year, huge shoals of pilchards set off from the cool Cape waters in search of warm spawning grounds. Moving with the north-flowing offshore current, the diminutive fish remain out of reach of the shore along the Cape coast. But somewhere around Natal's southern border, counter-currents sweep them landwards, and this is when the excitement starts, because there is always the chance that your spot of beach will be the one playing host to tons of fish driven onshore by permutations of wind, tide and predators. Sea birds provide one of the clues to finding the fish: wherever they are, wheeling, shrieking and diving into the waves, the sardines are sure to be. And so are the sharks and other large fish that prey on the pilchards, much to the delight of

countless game fishermen.

The sardines swim north in successive waves, swinging out to sea again in the vicinity of Durban. Their migration is an annual one, with the first sighting usually towards the end of June and continuing for about a month. The sardines can remain tantalisingly out of reach, but when they do hit the beaches, there is an immediate outbreak of sardine fever. Everyone who can, heads for the beach, and propriety is thrown to the winds as people scramble for a share of the spoils. In some years, fish have lain knee-deep on the sand in slithering, silver piles, to be scooped up in buckets, umbrellas, skirts, hats, even briefcases.

Just how many fish make it back to the Cape is uncertain. But with each female producing in the region of 100 000 eggs, it needs only two from each batch to survive in order to secure the sardine population, and the following year's run.

SAFEGUARDING THE SEAS

Taming the sea's finned fiends.

In the approximately 300-million years that the world's oceans have been prowled by sharks, these cartilaginous (rather than bony) fish have not changed much. Their bodies are as sleek and streamlined as ever (though their scaly skin feels like sandpaper), they have a keen sense of smell, good near vision, and jaws powered by strong muscles.

Above all they are famous for their teeth, often formed into serrated triangles sharper than any razor and unmistakeably part of the efficient killing equipment. The feared great white shark, for example, has five rows of teeth embedded in its jaws. Only the front rows are used, while the rear teeth are kept in reserve, moving forward like well-trained soldiers as the frontlines wear out or are lost. The older a shark, the larger and stronger its teeth, and a great white can go through an incredible 20 000 incisors in a lifetime.

It took a 'Black Christmas' in 1957 to convince authorities of the need for protective measures against sharks: that year five attacks — three of them fatal — occurred within the space of three weeks on Natal's south coast. In 1964, the Natal Anti-Shark Measures Board was established.

It was found that sharks do have a vulnerable spot. They have to keep moving to remain buoyant and for a constant flow of water over their gills. This is one of the reasons why the Natal Sharks Board nets, installed at intervals along the Natal coast, have proved effective. Nets almost 200 m long are laid in a double row beyond the surf line in about 12 m of water. If a shark heads towards the shore, it will blunder into the net; should the mesh entangle and immobilise it, drowning invariably follows.

Since 1964, Sharks Board field staff in powerboats have skimmed the nets daily, removing almost 13 000 sharks, which undoubtedly means that many human lives have been saved. Today attacks on bathers are fortunately infrequent.

as a railway siding called Middleton, but this was changed in 1910 to avoid confusion with a Cape settlement of the same name. A house called Lorna Doone stood on a hill overlooking the station, and its owner — an immigrant from Devon — suggested the derivation Doonside.

All the Kingsburgh resorts have link roads to the N2, but visitors who prefer a slower pace could reach them from the R102. It meanders beside the railway line, and through much of the borough it is identified as Kingsway.

8 Illovo sugar mill

Of all the sugar mills along the Natal coast, the only one almost consistently open to visitors is situated in Lower Illovo where the Lovu River flows through a scenic valley. To reach the mill, take the R78 which heads inland from the N2 at the turn-off to Winkelspruit. Surrounded once more by sugar plantations, take the turning to the left about a kilometre from the highway. As the road dips towards the river, the mill and its well-kept estates come into view.

Founded in 1850 by farmer William Pearce, the mill now produces 200 tons of sugar an hour. Once the mammoth transporters known as hilos offload their cargo of cane, it takes ten hours from the time the cane is crushed to its emerging as raw sugar crystals. The plant works around the clock, and its milling process takes place in a thundering crucible of noise, heat, fibre dust and the heady smells of a giant sweet shop! Nothing goes to waste. The bagasse (fibre) that is left as juice is squeezed from the cane is used to fuel the entire mill, and the fine mud that is thrown off as the juice clarifies is used on the fields as fertiliser.

The R78 is often used as a short cut from the south coast to Pietermaritzburg as it bypasses Durban and connects with the N3 at Camperdown. A single-lane tarred road, it passes through cane amd timber farming country, with the turn-off to Adams Mission lying about 8 km inland. Named after the American missionary, Dr Newton Adams, who founded it in the 1830s, the mission is a national monument and includes Adams' original church and his grave. The complex functions now as a Zulu training college.

9 Amanzimtoti

Situated only minutes on the N2 from Louis Botha Airport and Durban, Amanzimtoti is the largest holiday resort and also the largest commercial and business centre on the upper south coast. With its civic centre and library, central sporting complex, well-wooded residential areas, and numerous holiday flats and hotels, it caters for every need of both holiday-maker and resident.

An open sandy beach stretches for more than 7 km from the Manzimtoti Lagoon north to the borough's boundary with Umbogintwini. The main bathing area, protected by shark nets and manned by lifeguards, is located at Nyoni Rocks and offers ample parking, restaurants, picnic and braai sites, change-rooms, a mini waterworld (with supertube) and, set in the rocks, a filtered

Amanzimtoti's smooth gold sands trimmed by high-rise holiday accommodation.

turn-off from the R102 curves around a headland as Illovo Beach Avenue, which provides a scenic view over the Lovu Lagoon.

There is some doubt as to the origin of the name Winkelspruit, or Winklespruit as it is also spelt. One version holds that it is derived from the Afrikaans word for shop (*winkel*), referring to the impromptu store that was set up on the beach to sell groceries salvaged from the wreck of the *Tonga* in 1875. The beach stands out from the others in the Kingsburgh line-up. Reed windbreaks provide extra shelter on a narrow sunbathing lawn, and a prominent outcrop of rocks cradles two small

saltwater pools and an eye-catching lookout tower. A large shopping centre opposite the station supplements the usual village shops, and providing ample accommodation are several caravan parks tucked between the beach cottages.

A wide, almost level stretch of sandy beach is interrupted by the mouth of the Little Manzimtoti River. Here, with towering apartment blocks instead of sand dunes, Warner Beach lies on the south bank of the river with Doonside on the north. Beachgoers enjoy all the amenities from chair hire and lifeguards to lawns and even a soccer field on the Doonside bank. Doonside began life

The holiday hubbub dimmed, Amanzimtoti lies wrapped in tranquillity, with gay boats floating on the lagoon's still waters.

saltwater pool. A second bathing beach (known to locals as Pipeline) lies further north and is reached from Beach Road. Adding to the general appeal of sand and surf are boating facilities on the lagoon (including pedalboats for hire), the launch site and clubhouse of the local powerboat angling club (at Chain Rocks), and numerous rocky outcrops ideal for angling from the shore.

Two nature parks are situated on the inland side of the highway. The 4 ha Amanzimtoti Bird Sanctuary, close to the borough's border with Umbogintwini, attracts a number of wild ducks and geese as well as migrant birds. A small kiosk beside the dam serves tea to weekend visitors. The Ilanda Wilds Nature Reserve, with its picnic areas, marked trails among indigenous trees and abundant bird life, has retained the charm of an undisturbed natural river valley and is reached from Riverside Road.

To get the best out of Amanzimtoti, which means 'sweet waters' in Zulu, inquire about all its facilities at the active Visitors' Bureau, located close to the main beach.

10 Isipingo
Once farmed by some of Port Natal's earliest settlers, including Dick King, Isipingo is a residential township sliced in half by the N2 and colonised by the industrial monoliths of Prospecton. Yet it incorporates one of the more striking beachscapes near Durban.

With the main bathing area lying further south, the lagoon of the Sipingo River (named by the Zulu after a twining shrub that grew on its banks) meets the beach between two defined headlands, the northern promontory being the 'tail end' of Durban's Bluff. The somewhat sluggish river is home to a tangle of mangroves, and once surrounded an island. Except for some massive rocks where the mouth would be (should the river break through), the sands are flat and wide, and attract fishermen and strollers.

From the N2 turn-off before Louis Botha Airport, head south along Prospecton Road, left into The Avenue East, and left alongside the river on Beach Road, which ends in a small parking and refreshment area.

The crest of the southern headland overlooking the lagoon offers a superb view. From Delta Road, turn left into Third Avenue, then left again into Ocean Terrace and follow a narrow concrete road

THE CRAFT OF KEEPING TRADITION ALIVE

A riot of colourful beadwork at Umgababa.

The Zulu handicraft centres so popular with visitors to Natal are more than just commercial ventures: they turn back the pages of history by displaying skills handed down from one generation to another.

Simple pottery can be traced far back in Zulu culture, and although they had no potter's wheel, early craftsmen were able to coil almost perfectly symmetrical pots for everyday needs. These were fired in hollowed-out earth packed with wood and dried cow dung, then refired with grass so that the smoke would blacken the pots. Their sought-after ebony gloss would be obtained by rubbing them first with fat, then pebbles and finally gooseberry leaves.

The large, barrel-shaped baskets (*isilulu*) popular in modern homes as linen baskets or even plant holders, started life as grain storers. Woven from soft imbubu grass, they were often so big that they had to be carried to the fields on sledges. The flatter, bowl-shaped baskets (*iqoma*) were also used for grain. As these were carried on the head, however, their size was dictated by the weight that could comfortably be borne, and the width of an average pair of shoulders.

The bottle-shaped *isichumo* basket used so close-knit a grass-stitching technique that it could hold liquids. It usually had a snug lid fitting over the neck of the basket like a cap. Ilala palm leaflets were favoured in the making of these containers, as instead of rotting when damp, they would swell and make the basket watertight. The popular flat shoulder bag (*isikhwama*) is also woven from ilala palm leaflets, with dyed strips sometimes added for colourful decoration and a woven lid fitted.

Although once customary for men to make the baskets, as well as work in wood and horn, while the women took on beadwork, pottery and hut thatching, today it is almost all left to the womenfolk. Though many of the items for sale retain their pure, traditional form, some are beginning to show signs of Western taste and influence, and purely ornamental rather than practical pieces are now appearing.

Angling
Almost without exception, every resort along this coast rates a mention as a good angling spot, with the area's biggest claim to fame being the annual sardine run. As the sardines move inshore, they are tailed by snoek, kingfish, bonito and many more big fish. But at other times of year, there are also catches of shad (elf), kob (kabeljou), garrick (leervis) and bronze bream to keep the angler happy.

Beachcombing and shelling
Here, as anywhere else, the more people on a beach, the less likely you are to find shells. So head for the quieter, least developed spots such as Scottburgh's Back Beach, with its unspoilt rock pools; the sands on either side of Rocky Bay at Park Rynie; and the wilder shore between Clansthal and Widenham.

Birdwatching
The coastal evergreen forest and grasslands of the Vernon Crookes Nature Reserve are home to a good variety of birds. Species to look out for include the Knysna and purplecrested louries, the narina trogon and the grey cuckooshrike among the forested hillsides; birds of prey on the grasslands; and the cardinal woodpecker in patches of thornbush. Amanzimtoti has two good spots: Ilanda Wilds Reserve, with more than 300 identified bird species within the profusion of coastal forest, and the Umdoni Road sanctuary.

BELOW *Awesome jaws at Crocworld.*

up to a cul-de-sac with a panoramic outlook along the coast.

On the inland side of the N2, now designated Isipingo Rail, an echo of Dick King's house remains, now added to and altered as part of a community health clinic. Standing in grounds filled with trees planted by the celebrated King, the clinic is located at the rear of municipal offices in Old Main Road, with access during working hours. The house was built on the farm that was King's reward after his lifesaving ride to Grahamstown. A whitewashed memorial in a secluded cemetery some distance south marks his burial place. There is also a stone monument here to the lone woman and 21 children who died during the Anglo-Boer War in the Isipingo Concentration Camp. (Access is via the Old Main Road into Saunders Road, left and then right up a track signposted Cemetery Delhoo Road.)

LEFT *A showy cascade of bright bougainvillea so often associated with Natal.*

THINGS TO DO

Fish type	Season	Best area	Best bait
Bronze bream	Mar—Aug	Park Rynie, Clansthal, Warner Beach, Isipingo	Redbait, mussels, fishbait, chokka
Garrick (leervis)	May—Nov	Winkelspruit, Nyoni Rocks	Live bait
Kingfish	Nov—May	Kelso, Park Rynie, Scottburgh, Clansthal	Whole sardines, shad (elf), artificial lures
Kob (kabeljou)	All year	Karridene, Umkomaas	Sardines, squid, chokka
Shad (elf)	Dec—Aug	Kelso, Park Rynie, Umkomaas, Karridene, Warner Beach, Amanzimtoti	Chokka, fishbait, artificial lures and spoons

Boardsailing

The waves off Warner Beach attract boardsailors accustomed to open sea conditions, as does the Scottburgh surf. The Amanzimtoti beaches are considered tough, so only the seasoned launch from there. For inland boardsailors, there is the uMzinto Dam about 11 km from Scottburgh.

Boat trips

Small pleasure craft can be hired on the banks of the Manzimtoti Lagoon for a self-guided drift around the river mouth or as far upstream as possible.

Bowls

Clubs that welcome visitors include the Alexandra Memorial Country Club in uMzinto, Scottburgh and Umkomaas bowling clubs, and Hutchison Park, the AECI Country Club and Rockview Road in Amanzimtoti. Contact the relevant local municipality or publicity association for further details.

Camping and caravannning

Many of the resorts along this coast are crammed with privately run caravan and camping facilities, all within easy reach of the beach or, as with the municipal grounds at Scottburgh, within fishing distance of the surf. Contact the relevant municipality or publicity association for details.

Canoeing

White-water enthusiasts tackle the upper reaches of the Mkomazi River, but only if equipped with sturdy canoes and safety gear. Contact The Rivermen in Durban for details of organised outings. The calmer waters of the uMzinto Dam are better suited to pleasure paddlers.

Diving

The Landers Shoal off Park Rynie attracts skin divers and spearfishermen, but the diving honeypot of the south coast is the Aliwal Shoal. Because of its distance from the shore, a boat is essential. Dives and charters can be arranged through the Underwater World agency in Scottburgh or the Trident Dive Shop in Durban.

Drives and viewsites

The old south coast road (R102) is a scenic drive in itself, especially when it detours through the Kingsburgh hamlets (where it is identified for much of its passage as Kingsway). Good viewsites include the headlands at Amanzimtoti and Isipingo. The drive inland to Ixopo provides a pleasant contrast to the familiar sea vistas.

Golf

The are several fine 18-hole courses along this part of the coast (some with distracting sea views), including at Scottburgh and Umkomaas. Visitors are also welcome at the Amanzimtoti Country Club and the nearby AECI Club (Umbogintwini).

Horseriding

Rides can be organised by the Illovo Riding School any day of the week.

Libraries

The municipal library at Scottburgh (situated in the main street) welcomes temporary members, as does the Amanzimtoti library in the civic centre.

Museums

RICHMOND, BYRNE AND DISTRICT MUSEUM, cnr Chilley and Victoria Streets, Richmond: Focuses on the lives of the early settlers in the nearby Byrne Valley, and on sporting achievements.

Powerboating

Where there is good deep-sea fishing, there will be powerboat clubs and launching sites, but not all of them may be used by visitors. Scottburgh is one of the exceptions, provided boat-owners hold a skipper's ticket and submit to club inspections for a weekly fee of R10. Contact the local publicity association. Amanzimtoti Skiboat Club also accommodates visitors as long as their boats conform to Natal safety regulations and skippers are ticketed and familiar with handling surf conditions. The launch site is at Chain Rocks, just south of the lagoon.

Shipwrecks

No wrecks are visible along this section of coast, but it has had its fair share of casualties. The Aliwal Shoal in particular is a danger spot: the British steamship *Nebo* was one of the first recorded tragedies, sinking on its maiden voyage to Durban in 1884. In an ironic twist five years later, the crew of the Italian barque *Fidia Genoa* mistook the newly erected shoal beacons for Durban markers, and ran aground just north of Umkomaas.

The mouth of the Mkomazi itself claimed some victims during attempts to establish it as a small port. The *Natalie* sank there with a cargo of sugar in 1861, but was later refloated and repaired in Durban. The *Anthony Musgrave*, a steam lighter trading up and down the coast, was less fortunate. In 1873 it hit the rocks and was beached at the lagoon where it remained until being sold for £120.

Surfing

Scottburgh is the main surfing spot, with well-shaped waves that are particularly good in an easterly wind. Because the beach is so popular with bathers, however, you need to aim for early mornings, especially when an offshore breeze is blowing. Also popular are Rocky Bay at Park Rynie; Green Point with its almost perfect westerly swell (not for beginners); Widenham or High Rocks (just south of Umkomaas) with a good west swell; and the shark-netted waters of Warner Beach, Winkelspruit and Amanzimtoti.

Swimming

All the bigger resorts nave bathing beaches with shark nets and lifesavers on duty. Park Rynie has a shark-netted beach but the prettier spot, Rocky Bay, is unprotected. Scottburgh has an exceptionally inviting beach, complete with sweeping sunbathing lawns and tidal pool. Shark nets also bob behind the surf line at Umgababa, all the Kingsburgh beaches, Amanzimtoti and Isipingo, and there are tidal pools at Park Rynie, Pennington, Winkelspruit, Warner Beach, Amanzimtoti and Isipingo. Umkomaas has a saltwater pool.

Tennis and squash

For holiday tennis, visitors can play at uMzinto and Umkomaas (contact the local municipality), at the Scottburgh Country Club, and at the Country Club, Hutchison Park and AECI Club in Amanzimtoti. Squash courts are available at the last three venues.

Walks

Three well-marked trails (two of them requiring some effort) have been laid out in the river valley setting of the 14 ha Ilanda Wilds Nature Reserve on the Manzimtoti River. Guided walks can be organised through the Vernon Crookes Nature Reserve near uMzinto, and Crocworld has 3 km of very comfortable walks through its landscaped grounds. Nearly all the resorts have stretches of inviting sandy beaches for casual strolls.

INFORMATION
• Natal Parks Board, Elton Place, Congella, Durban 4001. Tel 031=251271.
• National Sea Rescue Institute, 28 Trust Building, Durban 4001. Tel 031=3040602; emergencies: 031=372011
• Scottburgh Publicity Association, PO Box 91, Scottburgh 4180. Tel 03231=22065.
• SA Tourism Board, 320 West St, Durban 4001. Tel 031=3047144
• Visitors' Bureau, 95 Beach Road, Amanzimtoti 4125. Tel 031=9032121
Nearest AA Office
• AA House, 537 Smith St, Durban 4001. Tel 031=3010341
• 35a Wooley Street, Port Shepstone 4240. Tel 0391=22503

A holiday haven under subtropical skies

THOSE EARLY SEAFARERS and settlers who encountered the charms of Natal Bay knew a good thing when they saw it. Now, only a few centuries later, a large and complex city sprawls north, west and south of that shallow, landlocked bay. For all its commercial success and sophistication as the country's premier holiday resort and a major African port, Durban retains a certain magic, a constant sense of its elemental nature. The city, textured with glass-walled skyscrapers alongside stately colonial façades and flinting minarets, rises from an earth luxurious with trees and flowers. The waters of the bay, bristling with activity during the day, soften in the long evening shadows. The warm, sandy beaches that draw the million-plus annual visitors to the sunshine city, are smoothed each night by the surging Indian Ocean. The rugged spirit of Africa is no more than a breath away.

1 The Bluff

A wooded promontory that is as much a geological landmark for Durban as it is for the Natal coast, the Bluff protects the harbour against prevailing south-easters, and boasts some pleasant beaches on its Indian Ocean flank. This residential area, with its northern end taken up by military installations, comprises two parallel, sandy ridges about 100 m in altitude and some 4 km in length. Cradled between these is a 45 ha nature reserve, featuring a freshwater vlei and birdwatching hide surrounded by reeds and the remains of coastal plain forest.

The Bluff was once the home of Lieutenant James Saunders King, a pioneering settler at Port Natal, and it remains his resting place. A humble and somewhat neglected stone bench in Lt King Crescent (off Bluff Road) commemorates his death in 1828, and the breezy site offers a panoramic view of the bay and city. No formal viewsite remains on the Bluff, but a drive northwards along Lighthouse Road (which forks off Bluff Road) shows a cityscape seldom featured

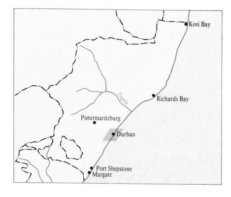

on postcards, and once the road becomes Marine Drive and heads south, the sea views on a clear day are breathtaking.

Towards the southern end of the Bluff is Treasure Beach, considered by botanists to be, literally, a treasure. Forming part of the unique 250 ha Treasure Beach Project, the area has a total of nine different habitat types with some of the finest examples of rock pool life in the country and

Sunrise over silvered seas.

dune vegetation believed to be the last piece of coastal climax grassland on the continent. The Environmental Education Centre in Marine Drive takes study groups through the area and offers plenty of information to the casual visitor.

To reach the Bluff's protected bathing beaches and popular rock angling spots, turn off Marine Drive into Anstey Road, then the Foreshore. The shore is narrow, with the Bluff sloping clifflike above it, so parking with immediate access to the beach can be a problem at peak times. Southernmost is Brighton Beach with paddling ponds, a tidal pool and nearby picnic area. Low tide reveals splendid rock pools. Next you reach a favourite spot for surfers: Cave Rock provides challenging rides for experienced surfers, thanks to an offshore reef that keeps the waves constant and strong. Anstey's Beach, with a private caravan park across the road, has a lawned paddling pool terrace, with surf swimming safest on weekends and holidays when lifeguards are on duty. Further north is Garvies Beach, reached by car via Sloane Road (from Marine Drive) but with vehicular access very limited and almost no parking. The beach is not geared for swimming but has some rich rock pools, and is favoured by divers during the garrick (leervis) season. Recommended access to Garvies Beach is on foot with a comfortable walk from Anstey's Beach.

2 Kenneth Stainbank Nature Reserve

Named after the man who gave this 214 ha tract of land and river to the province, the reserve (south of the city in Yellowwood Park) is an excellent example of coastal forest, well-populated with wildlife such as bushbuck, duiker, zebra and giraffe, and over 150 bird species. Members of the Stainbank family still live in a secluded part of the estate, but the rest is open to the public with several well laid-out trails and picnic spots that provide as authentic a bush experience as possible within a 15 km drive of the city centre. Also situated in the

LEFT *Swimmers splash in the surf at Durban's popular South Beach.*

The Bluff guards the entrance to Durban Harbour.

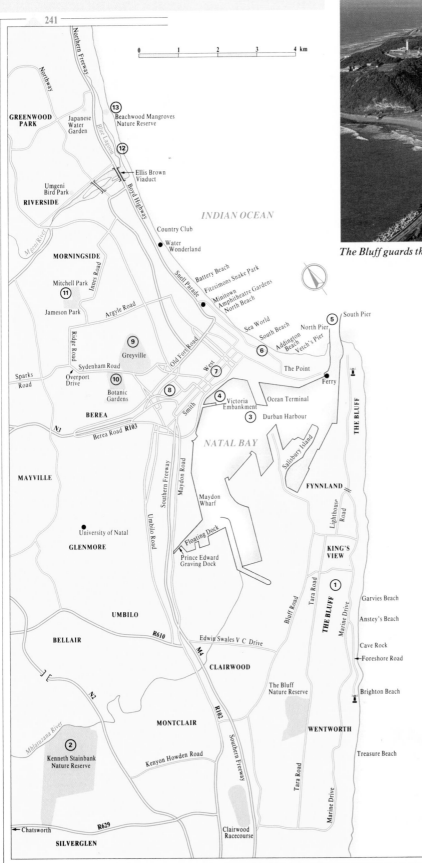

reserve are the headquarters of the Wilderness Leadership School, which uses the outdoors as a training ground.

3 Durban Harbour

For all the glamour and attention-grabbing appeal of Durban's beaches, the city's real pulse lies elsewhere … in the harbour, the very reason for Durban's existence. All early mention in recorded history of what is now Durban is due to its maritime location. Portuguese explorer Vasco da Gama, who named Natal in 1497, is said to have fished at the mouth of the bay. Some vessels even risked this dangerously shallow and narrow mouth to shelter in the lee of the Bluff, which was how the sloop *Julia*, with a reconnaissance party aboard under Lieutenants Francis George Farewell and James King, came to anchor in the bay in November 1823. What they saw impressed them: the landlocked harbour, conveniently close to Shaka's powerful Zulu nation, provided a natural trading base. So it was that in May 1824, the first formal group of white traders and hunters arrived to hack their way through the bay's bush-covered shore, and put down the roots of what is now a thriving harbour city.

Natal Bay's growth from a calm lagoon fed by two small rivers to the site of one of the ten largest harbours in the world was not all plain sailing. The harbour mouth in particular remained obstinately shallow from frequent siltings, and only at the turn of the century was the problem solved. The entrance's low-water depth of 2 m, recorded mid-19th century, is now an effective 12,8 m. Dredging and sandpumping still continue, and the harbour scrutinised by today's visitor has a water surface almost twenty times larger than that used by sailors 150 years ago.

Dockland access is sometimes awkward for security reasons, but the western edge of the harbour — Maydon Wharf with its grain elevator and sugar terminals — is usually easy to explore by car or on foot, provided you keep an eye out for trains and cranes. At the city end of Maydon Wharf, the fishing wharf bustles with boatbuilding and the comings and goings of deep-sea fishing cruisers. At the southern end is one of the largest dry docks in the southern hemisphere, the Prince Edward Graving Dock; this is worth a look, especially with a vessel or two lodged high and dry for repairs. Further along the quayside towards the Bluff is the Floating Dock, which also handles large ship repairs. Salisbury Island, once covered in mangrove swamps but now barely distinguishable from the rest of the harbour, serves as a busy container depot and naval base.

The northern edge of the harbour has its own attractions: Ocean Terminal, where luxury liners still occasionally berth, and the Small Craft Harbour. A no-frills harbour ferry operates from here, serving workers and fishermen, and a round-the-bay ticket is relatively cheap. Next to the ferry terminal is a well-preserved classic steam tug, the *JR More*, which serves as a museum. This sturdy craft was the last of its line to be built and is the only remaining example in the world of the powerful twin-screw model. On shore beside it, and also retired, is the 1927 pilot boat *Ulundi*.

4 Victoria Embankment

Outside the harbour but hugging the bay's northern shore is Victoria Embankment, or the Esplanade, a pleasant waterside stroll with gardens and shaded seats.

The Embankment has some historically interesting buildings, including the Old Supreme Court Building with its colonial courtyard design and neoclassical architectural details, and the exclusive Durban Club, built at the turn of this century. Other historical features include an equestrian statue in honour of Dick King's epic ride (1842) to Grahamstown to fetch help for the besieged British garrison in Durban; a humble

bronze statue acknowledging the courage of 15-year-old John Ross in walking more than 700 km north to Delagoa Bay to fetch medicines for the Port Natal settlers (1826); and the ornate Vasco da Gama clock, a gift from the Portuguese government in 1897 to commemorate his voyage.

Storing heaps of sweetness.

MOUNTAINS OF SWEET GOLD

Natal's 'green gold' — sugar — finds its way into a lot of cups and dishes around the world, and a vital link in the chain that stretches from grassy hillside to teaspoon is the Bulk Sugar Export Terminal at the western edge of Natal Bay.

Lying at the junction of Maydon Wharf and Victoria Embankment, three huge rib-backed silos stand 28 m high and almost 300 m long. Their outwardly bland, grey exterior is deceptive, for they comprise a sophisticated storage centre for much of the 24-million tons of sugar cut and refined in Natal

each year. Built with award-winning design and engineering techniques, the terminal's structure has been so effective that it has been copied by Brazil and Mauritius, two other major sugar exporters.

Since the first silo opened in 1965, approximately 20 000 people a year have visited the SA Sugar Association Terminal — and marvelled. For nothing quite prepares you for the sight of sugar in storage. Piled up to the roof are shadowy mountains of sweetness on a floor big enough to host two rugby games. Voices from the viewing gallery, which runs high up against the side of the silo, send avalanches down the slopes, and you are advised not to contemplate a playful leap onto the dunes below.

At full capacity, the whalelike trio can hold 520 000 tons of raw sugar on their 4,8 ha of combined floorspace. Once stored, the priority is to load the sugar onto ships as fast as possible. With a complex system of gravity-fed hoppers, weighing machines and 10,5 km of conveyor belts, the terminal can do just that, loading a ship at the rate of 1 000 tons per hour, whereas in pre-terminal days, it took fifty people three to four weeks. The operation is systematic to the end; it must be finished ninety minutes before high tide because tugs are standing by for the ship to sail on the tide.

Free tours of the terminal are conducted several times a week. Contact the harbour authorities for further details.

5 North Pier

Built off the Point in 1851 in an effort to improve the harbour entrance, North Pier is now a favourite fishing spot with a grandstand view of Durban's beachfront and the shoreline as far as Umhlanga Rocks. The concrete pier is surrounded by activity, with ships and yachts almost within touching distance on its south side, and powerboats and sailboards to the north.

A stone tablet on the pier, presented by the men and officers of the Royal Navy, commemorates the 'Lady in White', Perla Siedle Gibson. Standing at the dockside, Perla sang to hospital and troop ships through the war years from April 1940. Dressed in her white canteen uniform with red scarf and hat, her presence became an essential part of naval arrivals and departures in Durban, and she continued to sing to navy men until 1968.

6 The 'golden mile' and beachfront

The city's famous 'golden mile', with its phalanx of hotels overlooking sandy beaches, now stretches for nearly 4 km, built up with playgrounds and boulevards, parklike parking lots and entertainments. Over a million visitors revel in its pleasures each year, and the waves always beckon, even when winter in the subtropics drops to a bracing 16°C.

To explore the length of the beachfront, it is best to set off on foot from its southernmost point at

LEFT *Durban's golden beachfront curves away into the distance.*

A CENTURY OF SEASIDE FUN

Durban, even in the last century, was a holiday-maker's delight. As the writer of an early tourist pamphlet put it: 'Seen under a summer sky from the deck of a ship in the outer anchorage, Durban looks like a magnificent opal set in a pearly cloud of white, its lines of gold and green, purple and blue, changing every moment with the fleeting shadows of her glorious Bay and Bluff.'

Sheer beauty was not the only attraction. Durban was regarded as a healthy resort (the Medical Officer of Health reported that the death rate was 'probably the lowest in the world; the monthly rate frequently showing as low as 5,7 per thousand'). Bathing, ever popular on this coast, had its attendant health benefits, and gentlemen and ladies would take to the water — from decorously separate bathing tents.

There was always something to do, some entertainment to enjoy. From town, families could make their way by horse-drawn tram to the Botanic Gardens, fragrant with flowers, or take the omnibus to St Thomas Road, high up among the Berea homes with their croquet lawns. They could promenade along the handsome Victoria Embankment, or explore the sandy spit known as the Point — a throbbing pulse of Durban and site of the country's first railway, inaugurated amid great fanfare in 1860. The more energetic could go boating or fishing on the bay or Salisbury Island or take a turn on the roller-skating rink (although they could not hope to rival

Fun for all on South Beach at the turn of the century.

the heart-stopping performances of acrobatic skating by a certain Professor and Madame Wyman).

Come evening and the smartly uniformed Durban Borough Police would parade proudly down West Street, while music poured from the city bandstand. There was splendid entertainment to be had at the elegant Theatre Royal. Or, in a lighter vein, there was

a visit to the flea circus — although on one memorable occasion an escaped artiste was searched for (without success) in the chemise and camisole of a protesting lady spectator!

A century ago, Durban was the place to taste all the fun of a seaside resort. Today, although it might look different, nothing has really changed.

North Pier. Here, you will find seacraft and learner divers making the most of the sheltered waters off Vetch's Pier, which provides excellent protection to the inshore waters. Several watersport club-houses are located on the shore, which is not as developed as the rest of Durban's beaches, and is favoured by locals for just that reason. The beach is sandy and slopes gently to the water, making it an ideal base for the local control centre for the National Sea Rescue Institute. Monitoring the coast between Amanzimtoti in the south and Ballito in the north, the volunteer NSRI team works mainly with a powerful inshore rescue boat, and is drilled to launch the craft in six minutes.

Protected swimming starts with Addington Beach, a wide, sandy beach with sunbathing lawns and public facilities. In general there is little demarcation between beaches, so the only souls likely to know that the patch of beach following Addington is called Pumphouse would be the regular surfers and paddleskiers — because that bit is reserved for surfcraft.

Next comes South Beach, arguably the busiest beach in Africa and so popular that at peak times there is barely room to wield a bottle of tanning oil. South Beach offers a wide, level expanse of sunbathing sand punctuated by lifeguard towers and beacons, and backing onto a fairly built-up refreshment, toilet and shopping complex. Paddling pools and an adventure playpark are at

LEFT *The high-rise buildings of the city centre dwarf ranks of yachts.*

A FISH OUT OF WATER

An exception to the saying 'like a fish out of water' is the mudhopper (*Periopthalmus koelreuteri*), a creature equally at home on land as at sea. Its appearance would hardly excite interest — in fact, it is rather drab, with a stumpy head and bulbous eyes — yet this little fish has evolved a quite fascinating way of life.

It is found most often in the mangrove swamps of Natal's coast (in Durban, the Beachwood Mangroves Nature Reserve is the ideal habitat), where it moves freely from water to mud to the roots of the mangroves. To do this it must have a respiratory system capable of adjusting to two quite different environments. In the water it breathes through gills like any other fish, but when moving onto land, it gulps in a mouthful of oxygenated water, which is stored in the gill chamber. In addition, it 'breathes' through its skin by a network of superficial blood vessels which absorb oxygen directly from the air.

In water the mudhopper swims rather clumsily, but on the surface of the water it comes into its own. With its eyes projecting above the water, it flicks its tail to launch into a short 'flight' (a mere fraction of a second) and repeats the process immediately on 'landing', so that it seems to skip rapidly over the surface of the water. All the while the pectoral fins are extended sideways to stabilise it in 'flight'.

On land, or on a mangrove branch, it uses its pectoral fins as a type of crutch, extending them first, then swinging the weight of its body over. This slow crawl is not much use when pursuing a scuttling crab for supper, so the mudhopper then thrusts its tail against the mud and straightens its body — a lightning series of movements again rather like skipping. When, by contrast, it needs to steady itself on land, it uses its fused pelvic fins, which form a type of sucker, to cling to rocks and twigs.

street level, and add to South Beach's general appeal. At low tide the wreck of the *Ovington Court*, which ran aground in 1910, can be seen some 250 m off shore. An eye-catching landmark on South Beach is the Little Top, the stage area for open-air entertainments held each holiday season. It started life as a canvas tent — hence the name — but now resembles a brightly painted golfball.

At the junction of West Street and the beach is the dolphinarium and aquarium complex, providing entertainment and spectacle with an underlying educational and conservational intent. The dolphinarium stages several shows a day, all year round, featuring trained bottlenosed and dusky dolphins, jackass penguins and Cape fur seals. Feeding time at the aquarium, with sand-sharks, rays and turtles handfed by a diver, is always popular. The beach end of West Street is closed to traffic and is an attractive pedestrian mall with outdoor cafés, benches and flowerboxes.

North of West Street are more paddling pools, complete with fountains, stepping stones and bridges, and an aerial cableway and amusement rides alongside. The saltwater Rachel Finlayson Baths provide an opportunity for sheltered swimming and sunbathing.

North Beach with its promenading pier, and the Bay of Plenty are popular swimming beaches, and the shad season can find over 300 fishermen trying not to tangle their lines from the Bay of Plenty Pier. This section of the shore remains level and sandy, thanks to ongoing municipal sandpumping programmes, but bathers need to heed the safe swimming beacons: the topography underwater can change with little notice, adding to the effect of side- and backwashes. Parking, refreshment and toilet facilities stretch between Lower and Upper Marine Parade.

There are sunbathing lawns on the hotel side of

BELOW *Seine net fishermen are etched against a dramatic morning sky.*

Lower Marine Parade, and the landscaped Amphitheatre Gardens with their fountains and benches provide soothing respite from sun and sand. Zulu handicrafts are on sale from a shady pagoda nearby, and the ricksha-pullers start their rides in this vicinity. A beachfront ricksha ride has become symbolic of the tourist experience of Durban, but the ornately garbed men who pull their equally vivid carriages are a far cry from Natal's first rickshas. Imported from Japan by sugar baron Sir Marshall Campbell in 1893, the rickshas (originally known as jinrikishas) became so popular as to be Durban's main form of transport for a time. Local carriage-makers improved their design, swopping wooden wheels for steel, and in 1904, 2 000 Zulu were licensed as

Surf surges onto Durban's 'golden mile' with its backdrop of hotels and holiday flats — an ever-changing skyline to meet growing tourist demand.

pullers. Today, however, only a handful still offer the visitor a leisurely, two-wheeled jaunt.

Still heading north you pass Fitzsimons Snake Park, opened in 1939 as a base for snake serum production and today offering all the thrills and chills of staring a rinkhals in the eye or a Nile crocodile in the mouth without the danger. Oldest residents are Charles and Di, a romancing pair of crocodiles who were born in captivity, and most asked-about snakes are the mambas, of which several varieties are on show. Displays of indigenous and exotic snakes change frequently, as do the lizards and tortoises, and cage conditions attempt to create the natural environment.

Next you reach Battery Beach Number 1, whose

name recalls a gun battery built across the road by the British in anticipation of Russia threatening Indian Ocean ports. This beach has braai areas and sunbathing lawns. Reasonably safe bathing is possible between here and just south of Blue Lagoon at a string of less well-known beaches. These appear as a continuous ribbon of sand, with a slight incline to the ocean, and with nothing other than roadside change-rooms and refreshment kiosks to designate another official beach. Opposite one of these beaches, Country Club, is Water Wonderland, a spaghetti junction of landscaped waterslides. Highlights are the rampaging rapids and ski jumps, with the onus on fun-seekers to use the slides responsibly.

7 Historic city centre

Within a stone's throw of where Farewell and his men built their first wattle-and-daub camp in 1824, several blocks of buildings and attractive pedestrian malls demarcate what is known as the city's historic centre.

The City Hall, now a national monument, was opened in 1910 and its architecture closely resembles that of its counterpart in Belfast, Northern Ireland. Forming part of the complex is the oldest municipal museum in the country, as well as the Durban Art Gallery. Lunch-hour entertainment is often staged on the front steps overlooking Francis Farewell Square, which was used as a market square until late last century and

The sleek and graceful lines of Durban's countless pleasure craft at rest are reflected in a shimmering yacht basin.

is now busy with historic statues and war memorials. The Local History Museum backs onto the City Hall, and is well worth a visit for its visual records of life in early Durban.

At right angles to the City Hall (and facing West Street) is another national monument, the Post Office. Originally built and used as the city hall from 1885, the building hosted the National Convention of 1908 when the four colonies met to discuss unification. A wall plaque on its eastern steps commemorates a public speech given there in 1899 by a war correspondent ... the young Winston Churchill, newly escaped from the hands of the Boers.

Parts of the old Durban Station, opened in 1898, still remain (off Pine Street and Commercial Road). The main building, in decorative, red brick Victorian style, is due to become a plush hotel. A huge locomotive shed now serves as a stylish shopping centre, the Workshop, and further east (across NMR Avenue) a second clutch of buildings has been modernised into the Durban Exhibition Centre. 'The Coast of Dreams', which tells the story of Durban's past and present with dazzling audiovisuals and special effects, is screened in one of the DEC halls, and provides a good introduction to the city.

A little further afield (at the corner of Old Fort Road and NMR Avenue), informal gardens surround the remains of a British fort that was the scene of a ten-day siege in 1842. Trapped there by the Voortrekkers after the Battle of Congella, Captain Thomas Charlton Smith and his men were saved as a result of Dick King's rescue ride to Grahamstown. The gardens hold some interesting military artefacts, with the original barracks converted for use by war pensioners. The

ammunition magazine — now the chapel of St Peter in Chains — is much used for weddings.

A war museum with weaponry and memorabilia from local and foreign battles is housed in Warrior's Gate. Built like a Norman gatehouse, the Gate is also the headquarters of the Memorable Order of Tin Hats (Moths), a worldwide association of former soldiers that was founded in Durban after the First World War.

8 East meets West

Parts of Durban have a notably oriental flavour, like the lively Grey Street trading area. Two narrow

shopping arcades (between Grey Street and Cathedral Road), Madressa and Ajmeri, overflow with vitality and smallgoods traders, and convey a pungent sense of East meeting West. Also fun is the Indian Market (Warwick Avenue), a rather nondescript building from the street. As well as accommodating meat, fish and fresh produce, the market houses a myriad small stalls dealing in everything from exotic herbs and spices to jewellery, ornaments, clothing and handicrafts.

Adding dignity and character to the area is the Jumma Mosque (Grey Street), one of the largest in the southern hemisphere. Visitors enter the

A sense of architectural tranquillity is captured in the Temple of Understanding.

ablution rooms and prayer halls barefoot (women should not wear revealing garments), while a Muslim guide expounds on the teachings of Allah and his prophet, Muhammad.

Many of the members of the local Indian community are of the Hindu faith, and a variety of temples — each dedicated to a different god from among the wondrous pantheon of Hindu deities — can be found in and around Durban, colouring the urban landscape with their decorative architecture. Two complexes within easy city access are the Umgeni Road Temples, set in large, peacock-studded grounds, and the Durban Hindu Temple (Somtseu Road), which dates back to 1901.

9 Greyville

Greyville, venue for one of the country's premier horseraces, the annual July Handicap, was known as the Western Vlei and held its first meeting in July 1844. Tough farm steeds pounded along a makeshift track cut through coastal bush, and spectators ploughed through swampy, tick-infested terrain on wagons and ox-carts to watch the day's four races. Over the next half century the presence of British settlers and soldiers stimulated local horseracing, until on 17 July 1897, as part of the colony's celebration of Queen Victoria's diamond jubilee, the meeting that turned out to be the birth of the Durban July was held. Since then a mystique has grown around the race, added to by its reputation in recent years as a hothouse for spectacular race-day fashions!

With the landscaped, emerald links of the Royal Durban Golf Club in its centre, Greyville acts as the green heart of the city.

10 Durban Botanic Gardens

Virtually adjoining Greyville is another patch of green: the Durban Botanic Gardens. This, the

A CITY IN MINIATURE

The enchantment of a scaled-down city.

Gulliver, after his travels through Lilliput, would have felt at home — and much safer — in Minitown, South Africa's only city in miniature. Occupying less than a hectare of choice beachfront land, this is a charmingly landscaped fantasy park where knee-high Boeings taxi out for takeoff and civic buildings stop at a respectful shoulder level.

Opened in 1969, Minitown was inspired by the Dutch mini-scaled complex, Madurodam, and was researched and launched by local service organisations. (All proceeds from the complex are donated to charity.)

Built to a scale of 1/25th of full size, Minitown is not a replica of Durban, although many of its sponsored buildings and features are copied from city landmarks, like the City Hall and several hotels, banks and shopping centres. Other cities, like Cape Town and Johannesburg, have also provided 'model'

buildings for Minitown, so the out-of-town visitor might be surprised to find a little bit of home here.

A stroll around Minitown could take forever if you get hooked on the fun at the fair, the toings and froings at the airport, and the slick manoeuvres of a good half dozen trains. Even at a distance Minitown can be bewitching: the harbour, with lights glinting off its 218 000 ℓ of fresh water, has been known to disorient many a late-night reveller gazing mistily down from the heights of a beachfront hotel!

Every component is made in Minitown's own workshops by amateur enthusiasts, and theirs is a tall order, for the playground models have to withstand the elements as any real city would. Over a hundred features, including a game park and highway, currently make up Minitown, but there is space for more and, like any city with its eye on the future, it has plans for development.

city's prettiest park, started life in 1849 as an agricultural experimental station. The 20 ha grounds feature a variety of exotic and indigenous trees (including what is thought to be the country's first jacaranda), a highly rated orchid house which blazes with colour in springtime, a rare collection of cycads (notably *Encephalartos woodii*, believed to be the world's rarest plant) and a sunken garden. Facilities at the gardens include a refreshment kiosk and toilets.

11 Mitchell and Jameson parks

A favourite family spot on the slopes of the Berea is Mitchell Park in Innes Road, with its children's playgrounds, bird aviaries and wildlife. Some ancient, giant tortoises lord it over the animal corrals, and the buck may permit a velvety nose to be stroked. Shady paths wind past ponds and fountains to the open-air tea garden. Just across the way is Jameson Park, famous for its more than 200 species of roses.

LEFT *A vivid show of orchids against cool green growth in the Botanic Gardens.*

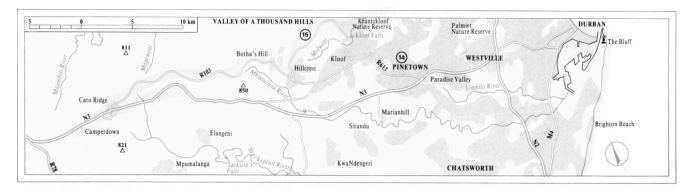

At the top of the map, from left to right: VALLEY OF A THOUSAND HILLS, Krantzkloof Nature Reserve, Kloof Falls, Palmiet Nature Reserve, DURBAN, The Bluff, 811, Mngweni, Botha's Hill, Molweni, Kloof, R613, 14, PINETOWN, WESTVILLE, R103, Hillcrest, 850, Mhlatuzana River, Paradise Valley, Umbilo River, Cato Ridge, N3, Marianhill, N3, Situndu, Brighton Beach, Camperdown, Elangeni, 821, Bucksspruit River, KwaNdengezi, N2, M4, Mpumalanga, Jackson's Falls, CHATSWORTH, Msaambiti River, R78, 15, Mvoti

12 Blue Lagoon and Umgeni Bird Park

The mouth of the Mgeni River is a popular rock and surf angling spot as well as the finishing line for the 'Duzi Canoe Marathon, which sees sportsmen paddling and portaging for three days each January between Pietermaritzburg and the coast. A model yacht pond, pleasure rides and a Putt-Putt course are located beside the Ellis Brown Viaduct on the river's south bank. Just inland, in Riverside Road, is the Umgeni Bird Park, a compact but beautifully landscaped park of walkthrough aviaries. Indigenous and exotic birds can be seen in as natural a (confined) setting as possible. The park also has a tea garden.

13 Beachwood Mangroves Nature Reserve

This sanctuary, on the northern bank of the Mgeni River, is a dense tropical forest of mangroves covering some 76 ha. These trees are unique in their adaptation to life in salty tidal waters and have developed special aerial roots that project above the mud. They have, in fact, 'colonised' the mudbanks, trapping silt and plant debris brought down by the river in their intermeshing root systems and creating an intricate web that supports other life — nesting birds, fish and crabs.

The reserve is controlled by the Natal Parks Board and arrangements can be made to visit it.

14 The Pinetown area

This town, some 25 km from the heart of Durban, developed around a staging post on the coach road to Pietermaritzburg in the mid-19th century. Its pleasant climate (it lies some 350 m above sea level and avoids the worst of Durban's humidity) and parklike surroundings have made it a popular residential area, with many opting to live here and commute to Durban to work.

The approach to Pinetown and the outlying areas offer a number of features of interest. The Palmiet Nature Reserve in the Westville municipality has some 7 km of walking trails crossing its craggy terrain and is home to about 150 bird species and numerous indigenous tree species. Guided weekend and winter sunset trails can be arranged through the the Wildlife Society. (To reach the reserve, take the Westville ramp off the N3; turn right from St James Avenue into Jan Hofmeyr Road after crossing the R103, and then left into David McLean Drive, which winds down into the Palmiet Valley.)

Still on the approach to Pinetown, just before the R103 joins the N3, is Paradise Valley, which is managed by the Natal Parks Board. Tucked under the tarmac of the highway are pleasant walks and picnic spots, set in 28 ha of coastal evergreen forest around the Umbilo River.

About 5 km south from the N3 at Pinetown is Mariannhill Monastery, a red brick monastery and church complex established by Trappist

---

TEMPLE OF UNDERSTANDING

Krishna Consciousness, a religious movement based on the Vedic scriptures, took root in India in the 16th century, but reached the West only this century and most people's knowledge of it is limited to the sight of chanting, orange-robed devotees proclaiming their faith in city streets. Internationally, however, the movement has established many retreats and institutes, and one of its latest projects is a temple in Chatsworth, south-west of Durban. The main objective of the Sri-Sri Radha-Radhanath Temple of Understanding is the spiritual upliftment of the community, but it is also a spectacular landmark, and visitors are welcomed along with the faithful.

Designed by Austrian architect Hannes Raudner (also known as Rajaram das), the temple is an exotic, multilevel structure surrounded by a million-litre moat. Every line and measurement in the three-towered building with its gold leaf highlights is spiritually symbolic and complies with ancient scriptural injunctions. Entrance is up a broad flight of steps with the building soaring above. Shoes must be removed before stepping into the foyer, with the pale pink and white Portuguese marble floor immediately cool underfoot.

The temple room interior is even more ornate and dazzling than the exterior aspect. A large, hexagonal room, it is filled with light and empty of chairs, and your gaze is drawn upwards to the ceiling. Eight large panels carrying colourful reproductions of Krishna paintings are surrounded by mirrors, lights, beading, and simulated gold and marble. Another 35 smaller pictures, illustrating Krishna's pastimes on earth, line the top of the windows, with breathtaking effect.

Lord Krishna and Radharani, the queen of devotion, are worshipped in the temple in the deity forms of Sri-Sri Radha-Radhanath, and their two figures stand upon an elaborate altar at one end of the room. These are bathed and freshly dressed, decorated and garlanded every day. Food is presented by devotees six times a day followed by a ceremony when lamps, flowers, incense and fans are offered to the accompaniment of chanting.

The temple complex, which has a vegetarian restaurant and snack bar, is open daily, and guided tours can also be arranged. (To reach it, take the Chatsworth-Mobeni turn-off from the N2 south, and drive inland on the Higginson Highway — R629 — then turn left to the Chatsworth Centre.)

BELOW *The brilliant face of Krishna Consciousness.*

monks in 1882 and now of considerable architectural and historical interest. Access is sometimes limited to a casual stroll around the grounds, so rather telephone beforehand. Included in the mission grounds is a guesthouse where, following the Benedictine tradition of hospitality, simple teas and lunches are available.

Perhaps the most scenic of the nature reserves around Durban is Krantzkloof, with its dramatically forested gorge and delightful picnic spots over the 90 m-high Kloof Falls, and some 20 km of trails to follow. Well stocked with wildlife such as mongoose, monkeys, bushbuck, otters and bushpigs, this is also home to the crowned eagle and numerous indigenous bird species. Natal Parks Board staff are on duty, and a small nature museum provides additional information. To reach the reserve, take the old Pietermaritzburg road through Pinetown, turn off at Kloof village and follow the signs.

15 Road to a Thousand Hills

History books do not reveal how the Valley of a Thousand Hills got its name, but one glance across its changing canvas of peaks, slopes and riverbeds confirms how apt it is. It is a reminder, within a half-hour drive from the city, of the rough-hewn face of Africa. The valley is believed to have taken its present form during the Pleistocene geological period when the ocean receded to about 100 m below the present sea level. That was when rivers, such as the Mgeni which meanders through the valley for over 60 km, gouged deep into the earth, and were subsequently refilled after the sea level began to rise again.

The valley is best viewed from the Old Main Road between Durban and Pietermaritzburg (the stretch from Botha's Hill to Cato Ridge), and the modern tarred road follows roughly the route

The timeless beauty of the Valley of a Thousand Hills, lightly brushed by human settlement.

taken by early transport riders and stagecoaches travelling inland. From the N3 to Pietermaritzburg, take the Pinetown R613 fork. Once up Field's Hill, the road passes through the plush garden suburb of Kloof, with the dramatic Kloof Falls about 4 km off to the north. Turn off to Hillcrest and Botha's Hill on the R103, and wind through a leafy country road that passes through Hillcrest village then climbs to Botha's Hill, with craft and produce stalls on either side to tempt the leisured traveller. Superb views of the valley are to be had from the terraces in front of the turreted Rob Roy Hotel, itself something of a landmark and a favourite stopping point. Continuing inland

on the R103 offers several excellent viewing points and tea stops.

The Valley of a Thousand Hills has long been home to the Zulu peoples. PheZulu Kraal at 168 Old Main Road maintains a simulated Zulu kraal, giving visitors a glimpse into traditional tribal life: dancing and drumming add excitement to household routines such as cooking, thatching, beading and knife-sharpening, all of which are explained by a guide. Life among these steep slopes is still a tough one, but the work done here by the Valley Trust has brought food, clean water and hope to many a family whose evening fires glow warm as dusk settles on ancient hillsides.

PLAYTIME AT THE PLAYHOUSE

Gone are the days when Durban's artists departed the banana coast in search of greener — and more appreciative — pastures. The most tangible evidence of the city's cultural renaissance is the Natal Playhouse. Standing opposite the City Hall in Smith Street, the Playhouse (formerly two cinemas) is home to the Natal Performing Arts Council, and behind its facade of two distinct architectural styles are five ultramodern performing venues, rehearsal rooms, restaurants and a souvenir shop.

The Moorish facade of the Natal Playhouse is what remains of Prince's, originally a de luxe picture palace. After its gala opening in July 1896, it hosted such silverscreen events as the first South African season of Charlie Chaplin's nine-reel comedy, and one of the first 'talkies' in town. Live entertainment included an Arthur Rubinstein recital, a Grand Jitterbug contest, and appearances by singer Richard Tauber and actor Lawrence Harvey. Modernised in 1965, and its name changed to the Colosseum, the cinema screened *My Fair Lady*, *The Sound of Music* and *Gone with the Wind* to packed houses for months

The heart of Durban arts.

on end — no doubt to the consternation of the two ghosts said to haunt the stalls!

The gables, wooden beams and leaded windows making up the rest of the Playhouse façade were the Tudor-style front to 'Ye Playhouse', opened in 1935 to high praise for its superior sound system and picture projection. War years saw the stage used for many a live show, with appearances over subsequent

years by such stars as Noël Coward, George Formby, Victor Borge, ballerina Alicia Markova, Maurice Chevalier, Cliff Richard, Spike Milligan, Charles Aznavour, the Supremes, Liberace and many more. But by the time Napac took over, the old Playhouse was in dire need of a facelift....

That it got, and more. Old has been blended with new, including the retention of the Playhouse's original 'starlit' ceiling and battlements as the setting for the plush 1 290-seat Opera house. The Drama theatre, the experimental Loft, the Studio recital room and the Cellar (for intimate supper theatre) can hold well over 2 000 patrons in stylish comfort.

Since it opened in 1986 — appropriately designated Heritage Year — the Playhouse has become home to the Natal Philharmonic Orchestra, the Loft Theatre Company, the Napac Singers and Dance Company. There is always something on at one or other of the venues, from lunchtime events to evening concerts and Sunday recitals. And adding to its attraction is its easily accessible situation in the pedestrianised city centre.

THINGS TO DO

Angling

The warm, south-flowing Agulhas Current ensures an abundance of fish species off Natal's coast, and Durban is a good place to fish all year round. Anglers make their biggest hauls from rock and surf fishing spots, but the bay and the mouth of the Mgeni are favoured zones, and deep-sea and powerboat fishermen usually do themselves proud. (Catches include king mackerel, spotted mackerel, musselcracker, slinger, soldier and rockcod.) Isle of Capri deep-sea fishing boats go out every day, equipped with tackle, bait and radar fishfinders. Rods and reels can be hired from Ride-a-While, where they will also advise on bait.

Fishing in the harbour and off North and South piers requires a permit, for which application forms are available at Kings Sports (West Street). It is illegal to fish from the harbour walls, and you need a registered dinghy or hired powerboat to get out onto the bay.

Art galleries

AFRICAN ART CENTRE, Guildhall Arcade (Gardiner Street): Traditional and transitional ethnic art, from Zulu bead- and basketwork, to tapestries, woodcarvings and screenprints; works by internationally acclaimed artists.
DURBAN ART MUSEUM, City Hall (Smith Street): Craft collection and Zulu folk art supplements French 19th-century paintings and South African works.
ELIZABETH GORDON GALLERY, Windermere Road: International graphics and works of top contemporary South African artists.
NSA GALLERY, Overport City, Ridge Road: Fortnightly exhibitions featuring the best of regional and national talent.

Beachcombing and shelling

The only chance of finding a shell anywhere near Durban is to try the less-frequented, undeveloped beaches such as the stretch between Anstey's and Garvies beaches on the Bluff, where low tide reveals good rock pools, and south of this the shoreline between Brighton and Treasure beaches. The last has rock pools that are the pride of local ecologists and are for observation and photography only.

Birdwatching

Port Natal a century ago was a favourite haunt of amateur and professional ornithologists, and although natural bird habitats have shrunk drastically as the city has grown, enough species remain to keep the birdwatchers happy. Inshore birds such as the greyheaded

Fish type	Season	Best area	Best bait
Garrick (leervis)	May – Oct	Sandy beaches	Live shad, mullet
Grunter	Oct – Apr	Sandy beaches	Sealice, squid
Kob (kabeljou)	Jun – Nov	Blue Lagoon (best at night)	Sardines, catfish
Shad (elf)	Dec – Aug (closed Sept – Nov)	Blue Lagoon, Bay of Plenty groyne, North Pier	Sardines
Stumpnose	Oct – Apr	Sunkist Beach north (near Battery Beach; best after dark)	Sealice, squid

gull and caspian tern frequent the beaches, while the Mgeni River estuary attracts the plover, fish eagle, osprey and mangrove kingfisher. Forest habitats such as those found in the city's nature reserves are home to birds like the blackcollared barbet, bulbul, crowned eagle, goldentailed woodpecker, Burchell's coucal and various hawks. Some dramatic offshore birds such as petrels, Antarctic terns and the huge wandering albatross can sometimes be spotted while deep-sea cruising. Seasonal outings are arranged by the Durban Museum.

Boardsailing

The small, sheltered bay between Vetch's Pier and North Pier is an ideal spot for beginners, with the Boardsailing Association Clubhouse on the spot for advice, and rescue boats on hand should a westerly blow you out to sea. Experienced boardsailors tackle the surf off 'Snake Park' beach. Easterly winds provide the most favourable conditions, and local experts rate May as the best time of year. For information on board hire and lessons, contact the association or sports shops.

Boat trips

Cruise around the bay or out to sea in one of the Sarie Marais pleasure craft which set off every day (weather permitting) from the Gardiner Street Jetty. The main booking office is at the corner of West Street and Marine Parade, opposite the aquarium. Charters are also available. The railways harbour ferry chugs around the bay on regular rounds, departing from a terminal near the tug museum.

Bowls

The Port Natal Bowling Association in Brand Road has information on clubs and fixtures.

Camping and caravanning

Anstey's Caravan Park, Brighton Beach, has sixty stands and is just a step away from the beach. Durban Caravan Park, Bluff, is the largest park

in Natal with 360 caravan and 325 camping stands.

Canoeing

Contact the Rivermen for details of organised canoeing and rafting trails on nearby rivers. Flatwater canoeing is possible on the bay or on Blue Lagoon when the tide is right, but it is best to check local conditions with the Natal Canoe Union.

Cycling

Social cycling and fun rides are possible along the beachfront and into the centre of town. Bicycles, including tandems, can be hired from Ride-a-While in Tyzack Street.

Information on more high-powered pedalling, racing and weekend rides can be obtained from Dave Wiseman Cycles in Berea Road, and trails are run by Funbikers.

Diving

Scuba diving requires a diving certificate before you go out, and divers using spearguns below the highwater mark need licences. Note that no spearfishing is allowed while using a scuba tank.

Favoured diving spots are Limestone Reef and Vetch's Pier (ideal for

beginner divers, and base for the Durban Undersea Club), Bluff Caves, Whaling Station Reef, and Number 1 Reef (in the region of the ships' outer anchorage). The DUC is a good source of advice on local conditions, while the Trident Dive Shop runs one-week training courses and hires out equipment to qualified divers.

Drives and viewsites

City views can be had from several urban routes. Try the crest of Durban's Berea with a drive along North and South Ridge roads, ending in King George V Avenue where the University of Natal commands an excellent outlook over the city. Parallel to the Ridge are Musgrave and Innes roads with similar views. The Bluff can almost be circled via Marine Drive, and heading north into sugarland on Umhlanga Rocks Drive presents a pleasing aspect of the city.

Golf

Natal Golf Union will help with information about local clubs, while Windsor Park Golf Club, on the banks of the Mgeni River, has a Pro Shop which hires out gear. Miniature golf can be played at Blue Lagoon Putt-Putt course and indoors at the Brickhill Road Sport Centre.

Horseriding

The Durban Pony Club at Newmarket Stables, Goble Road, gives lessons.

Libraries

The Central and Children's Library on the ground floor of the City Hall usually arranges temporary membership for a small fee. Of more specific interest is the Don Africana Library, Martin West Building, Smith Street, with a fine reference collection of Africana.

Maritime history is harboured in the sturdy body of this classic steam tug.

A diver explores the silent blue depths of the aquarium.

Museums

DURBAN NATURAL HISTORY MUSEUM, City Hall, Smith Street: Displays of geology, bird life and archaeology, including life-size (12 m-long) model of the extinct dinosaur, *Tyrannosaurus rex*.

J R MORE, Durban Harbour: A tour operates on board this classic steam tug and members of the Port Natal Maritime Museum are available to answer questions.

KILLIE CAMPBELL MUSEUM, cnr Marriott and Essenwood roads, Berea: Elegant Cape Dutch-style homestead holding a collection of Africana paintings, the William Campbell furniture collection, and the Mashu ethnology collection. Guided tours by appointment.

LOCAL HISTORY MUSEUM, Aliwal Street: Colonial double-storeyed building (Durban's courthouse until 1912) housing paintings and models of Durban's pioneer days, costumes, memorabilia and photographs.

OLD HOUSE MUSEUM, 31 St Andrews Street: Replica of a house first built on the site by settler John Goodricke in 1849 (later becoming the home of Natal's earliest prime minister, Sir John Robinson), containing furniture and artefacts from a colonial Victorian household.

WHYSALLS CAMERA MUSEUM, Brickhill Road: History of photography captured in a collection of old and rare cameras.

Music and theatre

DURBAN ARTS ASSOCIATION, Silverton Road: Contact the association for news of outdoor concerts, busking, music in the park and other arts events.

ELIZABETH SNEDDON THEATRE, King George V Avenue: Venue for university student productions, touring professional shows, and the International Durban Film Festival.

NATAL PHILHARMONIC ORCHESTRA: Regular concert seasons at the Natal Playhouse, but book early as most seats go to local subscribers.

NATAL PLAYHOUSE, Smith Street: Home of Natal Performing Arts Council with venues for opera, ballet, drama and cabaret theatre, as well as art exhibitions and fashion shows.

Powerboating

Activity is limited to harbour fishing and some waterskiing. Boats can be hired from Marine & Boating, with its own marina slipway. Durban Ski-Boat Club launches craft from the beach at Vetch's Pier, but boats go out only in the hands of a qualified skipper.

Shipwrecks

Dozens of ships — under sail, steampower and modern fuels — have sunk off Durban, but very little evidence of their fate is visible to the eye. During the 19th century, many wrecks were caused when ships were parted from their anchors in the outer roadstead and blown onto the beach or, in a few cases, onto the rocks at the foot of the Bluff.

The only wreck to be seen is that of the *Ovington Court* which went down off South Beach in November 1940, and can be seen at low tide some 250 m out.

In addition, anyone on the water in the vicinity of Vetch's Pier on a calm day might see the remains of Hunic, a diving chamber that was part of a University of Natal underwater experiment, and was abandoned after being overturned by a storm at sea.

Surfing

One of the world's top surfing contest spots, the Bay of Plenty, packs surf fans and professionals into Durban every July when several major competitions take place. Surfers wax lyrical over the waves, but beginners are advised to look rather than paddle out to join them.

Vetch's Pier and South Beach (as long as you keep at least 50 m clear of bathers) are best for beginners. The Wedge (next to the old West Street Jetty) breaks over a shallow reef so is better left to the experienced surfer, while Dairy (opposite the Paddling Pools) is very popular on 'smaller' days. More confident novices could try Snake Park but the breaks are decidedly bigger than those around South Beach.

Surf reports are broadcast on Capital Radio (between 06h00 and 06h30) and Radio Port Natal (07h15).

Swimming

Paddling pools at Brighton, Anstey's, South and North beaches ensure good swimming for children, as does a tidal pool at Brighton. Some of the calmest surf swimming is at Addington Beach. Bathing outside of designated areas — which are protected by shark nets, lifeguards and beach patrols — is to be avoided, as strong side currents and backwashes can catch the unwary. The saltwater Rachel Finlayson pool at North Beach is sheltered from wind and sand, and the Olympic-size freshwater pool at Kings Park offers scope for more serious swimming. Contact the Civic Information Office for details of suburban municipal pools.

Tennis and squash

Contact the Durban Lawn Tennis Association for details of nearby clubs and courts. Daytime and floodlit courts for hire at Westridge Park Tennis Stadium. There are squash courts at the Disc Squash Centre and 320 West Street in town.

Walks

Several self-guided trails have been established in protected natural areas that fall under the municipality's Metropolitan Open Space System. Close to the heart of the city are Burman Bush, a 50 ha patch of coastal bush on the Ridge just south of the Mgeni River, and the smaller Pigeon Valley, on the slopes of the Berea close to the University of Natal campus. Further afield is Virginia Bush, a birdwatchers' delight off Kensington Drive in Durban North. All these areas have shady, comfortable walks. (A visitors' centre at Burman Bush will provide free trail guides and pamphlets, or you could contact the Parks, Recreation and Beaches Department for more information.)

For more casual strolling, Durban's many parks provide the perfect venue. Particularly popular are the Japanese Water Gardens (in Tinsely Road, Virginia), an oasis of tranquillity with arched wooden bridges, winding paths and pagodas.

Guided city walkabouts are offered by the Durban Publicity Association on a daily basis. Duration varies from two to four hours (refreshments or lunch included), and themes are historical, maritime and oriental.

Yachting and dinghy sailing

The Royal Natal Yacht Club is located across the road from the yacht mole entrance, and the Point Yacht Club has its headquarters right on the edge of the yacht basin. Only members of clubs with reciprocity with either of these two clubs can launch a boat off the beach or onto the bay, so check here first.

The Ocean Sailing Academy offers five-day courses for beginners and more experienced sailors.

A burst of sails on a sparkling sea that laps the feet of the city.

INFORMATION
- Durban Municipality, City Hall, Smith St, Durban 4001. Tel 3040111
- Durban Publicity Association, Church Street Plaza/106 Marine Parade, Durban 4001. Tel 3044934/322595
- Natal Parks Board, Elton Place, Congella, Durban 4001. Tel 251271
- National Sea Rescue Institute, 28 Trust Bldg, Durban 4001. Tel 3040602; emergencies: 372011
- SA Tourism Board, 320 West St, Durban 4001. Tel 3047144

Nearest AA Office
- AA House, 537 Smith St, Durban 4001. Tel 3010341

The sweetest shores in all the land

SINCE THE EARLY 19TH CENTURY, when Natal's hills rang with the cries of Shaka's battle-scarred subjects, the coast that sweeps north from Umhlanga to the Tugela River has been colonised by sugar. Every vantage point presents a vista of green: hillsides, bathed in sunlight all year round, have their contours smoothed with the giant grass.

It is possible to take in this whole region by a circular drive, starting at Umhlanga and deflecting inland along the route known as the Sugar Way, which links towns that fluttered to life as sugar settlements. From Stanger rejoin the N2, skimming closer and closer to a coast with a Mediterranean feel, especially lovely during winter when the Indian Ocean rollers flatten out and turn an achingly beautiful aquamarine. The coastal resorts, punctuating the route known as Shaka's Way, began life as the seaside retreats of sugar planters whose cultivated acres were a fringe of coastal bush away from the tideline. Linger at the colourful resorts before completing the circuit at Umhlanga.

A glimpse of sea through waves of cane.

1 Umhlanga

This thriving coastal resort, just a twenty-minute drive from Durban, packs hotels and holiday apartments along an attractive beachfront, while residential garden suburbs spread inland. The borough has grown at a phenomenal rate since the 1970s; after amalgamating with the plush La Lucia to the south, its permanent population expanded to the present figure of 50 000. Umhlanga's sophisticated shopping malls and luxury accommodation can rival much of what Durban has to offer, yet despite this, a small village ambience prevails at the heart of the resort, and it is easy to get around on foot.

A paved walkway runs almost the entire length of Umhlanga Beach, providing quick access from one section to another (a welcome alternative to scorching summer sands), as well as an enjoyable promenade punctuated with benches. A well-known landmark along the way is the big Oyster Box Hotel, which was built on the site of an isolated beach cottage erected in 1869. Built of Burmese teak, corrugated iron and concrete, the cottage served for years as a useful navigation point for passing ships. Quite appropriately,

Umhlanga's distinctive red-and-white lighthouse is sited beside it.

Another beach landmark, one that can be seen at low tide, is the wreck of the *John Williamson*, a 100 ton corvette that went down in 1961 with no lives lost. The beach itself holds a special appeal, the shore alternating between slightly sloping sandy widths and rocky areas with inviting tidal pools. From the beach, powerboats are launched with great verve into the surf. Lifeguards and shark nets protect the swimmer, who is also catered for

with facilities like showers and change-rooms. Parking is a short distance off the beach. Umhlanga is also well supplied with sports facilities and restaurants, and the small bird park on Lighthouse Road offers pony rides and teatime treats among its attractions.

The modern headquarters of the the Natal Sharks Board stand on hill overlooking Umhlanga, amid a sea of sugar cane. Established in 1964, the board ensures that much of Natal's coast is safe from the threat of sharks. About 45 beaches, between the southern Natal border with Transkei and Richards Bay in the north, are protected by almost 400 shark nets. The board also runs a public education campaign and offers an interesting weekly lecture tour and demonstration.

2 Umhlanga Nature Reserve and Hawaan Forest

A tranquil lagoon forms the northern boundary of Umhlanga (the name means 'place of reeds'). The banks of the Ohlanga River are covered with a natural green belt of dense coastal forest, sprawling for some 86 ha on either side of the highway (the R627). To the east, embracing the lagoon and stretching northwards, is the 26 ha Umhlanga Lagoon Nature Reserve, a typical dune forest that changes from sand-binding creepers near the high-water mark to tall trees enveloped by undergrowth. To the west is the privately owned Hawaan (sighing in the wind) Forest, which extends inland along the south bank of the river.

Although so close to each other, the forests are very different: plants common to one are rare in the other. The lagoon reserve is characterised by red milkwood trees while the Hawaan is unique with its abundance of wild mango (*Cola natalensis*) and cavacoa trees. The reserve falls under the aegis of the Natal Parks Board, and two public trails meander through its density, taking in a picnic site en route. Casual access to the Hawaan is not possible, but the Wildlife Society regularly conducts walks through its tangled wilderness.

A walk through either forest is well rewarded. Branches and leaves form an almost unbroken

LEFT *Umhlanga blends a sophisticated urban lifestyle with the fun of a seaside resort.*

THE DOLPHINS THAT NAMED A COAST

Frolicsome bottlenosed dolphins.

One of the best sites to observe dolphins in the wild off the South African coast lies between Umhlanga and Zinkwazi Beach, hence the nickname the Dolphin Coast. They favour this stretch for its relatively clear and shallow water: the continental shelf off the Natal coast is very narrow, so the dolphins swim quite close to shore in order to feed.

It is mostly bottlenosed dolphins whose conspicuous fins and sleek black bodies are seen from the shore. The humpback dolphin is also found in these waters but is a much shyer creature, while the cold-water common dolphin usually visits these parts during the annual sardine run.

Surveys of these waters suggest that they are frequented by a school of about 200 dolphins. This breaks up into smaller groups averaging 15 animals, although when the water is dirty they stay in bigger groups and change their feeding strategy to be on the lookout for predators such as Zambezi, tiger and great white sharks.

Reported to be very friendly creatures, dolphins will follow boats and surfers, playing and swimming alongside the humans, and even turning over on their backs to get a better look at the landlubbers. They have a tremendous variety of spectacular leaps and jumps, and can out-surf any boardrider when the waves are breaking right. Ironically, it is man who poses the greatest threat to them: pollution, shipping traffic, careless boaters and perhaps even shark nets all put the amiable dolphin under pressure to survive.

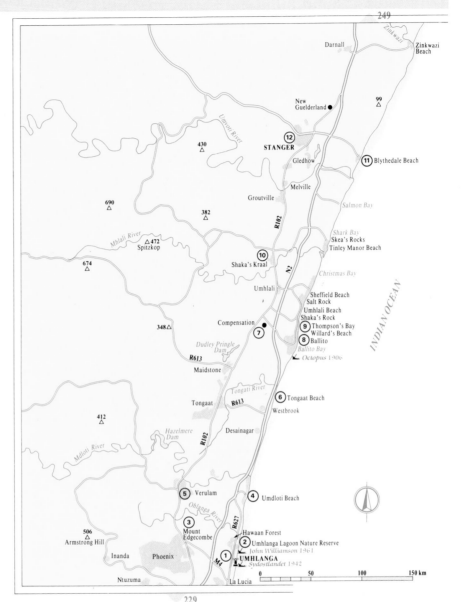

canopy overhead, so there is little light and the air barely stirs. The soil is well-drained and porous, but after a rainy spell, brightly coloured fungi flourish underfoot and on dead logs. These may be dainty mushrooms, brackets or wineglasses, or the bird's-nest fungus (*Cyathus*), looking like a small, grey cup with 'eggs' at the bottom. Always eye-catching is the chalice-shaped mushroom *Lentinus sajorcaju*, brilliant white and about 10 cm in size. Dozens of these crowd one another along fallen tree trunks. Pad softly along leaf-carpeted paths or be prepared to sit and watch and you may see some of the small forest animals and birds: a family of banded mongoose, a tiny *mpiti* buck, a monitor lizard, a rare crested guineafowl or the beautiful narina trogon.

3 Mount Edgecombe

About 6 km inland from Umhlanga is Mount Edgecombe, which can be reached by any of three northern routes: the N2 freeway, the R102 or old north coast road, and the M4 that turns inland from the sea shortly after La Lucia. Named after a Cornish earl, this was the site of one of Natal's pioneering sugar plantations where, following Edmund Morewood's successful sugar making at Compensation, William Smerdon built a steam sugar mill in 1861. Mount Edgecombe, its surrounding hills still swathed in cane, is today a major pulse in the sugar industry. The world-leading South African Sugar Association Experiment Station operates from here, as does one of the country's 16 sugar mills.

Although the sugar industry dominates the area, interesting textures to the small, dusty village are provided by an elegant country club and two Hindu temples. The small Ganesha Temple, thought to be the first work done in South Africa by master temple builder Kristappa Reddy, is a national monument. The Shri Emperumal Temple, which started out as a tin shanty in 1878, now houses a giant sacred chariot which is drawn by devotees during festivals.

Bordering on Mount Edgecombe is the Indian settlement of Phoenix, named by an early planter who rebuilt his farm on the ashes of his first failed sugar estate. It was on an *ashram* or farm settlement here that Mohandas (later Mahatma) Gandhi lived for several years at the turn of the century. Sadly, especially in the light of Gandhi championing the principles of passive resistance and nonviolence, his house, a small museum and a printing press were destroyed by fire during the 1980s disturbances.

4 Umdloti Beach

At the junction of the N2 and R627, some 25 km from Durban, is the turn-off to Umdloti Beach, a small but popular beach destination named after the wild tobacco that grew on the river banks.

THE ROOTS OF THE SUGAR INDUSTRY

Mount Edgecombe's sugar mill in 1918.

Natal in the 1850s was nicknamed the 'Colony of Samples'. The early settlers, most of whom knew nothing of farming but were determined to wrest a living from the soil, had tried just about everything that would grow — including cotton, mealies, coffee and even pumpkins. Arrowroot, introduced to Africa from Mauritius by Edmund Morewood, proved the most successful of these. In 1853 it was Natal's first agricultural export but was overtaken the very next year by another of Morewood's experimental products: sugar.

The sugar also originated in Mauritius, for the wild cane (*mpha* to the Zulu) that had long flourished in the region had too low a sugar content. The 40 000 tops of cane imported in 1847 were auctioned off to farmers and immediately planted. Hopes were pinned on the foreign cane, but it was Morewood who overcame all the odds and eventually established what has become the South African sugar industry.

Enterprising and well-travelled, Morewood was managing a cotton estate on the Mdloti River in 1848 when he predicted success for the sweet grass that had begun to take root in Natal.

A small patch of it was on Morewood's farm, Compensation, and this was added to in 1849 with the assistance of fellow settler Ephraim Rathbone. Having spent years in Mauritius, Rathbone knew good cane when he saw it, and he pronounced the Compensation crop to be excellent.

Even so, there were doubts about the wisdom of the enterprise, and money was not readily to hand. But Morewood persevered. More hectares were put under cane, including another two varieties, and by 1851 he was able to mill his first sugar. At the end of January 1852 Morewood walked into the office of the *Natal Times* in Durban with his first sample of sugar: fine, light brown crystals.

The sugar was well received, and great things were expected but still Morewood was unable to raise sufficient money to expand his venture, and he left Natal in 1853, disillusioned and frustrated. The Morewood Memorial Garden outside Tongaat was opened in December 1951, almost a hundred years exactly after he had crystallised the start of one of the country's greatest industries.

Served by hotels, shops and restaurants, the resort consists of a narrow strip of shore that extends for about 4 km between sea and headland.

Umdloti is a popular venue for powerboat anglers but the main attractions are the fairly safe bathing in a large chained tidal pool and a beach with interesting rock formations. This natural appeal is, however, somewhat overshadowed by the rank of holiday apartments crammed along North Beach Road. Parking is at a premium on busy days, and there is a choice between the fee-charging municipal lots or free parking some distance from the beach. The landscape opens out more attractively along South Beach Road where high-rise buildings give way to cottages and sugar cane set back from a sloping beach.

5 Verulam

Spreading south of the Mdloti River, Verulam is reached by the R102 or Sugar Way. Motorists cannot help but be aware that this is candyland for not only is the gently undulating landscape a smooth, swaying green, but the road almost trembles beneath powerful transporters loaded to the brim with harvested cane.

Verulam is one of the oldest settlements in Natal, established in 1850 by a party of English Methodist immigrants led by the Earl of Verulam. A shady old cemetery on the southern edge of the town holds a number of settler graves, including many of the first Mauritians who helped pioneer the sugar industry. The town was handed over in 1967 to the first local Indian authority.

A favourite recreational spot is nearby

BELOW *Luxuriant green sugar cane carpets Natal's hills.*

Hazelmere Dam, some 7 km from the main road signpost to Hazelmere/Canelands. Run by the Natal Parks Board, the wishbone-shaped dam with its picnic spots and 224 ha of water surface is popular with day visitors for inland watersports. A section of the dam laps against vertical rocky cliffs, while the rest of its banks are grassy and fairly level — ideal for launching watercraft. A thousand cars at most are allowed entrance (Sundays are very busy), and facilities include a walking trail with a bird list and tree names, as well as toilets and braai places.

6 Tongaat and Tongaat Beach

The name Tongaat is said to derive from two Zulu words — *utho* and *ngathi* — meaning 'something of importance to us', and the history of the town, ever since the first Tongaat sugar estate was established there in 1852, is synonymous with that of Natal sugar.

With an enterprising, multiracial town council, there is a subtropical bustle to Tongaat with its aggregation of small shops. Oriental architecture contrasts with the neo-Cape Dutch style of official buildings and sugar company residences. This architectural theme, which was initiated by artist Gwelo Goodman in 1936, is also seen in Maidstone, a self-contained village beside the sugar mill in north Tongaat. Set in lush, landscaped parklands, its All Saints Church was renovated in the Goodman theme and features a traditional slave bell set in a classic belfry. The handsome headquarters of the Tongaat-Hulett group are at Amanzimnyama Hill, and include valuable archives detailing the growth of the sugar industry. Access to these and the Saunders collection of antiques is by appointment.

A towering landmark of Tongaat is the unusual Juggernathi Puri Temple, which was built in 1901 as a copy of the Puri Temple in India. Now a national monument, the temple was once surrounded by a moat, and comprises only the windowless but atmospheric 21,6 m-high tower. The more conventionally built Vishwaroop Temple next door was erected in 1911.

The town of Tongaat is linked to Tongaat Beach by Watson Highway (R613), one of the few privately maintained public roads in the country. The Tongaat group is responsible for landscaping this tree-lined, 5,7 km road. Tongaat Beach is relatively undeveloped, except for a lane of cottages in the bush, discreet condominiums and a characterful hotel. Although the beach has shark nets, it is used more by anglers than bathers. There is a tarred parking area.

A few minutes' drive north of Tongaat is a small crocodile farm in a natural bush setting. The route convolutes along dirt roads through the cane, reaching Crocodile Creek on the banks of the Tongati River. Lecture tours of the crocodile pools are given seven days a week.

7 Compensation and Umhlali

About 7 km outside Tongaat is the turn-off (opposite Compensation station) to Morewood

The many pleasures of Umdloti Beach draw countless holiday-makers to soak up the fun.

THE WARRIOR KING WHO BUILT A NATION

The name U-Shaka means an intestinal beetle, and when given to the baby boy who was to become one of the mightiest Zulu kings, was a reference to his mother Nandi's illegitimate pregnancy. There was nothing small and insignificant about Shaka, however. He had to bear the brunt of much humiliation as a child but grew to be a commanding figure of a man. Broadly built, strong and almost 2 m tall, Shaka became an impressive warrior in Dingiswayo's regiment. He fought battle after battle, collected vast numbers of cattle, and by the time he wrested the kingship from his half-brother in 1816, already had a powerful army around him.

Shaka used military conquest to build the Zulu nation, and he ensured that his army was strictly disciplined, mobile and effectively armed. It was he who insisted on shields large enough to cover the whole body, and redesigned the old throwing spear into a close-quarters weapon with a broad blade and short handle — an ideal stabbing weapon in hand-to-hand fighting.

From his massive Zululand kraal, Bulawayo, Shaka conquered peoples to the north before subduing chiefdoms in the Tugela valley and along the coast. At his most powerful, he claimed allegiance over a huge area that stretched from the Drakensberg to the Indian Ocean, and from the Tugela River north to Pongola. He established two more military bases: one on the present-day site of Shaka's Kraal; the other on the road from there to Glendale, south of Stanger.

After the death of his mother in 1827, Shaka decided to move to a new royal kraal at Stanger —

The memorial to Shaka in Stanger.

Dukuza. There his own life ended as he had lived. On the afternoon of 22 September 1828, he was stabbed to death by his half-brothers, Dingane and Mhlangana, and a bodyguard called Mbopha, and buried upright in a grain pit the next day. The gravesite (in Couper Street) has been commemorated since 1932. In all, nine sites in and around Stanger, provisional national monuments, attest to the time that Shaka spent in the region. And although much of his reign was filled with fear, the monuments recall some of his quieter moments . . . like a favourite cave and bathing place, and a refreshing drinking spring.

Memorial Garden, the site of the country's first sugar mill, built in 1850 by settler Edmund Morewood on his farm Compensation. Today the garden is a pocket of peace cleared out of the caneland. A national monument since 1952, it incorporates the foundations of Morewood's storeroom, the site of his small factory, and a replica of the primitive wooden mills used to crush juice from sugar cane.

Umhlali, a small business centre patronised by local sugar planters, is 3,5 km beyond Compensation, and the Umhlali Country Club with its attractive 18-hole golf course lies on the link road between the R102 and Ballito, just north of Compensation. (A bust of Shaka on a stone column at the turn-off from the R102 to Shaka's Rock is a reminder that this territory was among the military monarch's stamping grounds.)

8 Ballito

Although not shown on the map, the coast from here is a series of small bays, each with its own charms and sheltered spots. The first of these is Ballito, meaning 'little ball' and named — perhaps rather oddly — after a brand of Italian silk stockings.

The settlement was transformed from sugar farm to coastal township in 1954. Originally known as Ballitoville, then Ballito Bay, it has grown steadily to include a hotel, dozens of holiday cottages, modern apartment blocks, shops and caravan parks. The attractive beach with a tidal pool is actually two small bays divided by a rocky outcrop, and lifesavers are on duty here all year round. A paved promenade attracts strollers at the southern end of the beach.

At the northern end of Ballito is Willard's Beach with protected bathing. From here, in fact from Ballito itself, it is possible to walk along the beach to Salt Rock.

9 Thompson's Bay to Sheffield Beach

North of Ballito, within a few twists and turns of

SHIPWRECKS OFF THE NORTH COAST

The first recorded shipwreck off the Natal coast involved two Portuguese galleons that fell foul of a savage south-wester in 1552. The *Sao Jeronimo* and *Sao Joao*, carrying more than 600 people between them, were wrecked off the Zululand coast, and only 22 of the castaways survived a desperate bid to walk to the safety of Delagoa Bay.

Of all the sailing vessels wrecked off the Natal coast since then, by far the most have been in the vicinity of Durban, but the elements have proved treacherous to the north as well. On 13 October 1906, the dredger *Octopus* left Durban for Australia, and sailed directly into a howling gale. It had taken on so much water by the next morning that the crew was forced to abandon ship. Two boats struggled towards the shore: one capsized as it was about to land just north of the mouth of the Tongati, and the captain's wife and two children were drowned; the second beached safely at the river mouth. The dredger eventually drifted onto rocks at Port Zimbali, south of Ballito.

It was probably a similar gale that drove the *Sydostlandet* aground off Umhlanga on 6 April 1942. The old whaler, converted into a minesweeper, was a total loss but all hands were saved.

One of the most dramatic of Natal's shipwrecks took place much further out to sea. On 13 June 1968, the Liberian oil tanker *World Glory* (then the largest in the world) snapped in two and sank, with the loss of 24 lives. According to one survivor, the wave that broke the tanker's back was over 21 m high and lifted the vessel right out the water, leaving the oil-laden bow and stern unsupported and opening a crack across the main deck. As the tanker began to tear in half, thousands of litres of oil poured over the sea and were ignited by sparks from the splintering steel, until an explosion shattered the ship. The oil spill spread over 200 km and got to within a short distance of Natal's north coast and nature reserves before a dozen ships and several aircraft were able to break up the slick with detergent.

the coastal road, you reach Thompson's Bay with a complex of luxury apartments on the headland above. A magnificent tidal pool is tucked into the southern edge of the bay, and is reached on foot from roadside parking. Toilets and change-rooms are available.

Folklore has it that the high rock dividing Thompson's Bay from Shaka's Rock was a place of execution during Shaka's reign: the king's enemies were apparently thrown to their sad fate from here. Today pleasure reigns supreme, and a popular hotel perches over a beach with natural tidal pools and fairly safe bathing.

Beyond Shaka's Rock is Umhlali Beach, which, in addition to being an umbrella name for all the beaches along this stretch, identifies a small bathing area with pleasant grassed picnic and braai facilities.

LEFT *The winning combination of deep gold sands and sparkling surf.*

Salt Rock follows, with its hotel set amid spacious lawns and a caravan park, and two striking, well-built tidal pools. Four concrete pillars remain from early fishing towers built by the Hulett family, who have the distinction of having run the hotel for three generations.

Salt Rock is thought to have taken its name from the Zulu practice of collecting salt from potholes in the rocks, where water would settle from the spring tides. Once crystallised, it would be used by local chiefs for trading with the settlers.

Sheffield Beach is more residential than resort but, with its secluded coves and rocky bays, is a delightful spot reached by a scenic drive. To the north of Sheffield Beach is Elephant Rock, something of a landmark for sailing vessels.

10 Shaka's Kraal and Groutville

Inland from Sheffield Beach is Shaka's Kraal, a straggling, single-street village just north of the Mhlali River and once the site of the Zulu military

ABOVE *Thompson's Bay, with its jewel of a tidal pool, lies in idyllic seclusion.* BELOW *Soft light and mist bathe the Ballito area.*

settlement, Hlomandini I. Less than 7 km further north, in the Groutville region, is a rock mass on which Shaka used to sit to inspect his *impi*. This spot, provisionally declared a national monument, is included in a programme of historical reconstruction being undertaken by the Stanger municipality.

A mission station and church are still in use at Groutville, which was named in the 1840s after its founder, American missionary Aldin Grout, and is now a KwaZulu settlement.

11 Blythedale and Zinkwazi beaches

Before reaching the two northernmost resorts along this coast you come to Tinley Manor Beach, a small resort where the main attraction for visitors is fishing.

Blythedale and Zinkwazi beaches are similar in style. Both are small and unspoilt, but access to the beach for casual day-trippers is controlled through

municipal car parks.

Blythedale Beach lies seaward of Stanger, about 72 km from Durban, and its camping facilities and cluster of holiday cottages are tucked into coastal bush and trees, with a length of sloping beach on the other side. The car park is almost on the beach, and a tidal pool lodges neatly among the rocks of the shark-netted bathing area.

The focus of Zinkwazi (85 km from Durban) is a typical Natal coastal lagoon used for watersports. A large caravan park and a bank of cottages have secured grandstand positions on the river's south shore, but the reed-rimmed lagoon can be reached on foot from the beach. Both car parks (the one to the south also accommodates picnickers) charge for entry. The beach itself is quite narrow and fairly rocky in places and offers only rudimentary toilet facilities.

12 Stanger

Stanger, with its hotels, sports facilities and business centre, was named in honour of Dr William Stanger, the first surveyor-general of Natal, in 1873.

But the site came to prominence before then, as it was here, in July 1826, that Shaka built what was to be his final capital, Dukuza. It was a convenient halfway point between Port Natal and Zululand, but was not long in service.

Following Shaka's assassination in September 1828, Dukuza was abandoned to the elements. It was only in 1932 that the Zulu people commemorated the former king's death with a monument erected over the grain pit into which Shaka had been cast. The memorial stands in Couper Street, and beside it is a rock on which Shaka used to sit, sharpening his spears in a groove that today is still visible in the stone.

Immigrant schemes subsequently brought small waves of settlers to the area, including Dutch farmers brought out by T C Colenbrander to New Guelderland, and Scots and Englishmen who laid the foundations for the surrounding sugar industry. The first Indian trader, a Mr Rampul, opened for business in Stanger in 1882. Memorabilia, weapons, household items and agricultural implements from those early pioneers are displayed in the Natal North Coast Museum.

Surf angling on Natal's north coast offers almost limitless rewards to the patient.

Angling

This stretch of coast is an angler's dream between August and December when the fish are reputed to take any bait that hits the water! All the spots between Umhlanga and Zinkwazi are well known for the hauls of garrick (leervis) that come in the wake of the shad (elf), but the rest of the year offers good pickings of pompano, stumpnose, grunter and cod. Gamefish such as barracuda, Natal snoek and yellowfin tuna are caught in the summer months, but you need a deep-sea craft to get to them. Light anglers can expect to find perch and salmon in any of the many lagoons, and best results for rock and surf anglers are at dawn or dusk when the tide is in.

Freshwater fishing is possible at Hazelmere Dam, which is stocked with such fish as bass, tilapia and scalies. Fishing licences must be obtained from the ranger's office.

Beachcombing and shelling

An Iron Age shell midden, dating back to AD 600, was found some years ago on the north bank of the Umhlanga Lagoon near Peace Cottage, an early beach house. Visitors are asked not to walk on the midden, but might be lucky enough to find the odd piece of ancient pottery dislodged from the dune and fallen onto the beach.

The beach north of here, between the lagoon and Umdloti, is a good beachcombing and driftwood spot, and shells are sometimes found among the rocks at the south end of the Umhlanga beach promenade, and at Christmas Bay, just north of Sheffield Beach.

Birdwatching

The Umhlanga 'Ponds' (the sewage disposal works landscaped into an attractive, parklike setting) are a popular birdwatching spot, and two hides have been built close to the water's edge. Commonly spotted are fish eagles, pelicans, kingfishers and a variety of wild duck. Ask for directions from the Municipal Offices in Lagoon Drive, where you can also get information on birding walks through the privately owned Hawaan Forest. The Umhlanga Lagoon Nature Reserve, controlled by the Natal Parks Board, has a host of estuary and coastal forest birds.

Boardsailing

The picturesque Hazelmere Dam is one of the most popular inland boardsailing spots on the Natal coast, and is divided into three watersport zones: sailing, powerboating, and skiing. Each sailboard must be registered at the

THINGS TO DO

ranger's office before launching and lifejackets are obligatory, even on the dam's placid waters. The turn-off to Hazelmere is a short distance out of Verulam on the R102, and the route inland is well signposted.

The sheltered lagoon at Zinkwazi is a haven for boardsailors but access to the shore is difficult unless through the caravan park or from private cottages.

Bowls
All Umhlanga hotel guests are automatically temporary members of the local country club and can use the greens. The Umhlali Country Club welcomes social bowlers, as does the Salt Rock Country Club. Check with the country clubs at Mount Edgecombe and Maidstone about greens.

Camping and caravanning
Caravan parks close to the beach are found at Umhlanga, Ballito and Salt Rock, and other resorts include Lala Lapha at Ballito and the Zinkwazi Park Resort with its prime lagoon-side location. Contact the Dolphin Coast Publicity Association for details.

Canoeing
Hazelmere Dam accommodates paddlers who must stay within 50 m of the shore or, if paddling across the dam, must remain close to the buoyed cables. Boats must be registered with the ranger's office.

Diving
The Dolphin Coast is good spearfishing territory. There are reefs off Umhlanga, Umdloti Beach (extending to the mouth of the Tongati River), Ballito, Salt Rock and Blythedale Beach. Tiffany's Reef (just north of Salt Rock) also attracts scuba divers. Spearfishing needs a licence, renewed annually and purchased from Natal Parks Board offices or the Natal Fisheries Licence Board in Durban.

Fish type	Season	Best area	Best bait
Garrick (leervis)	July — Oct	Umhlanga, Umdloti Beach, Ballito, Thompson's Bay	Live bait (e.g. pinkies), garrick popper lures
Kingfish	Feb — May	Ballito, Tinley Manor	Live bait, shrimps
Kob (kabeljou)	May — Nov	Umdloti Beach, Tongaat Beach	Live shad, sardines, squid
Shad (elf)	June — Aug, Dec	Umhlanga, Tongaat Beach, Salt Rock, Tinley Manor	Fresh fillets, spoons
Stumpnose	May — Sept	Umhlanga, Umdloti Beach, Tongaat Beach, Ballito	Shrimps, prawns

Drives and viewsites
Wind along tarred roads between Ballito and Sheffield Beach for an attractive coastal drive, with one of the prettiest coastline views of Natal to be had from Colwyn Drive at Sheffield. The road curves high over the sea, looking down on small bays and headlands with a distinct Mediterranean style.

Golf
A championship 18-hole course is open to visitors at Umhlali Country Club, and the Umhlanga Country Club also welcomes guests. The courses at the Huletts country clubs at Mount Edgecombe and Maidstone are highly reputed among local golfers, and can be used by fee-paying day members.

Horseriding
Wellesley Riding School at Umdloti Beach can arrange rides.

Libraries
Temporary membership can be arranged at the municipal libraries at Umhlanga and Ballito.

Museums
NATAL NORTH COAST MUSEUM, Gledhow Mill Street, Stanger: Local history and enthnological displays (especially pertaining to Shaka), housed in a small, redbrick, former railways home. Established in 1972, the museum features a number of domestic and agricultural artefacts from the 19th-century Dutch families who started New Guelderland. In pride of place is a parchment letter dated 1799 and penned by Lord Nelson to a shipbuilder, who was great-uncle to Sir Liege Hulett, the Natal settler whose family has become a cornerstone of the sugar industry.

Powerboating
Powerboats, fitted with regulation safety gear, use a section of Hazelmere Dam and must be registered at the Natal Parks Board office before launching. Another dam zone accommodates waterskiing.

Powerboats are launched from Umhlanga, Umdloti Beach, Tongaat Beach, Ballito and Salt Rock, but only by local licensed skippers.

Shipwrecks
The *Sydostlandet* (1942) and *John Williamson* (1961) are visible at low tide from Umhlanga, as is the *Octopus* (1906) at Port Zimbali.

Surfing
The surf is usually up at Umhlanga's main beach, at Umdloti Beach, Ballito and Salt Rock. Demarcated bathing areas must be avoided.

Swimming
Although the shore slopes quite abruptly from the high-water mark along much of this coast, there are delightful and fairly safe swimming spots. The beaches at Umhlanga, Umdloti Beach and Ballito (including Willard's Beach) are equipped with all facilities, including professional lifeguards. Shark nets cover Tongaat Beach, La Mercy, Thompson's Bay, Shaka's and Salt Rock, Tinley Manor, Blythedale Beach and Zinkwazi.

An inviting collection of tidal pools nestles among rocks at Umdloti Beach, Ballito, Thompson's Bay (this one rates a ten!), two at Shaka's Rock, another pair at Salt Rock, and a small one at Blythedale Beach.

Tennis and squash
Country clubs at Umhlanga, Mount Edgecombe, Umhlali, Maidstone and Salt Rock all have tennis and squash courts. There are additional squash courts at La Lucia, and in Umhlanga at Cabana Beach. Stanger has a squash centre in High Street.

Walks
For a civilised beachfront stroll, the Ken O'Connor Promenade runs the length of Umhlanga's beach, and several forest trails curl through the Umhlanga Lagoon Nature Reserve. Guided trails of one, two and three hours are run by the Wildlife Society in the Hawaan Forest, and details are obtainable from the Umhlanga Municipal Offices.

A do-it-yourself beach walk extends for a couple of kilometres north between Ballito and Sheffield Beach, and if taken at a leisurely pace could keep you outdoors a good half-day. The walk is overlooked alternately by beach cottages and dune bush dotted with strelitzia, and sometimes involves a clamber over headlands and around rock pools. Watch the tide as high water could trap you in a cove.

Yachting and dinghy sailing
Hazelmere Dam has a zone for inland sailors, and a storm-warning mast is used to alert sailors to approaching storms. One yellow buoy raised means everyone on the water must wear a lifejacket, and two buoys raised means all boats must return to shore.

The lagoon at Zinkwazi is used by small craft, and the caravan resort hires out boats to residents.

INFORMATION
- Dolphin Coast Publicity Association, PO Box 534, Ballito 4420. Tel 0322=61997
- Natal Fisheries Licence Board, Private Bag 15, Congella 4013. Tel 031=251294
- Natal Parks Board, Elton Place, Congella 4001. Tel 031=251271
- SA Tourism Board, 320 West St, Durban 4001. Tel 3047144
- Umhlanga Municipality, Civic Centre, Lagoon Drive, Umhlanga 4320. Tel 031=5611101

Nearest AA Office
- AA House, 537 Smith St, Durban 4001. Tel 031=3010341
- North Coast Agency, Stanger Enterprises, Couper St, Stanger 4450. Tel 0324=22424

Take a holiday ride alongside a blue lagoon.

Where history haunts a coastal kingdom

THE MIGHTY TUGELA is more than a symbolic boundary between Natal and KwaZulu. Crossing its sandy, often lazy expanse near the coast carries you into a new landscape. Towns and homesteads are more scattered, and cultivated spreads of sugar cane are interrupted by coastal scrubland, aloes and thorn trees. The roads stray inland, mostly paralleling a coast that, although wide and sandy, is almost empty of beach resorts for its steeply sloping shoreline makes swimming risky. Access to the sea is often difficult and, once on the beach, four-wheel drive could be the leisure-seeker's closest ally. In this wilderness atmosphere, the sophisticated harbour development at Richards Bay strikes an unexpected note.

The region as a whole has a special appeal. The green hills inland were the stage for the opening acts in King Shaka's awesome reign, and everywhere are the scars of the military might of Zulu, Brit and Boer. In rugged, alien valleys, early missionaries tentatively set up their stations, while sugar and timber planters began to colonise the coastal belt. Today the land is still brushed by shades from a vigorous history that has hardly had time to dry on paper.

1 Harold Johnson Nature Reserve

About 5 km south of the Tugela River is the turn-off to the 89 ha Harold Johnson Nature Reserve, its hillsides overlooking the Indian Ocean. The coastal vegetation, enriched by such flora as tree orchids and sprinkled with butterflies, can be enjoyed from three trails: the nGamanzi Tree Trail, a comfortable 5,3 km; the 9 km Bushbuck Trail, which offers sightings of zebra, grey duiker, impala and bushbuck; and the educational Remedies and Rituals Trail, about a forty-minute walk.

Favoured by day visitors, the reserve has a small educational centre, and a picnic and braai site (firewood can be bought from the ranger) with an excellent view of the Tugela flowing seawards. Camping stands are available but must be booked in advance.

2 Fort Pearson historical area

The turn-off from the N2 to the Harold Johnson Nature Reserve carries the traveller further down the banks of the Tugela — and back into Natal history. The major site is that of Fort Pearson, proclaimed a historical monument in 1950, but with not much remaining of the earthen hilltop

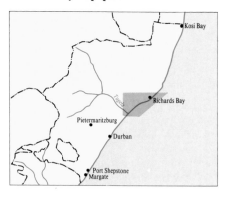

fortifications built by the British in 1878, just before the Anglo-Zulu War. The site is, however, well supplied with information markers and plaques, and at the cairn noting Fort Pearson's location, on a high bluff overlooking the river, points of historical significance in the vicinity can be established from their compass bearings. Pioneer hero John Ross is acknowledged in this line-up, as is John Dunn who lived with 49 Zulu wives on land given him in the area by Zulu king Cetshwayo.

A beach edged with lacy surf.

Fort Pearson, named after Colonel Charles Pearson who led the British during the first invasion of the then Zululand, housed some 5 000 men at various stages of the campaign, some of them buried in a military cemetery about a kilometre to the south.

The Pearson site includes naval graves and the earthworks of the naval redoubt on Euphorbia Hill, a small picnic area, and a viewing point that guides the eye across the mighty Tugela to the site of Fort Tenedos. This was built by Pearson as British forces began moving into Zululand, and a pontoon attached to a hawser linked the two fortified river banks.

A gnarled sycamore fig known as the Ultimatum Tree stands on a fenced-in site a short distance down-river of Fort Pearson. This is believed to be the tree under which a delegation from Cetshwayo was given a thirty-day ultimatum — effectively constraining Zulu rule — by the British in December 1878, thus precipitating war. This stately, natural monument can be reached on foot down a steep path from the marker at Fort Pearson, or by a car track (not advisable in wet weather) that turns left from the road heading to the river mouth.

3 Tugela Mouth north bank

The Tugela, or Thukela (the startling one), is South Africa's second largest river, and flows from the cool peaks of Mont-aux-Sources in the northern Drakensberg. The catchment area is vast, and the Tugela basin fans inland from the coast to serve 21 000 km² of Natal and 8 000 km² of KwaZulu. Water from the Tugela and its five main tributaries could provide power for six cities the size of Cape Town, six the size of Johannesburg, four the size of Durban, and four the size of Pretoria ... an impressive statistic to consider when gazing at the broad, muddy Tugela waters from the heights of the bridge.

Climbing north from the Tugela, the first, and rather sudden, turn-off to the right travels past the site of the Battle of Tugela. Here, in 1838, a Zulu impi almost annihilated a motley

LEFT *Fort Pearson, now a peaceful site.*

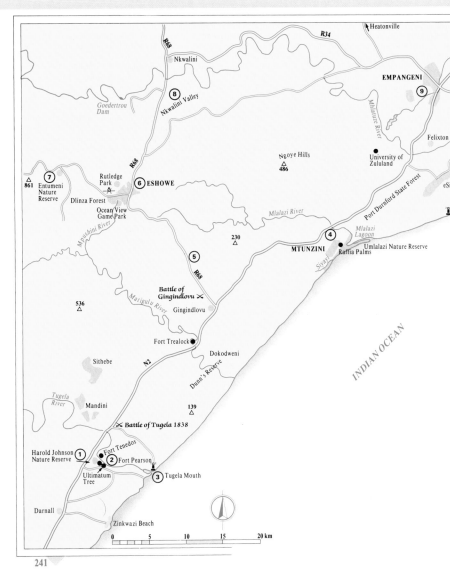

Durban force under Robert Biggar. A cairn, about 1,5 km from the N2, commemorates all those who fell.

From this spot, a corrugated gravel road winds past hillside settlements and mission schools to reach Tugela Mouth about 8 km further. A scattering of holiday cottages and a caravan park provide a base for keen surf fishermen and powerboat anglers. The sport fish *Lobotes* or tripletail, which is said to favour Tugela Mouth, is caught from the river bank and weighs in at an average of 4 to 7 kg. The beach north of the lagoon is wide, windswept and untamed (favoured for four-wheel-drive outings), and while there are no shark nets, beachgoers sometimes risk swimming in usually shallow surf.

4 Mtunzini and Umlalazi Nature Reserve
As it reaches the coast, the Mlalazi River (the place of the grinding stone) twists like a pipe cleaner into a long, narrow lagoon. Dune forest and mangroves blanket its banks, and wide, open beaches stretch north and south of the river mouth. On a low ridge west of the lagoon stands the village of Mtunzini, an unspoilt coastal retreat untouched by industrial development.

The only vehicular access to the lagoon and beach is through the Umlalazi Nature Reserve. Run by the Natal Parks Board, the 1 028 ha reserve is well serviced with log cabins, camp sites and picnic and parking areas, and is popular for boating and skiing. Three hiking trails are laid out: a 1 km walk through some of the best examples of mangrove swamp in the country; the Siyayi River Trail through dune forest where small game is sometimes spotted; and the more arduous 8 km River Mouth Trail that explores a wealth of river-edge forest, bird life and wild flowers, as well as colonies of mudhoppers and fiddler crabs.

The reserve also gives access to the Mtunzini Lagoon Resort at the last bend in the river, which

RIGHT *Fording the Tugela's muddy mouth.*

offers limited accommodation, refreshments and boat hire. Dunn's Pool, which was used as a holiday bathing spot by John Dunn and his wives, is tucked away near the parking lot.

South of the reserve is the enchanting national monument of raffia palms, and the municipality-run Mtunzini Chalets, providing attractive accommodation in serviced log cabins surrounded by natural dune forest. A limited number of day visitors can obtain access to the beach, dune walks and picnic sites. Additional accommodation is offered by a hotel in the village, and caravan and camp sites.

The Umlalazi River Resort lies immediately north of the river off the N2, and offers a range of boating, fishing and sports facilities to day visitors. Heading north to Empangeni, the road passes the Port Durnford State Forest (Port Durnford is simply an exposed roadstead watched over by a lonely lighthouse) and the University of Zululand in its Ngoye hills setting (there is a good roadside craft and curio stall shortly after the turn-off).

The monumental grove of raffia palms.

Surely one of the most unusual national monuments in the country is an awe-inspiring grove of giant raffia palms (*Raphia australis*), located off a dirt road east of the Mtunzini railway halt. A wooden boardwalk leads through tangled, swampy undergrowth and mangroves to the silent, churchlike heart of the grove.

The palms, with a lizardlike texture to their trunks and leaves that can reach 9 m long, soar to feathery heights of 18 to 20 m. These are so-called monocarpic trees, seeding only once in a 25-year cycle before dying off. They are common in East Africa, but their southernmost natural habitat is among the Kôsi Bay lakes, leaving the location of the Mtunzini palms something of a mystery.

Raffia palms have their uses: raffia from the dried leaves can be used for weaving, although the local application is limited to an unusual casing for a certain make of brandy! More importantly, they are closely associated with the palmnut vulture, which feeds extensively on the husk of the palm nut, and nests as close to the water as possible in a bulky nest built from palm fronds and sticks. In South Africa, these birds are seldom seen anywhere besides Mtunzini and Kosi Bay, and are among the rarer breeding species. With their boldly patterned black-and-white plumage, these distinctive birds frequent swampy river areas, and are often sighted feeding on fish, crabs and molluscs picked up from the mudflats beside the Mlalazi Lagoon.

A band of damp sand bars the broad Tugela, edged by patchwork lands, from the sea.

5 The route inland

The tongue-twisting Gingindlovu (swallower of the elephant) was named after Cetshwayo established a kraal there in 1856, having wrested leadership of the Zulu people from his brother Mbulazi. The N2 north bypasses the village, then forks, one route heading for the coast (and Mtunzini), the other a scenic road that climbs to the former capital of Zululand, Eshowe.

About 3 km after the fork to Eshowe, an inconspicuous monument on the left of the road commemorates the site of Lord Chelmsford's victory over a Zulu force in April 1879. Several war graves are located in a small, bleak cemetery situated half a kilometre along a farm road that curves into the sugar cane from beside the monument. It was the British soldiers of that battle who dubbed the place 'Gin gin I love you'.

From the memorial, the drive to Eshowe is about 21 km long, and the road cuts a swathe through canelands and small farmsteads before convoluting into a mountain pass that straightens out about 500 m above sea level. On a clear day, the view over the coastal plain below extends to the sea, and as the air cools and vegetation grows more dense, it is like entering another land.

Eshowe, with much of its admistrative role now in the hands of the KwaZulu Legislative Assembly in Ulundi, is no longer the vital heart of the region. In fact, the main road (R68) bypasses it en route to the moody hills of KwaZulu. Shortly after turning off to the town, Ocean View Game Park lies alongside the road. Cars have access to a picnic spot (with toilets), and a walking trail is laid out to the game hide. Wildlife on the 45 ha includes zebra, wildebeest, kudu and bushpig, with peacocks among the bird life.

6 Eshowe

Lodged on a ridge of hills, Eshowe was valued by Zulu kings and chiefs as a haven from summer heat, and 'the wind in the trees' is one suggestion for the origin of its name. Another suggested derivation is from the Zulu for the prolific *Xysmalobium* shrub — *itshongwe* — used in the preparation of cattle hides.

Cetshwayo, when still a prince, chose to build his main Esighwagini kraal on Eshowe's appealing uplands in 1860, and a memorial rock plinth in

LEFT *A swampy clearing in the Umlalazi reserve.*

William Chadwick Drive denotes the whereabouts of the kraal, which was also the king's deathplace. Norwegian missionary Ommund Oftebro was permitted to open his church station in the area at the same time. Called KwaMondi, it was transformed into a fort during the 1879 Anglo-Zulu War, when Pearson and his men were besieged within its temporary earthworks for ten weeks. Declared a historical monument in 1968, the overgrown remains of the fort and its cemetery lie on the eastern outskirts of Eshowe in a township called Gesinzila.

A second fort (also a national monument) on the opposite side of the town now serves as the Zululand Historical Museum. Fort Nongquai, with its whitewashed walls and neat parade court, was built in 1883 to house the Zululand Police who served in all the disturbances for the next quarter century. It is in excellent repair with natural history, military and ethnology collections housed in stone-floored former barracks. Pride of place goes to a three-handled silver mug presented to Cetshwayo in 1882 by Queen Victoria.

Eshowe has a tranquil, parklike air, with the annual rainfall of over 1 000 mm contributing to the lush vegetation. At its heart lies the 203 ha Dlinza Forest Nature Reserve (meaning a tomblike place of meditation), intersected by narrow gravel roads cut as early as the 1880s by soldiers garrisoned in the town. They also enlarged part of a stream bed as a swimming bath, and the modernised version still stands surrounded by forest. Picnic spots and marked trails branch off the roads, and small game such as bushbuck, red and blue duiker and vervet monkeys may be spotted. A clearing known as the Bishop's Seat is

used as an open-air setting for a nativity play, written by resident G S Moberly and performed every three years since 1953.

Adding to Eshowe's outdoor attractions is the small tumble of falls on the Mpusheni River (take the right-hand gravelled road from the end of Main Street; turn left before the bottom of the hill), where a wooded glade serves as a secluded picnic area. Two dams at Rutledge Park (reached respectively from Pearson and Oftebro streets) provide shady picnic and braai spots as well as good conditions for fishing and watersports.

7 Entumeni Nature Reserve

Travelling west out of Eshowe (on Kangella Street), a cemetery on the left houses a memorial to soldiers killed in the 1906 Zulu Rebellion, while on the right, as the road heads to Nkandla, are the grounds of the popular KwaZulu Agricultural Show, held every autumn.

The turn-off to Entumeni, a mist belt nature reserve of evergreen, indigenous forest, is about 12 km out of Eshowe, and from here there is a scenic 4 km drive on gravel road to the Natal Parks Board sign. The 436 ha reserve is undeveloped except for a small picnic spot and a rough-hewn walking trail. Its tangled recesses, with light barely filtering through the treetops, are home to a wealth of birds, butterflies, ferns and orchids, as well as small game.

8 Through the Nkwalini Valley

About 20 km north of Eshowe (on the R68) is the Nkwalini Valley, which early last century was overlooked by Shaka's huge military kraal, Bulawayo II. Today the sheltered basin is almost

THE WALKING DUNES OF MTUNZINI

The coastal dunes south of Mtunzini are unique: they are 'walking' into the sea. Aerial photographs taken of the dunes since 1937 show that the beach south of the Mlalazi River has advanced some 120 m in the last forty years — or at an average rate of about 3 m each year. This stretch of beach is thus rare in a world where most of the coastlines are either static or being eroded by rising sea levels.

Technically known as a prograding coast, the phenomenon stretches between the Tugela and Mlalazi rivers. The best place to observe it, however, is along the shoreline of the Umlalazi Nature Reserve where a series of at least 18 complete and unbroken dune ridges can be counted. All have developed in the last few decades, largely as a result of loads of sand being deposited in the sea from the Tugela, about 40 km south. Currents carry the sand northwards, dumping it on the beaches en route . . . and redrawing the map of the coast.

Vegetation changes according to the age of each dune. The young ones closest to the high-water mark are predominantly soft sweeps of drift sand. It is only once a sandtrapping plant takes root — such as the white-flowered, waxy-leaved *Scaveola plumieri* — that dune formation begins. The dune gradually stabilises, and other plants begin to colonise it. Grass appears, and woody plants such as *Passerina rigida*, then climbers and thicketlike growth that provides canopy cover. Finally, the oldest dunes boast fully fledged dune or riverine forest with tall, broad trees and abundant creepers and ferns.

Mlalazi Beach mirrors the sinking sun's gold glow at the end of a perfect day.

sleepily calm and the once-scarred land is richly cultivated with sugar, fruit and sisal.

The drive to Nkwalini heads towards a bank of hills that provide dramatic relief to the scrubland homesteads dotted on either side of the road. About 16 km out of Eshowe, a turn-off to the left is signposted Goedertrou Dam and KwaBheki-thunga. The latter is one of three establishments in the valley where guests can spend a night in a 'traditional' Zulu kraal.

Continuing west on a bumpy dirt road, the second of the kraal complexes is a short distance on, signposted to the left as Shakaland and

KwaLihl'izulu. It started life as a film production operation, its carefully built kraal a set for the television series, *Shaka*. Still further west and against an awesome backdrop of KwaZulu hills is the relatively new Goedertrou Dam on the Mhlatuze River, intended as a recreational area.

After Nkwalini, with its trading store and station, a tarred road (R34) turns right to Empangeni. Off this road (on the D132) is Stewart's Farm, established in the 1960s as a living museum of traditional Zulu life, with guided tours explaining aspects of family and cultural life, and comfortable accommodation available. The main

THE HEALING POWER OF NATURE

Natal's early inhabitants shared the need for food, shelter and medicine, and in many instances they went directly to nature for supplies. To the person familiar with the bush and veld, some fruit and berries became food. The wood of certain trees could be fashioned into yokes for oxen, knobkerries, chairs or farming tools. And leaves, bark and roots could be crushed or powdered into herbal treatments for all manner of ailments.

An hour's walk through the Harold Johnson Nature Reserve — on the Remedies and Rituals Trail — is a fascinating reminder of how far removed from nature modern lifestyles and medicine have become. Among the trees along the trail, 16 types have been marked for their historical or healing significance, some of them still used today by the Zulu medicine man. He — or she — could be either a herbalist (*inyanga*) or a diviner or witchdoctor (*isangoma*). Both are skilled in the preparation and prescribing of 'green medicines', but the *isangoma* has the greater status in the community. Having been 'chosen' by the spirits to become a diviner, the *isangoma* undergoes a ritualised training and always works in conjunction with the spirits.

Illness is often believed to be the result of wizardry and magic, and treatment of disease by traditional Zulu doctors can require a combination of medicine and countermagic. Against such a background, cures could well be psychosomatic but many of the leaves, bulbs, roots and bark have genuine medicinal value.

The coastal silver leaf, for instance, provided the Zulu and settler with an infusion to treat renal conditions and diabetes. Ashes of the plant were used by the colonists as alkali for soap-making, and domestic animals were treated for worms with a mixture of dried leaves and milk. Beautiful hardwood from the royal red ivory tree became exclusive knobkerries for the chiefs, while its bark was recommended for backache and rectal ulcers.

The root and bark of the prettily flowered white pear tree is used as a remedy for internal parasites, and the milky latex from the candelabra tree, or *Euphorbia ingens*, is still used by the Zulu to poison fish. This distinctively shaped tree often features in historical paintings of Dingane's kraal as it was under just such a tree that Piet Retief and his trekker party were killed in 1838.

road to Empangeni continues east towards the coast through undulating foothills and canefields.

Two privately owned game ranches are located north of this route, both catering for day visitors and bush camp stays. The 500 ha Nyala Game Ranch has a strong conservation education slant, with game and bird life to be viewed from hides and vehicles or on foot from one of several trails. About 7 km from Empangeni, the turn-off to Heatonville leads into the hills of the Lower Mfolozi district and to the 1 300 ha Windy Ridge

LEFT *Cane carpets a rise near Mtunzini.*

ABOVE *A still Richards Bay under a silver sky.*

Game Park, some 21 km later. Facilities include an airstrip, hunting lodge, guided bush trails and game-viewing drives (where you might spot the famous white rhino, or giraffe and nyala).

9 Empangeni and Enseleni Nature Reserve
Cradled by sugar estates, cattle farms and coastal timber plantations, Empangeni was formally surveyed and laid out in 1906, although Norwegian missionaries briefly ran a station there as early as 1851. Thought to be named after the *Olinia cymosa* (*mpange*) trees that lined the Mpangeni River, the town is now part of Richards Bay, 20 km east. The business centre includes shopping and sports facilities and two hotels, and is the base for the *Zululand Observer* newspaper.

The ultramodern Felixton sugar mill — with a crushing capacity of 3-million tons of cane a year making it the largest in the country — lies 8 km south of Empangeni on the N2. Opened in 1984, it was built on the site of one of Natal's first sugar mills, established in 1911 by Sir James Liege Hulett. A glance over hillsides smoothed by the big, sweet grass reveals the considerable role it has played in the development of this region.

The Enseleni Nature Reserve lies off the N2, 13 km north of the Empangeni turn-off, and is richly covered with coastal bush, fig tree forest, freshwater mangroves and papyrus swamps. The Umdoni Trail provides about an hour's meander around the banks of the Nseleni River. Bird life is abundant, as are warning notices about hippos and snakes in the river! Guided 5 km walks into the game park forming part of the 293 ha reserve can also be arranged.

MAKING A SAFE HARBOUR FOR ALL

Richards Bay started life as a vast natural harbour at the mouth of the Mhlatuze River, a drowned river valley that silted up over hundreds of years. This legacy of a turbulent geological past, surrounded by lakes and swamps, is thought to be the southernmost point in Africa where papyrus grows. It became home to flamingos, pelicans, giant herons and fish eagles, but it was not to be left undisturbed, for its potential as a shipping base was spotted as early as 1843, when the Voortrekkers contemplated an alternative to British-occupied Durban.

A hydrographic survey of northern Natal was carried out by the British in 1897, followed by a report in 1903 from harbour engineer Cathcart Methven. Richards Bay, he stated, had greater development potential than Durban. However, it was over half a century before action was taken. Selected above three other possible harbours to the north, the transformation of Richards Bay began in 1972.

Industry mushroomed around the area — a coal terminal, paper and fertiliser mills, dune mining, aluminium smelting — much to the dismay of conservationists. So the harbour was designed in an attempt to accommodate the needs of both industry and natural environment.

It was decided to divide the lagoon by means of a berm wall built across the bay. To the north the 1 600 ha working harbour with its tidal gates was established, with breakwaters limiting wave height to less than a metre to allow ships to enter in all weather conditions. Waters south of the berm wall remained a sanctuary for waterfowl and wildlife, and a whole new estuary was cut through dunes and coastal bush to allow lagoon floodwaters to flow directly into the sea.

Opened officially in 1976, the harbour with its vital rail links is visualised as the core of South Africa's city of the future. The environmentalists are reserving judgement on the outcome of the project, however, for a disturbed ecology cannot re-establish itself overnight. But signs are promising, with the bird species count in the area increasing, and the rare pinkbacked pelican being spotted once more among the reeds. . . .

10 Richards Bay
Lying at the sea edge of an ancient floodplain, Richards Bay is now a state-decreed development point with a highly industrialised deep-water port and the world's largest coal terminal. Named after Rear-Admiral Sir Frederick Richards, who landed British troops at the bay in 1879 to support Lord Chelmsford, Richards Bay was for many years a sleepy lagoon resort frequented by fishermen. Its biggest claims to fame had to do with wildlife: Huberta the peripatetic hippo was thought to have started her southwards trek to the eastern Cape from the bay in November 1928, and the honorary Zulu chief John Dunn shot a 6,7 m long crocodile (the largest recorded in South Africa) in the lagoon in 1891.

Long before you arrive at the residential area, ship superstructures and factory chimneys jut out

THE LEGEND OF JOHN ROSS

It was in 1825 that a 13-year-old ship's boy, known as John Ross but whose real name was Charles Rawdon Maclean, arrived at Port Natal. And what an arrival, for the brig *Mary* was wrecked on the sand bar at the harbour entrance.

More adventure followed when, on a visit to Shaka with some of the Port Natal settlers, the king took to the teenager. Ross was kept at the royal kraal like a 'rare, pet animal' for some months, growing quite close to the king.

During this time, the sailors off the *Mary* were attempting to build a new ship, but by 1827 their hopes were fading. Medical supplies were short and the schooner needed fittings unobtainable at Port Natal. Delagoa Bay, about 700 km to the north, seemed the only answer. And the robust John Ross, now 15, was chosen to undertake the journey.

Calling at Shaka's kwaDukuza kraal (where Stanger now stands) for permission to proceed through Zulu country, Ross was given an escort. Chief Langalibalele and about thirty warriors accompanied the boy, providing protection and food as the party trudged along the coast. They travelled approximately 35 km each day, fording rivers, skirting hostile settlements and malarial marshlands, and facing wild animals. Within three weeks they reached the Portuguese settlement, where Ross bought the supplies.

Returning to Natal, Ross was met by Nathanial Isaacs and Henry Fynn at the banks of the Tugela. They had come north for fear that Shaka might intercept and relieve the youngster of his booty. But all arrived safely at Port Natal, and the new ship, with Ross on board, was able to set sail in 1829.

John Ross went on to become a master mariner but his teenage heroism lives on in Natal, with a bridge over the Tugela (washed away in 1987's floods) and a road into Richards Bay named in his honour.

from the flat coastal plain. The bay's original cottages are surrounded by a meticulously laid-out residential township that includes two hotels, a caravan park, beach and boating facilities, and a country club on the shores of Lake Mzingazi. This 7 km long freshwater lake, which lies south of the airport, was used as a base for flying bombers in the Second World War, but today — as the sole source of the borough's water — it is out of bounds for recreation purposes.

What little remains of the Richards Bay Game Reserve — in the aftermath of the massive harbour development that has taken place here — is also not accessible to the general public, although the sanctuary on the southern side of the harbour is an attempt to re-establish an unpolluted marine habitat with waterfowl.

A viewsite on the headland next to the harbour control tower provides a panoramic perspective of the bay and its development. The main bathing beach, Alkantstrand (with facilities including shark nets and lifeguards on duty, a restaurant and picnic area and playgrounds), lies to the east, with yacht and powerboat clubs and a small craft harbour on the northern shore of the bay. Plans to develop a modern marina complex and recreational facility that blend into the environment are already under way.

North of this area are other beaches: Soetwaterstrand, with a freshwater pool, braai spots, toilets and change-rooms; Kleiklipklofie, a kilometre or so further, with toilets and a braai area beside the bush parking. This is a popular fishing rather than swimming spot, as is the next beach, Five Mile Beach, which has no facilities.

BELOW *Surf fans onto still sands, showing the wilder side of Richards Bay, where man and progress have not yet tampered.*

Angling
Lagoon, surf and deep-sea angling is always fruitful off this lower KwaZulu coast, but access to beaches often requires four-wheel drive or a beach buggy. The best times to be out are dawn or dusk, or at high tide.

No licence is needed for surf angling but Natal Parks Board permits must be obtained before going after crabs, mussels, oysters, rock lobsters, bait and rock life, as well as for spearfishing. Parks Board coastal resorts issue licences, as does the Durban office. There is a daily bag limit.

Richards Bay provides the best gamefishing, with marlin, barracuda and kingfish being caught with live bait all year round.

Art galleries
VUKANI ARTS AND CRAFTS, Main St, Eshowe: Locally made traditional Zulu handicrafts, with basketwork a speciality (especially the woven *ukhamba* beerpot that was used by Zulu royalty).

Beachcombing and shelling
Tidal action and turbulent rivers sometimes scatter interesting driftwood on the wide and sandy beaches, but most shells are usually broken by rough surf before reaching the shore.

Birdwatching
This is one of the richest areas for bird life in the country, with 230 species having been spotted between Eshowe and Richards Bay in a single 24-hour period. Habitats range from wetlands and coastal forest to thornveld and mist belt. Natal Parks Board terrain such as Dlinza Forest and the Harold Johnson, Entumeni, Enseleni and Umlalazi reserves are certain to produce sightings, with the palmnut vulture to be seen around the Mlalazi Lagoon at Mtunzini. Other spots are the Nkwalini Valley, and, near Empangeni, the game parks of Nyala and Windy Ridge (where the whitebacked vulture has been seen nesting), both of which provide lists of birds for visitors.

Richards Bay was a bird paradise before its programme of heavy industrialisation, but some birds — including rare and endangered species — are fortunately still attracted to the pans and wetlands around the harbour. Those known to have bred in the area are the African fish eagle, goliath heron, white-eared barbet, redwinged pratincole and purplebanded sunbird.

Boardsailing
Sheltered waters attract boardsailors to Eshowe's Rutledge Park, the northern shore of Richards Bay, the Mlalazi

THINGS TO DO

Lagoon at Mtunzini and a deepened stretch upriver.

Bowls

Members of clubs elsewhere can use the greens at Richards Bay Country Club; Eshowe Bowling Club and Empangeni Country Club also welcome visitors; as does Mtunzini Bowling Club, whose greens in Hely Hutchinson Street have a marvellous view of the resort.

Camping and caravanning

This stretch of coast provides a range of attractive outdoor accommodation, but it is advisable to check whether camping is allowed. Close to Tugela Mouth is the North Bank Caravan Park, while the Natal Parks Board has a tiny camp site at Harold Johnson Nature Reserve and a larger camp and caravan site at Mlalazi. Richards Bay Caravan Park lies between the beach and a freshwater pan. In and around Mtunzini are Casa Benri Camping Resort, Xaxaza Caravan Park, the Forest Inn Caravan Park (en route to Empangeni), and the Umlalazi River Resort.

Inland, near Empangeni, the Umvumvu Bush Camp at Nyala Game Ranch provides tents and rustic huts, and Windy Ridge Game Park has riverside camp sites that can hold caravans. Eshowe Municipal Caravan Park has sites on the edge of the Dlinza Forest.

Canoeing

Canoes can be hired at Umlalazi River Resort, and small fibreglass boats can be rented at the Mlalazi Lagoon but they must be powered by an engine. There is some canoeing off the northern edge of Richards Bay, between the shore and Pelican Island.

Fish type	Season	Best area	Best bait
Garrick (leervis)	July – Oct	Tugela Mouth	Live bait
Grunter	Aug – Dec	Mlalazi Lagoon, Richards Bay	Shrimps
Kob (kabeljou)	Mar – Oct	Tugela Mouth, Mlalazi River, Richards Bay, Five Mile Beach	Sardines, squid
Perch	All year	Mlalazi Lagoon, Richards Bay	Shrimps
Ray	All year	Mtunzini Beach, Richards Bay (four-wheel-drive access)	Sardines
Sandshark	All year	Mtunzini Beach, Richards Bay (four-wheel-drive access)	Sardines
Shad (elf)	June – Aug, Dec	Tugela Mouth, Richards Bay	Fresh fillet bait
Stumpnose	All year	Tugela Mouth, Mlalazi Lagoon	Sardines, shrimps

Diving

Local scuba divers favour the Tenedos Shoal, which lies between the mouth of the Mlalazi and Port Durnford lighthouse, and a spot just north of Glenton Reef, which is situated south of the small Siyayi Lagoon at Mtunzini. Access is awkward, however, and could require four-wheel-drive transport. The Natal Parks Board ranger at Umlalazi Reserve can advise, as can the Trident Dive Shop in Durban, which runs diving charters up the coast.

Drives and viewsites

The inland circuit from Gingindlovu to Eshowe, and from there via the Nkwalini Valley to Empangeni makes an attractive drive, with any number of detours to historic sites or other places of interest. A good example of this is one of the two possible routes to Empangeni from Nkwalini. A gravel road continues from Stewart's Farm on the D132 and rises into the hills south-east of the valley. At the junction of the D132 with the road from Eshowe (P230), turn left, to find a stone tablet (reached by concrete steps) on the left-hand side after about 1,7 km. What is now a peaceful, cultivated hilltop with sweeping views was once the site of Shaka's second Bulawayo Kraal (the place of the persecuted), with a massive circumference of 5 km enclosing some 1 400 huts and barracks for 12 000 soldiers. Less than a kilometre further, a monument and Kei apple tree to the right of the road recall another aspect of Shaka's life: here, at Coward's Bush, those who had displeased the king were executed. The gravel road continues as a rugged but scenic drive through this little-tamed corner of KwaZulu, meeting up with the tarred R34 to Empangeni about 17 km later.

Golf

An 18-hole course is open to visitors at Richards Bay Country Club, and Eshowe Country Club also welcomes holiday-makers.

Horseriding

Adult and children's rides are catered for at Umlalazi River Resort.

Libraries

Visitors are welcome at the municipal libraries at Eshowe and Richards Bay.

Museums

ZULULAND HISTORICAL MUSEUM, Nongqai Fort, Eshowe: A worthwhile introduction to the region's military, cultural and natural history.

Powerboating

Waterskiing is popular on the Mlalazi Lagoon with access to the river through the Umlalazi Nature Reserve, and powerboats are also launched from the beach off the reserve. Richards Bay Skiboat and Boating Club is active from a bayside launching site. Contact Z-Craft boatbuilders in Richards Bay for detailed local information.

Surfing

Surfing is limited to Alkantstrand at Richards Bay, immediately north of the harbour breakwater. Conditions are best when the south-wester is up.

Swimming

Beach swimming is risky as a result of the steeply sloping shoreline and limited shark nets. Lagoons such as Tugela Mouth and Mlalazi still recall crocodile sightings, although bathers have enjoyed the waters safely in recent times. Possible bilharzia sometimes also restricts lagoon bathing. The least risky beach bathing is at Richards Bay, and all the towns in the region have municipal pools.

Tennis and squash

Tennis courts are available to visitors on certain days at Richards Bay Country Club, while municipal squash courts in the town's Veldenvlei suburb can be booked. Floodlit courts are available at Umlalazi River Resort.

Temporary membership of Empangeni Country Club gives access to squash courts, and the Empangeni Tennis Club is in Pearce Crescent. Eshowe Country Club in Osborne Road has squash and tennis courts.

Yachting and dinghy sailing

Richards Bay provides one of Natal's few shelters for ocean-going yachts, and the Richards Bay Yacht Club has an active clubhouse near the small craft harbour. There is inland yachting on the Eshlazi Dam, situated on Eshowe's western outskirts.

INFORMATION

• Empangeni Municipality, Civic Centre, Union Street, Empangeni 3880. Tel 0351 = 21131
• Eshowe Town Board Offices, Osborne Road, Eshowe 3815. Tel 0354 = 41373
• Natal Parks Board, Elton Place, Congella, Durban 4001. Tel 031 = 251271
• Natal Parks Game and Fish Preservation Board, Umlalazi Nature Reserve, Mtunzini 3867. Tel 035322 = 136
• National Sea Rescue Institute, Richards Bay (PO Box 532, Empangeni 3880). Tel 0351 = 26971
• Richards Bay Municipality, Krewelkring, Richards Bay 3900. Tel 0351 = 31111
• SA Tourism Board, 320 West St, Durban 4001. Tel 031 = 3047144

Nearest AA office
• Zululand Insurance Brokers, Mimosa Court, 13 Turnbull Street, Empangeni 3880. Tel 0351 = 26921

Beach bathing is most popular at Richards Bay.

The magical lakeland where nature reigns supreme

NOTHING QUITE PREPARES YOU for the enchantment of St Lucia. Driving north of Richards Bay across a fertile alluvial plain, with carefully cultivated sugar cane and forests, the only clue to what lies ahead is a shadowy, mountainous ridge along the coast, which is finally revealed as a series of giant forested dunes. These, the highest of their kind in the world, provide an appropriate backdrop to a fascinating mosaic of lakes, rivers, freshwater pans, swamp forest, grasslands and long, empty beaches. All this adds up to what is popularly known as Lake St Lucia, although it is actually an estuary that parallels the sea for 61 km.

Shaped something like a battle-axe, St Lucia as a vital wetland is watched over by the Natal Parks Board. The public territory operates as four reserves: the lake with its 360 km² of water was proclaimed St Lucia Game Reserve in 1895; the land within 800 m of the lake shore (encircling St Lucia village and including the mouth of the estuary) became St Lucia Park in 1939; the western edge of False Bay became False Bay Park in 1944; and the wedge of land between lake and coast was proclaimed the Eastern Shores Nature Reserve in 1978. Jarring somewhat, the north-eastern portion of the complex is designated a missile testing site and areas in use are signposted as temporarily closed to the public.

1 Mfolozi Flats and Mtubatuba

The N2 north from KwaMbonambi noses between eucalyptus plantations and sugar cane, and passes west of the small (and as yet undeveloped) Lake Eteza Nature Reserve shortly before crossing the Mfolozi River.

Most of the time, the Mfolozi is well-behaved, meandering across a swampy plain before pouring into the sea almost within metres of the St Lucia Estuary. But the river's muddy mildness is deceptive. By the time it flows beneath the highway, its strength has been doubled because of the convergence of the White and Black Mfolozi rivers (named for the different coloured soils through which they flow) on the boundary of the Umfolozi Game Reserve. The river thus has the potential to become a tempestuous torrent, sweeping all before it when in flood.

Major damage was caused in 1984 when cyclone Demoina hit the KwaZulu coast, and again in 1987 with the region's worst floods in living memory. Roads and bridges were damaged or swept away, and valuable farmlands were lost. The river course has changed several times in the past, and although the Mfolozi Flats are considered among the most fertile in the world for sugar growing, the river gave early sugar pioneers

Off the beaten track at St Lucia.

severe headaches. A mill built injudiciously close to the river was damaged in 1917, and again in 1925, with many lives lost. Hence the site of the present mill at River View (between the river and Mtubatuba) and the development of an extensive system of drainage canals.

The R620 turns east about 7 km from the Mfolozi bridge, and within 2 km reaches Mtubatuba, which means 'he who was pummelled out'. This small town is a thriving regional centre, and with its hotel, shops and garages, it provides a pivotal point for motorists travelling both coastwards and inland.

2 Mapelane

Nature has the upper hand at Mapelane, southernmost camp in the cluster of Natal Parks Board resorts at St Lucia. Turning right from the N2 north, opposite the KwaMbonambi signpost, a rough, narrow road snakes for 45 km towards the sea. The road is so awkward in places — especially when it starts climbing the forested dunes close to the camp — that there is a size restriction on vehicle traffic and boats.

The effort is worth it, however, for Mapelane has an entrancing, hideaway atmosphere, with the camp situated on the southern bank of the Mfolozi River mouth. Log cabins and camp sites are almost hidden in thick bush, and behind them towers one of the giant dunes of the St Lucia coastline, with a dizzying expanse of sandy beach sweeping past. The massive hill Mjakaja, situated a short distance to the south, looms 182 m high and looks, from a distance, like part of a small mountain range.

Although the bustle and resources of St Lucia Resort are within virtual hailing distance on the other side of the estuary, Mapelane is quite cut off: no petrol is available and running out of groceries

LEFT *A rustic log cabin tucked in the wild dune vegetation at Mapelane.*

could mean a two-hour drive to 'civilisation' and back! But the attractions of excellent surf and powerboat angling, rich bird life and walks through 9 km of unique coastal forest keep visitors coming back for more.

Hutted camp bookings and inquiries are handled by Natal Parks Board reservations office in Pietermaritzburg, and camp site bookings by the officer-in-charge at St Lucia.

3 St Lucia village and resort

The hop from the N2 to St Lucia village is on a level, tarred road that passes first through the Dukuduku plantations, then coastal forest. The jade depths of the state forests are off limits, although a wooded spot about 13 km from Mtubatuba has been designated a picnic area. Three short, self-guided walking trails are marked out from here.

Another 16 km on is the first encounter with the estuary, spanned by a bridge that rises imperceptibly at its seaward end to allow dredgers to pass beneath. Turning right at the T-junction after the bridge takes you into the village of St Lucia. Its single business street is festooned with signs advertising a wide variety of holiday accommodation, which is swamped during the peak holiday seasons.

Operating independently of the village (and completely surrounding it) is St Lucia Resort. This is Natal Parks Board territory and includes caravan parks, a game park, walking trails and the Crocodile Centre. The centre, which besides its crocodile pools is a mine of information, is a useful starting point for first-time visitors to the area. The three caravan parks are Eden Park, with the short Loerie Trail starting next to it; Sugarloaf Camp, closer to the beach and complete with swimming pool; and Iphiva Camp in the St Lucia Game

Park. Visitors can walk unguided through this small reserve, or choose between three marked trails. The 4 km Hippo Trail leads to a hide on an estuary bank which provides excellent viewing, and all the walks allow you to get pretty close to the reserve's antelope, zebra and wildebeest.

All boating and angling in the vicinity of the mouth takes place from Parks Board ground, with jetties and parking lots at intervals around the southern bend of the estuary. Launch tours leave from the Parks Board jetty and visitors' boats must be registered at the office. Aluminium fishing boats can be hired by anglers with their own outboard motors.

Beach Road gives vehicle access to the mouth with its invitingly wide beach. It is here that the surf anglers crowd, every dawn and dusk, while behind

RIGHT *Shades of blue and grey in sky, sea and lakeland seem all to merge at St Lucia.*

them casuarina groves provide shelter from the wind, as well as picnic and braai sites. A boardwalk over the swampy Shark's Basin takes pedestrians back towards Sugarloaf Camp. An unprotected swimming beach (with showers and toilets) lies at the end of Beach Road's northern limb. No vehicles can pass through this 400 m length of beach.

4 Umfolozi Game Reserve

Inland but within pleasant driving range from St Lucia Estuary is one of the oldest and largest game reserves in Natal. The Umfolozi Game Reserve, proclaimed in 1895 and covering almost 48 000 ha of rugged African savannah, is famous for its Operation Rhino programme of the 1960s which helped save the white rhinoceros from extinction. Over a thousand of these square-lipped beasts now wander through what was once a hunting ground of Shaka's, together with shyer black rhino, elephant, lion, giraffe, buffalo and zebra, as well as thousands of blue wildebeest, impala and nyala.

The White and Black Mfolozi rivers almost double back on themselves as they twist and loop through the reserve, converging on the eastern boundary, south of the Mambeni entrance gate through which the visitor from the coast would arrive. (The reserve is reached from R618 which turns off the N2 about 3 km north of Mtubatuba. Signposted to Nongoma, this tarred road heads into the heart of KwaZulu for some 22 km before a turn to the left leads to the reserve.)

A detailed map is available of the roads, camps, picnic spots, viewsites and hides in the reserve. Wildlife experts are unenthusiastic about rushed day trips, but recommend instead soaking up the wilderness atmosphere by staying at least one night in a hutted or bush camp, and being primed to look for all manner of fascinating features in the environment. If, however, a day outing is all you can manage, the gates are open from sunrise to

THE LIFE OF A LAKE

The fascinating wilderness that is Lake St Lucia came about millions of years ago with a succession of dramatic changes to the landscape. The coastal terrace that holds the lake and its five rivers (Mkuze, Mzinene, Hluhluwe, Nyalazi and small Mpati) was once sea bed. The marine shoreline extended along the western edge of False Bay (as evidenced by the coral reef that caps Lister's Point). Then, sea levels changed — several times — and the rivers' drainage system was 'drowned'.

The lake or combined estuary took form, along with a distinctive border of dunes along the present coastline. These dunes were anchored by the rocky barrier at their feet and, protected thus from the erosive effects of the sea, they have been able to grow to astonishing heights.

Despite its ancient origins, Lake St Lucia is not unscathed by change. Sightings of the lake by early seamen suggest that it was deep enough to navigate, while today its average depth is a mere metre. Then, the orgy of game slaughter in the 19th century forever changed the pattern of life here, and modern translocation of animals has restored only a fraction of the wildlife. Man has interfered with the swamps that filter the fresh water draining into St Lucia, and the mouth of the Mfolozi has even been moved in an effort to avoid oversilting, with mechanical dredging attempting to keep it open.

Then there is the impact of drought and the scouring effect of a cyclone such as Demoina, adding up to extremes in the salinity of the lake and its steady sedimentation. This in turn affects the fish and bird and animal life, and sparks claims that St Lucia may be 'dying'. It could be that this coastal jewel has been irreparably damaged, and is being barely kept alive with the artifical pacemaker that is human management. Or it may be that St Lucia is a more resilient, elastic system than we thought, and is going through cycles of climatic change. Only time will tell.

sunset, and the 67 km Mosaic Auto Trail is recommended. It takes about five hours to complete, and is best enjoyed with an illustrated booklet available from the shop at Mpila Camp.

Booking for accommodation and trails through the reserve is done through the Natal Parks Board reservations office in Pietermaritzburg.

5 Eastern Shores Nature Reserve

This reserve, controlled by the Natal Parks Board, fills the strip of land between Lake St Lucia and the sea as far north as Sodwana Bay (about 13 000 ha), and is partly traversed by the gravel road to Cape Vidal. The high water table in the region requires that the road be packed with stones to prevent subsidence and, heading north beyond the Crocodile Centre, you are soon jolting along between pine plantations and grasslands teeming with reedbuck.

The forested areas are a source of ongoing

LEFT *Following a rugged trail through khaki-coloured Umfolozi Game Reserve.*

Lake fishing (generally from boats) is the constant lure at all the St Lucia resorts.

to dense forest and along hippo paths. Overnight accommodation is in the Mount Tabor base camp, a Royal Air Force observation camp during the Second World War.

The narrow dirt road to Mission Rocks provides views of Catalina Bay, with more wartime memories as this was used as a base for flying boats. At Mission Rocks, picnic sites have been laid out beside the parking area, while a few steps away green dunes collide with a tumble of rocks that becomes a fascinating marine shelf when the tide recedes. The energetic can clamber south to Perriers Rocks, or north — at low tide — to Bats Cave. This huge cavern is wall-to-wall bat, one of the few nesting colonies in South Africa of the large, migratory fruit bat.

6 Cape Vidal

Lying about 35 km from the St Lucia village, Cape Vidal, with its log cabins and camp sites nestling in the shelter of forested dunes, is a popular powerboat and surf angling spot. The sea looks bluer and the sand whiter than further south, and a reef-sheltered beach allows fairly safe bathing and excellent snorkelling. As with all the other St Lucia resorts, Cape Vidal is rich in bird life, and strolling through the dune forest is likely to bring you in sight of samango and vervet monkeys, red duiker, bushpig and bushbuck.

The St Lucia Wilderness Trail starts at Cape Vidal, and for three days a ranger leads a small group through a wilderness area where you can spot big game and magnificent bird life. Less arduous is the self-guided Mvubu Trail, which, in a few hours, takes in the freshwater Bhangazi Lake and follows hippo paths through the forest.

Camp site bookings are handled by the officer-in-charge, and trail and cabin bookings by the Parks Board in Pietermaritzburg. Firewood and petrol are obtainable, but all other supplies (including bait) must be provided, and pre-

controversy. Conservationists claim that the hectares of towering exotics reduce the fresh water available to the lake and threaten the wetlands. The timber producers, on the other hand, claim the trees are preventing dune erosion and that indigenous plants do flourish as forest undergrowth.

The height of the water table and the fact that the ground is below sea level account for the numerous freshwater pans in the reserve. It is here that waterfowl flock in profusion, that the animals come to drink and the crocodiles to breed. They are not easily viewed from the road, however, so it would be worthwhile to contact the Natal Parks Board about guided tours.

A rigorous alternative exists in the form of the self-guided Mziki Trail. This starts out from the Mission Rocks outpost (14 km from the village), and can keep hikers busy for three days, crisscrossing the reserve through a remarkable variety of habitats — from seashore and grassland

WAR ON THE LAKE

The hutted camp at Charters Creek looks out over a vast sheet of gently rippling water. Now and then the sound of an outboard stutters through the air, or a cormorant signals its flight path. Mostly it is still, but this was not always the case.

During the Second World War, air cover for shipping around the South African coast was limited, and vessels were at the mercy of prowling German U-boats. It was for this reason that the British Air Ministry decided to base 262 Squadron in Natal. From here they would undertake antisubmarine patrols and provide escorts for shipping.

The site for the base was the pocket of Lake St Lucia known now as Catalina Bay, with Charters Creek on its north-west shore and Eastern Shores Nature Reserve its eastern flank where barracks, workshops and a radar observation post were built.

For almost two years from December 1942, this wilderness wonderland was filled with the drone of aircraft, the occasional hammer of machine-gun fire

and the echo of depth charges exploding out to sea. But their presence was needed for within weeks of Flight-Lieutenant S J Wood arriving on the Eastern Shores to set up base, a German submarine attacked the auxiliary cruiser *Nova Scotia*, 50 km off St Lucia. It sank with over a thousand Italian civilian internees.

The Catalina flying boats went on regular patrols of the coast, frequently sighting and sometimes engaging the enemy. Survivors from ships sunk by the U-boats were often spotted on rafts and lifeboats, and by reporting their position, the Catalinas helped save many lives.

South African Air Force personnel took over from the British in November 1943, and the final air attack on U-boats in South African waters was in July 1944 when a submarine was hit by a Ventura aircraft. A grim reminder of those days, though, remains today. In June 1943, *Catalina H* crashed just after takeoff, killing eight of the nine crew. The wreck of the plane can still be seen near the shore of the lake.

THE TALE OF THE NILE CROCODILE

The Nile crocodile (Crocodylus niloticus).

Lake St Lucia is the only place in the world where three species with fearsome jaws share the same aquatic environment. The estuary's shallow, saline waters and mudbanks are home to crocodiles, hippopotamuses and Zambezi sharks, and they live together more or less peaceably.

Although the reserve was proclaimed mainly to protect the hippo from hunters and poachers, you would be forgiven for thinking St Lucia was largely a crocodile preserve. The lumbering and usually docile hippos are far outnumbered by their scaly, prehistoric neighbours — the Nile crocodile.

Although their numbers were decimated during the Second World War when flying-boat gunners would empty their magazines into colonies dozing on the sandbanks of the lake, the Nile crocodiles at St Lucia constitute over ninety per cent of the South African crocodile population in a natural environment. An aerial survey in 1987 counted more than a thousand, and that was just the big ones. So the Natal Parks Board leaflet titled 'How not to be eaten by a crocodile' is no joke!

Growing to an average length of 5 m, the Nile crocodile is the planet's largest living reptile. And it is as well to remember that every large crocodile has the potential to be a man-eater: a human leg or arm trailing from a fishing boat or playing in the water is nothing more to a hungry crocodile than a bite to eat. Crocodiles are able to remain underwater for up to three hours, and they will ambush large prey by lying immobile with just their eyes and snout tip showing above the water.

As feared as they are, they are also vulnerable, with only two per cent of their young hatching and maturing to adulthood. The female carries the hatchlings gently in her mouth to a river nursery — the only known instance among reptiles of maternal care for young.

The Nile crocodile is a vital cog in the balance of nature, providing an essential cleaning service with its scavenging. The Crocodile Centre in St Lucia is an excellent firsthand introduction to its role in life.

---

cautions should be taken against malaria.

The coast north of Cape Vidal is a marine reserve, and still further north — beyond Leven Point — is marine sanctuary area where vehicles are allowed access but stopping, fishing and boating are forbidden.

7 Charters Creek

On the western shore of Lake St Lucia, about in line with the halfway point between Mission Rocks and Cape Vidal, is the resort of Charters Creek. There is no direct road access from St Lucia village, but it is reached rather from the N2, about 34 km north of Mtubatuba, where a tarred road swings east through the plantations of the Nyalazi State Forest. The camp gates are 13 km from the highway, followed by another 5 km of dirt road to reach the lakeside retreat.

The small camp with its thatched rest huts and cottage stands in attractive grounds, looking out over a vast expanse of usually tranquil water. It has great family appeal, with the big attraction again being the good lake fishing. The gates are open for day visitors from sunrise to sunset, but keen salmon fishermen are known to arrive before dark, fish the night through, and depart early the next morning. All fishing is done from boats rather than the banks of the lake: crocodiles could be lurking in the shallows.

Other attractions include a daily jetboat tour around the nearby islands with their hippo colonies; walks and birdwatching; and table tennis and a swimming pool for residents. The self-guided Umkhumbe or Red Duiker Trail requires about an hour's walking, winding through coastal forest and along the lake shore. You can get a good look at the powderpuff tree, a member of the mangrove family with breathing roots and bark that can be powdered for use as fish poison. The longer Isikhova Trail (7 km) also penetrates the coastal forest, where the layers of trees shelter shy woodland creatures. A leaflet explaining the trail markers adds an extra dimension to the walk. Although hippos generally graze in the forest at night, keep an eye out for them by day as well.

Petrol and oil are sold at the camp, and visitors provide their own food, which is prepared by resident cooks. Accommodation is reserved through the Parks Board in Pietermaritzburg, and day visits and launch tours through the officer-in-charge at Charters Creek.

8 Fanies Island

Also on the water's edge, a short drive north of Charters Creek, is Fanies Island, another favourite angling haunt. With the island of the same name almost within casting distance of the shore, the self-catering resort comprises a cottage and rest huts, and camp and caravan sites.

Visitors launch their boats (which must conform to Parks Board regulations) from the lakeside camping ground, and can roam between Charters and False Bay in search of spotted grunter and salmon. Bait, petrol and outboard oil are sold at the camp office.

Picnic spots have been laid out beside the water, and the two-hour Imikhova Trail is a self-guided walk along the shoreline.

To get to Fanies Island, turn off from the Hluhluwe-Charters Creek road and drive a distance of about 13 km on gravel to the camp entrance. Tent and caravan bookings are done through the officer-in-charge on site, and hutted accommodation is booked through the reservations office located in Pietermaritzburg.

9 Hluhluwe

The N2 from Mtubatuba is almost completely straight, through a landscape beginning to sprout fever trees and spiky sisal plants. After about 50 km the road reaches the village of Hluhluwe, with a hotel, garage and handful of shops. This is a handy reference point for the couple of popular private game ranches close by.

Bona Manzi Game Park, 8 km south of Hluhluwe station, is distinguished by its novel accommodation: guests sleep in cosy, wooden, A-frame treehouses, complete with hot and cold

LEFT *From the mouth, the waters of St Lucia wander through tangled green shores.*

The shallow surf at Cape Vidal splashes ceaselessly into the countless little rock pools fragmenting this stretch of shoreline.

water! Visitors are expected to supply their own food and drinks, and are free to drive or walk along the park's game trails.

The Ubizane Game Ranch, west of the highway, promises good game viewing and guests have a host of drives and walks to choose from, including a night safari. The ranch takes a maximum of six guests who stay in a camp on stilts overlooking a fever tree forest. The Zululand Safari Lodge is located on the ranch's 1 200 ha, with the Kwa Umsasaneni Kraal and Zulu Museum (depicting a village from the 1870s).

10 Hluhluwe Game Reserve

With an entrance about 17 km from Hluhluwe, the 23 000 ha Hluhluwe Game Reserve is linked to Umfolozi Game Reserve in the south by an 8 km-wide game corridor.

Although the two reserves are so close, they are quite different in look and feel. Situated at a higher altitude (the Hilltop Camp and shop stand at 650 m), Hluhluwe is blessed with good rainfall, so its deep river valleys and grassy hillsides are greener and easier on the eye than the stark and dramatic Umfolozi landscape. Hluhluwe is also a lot cooler, even in summer, and April and May are rated among its best game-viewing months.

Hluhluwe provides habitats for more than 400 bird and 84 mammal species. Approximately 87 km of drives wind through the reserve,

RIGHT *The spreading view from the airy heights of Hluhluwe Game Reserve.*

punctuated by picnic spots and viewsites and a waterhole hide at Munywaneni. For advice on the best game viewing, talk to the ranger at the Information Centre, or arm yourself with an explanatory booklet from the Parks Board shop and take your chances with a leisurely drive along one of Hluhluwe's two planned car trails. The scenery from every elevated point gives that top-of-the-world feeling, and cameras and binoculars are essential equipment.

The hutted camp of cottages and rest huts is perched on the ridge of a hill with built-in,

panoramic views over the Hluhluwe valley. Guided walks lasting three to four hours set off from here every day, while a self-guided walking trail takes you into the nearby Mbhombe Forest. This type of semideciduous forest (growing on the south-eastern slopes of the surrounding hills) is becoming rare in South Africa. En route, look out for the white stinkwood, cabbage tree, strangler fig, and the thorny climber *Dalbergia armata*. Called *umHluhluwe* by the Zulu people, who have traditionally used the monkey rope as a muzzle to wean calves from their mothers, the plant has

given its sibilant name to the area as a whole.

Accommodation is reserved through the Natal Parks Board in Pietermaritzburg.

11 False Bay Park

From Hluhluwe village a tarred road leads after about 19 km to the gates of False Bay Park. This self-contained reserve of 2 247 ha runs along 23 km of lake shore, and with its somewhat remote location in the north-west of the St Lucia complex, it has frequently served as a breeding ground for the pinkbacked pelican.

Accommodation is limited to camp sites on the lakeside — usually filled with dedicated fishermen — and a couple of thatched wooden huts in the Dugandlovu Rustic Camp. The latter is tucked into the bush, about 8 km south of the camp entrance, and provides the bare minimum (including an outdoor bucket shower) for birdwatchers and walkers who are happy to rough it. A 'treehouse' platform provides a sweeping view over lake and pans, and there are numerous small mammals in the surrounding forest.

In addition to the Mphopomeni Trail, which offers a 7 or 10 km walk from the main camp, there is plenty of more casual walking available, with numerous picnic spots. The dry forest of False Bay is home to game such as nyala, porcupine, bushbuck, suni, spotted hyena and vervet monkey. Bird species abound, as do butterflies in the late summer. Of further interest are the remains of ancient fossil beds, which can be seen stetching a good 50 m inland from Lister's Point. These coral ridges are crusted with shells and molluscs, slowly fossilised in the thousands of years since the sea fell back from this level.

Visitors to False Bay Park should be fully equipped with supplies and fuel. Camp site bookings are handled by the office-in-charge, and other accommodation and trail booking by the Parks Board in Pietermaritzburg.

BELOW *A pinkbacked pelican* (Pelecanus rufescens) *surveys the shore at Lister's Point.*

A BED OF NEEDLES

'Weaving' a sleeping mat of needle grass.

A wiry rush that looks something like an elongated knitting needle and grows in the salty mudbanks of estuaries seems an unlikely material to use for bedding. But the dark green *iNcema* or needle grass is just that. With its stem an even thickness for a metre or more in length, and its smooth, round surface, it becomes, once cut and dried, a pliable weaving fibre which is used in the making of traditional Zulu sleeping mats.

The once-flourishing *iNcema* grass is now limited to only a few places, including St Lucia, and as a result the Natal Parks Board controls the quantity of grass that may be cut here. Visitors to St Lucia village during the winter months will see women wading from the water below the bridge, carrying dripping armfuls (seven per harvester a day) of this increasingly valuable commodity.

It is customary to give the sleeping mat (*iCansi*) as a wedding gift, and as it rolls up into a compact, light cylinder, many a traveller will carry one. It is usually about a metre wide and just under two long, made by tying the rushes together with fine, twisted fibres that appear as seams running the length of the mat. Patterns may also be created: pairs of rushes may be crossed over between the seams instead of lying side by side; long black oxtail hairs (or, these days, coloured wool) may be bound around sections of the mat to give a chequered effect; or the paler, root end of the rush may be alternated with the darker tip, giving the appearance of light and shade.

Angling

Fishing is the main reason why the St Lucia resorts came into being, and although their appeal has broadened to wilderness and nature lovers in general, the good catches in the lake, from powerboats and the shore are still the big attraction.

Regulations are strictly enforced by the Natal Parks Board, so make sure you are familiar with them. The Parks Board bait shop at the estuary mouth is open 24 hours a day, and bait can be bought from the other resorts as well (except Cape Vidal).

Lake fishing is generally done from boats (which again must conform to regulations), with Fanies Island the hot favourite. Powerboats are launched from Mapelane, St Lucia Estuary and Cape Vidal, with excellent hauls of game fish such as barracuda and marlin, and bottom fish such as rockcod and seventyfour.

Beachcombing and shelling

With the continental shelf dropping steeply along the St Lucia coastline, the wave action is often too severe for shells to survive intact. But try the beach north of Cape Vidal for cowries and, depending on the action of the Mfolozi River, the shore around the St Lucia mouth may have good driftwood.

Birdwatching

The St Lucia Complex is famous for its birds. Close on half the birds recorded in South Africa have been sighted around St Lucia, and over 360 species frequent the lake, seashore and pans, as well as the grasslands and the dense coastal forest.

Waterfowl is what St Lucia is really known for, and a launch trip may reveal species of pelican and flamingo, and the goliath heron and redwinged pratincole. The rare Woodwards' batis has been recorded at St Lucia village and near Cape Vidal. East of the road to Cape Vidal, look out for the pinkthroated longclaw and, in wet weather, the glossy ibis.

In the thick bush around Charters Creek, keep binoculars handy for the pinkthroated twinspot, and check among the reeds in summer for nesting brownthroated and yellow weavers. False Bay Park rates highly, and both the Mphopomeni and Dugandlovu trails (the latter with a viewing hide over the mudflats) are recommended. Watch for the narina trogon, purplecrested lourie, Rudd's apalis and African broadbill.

Inland, Umfolozi and Hluhluwe reserves are equally attractive prospects, with largely savannah woodland birds.

THINGS TO DO

Boat trips
Boat tours of the estuary depart daily (depending on demand) from the Natal Parks Board jetty near the mouth. Boats skim past clumps of mangroves, hippo colonies, crocodiles dozing on the banks, and fish eagles nesting high above the estuary banks. A similar tour operates from Charters Creek, with bookings taken at the respective Parks Board offices.

Bowls
Greens are available to visitors at the Mtubatuba Country Club.

Camping and caravanning
Facilities abound in the six Natal Parks Board resorts as well as St Lucia village. (Bookings for camp sites are made direct with the camp concerned, or contact the local publicity association.) It is wise to book well in advance, especially in peak season.

Diving
Cape Vidal is rated as a star-studded diving spot, with a reef close to shore teeming with underwater life. Further north (off St Lucia Marine Reserve) lie the southernmost coral reefs. Mapelane provides good rock lobster catches and the rocky ledge stretching south is a rich source of mussels (permits are necessary). Mission Rocks is another good source of rock lobsters, but it is recommended only for experienced divers.

Drives and viewsites
For a view of the Mfolozi Flats, try the turn-off to Monzi (south of the Mtubatuba-St Lucia road). A sea of sugar cane covers this former swamp plain, stretching to the line of forested

Fish type	Season	Best area	Best bait
Grunter	Sept — Feb	St Lucia mouth, Charters Creek, Fanies Island, False Bay Park	Shrimps, sardines
Kingfish	Nov — April	First Rocks, Mission Rocks, Cape Vidal	Squid
Mullet	April — June	St Lucia mouth, lake waters	Fresh bread
Salmon	April — July	St Lucia mouth, lake waters	Shrimps, sardines
Shad (elf)	June — Sept	St Lucia mouth, Cape Vidal, Mapelane	Sardines, shrimps

dunes along the coast: a vivid example of nature being temporarily tamed by man.

The drives to and through both Umfolozi and Hluhluwe reserves take in a canvas of contrasts. From thorn scrub and eroded soil, the scene changes around the next bend to plunging river valleys, euphorbias silhouetted against the sky and the wary eyes of a nyala peering through the undergrowth. Both reserves have self-guided auto trails, with maps and booklets available from camp office shops.

Golf
Local farmers have formed the Monzi Club, and visitors are welcome at their scenic 18-hole course. Monzi is a farming hamlet about 10 km inland from St Lucia village.

Museums
KWA UMSASANENI KRAAL AND MUSEUM, Ubizane Game Ranch: Reconstruction of a 19th-century village where visitors are introduced to Zulu traditions.
ST LUCIA CROCODILE CENTRE, St Lucia

Casting a hopeful line from the smooth sands at isolated Mapelane.

village: A centre for research into the Nile crocodile; also housing some illuminating natural history and ecological displays, and a chilling collection of confiscated poaching equipment.

Powerboating
Powered boats are the only sort allowed onto the lake, and must be registered with the Natal Parks Board office at the respective resorts before use. Check on minimum sizes: anything too small can be dangerous if faced suddenly by an angry hippo or on lake waters that roughen up in a squall.

All the resorts have launching facilities, and the St Lucia Ski Boat Club controls all powerboating activities at the estuary mouth. The clubhouse and slipway are close to the mouth, and are available for a small fee.

Shipwrecks
The reef off Cape Vidal got the better of the *Dorothea* during a storm in January 1898. It broke in two, with the bow sinking on the weather side of the reef, and the stern in the protected lee of the rocks. Although rumoured to have been carrying a secret load of gold and rough diamonds, salvage attempts have failed to raise any treasure. Remains of the wreck are visible to divers.

Surfing
Catching waves tends to be upstaged by fishing and diving, but some days when the south-easter is up, there are perfect waves off Mapelane, St Lucia mouth and Cape Vidal.

Swimming
There are no shark nets along this leg of coast, but visitors sometimes take their chances in the surf at Mapelane, St Lucia Resort and Cape Vidal. As for the lake itself, do not be fooled by its tranquil surface into a cooling paddle or swim: crocodiles abound, as do hippos. Stick to the pools at camps such as Sugarloaf (St Lucia Resort), Charters

Creek and Fanies Island, and in St Lucia village.

Tennis and squash
A public tennis court is available in St Lucia village (Hornbill Street), and tennis and squash courts serve visitors to Mtubatuba Country Club.

Walks
St Lucia provides plenty of scope for walkers, with each resort offering self-guided trails through a kaleidoscope of landscape, vegetation, and bird and animal habitats. Beware of hippos, even though they are seldom away from the water during daylight, and remember summer walking is strenuous.

The formal trails include: Loerie and Hippo trails (St Lucia Resort); Mziki Trail, which is self-guided and must be booked in advance (Eastern Shores Nature Reserve); Mvubu Trail (self-guided) and St Lucia Wilderness Trail, which is guided and must be booked (Cape Vidal); Umkhumbe and Isikhova trails (Charters Creek); Imikhova Trail (Fanies Island); Mphopomeni and Dukandlovu trails (False Bay Park); Wilderness and Primitive trails, which are guided and must be booked (Umfolozi Game Reserve); and guided camp trails and the Mbhombe Forest Trails (Hluhluwe Game Reserve).

INFORMATION
• Cape Vidal Officer-in-Charge, Private Bag, St Lucia Estuary 3936. Tel 03592=1104
• Charters Creek Officer-in-Charge, Private Bag 7205, Mtubatuba 3935. Tel 03352=1413
• False Bay Park Officer-in-Charge, PO Hluhluwe 3960. Tel 03562=2911
• Fanies Island Officer-in-Charge, PO Box 201, Mtubatuba 3935. Tel 03552=1431
• Mapelane Officer-in-Charge, Private Bag, St Lucia Estuary 3936. Tel 03592=20
• Natal Parks Board Headquarters (Reservations), PO Box 662, Pietermaritzburg 3200. Tel 0331=51514
• St Lucia Officer-in-Charge, Private Bag, St Lucia Estuary 3936. Tel 03592=20
• St Lucia Publicity Assocation, PO Box 106, St Lucia Estuary 3936. Tel 03592=225/143
Nearest AA Office
• Zululand Insurance Brokers, Mimosa Court, 13 Turnbull St, Empangeni 3880. Tel 0351=26921

A far, free coastline fringed by crystal blue seas

R EMOTE AND EXQUISITELY LOVELY, the final stretch of coastline up to the Mozambique border is a wilderness wonderland just waiting to be explored. A warm sea, the colour of blue ice, harbours coral reefs and tidal pools pulsing with marine treasures. Sensuous clean sands billow into majestic greened dunes; beyond them, a prehistoric floodplain stretches back to the foot of the Lebombo Mountains. Here human presence is more felt: vast plantations contrast with dust-powdered scrubland; freshwater pans and lakes are harvested by centuries-old fishing methods. Yet nowhere is nature diminished: this is a glorious aviary, a sanctuary for hippo, turtle and crocodile, a hothouse of rare palms, mangroves, ferns and orchids — all watched over closely by conservationists. This is also persistent mosquito territory, so be sure not to venture into the wilds without taking malaria precautions.

1 Mkuzi Game Reserve

From the Lower Mkuze region, just north of Hluhluwe, the N2 (which has followed the coastline fairly closely from Durban) veers off inland. Access to this remote stretch of coast is still via the N2, but now you follow little-used, fairly rough gravel roads over ever-increasing distances before reaching the sea.

The first real landmark in this region is situated inland, edging against the Ubombo Mountains. The recently enlarged Mkuzi Game Reserve (30 000 ha) is sometimes overshadowed by the more southerly Umfolozi and Hluhluwe reserves, but with its landscape of contrasts — pans flooded with water lilies, a river gorge embedded with marine fossils, dense acacia forest, red sand ridges almost 2-million years old — Mkuzi offers a scenic and distinctive treat to outdoor lovers.

Here summer temperatures and humidity soar to enervating heights, while winters are mild and dry. You can enjoy the reserve by travelling the 84 km of hard dirt roads, which include a 41 km-

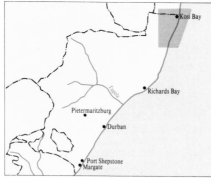

long Auto Trail. A highlight of this self-guided drive is the Nsumu Pan with its birdwatching hide. Mkuzi has recorded more than 380 bird species (including fish eagles, kingfishers, stilts and a host of ducks and waders), many of which can be seen around Nsumu. The Fig Forest Walk along the pan's southern shore winds through all that remains of a sycamore fig forest that was swept

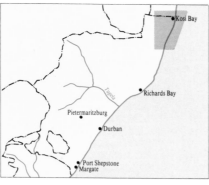

A river charts its corkscrew course through wide green lands near Lake Sibayi.

away by cyclone Demoina in 1984.

The wide variety of soil types in Mkuzi has produced over 700 plant species that in turn shelter more than seventy mammal species as well as dozens of reptile and amphibian species. Four game-viewing hides provide discreet windows on animals such as rhinoceros, giraffe, zebra, nyala, blue wildebeest, kudu, impala and even leopard coming to drink. Walks include the half-hour River View Trail, daily three-hour rambles with a game guard, and in winter the guided Nsumu Walk and three-day trails through the wilderness.

Adjoining the reserve's southern boundary is a 4 200 ha controlled hunting area, established in 1987 by the Natal Parks Board. Excess animals, which would otherwise have had to be removed from Mkuzi, stock the hunting ground, as part of the reserve's game management programme.

Accommodation at Mkuzi includes cottages, bungalows and rustic huts at eMantuma Camp, picnic sites for day visitors, and a camping and caravan site near the Emshopi entrance gate. (The entrance is about a 19 km drive through aloe-stubbled mountain pass after turning off the road between Hluhluwe and Mkuze village.)

2 Mkuze, Ghost Mountain and Ubombo

Lying in the lee of the Ubombo Mountains, and with cultivated plains stretching inland, is Mkuze village. This small but busy trading and transport centre is a useful base between Mkuzi Game Reserve and Ndumu further to the north.

The legendary Ghost Mountain, a jagged 529 m

LEFT *From the hides at Mkuzi you can watch the animals come down to drink.*

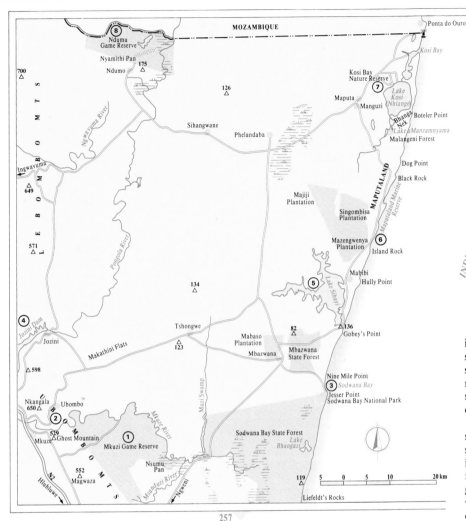

MOZAMBIQUE

Ponta do Ouro

8
Ndumu
Game Reserve
Nyamithi Pan
700 △
Ndumo △175

126 △

Kosi Bay

Kosi Bay
Nature Reserve
7
Lake
Kosi
Nhlange
Maputa
Manguzi
Boteler Point
Bhanga
Nek
Lake Manzamnyama
Malangeni Forest

Sihangwane
Phelandaba

649 △

Ingwavuma

Dog Point
Black Rock

MAPUTALAND

Majiji
Plantation

Singombisa
Plantation

571 △

Mazengwenya
Plantation
6
Island Rock

Mabibi
Hully Point

134 △

5

Maputaland Marine Reserve

INDIAN OCEAN

4
Jozini Dam
Jozini

Tshongwe
△123

Mabaso
Plantation
Mbazwana

82 △

Mbazwana
State Forest

△136
Gobey's Point

△ 598

598 △

Nkangala
650 △
Ubombo

Lake Sibaya

Nine Mile Point
3 Sodwana Bay
Jesser Point
Sodwana Bay National Park

2
Mkuze △529
Ghost Mountain

1
Mkuzi Game Reserve

Sodwana Bay State Forest

552 △
Magwaza
Nsumu
Pan

Mkuze River

Muzi Swamp

Lake
Bhangazi

119 △

5 0 5 10 20 km

N2
Hluhluwe
Mzinduzi River
Ngweti
Liefeldt's Rocks

LEBOMBO MTS

UBOMBO MTS

Ngwavuma River

Pongola River

Makathini Flats

257

peak to the south-east, towers over the Mkuze River and is said to be haunted. A taboo cave near its summit was for centuries the burial place for chiefs of a Ndwandwe family who clashed, bloodily, with Shaka. More bloodshed followed during the Anglo-Zulu War when a fierce battle took place in the river gorge at the foot of the mountain, and strange noises and lights have been reported on its slopes ever since....

A short distance north, a gravel road twists up into the Ubombos from Mkuze. Very narrow in parts, it provides stunning views over the plains before levelling out into the dusty trading post of Ubombo village. From this cloud-brushing eyrie, the road descends slowly along the eastern flank of the mountains before meeting up with the Jozini-Tshongwe-Mbazwana road.

3 Sodwana Bay

The nearest beach resort to Johannesburg is the angling and diving mecca of Sodwana Bay. To reach it, take the Sodwana Bay/Ngweni turn-off from the N2 about 10 km north of Hluhluwe. From here, the Lower Mkuze road — a hard, gravelled ride of some 60 km (to Mbazwana) — heads north-

east through landscape that is variously swamp, forest and dry thorn scrub. Game fencing parallel to the road demarcates private game ranches, some open in season. An alternative route to Mbazwana, from either Mkuze or Jozini and via Tshongwe, involves a slower drive on unrelenting gravel that is not always in good condition, and, if travelling from Mkuze, requires a dogged climb into the Ubombo heights before crossing the tail of the Muzi Swamp plain.

At Mbazwana (a forestry station with shop, petrol station and airstrip) keep your eyes skinned for the Sodwana Bay sign, directing you to a yellowish and very sandy road that deteriorates rapidly in wet weather. This undulates for about 20 km over old dunes until finally it reaches the sea.

Sodwana Bay National Park is 413 ha of beach and luxuriant dune forest that has exploded into a capacious and popular resort since the closure of Mozambican beaches to the north. With its numerous tent and caravan sites spread among 25 ha of coastal forest (new chalet accommodation

RIGHT *The dense coastal forest at Sodwana lends an air of seclusion.*

is in the planning stage), Sodwana swells into a small town of nearly 5 000 people during peak season. Powerboaters crowd in for some of the best marlin fishing in the world — and the southernmost coral reefs along Africa's eastern coast attract scuba divers all year round.

Part of Sodwana's magic is its sheltered situation. A rocky ridge called Jesser Point juts seaward from a dune headland, and although invisible at high tide, it protects the bay immediately to the north. Here, wide sands slope gently to water the colour of blue crystal. This is where most of the action takes place as hundreds of four-wheel-drive rigs muster along the shore, lines are cast, boats are launched, and swimmers

The deep blue sprawl of Lake Sibayi constitutes the largest freshwater lake in the country.

frolic in the inviting warm-water surf.

Those same four-wheel-drive vehicles — with a permit from Natal Parks Board — can drive 25 km north and south of the bay for fishing, beach walks and exploring rock pools at low tide. But because this is a reserve (the St Lucia Marine Reserve extends 11 km north of Sodwana, and the Maputaland Marine Reserve takes over from there), vehicles must ride within the high-water mark to protect the fragile dune vegetation, and

motorcycles are banned from the area.

Sodwana's landward face is equally attractive. A nearby stream gives Sodwana its name of 'little one on its own', and two small lakes gleam through a damp tangle of dune forest dotted with cycads. Once a shelter for hunters and gun-runners, this is now alive with small mammals such as red and grey duiker, reedbuck, bushpig, banded mongoose, and samango and vervet monkeys. A bird checklist includes the pied and giant kingfisher,

AN ANCIENT SEA BED TRANSFORMED INTO A WILDERNESS

Kosi Bay, just south of Mozambique, is not a bay but an 18 km chain of lakes parallel to the coast and opening to the sea as an estuarine basin. It was this estuary that was mistaken for the mouth of the Mkuze River by Royal Navy surveyors in 1823, hence one of the possible origins of the name: Mkuze misspelt as Kosi. Earlier still, Portuguese sailors knew the mouth as the 'River of the Sands of Gold' and the coastline as 'Land of Smoke' (from the camp fires).

Along with Richards Bay, Lake St Lucia and Lake Sibayi, the Kosi lakes were formed about 100-million years ago when some 7 000 km² of present-day land were under water. As the sea receded from its Lebombo Mountain shoreline and the coastal terrace tilted upwards, a vast, low-lying plain was trapped between sea and mountains, and its shallow depressions filled with water to become the unique swamp and lake wilderness of today.

Kosi Bay estuary, where fresh water meets salt, is a rich nursery for many fish species. The four interlinked lakes become progressively less saline from the mouth inland, until the southernmost lake — aManzamnyama or 'dark water', stained as it is by peat — is entirely fresh. These different salinities and the unusual temperature variations (water at the bottom of a lake is sometimes warmer than the surface) give an individual character to each lake. Rare orchids, mangroves and raffia palms luxuriate alongside cycads, spectacular swamp figs and marsh sedges, while about a third of the 250-odd bird species in the region are associated with water.

Of all the valuable wetlands on this former sea bed, Kosi Bay is the only one still unscathed by human hand. The lakes remain unsilted, the mouth is left to forge its own course, and the delicate interdependence of bush and beast, fish and fowl, is safe . . . for now.

THE TRADITION OF FISH KRAALS

An ages-old fishing method is still being used to harvest the waters of three Kosi lakes. The estuary serves as a perfect marine nursery: fish spawn in the ocean and escape into the Kosi system, where they fatten and mature, and then must return to the sea to complete their cycle. It is on this return trip, along clearcut channels, that countless generations of Thonga families have successfully set their fish kraals.

These stick fences and woven baskets are carefully placed, seeming from above rather like chains of giant fish-hooks on the lake surface. If fish swimming to the ocean miss the channel between the traps, a fish kraal fence will guide them into a funnel with a basket 'valve' at its mouth. This allows fish to enter but not to escape, unless they are very small.

Two types of basket are used, one a self-contained trap fastened each night to the funnel with wild banana fronds, and removed to the bank next morning complete with catch. This has proved vulnerable to poachers, however, so another method has developed, requiring the kraal owner to spear the live fish in their wooden enclosures.

There are between sixty and eighty fish kraals at Kosi Bay, each with several baskets. It is usually the old folk and children of a particular family who work the kraals, using the winds and tides to judge when good catches are likely.

Knysna lourie and pygmy goose.

Facilities at the camp include a supermarket, community hall, curio shop, helipad, first aid post, boat lockers and deepfreeze drawers. Petrol, bait, wood, oil and ice are sold. Bookings are made through the officer-in-charge, who will also answer your queries about trails and visits to the turtle breeding grounds north of Sodwana.

4 Jozini Dam and Maputaland

A huge dam on the Pongola (Phongolo) River provides a majestic entrance to Maputaland. The Jozini or Pongolapoort Dam lies in a dramatic setting between the Ubombo and Lebombo mountains, overlooked by Jozini village, which originally housed the dam's construction workers. Its waters teem with freshwater fish such as tilapia and tigerfish, and slipways near the wall are used by anglers to launch their powerboats. (You need a permit from the Department of Water Affairs to use the official slipways.)

Once over the dam wall, a good tarred road strikes north through the usually steamy Pongola floodplain with the equally swampy Makathini Flats to the east. As with the plains to the south, this sandy, tree-studded expanse was sea floor when waves broke against the sides of the Lebombo Mountains, 100-million years ago. The north-flowing Pongola river system now supports a rich diversity of freshwater fish, and is important to the existence of many species of waterfowl.

The Tembe-Thonga people living on the plain have adapted their subsistence to the river's resources. Fish is the staple food, and a colourful

WHEN THE ODDS AGAINST SURVIVAL TURN TURTLE

A clutch of loggerhead turtles.

The loggerhead turtle has survived almost unchanged for over 100-million years, a challenge equalled by few other species. Every year, these turtles brave incredible dangers to swim the vast seas until they reach their nesting grounds at Bhanga Nek.

In the early 1960s it was found that only a handful of females lumbered onto the Maputaland sands to lay their eggs. Of their companions, the rare leatherbacks, there were even fewer. An urgent cry went up to save these little-known creatures.

The main problem lay with predators, and man in particular. Female turtles, once their egg-laying instincts are roused, are extremely vulnerable, becoming oblivious to surroundings that are furthermore not their natural environment. It is then that the hunters strike.

Nesting is a sensitive business and begins in early summer. A female can lay up to 600 eggs a season (or 3 600 over 18 years), burying them carefully in the warm, golden sand. Incubation lasts about two months, and conditions must be just right — if the beach temperature exceeds 29,6°C in the early stages, most of the hatchlings will be male! The tiny newborns dig their way out of the nest, and set off on what for them is a marathon trek to the sea. The odds against their survival are high, with only two hatchlings in every thousand making it to adulthood.

So, when the already high odds against survival were increased by indiscriminate hunting, the time had come for strict conservation measures. The Natal Parks Board mobilised protection and research teams, and eventually succeeded in halting the killing. Today the numbers of nesting females have happily climbed (by the mid-'80s, more than a hundred female leatherbacks were recorded, and almost 400 loggerheads), and the Parks Board has now initiated another scheme to help nature along. By translocating thousands of eggs to a site south of Sodwana Bay, a second breeding beach is being established to attract future generations of turtles — and keep history alive.

6 Maputaland Marine Reserve

This reserve extends from a beacon 11 km north of Sodwana to the Mozambique border, and access to these clean, empty swathes of gleaming sand and sparkling surf is very tightly controlled. Guardian of the reserve is the Natal Parks Board, and permits for day visits (the only access is from inland) must be obtained from the KwaZulu Forestry Department at Mbazwana. (Beach permits for Mabibi are obtainable from the Natal Parks Board at Sodwana.)

From Sodwana Bay, twenty vehicles a day are allowed to drive between Nine Mile Point and Mabibi, a tantalising shore with deep tidal pools for sheltered swimming and snorkelling. Between Mabibi (Hully Point) and Kosi mouth, the beach is reserved for the turtles (and their researchers), with pedestrian access at only three points.

The forestry office at Mbazwana issues limited permits for Island Rock and Black Rock. Visitors have to travel back roads through the plantations, park off the beach, and walk onto the sand.

Permits for Bhanga Nek and Kosi mouth are issued only to residents at the Kosi Bay Nature Reserve. (Local residents may fish in the area.) Bhanga Nek, focus for the turtle monitoring programme, is a boat ride and short walk from the reserve camp site. Kosi mouth can be reached by boat (as far as the top of First Lake) and then on foot (3 km); by walking the full 12 km from the camp; or by a slow four-wheel drive along 17,4 km of spine-jarring sand track.

Five vehicles a day (seven passengers each) may drive to Kosi mouth. From the small parking and braai area, you reach the beach on foot — either around the edge of the lagoon or, if the tide is out, across its sandbanks. Surf fishing at the mouth is good, and a coral reef in the lagoon is a snorkelling delight (but there are no shark nets here and there

feature of daily life is the *fonya* or thrust fishing basket used by groups of women and boys wading through the pans, driving fish before them and finally trapping them in their conical baskets.

5 Lake Sibayi

The largest freshwater lake in South Africa is located about a 15-minute drive north of Mbazwana, and its unspoilt delights are now accessible to visitors. (Though not essential, four-wheel drive is recommended for the journey through the ordered ranks of Mbazwana State Forest and then over grassland tracks.) Falling under the jurisdiction of the KwaZulu Bureau of Natural Resources, a small wedge of the lake shore has (in conjunction with the local tribal authority) been developed into an atmospheric rustic camp.

At Baya Camp thatched, comfortable cabins nestle under splayed umdoni trees, and a wooden boardwalk links them to a communal eating lodge and sundeck. From here — as well as from the cabins — you look out over a sheet of water that barely ripples against reedbanks and powdery, white sand. The counterpoint of hippo grunt and fish eagle cry underscores the beauty and tranquillity of the area.

The lake once flowed into the ocean but is now landlocked with a narrow ridge of forested dunes separating it from the sea. Sea fish trapped in its clear, chill depths (averaging 13 m and believed to be fed by an underground source as well as

generous rains) have adapted to fresh water. The raggedly shaped lake, which was first mentioned in recorded history when shipwrecked Portuguese were killed here in 1554, covers an area of 18 km². Its myriad coves and channels are home to flamingo flocks and over 250 other bird species, and these can be enjoyed by boat (which can be hired by camp residents) or from walking trails.

RIGHT *Punting through the unruffled peace of lily-dappled Kosi Bay.*

is also a large stonefish population). Wandering more than a kilometre or two north of the mouth is courting trouble: the Mozambican border post of Ponta do Ouro is a short distance beyond.

7 Kosi Bay Nature Reserve

The northernmost bush resort on South Africa's east coast is Kosi Bay Nature Reserve, a small camp on the shores of Lake Nhlange. This is the third, and deepest, in a chain of lakes known collectively as Kosi Bay. The reserve was taken over by the KwaZulu Bureau of Natural Resources in 1984, who strictly control the estuary and beach.

The camp consists of a few tent and caravan sites, and picturesque, thatched lodges. The appeal of this secluded camp is primarily fishing, with boating on the three central lakes bringing in good catches. The pristine Kosi estuary and lake system also offers a seasonal feast for wilderness lovers. Fringing the shoreline are marsh forests, five species of mangrove, and a profusion of ferns and orchids beneath giant swamp figs and umdoni trees. The Sihadhla River, its banks covered with reeds and water lilies, hosts hippo, crocodiles and waterfowl in its shallows. The famous turtle nesting beach is a dip in the dunes away at Bhanga Nek, and just a comfortable walk away (with a guide) are the raffia palms and their palmnut vultures at Lake aManzamnyama. To the south, a cluster of Thonga-style huts on the Sihadhla River is the base camp for a four-day walking trail.

Getting to Kosi Bay is a long haul, and the easiest route is inland via Mkuze and Jozini. Once across the Jozini Dam wall, keep heading north over the Pongola floodplain on almost dead straight road. About 40 km from the dam you reach a T-junction, where you turn right towards Phelandaba and Manguzi. As you draw closer to the coast, look for the stripped clumps of lala palms being tapped for their potent wine.

A colourful colony of coral.

THROUGH CORRIDORS OF CORAL

Compared with the famous coral reefs in the world's warm oceans, the reefs along the Maputaland coast are modest in size; they are also not composed purely of coral and grow from a sandstone base quite close to the surface of the sea. This in no way detracts from their beauty, as anyone who has dived in Sodwana's unspoilt extravaganza will confirm.

Corals belong to an animal group known as coelenterates. These small polyps, related to creatures such as jellyfish and sea anemones, grow mostly in colonies, creating a dazzling array of shapes and colours. According to what function the polyps perform in the colony (such as defence or reproduction), they will assume shapes suggesting anything from mushrooms and flowers to staghorns and fans, although close-up, the coral body is simply cuplike, with a rim of waving tentacles around its single body opening.

The competition for food, light and space on a coral reef takes on aggressive proportions not immediately discernible to the observer. Rival colonies can even smother or sting each other in their fight for survival. The polyp absorbs calcium from the water to form its cup-shaped shell or limestone skeleton, and this not only provides protection when danger threatens, but is left behind when the polyp dies. Much of what you see as a coral reef is actually a limestone graveyard, with the shell of each dead polyp adding to the foundation for future coral generations and helping to give life to countless other exotically beautiful marine creatures, perhaps by sheltering or by feeding them.

Manguzi/Kwangwanase is the last stop for supplies and petrol. After 13 km on hard dirt road, you reach the reserve gate.

8 Ndumu Game Reserve

With its camp of thatched huts 6 km south of the Mozambique border, Ndumu Game Reserve is one of the more remote Natal Parks Board spots and until the road from Jozini was tarred, its outpost situation tended to discourage all but the

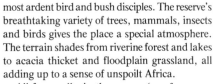

BELOW *Nyamithi Pan mirrors the natural assets of Ndumu Game Reserve.*

most ardent bird and bush disciples. The reserve's breathtaking variety of trees, mammals, insects and birds gives the place a special atmosphere. The terrain shades from riverine forest and lakes to acacia thicket and floodplain grassland, all adding up to a sense of unspoilt Africa.

All four walks in the reserve (one for game-viewing, two for birding, and an enchanting one for trees along the Pongola River) are guided, as are daily four-wheel-drive tours. These meander through some of the thickest bush on the continent and linger at freshwater pans that are home to countless birds. Almost 400 species have been recorded on Ndumu's 10000 ha — almost as many as the Kruger National Park which is nearly 200 times larger. Nyamithi Pan, its fever tree forest wreathed with early morning mist, is what wilderness memories are made of. Many of the reserve's 500 crocodiles and 300 hippo are safe here, and feeding nonchalantly among them are white pelican, black heron, hamerkop, spoonbill, blacksmith plover and common sandpiper.

A lookout tower near the entrance provides a panoramic overview of the whole reserve, and is one of the stops on the self-guided Auto Trail. This includes a sweep through grasslands south of the Usutu River where game such as giraffe, rhino, reedbuck, buffalo, zebra, kudu and nyala may be sighted. Closer to the camp, the sandy woodland with its marula, silverleaf and black monkey-thorn usually shelters skittish bushpig, the solitary grey duiker, and suni.

To reach Ndumu, turn right at the T-junction of the Jozini and Ingwavuma-Phelandaba roads, then left onto a signposted dirt road, a few kilometres on. From here, the run is about 15 km to the entrance gates, passing a small military camp and a shop selling petrol en route.

THINGS TO DO

Angling
The reserve status of this coast (St Lucia Marine Reserve stretches — for three nautical miles out to sea — from 1 km south of Cape Vidal to 11 km north of Sodwana, and Maputaland Marine Reserve continues from there to the Mozambique border) means certain restrictions apply. While no bait may be collected, fishing is permitted (except in the demarcated sanctuary areas), and only game fish may be fished from powerboats.

Beachcombing and shelling
The reserve and sanctuary status of the shore between Sodwana and Kosi Bay means that only dead shells on the beach may be collected. But some beautiful specimens — including cowries — can be picked up off almost pristine sands when the tide goes out, and there is many a vivid rock pool to admire at low tide.

Birdwatching
This chunk of coast with its tapestry of floodplain, mountain and dry thorn scrub is surely one of the most exciting birding areas in the country. Ndumu Game Reserve is rated a birding paradise but Mkuzi comes a good second, and each has several viewing hides and walks geared to this purpose. A reed (*Phragmites australis*) that grows around Ndumu pans provides one of two known South African breeding spots for the rare openbilled stork, while flocks of white pelicans, which usually breed at Lake St Lucia,

Fish type	Season	Best area	Best bait
Barracuda	Summer	Sodwana	Shad, live bait
Kingfish	Summer	Sodwana	Live bait, artificial lures
Marlin	Summer	Sodwana	Live bait, artificial lures
Shad (elf)	Winter	Shoreline around Sodwana, Kosi mouth	Sardines, shrimps, fresh fillets
Stumpnose	Winter	Shoreline around Sodwana, Kosi mouth	Sardines, shrimps, fresh fillets

frequently feed on the Pongola pans. The Kosi lakes themselves have long been described as a 'gorgeous aviary' with over 250 species sighted.

Camping and caravanning
Mkuzi, one of the few game reserves with camping facilities, can accommodate sixty people in tents and caravans, while the mammoth 600-site camp at Sodwana Bay takes up 25 ha of dune bush. (Contact the Natal Parks Board.) Kosi Bay Nature Reserve has 15 camp sites on the lake shore recommended more for tents than caravans. (Contact the KwaZulu Bureau of Natural Resources.)

Diving
The marine reserves here contain the southernmost coral reefs in the world, drawing divers from all over the country. Marine life at Two Mile Reef is intact, and its inhabitants — especially a moray eel named Monty and a potato bass called Archie — are fearless and friendly. A dive shop and school are planned for the camp, to provide tuition, equipment and boats for all

levels of scuba diver. Keep snorkel and flippers handy for any of the deeper rock pools north and south of Sodwana.

Drives and viewsites
Both Mkuzi and Ndumu game reserves have self-guided Auto Trails that, with the help of trail booklets, become leisurely conservation classes on wheels. From Mkuze, it is possible to make a round trip through the mountains that takes in Jozini Dam as well as a hair-raising, gravel road climb to Ubombo. Perched at an altitude of 610 m, this dust-shrouded hamlet has views over the plains reaching east and west.

Libraries
A tiny provincial library is located in the camp office at Ndumu Game Reserve.

Powerboating
Powerboats are to Sodwana Bay what skis are to the Alps — you can enjoy the place without them, but why bother! The boats launch from the beach at Jesser Point, and petrol and oil are available at the camp. Most of the fishing in the Kosi lakes is from

powerboats, and camp residents must bring their own craft.

Shipwrecks
Survivors from the Portuguese carrack *Sao Thomé* are thought to have come ashore in the vicinity of Lake Sibayi, following a dramatic voyage from India in 1589. The vessel, laden with riches, was disabled, adrift with its pumps clogged by pepper, when the Maputaland coast was spotted. Officers and crew together with aristocratic passengers, clergy and a few slaves set off in the only longboat, abandoning everyone else on the sinking ship. Several longboat passengers were tossed overboard to lighten the load, and of the 98 who made it to the beach, only a handful eventually survived the trip to Mozambique.

Surfing
Surfers often manage a good wave around Jesser Point and off the beach in the bay at Sodwana.

Swimming
This line of coast has no shark nets but swimmers venture into the shallow, sheltered waves at Sodwana Bay and at the mouth of Kosi Bay. The prevalence of crocodiles and hippo in the inland lakes and pans rules out even paddling.

Tennis and squash
The Mkuze Country Club welcomes guests from the Ghost Mountain Inn in the town.

Walks
Three- and four-day trails set off from Mkuzi Game Reserve and Kosi Bay Nature Reserve. These entail overnight stays in rustic huts or tents, and are led by experienced rangers. Ndumu Game Reserve offers a selection of guided game, birding and tree-spotting walks, and there are several interesting beach and bush walks in the vicinity of the camps at Sodwana Bay, Kosi Bay Nature Reserve and Lake Sibayi.

Sodwana's warm waters, crammed with powerboats, are still good for a splash.

INFORMATION
• KwaZulu Bureau of Natural Resources, Private Bag X23, Ulundi 3838. Tel 0358＝209111
• Natal Parks Board, PO Box 662, Pietermaritzburg 3200. Tel 0331＝51221
• Sodwana Bay Officer-in-Charge, Private Bag 310, Mbazwana 3974. Tel Jozini 1102
Nearest AA Office
• Zululand Insurance Brokers, Mimosa Court, 13 Turnbull Street, Empangeni. Tel 0351＝26921

PART THREE

Seaside sense

A HOLIDAY AT THE SEASIDE begins with common sense: however inviting the sea may look, it is not man's natural medium and it can be hostile, even dangerous. The best way to ensure your safety is to treat the sea with respect. Heed the advice of lifeguards and the warning signs on the beach. Make sure you know what to do should you get into difficulty in the water — how to signal for help, how to keep up your strength. Learn the basics of lifesaving and first aid, for there might be no one else to turn to in an emergency.

Remember, too, that certain laws and regulations apply specifically to the coast, such as angling and bait restrictions, protective measures for certain marine species (including shells), and laws governing 'treasure' from shipwrecks. Make a point of observing these: they are aimed at preserving the coast for everyone to enjoy, now and in the future.

RIGHT *Sharing the watercolour splendour of sunrise over a serene sea.*

Where you may go, what you may do

The seashore is there for all to enjoy — but know its laws, and protect its assets.

IN SOUTH AFRICAN LAW, ownership of the sea and the seashore rests with the State President for the benefit of the public.

This means the state has jurisdiction over the country's territorial waters (extending a distance of 12 nautical miles); over the water and land between the low-water mark (the lowest line to which the sea recedes during ordinary spring tides) and the high-water mark (the highest line reached by the sea during ordinary stormy periods); over tidal rivers and lagoons; and over internal waters (including harbours and other approaches to and exits from the country by sea).

People using the coast must be aware of the relevant laws and regulations. Some brief pointers are given here, but it is best to consult the local authorities for the latest rulings.

Trespass
While you have a common law right to be on the sea or seashore, you must take care when getting there not to breach any trespass laws. The Trespass Act of 1959 makes it an offence for anyone to be present on land or in a building without permission of the owner or occupier. In some circumstances permission is not required (e.g. in the course of your job, such as postmen), but merely gaining access to the sea is not one of these. The crime of trespass is also punishable under the Prevention of Illegal Squatting Act of 1951, which prohibits trespass and squatting without permission and also makes the refusal of illegal squatters to vacate land a criminal offence.

Defence Force restricted areas
Certain sections of the coast are set aside for South African Defence Force purposes, and your access as a member of the public is restricted.

In terms of the Defence Act of 1957, the Minister of Defence may designate any area of land for military exercises without the consent of anyone affected, and he may also determine the amount and conditions of compensation. When military exercises are taking place, the officer commanding the SADF personnel may stop all traffic by land, air or water in, or in the vicinity of, the area. The same applies to an area used for range practice or other military training.

The act also empowers the minister to prohibit or restrict access to any military premises or installations, or any land or area of water used for military or defence purposes or under military control; it also prohibits the taking of photographs or the making of sketches, plans or models of military premises or installations or land or water used for military purposes without ministerial permission. Merely being in possession of a camera or drawing materials in such an area is also prohibited, and any member of the SADF may confiscate a camera and film, which may then be declared as forfeit to the state.

Beachcombing and treasure
Articles found in and on the sea or on the seashore are often thought to belong to the finder, but this may not be so. Items lost by other people continue to belong to them. A finder may keep property he finds only if the items were abandoned by the previous owner. As it is presumed that the owner of a valuable thing does not intend to abandon it, the finder has a duty to advertise his find in the local newspaper or to hand it in at the nearest police station. If the owner cannot be traced, the finder (who must have found the item by accident and not as a result of a deliberate search) may keep half the property, the other half going to the owner of the land on which it was found. The finder is the legal owner only after thirty years.

Special rules exist in the National Monuments Act of 1976 and the Merchant Shipping Act of 1951, concerning wrecks or parts of wrecks, flotsam and jetsam. Such items cannot be appropriated but must be handed over to a salvage officer (based at most large ports) or to a customs or police official. As the finder you are entitled to claim a reward — salvage — from the owner if you helped to save the property. If you find and save a wreck at expense to yourself, you are entitled to repayment of all reasonable expenses, as well as salvage. You may not dive for treasure or any other items on old wrecks without the necessary permit from the National Monuments Council and the Department of Customs and Excise.

Off-road vehicles
A pastime growing in popularity is to take vehicles, particularly four-wheel drives, onto the beach. Besides damaging the beach and dunes, this can be a nuisance to other beachgoers and it is therefore controlled. In terms of the Seashore Act of 1935 local authorities may pass regulations either prohibiting or restricting such activities. In Natal uniform regulations prohibit the introduction of a vehicle to an area of seashore falling within the jurisdiction of a local authority; in the Cape individual local authorities have passed similar regulations, but the lack of uniformity means you should check first with the relevant authority.

Responsibilities of boating
Detailed regulations made under the Merchant Shipping Act of 1951 came into force in 1986 to govern small boats used for sport and recreation and thereby to ensure safety. As a boating enthusiast, you must familiarise yourself with these and also recognise your common law responsibility to take reasonable care while handling your boat to avoid possible injury or damage.

If you injure a swimmer or damage another boat through negligence, you will be liable for compensation and could be sued for damages. There is no legal obligation to insure a private pleasure vessel, but it is a wise precaution. Ensure that the policy covers all risks, including injury or damage to third parties.

If you fail to observe navigation rules, particularly in ports and at sea, it could lead to a collision and result also in a claim for damages. The rule for sailing vessels is that a boat with the wind on its right-hand side or quarter (starboard) has priority, and a boat with the wind on the left-hand side (port) must give way to it. When both vessels have the wind on the same side, the craft that is to windward (on the side from which the wind is blowing) must keep out of the way of the leeward vessel. Power-driven craft usually give way to sail, but if there is a risk involved (e.g. a larger vessel running aground by changing course) the sailing craft should give way.

Navigation lights must be carried at night: a red light on the port side and a green light on the starboard side. Certain larger vessels must also carry white masthead lights.

● Powerboating:

Powerboats used for waterskiing, racing or simply for pleasure are allowed on most public stretches of water, although local authorities may restrict the area of use and there may also be regulations governing horsepower, noise level and levy fees for the use of launch-ramps. You do not need a licence. When undertaking a voyage you must ensure that you have enough fuel.

● Offshore sailing:

Before you buy a yacht, make sure that mooring is available because the space at harbours (even the larger ones, where offshore yachting is concentrated) is very limited. You are under no legal obligation to have particular qualifications or experience for sailing, but harbour authorities and the port captain may apply discretionary regulations, which vary from port to port and are usually enforced through the local yacht club. Novices can be instructed in the theory of sailing and gain offshore experience through training schools based at the larger ports. There is also a system of national examinations run by the Cruising Association of South Africa which offers certificates of competence in five grades.

If you are sailing between South African ports you generally have to inform the port captain at your departure point of your destination and estimated time of arrival at the next port. If you are leaving for abroad you must comply with certain customs and immigration requirements.

Various other regulations apply to navigating, including distance and time limits depending on the category of vessel; boat design and maintenance safety measures; rules for colouring vessels for ready visibility; and restrictions regarding the number of people on board and the wearing of lifejackets in certain conditions.

Transporting a boat

When transporting a boat by car, you must ensure that the boat is secure and you must comply with the law governing the transport of boats on roof racks and trailers. You will be liable for any damage resulting from your negligence.

A roof rack on an average family car can safely carry about 50 kg, but remember that the load could affect the handling of the car, especially in windy conditions. If the boat projects more than 30 cm beyond the rear end of the vehicle, you must make the end of the boat clearly visible by fitting a red flag at least 30 cm² to the end of the projection during the day, and by fitting reflectors at night.

No load may project more than 1,8 m beyond the rear end of the vehicle (particularly applicable to dinghy masts), or more than 30 cm beyond the front of the car. No vehicle with a maximum width of more than 2,5 m may be used on a public road, and no load may project more than 1,2 m from the middle line on either side of any vehicle. These limits are large enough to accommodate most small boats, but in cases of doubt, consult you local traffic department. If you are transporting a large boat, you might have to make special arrangements with either the provincial or the municipal traffic authorities.

Trailers used for towing boats must comply with the regulations governing brakes, lighting, registration and licensing. While most boats fit onto trailers that comply with road regulations, you should always check that this is the case and that the trailer does not exceed the legal width. As far as maintenance is concerned, remember periodically to check the wheels of the trailer for wear, as regular immersion in water (particularly salt water) has a corrosive effect.

PROTECTION OF SEA BIRDS AND SEALS

Certain species and resources also enjoy protection, for example under the Sea Birds and Seals Protection Act of 1973. You may be prosecuted for setting foot on any island without a licence, for wilfully damaging the eggs of a sea bird on an island, or collecting or removing eggs or bird feathers or guano. It is also an offence, within South Africa's territorial waters, to pursue or shoot at or wilfully disturb, kill or capture any sea bird or seal without a licence.

The following species are protected:

● Any penguin (Spheniscidae), gannet (Sulidae), cormorant (Phalacrocoracidae), gull (Laridae), tern (Sternidae), pelican (Pelicanidae), albatross (Diomedeidae), petrel (Procellariidae, Thalassidromidae or Oceanitidae), dabchick (Podicipidae), ibis (Threskiornithidae), skua (Stercorariidae), wader (Charadriidae), oystercatcher (Haematopodidae), phalarope (Phalaropidae), flamingo (Phoenicoperidae) or sheathbill (Chionidae).

● Any Cape fur seal (*Arctocephalus pusillus*), Antarctic or southern elephant seal (*Mirounga leonina*), leopard seal (*Hydrurga leptonyx*), Weddel seal (*Leptonychotes weddeli*), Craeater seal (*Lobodon carcinophagus*), Ross seal (*Ommatophoca rossi*) and southern fur seal (*Arctocephalus* spp).

Marine conservation

To help conserve marine resources, remember the following rules.

Don't . . .

● remove any aquatic plants or shells from the sea or seashore, except for your own use and in quantities not exceeding 10 kg of plant and 1 kg of shells per day.

● collect a marine organism for anyone else.

● damage, uproot or collect any coral (unless it has washed ashore).

● catch or disturb any live pansy (*Echinodiscus* spp), but you can collect the pansy shells that wash ashore.

● catch or disturb any sea horse (*Hippocampus* spp) or pipefish (*Syngnathus* spp) or uproot, pick or collect any aquatic plant in the Knysna River area.

● disturb or catch any species of turtle, or remove turtle eggs.

● disturb or catch any dugong.

● catch, disturb or be in possession of any dolphin or any part or product of a dolphin, without written authority.

● disturb any whale at any time.

Angling regulations

Fishing in coastal and tidal waters is controlled in each province by the Chief Directorate of Nature and Environmental Conservation; it is important always to check locally for any new regulations.

● Cape

Licences are not required for coastal fishing for your own consumption in the Cape, and only licensed commercial and semicommercial fishermen may sell their catch.

You may not fish by sole means of gaffs, spears, clubs, flails, sticks, stones or similar instruments. Snatching — the impaling of a fish by jerking a hook in the water — is allowed only when catching octopus or squid (chokka). Crabs may not be caught from a fishing boat by means of traps. No artificial light or breathing apparatus, other than a snorkel, may be used while spearfishing.

No semicommercial, surf, speargun or sportfisherman may catch on any day more than five fish of the protected species. These include elf, galjoen, leervis, red steenbras, dageraad, seventyfour, musselcracker and bronze bream. No sport, rock, surf or speargun fisherman may on any day catch more than ten fish in total (not providing for fish listed as restricted).

A closed season applies to a few of the more popular protected species: elf, red steenbras and seventyfour (1 September to 30 November) and galjoen (15 October to 28 February). Oysters also have a short closed season (1 December to 15 January). Prescribed minimum sizes govern the catching of several species, and various limitations apply to the catching of bait and shellfish. Check with the local authorities for details.

Marine sanctuaries in the Cape Province

include those at Langebaan Lagoon, False Bay, Betty's Bay, De Hoop, Goukamma (Knysna), Knysna Lagoon, Robberg (Plettenberg Bay) and Sardinia Bay (Port Elizabeth).

● Natal

Unless you have a licence (contact the Natal Parks Board for details), the only instruments you may use for fishing are a rod and line with a gaff or landing net. All bait collection requires a licence as well, except for redbait and sea urchins where 'bag' limits apply.

Other restrictions include that no fish, other than sharks, may be caught or killed by means of poison, immobilising drugs, firearms or other explosives. Spearfishermen may not use underwater breathing apparatus (other than snorkels) and may load and carry spearguns only in the water, and then not within 25 m of anyone not spearfishing. Jigging (the use of a hook without bait), rock-stripping and digging for mud or sand prawns, except by means of an approved pump, are prohibited. Nets for bait collection may be used provided they are licensed. Artificial light may be used only in the following instances: for baiting

hooks, gaffing or the landing of fish with a net.

A daily bag limit of five fish per person (regardless of the number of licences held) applies to the following species: baardman, bronze bream, dageraad, Englishman, galjoen, garrick (leervis), grunter, knifejaw, musselcracker, perch, poenskop, red steenbras, Scotsman, seventyfour, shad (elf), slinger, soldier, spotted rockcod, white-edged rockcod and yellowbelly rockcod. This is subject to the provision that no angler may catch more than a total of ten fish per day from the species listed above.

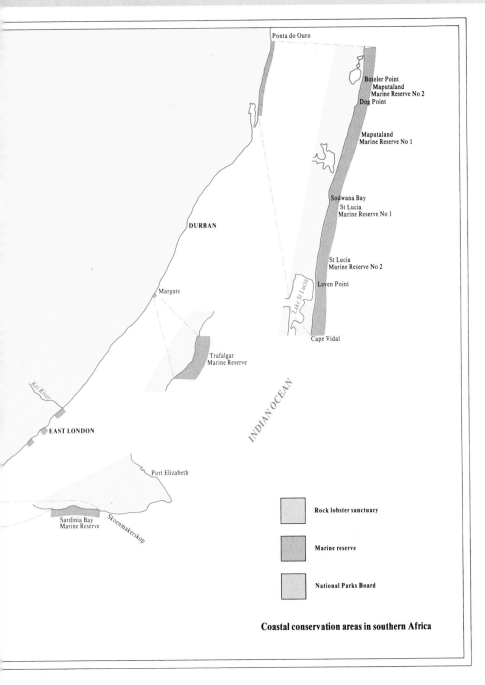

Coastal conservation areas in southern Africa

day for your own use; 16 rock lobsters may be transported at a time, provided that all the people who captured them are present. In Natal you must first obtain a licence from the Natal Fisheries Licensing Board, which limits you to a maximum catch of eight per day for your own use (general bait licence-holders are limited to three per day).

The minimum size in the Cape is a carapace length of 8,89 cm and in Natal it is 6,5 cm. Where the tail has been severed, you may not be in possession of a tail where the second segment is less than 2,38 cm (along the middle dorsal line) in the Cape, and 2,2 cm in Natal. No female rock lobster in berry (carrying eggs) or any rock lobster in a soft-shell condition (about to or having just cast its shell) may be removed from the water.

In the Cape, rock lobsters may be caught between sunrise and sunset from a boat not licensed for catching rock lobster or from the shore using a ring-net or scoop-net; they may also be caught by diving from the shore without artificial breathing apparatus (other than a snorkel). You may not dive for rock lobster from a boat, nor may you use a gaff, speargun, harpoon, flail or any sharp instrument. Rock lobsters must be landed whole and no part or offal of any rock lobster may be returned to the sea.

In Natal, rock lobsters may be caught by hand, by baited hooks or by any implement approved by the licensing board. You may not dive for rock lobster off any floating object, and when diving from the shore, you may not use scuba gear.

In the Cape rock lobsters may be sold only by registered quota holders, and businesses selling rock lobsters must be in possession of invoices from the factory that supplied them. It is illegal to buy or sell Natal rock lobsters. Businesses may buy only Cape rock lobsters, and they must be able to show proof of the factory that supplied them. No east coast rock lobster may be imported into Natal without a permit.

Among the marine sanctuaries where it is illegal to disturb or catch rock lobsters are those in the following areas: St Helena Bay, Saldanha Bay and Langebaan Lagoon, Melkbos to Hout Bay, False Bay, Betty's Bay, De Hoop (Cape); Trafalgar, Durban to Mgeni River mouth, St Lucia and Maputaland (Natal). Severe penalties are imposed for contravening these regulations.

Note that Cape perlemoen regulations impose a daily bag limit of five (twenty transported at a time), and for selling the same restrictions apply as for rock lobster. Perlemoen may be caught only between sunrise and sunset and without the aid of artificial breathing equipment (other than a snorkel), but they may only be dived from the shore and collected by hand or using an implement with a blade or flat edge not exceeding 3,8 cm. The minimum size is 11,43 cm (measured by a ring), the season is 1 November to 31 July, and sanctuary areas include False Bay, Betty's Bay, Dyer Island, De Hoop and Sardinia Bay ●

There is no closed season for oysters, but they may be taken only by licence. The only closed season with regard to coastal fishing applies to shad, which may not be caught between 1 September and 30 November.

Check with the Natal Parks Board about prescribed minimum sizes governing the catching of several species, and the limitations applying to the catching of bait and shellfish. The Parks Board also has details of specific regulations pertaining to fishing and bait collection in the Trafalgar Marine Reserve, the area north from Durban to

the Mgeni mouth, and the St Lucia and Maputaland marine reserves north to Mozambique.

Rock lobster regulations

Regulations may vary from time to time, so check first with the relevant local authorities.

The open season for catching rock lobster (also known as crayfish) is 15 November to 15 April (Cape) and 1 March to 30 October (Natal). In the Cape (where you need a permit, obtainable from magisterial offices) the maximum catch is four per

Safety on land and in the water

THE SEASIDE OFFERS endless possibilities for fun . . . rambling along the shore and fossicking among rock pools; tossing a beachball about or simply suntanning; or more active pursuits like surfing, boardsailing or boating. It is easy to be lulled by the sound of the surf and a good salty breeze into forgetting that beneath all this charm lurks danger, for the coast is an untamed element. Make sure no dark clouds blot out the pleasure of your day at the seaside by at all times treating the sea with respect, using your common sense and obeying a few basic rules.

Sunbathing

The sun is at its fiercest between 10h00 and 15h00; either avoid the beach then or take a hat, sunglasses and light, long-sleeved shirt.

Use suntan lotion, and remember that the higher the protection factor number, the stronger it is (e.g., a factor five lotion means it will take five hours to burn to the extent you would in one hour without protection). Renew your lotion regularly because sweating and swimming wash it off. Remember that salt water intensifies sunburn, and that you also burn on overcast days and when a cool wind is blowing.

Beach hiking

Before taking a gentle seaside stroll or a major coastal hike, check local conditions and tides. For rambles, always allow enough time to get back before the tide turns, while on long hikes, remember that high tide occurs about half an hour later each day, with the water level fluctuating by up to 2,5 m between high and low tide. It is easier to walk along firm, damp sand at low tide than soft, thick sand at high tide.

If you do get stranded, but are sufficiently high

ABOVE *The right equipment and supplies are essential for beach hiking.*

above the high-water mark and the weather is not too cold, it may be best to wait until the tide turns. Be wary of swimming or paddling between rocks as currents may overwhelm you; if you do decide to swim to safety, keep your shoes on for protection. Take particular care when crossing river mouths, and never cross a river in flood, or when the tide is flowing out to sea.

On a long hike take sensible clothing, suntan lotion, a basic first aid kit and sufficient water. Always inform someone of your trip.

Make sure the coastline you intend to cross is open to the public, and familiarise yourself with local regulations concerning camping, making fires and gathering seafood.

Angling

The rocky areas of the southern African coastline are particularly treacherous, making it vital never to turn your back on the sea. When rock angling, check tide tables and at the site itself spend some time watching your chosen rock for flooding. (You should be wearing nonslip shoes.) Note wave patterns and currents and work out an escape route to shore should you fall in.

When casting, always check that no one behind you will be hit. Never put your hand into a fish's mouth to remove the hook; rather use a pair of pliers. Use a barbless hook when fishing for snoek

Lifejackets, suitable for watersports (ABOVE); *sailing and fishing* (RIGHT); *canoeing, boardsailing and waterskiing* (BELOW); *and sailing* (BELOW RIGHT).

and red steenbras: their teeth have an anti-coagulant that causes profuse bleeding.

Avoid poisonous fish such as puffers (blaasops), which have a sixty per cent fatality rate. The livers of some fish (red steenbras, kabeljou, etc.) contain high concentrations of vitamin A, which can cause hair or skin loss.

Swimming

Swimming in the sea is very different from swimming in a pool, affected by factors such as waves, currents and the water temperature. Always obey warning signs or flags on a beach, and the instructions of lifesavers: they are there to protect you.

Never swim alone or in very cold water: below 10°C, your swimming ability will fail in less than 15 minutes. Never dive headfirst into a rock pool or the waves; if you must enter in a hurry, jump. Stay within your depth, swimming parallel to the beach and keeping a landmark in sight.

To avoid cramp, never swim on an empty stomach or after a meal. (If you do, float on your back, stretching the cramped muscle, then swim ashore using a different stroke.)

Study the wave patterns. 'Dumpers' (steep-faced waves that collapse from their crest) can fling you onto the sea bed, winding you. Smooth water in the midst of choppy water or surf indicates strong currents below the surface, and a fast-moving channel sweeping out to sea a rip current. (Never swim against a rip, but diagonally across it or parallel to the shore until clear of it — a rip current usually weakens considerably after a few hundred metres.)

Be particularly careful when swimming in river mouths, avoiding them altogether when the tide is running out.

Should you get into trouble, above all keep calm. Raise one arm above your head and wait for help. Conserve energy by floating on your back rather than treading water, and do not shout for help unless someone is nearby.

Swimming in the sea could mean contact with any of a number of dangerous marine creatures (such as sharks, bluebottles and stonefish). Check with local sources as to the particular dangers of an area, and take precautions. You should also be aware of basic emergency treatment.

Surfing

For surfing you need a board with an ankle strap, to make sure you and it are not parted, and a wetsuit for protection in cold water.

Before surfing in a new area, make sure there are no submerged rocks or obstacles, and find out about local currents and rips. (Should you be caught in a rip, paddle across the current until you are free.)

Obey the 'rule of the wave': the surfer closest to the break has the right of way. When paddling out, avoid the surfing area and incoming surfers, and

KEEPING AN EYE ON CHILDREN

Respect the sea and its creatures.

Children tend to become totally absorbed in what they are doing, and have little idea of what dangers the seaside might hold. While adults may be aware of the hazards of sunburn, incoming tides and swimming in too-deep water, they often do not realise that a young child can drown in just a few centimetres of seemingly safe water. They also generally do not realise the danger of children throwing sand: there have been a number of incidents of children having to be resuscitated after sand has lodged in their throats.

Never let a child out of your sight on the beach or near any exposed stretch of water; they can drown quickly and surprisingly quietly. While they may be taught to swim when very young, this ability should not be allowed to give them or their parents a false sense of security.

Children who cannot swim should use some form of buoyancy aid at the beach. Experts recommend the type that is built into a bathing suit rather than 'add-on' aids (such as water wings or a ring). The suit is worn both in and out of the water, without restricting movement, and protects the child should he or she fall into the water. The variable buoyancy of such a suit means that as the child learns to swim and gains confidence, the degree of buoyancy can gradually be reduced until finally the suit is no longer required.

in crowded conditions beware of loose boards. Always keep within restricted surfing areas where these apply.

Leave the water before you are tired and cold.

Boardsailing

Always check tides and the weather forecast, and do not sail in an offshore wind unless you are very experienced. Wear a wetsuit and a light buoyancy aid (which, unlike a lifejacket, does not restrict movement and is suitable for competent swimmers taking part in active watersports).

Keep well clear of swimmers, surfers, anglers and busy harbours, and also keep a sharp lookout for other boardsailors.

It is wise to carry a flare and a spare length of line. If you should get carried out to sea, undo the sail from the boom, roll and tie it to the mast, collapse the rig onto the sailboard, and paddle ashore. If you need help, raise one arm.

Canoeing and paddleskiing

In the sea these sports require strength and skill. You should be familiar with local conditions and at all times should wear a buoyancy aid.

Never launch your craft in an area where there are rip currents, rocks or swimmers. If caught in surf, meet the waves head on, paddling to keep the craft straight. Never get broadside to the waves, or you could capsize. When heading for shore, if you have no experience of riding waves, face into them, turning around if necessary.

Boating

Never take to the sea before you can handle your craft well, and know local conditions, including the tides and weather. Always tell someone where you are going and when you will be back, and inform them of your safe return.

Keep lifesaving gear for everyone within easy reach, and carry distress flares and plenty of water. Poor swimmers and children should wear their lifejackets all the time, and everyone should wear them in rough water or while crossing surf.

Remember the basic rules of navigation: a powerboat gives way to a rowing boat and both give way to a sailing boat. When passing or in a restricted area, keep to the right.

Should you capsize and be unable to right your craft, stay with it: the shore is invariably further away than it looks and it is also easier for rescuers to spot a boat than a head bobbing in the water.

In the case of sailing boats, if you are launching from the beach or a slipway an offshore wind will speed you on your way, but may cause difficulty in turning back. If you are not experienced in sailing into the wind, launch in an onshore wind.

Powerboats should always carry a pair of oars, and the outboard engine should be matched to the boat and properly secured to the transom. Always ensure that you have enough fuel. Never play around in a powerboat: it is easy to fall overboard and propeller injuries can be very severe.

Waterskiing

Always wear a lifejacket or buoyancy aid, even if you can swim well, and check that your skis are in good order.

Look out for submerged rocks, obstacles and swimmers, and never ski in water less than a metre deep or closer than 200 m to the shore.

Try not to fall forwards: either sit down or fall sideways. Let go the towline as you fall and retrieve your skis quickly to help you stay afloat. Signal that all is well by raising a ski or a hand. There should always be two people in the boat, one to drive and one to watch the skier ●

A portable holiday

A holiday 'home' on the edge of the beach — or anywhere else you might choose to move it — is a dream within reach of many.

TUCKED AMID NATAL'S subtropical groves, perched high on craggy cliffs above Transkei's battering surf, sheltered snugly in the forests of the Garden Route, lying in the lee of giant dunes on Namibia's desert coast . . . all along the southern African shoreline, camping and caravan sites abound, drawing outdoors enthusiasts from across the land. These are holidays everyone can enjoy: healthy and relaxing, relatively inexpensive but not without comfort, and best of all, set wherever your wanderlust takes you.

Camping checklist

The most important item for camping is, of course, the tent. When choosing your tent consider the size of your family and of your budget, the likely length of trips and the expected weather conditions in the places you want to visit.

There are many practical and attractive designs to choose from: backpackers generally opt for a lightweight hiking tent and separate fly sheet, but for longer stays, semiframe tents with dividing sections and robust full-frame tents are more popular. Whatever tent you choose, it should be made of a durable, weather-resistant fabric, be well-ventilated and easy to assemble, with strong guy ropes and tent pegs. Remember that many resorts do not allow the use of solid groundsheets, as they may damage the groundcover, so it is best to choose a tent with a separate open-weave sheet that can be lifted during the day.

When planning a camping trip, make a list of all the equipment and goods to take along, and anything else you need to do to ensure your trip is enjoyable. Essentials include:
- Good quality sleeping bags and stretchers or folding mattresses.
- A table and chairs.
- A gas or paraffin stove.
- Matches, a fire extinguisher and a good torch.
- Cooking and eating utensils, cleaning materials and refuse bags.

Food and other provisions. (Do not assume you will be near a shop; always check.) You should take enough tinned and dried goods for the whole trip; perishables may be stored for up to a week in a chilled cooler bag packed with dry ice (and opened as little as possible). For longer trips you could buy a small camping refrigerator, with a three-way power source: it is cooled at home using the 220 V electric facilities, connected to the car battery while travelling and linked to a gas cylinder on arrival at the resort.

- A first aid kit that includes insect repellant, suntan lotion, disinfectant and snakebite serum (and also malaria tablets in high-risk areas).

Before you set out, remember to leave your

home securely locked and under the watchful eye of a caring neighbour, cancel newspaper and milk deliveries, and leave your pet in safe hands.

Making camp

Organised camp sites have their own regulations which must be complied with, and while it is often possible to camp on private land, you must first obtain permission from the owner.

Wherever you set up camp, a number of factors should be taken into account (such as the availability of water and the likelihood of rain). If you are a first-time camper, practise pitching your tent at home first; a struggle with a tent at the end of a tiring journey is not a good start to a holiday.

Avoid settling too close to a river's edge or at the foot of a slope; a sudden downpour could swamp your site. Rather pitch your tent on a slight slope, where water runoff will not collect. Also make sure to position the tent so that the prevailing winds do not howl through the flap.

The camp site ground should provide a secure bed for your tent pegs. Grass is ideal, while sand compacts into a relentlessly hard sleeping surface.

A home on wheels

The caravan — representing the ideal alternative to conventional holiday accommodation — is used by thousands of South Africans who, every year, hitch up their portable homes and head for the sun-drenched coast.

As with tents, the range of caravan models to choose from is enormous and your choice should be based on the size of your family and the size of your car. If your budget is limited, consider a good second-hand caravan. Light models include the folding caravan, which has solid walls and fittings that fold down to form a compact trailer; the collapsible version with canvas walls supported by a solid roof and floor; and the tent trailer, which comprises a frame tent on a trailer base. (The latter version usually comes equipped with a separate awning that is attached to the side of the tent once parked.) Luxury touring caravans, fitted with all the mod cons, come in all shapes and sizes. Here the degree of comfort you require will determine the model: it may be fairly simple and fitted with gas or electrical outlets for appliances such as refrigerators and stoves, or it may be more sophisticated, with such features as air conditioning, a fitted hot and cold water shower, a deepfreeze and 220 V electricity for the television, hairdryer or toaster.

While small caravans are obviously easier to tow, the size of the towing vehicle is of vital importance. Generally, the gross mass of the caravan should not exceed 75 per cent of the unloaded weight (tare) of your towing vehicle. If the proportion is greater than this, your stability becomes dangerous, especially if you need to stop quickly. Also, excessive strain will be placed on your car, and you run the risk of breaking down

far from your destination.

An alternative to buying your own caravan is to hire one, either to tow on holiday yourself or already on the resort site. You should pay careful attention to the conditions of hire — they often absolve the owner of all responsibility and place the burden on you. Check that the caravan is in good order and report any defects to the owner (including superficial ones such as scratches on the bodywork, which will not detract from your holiday but which you do not want to be held responsible for). For your own protection, also insist on an inventory of the contents of the caravan. (Note that caravans must be covered by third party insurance.)

Caravanning in safety

When you buy or hire a caravan, it is best to take it for a test run with the towing vehicle to make sure you can handle it on the open road, and can control its vagaries in traffic and when reversing (you will find you have to turn the steering wheel in the 'wrong' direction). The caravan should be stable and stability is affected by numerous factors such as weight distribution of the contents of the caravan, tyre pressures, travelling speed and — most common of all — weather conditions.

Before setting off on your journey, go through a checklist:

● Check roadworthiness: all caravanners are regarded as responsible road users.

● Set the headlights of the towing vehicle lower than usual, as the caravan tends to pull down the back of the vehicle.

● Fit extendable wing mirrors to facilitate overtaking and give you a clear view to the left and right rear.

● Ensure that the tyres are pumped according to the manufacturer's specifications. The pressure in the rear tyres of the towing vehicle will have to be adjusted to cope with the extra weight.

● Tighten all wheel nuts and check the tyre tread.

● Check the towing bracket. The caravan should be safely coupled and the safety chain connected. (Equaliser bars help to cope with the extra load and stability.)

● Check that all appliances inside the caravan are switched off, that the windows are closed, the jacks and jockey wheel raised and clamped, and the brakes released.

● Make sure that you are carrying two warning triangles to be placed to the front and rear of the caravan should you break down. (Remember that no vehicle may stop within a metre of a public road unless in a parking area or lay-by.)

Once you set off on your journey, drive courteously and with care — for your own sake and that of others — and remember that it is illegal (and extremely dangerous) to carry any passengers in the caravan ●

BELOW *Taste the freedom of the coast by hiking.*

THE CARING CAMPER

An attractive spot to camp will remain so as long as you show appreciation for your natural surroundings and for those who share it with you.

Beat the bother of litter by placing all refuse in plastic bags and throwing them either in bins provided at the site, or taking the bags home with you for disposal. Never burn rubbish without the permission of the authorities, and bury only biodegradable refuse. If no sanitary facilities exist, latrines should be dug at some distance from the camp site and waste buried as deep as possible.

Noise is an equally offensive form of pollution: keep the volume of radios, tape recorders and portable televisions down, because other people might not want to share your entertainment.

Campfires are an essential part of enjoying life outdoors. Do not denude the indigenous vegetation to make your fire: take along your own firewood and use only fallen twigs as kindling. Choose a sheltered, secluded spot where there is no risk of damaging the surrounding vegetation or inconveniencing your fellow campers. Keep a bottle of water, a bucket of sand or a fire extinguisher at hand to douse any shooting sparks, and be sure that there are no gas cylinders or paraffin containers near the flames.

Canoeing, sailing and powerboating

'MESSING' ABOUT IN BOATS is the dream holiday ingredient for hosts of South Africans, whether drifting slowly down a sun-dappled river, or roaring across a sheet of water in a thrilling explosion of speed and sound.

Before you take to the water, in whatever vessel, you must be acquainted with basic safety precautions. Firstly, at most water resorts certain areas are set aside for different types of recreation; you should never overstep the limits as someone — and it might be you — could get hurt. Then, find out about weather conditions (particularly at sea), and never set out unless you are confident of your ability to handle them. An important precaution is always to tell someone on shore where you are going and when you expect to be back. Make sure you know what safety equipment you should carry at all times: from lifejackets, spare paddles, hand bailers, tow ropes and tool kits, to distress flares and suitable anchors.

The best way to learn about your responsibilities as a boater is to join a club: local expertise is invaluable, and besides, it can be fun to share your sport with fellow enthusiasts!

Canoeing and rafting
Paddling along southern Africa's watercourses is rapidly gaining in popularity: this is a relatively cheap sport, it is quiet and clean, and it can be as leisurely or energetic as you choose. In calm

Harnessing the power of the wind with spinnaker set on a fleet yacht.

conditions, two-seater, flat-bottomed canoes are ideal for lagoon and river trips, with either one or both occupants paddling. For the more

adventurous, there is a range of streamlined single-seaters designed for speed and fairly rough conditions, ideal for the more experienced or

Canoeing is growing in popularity, both on a competitive and a recreational basis.

KNOTS

Every boat owner worth his or her salt should know a few basic knots. A good knot is one that can be tied and released rapidly, and will stay firm whether the rope is wet or dry, slack or taut. Remember always to make allowance for the slipperiness of modern synthetic ropes by leaving a longer free end and encouraging slip by pulling hard until the knot jams. If correctly tied, it will still be easy to release, and a correctly tied knot may make the difference between safety and disaster.

Reef knot: Commonly used for joining two ropes of equal diameter.

Figure of eight: Useful for creating a knob or stop at the end of a rope, to prevent it slipping through eyes, or through your fingers.

Bowline: A nonslip loop, usually used at the end of a line, for dropping over bollards, or as a stirrup.

Sheepshank: Used for temporarily shortening a rope without cutting it. (If a synthetic rope slips, it can be secured by passing the free ends through the protruding loops.)

Round-turn and two half-hitches: Used for securing a rope to small fixtures such as jetty rings and eyes.

Clove hitch: The original cowboy hitching-post knot, for tying up to a bollard or mooring post.

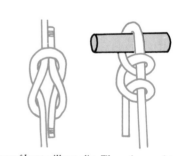

The reef knot will not slip. The safe round-turn.

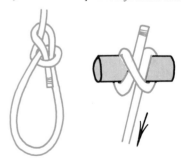

The nonslip bowline.   *The simple clove hitch.*

serious race competitors. Whatever the level of your expertise, you should be quite a strong swimmer, and you should always wear a buoyancy aid, which does not impede movement but will keep you afloat if you take a ducking.

Canoe trails along the several navigable rivers present a novel way of seeing the countryside. The best way to do this is through recognised canoeing organisations, as they will take care of details like permission from landowners, and transport and equipment, as well as providing the necessary know-how to ensure your safety. If you are an experienced canoeist and have a suitably light but spacious canoe, you can plan your own trip using surveys maps (the 1:50 000 scale is best). You should never, however, set off on your own but always travel in a party. Remember, too, that canoeing is seasonal because of different rainfall patterns, so check first about the water level of your chosen river.

Rafting is more limited than canoeing, because of the difficulty in manoeuvrability, and it is best suited to still waters, such as dams or lagoons. Rafts can carry an elementary mast and sail, or — if the water is shallow enough — they can be poled. Apart from the usual safety equipment, they should carry an anchor as its judicious use is the most effective way of avoiding collisions. In choppy water, swimmers should approach rafts with caution as they can slap down unexpectedly into troughs, causing injury.

Dinghy and offshore sailing
The range of sailing craft available is enormous, and what you choose will depend very much on what kind of sailing you are interested in, and the limitations of your budget. Offshore sailing usually means you must belong to a recognised yacht club, and comply with harbour regulations. While for inland dinghy sailing (i.e., generally a craft under 6 m with a raiseable centreboard rather than a fixed keel) you can go it alone, turning it into a sociable affair by joining a club could mean much more fun, as well as the advantages of club facilities, such as a rescue launch.

Clubs generally welcome visitors and prospective members, and a good way to determine what class of dinghy would best suit your requirements is to chat to owners and, if possible, be taken out on the water in the various types. At the outset you must be clear as to whether you intend sailing alone, or with a crew, although there are some two-man dinghies that can be sailed singlehandedly.

If you are buying a dinghy primarily to race, it is important to buy a recognised class (there are more than thirty, from Optimist up to Olympic classes). Some clubs cater for almost all classes, while others tend to concentrate on just a few. Clubs usually hold races over weekends, and class regattas are also held at provincial and national level, usually taking place during the mid-year

or end-of-year holiday seasons.

Offshore sailing vessels range from small overnight trailer-sailers, which you could use for short weekend trips without feeling too cramped, to the large, spacious craft that could be a floating home for as long as you choose to sail the wide seas. Motorsailers, with their wheelhouse and powerful engines, are becoming increasingly popular as they offer shelter for the crew and a virtually guaranteed means of getting back to base, even in rough conditions.

Besides the obvious financial restrictions dictating your choice, it is again important to decide whether you intend racing or cruising: the no-frills approach of the modern racing yacht would certainly not fit the requirements of a family. Most yachts in South Africa belong to the cruising category, in the 10 to 15 m range, with many designed and built in the country to meet the often demanding local conditions. (Projects are underway to develop more cruising harbours to meet increasing demand; as it is, there are already several small craft harbours and marinas providing mooring and launching facilities.)

While yacht ownership may be the preserve of relatively few, experienced sailors stand a good chance of being invited to crew, either for regattas or for the more gruelling offshore races, for instance, the Agulhas Race, or the prestigious Mauritius to Durban race, held every two years. Obviously, it is vital for any aspirant sailor to be well versed in the 'rules of the road' governing navigation, and again, the best way to learn what is expected of you is to join a club or take one of the many courses offered by private sailing schools. To meet international standards, the Cruising Association of South Africa officiates in the

examination of candidates, from 'crew hand' up to 'yacht master'.

Powerboating
As with other forms of boating, the scope here is enormous, from 'putting' motors clamped to the stern of rowing boats, through inflatables with outboard engines of varying ferocity, to luxuriously appointed cabin cruisers. You might want a powerboat for angling, for towing waterskiers, or for high-speed racing, and broadly speaking, the principal difference would be in the hulls: planing (for skimming the water surface at speed) and displacement (where the hull pushes through the water, whatever the speed).

In general, small powerboats or little runabouts should never put out to sea, having an open cockpit and, usually, only one motor. (Should the motor fail, the lighter bows would swing with the wind, presenting the stern to the seas — especially dangerous with crew members working on the motor, adding still more weight to the stern and lowering the transom so that waves might easily break over it and leave the boat awash.) You should always carry oars or paddles for use in the event of engine failure.

Of particular importance with powerboats is that passengers should never be carried on the foredeck, where even a moderate bump could dislodge them into the water and expose them to churning propellers. For the same reason the greatest caution should be used in the vicinity of swimmers or canoeists. If it is necessary to pass among people — when coming to the bank, for instance — the motor should be cut before reaching them, and the boat propelled slowly and carefully by paddling ●

Powerboating has an enormous following, particularly among anglers.

Riding the waves

Wavejumping stretches the ability of the boardsailor to the limits but it takes a good deal of practice and determination to master.

THERE IS NOTHING to beat the quality and variety of sporting waves off the southern African shoreline . . . or so the enthusiasts boast. The dynamic combination of winds and currents creates waves that, for the surfer and boardsailor, offer everything from the gentleness of the nursery to the heroic tumult of the kamikaze. In fact, almost every wave can be exploited to some extent.

Quite apart from the mental exhilaration of surfing and boardsailing, both sports are excellent for physical fitness. Although the skilled surfer, even when moving fast, appears to be standing more or less motionless on the board, he is using a lot of muscle power to achieve that. He generally spends only about twenty per cent of his time actually riding the wave, and the rest paddling out to catch the wave. The boardsailor enjoys a balanced and sustained level of exercise, one that works the spine and back muscles healthily, while also finding employment for arms and legs.

Riding the waves is among the cleanest and most natural of sports, leaving in its wake only memories of time well spent.

Surfing

The best conditions for surfing occur where large, smooth swells in deep water peak into steep breakers as they meet shelflike reefs or sand bars between 1 000 and 100 m offshore. A good surfing wave should have a speed of between 25 and 32 km/h, it should have 'muscle' (strength), weight and height (at least 3 m), and perhaps most important, it should be potent enough to be able to dump the surfer . . . to give that thrilling edge to an already exciting sport.

At its most basic level, the sport consists of the surfer swimming or paddling beyond the breaking waves to the point where the large rollers peak. As the wave of his choice approaches, he paddles his board shorewards to pick up enough speed to drop down the face of the wave. Once he has caught the wave, he stands on his board and rides it to shore, usually diagonally to get the most speed and distance out of the ride.

However simple it may sound, surfing — feeling the very pulse of the sea beneath you — has a magic all of its own. Part of its mystique lies in the sheer unpredictability of the right conditions: a magnificent break today may be gone tomorrow, because of variations in weather, tide and topography. But the more elusive the wave, the more magnetic the attraction. The legendary St Francis Bay wave known as Bruce's may work on as few as 25 winter days a year, but when it does,

barrelling 4 m-high waves allow one of the longest rides possible. Perhaps as consolation for those who miss this wave, nearby Jeffreys Bay produces the far more consistent Super Tubes, a breathtaking ride inside a vortex of clear water.

Right around the country there are spots that draw surfers daily to take up the challenge of the waves: tiny Elands Bay on the lonely west coast; Cape Peninsula beaches such as the seemingly endless Noordhoek and the beach next to Muizenberg, popularly known as Surfers' Corner; Victoria Bay east of George where perfect waves funnel through the narrow inlet; East London's Nahoon, with a fine reef wave; and the glorious beaches in and around Durban, which have spawned so many of the country's champion surfers.

Several of these beaches have been the venue of national and international surfing contests, where riders are judged on their takeoff and turns, the length of their ride and the difficulty of the wave they select. Amateur surfing in South Africa is administered by the South African Surfriders Association through seven affiliated provincial organisations, and the national association in turn is affiliated to the International Surfriders Association.

ABOVE *Riding the surging waves at Camps Bay, Cape Town.* TOP *Calm conditions at Struisbaai.*

Boardsailing

Unlike surfing, which originated hundreds of years ago when the kings of Hawaii took to the waves on massive plank boards, boardsailing is a very new sport. It had its beginnings in the mid-1960s, and the basic board design was registered only in 1969. After a fairly slow start in South Africa, it blossomed into one of the country's most popular watersports, echoing the world trend that saw boardsailing included as an Olympic sport in 1984.

One of the beauties of boardsailing is that almost any stretch of water is suitable, in light or strong winds (depending on the level of your experience and ability). It is also a highly mobile sport, with boards easily transportable by car, and anyone — man, woman or child — can take part.

On the sea, however, special precautions should be taken. Offshore winds (which frequently occur in the late afternoon, as the land cools off faster and a stream of air is drawn towards the sea) can be very dangerous and should be left to the real experts: people have been blown out to sea from these shores, and never seen again. Beginners should also not put to sea in any wind over force 3 (when the wind speed exceeds 10 knots, and the surface shows white horses).

Basic common sense should also dictate what safety measures to take. Before launching at a new spot, ask locals about currents, reefs and rescue facilities. Wear a buoyancy aid and carry flares, and make sure someone on shore is watching you, so that if difficulties arise, the alarm can be given promptly. If you should be blown out to sea, always stay with the board: it will keep you afloat; with the mast down the sail will act as a sea anchor to reduce drift; and you will also be easier to spot.

Although the tradition of seamanship is that power gives way to sail, this does not always apply in a practical way to boardsailing. If a sailboard is on a converging course with a yacht under power, it is much simpler for the boardsailor to take evasive action rather than for the yacht to have to change course. Another rule is that pleasure craft, including sailboards, give way to commercial and naval vessels, like trawlers and strikecraft. Courtesy, rather than any actual rule, generally extends the right of way to people who are taking part in organised competitions.

The equipment

The old Hawaiians surfed on mahogany boards that had no directional stability and weighed something like 50 kg, so a wipeout had very real potential for doing serious damage. Today a surfboard weighs about 3,6 kg and consists of a core of rigid plastic foam encased in a thin shell, usually made of either polyethylene or GRP (glass-fibre reinforced plastic). The polyethylene type of board, although easier to repair, is also more sensitive to damage: it may suffer minor distortion if it is overexposed to heat (by being left on the sand

for long periods under a glaring sun, for instance).

Most standard sailboards, which closely resemble the surfboard in shape, have a mass of around 8 to 10 kg and will support people of normal weight, up to about 85 kg. 'Sinkers' or fun boards are extremely light, short and thin, and some are so lacking in buoyancy that they can be used only in a force 4 or stronger wind.

The problem of tail slip in surfboards was solved by the addition of a fixed, rudderlike projection — the skeg — near the stern, and this was translated to the sailboard. This little underwater fin, sometimes fitted in pairs, gives the board the ability to make tight turns at speed. In addition to the skeg, the sailboard has a small keel, or daggerboard, fitted in a slot (called the case or trunk) just astern of the mast step. The function of the daggerboard is to prevent the board being blown sideways, and its size and proximity to the skeg determine the board's directional characteristics. In general, placing the skeg closer to the daggerboard gives a high degree of manoeuvrability but reduces directional stability.

Care should be taken to avoid damage to skeg or daggerboard, which can be caused by running ashore at speed or by resting the board on them. Most skegs are fixed, while the daggerboard can

be raised or lowered at will, sometimes by foot-operated levers that will draw it up fully or determine the length that protrudes. A dagger-board that pivots can save damage to the housing, as it automatically swings up and aft on being struck from the front.

The sail is attached to the mast (usually of GRP) by a sleeve through which the mast is threaded, and passes between the arms of a wishbone boom. There are three basic sizes, ranging down from the standard, to the all-weather sail and the storm sail. (The last is for use not only in strong winds, but is also suitable for children and beginners.)

Most masts are attached to the board by a flexible, solid rubber joint that allows the mast to fall or be moved in any direction. It is important to keep joint and socket free of sand, as this may prevent proper locking into place, and the grit will cause a rapid rate of wear. Some masts are designed to 'pop out' of the socket when under a certain amount of pressure, primarily to prevent injury (as when a leg is trapped between board and mast). Boards may be fitted with a double step, giving a choice of where to position the mast, the unused socket being used to attach the safety cord that prevents board and mast from parting company completely ●

Hints on hooking your catch

Rock angling has become one of the most popular — and rewarding — outdoor pursuits.

THOUSANDS OF PEOPLE, lured by the thrill of playing and landing fighting fish, stream to southern Africa's shoreline with rods and tackle every year — participants in what has become one of the country's largest outdoor sports. Rock and surf angling enjoys a greater following than deep-sea angling, because of easier accessibility.

The role of luck in fishing cannot be discounted, but by learning as much as you can about the sport, you will certainly increase your chances. If you are new to angling, and need advice about what equipment is suitable, consult an angling friend or a professional at your nearest sports shop. Remember that angling conditions along the coastline vary considerably; so do the sizes and types of fish, and the restrictions governing catches and bait. Study the area where you intend to fish; join an angling club and find out about local conditions as well as favourite spots and baits; and check regulations with the Sea Fisheries Institute.

Tackle

There are three basic divisions of tackle: light, medium and heavy, each of which is used for specific fish or particular areas or conditions.

● Light tackle

This is used for angling in gullies for bank fish, and also in estuaries, lagoons and coastal rivers. Choose a soft, flexible glass fibre rod with a whippy shaft about 2,5 m long. Look for a rod with rust-resistant runners, a tungsten steel tip and a chrome steel winch fitting on which the reel can be clamped securely. Make sure your rod is fitted with felt, cork or rubber hand grips above and below the winch fitting.

For a reel, use either a fixed-spool ('coffee grinder') reel or a small, open-spool reel. Coffee grinders have become increasingly popular in recent years, not only for gully fishing, but also for spinning with ultralight spoons and lures.

For your line, choose a lightweight nylon, with a breaking strain of about 5 kg (ideal for using drift bait in gullies close to rocks). The line should be soft and thin, and more or less invisible to fish. You do not need a great deal of nylon, unless you are angling from rocks high above the water.

Use a round, ball-type sinker weighing 5 or 10 g, a small swivel (No 8) and a 1/0 hook. If you intend fishing for gully fish such as galjoen and hottentot, use a thin, lightweight hook.

Once you have passed the nylon through the runners on your rod, thread it through the sinker and tie it to one end of the swivel. To the open end of the swivel attach a thin nylon trace (about 60 cm long) with a hook at the end of it.

● Medium tackle

This is the tackle the average angler will need for rock and surf angling, where he is after fish weighing anything from 5 kg upwards. A wide range of rods of various makes is available, but look for one that has a quick taper, a light tip and is between 3,5 and 4 m long.

Do not try to save money by buying an inferior quality rod. It should be strong, durable and made up of about seventy per cent glass fibre and thirty per cent resin. As with light rods, inspect the guides and ensure that they are rust-resistant. Guides with an inner ring of polished aluminium oxide ceramic are recommended.

The most popular reels for rock and surf angling are the conventional geared reels with glass fibre spools. Because of the wide variety available, seek professional advice in matching your reel to your rod.

When choosing line look for thin, durable nylon with a breaking strain of between 8 and 14 kg. The thinner the line, the easier it is to cast and reel in.

The sinkers you use will change according to the conditions. If you are fishing from the shore and the sea bed is sandy, use a pyramid sinker; if the sea bed is rocky, use a pear-shaped sinker. From a boat, use sliding barrel or ball sinkers. Depending on the strength of the wind and the size of your bait, your sinker should weigh between 75 and 125 g.

Before you buy hooks, it is important to

distinguish between long- and short-shank hooks. Short-shank hooks are used mainly to catch the smaller bottom feeders (dassie, hottentot, galjoen, etc.), when a little piece of bait is being used. The short shank enables shy feeders to swallow the hook more easily and to be hooked securely in the gullet or stomach. The long-shank hook is used for sharp-toothed fish such as elf (shad) or snoek, or the bigger species such as kabeljou (kob), musselcracker, dageraad and red steenbras. The long shanks are more suitable for baiting with live bait, or strips of fishbait or chokka.

For rock and surf angling take a selection of hooks with you, ranging from the 1/0 to the 6/0 and 8/0 hooks. Keep two or three medium-sized spinners in your tackle box in case there are elf or yellowtail about. For swivels use the well-known barrel or 'two-way' swivel. (A No 2 swivel should suit your purposes.) Other accessories are a roll of elastic cotton for tying on the bait, a few cork floats (used to keep your bait off the bottom or near to the surface of the water), and some wire traces to prevent large fish severing the line.

When you come to tying the traces to your sinker and swivel, make sure that the sinker trace has a lower breaking strain than the line on your reel so that if your sinker gets snagged, you will not lose a great deal of line.

- Heavy tackle

This division of tackle applies exclusively to shark fishing, a pastime that is becoming more and more popular in southern Africa's shark-infested waters. Hooking and playing a large shark can impose enormous strain on your equipment, so go for quality, strength and durability when choosing heavy tackle.

Buy a sturdy rod between 3,5 and 4 m long without a quick taper; match it with a strong, geared reel that can take at least 200 m of nylon. The nylon should have a breaking strain of between 20 and 27 kg.

Use a wire trace about a metre long, with a breaking strain of about 40 kg. Attach the trace at one end to an 8/0 to 12/0 steel hook, and to a tough swivel at the other end. A sinker will not be necessary if your bait is heavy, but if used, attach it to the hook trace's swivel with a short line.

Sharks are notorious for breaking up fishing line, either by becoming entangled in it or by severing it with their fins or tails. To avoid this, attach a 5 m-long nylon leader line of 40 to 60 kg breaking strain to the open end of your swivel and join it to the thinner line on your reel.

The right bait

The best tackle in the world will not help you if you use the wrong bait. The southern African coastline is a storehouse of dozens of types of bait, with those listed here among the most successful.

- Chokka

Caught by trawler but available at most bait or fish shops, chokka (squid) is an excellent bait when fresh. This eight-armed creature with two sucker-bearing tentacles should be cut open, and its soft backbone and entrails removed. Skin the body and slice into long, thin strips, which you can then use singly or together hanging like tassels from the hook. Some anglers like to use the head, while others use strips in combination with fishbait to make a 'mixed grill'.

- Fishbait

The flesh of most species of young fish can serve as bait, but the most commonly used are pilchards (sardines), mackerel, mullet (harder), maasbanker and steentjie. If you are using mackerel or elf, cut fillets off the bone and, using an elastic cotton, tie them to the hook in long strips. For the larger predators, use live bait if you can, inserting the hook through the back of the fish (just below the dorsal fin).

- Octopus

Fresh octopus (sea cat) is a highly prized bait and, with luck, can be found in rocky pools at low tide or alternatively at fishing harbours. Use the tentacles (unskinned) as bait, slicing them into strips to be threaded on the hook. You can also use the head, cleaned and cut into strips, or the whole octopus, if small.

- Prawns and shrimps

There are four main varieties: mud prawns (also known as cracker prawns or shrimps), sand prawns, swimming prawns and shrimps. Mud and sand prawns are collected by means of a prawn pump, which sucks or blows them out of their holes in mud and sandbanks flanking lagoons, rivers and estuaries. Swimming prawns and shrimps are caught with a hoop net.

Bait prawns and shrimps by inserting the hook into the rear end of the creature and bringing the point through the body and out of its mouth. If small, use two or three on one hook.

- Redbait

Popular in pursuit of bottom feeders such as galjoen and hottentot, redbait is found all along the rocky coastal regions, but it is usually difficult for all but skin divers to reach (except at a low spring tide).

Its outer body is a hard, cellulose 'pod' crowned by two nipple-shaped spouts. To get to the soft, orange flesh within the pods, take a strong, sharp knife and cut vertically downwards between the two spouts. Remove the flesh with your index finger, trying not to damage the nipples — they give the bait a firm hold on the hook. Most rock fish, excluding galjoen, prefer redbait fresh.

- White mussels

These are available at some bait and angling shops along the coastline, but they are scarce, owing to overexploitation. White mussels live beneath the sand in greatest abundance near the low-water mark or beyond it, and can be found by shuffling

Casting a line from Natal's sandy shores.

your feet into the sand and 'feeling' for them.

Bait white mussels fresh from the shell, threading the hook first through the two tubes, or siphons, and then through the fleshy tongue, and tie to the hook with elastic cotton.

- Worms

The worms most commonly used for bait include bloodworms, musselworms, wonderworms, moonlight worms and coral worms, which are all excellent for catching bottom feeders in the sea, and for fishing in rivers, lagoons and estuaries.

Bloodworms live under the sand on the beach, along river banks and around estuaries, and can be extracted with a prawn pump. Musselworms live among beds of black mussels and you can find them by gently prising a batch of mussels upwards with a strong knife. Wonderworms live under rocks and stones, and in sandy pools near the low-water mark; they can be found by overturning the stones. Look for moonlight worms at low tide in the sand or mud of riverbanks, or on sandy stretches of coastline.

With the exception of bloodworms, which may be cut into smaller pieces for baiting, you can thread two or three worms onto your hook ●

RIGHT *A deep-sea angler hauls in a gaffed long-fin tuna, a popular south coast catch.*

Reaping the harvest of the shores

YOUR ENJOYMENT of the beautiful southern African coastline can be enhanced by the treasure chest of mouthwatering culinary delights, there for the taking if you know where to look and what to do with your find. Use this guideline as an introduction to the sea's bounty, but remember that to conserve it for all to enjoy, now and in the future, it is important to respect the various restrictions that apply to marine life. (These may change from time to time, according to prevailing conditions, so always check with the relevant local authorities.)

Alikreukel

LOCATION These giant sea snails are found in rocky pools, gullies, coves and bays along the eastern seaboard.

COLLECTION Pluck from the rocks with gloved hand as protection against the spiny sea urchins that usually live nearby.

RESTRICTIONS Ten per person per day. Shells must be a minimum of 6,35 cm across.

PREPARATION Boil for twenty minutes, remove the operculum or 'trap door', and cut out the stomach. Then mince, and serve with lemon, butter, black pepper and nutmeg.

Black mussel

LOCATION Beds are found particularly on rocks between the high-water and low-water marks.

COLLECTION Pluck from the rocks with a gloved hand (for protection).

RESTRICTIONS If using a knife, the blade width may not exceed 3,8 cm. The bag limit is 25 per person per day in the Cape.

PREPARATION Scrape the shells clean, and leave in cold water for about 45 minutes (to eject particles of sand). Place in a little water in a large pan; cover and shake for six to eight minutes, until the shells open. Discard unopened mussels. Serve with bread, lemon juice and pepper.

Crab

LOCATION Found all along the coast in a variety of shapes and sizes, with the most sought-after being the tasty, giant estuarine crabs that live in mud holes along rivers and estuaries.

COLLECTION Use baited fishing line, or dive for crabs in rocky pools or on the sea bed. Use a long gaff to remove estuarine crabs (illegal in Natal).

RESTRICTIONS The bag limit in the Cape is 15 sea crabs per person per day, but no crabs in berry may be taken and traps may not be used. Knysna crabs are restricted to two per person per day, with a minimum shell size of 11,43 cm across. In Natal a licence is required; the bag limit on swimming crabs is six per person per day with a minimum size of 11,5 cm across; and the bag limit on other Natal crabs is ten per person per day.

PREPARATION Immerse in water for a few hours, then plunge into boiling salted or sea water. Bring back to the boil and simmer for about ten minutes, then drain and cool. Twist off the legs and claws and remove the flesh. Remove the abdomen flap and upper shell, discard intestines and gills, and scoop out all the yellow-brown meat from the shell. Serve with lemon juice and pepper, or in a salad with a seafood sauce.

Limpet

LOCATION These molluscs are found on the rocks in the intertidal and subtidal zones.

COLLECTION Prise from the rocks with a strong-bladed knife.

RESTRICTIONS The knife blade may not exceed 3,8 cm in width. The bag limit in the Cape is 15 per person per day, and in Natal (where you need a licence) 25 per person per day.

PREPARATION Steam out of their shells in a pot, remove the radula (the horny strip on the tongue) and serve with garlic butter or French dressing. Alternatively, brush limpets with butter and grill in their shells over hot coals.

Octopus

LOCATION Inhabits rocky pools and reefs, and is usually found under rocky ledges.

COLLECTION Use a gaff with strips of red cloth tied near the hook to entice it from its lair.

RESTRICTIONS The bag limit is two per person per day, and in Natal a licence is required.

PREPARATION Turn the octopus inside out; remove the mouth, stomach and transparent plastic-like pen. Pound thoroughly against a rock, then peel off the skin, working it away between the fingers and thumb. Rinse in cold water. Beat the tentacles with a sharp mallet. Soak in milk with a sprinkling of lemon juice for five hours. Slice and fry in oil or butter. Serve the hot dish with a lemon butter or a garlic sauce.

Oyster

LOCATION These are distributed in rocky pools, along reefs and among rocks on the sea bed along the south and east coasts.

COLLECTION Prise from the rocks with a strong knife, without damaging them.

RESTRICTIONS The knife blade should not exceed a width of 3,8 cm. In the Cape the bag limit is 25 per person per day with a minimum shell size of 5,08 cm across and a closed season from 1 December to 15 January; in Natal certain areas are closed annually, you need a licence and the daily bag limit is eight dozen.

PREPARATION Prise the shell open at the hinged end and serve raw with lemon, salt and pepper (or tabasco sauce), bread and butter. You can also bake or grill oysters quickly in their shells.

Periwinkle

LOCATION Small sea snails found in rock pools all along the coast.

COLLECTION Pluck from the rocks.

RESTRICTIONS There is a bag limit of fifty per person per day in the Cape (they are protected in Natal).

PREPARATION Soak in water for forty minutes, rinse and drain. Boil for five minutes in salted or fresh sea water. Drain, cool and remove from shells with a pin. Remove the operculum and the stomach, and serve with French dressing or butter.

Perlemoen (abalone)

LOCATION Found mainly between Saldanha Bay and Cape Agulhas.

COLLECTION Taken only by skin divers. Approach a perlemoen swiftly and quietly, and slip the blade of your diving knife between its suction pad and the rock face, prising it off before it can sense danger and clamp down.

RESTRICTIONS The knife blade may not exceed 3,8 cm in width, the bag limit is five per person per day, the minimum size shell is 11,43 cm across, and there is a closed season between 1 August and 31 October. (For further restrictions, see 'Laws of the seashore'.)

PREPARATION Use a steel scouring brush to clean the suction pad, and a strong, sharp knife to lever the perlemoen out of its shell. Slice off the beard, the head and the entrails, and slice the meat into thin steaks. Tenderise both sides of these with a mallet, and fry in a batter for a minute or two, or

LEFT *A Cape rock lobster* (Jasus lalandii).

Oysters — delectable bounty from the sea — crust a maze of rock pools on the Natal coast.

until the steaks are lightly browned. Some people prefer perlemoen boiled in salt water for twenty minutes, and then minced, or prepared as before as steaks.

Rock lobster (crayfish)

LOCATION Found in shallow and deep water, with the greatest concentrations off the west coast.

COLLECTION If you are above the surface, use a ring net or a trap baited with fish heads. (Both methods are illegal in Natal.) If you are skin diving, look for lobsters in crevices and beneath rocky ledges on the sea bed. Avoid grabbing the lobster's feelers (they will break), but grasp its body quickly and firmly (with gloved hands) and pull it out.

RESTRICTIONS Rock lobsters may not be caught in sanctuaries or if they are soft-shelled (not applicable in Natal) or in berry. In Namibia the bag limit is five per person per day in the open season (1 November to 30 April); in the Cape it is four a day (15 November to 15 April); in Natal (where you need a licence) it is eight in the open season (1 March to 31 October). The minimum carapace length in the Cape is 8,89 cm, in Namibia and Natal (and for the east coast lobster) it is 6,5 cm. (For further restrictions, see 'Laws of the seashore'.)

PREPARATION Plunge into boiling salted or sea water for about 15 minutes or until it turns bright red. Slice down the back of the carapace to remove the alimentary canal. If serving cold, leave to cool; if serving hot, brush the opening in the carapace with butter and flash under a hot grill before serving with lemon and garlic sauce.

Sea urchin

LOCATION Found mostly in rock pools, and clustered around rocks in bays and coves.

COLLECTION Picked off the rocks with gloved hands as protection from the spines. Make sure the sea urchins are under water.

RESTRICTIONS In the Cape the bag limit is twenty per person per day, and 25 in Natal.

PREPARATION Sea urchins must be fresh: do not refrigerate or leave in the sun. Cut around the shell, and discard the top. The edible (red) part should be seasoned with lemon juice and cayenne pepper and eaten raw.

Seaweed

LOCATION Found along the entire coastline. The two popular edible varieties (*Gelidium pristoides*, a dark brown seaweed growing in tufts on rocks and limpets in the intertidal zone, and *Suhria vittata*, a maroon-coloured seaweed growing on certain species of kelp) are both found along the western and southern Cape coastline.

COLLECTION Gather by hand.

RESTRICTIONS A maximum of 10 kg (wet weight) per person per day.

PREPARATION: These are most popular as a jelly. Boil a handful in water for about three hours, cool, then boil again until reduced to a jelly. Strain, flavour with sugar, cinnamon or fruit juices, and leave to set.

White mussel

LOCATION Beds are found in intertidal sands along the west, southern and eastern Cape coast.

COLLECTION Look for small holes just above the tideline, then use your hands to scoop out sand to a depth of 50 cm. Alternatively, wade into the surf and feel for mussels with your feet, sliding them under the sand.

RESTRICTIONS You may not use a plough or spade. The bag limit is fifty per person per day and the minimum size shell 3,5 cm across. White mussels are protected in Natal.

PREPARATION As for black mussels, without having to scrape the shells or remove a beard ●

Exploring the world beneath the waves

Displays of brightness by a couple of clownfish — and the visiting scuba diver in full kit.

WASHED BY THE waters of two mighty oceans, the rugged coastline of southern Africa tapers off into a submarine world of enchanting beauty, a natural playground for an astonishing diversity of living creatures. This silent region, isolated for so long from the adventurous spirit of man, now draws to its depths thousands of divers, seeking its peace, its multicoloured splendour, and its ancient secrets buried beneath the waves. By snorkelling or scuba diving, you too can become an explorer of this magical 'underworld'.

Snorkelling

Skin diving or snorkelling, one of the fastest growing sports in southern Africa, requires only that you are reasonably fit, that you can look after yourself in the water and that you can afford the basic gear. It is best that professional instructors evaluate your fitness and ability (swimming certain distances both in and under water, and using survival techniques to stay afloat), and teach you to recognise your limitations.

Standard snorkelling gear consists of a mask for clear vision, fins for easy propulsion and a snorkel. If you are diving in the colder waters of southern Africa, you will probably need the protection of a wetsuit. The suit allows a thin layer of water to seep between the nylon lining and the diver's body, and this quickly warms to body temperature. In particularly cold water, wear a three-piece wetsuit:

RIGHT *A coral rockcod dominates a shoal of smaller fish in the aquamarine depths.*

a vest, with hood attached, under a zip-up jacket (and optional extras of rubber gloves and rubber booties, worn inside your fins). The wetsuit's buoyancy is counteracted by a weightbelt, which fastens with a quick-release buckle.

Take great care in choosing your diving equipment: your mask, in particular, should cover your eyes and nose comfortably, and should provide you with a broad field of vision. The tempered glass should be firmly encased in a rubber or silicone frame. The snorkel's

mouthpiece should fit comfortably under your lips and between your teeth. Fins, whether they have foot pockets or open straps, should fit like shoes.

A diving knife is an important accessory; besides its usefulness as a tool (for instance, in prising perlemoen off rocks), it could save your life should you become entangled in line or mesh underwater. Make sure your knife has a rugged, stainless steel blade about 15 cm long, and a strong plastic handle with a stainless steel pommel at the end. If you want to join the growing ranks of spearfishermen (restricted to skin divers), you will need a reliable speargun. The spear is attached either directly to the gun or to a reel beneath the shaft by means of a heavy nylon cord, and is powered pneumatically, by tough rubber, or by a spring. Remember that if you intend taking any organism out of the water (from rock lobster to redbait), you should familiarise yourself with local regulations governing seasons and quotas; if in doubt, consult your nearest Sea Fisheries or Nature Conservation office.

Scuba diving

Developed by one of the world's great pioneers of the deep, Jacques Yves Cousteau, scuba equipment enables a diver to breathe underwater. Scuba (self-contained underwater breathing apparatus) gear generally consists of one or two compressed-air cylinders, and a demand valve that controls the flow of compressed air from the cylinders to the diver. Important accessories for scuba diving are an adjustable buoyancy lifejacket (ABLJ), a depth and pressure gauge, and a waterproof watch to record the length of time you have spent underwater.

Scuba diving is for the fit and the adventurous, and it requires proper training. Diving shops will generally refuse to fill your tanks or rent you equipment without proof that you have completed a recognised diving course. The South African Underwater Union has established certified scuba diving courses which you can enrol for at any affiliated club (in Cape Town, Durban, East London, Port Elizabeth and on the Witwatersrand). Courses in scuba diving are also offered by the National Association of Underwater Instructors (NAUI) and the Professional Association of Diving Instructors (PADI), where subjects include diving, equipment and planning, as well as physics and physiology, and rescue and resuscitation.

Diving precautions

Diving is fun, but it can be dangerous unless you observe some cardinal rules.

● Most importantly, never dive alone; always dive with a friend, where each is responsible for the other's safety.

DIVING FOR 'TREASURE'

From the icy west coast waters to the subtropical east coast, the lure of more than 2000 species of fish entices an army of spearfishermen and fun divers into the shimmering depths of the sea.

Beneath the Atlantic's chill surge on the west coast, mighty kelp forests sway gently in the current, their leafy fronds shading multihued algae and anemones. In these waters millions of microorganisms, tossed around by the upwelling of the cold Benguela Current, attract vast shoals of pelagic fish and their carnivorous predators. Here, and around Cape Point to the vicinity of Hermanus, divers harvest mouthwatering galjoen, hottentot, rock lobster, perlemoen, alikreukel and black mussels.

Further along the coast, the influence of the warm Agulhas Current begins to be felt. In the translucent waters of the Tsitsikamma coast, divers can follow an underwater trail and marvel at the rainbow-coloured world of flame coral, starfish and feather stars. Up the east coast, off the great Agulhas Bank, and further north towards the subtropical waters of Mozambique, the warm waters brim with a wondrous variety of fish, darting about enchanted coral gardens. At premier spots from Hermanus onwards up the coast — including Struisbaai,

Waenhuiskrans, Cape Infanta, Knysna, Plettenberg Bay, Jeffreys Bay, Port Elizabeth, East London and Sodwana Bay — spearfishermen bag booty such as leervis, elf, kabeljou, bream, musselcracker, stumpnose and steenbras.

Shipwrecks are another major drawcard and all along the coastline underwater explorers cruise through the rusted bones of ships that went down long ago. More than a thousand ships are believed to have sunk off the southern African coastline since the mid-16th century, creating artificial reefs for novice divers in some places, and providing daunting — even dangerous — challenges to the most experienced scuba divers in others. It is always best to check diving conditions with local experts and be sure to familiarise yourself with any relevant regulations.

Note that certain sections of the coast are out of bounds to the public. These include the restricted diamond area of the west coast, a military zone near Saldanha Bay, the Koeberg Nuclear Power Station north of Cape Town, a missile testing zone between Waenhuiskrans and Cape Infanta, parts of the Kosi Bay coastline, various protected islands off both west and east coasts, and all harbours or other waters appropriated for military or naval use.

ABOVE *Swimming among coral reefs, a butterflyfish (top) and a lyretail.*

● Before entering the water, rehearse any signals you might need underwater. Check your own equipment thoroughly, and check that each other's harnessing straps and buckles are fitted properly, and that the cylinders, valves, regulator and pressure gauge are in good working condition.
● Observe entry and exit points in the sea before a dive, noting whether the tide is coming in or going out, and at what point it is likely to be when you finally exit the water. Also note the size and strength of the swell.
● Do not hyperventilate (breathe in and out deeply a number of times) before a dive; this may extend the time you can stay submerged, but it could also lead to loss of consciousness and then to drowning. In the water, always follow the advice in the letters scuba: Stay Calm Underwater, Breathe Always. Panic is your worst enemy.
● As you descend, equalise the pressure in your ears by pinching your nose and blowing air against your closed nostrils. If at this stage — or any other — you have any doubts about the visibility, depth, currents or your standard of fitness, abort the dive.
● Be on the lookout for underwater hazards. Should you get caught in a rip current, go with it, and then ease out of it gently at right angles to the direction in which it is flowing. Should you see a shark, and it seems to be showing an interest in you, back off from the area and leave the water as quietly as possible, without creating a disturbance

RIGHT *A close encounter with a honeycomb moray and bluebanded snappers.*

that could increase its interest. If it actually heads for you, face it and give it a bang on the snout with your speargun or diving knife. Remember that your best defence is to keep calm in the water.
● When you have been in the water for a while, assess how you feel. If you are tired or cold, or feel at all faint, tell your friend and leave the water immediately. Exhaustion is a small step away from drowning. If you get into difficulties and are battling to keep your head above the water, release

your weightbelt immediately; the buoyancy of your wetsuit will keep you afloat.

Always surface from the bottom in a spiral, giving yourself a 360° view of possible obstacles. Ascend slowly: a too rapid ascent using scuba gear could cause nitrogen bubbles to expand in your bloodstream, leading to the 'bends', a painful and possibly fatal affliction of the joints. Also breathe out as you ascend, to prevent air from expanding in your lungs and rupturing the lung tissue ●

A visual record on land and under water

EVEN AFTER YOUR HOLIDAY is over, there is still something to look forward to: your photographs, a treasury of memories. The coast provides some excellent subject matter, from moody seascapes to children romping on the sands. Remember, however, to take special care of your camera, keeping it in a properly sealed bag or wrapped in plastic in your beach bag when not in use; sand and water can damage the delicate lens surfaces and electronics. Protect your lens against scratches by fitting a lens cap or an ultraviolet filter (which also helps prevent a blue cast to your pictures). To protect film, never leave your camera in direct sunlight or in a hot car, and keep all film, especially once it has been used, in a dark place or cool bag.

Before you start shooting, consider the following points, which could help to make your holiday photographs really special.

Light
The light at the coast is bright, even on overcast days, because of reflection from sand and sea. To prevent exposure problems, use a film with a low ASA rating, and to reduce flare when shooting towards the sun, use a lens hood. Take your exposure reading of the area in which you would like visible detail. It is often useful to move close to the object (e.g., a face), fill the frame with the object, take an exposure reading and then move back to compose the photograph. Large light (sky) or dark areas can cause exposure faults — if you take a reading from a light sky, you are likely to underexpose any foreground/low detail.

Early mornings and late afternoons provide the best natural light, when a slanting sun gives the image greater texture and creates a more mellow picture than the hard, flat image with stark shadows that the overhead sun tends to produce. Note, though, that in the morning and evening the light changes rapidly, so check your light meter every few minutes.

A popular coastal subject is the sunset, but note that an exposure that will record all the colours of the sky, will tend to leave other objects in the picture underexposed. A popular solution is to choose a foreground that will be effective in silhouette, or one like water that will reflect and continue the tones of the sky. Underexposure can be solved technically by using a graduated filter or by taking a reading from the sky immediately above the camera.

In general, remember that while the eye will often not register a shadow falling partly across the subject, the camera will, perhaps spoiling what would have been a good picture.

Landscapes and viewpoint
Lovely landscapes, when photographed, often turn out as dull, flat pictures. Often the reason is that the average camera lens does not have the wide-angled facility of the human eye, so try to picture the end product through the viewfinder.

A landscape is essentially static, so good composition is vital. Find a point of interest (a building, a boat, an area of colour or shadow or texture) around which to compose the picture. One of the major divisions in a landscape is the horizon, and positioning it is important for the outcome of your picture. Rather than divide the picture in half, position the horizon two-thirds of the way down when featuring an interesting sky, or a third when you want to emphasise the land. Similarly, placing your main area of interest slightly to one side will strengthen the composition; you can then use any elements in the scenery (a fence, a line of surf) to lead the eye to it. Putting an item of interest in the foreground of a broad view also leads the eye into the picture, at the same time creating a sense of depth and distance.

Also consider your viewpoint: instead of taking

BELOW *A perfect seaside picture: the eye is drawn through a field of colour to the simple cottage, placed off centre and in stark contrast to the moody sky.*

the picture at eye level, try viewing the scene from ground level, or from a vantage point above (a rock or sand dune).

People and animals

Including a human figure in a landscape is a simple way of creating a centre of interest, while at the same time giving a sense of scale. A figure in a scene, not looking at the camera, can make a more interesting picture than someone posing for the camera with the view in the background.

Children are natural subjects to photograph, but the most important rule here is patience. Wait until the child is absorbed in something (building a sand castle, hunting for shells), and you will get natural poses with a variety of facial expressions. A telephoto lens is a useful device as it enables you to be less obtrusive.

It may also be effective to take a picture from a child's point of view; hold the camera at the child's eye level occasionally, and ignore the fact that adults may be cut off at the waist.

As with children, photographing animals and birds requires patience, for you have little control over their movements. When the animal is in range, try to track it for a minute or two through the viewfinder, as it may yawn, look directly at you, or do something to make a really good picture.

Again, a telephoto lens is a useful accessory, particularly when photographing coastal birds. Remember that if there is a large expanse of sky in your picture (for instance, when photographing a bird in flight), you should set your light meter for the subject, or you could get a series of silhouettes.

Water

Water is always a good photographic subject, providing a serenely limpid image or one of surging power. A slight ripple on water can produce a picture of abstract colours and shapes, while a photograph of a flaming sunset may be enhanced by capturing its reflection. (This is one time when it may be effective to place the horizon in the middle of the picture to achieve a symmetrical image.)

When photographing reflections in still water, remember to focus on the reflection itself, not on the surface of the water. To capture the cool, clear colours of a calm sea, try using a polarising filter, which removes unwanted reflections or highlights. A starburst filter will add sparkle to a picture of water, changing the flickering highlights into bright stars.

The sea alone must be dramatic or your picture will be dull. Include the sun with a sparkling light path across the water, or some foreground detail such as a rock or boat, which will also give perspective and a feeling of depth.

There are two ways to approach photographing fast-moving water. One is to use a fast shutter speed to freeze the motion, so that every drop is suspended distinct; the other is to use a slow speed,

for a flowing effect. To freeze the motion use the fastest speed light conditions allow; to blur it use the slowest, and if necessary use a tripod.

Seashore features

The seashore offers a range of photographic opportunities, from nature's weirdly shaped rocks and abstract wind patterns on sand, to rusting old piers and bright umbrellas against an expanse of silver sand. The biggest problem here is exposure, with reflected light misleading an exposure meter, so take your close-up readings from a midtone detail. A polarising filter helps to reduce glare and

increase the colour of sky and sea.

Harbours are particularly good subjects, but however picturesque, avoid clutter or you will reduce the impact of the picture. It may be more satisfying to look for unusual detail or different viewpoints — a collection of lobster pots as an abstract composition, or the reflections of bright hulls in oily water. Boating photographs (be it of a yacht race or a group of waterskiers) are most successful if you get as near the action as possible, so try to go out in a boat yourself. This landward perspective is also excellent for unusual pictures of a harbour or beach ●

UNDERWATER PHOTOGRAPHY

Make your photographic record extra special by exploring the world under the water, where glowing coral, bright fish and delicate sea anemones are easily as photogenic as what you see from the shore.

All cameras can be used underwater, if completely protected from the water, so do not buy an expensive underwater camera until you are sure it is warranted. The easiest (but riskiest) way of waterproofing an ordinary camera is to put it into a plastic bag, keeping the opening above the water while you point the lens underwater. It would, however, be more sensible (and not much more expensive) to buy a custom-made sealable heavy-duty vinyl bag, where you operate the controls through a glove-shaped insert. More expensive and sturdier housings made from perspex, injection-moulded plastic and cast-metal alloys are available, and you can also buy connecting housings for your flash.

Because water is more dense than air, underwater photography presents special problems:

● **Refraction**

Water acts like a prism and bends light, so all objects appear a third larger than they are. This narrows your field of view (a wide-angle lens can be useful here), so focus for what the distance between the camera and the object appears to be, not the actual distance.

● **Colour absorption and contrast**

Even the clearest water acts like a strong green-blue filter. The deep blue of the sea is caused by the absorption of first red light, then yellow and finally green, according to depth. Little red light will travel through 3 m of water, and by 12 m there is no red light left. Yellow light travels further, but by about 20 m this is lost as well and below 30 m a flash is needed. The simplest way to avoid the problem of colour absorption is to work in very shallow water, where the light is brightest and colours strongest.

Water also affects contrast, with the clarity and saturation of colours being reduced. Try to get as near to your subject as possible (using a wide-angle lens if necessary), and use good lighting (i.e., work in shallow water or use a flash). Another way of obtaining higher contrast is to use a relatively slow film, which is underexposed (by exposing it for a higher

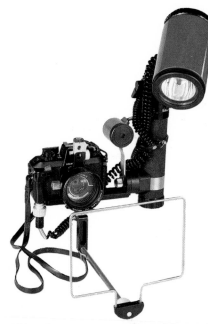

This underwater camera and powerful flashgun can be taken to a depth of 50 m without a special housing.

ASA value) and then 'push processed' or over-developed to increase the contrast.

To correct water colour (inshore water tends to be greener or yellower than sea water, but even the blue of the sea can be altered by the presence of a river mouth), you will have to experiment with various filters for the best result.

● **Flash**

Flash can be extremely difficult to use underwater, because its useful range is restricted and because light tends to be scattered by the various bits of vegetation and small organisms floating in the water. Before using a flash under water, familiarise yourself with the method of calculating exposure, which differs from that on land. To reduce scatter (which is most obvious when the flash is close to the lens), hold your flash to one side to give sidelight to your picture.

In search of adventure and hidden treasure

The wooden hull of the Colebrooke, *an English East Indiaman that sank in False Bay in 1778.*

LASHED BY VICIOUS STORMS, and battered by waves that roll in from the seething wilderness of the southern oceans, the coast of southern Africa has been a graveyard for ships and men. Over the centuries, more than 1 300 ships, overwhelmed by the fury of this cruel sea or ensnared by its reefs, have broken up and sunk, some taking with them untold treasures.

The odds against the early navigators were enormous. They were sailing uncharted waters and their knowledge of sea routes, currents and winds, reefs, sandbanks and islands was hopelessly inadequate. In addition, the vessels they pitted against the might of the ocean were frighteningly flimsy and — more often than not — overloaded to satisfy their avaricious owners.

As the technology of shipbuilding advanced, as equipment improved and navigational aids like lighthouses were established, and as the skills and experience of the seamen grew, so the hazards of a life at sea diminished. But they did not vanish entirely. Negligence and human error still constitute a very real threat; even the most sophisticated machinery can break down; and above all, the sea and the weather remain stubbornly unpredictable.

Every wreck tells a story
Of all the ships devoured by the sea off the southern African coastline, a little more than a

WRECK DIVING AND THE LAW

To prevent wholesale plundering of wrecks by amateur and professional divers, any diver wishing to salvage any part of a wreck more than fifty years old must fulfil certain requirements.

Firstly, the diver must be affiliated to a museum that is approved by the National Monuments Council; secondly, he must acquire a permit from the council, allowing him to salvage items on a wreck; thirdly, he must take out a salvaging licence from the Department of Customs and Excise. The prospective salvor must also allow the council to advertise in the Government Gazette for objections to the permit.

If the wreck lies in a security or nature conservation area, the approval of the authority controlling that area must also be given.

All material recovered from a wreck must be handed over to the museum, which, in consultation with the National Monuments Council and the salvor, will then decide on the apportionment of the material. It is expected that fifty per cent will go to the state and fifty per cent to the salvor, and that should there be only one item under consideration, compensation will be decided by arbitration or negotiation.

Anyone found removing items from or disturbing a wreck without a permit, or found obstructing a permit holder, will be liable to a fine of up to R10 000 or a prison sentence of up to two years.

hundred have been found, including Portuguese caravels and galleons, Dutch merchantmen and British tea clippers. Some of these have yielded treasure in the form of gold bullion, silver and jewels, and priceless pottery. Still buried beneath the sand, though, is a fortune in gold and gems estimated at R100-million.

Divers and salvage teams lured to these ships by their extraordinary cargoes and by the promise of adventure have brought up astonishing finds, some linked to the destinies of kings, the outcome of wars and the bankruptcy of nations: cannons from Goa, bullets bound for the Boer War, Ming vases from China. . . .

Wrecks lie strewn along the entire coastline, but the east coast proved particularly fatal to the Portuguese, returning groaning with booty from the East. The *Sao Bento*, one of the grandest ships of the 16th century, sank off the Mtata River mouth (Transkei) in 1554, sending 144 people to a watery grave — along with a fortune in gold, rubies and sapphires gleaned in exotic Cochin. The treasure-laden *Sao Thomé* broke up off the northern Natal coast in 1589, and just four years later another treasure ship, the *Santo Alberto*, broke up within 16 km of the wreck of the *Sao Bento*. Evidence of the vast wealth of these and other ships has washed ashore in the form of coins, beads and jewellery, but the exact location of many of them has not been pinpointed.

Even when the location of a wreck is known, the sea will not necessarily relinquish its hold. The most famous example of this is the British *Grosvenor*, which has captured the imagination of divers throughout South Africa. Homeward bound from India in 1782, and carrying a cargo of gold bullion, jewels and other precious goods, it went down in a deep bay known as Lwambazi on the Transkei coast. Ever since, it has been an irresistible magnet to fortune hunters, divers and salvage experts. Dykes have been built to cordon off the bay's water, tunnels have been dug in an attempt to reach the wreck beneath the sea, even cranes have been used. But although thousands of coins, beads and fragments of crockery have been recovered, the bulk of the ship's treasure remains intact, protected by the raging surf.

Further down the coast, in Algoa Bay (where one particularly vicious storm claimed 18 ships on a spring day in 1902), there are so many wrecks that divers sometimes report difficulty in telling them apart. Some, like the *Dodington*, wrecked with the loss of 247 lives off the jagged reefs of Bird Island in 1755, have yielded breathtaking bounty to adventurous divers, including incomparable silver and gold coins. Not far from the *Dodington* lies one of the great men o'war of the 17th century, the *Sacramento*, which was en route from Goa to Europe in 1647 when it broke up on the rocks near

SAFETY UNDER THE SEA

Diving at shipwrecks is an adrenaline-charged adventure, one that has few equals on land. But wreck diving must be accompanied by common sense, adherence to some basic rules, and consideration for the underwater environment.

As with any diving expedition, your standard gear should all be carefully checked. In addition, you should take along:

● A marker buoy to indicate the presence of divers to other boats.

● A floater or shot line, weighted and attached to the marker buoy or to the boat, and let down to the sea bed to mark the line of descent.

● A search line (optional) to keep you connected to the shot line if you are diving in a dark or strange environment.

● A torch for exploring dark chambers, corridors and cabins.

Wreck diving often involves exploring a changing and sometimes unpredictable environment, so be on the lookout for the unexpected, especially cables and moving articles. Some divers have reported being smashed in the face by wreck doors swinging open and closed in the current, or becoming entangled in wires or fishing line. Other divers have told of dangerous currents sucking them through holes in the submerged carcasses of old ships.

As with all diving, never go onto a wreck alone, and make sure your diving companion is at your side all the time. If you are diving a wreck for the first time, go with someone who has dived that particular wreck already.

and Christmas puddings for the Allied troops; and the *Nolloth*, a Dutch coaster that broke up on a reef less than a kilometre away, with a cargo of wine, brandy, soap and candles in April 1965.

Other less accessible wrecks are no less compelling. The Dutch East Indiaman *Meresteijn* was wrecked off Jutteneiland at the entrance to Saldanha Bay in 1702, apparently carrying a fabulous cargo. It was only in 1971, however, that two Cape Town salvage divers were finally able to descend successfully into the murky depths surrounding the ship and recover bronze cannons, lead ingots, and Dutch and Spanish coins.

The wreck of the British troopship *Birkenhead*, which struck a reef off Danger Point near Gansbaai one night in 1852, has a romance all of its own. This is the wreck that began the tradition of 'women and children first', where brave soldiers went to their death rather than overburden the lifeboats carrying the women and children to safety. Rumours that the *Birkenhead* was carrying a fortune in gold have long drawn divers, but there is no official record of any such find being made.

The fascination of all shipwrecks is an enduring one, perhaps symbolised best by the *Waratah*, the liner that in 1909 vanished without a trace somewhere between Durban and Cape Town. No

Booty from the Birkenhead*: a cannon, rusted from long years under water.*

wreckage has ever been found, nor any of the bodies of the 211 people on board. But as long as man remembers its disappearance, he will search the sea to uncover the secret ●

Skoenmakerskop, going down with an estimated R2-million in jewellery. It was discovered after a persistent search by two Port Elizabeth divers, who eventually brought up forty of the ship's bronze cannons, cast in Macao for the defence of Portugal.

By far the greatest concentration of shipwrecks, however, is off the vicious reefs of the south-western Cape. Known to the Portuguese as the Cape of Storms, these frenzied waters, whipped up by north-west storms in winter and screaming south-easters in summer, have swallowed countless ships. These are the waters that draw so many divers, for the thrill of both hidden treasure and buried history.

In Table Bay alone, an estimated 350 ships have been sunk, taking with them cargo valued at more than R40-million. Further south, along the jagged fringes of the Cape Peninsula towards Cape Point, scores of ships have broken their backs on the ragged reefs flanking the coastline. These include the steamer *Maori* (1909), which has delighted divers with such finds as intact bottles of champagne; the *Thomas T Tucker*, a United States Liberty ship torpedoed in the Second World War and beached with its cargo of Sherman tanks

The iron-hulled Birkenhead, *with steam-powered paddle wheels, reflected 19th-century shipbuilding.*

Identifying ships and signals

WHENEVER YOU VISIT THE COAST, you can expect to see ships of all sizes and descriptions plying one of the most significant sea routes in world history: the link between West and East around the tip of Africa. The nature of the shipping in any given area depends largely on the major port serving that area: Durban is South Africa's foremost port in terms of general cargo; the deep-water port of Richards Bay handles bulk cargo; the magnificent natural harbour at Saldanha Bay is primarily an ore-export port; Simon's Town in the lee of the Cape Peninsula has a long and proud history as the country's premier naval base.

Wander through any of the bustling harbours embraced by this long coastline, head off for a good vantage point with a pair of binoculars, or take to the waves yourself: the richness and diversity of the shipping tradition is just waiting to be discovered.

Tugs are the workhorses of any fleet. The Voith-Schneider propulsion system of this tug means it can move in any direction instantly, greatly facilitating ship handling.

The luxury passenger liner has, because of spiralling costs and the competition of air travel, become a rare — but no less romantic — sight.

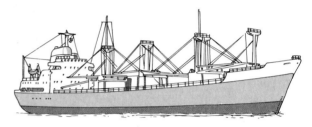

Freighters must be adaptable to the widely varying needs of carrying general cargo.

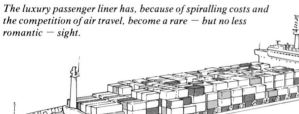

Container vessels, their decks stacked with large, standard-sized, general cargo-carrying containers, crisscross the world's oceans.

Trawlers, ranging greatly in sophistication and size, are common in rich fishing waters.

ABOVE *The ro-ro (roll on/roll off) is a cargo vessel designed so that lorries and trailers can be driven straight on and off the ship for easy loading and offloading.* BELOW *The VLCC (very large crude carrier) is, as the name implies, a very large tanker built to carry crude oil from source to oil refineries around the world.*

Commercial shipping

The role of commercial shipping in southern Africa has long been a vital one: even Dias and Da Gama, thrusting towards the East, were intent on nothing more than opening up the rich trade route. Since then there have been great advances in shipbuilding: from the replacement of sail by steam, diesel and nuclear power, to the development of container vessels and the giant crude carriers making cargo handling as straightforward and mechanised as possible.

Foremost among the half a dozen or so groups making up the South African Shipowners' Association is Safmarine, the national shipping line. Besides its traditional business — the liner and the bulk divisions, transporting containerised cargo and bulk commodities around the globe — Safmarine's main contribution is to coastal safety. Its ocean-going tugs, among the most powerful in the world, are well known for their salvage and towing work, while the Kuswag antipollution vessels are equipped to counter oil pollution.

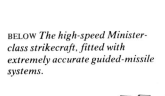

Powerboats — from simple runabouts to throaty cruisers — are a popular sporting choice, particularly with deep-sea anglers.

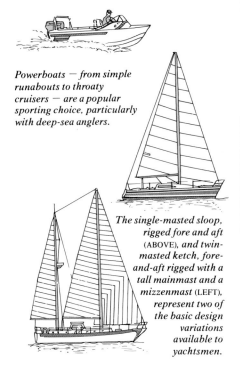

The single-masted sloop, rigged fore and aft (ABOVE), and twin-masted ketch, fore-and-aft rigged with a tall mainmast and a mizzenmast (LEFT), represent two of the basic design variations available to yachtsmen.

Pleasure craft

South Africa's sunny skies and its long coastline make it easy to understand why boating is such a popular pastime. The two basic divisions of pleasure craft — powerboats and yachts — are composed of a bewildering array of different designs. From the simplest of powerboats, with their single, outboard engines, to the sophisticated motor cruisers, with their navigational aids and spacious accommodation; and from the tiny singlehanded dinghies for racing or simply pottering about, to the sleek sailing yachts for round-the-world voyages, the choice is endless. Whatever the particular design, these are the vessels most frequently seen on any body of water, in or around the country ●

SIGNALS AT SEA

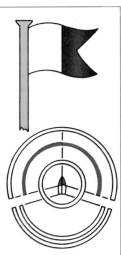

Messages are written with alphanumerical International Code flags. Vital among these are distress signals: for instance, flying the N flag above the C flag (shown left), or a square flag with any ball-like object above or below it (below left). Another signal is the blue-and-white flag (above right), attached to a buoy to indicate a diver's presence.

Lights are also used to indicate direction. In the most basic configuration (shown right), a white masthead light over the fore and aft centreline of the vessel shows an unbroken light over an arc of the horizon of 225°; a green light is placed on the starboard side and a red light on the port side (112,5° arc); and a white light at the stern (135° arc). In addition are the yellow towing light and the white all-round light.

BELOW *The high-speed Minister-class strikecraft, fitted with extremely accurate guided-missile systems.*

RIGHT *Besides their role in countering mines, the sturdy, wooden-hulled minesweepers carry out numerous other tasks, notably guardship duties.*

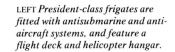

LEFT *President-class frigates are fitted with antisubmarine and anti-aircraft systems, and feature a flight deck and helicopter hangar.*

Naval vessels

The South African Navy is responsible for coastal defence and the protection of sovereignty of territorial waters. It performs these duties with its fleet of strikecraft, submarines, mine countermeasures vessels, and support vessels such as fleet replenishment and hydrographic survey vessels. This physical presence is backed by sophisticated armaments, and tracking and communications systems. In addition to the main naval base at Simon's Town, there are advanced bases on the west coast (Walvis Bay) and the east coast (Durban), as well as support facilities at other commercial harbours.

RIGHT *Fleet replenishment vessels can supply warships with fuel, fresh water, stores and ammunition under any conditions, so that they need not leave their station during emergencies.*

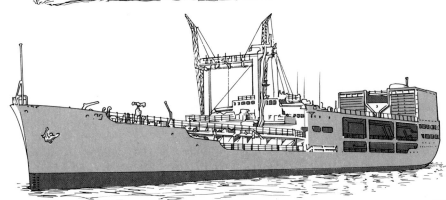

Helping to prevent an attack

In spite of its awesome jaws, the spotted ragged-tooth shark is not regarded as a man-eater.

MODERN MAN has come to terms with much of the natural world around him and today he has far less to fear from it than from his own man-made environment. A dreadful exception still remains, however: sharks, the animals man has been unable to tame or confine.

The thought of being attacked by a shark, with its razor-sharp teeth and powerful jaws, is spine-chilling, but fortunately the chance of it happening is very slight. More people die of humble bee stings than of shark attacks every year; in fact, the chance of drowning along the South African coastline is 600 times greater than the chance of being attacked by a shark.

To help prevent shark attacks, it is important to try to understand why, how and where they may occur.

The incidence of shark attacks

Not all sharks pose a threat; most sharks are, in fact, not man-eaters. Of the eighty species found in local waters, only three are responsible for the majority of attacks: the great white, tiger and Zambezi sharks.

While most shark attacks occur in warm waters, this is not because sharks favour them, but rather that more people go into the sea when it is warm. Natal's beaches are the most popular in the country, and as a result, Natal has the highest incidence of attacks. This does not mean that the cold Cape waters are any safer for swimmers.

Statistics have shown that more men than women are attacked by sharks (a ratio of 13,5:1), but again this is not the sharks' preference, but rather that more men than women participate in watersports such as surfing, angling and diving. When men go swimming, they generally stay in the water longer and venture deeper than women, thus increasing the chances of attack.

It seems that divers are particularly vulnerable to attack, because they go into deep water and often handle bleeding fish that might attract sharks. If wearing wetsuits, they have some measure of protection from sharks especially during investigatory attacks, when the shark may bump or brush against its 'prey' and its sharp scales tear the unprotected skin. Wetsuited divers also have the advantage of flippers, which increase their speed; goggles, which give them clear underwater vision; and perhaps also a speargun, which could be a useful weapon.

Keeping out of deep water, however, is no guarantee of keeping out of trouble. Although

most attacks on swimmers, bodysurfers and boardriders have taken place in waist-deep water, there have been cases in which the attack occurred in very shallow water. At least if the victims are closer to the shore, they are closer to first aid.

Why sharks attack people

Sharks are carnivorous animals and quite voracious eaters, so much so that some species will swallow almost anything. They are efficient predators, and people who enter their natural hunting ground run the risk of being attacked.

Sharks do not prefer humans to their normal diet, but they can be confused by the behaviour of people in the sea, particularly when conditions are murky. The great white and tiger sharks eat seals and dolphins, and researchers point out that a diver in a wetsuit and flippers resembles a seal or dolphin. An attack on a diver could simply be an error in recognition. Likewise, a surfer lying on a board with arms and legs dangling in the water could be mistaken for a turtle; and the V-shape of a man's dark bathing suit against pale skin could create the impression of a skate or ray.

Aside from any confusion in recognising the exact nature of their prey, sharks actually have good near vision, and are ten times more sensitive to contrasts between light and dark than humans are. They are also attracted to bright objects, and some divers believe they respond to certain colours under water.

Their sense of smell is acute, and they are able to detect odours nearly a kilometre from their source. Some species are so sensitive they are able to detect blood in a dilution of one part to a million parts of water.

To make them even more efficient hunters, sharks are able to detect distant vibrations in water with their ears and their well-developed lateral line (gel-filled canals running the length of the body). This enables them accurately to locate a struggling fish, swimmer or surfer in the open sea.

Safeguarding swimmers from attack

A concentration of shark attacks in an area can have a dramatic effect on the tourist industry and economy of that region, which is one of the reasons why vast sums of money are spent on researching measures to safeguard people from attacks.

The first local attempt to keep sharks at bay was made in 1906, when a Durban bathing area — Scotsmans Pool — was fenced off. This small enclosure could not withstand the pounding of the waves and the corrosive effects of salt water and after twenty years it disappeared from view.

In the 1950s a new approach was taken. Along the Margate-Uvongo coastline, depth charges were dropped in a bid to blast the sharks away. More than sixty explosions succeeded in killing only eight sharks, and the huge number of other fish killed drew all the more sharks to the area. Equally unsuccessful was the powerboat patrol instituted in Margate, when police were authorised to bombard sharks with hand grenades.

Around the world numerous other methods were being tested, and mostly found wanting. Chickenwire fences were erected; would-be shark repellants like stains, poisons and sound waves were used; even 'bubble curtains' were created (by pumping air through a perforated hose on the sea

RIGHT *Natal Sharks Board field staff retrieve a shark from the nets.*

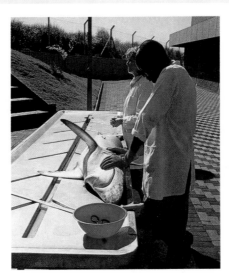

Shark dissection at the Sharks Board headquarters in Umhlanga.

bed). What did prove effective was the erection of electric barriers, but their cost was prohibitive.

The all-round most effective method of keeping sharks away from the shore is the current one of netting, discovered by chance by an Australian fisherman in 1937. After reporting to the authorities that his large diamond-mesh nets trapped sharks, rather than the large fish he had hoped for, several experimental nets were set.

The system used in South Africa today is based on the Australian model. Two rows of nets (each about 200 m long) are set at intervals parallel to the beach. The nets are suspended vertically in the sea and secured at the ends by anchors with marker buoys (sometimes visible from the shore). The nets do not form an impassable barrier as they do not stretch from the sea bed to the surface, and nor do they constitute a continuous line. The nets in the second row, however, overlap the gaps in the first row by about 20 m. The nets are invisible to the shark and it is captured soon after venturing into the area. Once immobilised, water no longer ventilates its gills and the shark suffocates and dies.

By reducing the numbers of sharks, the

EMERGENCY TREATMENT

Should someone be attacked by a shark, correct treatment on the beach is vital. The most important factor to ensure survival is to stop the loss of blood, and efforts to reconstitute blood supply should start as soon as possible.

While carrying the victim from the sea, keep his head lower than the rest of his body. Place him on his back on a towel or blanket at the nearest dry place from the water's edge. The victim must be kept in the head-down position, elevating both legs.

Keep the wound free of sand and stop bleeding by applying pressure with the hand on the wound or by placing a pad of any material over the wound and binding it tightly with a bandage. If there is more than one wound, indirect pressure must be applied at pressure points (the points where major arteries flow over or along large bones). To stop bloodflow to the arm or leg, press the artery against the bone in the upper arm or thigh.

Call a doctor and notify the hospital to prepare for a shark attack victim. The victim cannot be moved until the blood system has been stabilised (normally thirty minutes).

Do not give the victim anything to eat or drink as he is likely to require surgery. Alcohol in particular should not be given as it dilates the arteries.

Shade the victim from the sun and cover him with a light blanket, if available. Above all, constantly reassure and comfort the victim: several shark attack survivors have ascribed their recovery to the people who urged them not to give up hope.

probability of attack is reduced. This does not mean that attacks have not occurred within netted areas, but generally only in instances when the nets have been damaged. To prevent this, the nets are checked daily by the Natal Sharks Board. Dead sharks are removed and the nets are repaired, and replaced every three weeks.

If rough weather and seas damage the nets, bathing is banned temporarily while repairs take place. Bathing is also banned during the annual sardine run, when nets are lifted •

What to do in an emergency

WITH AS MANY AS 2000 deaths by drowning taking place in South Africa every year, it is essential to be equipped to deal with such emergencies. Always seek professional assistance: from lifesavers on duty, or by contacting the John Rolfe Rescue Helicopter Service (in major coastal cities) or the National Sea Rescue Institute. Remember, though, where instant action is required, your recognition of distress signals and knowledge of livesaving techniques and first aid could help to save lives.

Rescuing someone from a river, lagoon or dam
Two-thirds of all drownings occur in inland water, and in many cases you can rescue the victim without actually entering the water yourself. You should, in fact, never enter the water unless there is no alternative and you are a strong swimmer: the potential for getting into difficulty yourself is far too great.

Lifesaving experts use a four-word rhyme to summarise the safest ways of rescuing someone from the water: reach, throw, wade, row.

- If the victim is not far from reach, lie on your stomach at the water's edge, anchoring yourself however possible. Then stretch out a stout stick to the victim, or throw him the end of a rope or a piece of clothing and haul him in steadily.
- If the victim is out of reach, throw him some kind of buoy (even a child's rubber tube) to keep him afloat while you go for help.
- If you can approach the victim by wading, first test the temperature of the water and note any currents. Also probe the bottom with a stick before each step to discover any depth changes or submerged obstacles that could land you in unexpected trouble.
- When using a boat to rescue someone, be careful not to get too close — or you might accidentally push him under, knock him out or injure him. To lessen the risk of capsizing, haul him aboard over the stern.

Lifesaving techniques in the water
Not all of South Africa's beaches or public swimming places are protected by lifesavers, and even those that are may have lifesavers on duty only during peak seasons and at weekends. (Lifeguards may be recognised by their standard green-and-gold or professional red costumes.) Your own training (certificates can be obtained through SA Lifesaving) could thus mean the difference between life and death.

It is vital to remember that a person in difficulty in the water is often panic-stricken and may cling desperately to his rescuer, putting both at risk. Make sure that you stay out of the swimmer's reach until he is calm enough to understand your instructions; if he should make a grab for you, avoid his grasp by reversing immediately into backstroke and swimming vigorously away.

From a safe distance, offer him one end of a piece of clothing or towel or one side of a lifebuoy and tell him to hold onto it. With him floating face up in the water, you can then tow him to shore holding the other end. If he starts to pull himself towards you, let go and swim out of reach until he calms down.

If you are forced to make contact with the swimmer because he is not responding to your instructions, approach him from behind, grasping him firmly and supporting him in the water. Calm him by talking and tow him to shore by one of the following methods.

- If the swimmer is nervous and you need firm control, take him by the chin and pull him, face upwards, until his head is alongside yours (ear to ear). Clamp his shoulder with your elbow and if necessary, restrain him with your other arm as well. Keep talking reassuringly to try to keep him calm while you tow him to shore.
- If the water is calm and the swimmer is passive or unconscious, put your hand around his chin from behind. Then straighten your arm, locking your elbow, and make for the shore using sidestroke. This means that your legs are clear of the victim and that you can look forwards regularly to see where you are going.
- If the water is rough (e.g., through breaking surf) and you need to keep the swimmer's head well above water, put your arm across his chest and hold him round the lower ribs, with your hip positioned in the small of his back. This enables you to swim on your side, breathe more easily, and see where you are going.

Reviving a drowning person
Death by drowning results when the victim struggles for breath, and water enters the airway. The water causes a spasm of the epiglottis, a cartilage flap at the back of the tongue, and this spasm blocks the air supply.

To restore the air supply you must begin artificial respiration as soon as possible. While towing the victim to shore, you can give him the occasional breath (after first removing any obstructions — such as seaweed — from his mouth). Once you are within your depth, you can begin

---

SIGNALLING FOR HELP AT SEA

The internationally recognised distress signal Mayday (from the French phrase *m'aidez*, meaning 'help me') should be used only when you are in grave danger and require immediate assistance. If you urgently need help but are not in imminent danger, use the signal Pan Pan (from the French *panne*, meaning 'breakdown'), which is also the correct signal for man overboard.

To transmit the Mayday signal by radio, tune into the international distress frequency (channel 16 VHF or 2182 kHz SW) and follow this sequence. Repeat the word 'Mayday' three times, give the name of your craft three times, repeat 'Mayday' once more and then the name of the craft again. Give the craft's position as accurately as possible, a brief description of the emergency and the help needed. Say 'over' at the end of the message and listen for acknowledgement before sending out the distress call again.

In order to clarify a radio message, phonetic alphabets using specific words to identify individual letters are used. One internationally recognised alphabet reads as follows:

Alpha	Golf
Bravo	Hotel
Charlie	India
Delta	Juliet
Echo	Kilo
Foxtrot	Lima
Mike	Tango
November	Uniform
Oscar	Victor
Papa	Whisky
Quebec	X-ray
Romeo	Yankee
Sierra	Zulu

Under the International Convention for the Safety of Life at Sea, there are several recognised ways of calling for help other than by the Mayday signal. A ship's captain who sees any of these distress signals is legally obliged to respond to them.

- Gun or other explosive signal fired at intervals of about a minute.
- Continuous sounding of a hooter, such as a foghorn.
- Rockets or shells throwing red stars fired one at a time at short intervals.
- Morse code SOS (three dots, three dashes, three dots) transmitted by any means.
- International Code flags NC (flag N above flag C), or a square flag with above or below it anything resembling a ball.
- Flames on a vessels (e.g., burning tar, oily rags).
- Red parachute or hand flare.
- Orange-coloured smoke.
- Slowly raising and lowering outstretched arms.

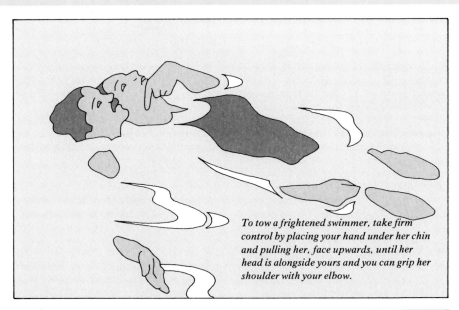

To tow a frightened swimmer, take firm control by placing your hand under her chin and pulling her, face upwards, until her head is alongside yours and you can grip her shoulder with your elbow.

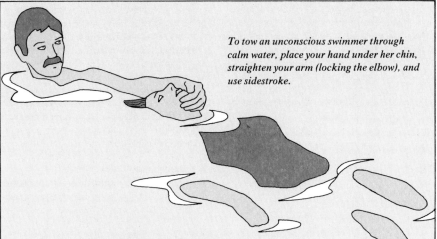

To tow an unconscious swimmer through calm water, place your hand under her chin, straighten your arm (locking the elbow), and use sidestroke.

To tow a swimmer through rough water, put your arm across her chest, holding her around the lower ribs and placing your hip in the small of her back. Sidestroke to shore.

the correct treatment: use one arm to support the victim's body and the other hand to support the head, at the same time sealing the nose while you perform artificial respiration.

Once the victim is ashore, check his breathing and heartbeat, and continue resuscitation if necessary. At this stage he should be dried and kept warm. All casualties rescued from drowning must be sent to hospital to check for congestion of the lungs, as secondary drowning can still occur ●

NATIONAL SEA RESCUE INSTITUTE

An NSRI vessel patrolling the coast.

Founded in 1967, the NSRI provides a 24-hour rescue service, operating from 22 full stations on the coast between Walvis Bay and Richards Bay and also from various inland dams. It has some 46 rescue boats ranging in size from 5 to 15 m, and boasts a proud average of a mere 15 minutes in getting a boat out to go to a craft in distress.

The service is operated by voluntary, unpaid crews of more than 500. These are all highly trained men and women, who must be excellent sailors, strong swimmers, capable of withstanding the rigours of cold seas and hazardous conditions, and well-versed in first aid. In addition, they are always endeavouring to improve their own high standards of efficiency.

By mid-1987, NSRI craft had undertaken 5 236 search and rescue operations, rescuing 8 550 people and 2 782 craft. The latter is normally the task of the harbour authorities to arrange, but where it is expedient to do so, the NSRI will also tow in the craft. The NSRI never claims salvage but donations are always welcomed to help meet its high running costs (about R650 000 a year). Donations from the private sector and individuals in fact cover three-quarters of the total costs, with a government grant providing the balance.

Besides its rescue function, the NSRI has the task of encouraging small boat owners to accept safety standards and carry proper equipment to prevent disasters at sea, and of fostering an adherence to the practice of sound seamanship. It is not a policing organisation and exercises no authority to prevent people from putting out to sea when ill equipped — it merely advises them not to do so.

Cuts, bites, burns and other injuries

EVEN AN ISLAND PARADISE — blue seas, white sands, swaying palms — has its fair share of 'serpents', from sunburn to shark bites. Quick and effective action can help to relieve pain or distress, so be prepared to meet any holiday emergency. Do remember, though, that first aid is no substitute for proper medical treatment.

Travel sickness

Many people suffer from travel sickness, whether it be sea, car or air sickness. The symptoms include sweating, faintness, nausea and vomiting.

If you anticipate being sick, it is best to take travel sickness tablets in advance, but they may cause drowsiness so avoid driving. To alleviate the symptoms, get fresh air, lie flat on your back and sip water to avoid dehydrating.

Stomach upsets

Drinking water is often the cause of stomach upsets on holiday. If you have doubts about the purity of the water supply, boil all your water or use water-purifying tablets.

Should you suffer from a stomach upset, eat no solids for 24 hours, but drink plenty of pure water to prevent dehydration. Take the appropriate medicine to relieve diarrhoea, and if the symptoms do not abate in a day's time, call a doctor.

Food poisoning

This may be caused by eating food that is not fresh or not properly cooked or reheated, or by unhygienic cooking conditions. Food poisoning manifests itself within a couple of hours by stomach cramps, nausea and vomiting, diarrhoea, weakness and shallowness of breath. Make the patient rest and give him plenty of liquids and antidiarrhoeal medicine, but if the symptoms appear to get worse, call a doctor.

'Red tide' poisoning occurs after eating mussels or other filter-feeders gathered during a red tide (when particular plankton are present in the ocean). The victim experiences numbness in the lips and face, spreading throughout the body and inhibiting swallowing and breathing. Seek urgent medical assistance, and be prepared to administer mouth-to-mouth resuscitation if breathing stops.

The flesh of some fish is poisonous and should never be eaten. Notable among these is the blaasop, where symptoms include numbness spreading from the lips and face, nausea and vomiting, convulsions and respiratory paralysis. Victims must be admitted to hospital at once.

Shock

Injuries of one kind or another often induce varying degrees of shock, the condition of circulation becoming sluggish. With an in-adequate supply of blood, the body concentrates on the vital organs — the heart, brain and kidneys — and less important areas, such as the muscles and skin, are consequently starved of blood. The symptoms (which need not manifest themselves until a few hours after the accident) include pallor, giddiness and faintness, sweating, nausea and vomiting, shallow breathing, and a weak and irregular pulse rate.

Treat shock by reassuring the victim, resting him with his head low and legs raised, and loosening his clothing for easier breathing and circulation. Keep the victim covered to maintain his body temperature and moisten his lips if he complains of thirst.

Sunburn, heat exhaustion and sunstroke

Adopt a sensible attitude towards spending time in the sun and you should suffer no ill effects. Limit your exposure and always use a good suntan lotion, choosing the protection factor best suited to your skin (usually a stronger one on the delicate skin of your face). Wear a hat to protect your face and neck, and a light, long-sleeved shirt if you are going to spend longer than usual in the sun. Drink plenty of water to replace loss by perspiration, and

---

FIRST AID KIT

A holiday first aid kit, kept in a waterproof container, should contain at least the following basic items:

- Paracetamol.
- Travel sickness tablets.
- Suntan lotion and sunburn balm.
- Patent remedies for stomach complaints (diarrhoea, indigestion, constipation).
- Antiseptic lotion and cotton wool for disinfecting wounds.
- Bandages: different width rolls of gauze and crepe bandages, triangular bandages; safety pins for fastening.
- Sterile dressings: various sizes to cover wounds, eye pad with bandage.
- Adhesive dressings: box of assorted plasters, role of plaster; blunt-ended scissors for cutting plaster.
- Insect repellant.
- Antihistamine cream for insect bites.
- Vinegar or meat tenderiser for mild marine stings.
- Witch hazel for bruises and inflammation.
- Bicarbonate of soda for stings.
- Sharp-pointed tweezers and a needle for removing thorns or stings.
- Thermometer.

If visiting a malaria area, consult your doctor about the correct precautions.

---

take salt tablets if the heat is extreme. Remember, too, that wind and cloud cover are no defence against burning.

The discomfort of mild sunburn can be eased by taking a cold shower or bath, applying a cool compress, resting in a cool place and drinking plenty of fluid. Do not apply oils or moisturisers to the skin as they retain heat. Should the skin begin to blister, immerse it in cool water, pat dry and cover lightly with a sterile gauze dressing.

Symptoms of heat exhaustion, which is caused by overexertion in hot conditions, include a headache, dizziness, faintness and stomach cramps. Lay the victim down with his feet slightly raised, sponge him down with cold water, and give him regular drinks of salted water (half a teaspoon to one glass).

Sunstroke can be very serious. Symptoms include dizziness, a high temperature and increased pulse rate, and even unconsciousness. The treatment for sunstroke is similar to that for heat exhaustion, but make sure the victim's head and shoulders are slightly raised. You could also keep him cool by wrapping a wet towel around him. Should the victim start to lose consciousness, place him in the recovery position (relaxed on his side, with one arm tucked under him and the other supporting his chin — keeping the neck extended to ensure an open airway) and call a doctor.

Burns and scalds

Burns are caused by dry heat, friction, electricity or acids and alkalis; scalds are caused by moist heat (boiling water, hot fat, etc.). You should not attempt to treat a serious burn, but should simply cover it with a sterile, nonfluffy dressing, calm the victim and seek medical help at once.

For minor burns, do not remove clothing that is stuck to the burnt area, but cut carefully around it. Immerse the injured area in cold water for as much as half an hour, then cover with a sterile gauze dressing.

Marine stings and stabs

The most common marine stings are from bluebottles, whose long, stinging tentacles can cause intense local pain and generalised joint and muscle pain. The sting can prove fatal to those allergic to the venom, and where the victim's reaction is severe, call a doctor. Remove the sting with the blade of a knife and rinse the affected area with vinegar, methylated spirits or — surprisingly — meat tenderiser (its protein-digesting enzyme destroys the protein-based venom).

Jellyfish in southern African waters have only mild stings that set up minor skin irritations. Treatment with meat tenderiser usually helps to relieve the discomfort.

RECOVERY POSITION

The recovery position prevents the airway from being blocked and vomit from entering the lungs.

To place the victim in the recovery position, kneel at his side and pull the leg further from you over the nearer leg.

Then place his further arm across his chest to the shoulder area. The arm nearer to you should be positioned down along the victim's body, with the palm upwards.

Pull the victim towards you and onto his side, tucking the arm now beneath him behind his back and bending his top leg. Put the hand of the crossed arm under his chin, away from the mouth, and tilt his head back to keep the airway clear.

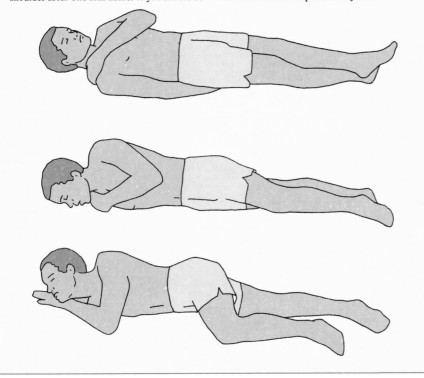

Sea urchins are seldom dangerous, usually simply inflicting splinters that can easily be removed with a pair of tweezers. However, along the Natal coast two sea urchin families have hollow, brittle spines (like sharp needles) that release venom. The stinging is intense and the victim may experience shortness of breath, faintness and muscular paralysis. Treatment involves removing the urchin spine and immersing the wound in very hot water (which neutralises the protein in the venom).

Fireworms, whose hollow, serrated bristles contain venom, can inflict stings that cause redness and burning, swelling, numbness or itching. Remove the bristles with adhesive tape or plaster, apply meat tenderiser and seek medical advice on further treatment.

Stingrays, which may bury the spines at the base of their tails in your flesh, inflict a painful stab causing vomiting, diarrhoea, accelerated heartbeat and muscular paralysis. In some cases the stab may be fatal. Immediate treatment involves immersing the wound in hot water and cleansing it thoroughly. Medical assistance should be sought. (The electric ray may give a shock intense enough to knock a man over, but the effect is not dangerous.)

Probably the most venomous fish in the world is the stonefish, found among coral reefs and rocks and blending so perfectly with its surroundings as to be virtually undetectable. Its sharp, stout spines contain a venom that attacks principally the nervous system, causing excrutiating pain and possibly resulting in death. For immediate relief, immerse the wound in very hot water and seek urgent medical help.

Insect and spider bites and stings
The most common insect bites are from mosquitos, bees and wasps. Mosquito bites are generally not serious (in a malaria area you should be taking the appropriate medicine), but to relieve the irritation apply a layer of damp soap to the bite. Alternatively, you could apply a little anti-histamine cream.

Bee and wasp stings are usually more painful, and can pose a serious threat to those allergic to them. In mild cases, remove the sting with a sterile needle (do not squeeze the poison sac) and apply ice, a sterile dressing soaked in a solution of bicarbonate of soda, or a layer of antihistamine cream. In an allergic reaction, symptoms to look out for include a rash or swelling, faintness and a feeling of weakness or paralysis, wheezing and breathing difficulties. Apply mouth-to-mouth resuscitation if it is necessary, and seek urgent medical assistance.

Tick bites are characterised by redness and itching. If the tick has burrowed into the skin, cover it with paraffin or petroleum jelly to force it to withdraw. Relieve the itching with a block of ice, calamine lotion, alcohol or antihistamine cream. Should the bite develop into a raised red bump with a black centre, consult a doctor to check for tick bite fever.

In South Africa, bites by spiders of only four genera are known to have a harmful effect. These include the button spider, with a neurotoxic (affecting the nervous system) venom, and the violin spider, with a cytotoxic (attacking cells) venom. (You should always try to keep the spider for identification.) In the first case, symptoms include cramps, difficulty in breathing, a headache, nausea and vomiting. Ice should be applied to the bite, the victim should be kept still and a doctor should be called. In the second case, pain sets in only two to eight hours after the bite, when the spot becomes inflamed. The tissues around the bite die, leading to an ulcerating crater. Again, treatment involves applying ice and seeking medical assistance.

Scorpion stings, which are treated the same way as spider bites, are indicated by a burning sensation for about thirty minutes. Other symptoms include a headache, dizziness, excessive sweating and salivating, laboured breathing and perhaps even convulsions.

Snakebites
Snakebite victims should be kept as calm as possible: the effects of fear and shock can sometimes be more damaging than the bite itself. Symptoms may include sharp pain and swelling around the bite, disturbed vision, nausea and vomiting, and difficulty in breathing. Keep the victim still and try to ensure that the area of the bite is below the level of the heart. Remove venom from around the wound by wiping outwards. Apply a sterile dressing and bandage securely, and seek urgent medical assistance. As with spider bites, positive identification of the snake will help the doctor in his course of treatment.

Only one sea snake (*Pelamis platurus*) is found in southern African waters and sometimes washed ashore. It is not aggressive but its venom is very potent and has no specific antiserum. Symptoms may appear only after an hour or so, and include convulsions, paralysis, respiratory distress and unconsciousness. Keep the victim very still and call a doctor immediately.

Shark bites

Shark attacks are rare, but quick action on the beach could mean the difference between life and death. Lifesaving and medical assistance should be summoned immediately.

Carry the victim from the sea in the head-down position, with the wounded limb elevated if possible. Keeping the head lower than the body, lay him down — no more than a few metres from the water's edge — on a towel or blanket to prevent sand from entering the wound. (He should not be moved from here for at least thirty minutes.) Prevent blood loss by pressing a hand firmly on the wound until the bleeding stops, and then cover with a sterile gauze bandage.

Calm and reassure the victim, and keep him cool and shaded, as heat promotes bleeding. Do not give him anything to eat or drink (other than moistening his lips), as he may require surgery.

Choking

At the coast, choking is often caused by swallowing sand. Remove any objects (such as food or false teeth) in the mouth of the victim, and give four sharp smacks between the shoulder blades. If this does not work, stand behind him and clasp your hands under his rib cage, forming a fist with one hand. Jerk the fist sharply upwards and inwards into the diaphragm, forcing the air in the windpipe up sharply and thus dislodging the obstruction. If the patient is not breathing, remove the obstruction and apply artificial respiration.

Young children should not be treated this way. Encourage the child to cough, and if this does not dislodge the obstruction, place him face downwards across your knees and smack sharply between the shoulder blades.

Foreign objects in eyes, ears and nose, and nosebleeds

Foreign bodies in the eye are usually washed away by tears. If not, carefully separate the eyelids and remove the object with a piece of sterile gauze or any clean cloth. If the object cannot be removed, cover the eye with a gauze pad and a light bandage and seek medical help.

Do not try to prise a foreign object from the ear. Olive oil may dislodge it, but if not, see a doctor. An object in the nose should also not be prised out. If hard blowing does not dislodge it, see a doctor.

Nosebleeds are often caused by heat, changes in air pressure or blowing the nose too hard. Sit upright with your head angled slightly forwards. Pinch the nostrils closed for about 15 minutes, while breathing through your mouth and spitting out any blood that may run down the back of your throat. Repeat if bleeding recurs. When the flow has stopped, rest and do not blow your nose for at least three hours.

Blisters and wounds

Blisters are usually caused by friction from ill-fitting shoes and they can thus be avoided. If a tender spot develops on the skin, protect it with a plaster. If a blister has already formed, cut a hole the same size as the blister in a plaster and place it over the sensitive area so that the blister shows through the hole but is protected from further friction. Never pierce blisters; should they burst, clean the area with antiseptic lotion.

If splinters are accessible, remove them with a sterile pair of tweezers or a needle and apply antiseptic cream. If the splinter is too deeply embedded, consult a doctor.

Cuts and grazes should be rinsed with warm water containing salt or a disinfectant. Cover the wound with a gauze dressing or plaster, and check regularly for infection.

Treat open wounds with utmost attention to cleanliness. For minor cuts, stop the bleeding by pressing on the wound with a piece of clean cloth. Gently wipe away any dirt using clean gauze and lukewarm water or a disinfectant solution. Cover the damaged skin with antiseptic cream and a sterile dressing, and hold it firmly in position with a bandage.

In the case of severe wounds, firmly apply direct pressure to stop the bleeding (unless something is protruding from the skin), raise the affected area and cover the wound with a cold compress. Call a doctor immediately.

Wounds are often caused at the coast by fish-hooks penetrating the skin. If the barb itself has not penetrated the skin, remove the hook gently and clean the skin with antiseptic lotion. If the barb is caught below the surface of the skin, it is best to seek medical assistance, but if none is readily available, follow this procedure.

Cut the fishing line from the hook and push the hook gently through the skin until the barb shows. Cut the shaft behind the hook and carefully withdraw the hook from the skin. Disinfect and bandage the wound. If there is any chance at all of damaging internal organs, do not even attempt to remove the hook.

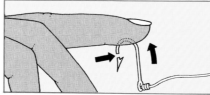

Cut line from the fish-hook. Pull the hook through the skin until the barb shows, then cut the shaft between barb and skin.

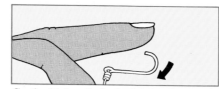

Gently withdraw the hook, disinfect the wound and bandage it. Check for infection.

Strains, sprains and fractures

Treat strains (stretched muscles) by covering the injury with a hot compress or immersing it in hot water to ease the discomfort. Treat sprains (when muscles and tendons around a joint are torn) by elevating and resting the injured limb and applying a bandage soaked in cold water to reduce the swelling. Strap the joint firmly to support it and prevent unnecessary movement. Seek medical advice if the swelling persists.

Fractures (which may be difficult to distinguish from sprains) manifest themselves in swelling and localised pain, immobility of the limb and irregularity in its shape. Support the limb comfortably and immobilise with splints made from strips of wood, cardboard or folded paper. Pad the splints to fit the limb and bandage them in place. Skull and spine fractures are the most serious and the patient should never be moved, unless absolutely essential. In all cases, call a doctor immediately.

Mouth-to-mouth resuscitation and heart massage

If someone has been rescued from drowning, his breathing and heartbeat may stop but he can still be revived by applying mouth-to-mouth resuscitation. Place the victim on his side on a firm, level surface and tilt his head to clear the airway. Remove all obstacles (including mucus) from his mouth.

Once the airway is clear, turn the patient on his back with the head tilted back. Pinch his nostrils closed. Take a deep breath, hold it, then put your mouth firmly over his (and over the nose, if a child). Exhale one hard breath every five seconds into an adult, and one shallow breath every three

Take the wrist pulse by placing two fingers just below the base of the thumb, in the hollow between two bones.

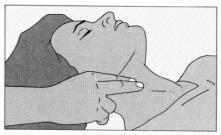

Take the neck pulse by placing two fingers to one side of the Adam's apple, below the angle of the jaw.

seconds into a child. Watch for the chest to rise, but do not wait for it to sink completely before refilling during the first four breaths. Continue inflating the lungs until the patient is breathing on his own, or until a doctor arrives. Keep checking his pulse rate.

Under no circumstances leave the patient alone, even if he has resumed breathing, as he may easily slip into unconsciousness again.

Cardiopulmonary resuscitation (heart massage) is best left to the experts and should be applied only if it has been established conclusively that the victim's heart has stopped. (Check by feeling the neck pulse after giving the first four breaths in mouth-to-mouth resuscitation. If there is no pulse, begin heart massage. Check the pulse again after one minute, and then after every three minutes. If the pulse returns, the heart has resumed beating.)

To apply heart massage, gently roll the patient onto his back, making sure that there are no obstructions in his mouth. Place the heel of one hand just above the base of the breastbone, and the other hand over the first. Press down 3,5 cm, keeping your thumbs and fingers raised. Let the chest rise again. Give 15 presses at normal pulse rate (sixty per minute), then inflate the lungs twice by mouth-to-mouth resuscitation. Repeat the sequence if necessary until medical help arrives.

If the patient is a child, you should press down between 2,5 and 3,5 cm and at a slightly faster rate than for adults. In the case of babies, support the body along one arm and cradle the head — tilted slightly backwards — in your hand. Using only two fingers, press down 1,3 to 2,5 cm on the middle of the breastbone ●

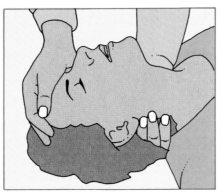

Start resuscitation by tilting the victim's head back (lift with one hand under the neck and press down with the other on the forehead).

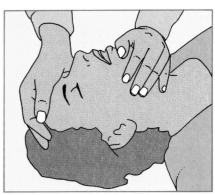

Push the chin up to lift the tongue away from the opening to the windpipe. The airway should now be unobstructed.

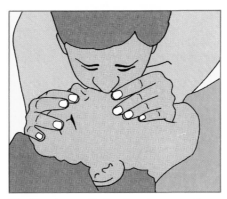

Pinching the nostrils closed, seal your mouth over the victim's and deliver four quick, full breaths.

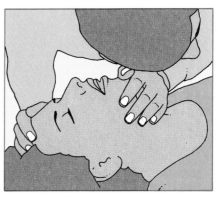

Remove your mouth and check the rising of the chest. Take a fresh breath and resume artificial respiration as necessary.

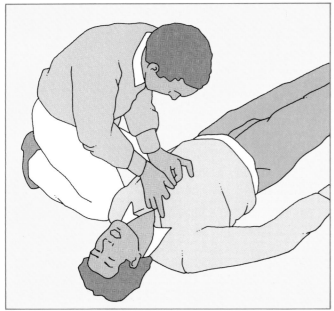

Before beginning heart massage, locate the lower half of the victim's breastbone. Find the sternal notch at the top and the intersection of the rib margins at the bottom. Apply pressure between these points.

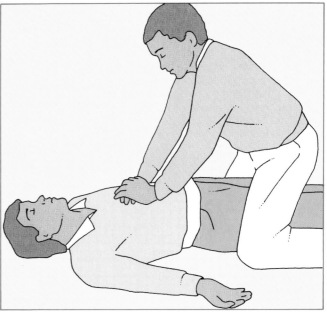

Place the heel of one hand on the breastbone, and the other hand over the first. Press down 3,5 cm — keeping fingers and thumbs raised — and let the chest rise again. Repeat sequence at pulse rate.

A

B

C

E

F

G

J

K

N

O

P

Q

R

S

Page numbers in bold type indicate illustrations.

Photographic credits

Photographic credits for each spread read from top to bottom, using the top of the picture as the reference point. Where the tops of two or more pictures are on the same level, credits read from left to right.

8-9 Walter Knirr 10-11 Anthony Bannister, Dave Snook (illustrations) 12-13 Walter Knirr, Dave Snook (illustrations) 14-15 Herman Potgieter, Dave Snook (illustrations) 16-17 Herman Potgieter, Dave Snook (illustrations), Anthony Bannister 18-19 Anthony Bannister, David Thorpe (illustrations) 20-21 Herman Potgieter, David Thorpe (illustrations) 22-23 Anthony Bannister, David Thorpe (illustrations) 24-25 Anthony Bannister, David Thorpe (illustrations) 26-27 David Thorpe (illustrations), Anthony Bannister, David Thorpe (illustrations) 30-31 Anthony Bannister, Anthony Bannister, Anthony Bannister 32-33 Gerald Cubitt, Anthony Bannister, Gerald Cubitt 34-35 Gerald Cubitt, Gerald Cubitt, Tobie Beele (illustration), Anthony Bannister 36-37 David Bristow, David Bristow, Anthony Bannister 38-39 David Bristow, David Bristow, David Bristow 40-41 Jean Laurie/Photo Access, David Bristow, David Bristow 42-43 Herman Potgieter, David Bristow, David Bristow 44-45 Herman Potgieter, Herman Potgieter, Herman Potgieter 46-47 Tobie Beele (illustration), Herman Potgieter, David Bristow 48-49 Anthony Bannister, Neville Poulter 50-51 Neville Poulter, David Steele/Photo Access, David Steele/Photo Access 52-53 Gerald Cubitt, David Steele/Photo Access 54-55 Neville Poulter, Anthony Bannister, Anthony Bannister 56-57 Herman Potgieter, Cape Archives, Herman Potgieter 58-59 David Steele/Photo Access, David Steele/Photo Access, Herman Potgieter 60-61 David Steele/Photo Access, David Steele/Photo Access 62-63 Glynn Griffiths/Photo Access 64-65 Walter Knirr, Jean Morris, Gerald Cubitt 66-67 South African Library, Walter Knirr, Herman Potgieter, Africana Museum 68-69 South African Library, Walter Knirr 70-71 South African Library, Tobie Beele (illustration), Walter Knirr, Mark van Aardt, Walter Knirr 72-73 Herman Potgieter, Walter Knirr, Gerald Cubitt 74-75 Glynn Griffiths/ Photo Access, Gerald Cubitt 76-77 Neville Poulter, Mark van Aardt, David Steele/Photo Access, Herman Potgieter 78-79 Mark van Aardt, Tobie Beele (illustration), Jean Morris 80-81 Herman Potgieter, Jean Morris 82-83 David Steele/Photo Access, Jean Morris,

Walter Knirr, Tobie Beele (illustration) 84-85 Herman Potgieter, David Steele /Photo Access, Ken Gerhardt/Photo Access, Ken Gerhardt/Photo Access 86-87 Herman Potgieter, Herman Potgieter, Herman Potgieter 88-89 Walter Knirr, Tobie Beele (illustration) 90-91 Herman Potgieter, Walter Knirr 92-93 Walter Knirr, David Steele/Photo Access, Herman Potgieter 94-95 Herman Potgieter, Gerald Cubitt, Walter Knirr 96-97 Herman Potgieter, Herman Potgieter, John Paisley/Photo Access 98-99 Walter Knirr, David Thorpe (illustration), Walter Knirr, Gerald Cubitt 100-101 Mark van Aardt, Ken Gerhardt /Photo Access 102-103 Herman Potgieter, Mark van Aardt, Mark van Aardt 104-105 Neville Poulter, Tobie Beele (illustration), Herman Potgieter, David Steele/Photo Access, Mark van Aardt 106-107 Mark van Aardt 108-109 David Steele/Photo Access, Mark van Aardt 110-111 Herman Potgieter, Herman Potgieter, Janek Szymnanowski 112-113 Dr F Leroux/Photo Access, Africana Museum, Janek Szymnanowski, Janek Szymnanowski 114-115 Herman Potgieter, Herman Potgieter, Neville Poulter 116-117 A S Bosman, A S Bosman, Herman Potgieter 118-119 Dr F Leroux /Photo Access, David Thorpe (illustration), Mark van Aardt 120-121 Herman Potgieter, John Paisley/Photo Access, A S Bosman 122-123 Herman Potgieter, Mark van Aardt, Herman Potgieter 124-125 David Steele/Photo Access, David Thorpe (illustration), Herman Potgieter, Ken Gerhardt/ Photo Access, Herman Potgieter 126-127 Gerald Cubitt, David Steele/Photo Access 128-129 David Steele/Photo Access, Zane Erasmus/Photo Access, David Steele/Photo Access 130-131 Gerald Cubitt, Mark van Aardt, Herman Potgieter 132-133 Gerald Cubitt, Herman Potgieter 134-135 Gerald Cubitt, Walter Knirr, Mark van Aardt 136-137 Walter Knirr, Herman Potgieter, Herman Potgieter 138-139 Gerald Cubitt, Mark van Aardt 140-141 Herman Potgieter, Herman Potgieter, Anthony Bannister 142-143 Gerald Cubitt, Walter Knirr 144-145 Anthony Bannister, Anthony Bannister, Herman Potgieter, Anthony Bannister 146-147 Walter Knirr, Gerald Cubitt 148-149 Herman Potgieter, Mark van Aardt 150-151 Herman Potgieter, David Steele/Photo Access, Herman Potgieter 152-153 David Bristow, David Steele/Photo Access, David Bristow 154-155 David Bristow, David Steele/Photo Access 156-157 Herman Potgieter, David Steele/Photo Access 158-159 David Steele/Photo

Access, Herman Potgieter, Herman Potgieter 160-161 J Alves/Photo Access, Gerald Cubitt 162-163 Herman Potgieter, David Steele/Photo Access 164-165 Ken Gerhardt/Photo Access, Gerald Cubitt, South African Library 166-167 Herman Potgieter, Herman Potgieter 168-169 David Bristow, Herman Potgieter, David Steele/Photo Access 170-171 J Alves/Photo Access, Alex de Gouveia/Photo Access, David Bristow, David Bristow, David Bristow 172-173 David Bristow 174-175 Herman Potgieter, David Steele/Photo Access, Herman Potgieter 176-177 David Steele /Photo Access, Tobie Beele (illustration), Herman Potgieter 178-179 Herman Potgieter, Brian Johnson Barker, David Steele/Photo Access, Herman Potgieter 180-181 Herman Potgieter, Neville Poulter, Gerald Cubitt 182-183 Neville Poulter, Walter Knirr, Herman Potgieter, Walter Knirr 184-185 Tobie Beele (illustration), Herman Potgieter 186-187 Herman Potgieter, David Steele/Photo Access, Herman Potgieter 188-189 Reader's Digest, David Steele/Photo Access, Anthony Bannister, David Steele/Photo Access 190-191 David Steele/Photo Access, John Paisley/Photo Access, Herman Potgieter, David Bristow 192-193 Lex Hes, A S Bosman 194-195 David Bristow, David Bristow 196-197 David Bristow, Herman Potgieter 198-199 Herman Potgieter 200-201 Herman Potgieter, David Bristow 202-203 David Bristow, David Bristow, David Bristow, Chris van der Merwe 204-205 Gerald Cubitt, Herman Potgieter, Gerald Cubitt 206-207 Herman Potgieter, David Steele /Photo Access, Walter Knirr 208-209 David Steele/Photo Access, Tobie Beele (illustration), David Steele/Photo Access 210-211 Monica Fairall, Walter Knirr 212-213 Walter Knirr 214-215 Herman Potgieter, David Steele/Photo Access, Monica Fairall 216-217 David Steele/ Photo Access, David Steele/Photo Access, Herman Potgieter 218-219 David Thorpe (illustration), David Steele/ Photo Access, David Steele/Photo Access 220-221 Herman Potgieter, David Steele/Photo Access, Herman Potgieter 222-223 Monica Fairall, David Steele /Photo Access, Herman Potgieter, Oceanographic Institute (Pat Garratt) 224-225 Natal Sharks Board, David Steele/Photo Access, Walter Knirr 226-227 Monica Fairall, Jay Matthews /Photo Access, David Steele/Photo Access 228-229 Durban Publicity Association, Herman Potgieter, David Steele /Photo Access 230-231 Sugar Association, Local History Museum, Herman Potgieter, Herman Potgieter 232-233

Walter Knirr, Pat Royal/Photo Access 234-235 Walter Knirr, Durban Publicity Association, Tobie Beele (illustration), David Steele/Photo Access 236-237 Herman Potgieter, Durban Publicity Association, Tobie Beele (illustration) 238-239 Durban Publicity Association, Neville Poulter, Herman Potgieter 240-241 Neville Poulter, Tobie Beele (illustration), Herman Potgieter 242-243 Local History Museum, Walter Knirr, Walter Knirr, Monica Fairall 244-245 Herman Potgieter, Anthony Bannister, Herman Potgieter 246-247 Walter Knirr, Herman Potgieter 248-249 Herman Potgieter, David Steele/Photo Access, Herman Potgieter 250-251 Monica Fairall, Herman Potgieter, David Steele /Photo Access 252-253 David Steele /Photo Access, Herman Potgieter, David Steele/Photo Access 254-255 Herman Potgieter, David Steele/Photo Access 256-257 Herman Potgieter, Monica Fairall, Herman Potgieter 258-259 Natal Parks Board, Natal Parks Board (R Gush) 260-261 Natal Parks Board, David Steele/Photo Access, Herman Potgieter, Monica Fairall 262-263 Tony Cunningham, Natal Parks Board, Natal Parks Board 264-265 Herman Potgieter, Natal Parks Board, Herman Potgieter 266-267 Herman Potgieter, Anthony Bannister, Natal Parks Board 268-269 Anthony Bannister, Monica Fairall, Herman Potgieter 270-271 Val Johnson /Photo Access 272-273 David Steele/ Photo Access 276-277 Chris van der Merwe, Herman Potgieter, Reader's Digest 278-279 Camping and Outdoor Life, Chris van der Merwe 280-281 Ken Gerhardt/Photo Access, Glynn Griffiths /Photo Access, Neville Poulter (illustrations), Herman Potgieter 282-283 Herman Potgieter, Ken Gerhardt/ Photo Access, Herman Potgieter 284-285 Ken Gerhardt/Photo Access, Kevin Rudham, A S Bosman 286-287 Tobie Beele (illustration), Anthony Bannister 288-289 Herman Potgieter, Herman Potgieter, Hans Gräspointer, Herman Potgieter 290-291 Walter Knirr, Reader's Digest 292-293 Charlie Shapiro, Charlie Shapiro, Charlie Shapiro 294-295 Dave Snook (illustrations) 296-297 Oceanographic Research Institute, Neville Poulter, Natal Sharks Board 298-299 David Thorpe (illustrations), NSRI 300-301 David Thorpe (illustrations) 302-303 David Thorpe (illustrations)

The publishers would like to thank pilots C Briers and J Navarro for their contribution to Herman Potgieter's aerial photography, commissioned for this book ●

Bibliography

The publishers acknowledge their indebtedness to the following publications, which were used for reference.

Abnormal waves on the south-east coast of South Africa by J K Mallory (University of Cape Town); *Annual report 1985/86 of the Institute for Coastal Research* (University of Port Elizabeth); *The application of the Sea-Shore Act and related legislation on the Natal coast* by A J Oosthuizen (Natal Town and Regional Planning Commission); *Atlantic Ocean fisheries* edited by G Borgstrom (Fishing News); *Atlas of southern Africa* edited by C Walton (Reader's Digest); *Ballito: The story of a township 1953-1963* by J Nash (Jack Nash); *101 Beaches in and around the Cape Peninsula* by R Torr and A Wood (Capricorn); *Birdlife in southern Africa* edited by K Newman (Macmillan SA); *Boardsailing Africa* by Bob Molloy (Molloy Publications); *The book of shipwrecks* by K Hudson and A Nicholls (Macmillan); *Break away* edited by C Gordon (Keddem); *Cape drives and places of interest* by J Burman (Human & Rousseau); *Cape Point* by N Lee and E Odden (Don Nelson); *Caravanning in South Africa* (SA Tourist Corporation); *Coastal holiday* by J Burman (Human & Rousseau); *Coastal sensitivity atlas of southern Africa* compiled by L Jackson and S Lipschitz (Dept of Transport); *The coast of southern Africa* by J Kench (Struik); *Coasts, waves and weather* by J Q Stewart (Princeton University); *Conolly's guide to southern Africa* by D Conolly (Conolly); *The cradle days of Natal* by G MacKeurtan (T W Griggs & Co); *Dainty Durban* (SAR and Durban Corporation); *52 Day walks in and around Cape Town* by T Anderson (Struik); *Dictionary of southern African place names* by P E Raper (Lowry Publishers); *Dinghy sailing in South Africa* by R Preedy (Purnell); *Discovering southern Africa* by T V Bulpin (Books of Africa); *Durban at your feet* by B van Niekerk (Overport); *Early railways at the Cape* by J Burman (Human & Rousseau); *Ebb and flow* by A Defaut (University of Michigan Press); *Estuarine ecology* edited by J H Day (Balkema); *Everyone's guide to trailing and mountaineering in southern Africa* by J Levy (Struik); *Explore the seashore of South Africa* by M Branch (Struik); *A field guide to the birds of the South African sea-shore* by G J Broekhuysen (Timmins); *Field guide to the birds of southern Africa* by I Sinclair (Struik); *A field guide to the seabirds of southern Africa and the world* by G Tuck and H Heinzel (Collins); *Fish cook book for South Africa* by S Ross (Southpoint Publishing); *Free from the sea* by L Snyman and A Klarie (Don Nelson); *Get up and go* (SA Tourism Board); *Great shipwrecks off the coast of southern Africa* by J Burman (Struik); *Guide to the Australian coast* (Reader's Digest); *A guide to the common sea fishes of southern Africa* by R van der Elst (Struik); *A guide to marine life on South African shores* by J H Day (Balkema); *Guide to the museums of southern Africa* compiled by H Fransen (Galvin and Sales for the SA Museums Association); *Handbook of instruction* (SA National Water Safety Council); *The historical monuments of South Africa* by J J Oberholster (Rembrandt van Rijn Foundation for Culture for the National Monuments Council); *Hitting the lip* by C Barnett (Macmillan); *Illustrated guide to Britain's coast* (Drive Publications for the Automobile Association); *Illustrated guide to the game parks and nature reserves of southern Africa* edited by A Duggan (Reader's Digest); *Illustrated guide to southern Africa* edited by G Maclay (Reader's Digest); *Landforms in Africa* by C Buckle (Longman); *International lights, shape and sound signals* by D A Moore (Stanford Maritime); *International regulations for preventing collisions at sea* (SA Navy Hydrographer); *The letters of Lady Anne Barnard written to Henry Dundas from the Cape of Good Hope 1793-1803* (Balkema); *The living shores of southern Africa* by M and G Branch (Struik); *Looking back on George* by C O Sayers (Herald Phoenix); *The mammals of the southern African subregion* by R H N Smithers (University of Pretoria); *Marine life along the shores* by P Harding (Tafelberg); *Maritime South Africa* by B Ingpen and R Pabst (Struik); *Medicinal and poisonous plants of southern and eastern Africa* by J M Watt and M G Breyer-Brandwijk (E&S Livingstone); *Modern water skiing* by R J Prytherch (Blandford Press); *Monitoring beach and dune advancement and vegetation changes 1937-1977 at the farm Twinstreams, Mtunzini, Natal, South Africa* by P J Weisser and A P Backer (Botanical Research Institute); *Myths and legends of southern Africa* by P Miller (T V Bulpin Publications); *Namibia, the untamed land* by G Cubitt (Don Nelson); *Natal and the Zulu country* by T V Bulpin (Books of Africa); *The new boatman's manual* by C D Lane (Adlard Coles); *Official place names in the Republic of South Africa and in South-West Africa* (Dept of National Education); *1985 Official South African municipal yearbook* edited by D Kevan (Melton); *Off the beaten track* edited by Alfie Steyn (AA The Motorist Publications); *An ornithological expedition to the Namib coast* by L G Underhill and D A Whitelaw (Western Cape Wader Group); *Outdoor holiday guide of SA* (Automobile Association of SA); *Oxford companion to ships and the sea* (Oxford University Press); *Photographer's handbook* by M Busselle and J Freeman (Octopus); *Port Natal* by J Malherbe (Howard Timmins);

Portrait of Plettenberg Bay by P Storrar (Centaur); *The private diary of the village harbour-master 1875-1897 (John F Sewell)* edited by C D Storrar (Ladywood Publishers); *Quality rating by the SA Caravan and Camping Council* (SACCC); *A rapid survey of forest succession at Mlalazi Nature Reserve* by J C van Daalen, C J Geldenhuys, P G H Frost and E J Moll (CSIR); *Report on drift-sands in South Africa* by J M Keet (Dept of Agriculture and Forestry); *Report of the interdepartmental committee of inquiry into shipwrecks* (Dept of Transport); *Report on the SA commission of inquiry into the control of small craft* (The Commission); *Review of coastal currents in southern African waters* by T F W Harris (CSIR); *Review of existing wave data, wave climate and design waves for South African and South West African (Namibian) coastal waters* by J Rossouw (CSIR); *Riches of the sea* by J R Grindley (Caltex); *The rise and fall of the seas* by R Brindze (Constable Young Books); *Roberts' birds of southern Africa* by G L Maclean (Trustees of the John Voelcker Book Fund); *Safety on small craft in South Africa* by R Preedy (Timmins); *Den sagen van den Vliegenden Hollander* by G Kalff (W J Thieme); *The Saldanha Bay story* by J Burman and S Levin (Human & Rousseau); *The sea* by L Engel (Time-Life International); *Sea and shore dangers* by M M Smith (J L B Smith Institute of Ichthyology); *Secrets of the seashore* (Reader's Digest); *Sedgwick's Old Brown rock and surf angling guides* by Dr V Taylor (Stellenbosch Farmers Winery); *Ships* by E Angelucci and A Cucuari (Macdonald and Jane's); *Ships and South Africa* by M Murray (Oxford University Press); *Ships of the South African Navy* by A K du Toit (SA Boating Publications); *Shipwreck and survival on the south-east coast of Africa* by A R Willcox (Drakensberg Publications); *Shipwrecks of the western Cape* by B Wexham (Timmins); *Skeleton coast* by A Schoeman (Macmillan SA); *Smith's sea fishes* edited by M M Smith and P C Heemstra (Macmillan); *The social system of the Zulus* by E J Krige (Shuter and Shooter); *South African angler's guide* by R Wegener (T W Hayne); *The South African backpacker* by H Hennig (Purnell); *South Africa's coastal resources: Their management requirements* by A E F Heydorn (CSIR); *The South African first aid manual* by the St John Ambulance and SA Red Cross Society (Struik); *SA National Committee for Oceanographic Research programme for coastal processes* April 1982 - March 1986 (CSIR); *SA 1985: Official yearbook of the Republic of South Africa* compiled by the Dept of Foreign Affairs and Information (Chris van Rensburg Publications); *South African shells: A collector's guide* by D Richards (Struik); *South African shore-life* by K H Barnard (Maskew Miller); *Southern Africa: Land of beauty and splendour* by T V Bulpin (Reader's Digest); *Southern Africa's weather patterns* by L Hurry and J van Heerden (Via Afrika); *So you want to be a skindiver* by L Plumridge (Laurie Plumridge); *Standard Encyclopaedia of Southern Africa* (Nasou); *The story of the 'Natal' engine* by T J Espitalier (SAR); *Strike! Handbook of coastal and offshore angling in South Africa* by S Schoeman (Balkema); *A tavern of the ocean* by P W Laidler (Maskew Miller); *Tavern of the seas* by L G Green (Timmins); *Threatened species* (Cape Provincial Dept of Nature and Environmental Conservation); *Thornton Cox travellers' guides, southern Africa* (Thornton Cox); *Touring in South Africa* by M Leigh (Struik); *Traditional Hindu temples in South Africa* by M Mikula, B Kearney and R Harber (Hindu Temple Publications); *Transvaal lowveld and escarpment* by J Onderstal (Botanical Society of South Africa); *The treasure diver's guide* by J S Potter (Robert Hale & Co); *Trees of southern Africa* by K C Palgrave (Struik); *Tsitsikama shore* by R M Tietz and Dr G A Robinson (National Parks Board); *Uitenhage past and present* by W J S Sellick (Uitenhage Times); *Underwater Africa* by A J Venter (Purnell); *The underwater photographer's handbook* by P Rowlands (Macdonald and Co); *The unquiet landscape* edited by D Brundsden and J C Doornkamp (David & Charles); *Veld types of South Africa* by J P H Acocks (Botanical Research Institute); *Valiant harvest: The founding of the SA sugar industry 1848-1926* by R F Osborn (SA Sugar Association); *What to do in an emergency* (Reader's Digest); *When in Durban* by M Fairall (Struik); *Wild flowers of Table Mountain* by W P U Jackson (Timmins); *The windsurfing funboard handbook* by C Boden and A Chater (Centaur); *The wonder of Richards Bay* by Dr J C van der Walt (Richardsbaai Afrikaanse Sakekamer); *Zulu crafts* by J W Grossert (Shuter and Shooter); *Zulu medicine and medicine men* by A T Bryant (Centaur).

Periodicals consulted include: *Africana Notes and News; African Wildlife; Backpacker; Boardsailor; Caravan and Outdoor Life; Custos; De Goede Hoop* (1911-13); *Government Gazette* (December 1985 No 10042); *Great Outdoors; SA Yachting; Underwater; Vagabond; Veld and Flora.*

Use was also made of pamphlets from various publicity associations ●

Acknowledgements

PRODUCTION ARTIST   Clarence Clarke
TYPESETTERS   Mary Lacey, Dalene Newbould, Elizabeth Brookes
PROOFREADER   Jack Early
INDEXER   Ethleen Lastovica
MAPS   Institute for Cartographic Analysis, University of
Stellenbosch: Chris Vlok, Ralene van Staden

Many people and organisations assisted in the preparation of this book. The publishers would like to acknowledge the generous contribution of the numerous municipalities, publicity associations and tourist information bureaus.

The following people and organisations have been particularly helpful:
J Barkly; Y Booysens; Prof G Branch; H Brümfield; G Castle; N Chandler; R Cooper; T Dearlove; A J de Jager; L de Klerk; R de Kock; Dept of Nature Conservation and Holiday Resorts (Namibia); A Diplock; I Dixon; L du Randt; D Engelbrecht; R Fourie; C Gaigher; J Glazewski; R Harding; J Herdman; D Hersch; J Hugo; R Jameson; M Johannson; J Joubert; P Joubert; Kaffrarian Museum; J Katz; D Keet; A Kotze; KwaZulu Bureau of Natural Resources; K P Liebenberg; D Lavender; B Mackenzie; G G S Madyibi; C J Malan; B Molyneux; Natal Parks Board; Natal Sharks Board; National Parks Board; National Sea Rescue Institute; Office of Surveys and Mapping; J Paarman; J Paisley; J Payn; P Price; P Prins; L Quinn; J Rudner; N Rusch; Safmarine; St John Ambulance; A Schoeman; L Schoeman; M Scott; Sea Fisheries Research Institute; R Solomon; SA Library; SA Tourism Board; N Steele; H Steyn; M Stott; P Swanepoel; Dr V Taylor; P Thomas; I Thompson; K van Zyl; G Ward; D A Webb; L R Wingate; G Wright; N B Wynne.

Colour separations by Unifoto, Cape Town.
Printed and bound by Printpak Books, Cape Town.